HUM

IN

PERSPECTIVE

The Thinker's Handbook

of

Insightful Quotations

JAMES D. COHOON, EDITOR

SAGES PRESS

VANCOUVER, B.C.

2000

First Edition

Canadian Cataloging in Publication Data:
Humanity in perspective
Includes index.
ISBN 0-9684953-0-3
1. Quotations, English.
I. Cohoon, James D. (James Douglas), date-
PN6081.H85 1999 082 C99-910250-8

Book designed and typeset by Robert D. MacNevin

Printed in Canada by Hignell Printing Ltd.

SAGES PRESS
VANCOUVER, B.C.
CANADA

To my mother, born Florence Sophia Larkin, whose middle name means wisdom, and whose life was a testament to the unassuming wisdom of motherhood.

ACKNOWLEDGEMENTS

I wish to acknowledge all those whose efforts or ideas have contributed in any way to the end product that is this book. I include all those, living or dead, whose quotations are cited in the following pages, as well as all associated publishers and translators, where applicable. A more personal acknowledgement must go to all those who have directly contributed to the book's production and completion. In particular, I must express my gratitude to Robert MacNevin, not only for his work in the design and typesetting of the book, but for all the countless ways in which he provided valuable feedback on the difficult journey to the successful completion of this project.

Contents

Contents

Preface

A new millennium is dawning, and with it monumental challenges and responsibilities for Mankind. Human civilization, the human soul, and life itself will all be tested in unprecedented ways. The stakes are supremely high. We will learn whether Mankind can rise to the highest challenges, or whether it is doomed to be swept along by mistakes and myopia to catastrophic results. To successfully meet the challenges ahead I believe scientific knowledge alone will prove grossly insufficient. We need something more, something that provides the basis for a broad and deep vision, something that identifies the truly vital issues and addresses them courageously in their totality. We will need something which recognizes the importance of the moral, philosophical and *human* element in all future decisions that affect the fate of Mankind. That something is, quite simply: *human wisdom*. By "human wisdom" I essentially mean an optimal partnership of reason, knowledge and morality, all directed towards the common goal of human welfare. The very notion of "wisdom" is under constant attack in postmodern culture. This is a dangerous trend. Wisdom in the future will not simply be about living the philosopher's "good life": it will be about the fate of human life, and all life, on this planet.

Wisdom joins together knowledge of life and an understanding of what it means to be *human* into an ethos of care and concern for what is best for our individual and collective existences on this unique planet. The pursuit of wisdom will take us down the intersecting paths of mind, spirit, and conscience. This book attempts to shine light on all these aspects of human wisdom, from a myriad of perspectives, past and present. It does so primarily through the insights of reasoned thought, captured here in a very diverse and distinctive collection of quotations. Its contents are derived principally from the works and minds of great thinkers, but it is a book that does not evade controversial ideas or unorthodox views; it does attempt, however, to put them all "in perspective"—the perspective of humanity as a whole.

Humanity in Perspective is intended not merely as a collection of quotations, but as a thought-provoking book in its own right. The 125 keywords have been selected to emphasize the most fundamental concepts underlying a solid understanding of the emotional, intellectual, social and spiritual dimensions of human existence, and thus of *wisdom* itself. Each of these keywords is explored in a wide range of ideas, opinions, and viewpoints. The quotations under each keyword have been specially arranged in a *dialectical* order permitting the reader to begin with a set of introductory notions and to sequentially read through a series of conflicting ideas to a number of often profound concluding statements. It is my hope that, within the scope of each keyword, and in the process of following the winding course of interconnected quotations, the reader will be led on an intellectually stimulating and a possibly morally challenging journey.

Preface

This is a book of ideas. Ideas are the building blocks of knowledge and reason. But not all ideas contribute equally to wisdom; somehow, they must be tested. A dialectical juxtaposition of ideas provides such a test. It may be appropriate that I attempt to explain this with the aid of quotations. Walter Lippmann: "The method of dialectics is to confront ideas with opposing ideas in order that the pro and the con of the dispute will lead to true ideas." Erich Fromm: "It is one of the peculiar qualities of the human mind that, when confronted with a contradiction, it cannot remain passive. It is set in motion with the aim of resolving the contradiction. All human progress is due to this fact." George Santayana: "The principle of dialectic is intelligence itself.... But the direct purpose of dialectic is not its ultimate justification. Dialectic is a human pursuit and has, at bottom, a moral function; otherwise, at bottom, it would have no value. And the moral function and ultimate justification of dialectic is to further the Life of Reason, in which human thought has the maximum practical validity, and may enjoy in consequence the richest ideal development." I would add that dialectical thought forces us to question our basic ideological and philosophical assumptions; this is increasingly vital, for as Socrates—the archetypal "wise man"—emphasized, unquestioned assumptions and premises are the enemy of true reason and wisdom. Unquestioned assumptions are thus an enemy of Mankind's future.

In this age of "information overload" it is seldom obvious how we may most fruitfully apply our ever-expanding knowledge to the profound challenges that will confront humanity. The increasingly computerized foundations of both our learning and information processes have produced an accelerated emphasis on data, artificial memory and linear logic, often at the expense of general comprehension, human understanding, and wisdom itself. The fundamental human meanings that underlie a broad and authentically rational comprehension of accumulated knowledge have become both less certain and less respected. I suspect that this trend is intimately associated with a decreasing respect for, and a weakening integrity of, both the human mind and human conscience. Any attempt to foster reason and wisdom will therefore have to emphasize an understanding of the many human factors that underlie the health and integrity of both mind and conscience. The concepts that I have tried to elucidate through the use of insightful quotations highlight many of these factors.

It is my hope that this book will find its place on the bookshelves of all those who enjoy mental stimulation. But while I hope that the reader will challenge his or her mind, I also hope that he or she will find the experience of reading these pages a rewarding experience on a variety of levels. For ultimately wisdom is not only about stretching the intellect; it is also about understanding, integrating, and respecting the full range of those qualities that define and foster our *humanity.* In Mankind's future, *humanness* itself will be increasingly at issue, and at risk. Never before has the ancient oracle's injunction to "Know thyself" had such important ramifications.

Ultimately, human existence is not comprehensible solely within an objective understanding of human nature, but must also be viewed through the subjective lens of what it *means* to be human. If this book does contribute to a heightened understanding of what it means to be human, and an increased appreciation of the importance of such understanding, it will have been a worthwhile project.

James D. Cohoon

Aggression / Violence

Numbed violence of varied dimensions has become a kind of métier of our century. 1
Robert Jay Lifton

Violence is ostensibly rejected by us as a part of the American value system, but ... violence has truly become a part of our unacknowledged (or underground) value structure.... We must recognize that, despite our pious official disclaimers, we have always operated with a heavy dependence upon violence in even our highest and most idealistic endeavors. 2
Richard M. Brown

The modern American reacts to aggression the way his Puritan ancestor reacted to sex. He likes to engage in it without admitting to the world what he is doing. 3 *William Blanchard*

I say violence ... is as American as cherry pie. 4
H. Rap Brown

It is curious that Americans show such a preference for violence in their television programs and movies while, at the same time, becoming ever more frightened by the rising rate of violent crimes in their streets. 5
P. Zimbardo & C. Maslach

Certainly my interpretation is that there is a causative relationship between television violence and subsequent anti-social behavior, and that the evidence is strong enough that it requires some action on the part of responsible authorities.... 6 *U.S. Surgeon-general*

Violence has always been acceptable to middle-class Americans when it was (1) nonpolitical and (2) confined to poor neighborhoods. These two conditions are related in that they both protect the advantaged from the anger of the disadvantaged. 7 *Philip Slater*

It isn't so much the *increase* in violence that upsets middle-class Americans as the *democratization* of violence.... 8 *Philip Slater*

The less respect there is for individual persons, the more they are exposed to violence, while this violence at the same time appears less criminal. 9 *Émile Durkheim*

Violence follows readily from victimization. 10
Robert Jay Lifton

A person who is not inwardly prepared for the use of violence against him is always weaker than the person committing the violence. 11
Alexander Solzhenitsyn

[T]he tendency to aggression is an innate, independent, instinctual disposition in man ... constituting the most powerful obstacle to culture.... This aggressive instinct is the derivative and the main representative of the death instinct.... In consequence of this primary mutual hostility of human beings, civilized society is perpetually threatened with disintegration. 12 *Sigmund Freud*

I believe ... that present-day civilized man suffers from insufficient discharge of his aggressive drive ... for which in the social order of today he finds no adequate outlet. 13
Konrad Lorenz

One of the most effective ways of getting rid of anxiety is to become aggressive. 14
Erich Fromm

Aggression is always a consequence of frustration. 15 *John Dollard et al.*

Aggressive behavior without hostile content is a natural reaction to the frustration of the need for love. Aggressive behavior that is hostile is learned.... It is probable that there is not an iota of innate hostile aggressiveness in human beings.... 16 *Ashley Montagu*

Violence is a product of cultural environment. ... 17 *José Delgado*

[I]n humans ... the capacity for aggression is inherited, but the ability to be aggressive has to be learned.... [D]estructive aggression is, in most cases, a response to the experience of rejection, frustration, or aggression in infancy and childhood. 18 *Ashley Montagu*

The recent growth of violence toward women ... often indicates that the offender is striking out against an incorporated, hated mother-image. 19 *Natalie Shainess*

Aggression / Violence

Many aggressive actions are instrumental.... The behavior can be learned much as other instrumental actions are learned—because the actor has found that the behavior pays off. 20
Leonard Berkowitz

Is aggression in man adaptive? From the biologist's point of view it certainly seems to be. 21
E. O. Wilson

[V]iolent men play violent games because their non-violent repertoire is restricted.... [W]e must help him arrive at the discovery of new strategies for satisfying needs. 22
Hans Toch

The rewards and punishments of violence are measured in increments and decrements to the ego rather than in terms of future well-being. The perspective of violence is short-term.... Probably the hardest task we face in the rehabilitation of Violent Men is that of developing their interpersonal maturity, or—in psychoanalytic parlance—of building their ego. 23
Hans Toch

Deeds of violence in our society are performed largely by those trying to establish their self-esteem, to defend their self-image, and to demonstrate that they too, are significant. 24
Rollo May

Violence is ... the ultimate and most primitive way for people to assert their significance, to have impact on others.... But our conception of masculinity does more than recognize this aspect of the human condition. It makes the experience of the ecstasy of violence a mythic prerequisite of men's self-esteem.... 25
Marc Fasteau

Violence is the ultimate destructive substitute which surges in to fill the vacuum where there is no relatedness. 26 *Rollo May*

I understand violence as a substitute for productive activity occurring in an impotent person. 27 *Erich Fromm*

Men must come to terms with violence because it is the prime component of male identity.... Violence is male. 28 *Andrea Dworkin*

[V]iolent behavior is most common among 15-25 year old males, the ages at which testosterone levels are highest. 29 *James W. Kalat*

[H]uman aggression in its social organizational sense is a propensity of males. It is most efficiently and effectively "released" or stimulated by association with other males.... [A] particular characteristic of the male bond is its close interconnection with aggressive and possibly violent action. 30 *Lionel Tiger*

[G]roups of men banded together in some interest will readily resort to violence against other groups of men who are seen as opposed to that interest. 31 *Lionel Tiger & Robin Fox*

[T]he most brutal forms of violence can be committed in the name of defending the "territory" or "cherished values." ... Shared violence is not only unitary but unifying. 32
Robert Jay Lifton

Yes, men are destructive, and every boy on his way to manhood must learn how to master the violent side of himself.... [But] there is no construction without destruction ... [and] the survival of our species ... required at times not only living in and with [nature], but also opposing her.... What needs to be destroyed is, in human society, a matter of judgment; but a man who could not destroy, be he architect, lawyer, or farmer, could not protect and provide. He could also not create; he would hardly be worth his keep. 33 *Wolfgang Lederer*

[I]t is highly probable that the undoubted superiority of the male sex in intellectual and creative achievement is related to their greater endowment of aggression.... [A]ggression in the female is only fully aroused in response to threat, especially if the young are involved. 34
Anthony Storr

In a tragic way we are indebted to aggression for the rapid development of our intellect. Yet this same aggression has encouraged our astonishing capacity for cooperation. 35
Irenäus Eibl-Eibesfeldt

[T]he nonviolent approach does not immediately change the heart of the oppressor. It first does something to the hearts and souls of those committed to it. It gives them new self-respect; it calls up resources of strength and courage that they did not know they had. Finally, it reaches the opponent and so stirs his conscience that reconciliation becomes a reality. 36 *Martin Luther King Jr.*

Nonviolence ... offers a unique weapon which, without firing a single bullet, disarms the adversary. It exposes his moral defenses, weakens his morale, and at the same time works on his conscience. 37 *Martin Luther King Jr.*

Non-violent opposition has nothing to do with passivity.... [It] is an expression of spiritual, physical and moral strength. 38 *Petra Kelly*

It is no longer a choice between violence and nonviolence in this world; it's nonviolence or nonexistence. 39 *Martin Luther King Jr.*

[N]onviolent action ... has become, in the age of scientific progress, humanity's only practical substitute for hopeless revolution and self-stultifying or suicidal war. 40 *Aldous Huxley*

Violence cannot lead to real progress unless, by way of compensation and reparation, it is followed by nonviolence, by acts of justice and good will. In such cases, however, it is the compensatory behaviour that achieves the progress, not the violence.... 41 *Aldous Huxley*

Absolute non-violence is the negative basis of slavery.... [S]ystematic violence positively destroys the living community.... To be fruitful, these two ideas must establish final limits. 42
Albert Camus

A society where all were invariably aggressive would destroy itself by inner friction, and in a society where some are aggressive, others must be non-resistant, if there is to be any kind of order. This is the present constitution of society, and to the mixture we owe many of our blessings. 43 *William James*

[V]iolence against a being one really confronts is better than ghostly solicitude for faceless digits! From the former a path leads to God, from the latter only to nothingness. 44 *Martin Buber*

Human aggression is most dangerous when it is attached to the two greatest absolutarian psychological constellations: the grandiose self and the archaic omnipotent object. And the most gruesome human destructiveness is encountered ... [when] the perpetrators' destructiveness is alloyed with absolute conviction about their greatness. 45 *Heinz Kohut*

Any violence which does not spring from a firm, spiritual base, will be wavering and uncertain. It lacks the stability which can only rest in a fanatical outlook. 46 *Adolf Hitler*

History teaches perhaps few clear lessons. But surely one such lesson learned by the world at great cost is that aggression unopposed becomes a contagious disease. 47
Jimmy Carter

Most Americans would say that they disapproved of violence. But what they really mean is that they believe it should be a monopoly of the state.... In the modern world, nearly all the violence that occurs is lawful violence. 48
Edgar Friedenberg

Life, based on principles of violence, has culminated in the negation of the basis on which it was founded. The organization, on principles of violence, of a society whose object was to insure the happiness of the individual and the family, and the social welfare of humanity, has brought men to such a pass that these benefits are practically annulled. 49
Leo Tolstoy

[A]ccording to the measure in which people renounce violence and establish their relations upon rational persuasion—only in that measure is true progress in the life of men accomplished. 50 *Leo Tolstoy*

Alienation

Alienation is a mark of man's uniqueness among all the forms of created existence.... To be human is to be alienated; without alienation there is simply no humanness. 1
Lloyd J. Averill

ALIENATION

The condition of alienation ... is the condition of the normal man.... We are born into a world where alienation awaits us.... In a world where the normal condition is one of alienation, most personal action must be destructive both of one's own experience and of that of the other.... If our experience is destroyed, our behaviour will be destructive. If our experience is destroyed, we have lost our own selves. 2

R. D. Laing

[A]lienation [is] the deadening of man's sensitivity to man.... Wherever non-human elements—whether revolutionary doctrine or material goods—assume greater importance than human life and well-being, we have the alienation of man from man, and the way is open to the self-righteous use of others as mere objects. 3 *Theodore Roszak*

The *alienation* of the worker in his product means not only that his labour becomes an object, assumes an *external* existence, but that it exists independently, *outside himself*, and alien to him, and that it stands opposed to him as an autonomous power. The life which he has given to the object sets itself against him as an alien and hostile force.... [A] relationship of the worker to his own activity as something alien ... as an activity which is directed against himself, independent of him and not belonging to him. This is *self-alienation*. 4

Karl Marx

The word alienation as Marx and Hegel used it means precisely the same thing as the idea of idolatry did for the prophets: a subjugation of self to things, a loss of the inner self, of freedom, and a self-preoccupation produced by that subjugation. 5 *Erich Fromm*

The alienation of the internal proletariat is ... the most conspicuous symptom of the disintegration of a civilization.... 6

Arnold Toynbee

To separate labor from other activities of life and to subject it to the laws of the market was to annihilate all organic forms of existence and to replace them by a different type of organization, an atomistic and individualistic one. 7

Karl Polanyi

[A]lienation ... is the feeling that there is little if anything of value and worthy of respect in society, combined with profound pessimism as to the chances of improvement. 8

Paul Hollander

[T]he central issue of the effects of Capitalism on personality [is] the phenomenon of alienation.... In the nineteenth century inhumanity meant cruelty; in the twentieth century it means schizoid self-alienation.... This alienation and automatization leads to an ever-increasing insanity. Life has no meaning, there is no joy, no faith, no reality. Everybody is "happy." ... 9 *Erich Fromm*

When we refuse to hear the voices of our inner selves we become strangers to ourselves. At some point, this alienation puts us into flight from ourselves and thus from our conscience and humanity. 10 *Joseph Amato*

Guilt can teach [us] how utterly a man can be alienated from the very sources of his being. But the recognition may point the way to a reunion and a reconciliation.... Atonement will become for him not an act of faith or a deed, but a life, a life devoted to strengthening the bonds between men and between man and nature. 11 *J. Glenn Gray*

[E]very step towards greater consciousness is a kind of Promethean guilt: through knowledge, the gods are as it were robbed of their fire, that is, something that was the property of the unconscious powers is torn out of its natural context and subordinated to the whims of the conscious mind. The man who has usurped the new knowledge suffers, however.... He has raised himself above the human level of his age, but in so doing has alienated himself from humanity. The pain of his loneliness is the vengeance of the gods, for never again can he return to mankind. 12 *Carl Jung*

[T]he distinction between self and not-self ... remains the source of our existential uneasiness.... Selfhood presents itself, at first, as a painful separation [which] ... becomes the basis of all subsequent experiences of alienation, of historical myths of a lost golden age. 13

Christopher Lasch

[T]he alienation of myself, which is the act of being-looked-at, involves the alienation of the world which I organize.... If there is an Other, whatever or whoever he may be, whatever may be his relations with me ... then I have an outside, I have a *nature*. My original fall is the existence of the Other. 14 *Jean-Paul Sartre*

[T]he experience of self-alienation and the feeling of being alienated from reality, from the world around one, proceed from the same cause: one's default on the responsibility of thinking. The suspension of proper cognitive contact with reality and the suspension of one's ego, are a single act. A flight from reality is a flight from self. 15 *Nathaniel Branden*

We may say that in the eighteenth century the alienation was chiefly political, in the nineteenth chiefly economic, and in the twentieth chiefly technical, that is, due to the application of rational, effective methods. 16

Jacques Ellul

Just as our scientific knowledge is becoming alienated from human experience, so are its technological applications becoming increasingly alienated from human needs. 17

René Dubos

To be "a part of" is a fundamental prerequisite of every human being.... Yet as modernization and ... technology envelops us further, these longings are doomed to even greater degrees of frustration ... to the point of alienation from our deepest needs and wishes. 18

Kent G. Bailey

All existents need other existents around them to enable them to experience their own transcendence. But men experience the freedom of other men as continually threatening, while at the same time they feel in their own free existence a disquieting nothingness, a painful alienation from nature.... Hence man dreams of finding in woman ... a bridge between himself and nature, through the possession of which he will regain his wholeness. 19

Mary Anne Warren

The "feminist revolution" is fighting today to give women greater influence and power over the formation of attitudes in society.... This dispute over humanity's self-alienation is the focal point of women's struggle. 20

Margarete Mitscherlich

[A]lienation can be avoided only to the extent that personal projects and individual action can be harmonized with universal requirements.... They are not imposed from outside, but reflect our own disposition to view ourselves, and our need to *accept* ourselves, from outside. Without such acceptance we will be in a significant way alienated from our lives. 21

Thomas Nagel

Alienation today is no longer a matter of being dispossessed of the value produced by labor. It consists, rather, in a breakdown of the personality, a dispersal of needs and capacities.... In short, alienation now touches man at his deepest level. Consequently, it is at that level that the revolution must take place. 22

Jacques Ellul

Altruism / Sacrifice

When a person (or animal) increases the fitness of another at the expense of his own fitness, he can be said to have performed an act of *altruism*. 1 *E. O. Wilson*

Altruism is ... one person's utility being positively affected by another person's welfare. 2

Robert Axelrod

[P]revention of future catastrophes is hardly possible without some fundamental change of man's motivations in the direction of altruism. 3

Pitirim Sorokin

Every society is a moral society.... Thus, altruism is not destined to become ... a sort of agreeable ornament to social life, but it will forever be its fundamental basis. 4

Émile Durkheim

In love and by love we seek to perpetuate ourselves, and we perpetuate ourselves on the earth only on condition that we die, that we yield up our life to others. 5 *Miguel de Unamuno*

Altruism / Sacrifice

The foundation of everything sublime in man is sacrifice.... Man does not know his humanity until he proves it by courage and by contempt of death. 6 *Karl Jaspers*

For the willingness to sacrifice, like the attraction of the sublime, is what makes possible the higher reaches of the spirit.... 7 *J. Glenn Gray*

Greater love hath no man than this, that a man lay down his life for his friends. 8
Jesus Christ

In giving one's own life for the existence of the community lies the crown of all sense of sacrifice. It is this alone that prevents what human hands have built from being overthrown by human hands or destroyed by Nature. 9
Adolf Hitler

Many people believe that altruism means kindness, benevolence, or respect for the rights of others. But it means the exact opposite: it teaches self-sacrifice, as well as the sacrifice of others, to any unspecified "public need"; it regards man as a sacrificial animal. 10
Ayn Rand

Agitators are indispensable, but an agitator mad with altruism is as dangerous as any other madman. 11 *Shailer Matthews*

"Every major horror of history was committed in the name of an altruistic motive. Has any act of selfishness ever equalled the carnage perpetrated by disciples of altruism?" 12
Ayn Rand

Altruism is incompatible with freedom, with capitalism and with individual rights. One cannot combine the pursuit of happiness with the moral status of a sacrificial animal.... Altruism holds *death* as its ultimate goal and standard of value.... If civilization is to survive, it is the altruistic morality that men have to reject. 13 *Ayn Rand*

"Selflessness" has no value either in heaven or on earth. All great problems demand *great love*, and of that only strong, round, secure spirits who have a firm grip on themselves are capable. 14
Friedrich Nietzsche

As the degree of dependence of [an] other person increased, men became less altruistic and women much more so. 15 *Derek Wright*

[A]ll altruistic conduct has its root and origin in the maternal instinct. 16
William McDougall

Altruism comes ... *if the child is not taught to be unselfish*. It probably never comes at all if the child has been forced to be unselfish. By suppressing the child's selfishness, the mother is fixing that selfishness forever. 17
A. S. Neill

As a rule, the altruization of an individual is possible only through the altruization of his groups or institutions.... [T]he family ... has been the most efficient agency in human altruization. 18 *Pitirim Sorokin*

The most basic social problems of modern society arise from a fundamental mismatch between the large size of the present social environment and the limited range of human altruistic social motivations. 19
George E. Pugh

We sanctify true altruism in order to reward it and thus to make it less than true, and by that means to promote its recurrence in others. 20
E. O. Wilson

[A]ltruism is an *essential* part of the nature of evolution. Evolution would have long ago come to a halt if it were not endowed with altruism as its *modus operandi*. 21
Henryk Skolimowski

[I]n order for altruistic behavior to evolve, the net risk to the altruist must be less than the net benefit to the recipient multiplied by the relatedness. 22 *Richard Dawkins*

The evolution of society fits the Darwinian paradigm.... No hint of genuine charity ameliorates our vision of society, once sentimentalism has been laid aside. What passes for cooperation turns out to be a mixture of opportunism and exploitation.... Scratch an altruist and watch a hypocrite bleed. 23
Michael Ghiselin

Altruism / Sacrifice

[A]ccounting for the altruism of moral behavior in genetically selfish terms ... can be done by interpreting moral systems as systems of indirect reciprocity.... [I]t can pay to give the impression of being an altruist even if you are not. 24 *Richard Alexander*

The theory of group selection has taken most of the good will out of altruism. When altruism is conceived as the mechanism by which DNA multiplies itself through a network of relatives, spirituality becomes just one more Darwinian enabling device. 25 *E. O. Wilson*

[O]nce population survival is recognized as the true criterion in terms of which the function of instinctive behaviour is measured, some old-standing problems evaporate.... Whether classified as "egotistic" or as "altruistic" the ultimate function is the same. This means that altruistic behaviour springs from roots just as deep as does egotistic, and that the distinction between the two, though real, is far from fundamental. 26 *John Bowlby*

[E]ven if we look on the dark side and assume that man is fundamentally selfish ... [we] have the power to defy the selfish genes of our birth.... We can even discuss ways of deliberately cultivating and nurturing pure, disinterested altruism—something that has no place in nature, something that has never existed before in the whole history of the world. 27
Richard Dawkins

In the absence of competition between tribes the survival value of altruism in a crowded world approaches zero because what ego gives up necessarily goes into the commons.... So if we desire a world in which altruism can persist we must reject the ideal of One World.... 28
Garrett Hardin

Really voluntary work is not fundamentally about generalized good will. It's about individual and continuing effort. It's about doing something one's self. 29 *Margaret Thatcher*

All the members of human society stand in need of each other's assistance.... Where the necessary assistance is reciprocally afforded from love, from gratitude, from friendship and esteem, the society flourishes and is happy. 30
Adam Smith

From our study of the private market in blood in the United States we have concluded that the commercialization of blood and donor relationships represses the expression of altruism, erodes the sense of community.... 31
Richard Titmuss

The value of a man ... should be seen in what he gives and not in what he is able to receive. 32
Albert Einstein

[W]e receive but what we give.... 33
Samuel Taylor Coleridge

Giving is more joyous than receiving ... because in the act of giving lies the expression of my aliveness. 34 *Erich Fromm*

It is more blessed to give than to receive. 35
Jesus Christ

You are good when you strive to give of yourself. 36 *Kahlil Gibran*

[T]he integrity of personality is far better preserved by the faith of self-giving than the shattering anxiety of self-preservation. 37
Alan Watts

What denies both the individual and his natural egotism is what constructs a person. 38
Denis de Rougemont

Agape is a love that loves to give, freely, selflessly.... Agape means the death, not of the self, but of selfishness; it is the antithesis, not of selfhood, but of self-centredness, which is the deadliest enemy of true selfhood. Man realizes his true self in so far as he lives by and in Agape. 39 *Anders Nygren*

Sacrifice signifies neither amputation nor repentance.... It is the gift of oneself to the being of which one forms part. 40
Antoine de Saint-Exupéry

[Our] civilization ... has forgotten [that a] man's life should be sacrificial, that is, offered up to an idea greater than man. 41 *Carl Jung*

Altruism / Sacrifice

Animal Liberation will require greater altruism on the part of human beings than any other liberation movement.... Will our tyranny continue?... Or will we rise to the challenge and prove our capacity for genuine altruism by ending our ruthless exploitation of the species in our power, not because we are forced to ... but because we recognize that our position is morally indefensible? 42 *Peter Singer*

Anxiety / Fear Neurosis

Man's quest to avoid anxiety not only explains much about motivation; it explains almost everything. 1 *Ernest Becker*

Anxiety seems to be the dominant fact ... of modern life ... [which] is almost universally regarded as the Age of Anxiety.... It speaks of man's dreaded loss of identity, of a desperate need to make contact with his fellow man, with the world and with whatever may be beyond the world. Above all, it speaks of God gone silent. 2 *Time cover story*

[M]ay we not be justified in reaching the diagnosis that, under the influence of cultural urges, some civilizations, or some epochs of civilization—possibly the whole of mankind—has become "neurotic"? 3 *Sigmund Freud*

Ours ... is a generally neuroticizing civilization, in which most people are more or less emotionally disturbed because they are brought up to believe, and then to internalize and to keep reinfecting themselves with, arrant nonsense which must inevitably lead them to become ineffective, self-defeating, and unhappy. 4 *Albert Ellis*

The amount of energy that is wasted in consequence of unresolved neurotic conflicts is unfathomably great. Since neuroses are ultimately a product of the particular civilization, such a thwarting of human gifts and qualities stands as a serious indictment of the culture in question. 5 *Karen Horney*

[It was] once found that neurotic anxiety was a good predictor of success and achievement, both for individuals and for nations, thus confirming a long-felt suspicion that something sick forms the driving force for our civilization. 6 *Philip Slater*

Foreign commentators have often remarked that America seems to be one vast mental hospital.... 7 *Max Lerner*

The American culture is an insane asylum. 8 *Timothy Leary*

Psychosis is the final outcome of all that is wrong with a culture. 9 *Jules Henry*

If it is true that every civilization has its characteristic culture style and social structure, it will also have its characteristic pattern of neuroses.... The neurotic-personality–as–American may feel caught in the conflict between the stated ideals and operative drives of his society. Because of this gap he may feel guilty, anxious, and insecure, and may seek to build himself up in the mirror of other people, or may seek the elusive inner security in the feverish effort to achieve money, power, and an outer security. 10 *Max Lerner*

Men have gained control over the forces of nature to such an extent that with their help they would have no difficulty in exterminating one another to the last man. They know this, and hence comes a large part of their current unrest, their unhappiness, and their mood of anxiety. 11 *Sigmund Freud*

But the driving force in human minds is fear, which begets an imperious demand for security in the world's confusion: a demand for a world-picture that fills all experience and gives each individual a definite *orientation* amid the terrifying forces of nature and society. 12 *Susanne Langer*

Man's fears are fashioned out of the ways in which he perceives the world.... Reality and fear go together naturally. 13 *Ernest Becker*

Our civilization is held together by fear rather than by good will. 14 *Harold Laski*

Fear is the basis of the whole thing—fear of

Anxiety / Fear / Neurosis

the mysterious, fear of defeat, fear of death. Fear is the parent of cruelty, and therefore it is no wonder if cruelty and religion go hand–in–hand. 15 *Bertrand Russell*

A man's life is the story of his fears. 16 *A. S. Neill*

Anxiety is a flood of utter chaos, of annihilating destruction. 17 *Ernest Becker*

A neurosis is the result of a conflict between the ego and the id; the person is at war with himself. A psychosis is the outcome of a similar disturbance in the relation between the ego and the outside world. 18 *Sigmund Freud*

Fear is always egoistic.... Fear must be egoistic, for every fear is ultimately a fear of death. 19 *A. S. Neill*

True neuroses ... are best defined as stubborn self-centeredness. 20 *Gordon W. Allport*

Neurosis is ... nothing less than an individual attempt, however unsuccessful, to solve a universal problem. 21 *Carl Jung*

[T]he three basic types of fear [are]: the fears of abandonment, of engulfment, and of nonbeing.... Almost all of man's constructive and destructive efforts ... derive from his efforts to cope with anxiety ... as part of his desperate search for emotional security. 22 *Reuven Bar-Levav*

The scars left from the child's defeat in the fight against irrational authority are to be found at the bottom of every neurosis. 23 *Erich Fromm*

A tendency to react with fear ... [is] present throughout the whole span of life.... Whether a child or adult is in a state of security, anxiety, or distress is determined in large part by the accessibility and responsiveness of his principal attachment figure.... [C]hildren who have been well mothered, and therefore, in all likelihood, have been protected from the experience of both intense distress and of intense fear, are those least susceptible to respond with fear to situations of all kinds.... 24 *John Bowlby*

The primary ties offer security and basic unity with the world.... [Therefore one] aspect of the process of individuation is [a] growing aloneness ... [which is] often threatening and dangerous.... This separation ... creates a feeling of powerlessness and anxiety. 25 *Erich Fromm*

[T]he main prerequisite of healthy growth is gratification of the basic needs, especially in early life. Neurosis is very often a deficiency disease.... 26 *Abraham Maslow*

Missing someone who is loved and longed for ... [is] the key to an understanding of anxiety. 27 *Sigmund Freud*

Driving neurosis is ... the need to be loved. 28 *Arthur Janov*

Fears are all related to and derived from early experiences of helplessness. That is why it is so important to protect the young child from traumatic experiences. 29 *Calvin S. Hall*

[In unhealthy homes there is] an insidiously increasing, all-pervading feeling of being lonely and helpless in a hostile world.... Because of the fundamental role this attitude plays in neuroses I have given it a special designation: the basic anxiety; it is inseparably interwoven with a basic hostility. 30 *Karen Horney*

The fading of a durable, common, public world ... intensifies the fear of separation at the same time that it weakens the psychological resources that make it possible to confront this fear realistically. It has freed the imagination from external constraints but exposed it more directly than before to the tyranny of inner compulsions and anxieties. The inescapable facts of separation and death are bearable only because the reassuring world of man-made objects and human culture restores the sense of one's connection.... When that world loses its reality, the fear of separation becomes almost overwhelming and the need for illusions, accordingly, more intense than ever. 31 *Christopher Lasch*

Neurosis separates the individual from his fellows and connects him with his own infantile images. 32 *Géza Róheim*

Anxiety / Fear / Neurosis

The other-directed person is cosmopolitan. For him the border between the familiar and the strange ... has broken down.... As against guilt-and-shame controls ... one prime psychological lever of the other-directed person is a diffuse *anxiety*. This control equipment ... is like a radar. 33
David Riesman

It is by evading anxiety that we convert it, unawares, to neurotic forms, which return to haunt us. 34 *Charles Hampden-Turner*

It seems, then, that these "good," "nice" scientific words—prediction, control ... orderliness, lawfulness, quantification, proof ... rationality, organization etc.—all are capable of being ... primarily anxiety-avoiding and anxiety-controlling mechanisms ... for detoxifying a chaotic and frightening world.... 35
Abraham Maslow

Information anxiety is produced by the ever-widening gap between what we understand and what we think we should understand.... It happens when information doesn't tell us what we want or need to know. 36 *Richard Saul Wurman*

If you overload an environment with novelty, you get the equivalent of anxiety neurotics—people who have their systems continually flooded with adrenaline. 37 *Ardie Lubin*

Neurosis is frozen Pain. 38 *Arthur Janov*

Neurosis is a substitute for legitimate suffering. 39 *Carl Jung*

Neurosis ... is illogical behavior by a potentially logical individual. 40 *Albert Ellis*

[M]en are consumed by the silent fear of other men. 41 *Phyllis Chesler*

Scapegoats are often used to give a group cohesion.... Politicians arouse both fear of enemies and fear of chaos—for order gives us orientation and with it security.... Establishing a bond through fear is ... a strategy for tyrants. 42
Irenäus Eibl-Eibesfeldt

Fear is the foundation of most governments. 43
John Adams

Fear of one's neighbors, one's friends and even one's relatives seems to be the rule within all mass movements.... The true believer is eternally incomplete, eternally insecure. 44
Eric Hoffer

In general it can be stated that those who strive passionately for power and prestige are unconsciously frightened persons trying to overcome and to deny their anxiety. 45 *Otto Fenichel*

Fear is sometimes defined as the anticipation of evil. 46 *Aristotle*

Anxiety leads us to the door; fear opens the door and makes us look at the abyss where death meets life. 47 *Karl König*

Anxiety may be the tension exhibited by the organized concept of the self when these "subceptions" indicate that the symbolization of certain experiences would be destructive of the organization. 48 *Carl Rogers*

Neurosis ... both saves and kills. It protects the real self from further disintegration, but in doing so, it buries the real self. 49 *Arthur Janov*

Anxiety strikes at the very "core" of ourselves: it is what we feel when our existence as selves is threatened. 50 *Rollo May*

Anxiety is the experience of the threat of imminent *non-being*. 51 *Rollo May*

The first assertion about the nature of anxiety is this: anxiety is the state in which a being is aware of its possible nonbeing. 52 *Paul Tillich*

Neurosis is the way of avoiding nonbeing by avoiding being. 53 *Paul Tillich*

That which fear fears *about* is that very entity which is afraid—Dasein. Only an entity for which in its Being this very Being is an issue, can be afraid. Fearing discloses this entity as endangered and abandoned to itself. 54
Martin Heidegger

Anxiety makes manifest in Dasein its *Being towards* its ownmost potentiality-for-Being—that is, its *Being-free for* the freedom of

choosing itself and taking hold of itself. 55
Martin Heidegger

Neurosis is an inner cleavage—the state of being at war with oneself.... Healing may be called a religious problem. 56 *Carl Jung*

Neurosis itself is, in the final analysis, a symptom of moral failure. 57 *Erich Fromm*

Even if permanent fear constitutes a latent state only, so that its painful effects are only rarely experienced directly, it remains always a disease. It is a semi-paralysis of the soul. 58 *Simone Weil*

From birth on, anxiety lives in every human being.... It is a mist rising in our soul, a haze covering the horizon and gradually filling the whole land.... Darkness envelops us; we are cut off from other beings.... Out of the depths of the unconscious it overtakes us and we become its slave. 59 *Karl König*

No passion so effectively robs the mind of all its powers of acting and reasoning as fear. 60
Edmund Burke

Fear, irrational and capricious ... is epidemic among women today. Fear of being independent.... It has been built up over long years by social conditioning.... Women will not become free until they stop being afraid ... until we begin the process—almost a de-brainwashing—of working through the anxieties that prevent us from feeling competent and whole. 61
Colette Dowling

Every neurosis is the result of a conflict between man's inherent powers and those forces which block their development. 62 *Erich Fromm*

The first duty of man is that of subduing fear. We must get rid of fear; we cannot act at all till then. 63 *Thomas Carlyle*

The only thing we have to fear is fear itself. 64
Franklin D. Roosevelt

A man shall and must be valiant.... Now and always, the completeness of his victory over Fear will determine how much of a man he is. 65
Thomas Carlyle

I do not wish to suggest that absence of fear is alone enough to produce a good human being.... But I do suggest that freedom from fear is *one* of the most important things to aim at. ... 66 *Bertrand Russell*

[A]s long as man is an ambiguous creature he can never banish anxiety; what he can do instead is to use anxiety as an eternal spring for growth into new dimensions of thought and trust. Faith poses a new life task, the adventure in openness to a multi-dimensional reality. 67
Ernest Becker

Everything great in the world comes from neurotics. They alone have founded our religions and composed our masterpieces. Never will the world know all it owes to them nor all they have suffered to enrich us. 68 *Marcel Proust*

The person who gives in eagerly to the distorting forces in his culture, i.e., the well-adjusted man, may be less healthy than the delinquent, the criminal, the neurotic who may be demonstrating by his reactions that he has spunk enough left to resist the breaking of his psychological bones. 69 *Abraham Maslow*

[N]eurosis represents the striving for an "individual religion," a self-achieved immortality.... There is no embracing world-view for the neurotic to depend on or to merge with ... so the "cure" for neurosis is difficult in our time. 70
Ernest Becker

[N]eurosis reaches its peak not when biological survival but rather when the symbolic superstructure is at stake. When life becomes intolerably dull, void, and meaningless—what can a person do but develop a neurosis? 71
Ludwig von Bertalanffy

In every case ... fear is a cerebral interpretation of reality.... Knowledge of intracerebral mechanisms of anxiety and fear will permit the establishment of a more rational pharmacological and psychiatric treatment of many suffering patients, and may also help us to understand and ameliorate the increasing level of anxiety in our civilization. 72 *José Delgado*

Art

Art is action which transcending the body makes the world a more congenial stimulus to the soul. 1 *George Santayana*

[The] fertilisation of the soul is the reason for the necessity of art.... It transforms the soul into the permanent realisation of values extending beyond its former self. 2 *Alfred N. Whitehead*

[A]rt has been, and still is, the essential instrument in the development of human consciousness. 3 *Herbert Read*

All art is concerned with coming into being. 4 *Aristotle*

[T]o see through the fragments of time to the full power of original being—that is a function of art. 5 *Joseph Campbell*

[A]rt is essentially the affirmation, the blessing, and the deification of existence. 6 *Friedrich Nietzsche*

Art is an attempt to transport into a limited quantity of matter, modelled by man, an image of the infinite beauty of the entire universe. 7 *Simone Weil*

Art always serves beauty.... 8 *Boris Pasternak*

The first act of awe when man was struck with the beauty or wonder of nature was the first spiritual experience.... All great art, in its creation and in its reception, is a living expression of human spirituality. 9 *Henryk Skolimowski*

[A]ll art belongs to the life of the spirit, though its greatness is derived from its being also intimately bound up with the life of instinct. 10 *Bertrand Russell*

We are alive or dead to the eternal inner message of the arts according as we have kept or lost [our] mystical susceptibility. 11 *William James*

The canons of art are merely the expression, in specialized forms, of the requisites for depth of experience. 12 *Alfred N. Whitehead*

In short, the history of human experience is a history of the development of arts. 13 *John Dewey*

We need art ... to help explain life to us, to show us meanings, to illuminate the relationship between the life that each of us embodies and the life around us. We need art most, perhaps, to reassure us of our own humanity. 14 *Jane Jacobs*

[T]he function of art is to make life better. 15 *George Santayana*

[A]rt gives us the highest pleasure, perhaps the most durable and intense pleasure of which human nature is capable. 16 *Ernst Cassirer*

Only in art does it still happen that a man who is consumed by desires performs something resembling the accomplishment of those desires.... 17 *Sigmund Freud*

Art challenges the prevailing principle of reason: ... it invokes a tabooed logic—the logic of gratification as against that of repression. Behind the sublimated aesthetic form, the unsublimated content shows forth: the commitment of art to the pleasure principle. 18 *Herbert Marcuse*

[T]he works of art and literature that still express without compromise the fears and hopes of humanity stand against the prevailing reality principle: they are its absolute denunciation. 19 *Herbert Marcuse*

[A]rt is not the mere reproduction of a ready-made, given reality ... but a discovery of reality.... Language and science are abbreviations of reality; art is an intensification of reality. 20 *Ernst Cassirer*

The highest mission of all art is to project a pretended semblance of a higher reality. 21 *Goethe*

[A]rt is a means of seeing truth that cannot be observed directly.... 22 *Katherine Paterson*

Art survives only where it cancels itself, where it saves its substance by denying its traditional

form and thereby denying reconciliation: where it becomes surrealistic and atonal. Otherwise, art shares the fate of all genuine human communication: it dies off. 23
Herbert Marcuse

For all art is a process of making the world a different place in which to live, and involves a phase of protest.... It is owing to frustration in communication of meanings that the protest becomes arbitrary.... 24 *John Dewey*

[A]rt has ... magic power only as the power of negation. It can speak its own language only as long as the images are alive which refuse and refute the established order. 25 *Herbert Marcuse*

The artist is the man who refuses initiation through education into the existing order, remains faithful to his own childhood, and thus becomes "a human being in the spirit of all times." 26 *Norman O. Brown*

Art, if its object is to undo repressions, and if civilization is essentially repressions, is in this sense subversive of civilization. 27
Norman O. Brown

Societies that have been conventionally virtuous have not produced great art.... Art in the past has had a popular basis, and this has depended upon joy of life. 28 *Bertrand Russell*

Traditional modernism sought to substitute for religion or morality an aesthetic justification of life; to create a work of art, to be a work of art—this alone provided meaning in man's effort to transcend himself.... Today modernism is exhausted. There is no tension. The creative impulses have gone slack. It has become an empty vessel. The impulse to rebellion has been institutionalized by the "cultural mass" and its experimental forms have become the syntax and semiotics of advertising and haute couture. 29 *Daniel Bell*

Post-modernism overflows the vessels of art. It tears down the boundaries and insists that *acting out*, rather than making distinctions, is the way to gain knowledge.... [A]gainst the aesthetic justification for life, post-modernism has completely substituted the instinctual. Impulse and pleasure alone are real and life-affirming; all else is neurosis and death.... [T]he autonomy of culture, achieved in art, now begins to pass over into the arena of life.... Anything permitted in art is permitted in life as well. 30 *Daniel Bell*

Modern art has moved ... towards the exploration of increasingly radical negations.... It regards easiness as vulgar and intelligibility as dishonest. Fragmentation alone can then be trusted; only an aggregate of fragments can carry a meaning that is wholly ineffable and protected thereby against self-doubt. 31
Michael Polanyi

Art can be described as a psychopathic reaction of the race to the stresses of its existence. 32
Alfred N. Whitehead

What society requires from art ... is that it function as an early warning system. 33
Elizabeth Janeway

If art is the barometer of a society, then madness in the realm of art portends certain existential consequences. 34 *Leonard Peikoff*

The creators of modern art have been able to see the meaninglessness of our existence; they participated in its despair. At the same time they have had the courage to face it.... They had the courage to be as themselves. 35 *Paul Tillich*

[N]eurotic conflicts ... may at best mobilize a temporary incentive, but the creative urge itself and the creative power can stem only from [a] desire for self-realization.... *An artist then creates not because of his neurosis but in spite of it.* 36
Karen Horney

Arguments with one's self make art. 37
Camille Paglia

Indeed, the works of an artist are the outward and visible signs of his inner development as a person. 38 *Anthony Storr*

Outside art, the numinous experience is not ordinarily available to modern men of culture. In this sense, all great art is therapeutic. 39
Philip Rieff

Art

In compensation, and in place of where faith once was, men are offered Art.... Confronted thus with a picture gallery as the new center of self-worship, civilized men must become again anti-art, in the hope of shifting attention toward modalities of worship wholly other than that of self. 40 *Philip Rieff*

Art is a lie that makes us realize truth. 41 *Pablo Picasso*

Truth is ugly.... We have art in order not to perish of truth. 42 *Friedrich Nietzsche*

Ugliness is the contradiction of art. 43 *Friedrich Nietzsche*

[T]he transformation of a natural object ... to an object of art is closely related to our impact on matter. Artistic activity breaks the temporal symmetry of the object. It leaves a mark that translates our temporal dissymmetry into the temporal dissymmetry of the object. 44 *Ilya Prigogine*

Any operation which ... humanizes and rationalizes objects is called art. Of all reason's embodiments art is therefore the most splendid and complete. 45 *George Santayana*

Art is ... pattern informed by sensibility. 46 *Herbert Read*

Art is the imposing of a pattern on experience, and our aesthetic enjoyment is recognition of the pattern. 47 *Alfred N. Whitehead*

Art means "the skillful realization of humanly satisfying or challenging special case applications of the theoretical schemes of applied science." 48 *R. Buckminster Fuller*

[A]rt lies half-way between scientific knowledge and mythical or magical thought. 49 *Claude Lévi-Strauss*

[A]mong many primitive tribes decorative art for its own sake does not exist.... Among primitive people the aesthetic motive is combined with the symbolic, while in modern life the aesthetic motive is either quite independent or associated with utilitarian ideas. 50 *Franz Boas*

[P]rimitive art is the opposite of professional or academic art. Professional or academic art internalizes execution (which it ... believes itself to have mastered) and purpose.... As a result, it is impelled to externalize the occasion.... Primitive art, on the other hand, internalizes the occasion (since the supernatural beings which it delights in representing have a reality which is timeless...) and it externalizes execution and purpose.... 51 *Claude Lévi-Strauss*

The functional context of art in band societies is religious ritual; the forms of art are limited in kind, and the aim is control.... [T]he style or pattern must be followed exactly simply because it is ritualized—any deviation breaks the spell just as surely as it does in an act of magic or sorcery. 52 *E. R. Service*

Art is a *shutting in* in order to *shut out*. Art is a ritualistic binding of the perpetual motion machine that is nature. 53 *Camille Paglia*

The process of artistic creation is the prototype of synthetic solution.... Such a tendency toward "order" is inherent in every work of art, even when its content or intent represents "disorder." This is, then, another case of "regressive adaptation": a mental achievement (whose roots are archaic) gains a new significance both for synthesis and in relation to the external world, precisely because of the detour through the archaic. 54 *Heinz Hartmann*

Art is form struggling to wake from the nightmare of nature. 55 *Camille Paglia*

I feel that art has something to do with the achievement of stillness in the midst of chaos. A stillness which ... has something to do with an arrest of attention in the midst of distraction. 56 *Saul Bellow*

The artists's voice owes its power to the fact that it arises from a pregnant solitude that conjures up the universe so as to impose on it a human accent.... 57 *André Malraux*

Art is the revelation of man; and ... the revelation of nature, speaking through man. 58 *Henry Wadsworth Longfellow*

Art

At bottom nature and a true artist agree. 59
Vincent van Gogh

[A]rt is simply nature unravelling its potentialities, both in the world and in the mind, and unravelling them together, in so far as they are harmonious in the two spheres. 60
George Santayana

In art we can recover something of the harmony of the universe. 61 *Katherine Paterson*

In esthetic and symbolic terms, it is our present culture that has become painfully uninventive.... The end products in painting and sculpture, at least those most exploitable commercially, are now deliberately degraded to a level far below the earliest paleolithic carvings. 62 *Lewis Mumford*

As soon as any art is pursued with a view to money, then farewell, in ninety-nine cases out of a hundred, all hope of genuine good work. 63
Samuel Butler

In art there are those who strive after novelty at all costs and have lost all interest in beauty.... 64
Kenneth Boulding

The artist appeals to the part of our being which is not dependent on wisdom; to that in us which is a gift and not an acquisition—and therefore, more permanently enduring. 65
Joseph Conrad

Most of the faint intimations of immortality of which we are occasionally aware would seem to arise out of Art.... 66 *James Thurber*

[M]ore than any other activity, art escapes death. 67 *André Malraux*

All art is a revolt against man's fate.... For every masterpiece, implicitly or openly, tells of a human victory over the blind forces of destiny. 68
André Malraux

Art is hope. 69 *Thomas Mann*

Art is the objectification of feeling, and the subjectification of nature. 70 *Susanne Langer*

Art is an organ of human life transmitting man's reasonable perception into feeling. 71
Leo Tolstoy

[T]he task of art is to transform not perception into feeling, but feeling into perception. 72
Herbert Read

Art does not reproduce the visible; rather, it makes visible. 73 *Paul Klee*

The arts give back only so much of nature as the human eye has been able to master. 74
George Santayana

It is not possible that any nature should be inferior to art, since all arts imitate nature. 75
Marcus Aurelius

Art supplies constantly to contemplation what nature seldom affords in concrete experience—the union of life and peace. 76 *George Santayana*

If happiness is the ultimate sanction of art, art in turn is the best instrument of happiness.... Thus the emergence of arts out of instincts is the token and exact measure of nature's success and of mortal happiness. 77 *George Santayana*

The essence then of true human art is that it should convey the emotions of one man to another.... [I]t is the medium through which men express their deep, real feelings. 78
D. H. Lawrence

[S]orrow, being the supreme emotion of which man is capable, is at once the type and test of all great art. What the artist is always looking for is the mode of existence in which soul and body are one and indivisible: in which the outward is expressive of the inward: in which form reveals. 79 *Oscar Wilde*

Art heightens the sense of humanity.... It requires Art to evoke into consciousness the finite perfections which lie ready for human achievement. 80 *Alfred N. Whitehead*

Music is the art ... which most completely realizes the artistic idea, and is the condition to which all the other arts are constantly aspiring. 81
Oscar Wilde

Art

Until art arises, all achievement is internal to the brain, dies with the individual, and even in him spends itself without recovery, like music heard in a drum. Art, in establishing instruments for human life beyond the human body, and moulding outer things into sympathy with inner values, establishes a ground whence values may continually spring up.... 82

George Santayana

What is to-day obvious to all is a decay in the essence of art.... Instead of effecting the liberation of the consciousness in contemplation of the being of Transcendence, it becomes a renunciation of the possibility of selfhood in which Transcendence can first disclose itself.... Art of this kind voices the opposition to man's true nature as man, in favour of an immediate and crude present.... To the extent that art has lapsed into this function, it has become unprincipled.... It necessarily lacks what used to be its unquestionable moral substance, the tie of intrinsic value. 83 *Karl Jaspers*

If art does not enlarge men's sympathies, it does nothing morally. 84 *George Eliot*

Art is the indispensable medium for the communication of a moral idea. 85 *Ayn Rand*

Art remains an avenue of escape from morality. 86 *Camille Paglia*

All art is immoral. 87 *Oscar Wilde*

Art has nothing to do with morality.... The artist makes art not to save humankind but to save himself. 88 *Camille Paglia*

The task which the artist implicitly sets himself is ... to make of the chaos about him an order which is his own.... 89 *Henry Miller*

As manipulators of the mass market tyrannized over the artist, the artist in isolation achieved a new clairvoyance concerning the crucial role of design and of art as a means to human order and fulfilment. 90 *Marshall McLuhan*

I see little of more importance to the future of ... civilization than full recognition of the place of the artist. If art is to nourish the roots of our culture, society must set the artist free to follow his vision wherever it takes him. 91

John F. Kennedy

Creation for the joy of creation is the aim of the artist, and that is why the artist is a more divine type than the saint. 92 *Oscar Wilde*

A gradual process extending over many centuries has succeeded in de-functionalizing art and making it more and more a free and independent occupation for individuals called artists.... Art became more intimate, but also more isolated; it became an affair of the individual and his taste. 93 *Johan Huizinga*

[I disagree with] the belief, held even by artists, that modern art has nothing to do with values.... For there *is* a fundamental value of modern art, and one that goes far deeper than a mere quest of the pleasure of the eye. Its annexation of the visible world ... stands for that immemorial impulse of creative art: the desire to build up a world apart and self-contained, existing in its own right: a desire which, for the first time in the history of art, has become the be-all and end-all of the artist. 94 *André Malraux*

There is in fact no such thing as art for art's sake, art that stands above classes, art that is detached from or independent of politics. 95

Mao Tse-tung

At the dawn of history, the arts were strictly functional; and functional for the community, not for the individual artist.... Art has [now] become an individual statement and, for the artist himself, a means whereby he can pursue his own self-realization. 96 *Anthony Storr*

A work of art has no importance whatever to society. It is only important to the individual. ... 97 *Vladimir Nabokov*

It is true that in late phases of civilization a desire to be artistic, or, individually, to be an artist, does exist, but by that time art is already decadent. 98 *Herbert Read*

[T]he end of history will mean the end ... of all art that could be considered socially useful.... 99 *Francis Fukuyama*

[W]hen life itself becomes fully conscious, art as we know it will vanish. Art is only a stopgap, an imperfect effort to wrest meaning from an environment where nearly everyone is sleepwalking. 100 *Marilyn Ferguson*

Art, so long as it needs to be a dream, will never cease to be a disappointment.... In the mere artist, too, there is always something that falls short of the gentleman and that defeats the man.... Art, like religion, needs to be absorbed in the Life of Reason. 101 *George Santayana*

Art and Religion are means to similar states of mind. 102 *Clive Bell*

Art ... is the soul of the past in the same sense that each ancient religion was a soul of the world. In times when man feels stranded and alone, it assures to its votaries that deep communion which would else have passed away with the passing of the gods. 103
André Malraux

Art, in its nobler acceptation, is an achievement, not an indulgence. It prepares the world in some sense to receive the soul, and the soul to master the world; it disentangles those threads in each that can be woven into the other. 104 *George Santayana*

[T]o be art and not merely propaganda [works] must have that deep connective quality that links soul to soul. 105 *Katherine Paterson*

What is essential in a work of art is that it should rise far above the realm of personal life and speak from the spirit and heart of mankind.... When a form of "art" is primarily personal it deserves to be treated as if it were a neurosis. 106 *Carl Jung*

A work of art is a public possession; it is addressed to the world. 107 *George Santayana*

To try to understand the real significance of what the great artists, the serious masters, tell us in their masterpieces, that leads to God. 108
Vincent van Gogh

Art is a step from nature toward the Infinite. 109
Kahlil Gibran

Authority

[W]e are born in need of authority.... 1
Otto Rank

[M]y analysis leads me to place my hopes for the long-term survival of man on his susceptibility to appeals to national identity and to his willingness to accept authority.... [A]uthoritarianism will be necessary to cope with the exigencies of the future.... 2 *Robert Heilbroner*

Without ties of loyalty, authority, and fraternity, no society as a whole, and none of its institutions, could long function.... [But the] dominant forms of authority in our lives are destructive; they lack nurturance ... [which is] a basic human need, as basic as eating or sex. Compassion, trust, reassurance are qualities it would be absurd to associate with these figures of authority in the adult world. 3
Richard Sennett

The nurturant, protective, benevolent side of social and parental authority no longer tempers its punitive side. 4 *Christopher Lasch*

[A] basically hierarchical, authoritarian, exploitive parent-child relationship is apt to carry over into a power-oriented, exploitively dependent attitude toward one's sex partner and one's God and may well culminate in a political philosophy and social outlook which has no room for anything but a desperate clinging to what appears to be strong and a disdainful rejection of whatever is relegated to the bottom. 5 *T. W. Adorno et al.*

The principle which ... [must be] the principle of the construction of our whole State constitution: Authority of every leader towards below, and responsibility towards above. 6
Adolf Hitler

We find that the highest achievement of the Fascist reform consists in having shorn the People of all power, and in having conferred this upon a central organ which in turn delegates its authority to secondary and derivative organs of control.... The true essence of the Fascist constitution of the state lies thus with the

Authority

derivation of authority from above rather than from below. 7 *Mario Palmieri*

Perhaps the biggest obstacle to the improvement of human relations is the amazing ease with which the human mind creates categories.... [T]he authoritarian personality is one that feels insecure and threatened; as a result, it creates safe little islands of self-esteem. Mental hierarchies are formed, with most groups standing below one's own. Human relations are regarded chiefly not in terms of love, but of power. 8 *Gordon W. Allport*

The convenient feature of authoritarians ... is not that they accept authority directly but that they accept some simple-minded way in which the world has been divided up for them into categories of people whose conflicting self-interests are major determinants of life as it has to be lived. 9 *Chris Brand*

Rational authority is based upon the equality of both authority and subject.... The source of *irrational authority*, on the other hand, is always power over people. 10 *Erich Fromm*

[W]ithout the application of the scientific method to social organisation the crucial problem of democracy, the problem of authority—how we can obviate the arbitrary exercise of one man's will over another—cannot be solved. 11 *Sidney & Beatrice Webb*

Experience tends universally to show that the purely bureaucratic type of administrative organization ... is from a purely technical point of view, capable of attaining the highest degree of efficiency and is in this sense formally the most rational known means of exercising authority over human beings.... The purest type of exercise of legal authority is that which employs a bureaucratic administrative staff. 12 *Max Weber*

Organizations as well as individuals can suffer from hallucinations. It is the peculiar disease of authoritarian structures. 13 *Kenneth Boulding*

When for the first time Engels and I joined the secret society of communists, we did so on the condition *sine qua non* that everything that could favour a culture of authority be banished from the statutes. 14 *Karl Marx*

The masses themselves want to be led and seek a firm leadership.... Of course, the fact that a group of leaders emerged among us who rose too high and had great authority—this fact is in itself a great achievement of our Party. It is clear that without such an authoritative group of leaders it is impossible to lead a great country. 15 *Joseph Stalin*

Crimes by constituted authorities are worse than crimes by Madame Tussaud's private malefactors. Murder may be done by legal means, by plausible and profitable war, by calumny, as well as by dose or dagger. 16 *Lord Acton*

[W]hat makes authoritarian leadership necessary is the irrational character structure of the human masses.... No freedom program has any chance of success without an alteration of human sexual structure. 17 *Wilhelm Reich*

Abolish sex repression and youth will be lost to authority. 18 *A. S. Neill*

Authority does not come primarily from authoritative men and their values, that is from outside; it comes from the need for obedience driving within.... [T]he swing of the family into mother domination caused enough of a shift in disposition to crack the pillars of authority that supported the sublimations of civilized guilt.... Sublimation is learned through obedience to the authority of the accomplished. 19 *John Carroll*

[T]he essential fact about paternal authority, the fact that makes both sexes accept it as a model for the ruling of the world, is that it is under prevailing conditions a sanctuary from maternal authority. 20 *Dorothy Dinnerstein*

[A]ny particular symbol [that takes] root in any particular person's mind ... is planted there by another human being whom we recognize as authoritative. If it is planted deeply enough, it may be that later we shall call the person authoritative who waves that symbol at us. 21 *Walter Lippmann*

Authority

An intellectual may be defined as a man who speaks with general authority about a subject on which he has no particular competence. 22
Irving Kristol

[It is] through an ideal of authority that the conservative experiences the political world. 23
Roger Scruton

[A]uthoritarian or conservative principles are usually an expression of ethical nihilism; that is to say, of an extreme moral scepticism, of a distrust of man and his potentialities. 24
Karl Popper

The weakening of authority throughout society ... contributes to the weakening of the authority of government.... In the United States, the government is constrained more by the shortage of authority than by the shortage of resources. 25 *Michel Crozier et al.*

[T]he *authority* of a President is even more important than his *power*, because it is the authority that shapes and decides what the power shall be.... If he has grasp, contagion, political artistry, and a mastery of his purposes and methods, then he will carry authority no matter what powers he claims or forsakes, and his authority will work magic to bolster the claims he stakes out. If, on the other hand, he ... fails to carry authority, then even a limited view of the Presidential power will get him into trouble.... 26 *Max Lerner*

Authority is power plus legitimacy. 27
Robert E. Lane

If the right persons make the law in the proper manner, then the law will be considered good or just. Thus authority combines the functions of furnishing both legitimacy, and certainty and stability of expectations. It is the concept of authority which furnishes the link between law and myth. The myth structure from which legal authority is derived must justify the existence of a social hierarchy.... It must justify the right of certain persons to command, and of others to obey, and it must do so in terms that make it clear that this is the natural order of things. 28 *J. C. Smith*

It would ... be nearer the truth if we inverted the plausible and widely held idea that law derives from authority and rather thought of all authority as deriving from law—not in the sense that the law appoints authority, but in the sense that authority commands obedience because (and so long as) it enforces a law presumed to exist independently of it and resting on a diffused opinion of what is right. 29
Friedrich von Hayek

[T]he basis of every authority, and correspondingly of every kind of willingness to obey, is a *belief*, a belief by virtue of which persons exercising authority are lent prestige. 30 *Max Weber*

Prestige buttresses power, turning it into authority, and protecting it from social challenge. 31
C. Wright Mills

Prestige is the mainspring of all authority. Neither gods, kings, nor women have ever reigned without it. 32 *Gustave Le Bon*

Authority doesn't work without prestige, or prestige without distance. 33
Charles de Gaulle

The most important political distinction developed by Western civilization is that between power and authority.... It is the blindness of Libertarians to the distinction between power and authority that keeps them from seeing the difference between a gunman and a policeman. 34 *Shirley Letwin*

Few people like authority unless they exercise it themselves. Objective authority is always a diminution of personality, a restriction on freedom of expression and a continual and implicit threat to personal integrity. The policeman is the personal embodiment of this authority. 35
Brian Chapman

Some dismiss the Nazi example because we live in a democracy and not an authoritarian state. But, in reality, this does not eliminate the problem. For the problem is ... authority itself. 36
Stanley Milgram

It is one of the few "laws" of human relations that not only those who suffer from arbitrary authority, but also those who wield it, become alienated from others and thus dehumanized. 37 *Thomas Szasz*

Civilization ... means, above all, an unwillingness to inflict unnecessary pain. Within the ambit of that definition, those of us who heedlessly accept the commands of authority cannot yet claim to be civilized men.... 38
Harold Laski

As soon as we abandon our own reason, and are content to rely upon authority, there is no end to our troubles. 39 *Bertrand Russell*

Every great advance in natural knowledge has involved the absolute rejection of authority. 40
T. H. Huxley

How can happiness be bestowed? My own answer is: *Abolish authority*. 41 *A. S. Neill*

Society no longer expects authority to articulate a clearly reasoned, elaboratively justified code of law and morality.... It demands only conformity to the conventions of everyday intercourse, sanctioned by psychiatric definitions of normal behavior. 42 *Christopher Lasch*

[A]uthority is not merely made by us at some definite moment of origin, but continues to be so made by being interwoven, at each stage of the process of government with our own activities. These represent the wants we know as we only can know them. Authority, otherwise, has no profound roots in the soil of our own existence. 43 *Harold Laski*

When the appeal to authority is used as a *sole* method of gaining ethical wisdom it can become a roadblock to progress; but when used in conjunction with current judgment and experience it provides a systematic mechanism by which the principles of social ethics can evolve to more accurately serve the needs of a society. 44 *George E. Pugh*

[T]he claim of authority is worth just as much as it proves itself to be worth.... 45
Harold Laski

BEAUTY

THE SOUL SEEKS nothing so much as contact with the beauty of the world.... 1
Simone Weil

Love is the love of beauty. 2 *Socrates*

The soul's natural inclination to love beauty is the trap God most frequently uses in order to win it and open it to the breath from on high. 3
Simone Weil

No reason can be asked or given why the soul seeks beauty.... [But the] world thus exists to the soul to satisfy the desire of beauty. This element I call an ultimate end. 4
Ralph Waldo Emerson

Only beauty is not the means to anything else. 5
Simone Weil

The beauty of the world is not an attribute of matter in itself. It is a relationship of the world to our sensibility, the sensibility which depends upon the structure of our body and our soul. 6
Simone Weil

[B]eauty is precisely the unity of the psychical and the corporal. 7 *Søren Kierkegaard*

Our ability to perceive quality in nature begins, as in art, with the pretty. It expands through successive stages of the beautiful to values as yet uncaptured by language. 8 *Aldo Leopold*

The Beautiful implies effects of unspeakableness, indescribableness. 9 *Valéry*

Beauty is unbearable ... offering us for a minute the glimpse of an eternity that we should like to stretch over the whole of time. 10
Albert Camus

Beauty is eternity here below. 11 *Simone Weil*

Beauty is eternity gazing at itself in a mirror. But you are eternity and you are the mirror. 12
Kahlil Gibran

If for a brief moment our spirit finds peace and

rest and assuagement in the contemplation of the beautiful, even though it finds therein no real cure for its distress, it is because the beautiful is the revelation of the eternal, of the divine in things. 13 *Miguel de Unamuno*

What is the beauty of anything but its eternal essence, that which unites its past with its future, that element of it that rests and abides in the womb of eternity? Or, rather, what is it but the revelation of its divinity? 14
Miguel de Unamuno

Beauty therefore seems to be the clearest manifestation of perfection, and the best evidence of its possibility. If perfection is ... the ultimate justification of being, we may understand the ground of the moral dignity of beauty. Beauty is a pledge of the possible conformity between the soul and nature, and consequently a ground of faith in the supremacy of the good. 15
George Santayana

[W]e love the beauty of the world, because we sense behind it the presence of something akin to that wisdom we should like to possess to slake our thirst for good. 16 *Simone Weil*

The highest expression of the emotional side of human nature is the attainment of the beautiful and the good.... 17 *Beatrice Webb*

That which is beautiful is moral. 18
Gustave Flaubert

[E]ach masterpiece of beauty morally ennobles and mentally enlightens the members of the human universe. 19 *Pitirim Sorokin*

A thing of beauty is a joy for ever: / Its loveliness increases; it will never / Pass into nothingness.... 20 *John Keats*

Genuine beauty, which fills the soul, is an indication of life, and genuine ugliness, which blasts the soul, is an indication of morbidity. 21
D. H. Lawrence

[T]he experience of great beauty tends to unify the self: the object engages us immediately and totally in a way that makes distinctions among points of view irrelevant. 22 *Thomas Nagel*

Youth is happy because it has the capacity to see Beauty. Anyone who keeps the ability to see Beauty never grows old. 23 *Franz Kafka*

A man's life is most worth living in the contemplation of beauty itself. 24 *Aristophanes*

The world is only empty to him who does not know how to direct his libido towards things and people, and to render them alive and beautiful. 25 *Carl Jung*

Too late came I to love thee, O thou Beauty.... And behold, thou wert within me. 26
Saint Augustine

The key difficulty in recognizing the beauty of the world these days is that such teaching is rooted in the act of looking at the world as it is, while the dominant science is rooted in the desire to change it. 27 *George Grant*

Remember that the most beautiful things in the world are the most useless. 28
John Ruskin

Beauty has no obvious use; nor is there any clear cultural necessity for it. Yet civilization could not do without it. 29 *Sigmund Freud*

In upholding beauty, we prepare the way for the day of regeneration when civilization will give first place ... [to the] living virtue on which is founded the common dignity of man and the world he lives in, and in which we must now define dignity in the face of a world that insults it. 30 *Albert Camus*

BELIEF

MAN ... is a being born to believe. 1
Benjamin Disraeli

The momentous story of man is that of the framer of beliefs.... Man's mind is born as naked as his body. His beliefs [function in] ... serving its needs and covering its nakedness. 2
Joseph Jastrow

[The] mind is a belief-seeking rather than a fact-seeking apparatus. 3 *Joseph Jastrow*

BELIEF

And what, then, is belief? It is the demi-cadence which closes a musical phrase in the symphony of our intellectual life. We have seen that it has just three properties: First, it is something that we are aware of; second, it appeases the irritation of doubt; and, third, it involves the establishment in our nature of a rule of action, or, say for short, a *habit*. 4 *Charles S. Peirce*

[T]he action of thought is excited by the irritation of doubt, and ceases when belief is attained; so that the production of belief is the sole function of thought. 5 *Charles S. Peirce*

Thought in movement has for its only conceivable motive the attainment of belief, or thought at rest. Only when our thought about a subject has found its rest in belief can our action on the subject firmly and safely begin. Beliefs, in short, are rules for action; and the whole function of thinking is but one step in the production of active habits. 6 *William James*

One crucial law of mind is that belief precedes knowledge. New knowledge does not come without a leap of hypothesis, a projection of the intuitive sense. 7 *George Gilder*

Beliefs stand at the end point of much of our cognitive activity. 8 *Michael Gazzaniga*

[T]he presence of beliefs in our species results from the way the human brain is constructed. With the appearance of left hemisphere systems that allow for the making of inference, an act that freed humans from the endless tedium of advancing by trial and error, the system was inextricably committed to the construction of human beliefs. Once beliefs were in place, the organism no longer lived only in the present. 9 *Michael Gazzaniga*

[A]ll belief-disbelief systems serve two powerful and conflicting sets of motives at the same time: the need for a cognitive framework to know and to understand and the need to ward off threatening aspects of reality.... A person will be open to information *insofar as possible*, and will reject it, screen it out, or alter it *insofar as necessary*. 10 *Milton Rokeach*

[B]eliefs serve the rationalization function of bridging illogicalities. The beliefs are thus ... regularly "biased," by which we mean that they are systematically twisted in the one direction which fits them best for purposes of rationalization. 11 *Gunnar Myrdal*

In a rationalistic civilization it is not only that the beliefs are shaped by the valuations, but also that the valuations depend upon the beliefs. 12 *Gunnar Myrdal*

[A] belief is rational if it best serves the believer's needs and values.... 13 *Mike W. Martin*

[I]ndividuals will organize their beliefs and behaviors in ways that will serve to maintain and enhance their self-conceptions as moral and competent human beings. 14 *Milton Rokeach & J. Grube*

For what a man would like to be true, that he more readily believes. 15 *Francis Bacon*

The basic tenet of ... fundamentalist Christianity, is that we have one document on which we predicate everything we believe ... not only in matters of theology, but science, geography, history, etc.—totally and entirely, the very word of God. 16 *Rev. Jerry Falwell*

[T]he belief system ... confers upon the self a quality of "confirmation" as a member of the "elect"—a secular grace associated with ultimate truth, ultimate psychic power. 17 *Robert Jay Lifton*

The ego keeps its integrity only if it does not identify with one of the opposites, and if it understands how to hold the balance between them.... However, the necessary insight is made exceedingly difficult not only by one's social and political leaders alone, but also by one's religious mentors. They all want decision in favor of one thing, and therefore the identification of the individual with a necessarily one-sided "truth." Even if it were a question of some great truth it would still be a catastrophe, as it arrests all further spiritual development. Instead of knowledge one has only belief. 18 *Carl Jung*

Belief is the seed, received into the will, of

which the Understanding or Knowledge is the Flower, and the thing believed is the fruit. Unless ye believe ye cannot understand: and unless ye be humble as children, ye not only *will* not, but ye *can*not believe. 19

Samuel Taylor Coleridge

The believer does not seek to understand that he may believe, but he believes so that he may understand. For unless he first believes, he shall not understand. 20 *Saint Anselm*

[T]o believe is precisely to lose one's understanding in order to win God. 21

Søren Kierkegaard

[The] only people who ... feel safe are people with belief. 22 *John Irving*

It is startling to realize how much unbelief is necessary to make belief possible.... It is the true believer's ability to "shut his eyes and stop his ears" to facts that do not deserve to be either seen or heard which is the source of his unequaled fortitude and constancy. 23

Eric Hoffer

The true believer is eternally incomplete, eternally insecure. 24 *Eric Hoffer*

The man of belief is necessarily a dependent man.... He does not belong to himself, but to the author of the idea he believes. 25

Friedrich Nietzsche

The natural disposition is always to believe.... It is, perhaps, the instinct upon which is founded the faculty of speech ... [necessary in] leading and directing the judgments and conduct of other people. 26 *Adam Smith*

[T]he more open the belief system, the more should the person be governed in his actions by internal self-actualizing forces and the less by irrational inner forces. Consequently, the more should he be able to resist pressures exerted by external sources to evaluate and to act in accord with their wishes.... Conversely, the more closed the belief system, the more difficult should it be to distinguish between information received about the world and information received about the source. 27 *Milton Rokeach*

No real belief, however trifling and fragmentary it may seem, is ever truly insignificant; it prepares us to receive more of its like, confirms those which resembled it before, and weakens others; and so gradually it lays a stealthy train in our inmost thoughts, which may someday explode into overt action, and leave its stamp upon our character forever. And no man's beliefs is in any case a private matter.... Belief, that sacred faculty which prompts the decisions of our will, and knits into harmonious working all the compacted energies of our being, is ours not for ourselves, but for humanity. It is rightly used on truths which have been established by long experience.... Then it helps to bind men together, and to strengthen and direct their common action. It is desecrated when given to unproved and unquestioned statements, for the solace and private pleasure of the believer.... [Therefore] it is wrong always, everywhere, and for any one, to believe anything upon insufficient evidence. 28

William Clifford

For everybody ... it is more important that a statement be believable than that it be true.... The advertising world can never collapse so long as believability remains the test. 29

Daniel J. Boorstin

[P]eople act in certain ways because they *believe* that they should or must act in these ways.... The main problem of effective living, then, would seem to be not that of eradicating people's beliefs, but of changing them so that they become more closely rooted to information and to reason. This can be done, says the rational therapist, by getting people to examine, to question, to think about their beliefs, and thereby to develop a more consistent, fact-based, and workable set of constructs than they now may possess. 30 *Albert Ellis*

Complete rationality of action ... demands complete knowledge of all the relevant facts.... But the success of action in society depends on more particular facts than any one can possibly know. And our whole civilization in consequence rests, and must rest, on our *believing* much that we cannot *know* to be true. 31

Friedrich von Hayek

Belief

Innocently, we had trusted that we could be relieved of all personal responsibility for our beliefs by objective criteria of validity—and our own critical powers have shattered this hope. Struck by our own sudden nakedness, we may try to brazen it out by flaunting in it a profession of nihilism. But modern man's immorality is unstable. Presently his moral passions reassert themselves in objectivist disguise and the scientistic Minotaur is born. The alternative to this ... is to restore to us once more the power for the deliberate holding of unproven beliefs. 32 *Michael Polanyi*

We must now recognize belief once more as the source of all knowledge. Tacit assent and intellectual passions, the sharing of an idiom and of a cultural heritage, affiliation to a like-minded community; such are the impulses which shape our vision of the nature of things on which we rely for our mastery of things. No intelligence, however critical or original, can operate outside such a fiduciary framework. 33
Michael Polanyi

All the evidence ... supports [this] conclusion—that false beliefs result in evil and that true beliefs have fruits that are good. What we think determines what we are and do.... We see then that through ethics, all the activities of individuals and societies are related to their fundamental beliefs about the nature of the world. 34 *Aldous Huxley*

The great generalized beliefs are very restricted in number. Their rise and fall form the culminating points of the history of every historic race. They constitute the real framework of civilization. 35 *Gustave Le Bon*

General beliefs are the indispensable pillars of civilizations; they determine the trend of ideas. They alone are capable of inspiring faith and creating a sense of duty.... The weakening of general beliefs clears the ground for a crop of haphazard opinions without a past or a future. 36
Gustave Le Bon

The beginning of a revolution is in reality the end of a belief. 37 *Gustave Le Bon*

[M]en become civilized, not in proportion to their willingness to believe, but in proportion to their readiness to doubt. 38 *H. L. Mencken*

In education you can hand on to the child the beliefs that have meaning for yourself and that belong to the small cultural or religious area that you happen to be born into. But you will have success only in so far as the child has a capacity to believe in anything at all. 39 *D. W. Winnicott*

Nobody really believes in anything anymore, and everyone spends his life in frenzied work and frenzied play so as not to face the fact, not to look into the abyss. 40 *Allan Bloom*

Absolute certainty and absolute doubt are both alike forbidden to us. We hover in a vague mean between these two extremes, as between being and nothingness.... But it is not given to man to annihilate himself; there is in him something which invincibly resists destruction.... Whether he likes it or not, he must believe, because he must act, because he must preserve himself. 41
Miguel de Unamuno

Belief remains a fundamental social condition, nor is the will to belief erased, even as mankind loses a belief in gods.... [Our] beliefs become more and more centered on the immediate life of man himself, and his experiences as a definition of all that he can believe in. 42
Richard Sennett

We need to face one fact squarely: *What the future could hold, and what each of us could become, is limited mainly by what we believe.* 43
Gloria Steinem

If we succeed, it will ... [be] because of what we believe. For we are a nation of believers.... [W]e are believers in justice and liberty and union, and in our own Union. We believe that every man must someday be free. And we believe in ourselves.... For this is what America is all about. 44 *Lyndon B. Johnson*

Bonding

Man wins destiny only through ties: not through coercive ties imposed on him as an impotent creature by great forces that lie without;

Bonding

but by ties freely comprehended which he makes his own. Such ties hold his life together, so that it is not frittered away but becomes the actuality of his possible existence. 1
Karl Jaspers

Man's characteristic privilege is that the bond he accepts is not physical but moral; that is, social.... Because the greater, better part of his existence transcends the body, he escapes the body's yoke, but is subject to that of society. 2
Émile Durkheim

[W]hen guilty I see myself as a moral debtor in having broken the promise implicit in my membership in the human community or explicit in some particular relationship. I know that this breaking of the bond between myself and the other is a wrong which confers on the other a right, possibly to punish, certainly to judge. 3 *Merold Westphal*

By an internal negation we understand such a relation between two beings that the one which is denied to the other qualifies the other at the heart of its essence—by absence. The negation becomes then a bond of essential being since at least one of the beings on which it depends is such that it points toward the other, that it carries the other in its heart as an absence. 4
Jean-Paul Sartre

Territory, in the evolving world of animals, is a force perhaps older than sex.... [T]he bond between a man and the soil he walks on [is] more powerful than his bond with the woman he sleeps with. 5 *Robert Ardrey*

The principle of the bond formed by having something in common which has to be defended against outsiders remains the same, from cichlids defending a common territory or brood, right up to scientists defending a common opinion and—most dangerous of all—fanatics defending a common ideology. In all these cases, aggression is necessary to enhance the bond. 6 *Konrad Lorenz*

[A]nimals who bond are also animals who aggress. 7 *Lionel Tiger*

Unless there is something to force the animals apart, there is no reason to evolve complicated means of bringing them together.... This may reflect a biological principle: that the more highly developed the species, the more likely there is to be a high degree of individualism and aggression, and hence of mistrust, and consequently of bonding. 8
Lionel Tiger & Robin Fox

Unless you can make a strong co-operative bond, your society will be conquered and killed out by some other society which has such a bond. 9 *Walter Bagehot*

[T]he cohesion of the *Wehrmacht* [was] a direct result of soldiers' ability to identify their personal safety and survival with the advancement of Hitler and the Nazi cause on the battlefront.... When the image of a strong Hitler began to be discredited, the bonds between soldier and soldier and between soldiers and leaders weakened and military effectiveness and cohesiveness was undermined. 10
James MacGregor Burns

Fear strengthens the group bond—a fact exploited by demagogues throughout the ages. They encourage fear of enemies when desiring to consolidate group cohesion and loyalty to a protective ruler. 11 *Irenäus Eibl-Eibesfeldt*

[A] particular characteristic of the male bond is its close inter-connection with aggressive and possibly violent action.... In both violent and aggressive action male-bonding is the predominant instrument of organization.... [Indeed] the very existence of a male group may lead to an aggressive relation between the group and the outside environment. 12 *Lionel Tiger*

Male bonding stems from a contempt for women, bolstered by distrust, and is not, *per se*, homosexual. It is also, in this culture with its forced and exaggerated male/female polarities, an easier way to get along with other human beings than a male-female group bonding.... 13 *Susan Brownmiller*

Indeed, one of the earliest forms of male bonding must have been the gang rape of one woman by a band of marauding men. 14
Susan Brownmiller

Bonding

Male bonding and patriarchy were the recourse to which man was forced by his terrible sense of woman's power, her imperviousness, her archetypal confederacy with chthonian nature. 15
Camille Paglia

Male bonding is not a vehicle for male-male emotional relationships, but rather a substitute for them.... 16 *Joseph H. Pleck*

Females bond too, but in different ways, for significantly different purposes.... [M]ales bond for reasons of macrostructure, females for reasons of microstructure.... Their long-lasting bonds are largely kinship bonds ... but the female bonds are as crucial and heroic as the more political male bonds. If they fail, the system collapses, and no amount of male solidarity will be able to hold it together. 17
Lionel Tiger & Robin Fox

[T]he basis of all primate social groups is the bond between mother and infant. That bond constitutes the social unit out of which all higher orders of society are constructed. 18
Richard E. Leakey

[T]he emotional bond uniting mothers and their young ... may conceivably be the nucleus of emotion in general. 19 *Sidney Mellen*

Because ... emotions are usually a reflection of the state of a person's affectional bonds, the psychology and psychopathology of emotion is found to be in large part the psychology and psychopathology of affectional bonds. 20
John Bowlby

Simply on the basis of what we know about the social animals in general, we can predict that if the mother-child bond does not go right, the unfortunate youngster may never get any of his *other* bonds right. 21 *Lionel Tiger & Robin Fox*

Making the parent-child bond more intense and more exclusive, *in the face of the incest taboo*, creates erotic scarcity.... [T]he more we can bind up a person's erotic desires in a tabooed relationship, the less he will seek pleasure in those forms that are readily available. He will consume little and produce much.... [H]e will work without cessation into the grave. 22 *Philip Slater*

[T]hose who once worshipped at the shrine of "the mother-infant bond," that mystery which was beyond the grasp of behaviourism, now look on aghast as research suggests that it is fear—even fear of parental violence—that is one awful determinant of the human infant's attachment. 23 *Chris Brand*

The special tie women have with children is recognized by everyone. I submit, however, that the nature of this bond is no more than shared oppression. 24 *Shulamith Firestone*

Central to the structural weakness built into our species' life is ... [the] special and exclusive bond between women and children.... We lean heavily on the reliability of this bond; yet it is part of a congenital deformity that we must now outgrow before it kills us off.... [We need] full male participation in early child care. 25
Dorothy Dinnerstein

Primary bonds once severed cannot be mended; once paradise is lost, man cannot return to it. There is only one possible, productive solution for the relationship of individualized man with the world: his active solidarity with all men and his spontaneous activity, love and work, which unite him again with the world, not by primary ties but as a free and independent individual. 26
Erich Fromm

Bonding with animals—or rather, admitting the bond we work so hard to ignore—is one way of increasing health and strengthening a sense of self. 27 *Gloria Steinem*

The basic bond of any society, culture, subculture, or organization is a "public image," that is, an image the essential characteristics of which are shared by the individuals participating in the group. 28 *Kenneth Boulding*

A crucial problem for the world of the future will be a concern for generations to come. Where will such a concern arise?... On what private, "rational" considerations, after all, should we make sacrifices now to ease the lot of generations whom we will never live to see? There is only one possible answer to this question. It lies in our capacity to form a collective bond of identity with those future generations....

Indeed, it is the absence of just such a bond with the future that casts doubt on the ability of nation-states or socio-economic orders to take now the measures needed to mitigate the problems of the future.... Contemporary industrial man, his appetite for the present whetted by the values of a high-consumption society ... has but a limited motivation to form such bonds. 29
Robert Heilbroner

~ BUREAUCRACY ~

THE DECISIVE REASON for the advance of bureaucratic organization has always been its purely *technical* superiority over any other form of organization. The fully developed bureaucratic apparatus compares with other organizations exactly as does the machine with the non-mechanical modes of production. 1
Max Weber

Bureaucratic administration means fundamentally domination through knowledge. This is the feature of it which makes it specifically rational. 2 *Max Weber*

[A] bureaucracy knows no party lines. Its inherent nature is to professionalize the process of government, to achieve continuity of administration through all the changes in party power, to bring expertness to the technical problems of government, and to effect a fusion of legislative, executive, and judicial powers wherever necessary despite the formal separation of those powers. 3 *Max Lerner*

Bureaucratization offers above all the optimum possibility for carrying through the principle of specializing administrative functions according to purely objective considerations.... "Objective" discharge of business primarily means a discharge of business according to *calculable rules* and "without regard for persons." ... Bureaucracy develops the more perfectly, the more it is "dehumanized." ... This is appraised as its special virtue by capitalism. 4
Max Weber

In bureaucracy Weber saw the possibility for both freedom and despotism—for the liberation of mankind through collective reason, and for the dehumanization of people through the conversion of bureaucratic means into ends. 5
James MacGregor Burns

[T]he essence of totalitarian government, and perhaps the nature of every bureaucracy, is to make functionaries and mere cogs in the administrative machinery out of men, and thus to dehumanize them. 6 *Hannah Arendt*

It is the acculturation into a culture of compliance built on the willing adherence to prescription and the acceptance as normal of external control and management that makes bureaucracy possible. 7 *Ursula Franklin*

Internally, an absolute bureaucracy tends to keep all its secrets, extends its control over the entry to official positions, strictly enforces the rules of promotion and compensation, and rigidly imposes the bureaucratic code of honor.... The end of such a development is bureaucratic absolutism in which one bureaucrat becomes the dictator of the country. 8
Arthur Schweitzer

When Hitler said that a day would come in Germany when it would be considered a "disgrace" to be a jurist, he was speaking with utter consistency of his dream of a perfect bureaucracy. 9 *Hannah Arendt*

[A] leading aim of bureaucracy is to neutralize competition within its structure in order to compete successfully outside. 10
Maria Carmen Gear et al.

[A] well-organized bureaucracy is an integral part of the megamachine: a group of men, capable of transmitting and executing a command, with the ritualistic punctilio of a priest, the mindless obedience of a soldier. 11
Lewis Mumford

For the bureaucrat, there is only one sin, and that is to violate the established order, to break the established rules. 12 *Erich Fromm*

To be effective, organization must in some sense incarnate the founding father ... the hypnotic persecuting father, a figure not at all incompatible with a mammoth bureaucracy which

Bureaucracy

operates as an extension of his ego.... "I love Big Brother" is the perfected slogan of erotic submission. 13 *Philip Rieff*

[T]he narcissist has many traits that make for success in bureaucratic institutions, which put a premium on the manipulation of interpersonal relations, discourage the formation of deep personal attachments, and at the same time provide the narcissist with the approval he needs in order to validate his self-esteem.... [B]ureaucracy has made life predictable and even boring while reviving, in a new form, the war of all against all. 14 *Christopher Lasch*

[B]ureaucracy ... [was one of] the two main political devices of imperialist rule.... Race ... was an escape into an irresponsibility where nothing human could any longer exist, and bureaucracy was the result of a responsibility that no man can bear for his fellowman and no people for another people. 15 *Hannah Arendt*

This is what bureaucracy is: a mechanism for carrying on transactions between strangers. 16 *Philip Slater*

The inquiry part I do not like, for the main reason that there you have to deal with living material. But the judicial side—that's another thing! Here you deal only with paper. 17 *Soviet bureaucrat*

The Communists do not distinguish people as to whether or not they are functionaries—all persons are considered to be functionaries.... By means of collectivization, even the peasant gradually becomes a member of the general bureaucratic society. 18 *Milovan Djilas*

The workers, having conquered political power, will break up the old bureaucratic apparatus, they will shatter it from its foundations up.... To guard against their transformation into bureaucrats ... *all* shall fulfil the functions of control and superintendence, so that *all* shall become "bureaucrats" for a time, and no one should therefore have the opportunity of becoming "bureaucrats" at all. 19 *Vladimir Ilyich Lenin*

To destroy officialism immediately, everywhere, completely.... That is a utopia. But to *break up* at once the old bureaucratic machine and to start immediately the construction of a new one, enabling us gradually to abolish bureaucracy—this is not a utopia.... The specific "bossing" methods of the State officials can and must begin to be replaced—immediately ... by the simple functions of managers and clerks.... To organise our whole national economy like the postal system ... is our immediate aim. 20 *V. I. Lenin*

The antimony between bureaucracy and democracy is well known.... The illusion is to believe that bureaucracy can be controlled by democracy. 21 *Jacques Ellul*

Democracy as such is opposed to the rule of bureaucracy. 22 *Max Weber*

[To] have the tendency to become corrupt ... that is, privileged persons detached from the masses, *and standing above it*. That is just the essence of bureaucracy. 23 *V. I. Lenin*

As the barons used to be the king-makers, the bureaucrats now make the politicians. 24 *Jacques Ellul*

In the totalitarian case the bureaucracy is the servant of the party and its leaders.... In the democratic case the bureaucracy is largely recruited by civil service ... and is accountable to the Constitution and the people under the "rule of law." 25 *Max Lerner*

Legally, government by bureaucracy is government by decree, and this means that power, which in constitutional government only enforces the law, becomes the direct source of all legislation. Decrees moreover remain anonymous ... and therefore seem to flow from some over-all ruling power that needs no justification. 26 *Hannah Arendt*

Bureaucracy, the rule of no one, has become the modern form of despotism. 27 *Mary McCarthy*

It is not enough that the bureaucracy should be efficient.... It must also be strong enough to guide.... In order to be able to do this it must be in a position to evolve principles of its own and sufficiently independent to assert them. It

must be a power in its own right. 28
Joseph Schumpeter

In a modern state the actual ruler is necessarily and unavoidably the bureaucracy, since power is exercised ... through the routines of administration. 29 *Max Weber*

Once fully established, bureaucracy is among those social structures which are the hardest to destroy. 30 *Max Weber*

The reaction to increased bureaucracy in one institutional area ... increases the need for bureaucratization of other institutions.... 31
Seymour Lipset

It has proven not to be the case that industrial development necessarily implies bureaucracies of ever-increasing size.... Past a certain point, large bureaucracies become increasingly less efficient ... than a larger number of smaller organizations. 32 *Francis Fukuyama*

Since *homo sapiens* evolved in small, face-to-face groups, he may not be "programmed" to function well in impersonal bureaucratic structures; therefore, large-scale bureaucratic society may be doomed to fail. 33 *A. Somit & S. Peterson*

[T]he more familial a society, the less effective its administration.... In the case of every successful movement to institute an effective bureaucratic instrument of control, the human components of the instrument have been decisively estranged not from wives and children but from kith and kin. 34 *Germaine Greer*

Our revolt against bureaucracy is really a revolt of nature against antinature, of all our evolutionary skills against a system that is their negation. 35 *Lionel Tiger & Robin Fox*

The world has enough scientists, enough technicians, enough secretaries, enough organizers, managers, and co-ordinators. What it needs now are persons. A bureautechnocratic culture stands against man in the development of personhood. 36 *C. A. Tesconi & V. C. Morris*

Bureaucracy is the death of any achievement. 37
Albert Einstein

Capitalism

THE IMPULSE TO ACQUISITION, pursuit of gain, of money, of the greatest possible amount of money, has in itself nothing to do with capitalism.... Unlimited greed for gain is not in the least identical with capitalism, and is still less its spirit. Capitalism *may* even be identical with the restraint, or at least rational tempering, of this irrational impulse. 1 *Max Weber*

Capital is the condition precedent of all gain in security and power, and capital is produced by selection and thrift. It is ... the essential means of man's power over nature, and it implies the purest concept of the power of intelligence to select and dispose of the processes of nature for human welfare. 2
William Graham Sumner

How few men are content with the possession of what they need.... It is this excess of activity beyond that required for the satisfaction of all other material needs, that results in the accumulation of the capital which is a necessary condition for the development of civilization. 3
William McDougall

Capitalism accumulates the capital gains not only of its successes but also of its failures, capitalized in new knowledge. It is the only appropriate system for a world in which all certitude is a sham. 4 *George Gilder*

Capitalism succeeds because it accommodates chance and thus accords with the reality of the human situation in a fundamentally incomprehensible, but nonetheless providential, universe. Economists who attempt to banish chance through methods of rational management also banish the only sources of human triumph. 5 *George Gilder*

The capitalist process rationalizes behavior and ideas and by so doing chases from our minds, along with metaphysical belief, mystic and romantic ideas of all sorts. Thus it reshapes not only our methods of attaining our ends but also these ultimate ends themselves. 6
Joseph Schumpeter

Capitalism

[M]ale hegemony in the culture is expressed by the generalization of rationality. This would conceptualize one way in which male domination precedes and paves the way for capitalism. 7 *Jessica Benjamin*

Is male dominance a creation of capitalism, or is capitalism one expression of male dominance? 8 *Catherine MacKinnon*

[One] capitalist principle [is] that human beings are ultimately reducible to interchangeable objects.... In the resulting state of organized anarchy ... pleasure becomes life's only business—pleasure, however, that is indistinguishable from rape, murder, unbridled aggression. 9 *Christopher Lasch*

Within the capitalist system ... all means for the development of production become means of domination and exploitation of the workers; they distort him into a fragment of a man, they degrade him to the level of an appendage of a machine, they destroy the actual content of his labor by turning it into a torment ... they transform his life-time into working-time, and drag his wife and child beneath the wheels of the juggernaut of capital.... It makes an accumulation of misery a necessary condition, corresponding to the accumulation of wealth. 10 *Karl Marx*

The capitalist scheme of values ... transformed five of the seven deadly sins of Christianity—pride, envy, greed, avarice, and lust—into positive social virtues, treating them as necessary incentives to all economic enterprise; while the cardinal virtues, beginning with love and humility, were rejected as "bad for business," except in the degree that they made the working class more docile and more amenable to cold-blooded exploitation. 11 *Lewis Mumford*

Normally speaking, it may be said that the forces of a capitalist society, if left unchecked, tend to make the rich richer and the poor poorer. 12 *Jawaharlal Nehru*

Capitalist production is not merely the production of commodities; it is essentially the production of surplus value.... All surplus value ... is in substance the materialization of unpaid labor. 13 *Karl Marx*

[T]he socialist believes that the very basis of the capitalist system is scientifically unsound, as a means of organising the production and distribution of commodities and services, and fundamentally inconsistent with the spiritual advancement of the race.... [B]y its exclusive reliance on the motive of pecuniary gain to individual owners [it is] inimical to national morality and international peace; in fact, to civilisation itself. 14 *Sidney & Beatrice Webb*

The capitalist, without the slightest hesitation, will destroy masses of useful products, or close down his works and abandon his employees to starvation in order to keep up prices. That is flat sabotage; and sabotage is a force that now threatens the existence of civilisation. 15 *Sidney & Beatrice Webb*

The laws of capitalistic production prove stronger than ... all laws of bourgeois economics. Unrestricted competition—the alpha and omega of bourgeois society—is supposed to place those most capable at the helm of all enterprises. But experience shows that as a rule it places those at the helm who are most shrewd and cunning and least troubled by conscience. 16 *August Bebel*

Unlimited competition leads to a ... crippling of the social consciousness of individuals.... This crippling of individuals I consider the worst evil of capitalism. 17 *Albert Einstein*

Modern capitalism needs men who feel free and independent, not subject to any authority or principle or conscience.... What is the outcome? Modern man is alienated from himself, from his fellow men, and from nature. 18 *Erich Fromm*

It is not capitalism that teaches greed and alienation; it is our greedy and alienated conceptions of ourselves that lay the foundation for capitalist ideology. We must change ourselves before we change society.... 19 *Robert C. Solomon*

Religion was not objectively discussed till it was no longer the cultural trait to which our civilization was most deeply committed. Now for the first time the comparative study of religions is free to pursue any point at issue. It is not yet possible to discuss capitalism in the same way.... 20 *Ruth Benedict*

[Capitalism] is a system in which production is undertaken for private profit rather than for social need—or, to put it differently, in which private profit is the effective gauge of social need. 21 *R. Jeffrey Lustig*

Capitalism ... is individualism in the realm of economics. 22 *John Hospers*

Modern capitalist society not only elevates narcissists to prominence, it elicits and reinforces narcissistic traits in everyone. 23 *Christopher Lasch*

The whole tendency of modern capitalism is towards the destruction of such communities as do exist. We have seen the effects of the frenetic exploitation of the new which is so essential a part of the marketing strategy of mass production.... [The] pressure put on our citizens to compete for material possessions has already destroyed the concept of the extended family.... 24 *John Gummer*

I am inclined to the paradox that a society in which the noneconomic elements in life have a strong familistic or socialistic character the institutions of capitalism and the market economy will work very well.... On the other hand in societies where the sense of community is weak and where the sense of responsibility of each for all is poorly developed, the institutions of capitalism can be quite corrupting. 25 *Kenneth Boulding*

Capitalist rationality does not do away with sub- or super-rational impulses. It merely makes them get out of hand by removing the restraint of sacred or semi-sacred tradition. 26 *Joseph Schumpeter*

Capitalism has made impossible the construction of a meaningful cultural existence. Capitalism itself has become the symbol of a "self-sufficient finitude." ... Autonomous individuals cut off from their roots and from their nature find little support in a human community. The sacred is unfulfilling and unfulfilled in such a world. 27 *Richard Quinney*

Only the methodical way of life of the ascetic sects could legitimate and put a halo around the economic "individualist" impulses of the modern capitalist ethos. 28 *Max Weber*

Capitalist prosperity is best promoted by a strong work ethic, which in turn depends on the ghosts of dead religious beliefs.... 29 *Francis Fukuyama*

[T]he religious valuation of restless, continuous, systematic work in a worldly calling, as the highest means to asceticism ... [produced] the spirit of capitalism.... When the limitation of consumption is combined with this release of acquisitive activity, the inevitable practical result is obvious: accumulation of capital through ascetic compulsion to save.... [T]he Puritan outlook ... stood at the cradle of the modern economic man. 30 *Max Weber*

[T]he quality in modern societies, which is most sharply opposed to the teaching ascribed to the Founder of the Christian Faith ... consists in the assumption ... that the attainment of material riches is the supreme object of human endeavour and the final criterion of human success.... Compromise is as impossible between The Church of Christ and the idolatry of wealth, which is the practical religion of capitalist societies, as it was between the Church and the State idolatry of the Roman Empire. 31 *R. H. Tawney*

Ownership of property is biblical. Competition in business is biblical. Ambitious and successful business management is clearly outlined as a part of God's plan for His people. 32 *Rev. Jerry Falwell*

A correct organization of economic life requires the recognition and respect of the private ownership of the means of production. They are ordained by God.... 33 *Pope Pius XII*

The fundamental aim of Satan himself is the same as the fundamental aim of capitalism—to make himself *princips mundi* and *deus huins seculi*.... The structure of the entire kingdom of Satan is essentially capitalistic: we are the Devil's property. 34 *Norman O. Brown*

CAPITALISM

[A]scetic capitalism, with its gospel of thrift, repression, and self-denial, now requires for its own continuance orgies of indulgence and escalating appetite, an ethos that undermines its own foundations. 35
Charles Hampden-Turner

The one thing that would utterly destroy the new capitalism is the serious practice of deferred gratification. 36 *Daniel Bell*

State socialism tends to produce a single, centralized, totalitarian dictatorship.... Capitalism tends to produce a multiplicity of petty dictators, each in command of his own little business kingdom. 37 *Aldous Huxley*

[C]apitalist enterprise now enters the stage at which large-scale social integration and control become paramount interests in and of themselves: the corporations begin to behave like public authorities concerned with rationalizing the total economy. 38
Theodore Roszak

In fact, the new corporate capitalism, which is in one sense a "popular capitalism" is in another a new and peculiarly American collectivism—a form of business syndicalism.... For all its individualistic slogans, the business class in America has effectively substituted its own form of collectivism for the old individualism. 39
Max Lerner

The free enterprise system fully embraces the right to inflict limitless damage on itself. The mergers and acquisitions mania was, without doubt, the most striking exercise in self-destruction.... Under the broad and benign cover of laissez faire and the specific licence of the market, there are forces that ravage and even destroy the very institutions that compose the system.... That is an intrinsic feature of the uncontrolled market system ... still largely unrecognized. 40 *John K. Galbraith*

[C]apitalist economy is not and cannot be stationary. Nor is it merely expanding in a steady manner. It is incessantly being revolutionized *from within*.... This process of Creative Destruction is the essential fact about capitalism. 41
Joseph Schumpeter

Capitalism represents a sum of human choices about the good life and the good society. These choices inevitably have their associated costs, and after 200 years the conviction seems to be spreading that the costs have got out of line. 42
Irving Kristol

Why does American business insist on "growth" when it is demonstrably using up the three basics of life on our planet—land, water and unpolluted air? 43 *Barbara Tuchman*

Capitalism, in its effects upon cities, is like that aberration of human physiology known to medicine as the stomach that digests itself. 44
Lewis Mumford

The atmosphere is already poisoned. The waters are poisoned. The forests are being subjected to acid rain. The weather is getting warmer.... Capitalism developed the forces of production; it developed technology. But at the same time, it has been digging its own grave. 45
Fidel Castro

The market mentality which puts economic activity, irrespective of purpose, at the center of the universe is a product not of human instinct but social organization. Competitive individualism ... is increasingly incompatible with survival of the species. 46
R. J. Barnet & R. E. Muller

Capitalism ... is the system of the future—if mankind is to have a future. 47 *Ayn Rand*

Wars have occurred during the periods of capitalistic dominance, but they have been least frequent in the areas most completely organized under that system. 48 *Quincy Wright*

[T]he capitalist system had, incidentally, the merit of training the nation in the science and art of co-operative working.... Profit-making was, in fact, at the opening of the 19th century, the world's substitute for qualities which did not at the time exist, for self-discipline, for professional technique, for scientific knowledge, for public service, for the spirit of free association, for common honesty itself. 49
Sidney & Beatrice Webb

Capitalism is based on self-interest and self-esteem; it holds integrity and trustworthiness as cardinal virtues and makes them pay off in the market place, thus demanding that men survive by means of virtues, not of vices. 50
Alan Greenspan

[C]apitalism is the expression of the talented, socialism is the revenge of the unsuccessful. 51
Peter Steinfels

Capitalist production entails faith—in one's neighbors, in one's society, and in the compensatory logic of the cosmos. Search and you shall find, give and you will be given unto, supply creates its own demand. It is this cosmology, this sequential logic, that essentially distinguishes the free from the socialist economy. 52
George Gilder

The American economy, because of its power and prosperity, has become the last, best hope of free economies in the world. But by the same token the issues of its capacity for survival, its social costs, and its impact on the human spirit have called in question the nature and survival value of the system of capitalism itself. 53
Max Lerner

[W]hatever its economic strengths, the social ethos of capitalism is ultimately unsatisfying for the individual and unstable for the community. The stress on personal achievement, the relentless pressure for advancement, the acquisitive drive that is touted as the Good Life—all this may be, in the end, the critical weakness of capitalist society.... Affluence does not buy morale, a sense of community, even a quiescent conformity. Instead, it may only permit larger numbers of people to express their existential unhappiness because they are no longer crushed by the burdens of the economic struggle.... [M]an does not live by bread alone. 54
Robert Heilbroner

As a pure system, capitalism was humanly intolerable; what has saved it from violent overthrow has been the absorption of the heresies of socialism ... that have given it increasing balance and stability. 55 *Lewis Mumford*

The most important event in the recent history of ideas is the demise of the socialist dream.... The second most important event of the recent era is the failure of capitalism to win a corresponding triumph. 56 *George Gilder*

Socialism and capitalism are in the same boat, and the boat is sinking. 57 *Harold D. Lasswell*

Marx was wrong in his diagnosis of the manner in which capitalist society would break down; he was not wrong in the prediction that it would break down eventually. 58
Joseph Schumpeter

Chaos / Order

[T]he feeling of chaos, of disintegration ... I take to be closely related to the fear of death.... [T]he fear of annihilation by the destructive forces within is the deepest fear of all. 1
Melanie Klein

To the Biblical images of evil corresponds ... the purpose of man to overcome the chaotic state of his soul, the state of undirected surging passion.... 2 *Martin Buber*

The first of the soul's needs, the one which touches most nearly its eternal destiny, is order.... 3 *Simone Weil*

The psyche is exalted in rehearsing ... order; and quite intelligibly, since organisms exist only by enacting some form of order and defending it, and the psyche is but a name for the success of the organism in so doing. When spirit perceives order in the world, it is therefore quickened by a sort of ... applause electrifying all those impulses by which the soul itself and the spirit first came to exist. 4
George Santayana

We all need to find some order in the world, to make some sense out of our existence. 5
Anthony Storr

The benefits of order are incontestable. It enables men to use space and time to the best advantage, while conserving their psychic forces. 6
Sigmund Freud

Chaos / Order

[O]nly an ordered existence is productive—of happiness if of nothing else. 7 *Pearl S. Buck*

The impulse of Nature made for a world of order. All that now happens follows in the train of consequence.... This thought will often bring calm. 8 *Marcus Aurelius*

The chief lesson is that the world displays a lovely order, an order comforting in its intricacy. And that the most appealing part of this harmony, perhaps, is its permanence—the sense that we are part of something with roots stretching back nearly forever, and branches reaching forward just as far. 9 *Bill McKibben*

General evil can exist only in disorder.... [T]he love of order which produces order is called *goodness*; and the love of order which preserves order is called *justice*. 10
Jean-Jacques Rousseau

Good order is the foundation of all good things. 11 *Edmund Burke*

In a Roman family the boys ... were bred to a domestic despotism which well prepared them for a subjection in life to a military discipline.... They conquered the world in manhood because as children they were bred ... by the habit of implacable order. 12 *Walter Bagehot*

The psychological structure that corresponds to pseudoconservatism is conventionality and authoritarian submissiveness on the ego level, with violence, anarchic impulses, and chaotic destructiveness in the unconscious sphere. 13
T. W. Adorno et al.

Morality powered by the superego can be compared to the use of ever greater repressive police action in civil disorders. If the police perform well ... there will be law and order; if not, chaos reigns. 14 *Irving Bieber*

[D]isorder and chaos are the greatest enemies of freedom today. 15 *Richard M. Nixon*

Freedom cannot exist without the concept of order. 16 *Prince Metternich*

Those who won our independence ... did not fear political change. They did not exalt order at the cost of liberty. 17
U.S. Judge Louis Brandeis

The Negro's great stumbling block in the stride toward freedom is not ... the Ku Klux Klanner but the white moderate who is more devoted to order than to justice; who prefers a negative peace which is the absence of tension to a positive peace which is the presence of justice. 18
Martin Luther King Jr.

This type of thinking equates regularity and order with reason and reason with virtue. The "bad" people are those who upset the system.... 19 *William Blanchard*

[C]onfusion is anti-American.... To admit to anything that suggests chaos is subversive. But sometimes subversion is the way to understanding.... To entertain the radical idea that understanding might involve accepting chaos threatens the foundations of our existence. Maybe that's why so many people avoid the subject of understanding altogether. 20
Richard Saul Wurman

The transition from a life that is actually chaotic but gives the appearance of order to one that is genuinely ordered but, to the philistine, appears disordered cannot be achieved except by passing through a phase of grave upheavals. 21
Wilhelm Reich

[R]ather than chaos emerging from the breakdown of order, it is chaos that is the generative source of the universe. 22 *F. David Peat*

When into the womb of time everything is again withdrawn chaos will be restored and chaos is the source upon which reality is written. 23
Henry Miller

A new unity is emerging: irreversibility is a source of order at all levels. Irreversibility is the mechanism that brings order out of chaos. 24
Ilya Prigogine

Chaos is an order of infinite complexity; indeed, if one wanted to pin down a chaotic system, an infinite amount of information and detail would be required. 25 *F. David Peat*

Chaos / Order

Without "chaos," no knowledge. 26
Paul Feyerabend

[I]f there is to be progress beyond limited ideals, the course of history by way of escape must venture along the borders of chaos in its substitution of higher for lower types of order.... The right chaos, and the right vagueness, are jointly required for any effective harmony.... Thus chaos is not to be identified with evil.... 27
Alfred N. Whitehead

I tell you: one must have chaos in one, to give birth to a dancing star. 28 *Friedrich Nietzsche*

People with excessive need for order are usually ... afraid of life, because life is not orderly. 29
Erich Fromm

[A]n ordered world is not the world order. 30
Martin Buber

Technique is opposed to nature.... Technique integrates the machine into society. It constructs the kind of world the machine needs and introduces order. 31 *Jacques Ellul*

A radical paradigmatic shift took place in ancient Greece with the evolution of philosophy and science.... The universe was no longer conceived as a product of the will of the gods, or of magical and mystical forces, but was perceived as a rational natural order. 32
J. C. Smith

[A] new myth of man is developing.... It is a response to the divisiveness and destruction without and to the chaos within. 33
Philip Rieff

Does a child conclude that the world is intelligible, and proceed to expand his understanding by the effort of conceptualizing on an ever-wider scale, with growing success and enjoyment? Or does he conclude that the world is a bewildering chaos, where the fact he grasped today is reversed tomorrow, where the more he sees the more helpless he becomes.... Does a child ... grasp the distinction between consciousness and existence, between the mind and the outside world, which leads him to ... control over his mental operations? Or does he remain ... trapped between two unintelligible states of flux: the chaos within and without? 34
Ayn Rand

We live in a period of atoms, of atomic chaos. 35
Friedrich Nietzsche

[W]hen we affirm that we are imagining a chaos ... in which the physical world no longer obeys laws, what are we thinking of ?... In reality we have substituted *will* for the mechanism of nature; we have replaced the "automatic order" by a multitude of elementary wills. 36
Henri Bergson

We are not in fact facing the "new world order" today's politicians so constantly invoke. Rather, we are facing a *new world disorder*—no one can know for how long. 37 *Peter F. Drucker*

The laws of logic for the angels are written in the universal harmony. They need no text books. Man needs text books because he has brought his inner thought processes into disorder. 38 *Rudolf Steiner*

Human life, when it begins to possess intrinsic value, is an incipient order in the midst of what seems a vast ... chaos. This retreating chaos can be deciphered and appreciated by man only in proportion as the order in himself is confirmed and extended. 39
George Santayana

The eternal laws of nature and order do exist. For the wise man, they ... are written in the depth of his heart by conscience and reason. 40
Jean-Jacques Rousseau

Were one asked to characterize the life of religion in the broadest and most general terms possible, one might say that it consists of the belief that there is an unseen order, and that our supreme good lies in harmoniously adjusting ourselves thereto. 41 *William James*

It is ... certain that nature is the expression of a definite order with which nothing interferes, and that the chief business of mankind is to learn that order and govern themselves accordingly. 42 *T. H. Huxley*

CHRISTIANITY

THE CHRISTIANS WERE the first to consider human life and the course of events as a history that is unfolding from a fixed beginning to a definite end, in the course of which man achieves his salvation or earns his punishment. 1
Albert Camus

Christianity: A religious system attributed to Jesus Christ, but really invented by Plato, improved by St. Paul, and finally revised and corrected by the Fathers, the councils, and other interpreters of the Church. Since the foundation of this sublime creed, mankind has become better, wiser, and happier than before. 2 *Voltaire*

Christianity would have remained a Jewish sect had it not been made at once speculative, universal, and ideal by the infusion of Greek thought, and at the same time plastic and devotional by the adoption of pagan habits.... The eclectic Christian philosophy thus engendered constitutes one of the most complete, elaborate, and impressive products of the human mind. The ruins of more than one civilization and of more than one philosophy were ransacked to furnish materials for this heavenly Byzantium. 3 *George Santayana*

Christianity ... personified opposition against the beastly materialism that prevailed among the rich and mighty ones in the Roman empire; it represented rebellion against the oppression and disdain of the masses. 4 *August Bebel*

[T]he Christian myth ... provides ... a face saving excuse for those who must accept inferiority and impotence as their lot in this world.... 5
David Kipp

What is Christian altruism if not the mass-egoism of the weak, which divines that if all care for one another each individual will be preserved as long as possible?... What is "virtue" and "charity" in Christianity if not just this mutual preservation, this solidarity of the weak, this hampering of selection?... Genuine charity demands sacrifice for the good of the species— ... it needs human sacrifice. 6
Friedrich Nietzsche

Christian civilization has proved hollow to a terrifying degree: it is all veneer, but the inner man has remained untouched.... Yes, everything is to be found outside—in image and in word, in Church and Bible—but never inside. Inside reign the archaic gods, supreme as of old. 7
Carl Jung

Cruelty and barbarity were more frequent in the Christian Middle Ages than in any civilization prior to our own. 8 *Will & Mary Durant*

Christian warriors ... go and fight for the deliverance of the holy places.... If you must have blood, bathe your hands in the blood of the infidel!... Soldiers of Hell, become the soldiers of the Living God. God wills it. 9 *Pope Urban II*

The Christian exults in the death of a pagan, because Christ is glorified. 10
Saint Bernard of Clairvaux

For Christians ... there is such a thing as "righteous indignation." Thanks to this possibility of indignation being righteous, Christians have always felt themselves justified in making war and committing the most hideous atrocities. 11
Aldous Huxley

[F]or the last four centuries ... it has been Western Christendom that has invaded, robbed, exploited, killed, exterminated, pillaged and enslaved all the other parts of the human race; and these same Christians have been perpetrators of the bloodiest wars among themselves.... [T]he overt behavior of Christians exhibits little, if any, application of the Sermon on the Mount or the other teachings of Christianity. 12
Pitirim Sorokin

If all the world were composed of real Christians, that is, true believers, no prince, king, lord, sword, or law would be needed. 13
Martin Luther

Christianity is meekness, nonresistance, love. And, therefore, government cannot be Christian, and a man who wishes to be a Christian must not serve government. 14 *Leo Tolstoy*

The sanctification of political power by Christianity is blasphemy; it is the negation of

Christianity.... Christianity is subversive of every government. 15 *Leo Tolstoy*

A Christian, whose doctrine enjoins upon him humility, nonresistance to evil, love to all (even to the most malicious), cannot be a soldier; that is, he cannot join a class of men whose business is to kill their fellow-men.... But of true Christians there have always been but few. 16 *Leo Tolstoy*

The mystery of history since Jesus Christ ... is that it was in the West that Christianity developed.... For, the West is, in itself, the opposite of what God teaches us and bids us live in Christ. 17 *Jacques Ellul*

American culture is not only post-Christian but anti-Christian. 18 *Alan Watts*

[T]he dispensationalists say our future lies in war and annihilation.... Somehow in all the sermons of ... TV evangelists, I miss their telling us that Christ possessed a way that was not based on military strength. His way was not to obliterate property and people.... Rather, He came to advance and enhance life. 19 *Grace Halsell*

When the Western world accepted Christianity, Caesar conquered.... The Church gave unto God the attributes which belonged exclusively to Caesar.... The brief Galilean vision of humility flickered throughout the ages, uncertainly. 20 *Alfred N. Whitehead*

Christian culture survived because it superintended the organization of Western personality in ways that produced the necessary corporate identities, serving a larger communal purpose institutionalized in the churches themselves. 21 *Philip Rieff*

That the Church is, supposedly, *in* but not wholly *of* this world supplied a critical principle of renewal which is basic to all Christian therapies of commitment. The Church, as an institution, is vital only inasmuch as its symbolic is detached from the established social order, thus preserving its capacity for being the guardian critic of our inherited moral demand system. 22 *Philip Rieff*

I say quite deliberately that the Christian religion, as organized in its Churches, has been and still is the principal enemy of moral progress in the world.... 23 *Bertrand Russell*

It is now a well documented finding that, in the U.S. in particular, but also in other countries, those who believe in Christianity and go to church are on average more racially prejudiced than atheists and agnostics. 24 *Derek Wright*

Having experienced a form of male chauvinism among Christians that was devastating, I can see how women are controlled in a very un-godlike, un-Christian way.... There are some valid reasons why feminists are doing what they're doing. 25 *Anita Bryant*

The Western experiment in changing the face of nature by science and technology has its roots in the political cosmology of Christianity.... [N]othing is more important for Christianity than the subservience of nature to the commands of Christ, culminating in his victory over ... death itself. 26 *Alan Watts*

Christ came to solve two major problems, evil and death.... The night on Golgotha is so important in the history of man only because, in its shadow, the divinity abandoned its traditional privileges and drank to the last drop, despair included, the agony of death.... For God to be man, he must despair. 27 *Albert Camus*

This is the absolute crux of all traditional Christianity: the faith that Jesus ... was God himself become human. The point was to bring into the world a Second Adam. The First Adam had, by his Fall, tainted all humanity with sin. The Second Adam would ... unite all humanity ... with the divine nature. As St. Athanasius put it, "God became man that man might become God." 28 *Alan Watts*

It is not only impossible, but useless to know God without the intermediary of Jesus Christ.... Man's knowledge of God without an awareness of his own wretchedness leads to pride.... An awareness of his wretchedness without the knowledge of God leads to despair....

Christianity

The knowledge of Jesus Christ represents the middle state because we find in it both God and our wretchedness. 29 *Blaise Pascal*

It has been said that one of the great superiorities of Christianity … was that it gave value to suffering: transforming pain from a negative condition to an experience with a positive spiritual content. 30 *Mircea Eliade*

[S]ickness is the natural state of the Christian.… [H]e should always be in suffering and privation of all the pleasure of the senses, exempt of all passions … without ambition, without avarice, in a continuous expectation of death.… Is it not a great blessing when one finds oneself through necessity in a condition in which one … has no other choice but to submit humbly? 31
Blaise Pascal

For Christianity, the true end of Man … is not to extinguish suffering, but … to follow the lead of love, even if it leads to the Cross. As Christianity sees it, to incur suffering is a lesser evil than to extinguish love.… 32 *Arnold Toynbee*

Christian love is, so to speak, the extension of God's love.… In relation to God and his neighbour, the Christian can be likened to a tube, which by faith is opened upwards, and by love downwards.… A Christian is called to be a Christ to his neighbour. 33 *Anders Nygren*

Christ … is the leader of all the lovers. He saw that love was the first secret of the world for which the wise men had been looking, and that it was only through love that one could approach either the heart of the leper or the feet of God. 34 *Oscar Wilde*

Christianity teaches that love is a relationship between: man-God-man, that is, that God is the middle term.… For to love God is to love oneself in truth. 35 *Søren Kierkegaard*

Christianity's view is: forgiveness *is* forgiveness; your forgiveness is your forgiveness.… God forgives you neither more nor less nor otherwise than *as* you forgive your trespassers. 36
Søren Kierkegaard

[H]e who adopts the Christian, the true, conception of life, cannot shrink from the claims of his conscience. In this is the essence and peculiarity of Christianity, distinguishing it from all other religious teachings; and in this is its unconquerable power. 37 *Leo Tolstoy*

It is in Christianity that we first find egocentric religion essentially superseded by theocentric religion.… The Christian Religion is a thoroughly ethical religion and its ethic is a thoroughly religious ethic. 38 *Anders Nygren*

The whole effect of Christianity was to transfer the drama onto the moral plane. 39
André Gide

Christianity was thus a fundamentally new religion, a religion of the spirit. 40
George Santayana

Through experiencing the Christ Event on earth, man was able to ascend to creating in the Holy Spirit … of creating the right, beautiful and good in the course of his further evolution.… And the Christ Event has given man … the power that makes him capable of living on into the perspectives of the future and of increasingly creating out of relationships, out of all that is not predetermined.… [This] is connected with the profoundest thought in the whole of our evolution, the thought of creation out of nothingness. 41
Rudolf Steiner

The aesthetic experience is a simple beholding of the object.… [Y]ou then become aware of the relationship of part to part, each part to the whole, and the whole to each of its parts. This is the essential, aesthetic factor—rhythm, the harmonious rhythm of relationships. And when a fortunate rhythm has been struck … you experience a radiance.… This is the epiphany. And that is what might in religious terms be thought of as the all-informing Christ principle coming through. 42
Joseph Campbell

The universe fulfilling itself in a synthesis of centres in perfect conformity with the laws of union. God, the Centre of centres. In that final vision the Christian dogma culminates. 43
Pierre Teilhard de Chardin

Christianity

What is remarkable about Christianity is that in its system of dogma it anticipates a metamorphosis in the divinity, a process of historic change on the "other side." ... [But this] otherworldliness, the transcendence of the Christian myth was lost, and with it the view that wholeness is achieved in the other world. 44
Carl Jung

[Through] the dimension called heaven ... Christianity took creature consciousness—the thing man most wanted to deny—and made it the very *condition for* his cosmic heroism. 45
Ernest Becker

In Christ spirit did not need to be saved, it was free initially; yet it was inspired to love and willing to suffer; neither tempted, like the gods of Greece, to become an accomplice to human passions, nor like Lucifer to shut itself up in solitary pride. It was humble towards universal power, wisely respectful towards the realm of matter.... Humility, piety, is a prerequisite to spirituality. It is much more than a prudential virtue.... It enables spirit to recognize the truth and to be inwardly steady, clear, fearless, and without reproach. 46 *George Santayana*

The one, great positive idea which Christ repeatedly tried to express was the thought that no individual human being could know himself unless his inner honesty was complete.... No man, according to Christ, could know himself unless he knew all the negative and inferior aspects of himself.... A man, Christ also said, who did not know himself could not in any way trust what he thought about other men or the world. 47 *Philip Wylie*

Christianity paved the way for the social progress—political, economic, scientific—of the modern world, the social progress which is so dominantly characteristic of that world. For the Christian notion of a rational or abstract universal human society or social order... expanded to include all the other main aspects of concrete human social life.... 48
George H. Mead

The idea of freedom—the freedom that we in the U.S. know and love so well—is derived from the Bible with its extraordinary emphasis on the dignity of the individual. Democracy is the only true political expression of Christianity. 49 *U.S. Vice President Henry Wallace*

Christ is the most supreme of individualists.... 50 *Oscar Wilde*

Christianity is the "religion" of modern man and historical man, of the man who simultaneously discovered personal freedom and continuous time (in place of cyclical time). 51
Mircea Eliade

[T]he divine centre of Christianity actually threw man out of it in order that he might love it.... Love desires personality; therefore love desires division. It is the instinct of Christianity to be glad that God has broken the universe into little pieces, because they are living pieces.... No other philosophy makes God actually rejoice in the separation of the universe into living souls. 52 *G. K. Chesterton*

The incarnation of Christianity implies a harmonious solution of the problem of the relations between the individual and the collective. Harmony in the Pythagorean sense, the just balance of contraries. This solution is precisely what men are thirsting for today. 53
Simone Weil

They who praise Christianity as a great achievement of civilization, should not forget that to woman it owed many of its victories. 54
August Bebel

Christianity succeeded ultimately because it represented a return to the original goddess worship, which the Olympian gods had temporarily replaced.... 55 *Elizabeth Gould Davis*

Christianity is a woman's religion, invented by women and womanish men for themselves. 56
Samuel Butler

Christianity has waged a deadly war against the higher type of man. It has put a ban on all his fundamental instincts. 57
Friedrich Nietzsche

Christianity's contribution ... to the historical process was to make clear to the slave [a] vision

Christianity

of human freedom, and to define for him in what sense all men could be understood to have dignity. 58 *Francis Fukuyama*

One of the fundamental truths of Christianity is that progress towards a lesser imperfection is not produced by the desire for a lesser imperfection. Only the desire for perfection has the virtue of being able to destroy in the soul some part of the evil which defiles it. 59
Simone Weil

Christianity is inwardness, inward deepening.... [Thus] self-concern must be awakened in "the single individual" which infinitely gives him something other to think about than external forms.... Christianity is victorious inwardness ... [gained] by means of the vision of the ideals. 60 *Søren Kierkegaard*

The Christian ideal has not been tried and found wanting. It has been found difficult, and left untried. 61 *G. K. Chesterton*

Christ had powerful flashes of insight into the deep nature of man's consciousness and he used every device he could invent to try to reveal the process of that insight to those who would listen. He failed. 62 *Philip Wylie*

Civilization

[C]ivilization is passing away, and ... this is the meaning of the twentieth century. 1
Kenneth Boulding

[F]ew today have any sense of belonging to something bigger and better than themselves. There is a sick odor in the air. It is the smell of a dying Second Wave civilization. 2
Alvin Toffler

The three great revolutions of our age—the moral, political, and technical—have this in common: they support and strengthen each other and move in the same direction—that of a global conflagration. Their coincidence in time and their parallel development aggravate the threat to the survival of Western civilization which each of them carries independently. 3
Hans Morgenthau

Human beings seem to have an almost unlimited capacity ... to deceive themselves into taking their own lies for truth. By such mystification, we achieve and sustain our adjustment, adaptation, socialization.... Only by the most outrageous violation of ourselves have we achieved our capacity to live in relative adjustment to a civilization apparently driven to its own destruction. 4 *R. D. Laing*

No civilization can too long tolerate a cleavage between the professing rhetoric of its tradition and the possessive force of its frame of power. 5
Max Lerner

Civilizations die in the measure that they become conscious of themselves. They realize, they lose heart, the propulsion of the union motive is no longer there. 6 *Lawrence Durrell*

[I]t is lack of confidence, more than anything else, that kills a civilization. 7 *Kenneth Clark*

[H]igher civilization means an increase in the domain of the death instinct at the expense of the life instinct. 8 *Norman O. Brown*

[T]he entire progress of civilization is rendered possible only by the transformation and utilization of the death instinct or its derivatives. The diversion of primary destructiveness from the ego to the external world feeds technological progress, and the use of the death instinct for the formation of the superego achieves the punitive submission of the pleasure ego to the reality principle and assures civilized morality. 9
Herbert Marcuse

It is impossible to ignore the extent to which the existence of civilization is built up on renunciation of instinctual gratifications. 10
Sigmund Freud

[T]his primal guilt ... was also the beginning of civilization.... 11 *Sigmund Freud*

The saving of civilization is contingent upon the revival of something like the doctrine of original sin. 12 *Russell Kirk*

True civilization ... lies in the reduction of the traces of original sin. 13 *Baudelaire*

Civilization

Civilization originates in delayed infancy and its function is security. It is a huge network of more or less successful attempts to protect mankind against the danger of object-loss, the colossal efforts made by a baby who is afraid of being left alone in the dark. 14 *Géza Róheim*

[C]ivilization is a product of the Eros.... Having learned to accept substitute objects Eros remains only half-satisfied. Without giving up the desire to regain the original it is ever in search of new substitutes. In its eternal search the family, the tribe, and the nation are formed. 15 *Géza Róheim*

Eros is the center of the vitality of a culture—its heart and soul. And when the release of tension takes the place of creative eros, the downfall of the civilization is assured. 16 *Rollo May*

Civilization is nothing but tension. The head, in all the outstanding men of the Civilizations, is dominated exclusively by an expression of extreme tension. 17 *Oswald Spengler*

Civilization advances by extending the number of important operations which we can perform without thinking about them. 18 *Alfred N. Whitehead*

[C]ivilization rests on the fact that the individual benefits from more knowledge than he is aware of.... The more civilized we become, the more relatively ignorant must each individual be of the facts on which the workings of his civilization depends. 19 *Friedrich von Hayek*

[W]hat is civilization? Its first essential character, I should say, is *forethought*.... [W]e can distinguish more or less civilized nations and epochs according to the amount of it that they display. 20 *Bertrand Russell*

The precondition of a civilized society is the barring of physical force from the social relationships—thus establishing the principle that if men wish to deal with one another, they may do so only by means of *reason*. 21 *Ayn Rand*

Civilization is nothing else than the attempt to reduce the use of force to the last resort. 22 *José Ortega y Gasset*

Civilization and violence are antithetical concepts. 23 *Martin Luther King Jr.*

Rebellion in itself is not an element of civilization. But it is a preliminary to all civilization. Rebellion alone ... allows us to hope for the future.... 24 *Albert Camus*

To exert power in every form was the essence of civilization.... 25 *Lewis Mumford*

Civilization begins, because the beginning of civilization is a military advantage. 26 *Walter Bagehot*

[W]ar prepares the way for civilization ... [and] civilization prepares the way for war. 27 *Sir Arthur Keith*

The history of civilization, from the destruction of Carthage and Jerusalem to the destruction of Dresden, Hiroshima, and the people, soil, and trees of Vietnam, is a tragic record of sadism and destructiveness. 28 *Erich Fromm*

[I]t would take only one more exceptional personality like Hitler to put an end to most of human civilization.... 29 *G. M. Gilbert*

The recurrent problem of civilization is to define the male role satisfactorily enough ... so that the male may ... reach a solid sense of irreversible achievement.... 30 *Margaret Mead*

Civilized society is dependent upon the submission of the short-term sexuality of young men to the maternal horizons of women. This is what happens in monogamous marriage; the man disciplines his sexuality and extends it into the future through the womb of a woman. 31 *George Gilder*

The Positive Woman accepts her responsibility to spin the fabric of civilization, to mend its tears, and to reinforce its seams. No matter how wide or how narrow is the scope of her influence, this is her task. 32 *Phyllis Schlafly*

Woman's success in lifting men out of their way of life nearly resembling that of beasts—who merely hunted and fished for food, who found shelter where they could in jungles, in trees,

Civilization

and caves—was a civilizing triumph. 33
Mary R. Beard

If civilization had been left in female hands, we would still be living in grass huts. 34
Camille Paglia

[Since] love comes into opposition to the interests of civilization ... women soon come into opposition to civilization.... The work of civilization has become increasingly the business of men, it ... compels them to carry out instinctual sublimations of which women are little capable. 35 *Sigmund Freud*

What is called civilization may be defined as the pursuit of objects not biologically necessary for survival. 36 *Bertrand Russell*

When a civilization is analysed it is seen that, in reality, it is the marvellous and the legendary that are its true supports. Appearances have always played a much more important part than reality in history.... 37 *Gustave Le Bon*

As the essence of every Culture is religion, so—and *consequently*—the essence of every Civilization is irreligion.... It is this extinction of living inner religiousness, which ... [signifies] the turn from Culture to Civilization. 38
Oswald Spengler

Civilization ... is the stage of a Culture at which tradition and personality have lost their immediate effectiveness, and every idea, to be actualized, has to be put into terms of money. 39
Oswald Spengler

Naked greed has been the moving spirit of civilization from the first day of its existence to the present time; wealth, more wealth and wealth again.... 40 *Friedrich Engels*

Not only ... modern technology and economic organization, but all the features and achievements of modern civilization are, directly or indirectly, the products of the capitalist process. 41 *Joseph Schumpeter*

The bourgeoisie, by the rapid improvement of all instruments of production, by the immensely facilitated means of communication, draws all, even the most barbarian, nations into civilization. 42 *Karl Marx*

The difference between civilization and savagery ... is found in the degree to which previous experiences have changed the objective conditions under which subsequent experiences take place. 43 *John Dewey*

The virtues and arts of civilization are almost as disastrous to the uncivilized as its vices. It is really the great tragedy of civilization that the contact of lower and higher is disastrous to the former, no matter what may be the point of contact, or how little the civilized may desire to do harm. 44 *William Graham Sumner*

[W]hen civilization hits a precivilized society it cannot remain as it was. Either it must make an adjustment to civilization or it will disintegrate. 45 *Kenneth Boulding*

[S]avage and civilized man differ so much in the bottom of their hearts and inclinations that that which constitutes the supreme happiness of the one would reduce the other to despair. The savage man breathes only freedom and peace.... Civil man, on the contrary, being always active, sweating and restless, torments himself endlessly ... [and] renounces life in order to acquire immortality. 46 *Jean-Jacques Rousseau*

It is easy ... for a barbarian to be healthy; for a civilized man the task is a hard one. 47
Sigmund Freud

[T]he differences between civilized man and primitive man are in many cases more apparent than real.... [T]he fundamental traits of the mind are the same. 48 *Franz Boas*

Men have been barbarians much longer than they have been civilized. They are only precariously civilized, and within us there is the propensity, persistent as the force of gravity, to revert under stress and strain, under neglect or temptation, to our first natures. 49
Walter Lippmann

The bicameral mind is a form of social control.... The bicameral mind with its controlling gods was evolved as a final stage of the evolution of language. And in this development lies the origin of civilization. 50 *Julian Jaynes*

It can be argued ... that the phonetic alphabet, alone, is the technology that has been the means of creating "civilized man"—the separate individuals equal before a written code of law. Separateness of the individual, continuity of space and of time, and uniformity of codes are the prime marks of literate and civilized societies. 51 *Marshall McLuhan*

[A]n important change from primitive culture to civilization seems to consist in the gradual elimination of what might be called the emotional, socially determined associations of sense-impressions and of activities, for which intellectual associations are gradually substituted. 52 *Franz Boas*

"Civilization" must now be used technically to mean detribalized man for whom the visual values have priority in the organization of thought and action. 53 *Marshall McLuhan*

[T]he evolution of civilized human society from primitive human society has largely depended upon or resulted from a progressive social liberation of the individual self and his conduct, with the modifications and elaborations of the human social process which have followed from and been made possible by that liberation. 54
George H. Mead

"Civilization is the progress toward a society of privacy. The savage's whole existence is public, ruled by the laws of his tribe. Civilization is the process of setting man free from men." 55
Ayn Rand

The great advances of civilization, whether in architecture or painting, in science or literature, in industry or agriculture, have never come from centralized government.... Their achievements were the product of individual genius.... 56 *Milton Friedman*

To make a connection, however irrational or illogical ... was the first step in civilization.... 57
Herbert Read

The uniqueness of man lies in the fact that whatever ideal his "ought" enshrines, man by striving possesses the capacity to realize that ideal. Being human means working at it, and true civilization is the development of the art of being both intelligent and kind, the ability to work and the ability to love. 58
Ashley Montagu

When the individual becomes civilized he acquires a second nature. This second nature is made in the image of what he is and is living for and should become. 59 *Walter Lippmann*

The faith of civilization is built upon the assumption that by reason of its mechanisms an increasing number of human beings realise at their best their highest faculties. 60 *Harold Laski*

The guarantee of a stable civilisation is that men in general should have at least that minimum without which they cease to be men. 61
Harold Laski

Civilizations remain capable of surviving and growing only if they enable man to express the aspects of his nature that are still dormant. 62
René Dubos

I would define a civilized man as one who can be happily occupied for a lifetime even if he has no need to work for a living. This means that the greatest problem of the future is civilizing the human race. 63 *Arthur C. Clarke*

To be able to fill leisure intelligently is the last product of civilization. 64 *Bertrand Russell*

[R]eal civilization cannot exist in the absence of a certain play-element, for civilization presupposes limitation and mastery of the self, the ability not to confuse its own tendencies with the ultimate and highest goal, but to understand that it is enclosed within certain bounds freely accepted. Civilization will, in a sense, always be played according to certain rules, and true civilization will always demand fair play. 65
Johan Huizinga

I am stronger because ... civilization possesses power to bind into its unity all diversity without depriving any element of its individuality. 66
Antoine de Saint-Exupéry

Civilization

The libido attaches itself to the satisfaction of the great vital needs, and chooses as its first objects the people who have a share in that process. And in the development of mankind as a whole, just as in individuals, love alone acts as the civilizing factor in the sense that it brings a change from egoism to altruism. 67
Sigmund Freud

I should define civilization in spiritual terms. Perhaps it might be defined as an endeavour to create a state of society in which the whole of Mankind will be able to live together in harmony, as members of a single all-inclusive family. This is, I believe, the goal at which all civilizations so far known have been aiming unconsciously.... 68 *Arnold Toynbee*

Our present civilization is a gigantic motor car moving along a one-way road at an ever-accelerating speed. Unfortunately as now constructed the car lacks both steering wheel and brakes, and the only form of control the driver exercises consists in making the car go faster, though ... he has quite forgotten the purpose of the journey. 69 *Lewis Mumford*

[T]he direction of society has been taken over by a type of man who is not interested in the principles of civilization.... The simple process of preserving our present civilization is supremely complex.... Ill-fitted to direct it is this average man who has learned to use much of the machinery of civilization, but who is characterized by root-ignorance of the very principles of the civilization. 70
José Ortega y Gasset

We are a schizophrenic civilization which deludes itself that it is the greatest that has ever existed, while its people are walking embodiments of misery and anxiety. 71
Henryk Skolimowski

A great civilization is not conquered from without until it has destroyed itself from within. 72
Will & Ariel Durant

The great enemy of any civilization is the enemy within. 73 *Max Lerner*

Community

People need roots in a transnational world; they need community. 1 *Peter F. Drucker*

Any kind of community is more than a set of customs, behaviors, or attitudes about other people. A community is also a collective identity; it is a way of saying who "we" are.... [It] is born from [a] sense of shared action and a shared sense of collective self. But in times when public life is eroding, this relationship between shared action and collective identity breaks down. If people are not speaking to each other on the street, how are they to know who they are as a group? 2 *Richard Sennett*

Human aggregates are possible, or at least conceivable, without a sense of the sacred.... But it is the community that gives to the sacred its most vital expressions everywhere: birth, marriage, death, and other moments in the human drama. 3 *Robert Nisbet*

The sacred roots of community are contrary to the rights of individuals and liberal tolerance. 4 *Allan Bloom*

[W]hat threatens the possibility of meaningful community is not a force external to the community, but those very *principles* of liberty and equality on which they are based.... This suggests that no fundamental strengthening of community life will be possible unless individuals give back certain of their rights to communities.... 5 *Francis Fukuyama*

Individualism is social atomism; conservatism is community of spirit.... The leaders of yesteryear's liberalism assumed that man is sufficient unto himself; and that assumption was fallacious, for man cannot subsist without community. 6 *Russell Kirk*

I have no intention of urging a return to the simpler ways of ... community life. That route, alas, is blocked by the very forces that produce our civilizational climacteric. Until the forces of population growth, of nuclear danger, and, above all, of a runaway industrial order have been brought under control, there is very little

realistic likelihood of the establishment of the small ... communities that many would urge as the most welcome alternative to the present order. For a very long period there will be no escape from the necessity of a centralized administration for our industrial world. 7
Robert Heilbroner

In the time of public philosophies and social religions, the communities were positive. A positive community is characterized by the fact that it guarantees some kind of salvation to the individual by virtue of his membership and participation in that community. That sort of community seems corrupt to the economic man, with his particular version of an ascetic ideal tested mainly by self-reliance and personal achievement. The positive community was displaced ... by the neutral market. 8
Philip Rieff

Unquestionably a period of exceedingly rapid economic growth has contributed to the disturbance of communal integrity. 9 *Elton Mayo*

Common man, forever confusing progress with material gain, exploited and exploiting, begins at that point to undermine his own community. 10 *Philip Wylie*

By marketing the myth that the pleasures of consumption can be the basis of community, the global corporation helps to destroy the possibilities of real community—the reaching out of one human being to another. 11
R. J. Barnet & R. E. Muller

Compassionate communities, as distinct from welfare states, exist only where there is a rich symbolic life, shared, and demanding of the self a hard line limiting the range of desires. The symbolic impoverishment of the Western communities cannot be corrected by analysis, nor by analyses of other analysts. 12 *Philip Rieff*

Technological progress has reduced the number of physical contacts, [and thus] impoverished the spiritual relations between the members of a community. 13 *Aldous Huxley*

Because machines provide us with the power to flit about the universe, our communities grow more fragile, airy, and ephemeral, even as our connections multiply. 14 *Michael Heim*

Modern organization creates yet another tension for the community.... Its "culture" has to *transcend* community. 15 *Peter F. Drucker*

America is one vast, terrifying anti-community.... Protocol, competition, hostility, and fear have replaced ... affection which might sustain man against a hostile universe. 16
Charles A. Reich

Only in the continuous encounter with other persons does the person become and remain a person. The place of this encounter is the community. 17 *Paul Tillich*

[T]he sense of self obtained through the realization of a function in the community is a more effective and for various reasons a higher form of the sense of self than that which is dependent upon the immediate personal relations in which a relation of superiority and inferiority is involved. 18 *George H. Mead*

The relationship between white-collar crime and prevailing attitudes among the public as to trust has never been explored systematically. Yet, it is precisely public trust—trust in social institutions, groups, and particular persons—that may provide the social glue that *is* social cohesion in the community. Once that cohesiveness is weakened or broken, the social fabric itself suffers. 19 *R. Meier & J. Short*

[W]e reach the general conclusion: suicide varies inversely with the degree of integration of the social groups of which the individual forms a part.... [T]he more the family and community become foreign to the individual, so much the more does he become a mystery to himself, unable to escape the exasperating and agonizing question: to what purpose? 20 *Émile Durkheim*

There's probably no more important task ahead of us than finding a way for people to make a living being useful to the community. 21
Philip Slater

To have a good life in the fullest sense a man must have a good education, friends, love,

Community

children (if he desires them), a sufficient income … good health, and work which is not uninteresting. All these things, in varying degrees, depend upon the community.… The good life must be lived in a good society and is not fully possible otherwise. 22 *Bertrand Russell*

Only in association with others has each individual the means of cultivating his talents in all directions. Only in a community therefore is personal freedom possible. 23 *Karl Marx*

The community stagnates without the impulse of the individual. The impulse dies away without the sympathy of the community. 24

William James

[F]riendship patterns within a community are closely tied to patterns of participation in self-government. For democratic political systems are based in community, and community, in turn, is held together by friendships. 25

Diane Margolis

True community does not come into being because people have feelings for each other (though that is required too), but rather on two accounts: all of them have to stand in a living, reciprocal relationship to a single living center, and they have to stand in a living, reciprocal relationship to one another. 26 *Martin Buber*

All effective communities are founded upon the principle of unlimited liability. 27

Aldous Huxley

If man is to live in community with his fellows it is a necessary condition of his life that what he attains should, at least in the long run, involve benefit also to others. 28 *Harold Laski*

[The] state of mind, which subordinates the interests of the ego to the conservation of the community, is really the first premise for every truly human culture. 29 *Adolf Hitler*

People feel more comfortable when consensus prevails. Consequently … leaders can achieve considerable freedom for their policies as long as they are able to provide the people with a sense of belonging … the sense of community. 30

Lucian Pye

Community feeling formed by the sharing of impulses has the special role of reinforcing the fear of the unknown, converting claustrophobia into an ethical principle. 31

Richard Sennett

People in struggling to be a community become ever more absorbed in each other's feelings, and ever more withdrawn from an understanding of, let alone a challenge to, the institutions of power.… 32 *Richard Sennett*

Any community worthy of the name—one in which the relationships between people are regulated by the people themselves instead of by machines—would probably seem "totalitarian" to today's youth.… But there is no way for large numbers of people to coexist without governing and being governed by one another unless they establish machines to do it, at which point they risk losing sight (and understanding) of their interconnectedness—a loss well advanced in our society. 33 *Philip Slater*

The community is a fictitious *body* composed of the individual persons who are considered as constituting as it were its *members*. The interest of the community then is what?—the sum of the interests of the several members who compose it. 34 *Jeremy Bentham*

The *first* condition upon which the existence of a community … depends, is the power of an individual self to extend his life, in ideal fashion, so as to regard it as including past and future events which lie far away in time, and which he does not now personally remember. 35 *Josiah Royce*

Community exists when there are many connections between individuals so that every interaction builds upon those that went before and also prepares for the next. 36

Diane Margolis

To be rooted is perhaps the most important and least recognized need of the human soul.… A human being has roots by virtue of his real, active and natural participation in the life of a community which preserves in living shape certain particular treasures of the past and certain particular expectations for the future. 37

Simone Weil

Traditional communities no longer have much integrating power; they cannot survive the mobility which knowledge confers on the individual.... The community that is needed in post-capitalist society—and needed especially by the knowledge worker—has to be based on *commitment and compassion* rather than being imposed by proximity and isolation. 38

Peter F. Drucker

As a society we're at [a] crucial point now—we can either use what we've learned from our wanderings and ordeals to enrich our community, or disintegrate altogether. 39

Philip Slater

The decline of community life suggests that in the future, we risk becoming secure and self-absorbed last men.... 40 *Francis Fukuyama*

Computers

Because they stand on the line between mind and not-mind, between life and not-life, computers excite reflection about the nature of mind and the nature of life. They provoke us to think about who we are. 1 *Sherry Turkle*

I think what we have learned is that we are probably computers.... I think we'll be able to program emotions into a machine once we can do thoughts. 2 *Marvin Minsky*

Feelings and emotions ... can be built into the computer. 3 *Robert Jastrow*

[O]ften the attraction of the computer-man idea is the expression of a flight from life and from humane experience into the mechanical and purely cerebral.... When the majority of men are like robots, then indeed there will be no problem in building robots who are like men. 4 *Erich Fromm*

Some computer scientists with big computers are programming them to turn out poems, mystery stories, and other kinds of "literary works." Will there ever be a time when you won't be able to tell the difference between something written by a computer and something written by a person? 5 *Daniel Watt*

The computer can only process that which may be represented unambiguously.... The computer, one may say, is a mechanical "being" which logically, rationally and objectively deals with a reduced reality.... Though an artificial intelligence, it is, and this is important, liberated from ... emotions, senses and subjectivity. With this "cognitive" computer, then, the masculine ideal has been reached. 6 *Janni Nielsen*

The computer programmer ... is a creator of universes for which he alone is the lawgiver.... They compliantly obey their laws and vividly exhibit their obedient behavior.... The test of power is control. The test of absolute power is certain and absolute control. When dealing with the compulsive programmer, we are therefore also dealing with his need to control and his need for certainty. 7 *Joseph Weizenbaum*

[T]he computer brings with it a hidden curriculum.... [T]he computer lends itself all too conveniently to the subversion of democratic values. This threatening liability arises precisely from what has always been advertised as the technology's greatest power: the ability to concentrate and control information. 8

Theodore Roszak

When computers are set down in the front office, their valuable word-and number-juggling features are used to camouflage their monitoring functions. 9 *Barbara Garson*

For the manager ... the computer means greater and greater control.... It means the security of less and less dependency on other people. 10 *Corporate executive*

[T]he most serious threat of computer-controlled automation ... [is] the displacement of the human mind and the insidious undermining of confidence in its ability to make individual judgements that run contrary to the system.... 11

Lewis Mumford

The phrase "the computer does not impose" misleads, because it abstracts the computer from the destiny that was required for its making.... [C]omputers can only exist in societies in which there are large corporate institutions.... In this sense computers are not neutral

Computers

instruments, but instruments which exclude certain forms of community and permit others. 12 *George Grant*

[I]t is evident that microchip technology is not just a neutral tool: it is clearly society-forming as well as society-formed. It is a tool that contributes to the future shape of the society that utilizes it. 13 *Peter Singer & Deane Wells*

[L]ong-term value change can be induced by computers. 14 *Milton Rokeach*

One might say the computer is being used to program the child. 15 *Seymour Papert*

The translation of society into a form that can be represented electronically, and the abandonment of whatever cannot be so translated, represents a new variety of totalitarianism and a great dividing point in human history. 16
W. H. Stoddard

The computer will smash the pyramid: We created the hierarchical, pyramidal, managerial system because we needed it to keep track of people and things people did; with the computer to keep track, we can restructure our institutions horizontally. 17 *John Naisbitt*

Computers will be used more and more to produce the opinion-obsoleting answers to progressive crises-provoked questions about which way world society as a whole will enduringly profit the most. Computers will correct misinformed and disadvantaged conditioned reflexes, not only of the few officials who have heretofore blocked comprehensive techno-economic and political evolutionary advancement, but also of the vast majorities of heretofore-ignorant total humanity. 18
R. Buckminster Fuller

The computer will relegate all physical substances to their uniquely best functional uses.... Only the computer can cope with the astronomical complexity of integrating the unpredicted potentials of the millions of invisible technology gains in physical capabilities already accomplished. 19
R. Buckminster Fuller

The computer will also make it very clear that, freed of the necessity to earn a living, all humanity will want to exercise its fundamental drive first to comprehend "what it is all about" and second to demonstrate competence in respect to the challenges. 20 *R. Buckminster Fuller*

Today computers hold out the promise of a means of instant translation of any code or language into any other code or language. The computer, in short, promises by technology a Pentacostal condition of universal understanding and unity. The next logical step would seem to be, not to translate, but to by-pass languages in favor of a general cosmic consciousness.... 21
Marshall McLuhan

Several years or decades from now, when computers have the memory trace that will allow them to "enjoy" ... or "rejoice" in their accomplishments, they'll be no closer to having some mystical level of consciousness than we are. They'll just be high-speed computation machines like us—only they'll be made largely of silicon instead of carbon. 22 *Marvin Minsky*

[Y]our nervous system is being replaced by a computer.... After a while it begins to insert its own messages into the flow, gradually insinuating itself into your thinking, endowing you with new knowledge and new skills.... Ultimately your brain would die, and your mind would find itself entirely in the computer. 23
Hans Moravec

At last the human brain, ensconced in a computer, has been liberated from the weakness of the mortal flesh.... It is in control of its own destiny. The machine is its body; it is the machine's mind.... It seems to me that this must be the mature form of intelligent life in the Universe. Housed in indestructible lattices of silicon, and no longer constrained in the span of its years by the life and death cycle of biological organisms, such a kind of life could live forever. 24 *Robert Jastrow*

"Downloading" a human brain into a computer workalike has captured the imagination of those preoccupied with immortality.... 25
William H. Calvin

Computers

The era of carbon-chemistry life is drawing to a close on the earth and a new era of silicon-based life—indestructable, immortal, infinitely expandable—is beginning. 26 *Robert Jastrow*

Will we become the "contented cows" or the "household pets" of the new computer kingdom of life? Or will *Homo sapiens* be exterminated as *Homo sapiens*?... 27 *Ralph W. Burhoe*

Look about you and consider what human beings have done and are doing to the world.... Viewed in that manner, the succession of a computer-intelligence that is superior to the human variety and that is (perhaps) not associated with the emotions and with the judgmental incapacity of the latter is something that could be much to be desired.... It is with that thought in mind that sometimes, when I am asked if the computer will ever replace the human being, that I answer, "I hope so." 28
Isaac Asimov

To the extent that man fails to make the distinction between the intermediate operations of electric intelligence and the ultimate responsibilities of human decision and conscience, the computer could ... obscure man's awareness of the need to come to terms with himself. It may foster the illusion that he is asking fundamental questions when actually he is asking only functional ones. It may be regarded as a substitute for intelligence instead of an extension of it.... For the danger is not so much that man will be controlled by the computer as that he may imitate it. 29 *Norman Cousins*

The computer and its information cannot answer any of the fundamental questions we need to address to make our lives more meaningful and humane.... The computer is, in a sense, a magnificent toy that distracts us from facing what we most need to confront—spiritual emptiness, knowledge of ourselves, usable conceptions of the past and future.... 30
Neil Postman

What emerges as the most elementary insight is that, since we do not now have any ways of making computers wise, we ought not now to give to computers tasks that demand wisdom. 31
Joseph Weizenbaum

Sophisticated robots can overcome lots of problems. What they cannot do is provide vision, and political leadership.... 32
Paul Kennedy

[C]omputers can have a powerful influence on how people think. 33 *Seymour Papert*

There is the risk that the electronic computer—a product of Western thinking and technology—may prove most useful for perpetuating just those forms of intelligence that led to its devising in the first place. 34
Howard Gardner

[A] particular subculture, one dominated by computer engineers, is influencing the world of education to favor those school students who are most like that subculture. 35
Seymour Papert

Something essential to man's creativity, even in science, may disappear when the defiantly metaphoric language of poetry gives way completely to the denatured language of the computer. 36 *Lewis Mumford*

Learning to program and work with computers seems to mean learning to deal with ... reality reduced to its simplest possible elements.... Once reality has been reduced ... to data ... processing in a computer can only take place according to the rules and principles of the data logic.... And the road to knowledge and cognition has to pass through the computer.... The computer becomes the means through which knowledge of reality may be acquired. 37 *Janni Nielsen*

For now that language has become merely another tool, all concepts, ideas, images that [we] cannot paraphrase into computer-comprehensible language have lost their function and their potency.... No wonder, given this view of language, that the distinction between the living and the lifeless, between man and machine, has become something less than real.... In the process of adapting ourselves ... [we] have castrated not only ourselves (that is resigned ourselves to impotence), but our very language as well. 38 *Joseph Weizenbaum*

Computers

In the same way that technology was used to carry out mass murders in the Third Reich ... the more precise kind of knowledge of human behavior based on computer data and cybernetics can contribute to the more rapid, comprehensive, and effective soul murder of the human being.... 39 *Alice Miller*

The computer has raised the stakes both for our inaction and our action. 40
Seymour Papert

Conflict

Conflict is the essence of existence. Without it personal life has no meaning.... Oswald Spengler ... distinguishes two great destiny ideas: the Apollonian of the classical world and the Faustian of the modern world. Apollonian man conceived of his soul "as a cosmos ordered in a group of excellent parts." There was no place in his universe for will, and conflict was an evil.... On the other hand, the Faustian's picture of himself is as a force endlessly combatting obstacles. 1 *Ruth Benedict*

The normal human being is free neither of problems nor of conflicts. Conflicts are part of the human condition. 2 *Heinz Hartmann*

Without contraries is no progression. Attraction and repulsion, reason and energy, love and hate, are necessary to human existence. 3
William Blake

Conflict is the father of all things.... Everything originates in strife. 4 *Heraclitus*

Strife is the origin of all things.... Strife will always remain at the root of human nature, like a supreme fatality.... Peace is hence absurd.... The Christian and Socialist "men be brothers" is a mask for the eternal and immutable *homo homini lupus*. 5 *Benito Mussolini*

Americans tend to believe that conflict is unnatural, that people from all nations are basically alike, that differences are products of misunderstanding, and that permanent and perfect peace is a reachable goal.... [A] world without conflict is an illusion. It has never existed and will never exist.... [C]onflict is intrinsic to mankind. 6 *Richard M. Nixon*

Mankind has grown great in eternal struggle, and only in eternal peace does it perish.... [T]hose who do not want to fight in this world of eternal struggle do not deserve to live. 7
Adolf Hitler

[T]he ideal of a State co-extensive with humanity is no ideal at all.... The grandeur of history lies in the perpetual conflict of nations. 8
Heinrich von Treitschke

Conflict has become the stepchild of political thought. 9 *James MacGregor Burns*

The paramount question facing ... the world is the *global* organization and management of conflict. 10 *James MacGregor Burns*

It is ... useless for human-reality to seek to get out of this dilemma: one must either transcend the Other or allow oneself to be transcended by him. The essence of the relations between consciousnesses ... is conflict. 11
Jean-Paul Sartre

I call the project self versus other *Structure*.... [It] starts from the assumption of conflict and makes that a reason for establishing control. 12
Graham Little

The first class conflict that appears in history coincides with the development of the antagonism between man and woman in monogamous marriage. 13 *Friedrich Engels*

[I]t is in time of conflict that the emotional acknowledgment of male authority comes into male and female consciousness. 14
Steven Goldberg

[The] four psychodynamic conflicts leading to the development of male chauvinism [are] ... infantile strivings, power and dependency conflicts, Oedipal anxiety, and a hostile envy of women. 15 *Kenneth Solomon*

Intrapsychic conflicts ... reflect the power structures and value norms of a given society. 16
Margarete Mitscherlich

Conflict

It is not accidental that a conflict that starts with our relation to others in time affects the whole personality. 17 *Karen Horney*

[Women's] powers are more co-ordinated, more in harmony with each other, where [men's] are disjointed and in conflict.... So naturally we have a society made after his pattern—advanced in mechanical invention, but all involved in a whirling confusion and strife, which on its human side is an *utter failure*. 18 *Edward Carpenter*

[C]onflict and division experienced by an individual can give rise to a very subtle form of damage to the brain.... [A] person whose levels of meaning are incoherent and confused will develop a brain that becomes increasingly insensitive. When mind and body are no longer in harmony, confused meanings enter the body and cause illness and disease. The result is a muted response to life and even bizarre, destructive, and violent behavior. 19 *F. David Peat*

The "American Dilemma" ... is the ever-raging conflict between, on the one hand, the valuations preserved on the general plane ... [i.e.] the "American Creed," where the American thinks, talks, and acts under the influence of high national and Christian precepts, and on the other hand, the valuations on specific planes of individual and group living ... [where] all sorts of miscellaneous wants, impulses, and habits dominate his outlook. 20 *Gunnar Myrdal*

The psyche ... is a boiling caldron of contradictory impulses, inhibitions, and affects, and for many people the conflict ... is so insupportable that they even wish for the deliverance preached by theologians. 21 *Carl Jung*

[F]arming communities accumulate possessions, and ... they must protect them. This is the key to human conflict. 22 *Richard E. Leakey*

It is ... chimerical to build peace on economic foundations, which, in turn, rest on the systematic cultivation of greed and envy, the very forces which drive men into conflict. 23 *E. F. Schumacher*

[M]odern man suffers from his inability to make a choice, as he sees it, between renouncing freedom and individualism, or giving up the material comforts of modern technology and the security of a collective mass society. This, as I see it, is the true conflict of our times. 24 *Bruno Bettelheim*

[T]he crucial psychological battle we must wage is that against our own dependent needs, and our anxiety and guilt feelings which will arise as we move toward freedom. The basic conflict, in fine, is between that part of the person which seeks growth, expansion and health against the part which longs to remain on an immature level.... 25 *Rollo May*

[A]s our culture has grown less homogeneous, it gives much less support to the individual. He ... finds many of the basic issues and conflicts of life centering in himself. Each man must resolve within himself issues for which his society previously took full responsibility.... [I]n our modern culture, with its conflicting subcultures, and its contradictory sets of values, goals, and perceptions, the ... internal conflict is multiplied. 26 *Carl Rogers*

Conflict is the evil we most want to avoid, among nations, among individuals and within ourselves.... We must respect values, but they must not get in the way of peace.... Conflict, the condition of creativity for Nietzsche, is for us a cry for therapy.... 27 *Allan Bloom*

The increasing size of the group increases the difficulties of achieving a group self-consciousness, except as it comes in conflict with other groups and is unified by perils and passions of war. It is a rather pathetic aspect of human social life that conflict is a seemingly unavoidable prerequisite of group solidarity. 28 *Reinhold Niebuhr*

Communism ... is the *genuine* resolution of the conflict between man and nature and between man and man—the true resolution of the strife between existence and essence, between objectification and self-confirmation, between freedom and necessity, between the individual and the species. 29 *Karl Marx*

CONFLICT

Marxist philosophy holds that the law of the unity of opposites is the fundamental law of the universe.... Contradictions exist everywhere.... Between the opposites in a contradiction there is at once unity and struggle, and it is this that impels things to move and change. 30 *Mao Tse-tung*

[E]ach species behaves as if the general movement of life stopped at it instead of passing through it. It thinks only of itself, it lives only for itself. Hence the numberless struggles that we behold in nature. Hence a discord, striking and terrible, but for which the original principle of life must not be held responsible. 31 *Henri Bergson*

Opposition is not a hindrance to life, it is the necessary condition for the becoming of life. 32 *Havelock Ellis*

For the principle of life consists in the tension which connects spirit with the realm of matter, symbiotically joined. 33 *Ruth N. Anshen*

[C]onflict is not a bad thing in itself. It is indeed an essential element in that creative process by which evolution proceeds. 34 *Kenneth Boulding*

From the war of nature ... the most exalted object which we are capable of conceiving, namely, the production of the higher animals, directly follows. 35 *Charles Darwin*

The struggle for existence is the life of Nature, the basis of all healthy development. All existing things show themselves to be the result of contending forces. So it is in the life of man. The struggle is not merely the destructive but the life-giving principle. 36 *F. von Bernhardi*

The conflict of nature and mind is itself a reflection of the paradox contained in the psychic being of man. 37 *Carl Jung*

[T]he formation of personality is dominated by the search for a coherence and an organization of values that will prevent internal conflicts.... 38 *Jean Piaget & Bärbel Inhelder*

The heart of man is made so as to reconcile contradictions. 39 *David Hume*

[T]he only way out of human conflict is full renunciation, to give one's life as a gift to the highest powers. Absolution has to come from the absolute beyond. 40 *Ernest Becker*

Conflict engenders fire, the fire of affects and emotions, and like every other fire it has two aspects, that of combustion and that of creating light. 41 *Carl Jung*

CONSCIENCE

[O]F ALL THE DIFFERENCES between man and the lower animals, the moral sense of conscience is by far the most important.... It is the most noble of all the attributes of man. 1 *Charles Darwin*

The human being is nature's fall from a state of innocency; but it is not a decline, it is rather an ascent, in that a state of conscience is higher than a state of innocence. 2 *Thomas Mann*

[C]onscience ... —true fountainhead as it is of idealism and imagination—[has] produced an abundance of novel and amazing beauty and affirmation, and perhaps has really been the first to give birth to beauty at all. 3 *Friedrich Nietzsche*

Conscience may be defined as a means to discover meanings.... 4 *Viktor Frankl*

Conscience derives from the same root as *conscious*, namely *conscio*, or "I know together with (someone else)." Its origin is therefore the notion of sharing knowledge with someone ... [who] becomes the potential witness against me, the person who could make me ashamed. 5 *Derek Wright*

[I]n the fact of the conscience we are not only agents, but it is by this alone that we know ourselves to be such.... The result is the consciousness of responsibility.... But as without a Thou there can be no you, so ... it is evident that conscience is the root of all consciousness. 6 *Samuel Taylor Coleridge*

The conscience of man will necessarily think of itself as, in respect of all duties, another person—

as himself in the character of judge of his acts ... and this other person may either be a real or a mere ideal person, created by reason for itself. Such an ideal person ... must understand the hearts of men: for the tribunal is set up within the heart of man. 7 *Immanuel Kant*

There is ... at the bottom of our hearts an innate principle of justice and virtue ... and it is this principle that I call conscience. 8
Jean-Jacques Rousseau

[T]he mature person loves with both the motherly conscience and the fatherly conscience, in spite of the fact that they seem to contradict each other. If he would only retain his fatherly conscience, he would become harsh and inhuman. If he would retain only his motherly conscience, he would be apt to lose judgment and to hinder himself and others in their development. 9 *Erich Fromm*

The word *conscience* is used to express two phenomena which are quite different from each other. One is the "authoritarian conscience" which is the internalized voice of an authority who we are eager to please and afraid of displeasing.... It is also the conscience which Freud speaks of, and which he called "Super-Ego." ... Different from the authoritarian conscience is the "humanistic conscience." ... Humanistic conscience is based on the fact that as human beings we have an intuitive knowledge of what is human and inhuman, what is conducive of life and what is destructive of life.... It is the voice which calls us back to ourselves, to our humanity. 10 *Erich Fromm*

Women's conscience operates in terms of an internalized observer in whose eyes the self is judged.... Women's conscience involved an ideal of goodness—it was more benign.... Men's conscience felt "ego-alien"—it is more like an internal enemy. 11 *Helen B. Lewis*

Conscience manifests itself as the call of Care.... 12 *Martin Heidegger*

Increasingly, larger organizations—public and private—possess a Medea-like intensity to paralyze conscience.... Within the structure of the organization there has taken place an erosion of both human values and the broader value of human beings as the possibility of dissent within the hierarchy has become so restricted that common candor requires uncommon courage. 13 *Ralph Nader*

The Party is the Mind, Honor and Conscience of our epoch. 14 *V. I. Lenin*

The ordinary [Nazi] party member was being taught that grand policy was much too complex for him to judge it. Consequently, one felt one was being represented, never called upon to take personal responsibility. The whole structure of the system was aimed at preventing conflicts of conscience from even arising. 15
Albert Speer

The more severe the conscience ... [and] the greater the quantity of aggression channeled inwards through it, the higher the general level of tension within the system. The only way in which temporary relief from this tension can be achieved is by creating conditions under which this superego aggression can be turned outwards on to someone else. 16
Derek Wright

Conscience has ... been the conqueror's chief ally.... [It] organizes hatred as it organizes love.... And so conscience in human society becomes an essentially anti-rational power. Its symbols must not be questioned too closely: they will lose their magic.... The power of conscience, blind, anti-rational, and acting in alliance with the weapons fixation, will be the responsible force if self-annihilation be the human outcome. 17 *Robert Ardrey*

We can obey a cultural commandment when it conflicts with a biological commandment, but conscience reminds us of the conflict. Conscience will always conflict with a cultural command to kill.... 18 *Irenäus Eibl-Eibesfeldt*

The presence of conscience in men ... can be seen as a special case of the more general principle that any self-generating automaton must have an inhibitor to check its actions against its own kind, for without such inhibition, several automata cannot occupy a common territory. 19 *Stanley Milgram*

Conscience

[C]onscience ... [is the] voice that tells us how far we can go without incurring intolerable risks or costs to our own interests. 20
Richard Alexander

Conscience stands in striking contrast to any values that might be put forward by materialism. 21 *Friedrich Hebbel*

In recent decades "conscience" has lost much of its significance. It seems as though neither external nor internal authorities play any prominent role in the individual's life. Everybody is completely "free."... 22 *Erich Fromm*

[T]he consistent derogation of the superego as harsh, cruel and oppressive has filtered down to the public as a derogation of conscience, has helped to convert guilt into nothing but guilt feelings, and responsibility into ... neurotic feelings of obligation. 23
W. Lederer & A. Botwin

[A] movement away from the authoritarian and towards the humanist type of conscience is the moral effect of any increase in that kind of wisdom which consists in insight or self-knowledge. 24 *R. E. Money-Kyrle*

The distinguishing characteristic of selfhood ... is not rationality but the critical awareness of man's divided nature. Selfhood expresses itself in the form of a guilty conscience. 25
Christopher Lasch

[B]ad conscience is inseparable from freedom.... There is no freedom without an accompanying critical attitude of the self. 26 *Jacques Ellul*

Conscience, and particularly bad conscience, can be a gift from heaven; a genuine grace, if used as a superior self-criticism. Self-criticism ... is indispensable to any attempt to understand one's own psychology. 27 *Carl Jung*

Undoubtedly the bad conscience is an illness, but an illness as pregnancy is an illness. 28
Friedrich Nietzsche

[Man's] conscience is the voice which calls him back to himself ... in order to become himself; it helps him to remain aware of the aims of his life and of the norms necessary for the attainment of these aims. 29 *Erich Fromm*

Conscience is the voice of our true selves which summons us ... *to become what we potentially are....* Conscience judges our functioning as human beings ... in the art of living. 30
Erich Fromm

Our conscience is the call to ourselves. 31
Paul Tillich

The call of conscience has the character of an *appeal* to Dasein by calling it to its ownmost potentiality-for-Being-its-self.... [A]n authentic potentiality-for-Being is attested by the conscience. And conscience, as a phenomenon of Dasein, demands ... a genuinely existential interpretation. 32 *Martin Heidegger*

Conscience is the summary of the whole man.... It is the mirror of a man's depths.... Conscience is the face of the soul. 33
Thomas Merton

Conscience never deceives us; she is the true guide of man; it is to soul what instinct is to body; he who obeys his conscience is following nature.... Conscience is the voice of the soul. 34 *Jean-Jacques Rousseau*

Conscience is a man's compass.... 35
Vincent van Gogh

Conscience ... is one's capacity to tap one's own deeper levels of insight, ethical sensitivity and awareness ... [and] the individual's method of tapping wisdom and insight within himself.... 36 *Rollo May*

[T]he healthy conscience ... vigilantly guards the very best interests of our true self.... It is the reaction of our true self to the proper functioning or the malfunctioning of our total personality.... To put it in most general terms, our conscience is a moral agency serving our growth.... 37 *Karen Horney*

Conscience is a crucial agent in the growth of personality.... In proportion as the generic conscience becomes the monitor of growth, emphasis shifts from tribalism to individuality, from

opportunistic to oriented becoming. 38
Gordon W. Allport

Every strong state of conscience is a source of life; it is an essential factor of our general vitality. Consequently, everything that tends to enfeeble it wastes and corrupts us. 39
Émile Durkheim

[W]hat conscience (the highest forefeeling man possesses of the truth accessible to him) demands, is always, and in all respects, the activity most fruitful and most necessary for humanity at the given time. 40 *Leo Tolstoy*

Consciousness of failure to act in response to conscience can lead to the greatest revulsion, not only of oneself, but for the human species. 41
J. Glenn Gray

[T]he safest course is to do nothing against one's conscience. With this secret, we can enjoy life and have no fear of death. 42 *Voltaire*

[T]he very constitution of our nature requires that we bring our whole conduct before this superior faculty [of conscience]; wait its determination; enforce upon ourselves its authority, and make it the business of our lives, as it is absolutely the whole business of a moral agent, to conform ourselves to it. This is the true meaning of that ancient precept, *Reverence thyself.* 43 *Joseph Butler*

Be the master of your will and the servant of your conscience. 44
Maria von Ebner-Eschenbach

~ CONSCIOUSNESS ~

MAN'S CAPACITY FOR consciousness alone makes him man. 1 *Carl Jung*

What then is consciousness? It is as if the information processed by the senses becomes integrated to form an analogue of the energy patterns impinging upon them.... [I]t is precisely from this "being aware of having experience" and being able both to communicate its features to another and to distinguish between oneself as experiencing agent and another's reported experiences that the prime features of humanity arise. 2 *John H. Crook*

Nothing but consciousness can unite remote existences into the same person.... [W]ithout consciousness there is no person.... 3 *John Locke*

Since everything which exists or happens for a man exists only in his consciousness and happens for it alone, the most essential thing for a man is the constitution of this consciousness, which is in most cases far more important than the circumstances which go to form its contents. 4 *Arthur Schopenhauer*

[W]hile membership of a certain species is not a morally relevant characteristic, consciousness [is].... Research on the embryo therefore ought to stop—or at least should only be permissible under extremely strict controls—as soon as the embryo reaches the stage at which it may be conscious. 5
Peter Singer & Deane Wells

Mind denotes the whole system of meanings as they are embodied in the workings of organic life; consciousness in a being with language denotes awareness or perception of meanings.... 6 *John Dewey*

[C]onsciousness has developed only under the pressure of the need for communication.... In brief, the development of language and the development of consciousness ... go hand in hand. 7 *Friedrich Nietzsche*

[C]onsciousness is ... a sensory organ directed toward the outside world. 8 *Sigmund Freud*

Consciousness is the mere surface of our mind, of which, as of the earth, we do not know the inside but only the crust. 9
Arthur Schopenhauer

All experience is already interpreted by the nervous system a hundredfold—or a thousandfold, before it becomes conscious experience. When it does become conscious experience then it can be interpreted, more or less consciously, as a theory.... 10
Karl Popper & John Eccles

Consciousness

If consciousness has a role at all ... then it would seem to be that of general supervisor, something which, like the airline captain, keeps a fatherly eye on the black boxes. 11 *Norman F. Dixon*

[T]he conscious mind may on occasion, like the Queen of England, reign but not rule.... 12
Robert E. Lane

[P]rimitives are afraid of uncontrolled emotions, because consciousness breaks down under them and gives way to possession. All man's strivings have therefore been directed towards the consolidation of consciousness. This was the purpose of rite and dogma; they were dams and walls to keep back the dangers of the unconscious. 13 *Carl Jung*

[T]he apparent unity of consciousness is a deceit of artful nature. We are protected from the knowledge of our own conflicts and frequent inconsistencies by this wonderful mechanism. 14
Alberta Gilinsky

[T]he history of human consciousness is the history of human social life.... The form of consciousness is a product of the myth generating socio-economic forces of its time. 15
John H. Crook

Consciousness arises from the interrelation of the form and the environment, and it involves both of them.... Consciousness as such refers to both the organism and its environment and cannot be located simply in either. 16
George H. Mead

It is not the consciousness of men that determines their being, but, on the contrary, their social being determines their consciousness. 17
Karl Marx

Of all the qualities of human beings that are injured, narrowed or repressed in the Corporate State, it is consciousness, the most precious and the most fragile, that suffers the most.... Encounters with people are so many, so brutish and impersonal, so fleeting and harrowing that consciousness must be desensitized to reduce the pain.... [O]nly by an antisocial posture can people really be "alive"... in a society that is essentially dead. 18 *Charles A. Reich*

[T]he restricted and enclosed consciousness of the ego is really a spasm of fear.... Fully expanded, consciousness feels an identity with the whole world, but contracted it is the more inescapably attached to a single minute and perishable organism. 19 *Alan Watts*

[T]he old king of consciousness was kingly, continuous.... The old king had a role, not a job. He was an inclusive centre-without-a-margin. The new consciousness like the new prince is a harassed executive, exercising a job, applying knowledge to problems, and having only momentary contacts with his marginal subjects, who are all ambitious rival segments anyway. 20 *Marshall McLuhan*

The automatization of ordinary consciousness is a tradeoff: for the sake of survival, we lose much of the possible richness of experience. 21
Robert E. Ornstein

To despise the animal basis of life, to seek value only at the level of conscious intelligence and rational effort, is ultimately to lose one's sense of cosmic relationships; and without this sense a noble consciousness of human destiny, higher and wider than any merely human institution, has never arisen. 22 *Lewis Mumford*

[O]ur normal waking consciousness, rational consciousness as we call it, is but one special type of consciousness, whilst all about it, parted from it by the filmiest of screens, there lie potential forms of consciousness entirely different.... No account of the universe in its totality can be final which leaves these other forms of consciousness quite disregarded. 23
William James

Two new ethical commandments are necessary as man moves into the molecular age.... [:] I. Thou shalt not alter the consciousness of thy fellow man.... II. Thou shalt not prevent thy fellow man from altering his own consciousness. 24 *Timothy Leary*

A radical change in consciousness is the necessary first step towards radical social change. 25
Herbert Marcuse

Anything which changes consciousness is a

threat to the established order. 26
Timothy Leary

There is a revolution coming.... At the heart of everything is what we shall call a change of consciousness.... Consciousness I is the traditional outlook of the American.... Consciousness II represents the values of an organizational society. Consciousness III is the new generation. 27 *Charles A. Reich*

[A] person's consciousness is limited by his assumptions or available categories. 28
Robert E. Ornstein

In the split brain syndrome we deal with two separate spheres of conscious awareness.... 29
Roger Sperry

[I]n the minor hemisphere we deal with a second conscious entity that is characteristically human and runs along in parallel with the more dominant stream of consciousness in the major hemisphere. 30 *Roger Sperry*

Man has developed out of the animals ... where what we call "consciousness" is hard to believe in.... It is therefore natural to suppose that, whatever may be the correct definition of "consciousness," "consciousness" is not the essence of life or mind. 31 *Bertrand Russell*

[M]an, by the very fact of being man, of possessing consciousness, is, in comparison with the ass or the crab, a diseased animal. Consciousness is a disease. 32 *Miguel de Unamuno*

As soon as high consciousness is reached, the enjoyment of existence is entwined with pain, frustration, loss, tragedy. 33
Alfred N. Whitehead

For consciousness is now called upon to do what nature has always done ... [:] give a certain, unquestionable and unequivocal decision.... And here we are beset by an all-too-human fear that consciousness—our Promethean conquest—may in the end not be able to serve us in the place of nature. Problems thus draw us into an orphaned and isolated state where we are abandoned by nature and are driven to consciousness. 34 *Carl Jung*

Consciousness has made cowards of us all. 35
Camille Paglia

The upheaval of our world and the upheaval in consciousness is one and the same. Everything has become relative and therefore doubtful. 36
Carl Jung

And yet the attainment of consciousness was the most precious fruit of the tree of knowledge, the magical weapon which gave man victory over the earth, and which we hope will give him a still greater victory over himself. 37
Carl Jung

The time has come when psychology must discard all references to consciousness and need no longer delude itself into making mental states the object of observation; its sole task is the prediction and control of behavior; and introspection can form no part of its method. 38
John B. Watson

If there is anything "soul-like" or "mystical" or "supernatural" about human psychology, it is the *presence* not the absence of consciousness. It is consciousness, and not behavior without consciousness, which remains completely inexplicable. 39 *Norman F. Dixon*

"Existence exists—and the act of grasping that statement implies two corollary axioms: that something exists which one perceives and that one exists possessing consciousness, consciousness being the faculty of perceiving that which exists. If nothing exists, there can be no consciousness: a consciousness with nothing to be conscious of is a contradiction in terms." 40
Ayn Rand

We shall, sooner or later, arrive at a mechanical equivalent of consciousness. 41 *T. H. Huxley*

Today, after more than a century of electric technology, we have extended our central nervous system itself in a global embrace.... Rapidly, we approach the final phase of the extensions of man—the technological simulation of consciousness ... [and] the ultimate electronic goal of a collective consciousness. 42
Marshall McLuhan

Consciousness

[P]hysicists and neuroscientists have speculated that human consciousness itself is the direct manifestation of a holistic quantum system. Consciousness acts as a whole: Its manifestations are global and extend across the whole brain, and certain of its properties hint at some sort of global quantum process. 43

F. David Peat

Matter, being made of quanta of energy, is the vibrating, changing component of pure consciousness.... The thrust of evolution is toward more and more complex systems, implying higher and higher levels of consciousness. 44

Itzhak Bentov

Right at its base, the living world is constituted by consciousness clothed in flesh and bone ... and consciousness, in its turn, as we now know, is nothing less than the substance and heart of life in process of evolution. 45

Pierre Teilhard de Chardin

[I]t is consciousness, or rather supra-consciousness, that is at the origin of life. Consciousness, or supra-consciousness, is the name for the rocket whose extinguished fragments fall back as matter; consciousness ... subsists of the rocket itself, passing through the fragments and lighting them up into organisms. But this consciousness, which is a *need of creation*, is made manifest to itself only where creation is possible. It lies dormant when life is condemned to automatism; it wakens as soon as the possibility of a choice is restored. 46

Henri Bergson

Throughout the whole extent of the animal kingdom ... consciousness seems proportionate to the living being's power of choice. 47

Henri Bergson

It is only by making itself for-itself that being can aspire to be the cause of itself. Consciousness as the nihilation of being appears therefore as one stage in a progression toward the immanence of causality—i.e., toward being a self-cause.... Consciousness is in fact a project of founding itself; that is, of attaining to the dignity of the in-itself-for-itself or in-itself-as-self-cause. 48 *Jean-Paul Sartre*

Consciousness is not a mode of particular knowledge which may be called an inner meaning of self-knowledge; it is the dimension of transphenomenal being in the subject. 49

Jean-Paul Sartre

The distinguishing characteristic of consciousness ... is that it is a decompression of being. 50

Jean-Paul Sartre

[I]n conscious life cosmic being recurs as human becoming. 51 *Martin Buber*

Consciousness is a precondition of being. Thus the psyche is endowed with the dignity of a cosmic principle, which philosophically and in fact gives it a position co-equal with the principle of physical being. 52 *Carl Jung*

The subjectivity of consciousness is an irreducible feature of reality.... [W]e and our personal perspectives belong to the world. 53

Thomas Nagel

Human consciousness created objective existence and meaning, and man found his indispensable place in the great process of being. 54

Carl Jung

In the light of human consciousness, it is not man, but the whole universe of still "lifeless" matter that turns out to be impotent and insignificant. That physical universe is unable to behold itself except through the eyes of man, unable to speak for itself, except through the human voice, unable to know itself, except through human intelligence: unable in fact to realize the potentialities of its own earlier development until man ... emerged from the utter darkness and dumbness of pre-organic existence. 55 *Lewis Mumford*

Consciousness ... is the phenomenon whereby the universe's very existence is made known. 56

Roger Penrose

The very cosmos itself depends for its being on the uttermost mystery of consciousness. And thus the symbiosis, the union between the physical world and the mind, the great metaphysical dance by which each brings into being the other. 57 *George Greenstein*

[M]ove upwards towards greater consciousness and greater love. At the summit you will find yourselves united with all those who, from every direction, have made the same ascent. 58
Pierre Teilhard de Chardin

Man, if he is to remain man, must advance by way of consciousness. There is no road leading backward. 59 *Karl Jaspers*

The world is for consciousness. 60
Miguel de Unamuno

CONSERVATISM

GENUINE CONSERVATIVES know that man and society are not perfectible; they are realistically aware that Utopia—including the dream paradise of absolute, unfettered liberty to act just as the individual pleases—means literally Nowhere. It is one of the Conservatives principle functions to remind mankind that politics is the art of the *possible*. 1 *Russell Kirk*

The man of conservative temperament believes that a known good is not lightly to be surrendered for an unknown better. 2
Michael Oakeshott

The hard and fast conservative is the man who cannot conceive that existing constitutions, institutions and social arrangements are mechanisms for achieving social results. To him, *they* are the results; they are final. 3
John Dewey

One of the fundamental traits of the conservative attitude is a fear of change.... [T]hey lack [a] faith in the spontaneous forces of adjustment.... The conservative feels safe and content only if he is assured that some higher wisdom ... [or] some authority is charged with keeping the change "orderly." ... Order appears to the conservatives as the result of the continuous attention of authority.... 4 *Friedrich von Hayek*

[The] fear of change is at the root of conservative fondness for authority.... The conservative cannot accept that order can arise spontaneously.... 5 *David Green*

[A] conservative doesn't really trust anyone, much less himself.... Therefore he is always struggling to submit his bodily desires to the regimen of some external permanent standard of conduct. 6 *Jim Lucier*

The chances are somewhat better than even that a closed-minded person will be conservative rather than liberal in his politics.... 7
Milton Rokeach

Conservatives saw in foreign policy a version of the eternal struggle of good with evil, a conflict which recognizes no middle ground.... Regard for the purity of our ideals inspired conservatives.... There could be no compromise with the devil. 8 *Henry Kissinger*

Liberty has tended to be emphasized at the conservative end of the political spectrum and justice at the liberal end. 9
Richard Hutcheson Jr.

[T]he Right reflects the attitudes of those at the top of the heap, conservatives who are well satisfied with unequal privileges which they wish to retain. Their emphasis is on the liberty of the individual, meaning primarily themselves, which they consider threatened by the programs of the welfare state.... 10
Leslie Lipson

Political necessity compelled the conservatives to develop their own concept of liberty to oppose ... [and] distinguish it from the revolutionary egalitarian concept.... Men, they claimed, are essentially unequal ... at the very core of their beings. Freedom therefore can only consist in the ability of each man to develop without let or hindrance according to the law and principle of his own personality. 11
Karl Mannheim

[T]he conservative position rests on the belief that in any society there are recognizably superior persons ... who should have a greater influence on public affairs than others.... And since it does not really believe in the power of argument, its last resort is generally a claim to superior wisdom, based on some self-arrogated superior qualities. 12 *Friedrich von Hayek*

Conservatism

[I]n the same way that men cannot for long tolerate a sense of spiritual meaninglessness in their individual lives, so they cannot for long accept a society in which power, privilege and property are not distributed according to some more meaningful criteria.... So I conclude, despite Prof. Hayek's ingenious analysis, that men cannot accept the historical accidents of the marketplace—seen merely as accidents—as the basis for an enduring and legitimate entitlement to power, privilege and property. 13
Irving Kristol

[A]n elite is the major premise of a genuinely conservative ideology. 14 *C. Wright Mills*

The ideology of conservatism has frequently been based on elitist values which reject the idea that there is wisdom in the voice of the electorate. 15 *Seymour Lipset*

Even democracy—which corresponds neither to the natural nor to the supernatural yearnings of the normal citizen—can be discarded without detriment to the civic wellbeing as the Conservative conceives it. 16 *Roger Scruton*

[A neoconservative] assumption is ... that society is exceptionally brittle, that chaos is just below the surface.... For neoconservatism ... the bulwark it envisions against the forces of chaos is not a widened democracy but a new establishment. 17 *Peter Steinfels*

If one were to probe into the hearts of many potential and actual Tory supporters ... one might well discover that what worries them most about contemporary Britain was not so much a lack of freedom as its excessive abundance ... of something unpleasantly close to chaos.... The urgent need today is for the state to regain control over "the people." 18
Maurice Cowling

[T]he extreme conservative perceives the world as "falling apart," which leads him to seek and place value upon order, simplicity, and security. 19 *G. D. Wilson*

Though the discontents of our civilization express themselves in the "rhetoric of liberation" and "equality," one can detect beneath the surface an acute yearning for order and stability—but a legitimate order, of course, and a legitimate stability. 20 *Irving Kristol*

[Carl] Jung represents a conservative.... He is perhaps the most subtle of modern conservatives, trying to save not this tradition or that, but the very notion of tradition, which can be defined, in Jungian terms, as shared archetypes internalized. 21 *Philip Rieff*

The plea to preserve "tradition" as such, can appeal only to those who have given up or those who never intended to achieve anything in life. It is a plea that appeals to the worst elements in men and rejects the best.... If the "conservatives" do not stand for capitalism, they stand for and are nothing; they have no goal, no direction, no political principles, no social ideals, no intellectual values, no leadership to offer anyone. 22 *Ayn Rand*

A task for conservative leaders is to reconcile individualism ... with the sense of community.... 23 *Russell Kirk*

The prospects for conservatism are hardly bright. It became great by virtue of its fight against power, which now is being converted into a fight for the capture of power, central power. 24 *Robert Nisbet*

By its softening of the political will, this [conservative] mood enables men to accept public depravity without any private sense of outrage, and to give up the central goal of western humanism.... 25 *C. Wright Mills*

Humanism ... refers to *a commitment to the needs of man*. Only conservatives can be consistent humanists, because they alone recognize the eternally binding character of morality and ethics, which is the ultimate justification for humanism. 26 *Craig Schiller*

[The American founding fathers] were not soft-headed do-gooders, but they believed in moral and spiritual values. They would have been appalled by the philosophy that seems so dominant in the capitalist world today—when so many seem motivated only by selfish, materialistic values and for whom the only god is money.

They were conservatives, but their conservatism was leavened with compassion. 27
Richard M. Nixon

In sum, the object of conservatism is *social friendship*, the moderating of animosity by the tightening of the collective moral bonds, the depiction of a collective ethical purpose ... the renewal of social harmony ... [and] the rule of tranquility and benevolence. 28 *Donald Zoll*

The problem of moral and spiritual regeneration; the restoration of the ethical system and the religious sanctions upon which any life worth living is founded. This is conservatism at its highest; but it cannot be accomplished as a deliberate program of social reform.... If the conservatives' effort comes to no more than this, it will fail. Spiritual restoration cannot be a means to social restoration: it must be its own end. 29 *Russell Kirk*

How to restore a living faith to the lonely crowd, how to remind men that life has ends—this conundrum the twentieth century conservative faces. 30 *Russell Kirk*

Consumerism

[J]UST AS PRINT was the first mass-produced thing, so it was the first uniform and repeatable "commodity." ... As the Gutenberg typography filled the world the human voice closed down. People began to read silently and passively as consumers. 1 *Marshall McLuhan*

The cultural transformation of modern society is due, singularly, to the rise of mass consumption, or the diffusion of what were once considered luxuries to the middle and lower classes in society. In this process, past luxuries are constantly redefined as necessities.... 2
Daniel Bell

In an economic democracy there is no appeal from the decision of the consumers.... In the free market the consumer is king. 3
John Hospers

Consumption is the sole end and purpose of production; and the interest of the producer ought to be attended to only so far as it may be necessary for promoting that of the consumer. 4
Adam Smith

Consumption—to repeat the obvious—is the sole end and object of all economic activity. 5
John Maynard Keynes

While not every country is capable of becoming a consumer society in the near future, there is hardly a society in the world that does not embrace the goal itself. 6 *Francis Fukuyama*

Is your life empty? Consumption promises to fill the aching void; hence the attempt to surround commodities with an aura of romance; with allusions to exotic places and vivid experiences; and with images of female breasts from which all blessings flow.... [T]he propaganda of consumption turns alienation itself into a commodity.... The inner void, however, persists.... 7 *Christopher Lasch*

The state of mind promoted by consumerism is better described as a state of uneasiness and chronic anxiety. The promotion of commodities depends ... on discouraging the individual from reliance on his own resources and judgment: in this case, his judgment of what he needs in order to be healthy and happy.... The consumer experiences his surroundings as a kind of extension of the breast, alternatively gratifying and frustrating. He finds it hard to conceive of the world except in connection with his fantasies. 8 *Christopher Lasch*

Another facet of our economic system, the need for mass consumption, has been instrumental in creating ... the principle that every desire must be satisfied immediately, no wish must be frustrated.... Having fun consists mainly in the satisfaction of consuming.... The world is one great object for our appetite, a big apple, a big bottle, a big breast; we are the sucklers, the eternally expectant ones ... and the eternally disappointed ones. 9 *Erich Fromm*

Compulsive consumption compensates for anxiety.... [M]ost urges for pleasure, if they are compulsive, including sex, are not caused by the wish for pleasure but by the wish for the avoidance of anxiety. 10 *Erich Fromm*

Consumerism

The Consumption Ethic is now far more important to the success of the Global Shopping Center than the Work Ethic.... [I]ts message is simple and insistent: consumption is the key to happiness and the global corporation has the products that make life worth living. "Consumer democracy is more important than political democracy," the Council of the Americas suggests as a good slogan for its corporate members. 11 *R. J. Barnet & R. E. Muller*

The second modern commandment, "Thou shalt consume!" is the natural complement of the first—"Create more desire!" Together they lead the attack on the key bastion of the Indo-European, Islamic, and Hebrew traditions—the impulsive control system—for the desire for a million things cannot be created without stimulating a craving for everything. 12

Jules Henry

In a consumer society there are inevitably two kinds of slaves: the prisoners of addiction and the prisoners of envy. 13 *Ivan Illich*

Our present economic system is based on maximum production and maximum consumption.... [A person's] sense of self-worth is based on how much he has. And if he wants to be the best he has to have the most. 14

Erich Fromm

The basis on which good repute in any highly organized industrial community ultimately rests is pecuniary strength; and the [primary] means of showing pecuniary strength ... [is] conspicuous consumption. 15 *Thorstein Veblen*

Any consumer who might ... insist on the elimination of all honorific or wasteful elements from his consumption, would be unable to supply his most trivial wants in the modern market. 16

Thorstein Veblen

One might conclude ... that the American consumer would be approaching the satiation point. Thus far it has not happened. 17

Max Lerner

[T]he marketers, by promoting status striving through the purchase of goods, are giving people the sense that they are getting ahead. This, at the lower levels, is largely a consumption gain.... [But] by encouraging people constantly to ... equate possessions with status, what are we doing to their emotions and their sense of values? 18 *Vance Packard*

A final price that must be considered in assessing the ... impact of an economy based on ever-mounting consumption is the change it may be producing in the character of the people involved. What is the impact on the human spirit of all these pressures to consume? 19

Vance Packard

Modern consumer capitalism has brought us the ... ethic of indifferent fairness. So called love relationships in this society tend to deteriorate into mere exchanges of mutually profitable personality packages.... *Homo consumens* ... makes of himself a commodity. 20

Charles Hampden-Turner

Today the currency into which all values tend to be translated is no longer money but appraisal by the peer-group.... [T]he other-directed consumer seeks experiences rather than things.... That is, people themselves, friendships, are viewed as the greatest of all consumables; the peer-group is itself a main object of consumption. 21 *David Riesman*

[T]here is a fundamental opposition between the ethos of the family and the consumer economy. 22 *Germaine Greer*

The most effective medium of consumerism is the nuclear family.... As a consumer unit, the multigenerational family is unsatisfactory because of its economic efficiency.... The will of the [multigenerational] family is performed ... by its members, who have no personal accountability, so that they are immune to the techniques of manipulation that capitalism employs. 23 *Germaine Greer*

[The] concept of free will has been subverted and appropriated in the children of an efficient merchandising—consumer oriented economic system. 24 *Wilson Bryan Key*

The State is the body which seeks so to organize the interests of consumers that they obtain the commodities of which they have need.... The State, then, serves its members by organising the avenues of consumption on their behalf. 25 *Harold Laski*

The State works hard to keep the worker-consumer contented. But this is the contradiction under which it works: the overly persuaded consumer may no longer be a willing worker.... [T]he State itself is now bringing about its own destruction. 26 *Charles A. Reich*

[C]onsidering goods as more important than people and consumption as more important than creative activity ... means shifting the emphasis from the worker to the product of work, that is, from the human to the subhuman, a surrender to the forces of evil. 27
E. F. Schumacher

[C]onsumerism induces people to make moral compromises with themselves daily, and they lie to themselves ... in the name of ... ideas like "self-realization" or "personal growth." 28
Francis Fukuyama

The producer-consumer society in which we exist to make a profit from one another is not only inherently destructive of the physical world; basically it is morally disastrous. 29
D. Slusser & G. Slusser

[T]he incentive to scrupulous performance operates on all levels of a given field of production. It is a built-in safeguard of a free enterprise system and the only real protection of consumers against business dishonesty.... [I]t is precisely the "greed" of the businessman or, more appropriately, his profit-seeking, which is the unexcelled protector of the consumer. 30 *Alan Greenspan*

The consumer, so it is said, is the king.... [E]ach is a voter who uses his money as votes to get the things done that he wants done. 31
Paul A. Samuelson

Willingness to pay. What is wrong with that? The rub is this: Not all of us think of ourselves simply as *consumers*. Many of us regard ourselves as *citizens* as well. We act as consumers to get what we want *for ourselves*. We act as citizens to achieve what we think is right or best *for the community*.... I support almost any political cause that I think will defeat my consumer interests. This is because I have contempt for—although I act upon—those interests. 32
Mark Sagoff

[W]e have gradually drifted into a position of what amounts to calculated self-abasement, by actively forfeiting what the human animal needs most: a unitary, critical world view, infused by continuing moral awareness.... It is ... in the service of the new cynicism, blind to both spiritual and human values, a headlong, consumer race to "enjoy" while there is still time. 33
Ernest Becker

A culture organized around mass consumption encourages narcissism.... 34
Christopher Lasch

A society in which consumption has to be artificially stimulated in order to keep production going is a society founded on trash and waste, and such a society is a house built upon sand. 35 *Dorothy Sayers*

All societies influenced by Western civilization are at present committed to the gospel of growth—the whirling dervish doctrine which teaches: produce more so that you can consume more so that you can produce still more. One need not be a sociologist to know that such a philosophy is insane. 36 *René Dubos*

~ CONTROL ~

ALL MEN CONTROL and are controlled. The question of government in the broadest possible sense is not how freedom is to be preserved but what kinds of control are to be used and to what ends.... No one, I am sure, wishes to develop new master-slave relationships or bend the will of the people to despotic rulers in new ways. These are patterns of control appropriate to a world without science. They may well be the first to go when the experimental analysis of behavior comes into its own in the design of cultural practices. 1
B. F. Skinner

Control

The interest of the behaviorist is more than that of a spectator, he wants to control man's reactions as physical scientists want to control and manipulate other natural phenomena. 2

John B. Watson

Science has its meaning as the objective pursuit of a purpose which has been subjectively chosen.... Consequently, any discussion of the control of human beings by the behavioral sciences must first and most deeply concern itself with the subjectively chosen purposes which such an application of science is intended to implement. 3 *Carl Rogers*

[P]eople who believe in inherent evil prefer strong social constraints.... If we believe that people are basically bad, we often seek ways by which to control them. 4

Kenneth Gergen & Mary Gergen

Today the behavioural sciences are replete with "devilish" research findings on obedience, aggression, alienation, authoritarianism, anomie and cheating.... [C]ould it be that the devil we keep "finding" is but the cloven hoof-print of our controlling, all-determining god? ... It is my contention that modern doctrines of scientism, positivism and behaviourism ... are steeped in Calvinist ideology, having borrowed even its ... devastating lack of self-awareness. 5

Charles Hampden-Turner

Grounded still upon an impoverished view of human beings and a systematic denial of their potential, the search for total control consists in an ever more elaborate and costly effort to construct a profitable, militarily effective, and technically elegant apparatus that is not dependent upon the cooperation and resources of the mass of the population. 6 *David Noble*

Secret knowledge is the key to any system of total control. Until printing was invented, the written word remained largely a class monopoly. Today the language of higher mathematics plus computerism has restored both the secrecy and the monopoly, with a consequent resumption of totalitarian control. 7 *Lewis Mumford*

It has become clear ... that the paramount challenge to human liberty in the post-literate era is no longer that of resisting coercion ... but of withstanding persuasion.... The newer mechanisms of cultural control are aimed not at the pain reflex but at the pleasure bond; their appropriate symbols are no longer the dungeon and the rack but *TV Guide* and the 30-second commercial. 8

Ashley Montagu & Floyd W. Matson

[T]he new administrative elite have replaced the direct supervision of the labor force with a far more subtle system of psychiatric observation. Observation, initially conceived as a means to more effective forms of supervision and control, has become a means of control in its own right. 9 *Christopher Lasch*

Consciousness II believes in the central ideology of technology, the domination of man and environment by technique.... Throughout all of Consciousness II runs the theme that society will function best if it is planned, organized, rationalized, administered.... Consciousness II believes in *control*. 10 *Charles A. Reich*

[The] purpose that animates the entire megamachine [is] to reduce the human organism itself, its habitat, and its mode of existence, and life-purpose to just the minimal dimensions that will bring it under total external control. 11 *Lewis Mumford*

Nature has been objectified. Science ... has produced a system of knowledge that sanctifies our desire for prediction and control. No wonder the metaphors of physics were to spread out over all the sciences and into such disciplines as economics, sociology, and psychology. Rational analysis and mathematical modeling have become not simply a way of understanding the world but the tool used to control it. 12

F. David Peat

We would be unfaithful to the tradition of Western civilization ... if we failed to increase man's control over nature.... This duty led to the invention of the ... hydrogen bomb. 13

Edward Teller

[T]he necrophilous person is driven by the desire to transform the organic into the inorganic, to approach life mechanically.... He loves control, and in the act of controlling he kills life. He is deeply afraid of life, because it is disorderly and uncontrollable. 14

Erich Fromm

Modern science's definition of knowledge in terms of a controlling subject and an objectified world is one instance of the hegemony of male rationality. 15 *Jessica Benjamin*

And in time control superseded natural values; and as it did, men superseded women in value. 16

Marilyn French

Most initiations of boys symbolize rebirth as a man by men.... The rites are designed to detach the boy from natural affection and natural role, to teach him that a man does not act on feelings but rather on meeting an external societal standard of manliness that is focused on exhibiting self-control and control over others. 17

Marilyn French

We might call this the dialectic of control: If I completely control the other, then the other ceases to exist, and if the other completely controls me, I cease to exist. 18 *Jessica Benjamin*

It is the sense of impotence that is crucial to resentment, the sense of inferiority, and the goal of revenge and control that structures this morbid view of the world. 19

Robert C. Solomon

[T]he most intense experiences of shame and the most violent forms of narcissistic rage arise in those individuals for whom a sense of absolute control over an archaic environment is indispensable [to] the maintenance of self-esteem—and indeed of the self.... 20

Heinz Kohut

[T]he controlling male forfeits self-awareness, sensitivity to others and freedom to be honest. 21

James M. O'Neil

Investing all his energies in the control of nature, sensate man achieved a conspicuous degree of success. But in this process he lost his *self*-control. 22 *Pitirim Sorokin*

The good life cannot be lived without self-control, but it is better to control a restrictive and hostile emotion ... than a generous and expansive emotion such as love. Conventional morality has erred, not in demanding self-control, but in demanding it in the wrong place. 23

Bertrand Russell

One must "control himself" in order to be able to be spontaneous without cracking, without succumbing to inner pressure.... Control here means the preservation of meaning, *Gestalt*, the integrated functioning of the organism; that which is to be kept under control is a surging chaos.... 24 *Paul Kesckemeti*

The highest possible stage in moral culture is when we recognize that we ought to control our thoughts. 25 *Charles Darwin*

[Modern] man, with his present character structure, cannot regulate himself.... How do we achieve voluntary discipline in people without having to force them?... The healthy person is virtually without compulsive morality, but neither does he have any impulses that would require a restraining morality. 26

Wilhelm Reich

Inner controls are built up only on the basis of direct personal relations, not by obeying society's demands. They are only internalized when we directly identify ourselves with people we love, respect, or admire.... 27

Bruno Bettelheim

No culture of which we are aware has yet escaped the tension between the modalities of control and release by which every culture constitutes itself. Cultures achieve their measure of duration in the degree that they build releasing devices into the major controls. These are the devices that modern psychotherapy seeks to develop.... A cultural revolution occurs when the releasing or remissive symbolic grows more compelling than the controlling one.... 28 *Philip Rieff*

Control is not a need; it is the way we must function to fulfill our needs. 29

William Glasser

The attitude of control looks to the future, to production. 30 *John Dewey*

Control

The history of life on this planet is the history of the ways in which life has gained control over and freedom within its environment. 31
W. H. Auden

[T]he human unit of consciousness is slowly moving ... toward more control over one's environment and more happiness. 32
Itzhak Bentov

Yoga aims to free the individual from his bondage to the world. Self-help literature aims for mastery of the self as a stepping-stone to mastery of the environment.... Control of self would eventuate in shaping the world to the will of men. 33 *Samuel Klausner*

[P]hilistinism thinks it is in control of possibility.... [I]t carries possibility around like a prisoner in the cage of the probable, shows it off, imagines itself to be the master, [but] does not take note that precisely thereby it has taken itself captive to be the slave of spiritlessness. 34
Søren Kierkegaard

Man's advance in control over his environment is making it more and more difficult for him ... to lead a naturally good life, and easier and easier to lead a morally bad one. 35
W. H. Auden

The safety which is guaranteed by well-functioning mechanisms for the technical control of nature, by the refined psychological control of the person, by the rapidly increasing organizational control of society—this safety is bought at a high price: man, for whom all this was invented as a means, becomes a means himself in the service of means. 36
Paul Tillich

The twentieth century is unique in offering to men for the first time the opportunity to fashion social life according to their desires; and it is both hopeful and terrible for that reason. 37
T. B. Bottomore

The disastrous results of common sense in the management of human behavior are evident in every walk of life ... and we shall continue to be inept in all these fields until a scientific analysis clarifies the advantages of a more effective technology.... In the behaviorist's view, man can now control his own destiny because he knows what must be done and how to do it. 38
B. F. Skinner

Today, for the first time, humans have the opportunity to take control of their own evolution.... What should be the goal of human evolution?... What kind of creature should we desire to become? 39 *Michael Hutchinson*

Human beings can control their own acts, but not the consequences of their acts. 40
John Stuart Mill

Corporations

[T]he corporation occupies a place as important in our time as that of the Holy Roman Church in medieval Europe.... 1
Robert Lekachman

The myth that holds that the great corporation is the puppet of the market ... is, in fact, one of the devices by which its power is perpetuated.... Between the modern corporation and the modern state there is a deeply symbiotic relationship based on shared power and shared reward. 2 *John K. Galbraith*

The mature corporation has taken control of the market—not alone the price, but also what is purchased—to serve ... the goals of its planning. 3 *John K. Galbraith*

The global corporation is the first institution in human history dedicated to centralized planning on a world scale. 4
R. J. Barnet & R. E. Muller

In its modern form, the multinational corporation ... is a distinctly American development. Through such corporations it has become possible for the first time to use the world's resources with maximum efficiency.... But there must be greater unification of the world economy to give full play to the benefits of multinational corporations. 5 *George Ball*

In command of vast resources, corporations are in a position to either facilitate or slow

the transition to a sustainable society. 6
Lester Brown

Driven by the ideology of infinite growth, a religion rooted in the existential terrors of oligopolistic competition, global corporations act as if they must grow or die, and in the process they have made thrift into a liability and waste into a virtue.... The corporate vision depends upon converting ever-greater portions of the earth into throwaway societies. 7
R. J. Barnet & R. E. Muller

[I]t is obviously impossible for society to rely upon the benevolence of the large corporations; they ... have indefinitely expansible wants and will never be satisfied with their incomes, no matter how large. 8
Edwin H. Sutherland

The large corporations in time of war, when Western civilization was endangered, did not sacrifice their own interests ... but instead they attempted to use this emergency as an opportunity for extraordinary enrichment of themselves.... They are driven by self-interest and the desire to secure an advantage over others which makes them constitutionally unable to engage in the cooperative life of society. 9
Edwin H. Sutherland

In practice, those arrangements which underlie a functioning individualism ... —a stable community, free opportunities, dependable social relations, a sense of limits—have now begun to be destroyed by the workings of corporate capitalism. A political culture which had always reasoned as if community, tradition, family, and morality made no difference, now finds them disappearing in fact. 10
R. Jeffrey Lustig

The policy of corporations is general public adherence to the law and secret defections from the law. 11
Edwin H. Sutherland

To retreat from a vigorous effort to expose corporate criminality ... ensures that such injurious corporate behavior will continue to erode the moral texture of the world. 12
Stuart L. Mills

Many of the problems of "white-collar crime" and of relaxed public morality ... are problems of *structural* immorality. In the corporate era, economic relations become impersonal—and the executive feels less personal responsibility.... It is this mindlessness of the powerful that is the true higher immorality of our time; for, with it, there is associated the organized irresponsibility that is today the most important characteristic of the American system of corporate power. 13
C. Wright Mills

Few trends could so thoroughly undermine the very foundations of our free society as the acceptance by corporate officials of a social responsibility other than to make as much money for their stockholders as possible. This is a fundamentally subversive doctrine. 14
Milton Friedman

And yet who else is there to take care of society, its problems and its ills? These organizations collectively *are* society. It is futile to argue, as does ... Milton Friedman, that a business has only one responsibility: economic performance. Economic performance is the *first* responsibility of a business.... But economic performance is not the sole responsibility of a business. 15
Peter F. Drucker

As we have had in the corporation the classic shift from ownership to managerial control, so, on the symbolic level, we have the shift from "private property" to "enterprise" as the justification of power. And, as with any ideology, the symbol itself sometimes becomes a propelling force, and "performance" for its own sake has become a driving motive of the American corporate head. 16
Daniel Bell

Rationality is today considered the supreme virtue in the large corporation. The human managers are expected to be at all times absolutely logical and at no time humanely emotional.... [T]he expression of feeling becomes so suppressed that superiors often are only vaguely aware of the impact they create on their people when they wield power. 17
Vance Packard

[C]omplex hierarchical organizations routinely foster a pragmatic structural amorality—an

Corporations

ethical numbness—that can bring immense suffering to others.... In a capitalistic economy dominated by multinational corporations where the profit motive is supreme, where decentralized decision-making diffuses responsibility ... evil takes on a certain *banality*. 18
Stuart L. Mills

The nature of the large corporations is profoundly inhuman. 19 *Fritjof Capra*

Nietzsche never foresaw that in the American case the effort to reach to the godlike would apply to the creation not of the Superman but of Super-corporation. And the hero of this story, while seeing the evil and ruthlessness of the head man, is himself at the end half caught up in his fervor and asks only for a chance to be more ruthless himself and to make a victim of the man who has made victims of others—all in the name of the Corporation. 20
Max Lerner

[T]he corporation controls a trump—the manager's identity.... [M]anagers must depend on the corporation for their definition of self.... Just as an addict's need for his drug increases with use, a manager's dependence on his corporation deepens with continued affiliation ... [and] grows until other needs are eclipsed.... For those who stay, corporate policy becomes personal morality.... 21 *Diane Margolis*

[T]he reenchantment of the workplace constitutes the culmination of corporate control over work rather than an alternative to it.... [T]he self becomes a strategy ... [in which] workers can be made to see the corporation as the pathway not only to financial security but to personal growth and psychological identity.... 22
Robert Howard

[W]hile religion, the family and the nation are preservatives against egoistic suicide ... there is one other of which no mention has yet been made.... [T]he corporation has everything needed to give the individual a setting, to draw him out of his state of moral isolation.... But for it to have this influence it must be organized on wholly different bases from those of today.... [I]t is essential that it become a definite and recognized organ of our public life ... instead of expressing only various combinations of particular interests. 23 *Émile Durkheim*

[T]he great corporation ... can often impose its hierarchy of ranks—and symbols of differential status—upon the social structure of the surrounding community. 24 *Vance Packard*

The corporations have become, in a sense, private governments. 25 *Max Lerner*

Thus today giant corporations enjoy rights ... similar to persons, with virtually all the rights granted persons to keep them free from control by their government, but with virtually none of the restraints placed upon democratic governments to prevent oppression. 26
Diane Margolis

The greatest impediment to true democracy in the West is not socialism but the corporate world. 27 *Marilyn French*

[P]owerful corporations are at work shaping a new social order. The government (especially the military) as a prime customer and user of information technology is allied to the corporations in building that order.... 28
Theodore Roszak

[C]ontrol over scientific knowledge has become a central goal in the strategies of multinational corporations, strategies which, to a large extent, will determine national policies and prospects. 29 *David Noble*

The great danger posed by and to neoconservatism is that it will become nothing more than the legitimating ... ideology of an oligarchic America where essential decisions are made by corporate elites.... 30 *Peter Steinfels*

Corporations, by the very fact of their bigness, may achieve a strategic power that sometimes makes it unnecessary for them to pursue efficiencies which can cut costs. They become tired and unwilling to take risks, and in some cases grow backward in their response to technological change. 31 *Max Lerner*

[T]he modern corporation, although the product of the capitalist process, socializes the

bourgeois mind; it relentlessly narrows the scope of capitalist motivation; not only that, it will eventually kill its roots. 32
Joseph Schumpeter

With the rise of the great corporation there comes a contented accommodation to the larger errors of public life.... It is for others to do the worrying, take the action. In the world of the great organization, problems are not solved but passed on. 33 *John K. Galbraith*

Left to themselves, corporations tend to go toward more-of-the-same-only-bigger, and that isn't quite what we need right now.... What we want is to live decent lives, and for every move American corporations make to bring this about, they make two more to prevent it.... Putting our fate in the hands of corporations, in other words, has failed. 34 *Philip Slater*

The corporation with the technology it has organized seems a headless monster on the loose.... Human beings made the rules that govern corporate structures, and human beings can change the rules.... May our politics be equal to the task. 35 *Diane Margolis*

If the problem of the corporation is not the only one demanding public attention, there is certainly none more urgent, for the others can be considered only when this has been solved. 36
Émile Durkheim

CULTURE

A CULTURE IS BORN in the moment when a great soul awakens out of the proto-spirituality of ever-childish humanity, and detaches itself, a form from the formless, a bounded and mortal thing from the boundless and enduring.... It dies when this soul has actualized the full sum of its possibilities in the shape of peoples, languages, dogmas, arts, states, sciences, and reverts into the proto-soul.... The aim once attained ... the Culture suddenly hardens ... and it becomes *Civilization*. 1
Oswald Spengler

Man through his creation of culture has created himself. 2 *Ashley Montagu*

Man might ... be defined as a creature never found in a "state of nature," for as soon as he becomes recognizable *as* man he is already in a state of culture. 3 *Lewis Mumford*

[T]here is no such thing as a human nature independent of culture. Men without culture ... would be monstrosities with few useful instincts, fewer recognizable sentiments, and no intellect. 4 *Clifford Geertz*

Now, the end of all practical activity is culture: a maturing mind, a ripening character, an increasing sense of mastery and fulfillment, a higher integration of all one's powers in a social personality, a larger capacity for intellectual interests and emotional enjoyments, for more complex and subtle states of mind. 5
Lewis Mumford

Inevitably, the culture within which we live shapes and limits our imaginations, and by permitting us to do and think and feel in certain ways makes it increasingly unlikely or impossible that we should do or think or feel in ways that are contradictory or tangential to it. 6
Margaret Mead

Culture may be defined as the totality of the mental and physical reactions and activities that characterize the behavior of the individuals composing a social group.... [But] its elements are not independent, they have a structure. 7
Franz Boas

The goal of culture ... is to condition the most reliable conformity in its members.... The civilized person is, thus, "free" in only the most abstract sense. 8 *Kent G. Bailey*

Culture is another name for a design of motives directing the self outward, toward those communal purposes in which alone the self can be realized and satisfied. 9 *Philip Rieff*

Human culture taken as a whole may be described as the process of man's progressive self-liberation. Language, art, religion, science, are various phases in this process. In all of them man discovers and proves a new power—the power to build up a world of his own, an "ideal" world. 10 *Ernst Cassirer*

Culture

[T]here is perhaps no better definition of culture than that it is the capacity for constantly expanding the range and accuracy of one's perception of meanings. 11 *John Dewey*

[T]here is a desperate social need for the creative behavior of creative individuals.... Many of the serious criticisms of our culture and its trends may best be formulated in terms of a dearth of creativity. 12 *Carl Rogers*

[B]ehind every culture there are heroes.... These are the "nucleators," the bearers of viable mutant images.... These are the true entrepreneurs of society. 13 *Kenneth Boulding*

Cultures are but abstractions of common psychological elements in aggregates of human beings. 14 *Quincy Wright*

Culture ... [is] a screen on which the psyche projects itself in a grand repertory of "sublimations." 15 *Theodore Roszak*

Culture demands continuous sublimation; it thereby weakens Eros, the builder of culture. 16 *Herbert Marcuse*

Sublimation of instinct is an especially conspicuous feature of cultural evolution; this it is that makes it possible for the higher mental operations, scientific, artistic, ideological activities, to play such an important part in civilized life. 17 *Sigmund Freud*

[T]he incapacity in the sexual instinct to yield full satisfaction ... becomes the source ... of the grandest cultural achievements, which are brought to birth by even greater sublimation of the components of the sexual instinct. 18 *Sigmund Freud*

Culture develops not only out of the underlying economic dialectic, but also out of the deeper sex dialectic. 19 *Shulamith Firestone*

Woman's body is a labyrinth in which man is lost. It is a walled garden.... Men, bonding together, invented culture as a defense against female nature. 20 *Camille Paglia*

Culture (sublimation) leads the libido into ego-syntonic channels by the creation of substitute objects. The most important of these substitutions is a human being, the wife who replaces the mother. The basis of society is formed by these substitutions and therefore the psychology of growing up falls, in many respects, in a line with the psychology of culture. 21 *Géza Róheim*

[T]he function of culture is to make continued self-esteem possible. The main task of culture, in other words, is to provide the individual with the conviction that he is *an object of primary value in a world of meaningful action*. 22 *Ernest Becker*

Culture is the system of significances attached to behavior by which a society explains itself to itself. 23 *Philip Rieff*

Every advance in culture is, psychologically, an extension of consciousness, a coming to consciousness that can take place only through discrimination. 24 *Carl Jung*

The *modalities* of culture are few, and they derive from the existential situations which confront all human beings, through all times, in the nature of consciousness: how one meets death, the nature of tragedy and the character of heroism, the definition of loyalty and obligation, the redemption of the soul, the meaning of love and of sacrifice, the understanding of compassion, the tension between an animal and a human nature, the claims of instinct and restraint. 25 *Daniel Bell*

[A]ll cultural forms are *in essence sacred* because they seek the perpetuation and redemption of the individual life.... Culture *means* that which is super*natural*; all culture has the basic mandate to transcend the physical, to permanently transcend it. 26 *Ernest Becker*

[M]an aggressively builds immortal cultures and makes history in order to fight death. 27 *Norman O. Brown*

Eros creates culture in his struggle against the death instinct. 28 *Herbert Marcuse*

The meaning of the evolution of culture is ...

the struggle between Eros and Death, between the instincts of life and the instincts of destruction, as it works itself out in the human species. 29 *Sigmund Freud*

Of the psychological characteristics of culture two appear to be the most important: a strengthening of the intellect ... and an internalization of the aggressive impulses.... Now war is in the crassest opposition to the psychical attitude imposed on us by the cultural processes.... [W]hatever fosters the growth of culture works at the same time against war. 30
Sigmund Freud

Culture mediates between the inner world and the outer world. 31 *Christopher Lasch*

Passage from the state of Nature to the state of Culture is marked by man's ability to view biological relations as a series of contrasts.... 32
Claude Lévi-Strauss

Most of what is unusual about man can be summed up in one word: "culture." ... [M]an's way of life is largely determined by culture rather than by genes.... Cultural transmission is analogous to genetic transmission ... [and] can give rise to a form of evolution. 33 *Richard Dawkins*

Historians will have to face the fact that natural selection determined the evolution of cultures in the same manner as it did that of species. 34 *Konrad Lorenz*

Culture is not inherited through genes, it is acquired by learning.... In a sense, human genes have surrendered their primacy in human evolution to an entirely new, nonbiological or superorganic agent, culture. 35
Theodosius Dobzhansky

Culture is all the information man possesses except for that which is stored in the chemical language of his genes. 36 *Paul Ehrlich*

A culture survives by the power, plasticity, and fertility of its ideas.... [T]he *master ideas*—the great moral, religious, and metaphysical teachings ... *are based on no information whatever.* 37 *Theodore Roszak*

Culture is composed of ideas and only of ideas, and man is only Culture's instrument. 38
Miguel de Unamuno

We might say that human culture is the function of the corpus callosum. 39 *Carl Sagan*

Man is born without the equipment for appropriate action which the animal possesses.... Yet this very helplessness of man is the basis from which human development springs; *man's biological weakness is the condition of human culture.* 40 *Erich Fromm*

[D]efense systems against anxiety are the stuff that culture is made of and ... therefore specific cultures are structurally similar to specific neuroses. 41 *Géza Róheim*

[C]ulture consists in the sum total of efforts which we make to avoid being unhappy. 42
Géza Róheim

In general, all cultures have a therapeutic function, insofar as they are systems of symbolic integration—whether these systems be called religious, philosophical, ideological, or by any other name. 43 *Philip Rieff*

Culture ... has become the most dynamic component of our civilization, outreaching the dynamism of technology itself. There is now ... a dominant impulse toward the new and original, a self-conscious search for future forms and sensations, so that the idea of change and novelty overshadows the dimensions of actual change.... Thus, our culture has an unprecedented mission: it is an official, ceaseless search for a new sensibility. 44 *Daniel Bell*

The essence of culture is continuity and conservation of the past; craving for novelty produces only anti-culture and ends in barbarism. 45
Carl Jung

The living links between the individual and his culture are loosened. This culture was, in and for the individual, the system of inhibitions that generated and regenerated the predominant values and institutions. Now, the repressive force of the reality principle seems no longer renewed and rejuvenated by the repressed

Culture

individuals ... [and consequently] the less is the reality principle strengthened through "creative" identifications and sublimations, which enrich and at the same time protect the household of culture. 46 *Herbert Marcuse*

Today, the culture can hardly, if at all, reflect the society in which people live. The system of social relations is so complex and differentiated, and experiences are so specialized ... that it is difficult to find common symbols to relate one experience to another.... Insofar as experiences in the society can no longer be generalized into the culture, culture itself becomes private.... 47
Daniel Bell

The energy of culture-man is directed inwards, that of civilization-man outwards.... The present is a civilized, emphatically not a cultured time-period. 48 *Oswald Spengler*

Perhaps one day this civilization will produce a culture. 49 *Ludwig Wittgenstein*

Culture now signifies something which never acquires a form, but is to emerge with extraordinary intensity out of a vacancy into which there is a speedy return. 50 *Karl Jaspers*

Culture in America provides one more manifestation of the concept of impoverishment by substitution.... [In] American culture ... the genuine is replaced by the simulated. 51
Charles A. Reich

[C]ulture—is today a manufactured product. 52
Wilson Bryan Key

We have created a culture that systematically destroys quality. 53 *Henryk Skolimowski*

[W]hat is remembered by the aged seems to be what *sustains the culture*.... Thus, if primitive culture is an unchanging mountain, ours is an avalanche falling into a Sea of Nonexistence. Who can remember it? If, in primitive society, one's personal community is a rope fastened in a mythic past and continuing into a future without end, ours is a bit of string that falls from our hands when we die. 54 *Jules Henry*

Culture is on the horns of this dilemma: if profound and noble it must remain rare, if common it must become mean. 55
George Santayana

The concentration and death camps of the twentieth century, wherever they exist, under whatever regime, are *Hell made immanent*.... In locating Hell above ground, we have passed out of the major order and symmetries of Western civilization.... [W]e are now in a *post-culture*. 56 *George Steiner*

[T]here is no culture where there are no standards to which our fellow-men can have recourse. There is no culture where there are no principles.... [When] there is no culture, there is ... barbarism. 57 *José Ortega y Gasset*

We know that a deep cleavage exists between our mechanical and materialistic civilization and the aesthetic and spiritual values that constitute a culture. We have no unique and typical culture in our time because of that cleavage. 58
Herbert Read

[C]ulture certainly means something quite different from learning or technical skill. It implies the possession of an ideal, and the habit of critically estimating the value of things by comparison with a theoretical standard. Perfect culture should supply a complete theory of life, based upon a clear knowledge alike of its possibilities and of its limitations. 59
T. H. Huxley

The great law of culture is, Let each become all that he was created capable of being. 60
Thomas Carlyle

No individual can arrive even at the threshold of his potentialities without a culture in which he participates. 61 *Ruth Benedict*

Culture founds the dignity of man. Culture as a form of community is the fabric of relations in which the self finds its diverse and elaborate expression. It is the house of the self, but also its product. 62 *Allan Bloom*

Summed up, the two outstanding qualities of the cultured man are humanity and reason ... but both work in harmony and balance together....

It is one of the marks of the cultured man that he presents a unity.... He is a person who having had loving order made in himself makes loving order in the world. 63 *Ashley Montagu*

[W]hile appetites are guided by standards of private satisfaction, a passion for mental excellence believes itself to be fulfilling universal obligations. This distinction is vital to the existence of culture. If it is repudiated, all cultural life becomes sub-ordinated in principle to the demand of our appetites and of the public authorities responsible for the advancement of material welfare. 64 *Michael Polanyi*

Genuine culture consists in being a citizen of the universe. 65 *Bertrand Russell*

DEATH

THERE IS AN AMAZING DEMOCRACY about death.... Death is the irreducible common denominator of all men. 1
Martin Luther King Jr.

Man has created death. 2 *W. B. Yeats*

Man is the only being that knows death; all others become old, but with a consciousness wholly limited to the moment. 3
Oswald Spengler

Consciousness of death is the primary repression, not sexuality.... *[T]his is* the repression on which culture is built, a repression unique to the self-conscious animal.... [T]he final terror of self-consciousness is the knowledge of one's own death.... This is the meaning of the Garden of Eden myth and the rediscovery of modern psychology: that death is man's peculiar and greatest anxiety. 4 *Ernest Becker*

If in the strictest sense we are to speak of a sickness unto death, it must be one in which the last thing is death, and death the last thing. And this precisely is despair. 5 *Søren Kierkegaard*

One of the main factors underlying the need for integration is the individual's feeling that integration implies being alive, loving, and being loved by the internal and external good object; that is to say, there exists a close link between integration and object relations. Conversely, the feeling of chaos, of disintegration ... I take to be closely related to the fear of death. 6 *Melanie Klein*

Autonomy [is] literally *control of the self....* Death is ... the destruction of autonomy. 7
Gregory Bateson

A deep relation, and one which is early felt, exists *between space and death....* The child *suddenly* grasps ... itself as an individual *being* in an alien extended world.... Here, in the decisive moments of existence ... man first becomes man and realizes his immense loneliness in the universal. 8 *Oswald Spengler*

[F]or the patient death itself is not the problem, but dying is feared because of the accompanying sense of hopelessness, helplessness, and isolation.... Maybe instead of cryo-societies we should develop societies for dealing with the questions of death and dying, to encourage a dialogue on this topic and help people to live less fearfully until they die. 9
Elizabeth Kübler-Ross

I believe that the fear of death concerns an interplay between the ego and the super-ego.... To the ego ... living means ... being loved by the super-ego. 10 *Sigmund Freud*

Fear of the superego is finally transformed into fear of death. 11 *Manuel Furer*

[T]he fear of death, like the fear of conscience ... [is] a development of the fear of castration. 12
Sigmund Freud

I taught myself as a boy: defeat the fear of death and welcome the death of fear. 13
G. Gordon Liddy

Hatred of death ... will lead ... if not to the exercise, at least to the vindication, of evil and murder. 14 *Albert Camus*

[I]n the blindest fury of destructiveness, we cannot fail to recognize that the satisfaction of the [death] instinct is accompanied by an extraordinarily high degree of narcissistic enjoyment,

Death

owing to its presenting the ego with a fulfilment of the latter's old wish for omnipotence. The instinct ... must, when it is directed towards objects, provide the ego with the satisfaction of its vital needs and with control over nature. 15
Sigmund Freud

Freud was right in positing a death instinct, and the development of weapons of destruction makes our present dilemma plain: we either come to terms with our unconscious instincts and drives—with life and with death—or else we surely die. 16 *Norman O. Brown*

In Western Culture today one must make a distinction between the culture of life and the culture of death.... It is impossible to calculate just how much American scientific talent has been put out to pasture on the rank grasses of death.... Thus the forces of death are confident and organized while the forces of life [are] ... overwhelmed by their own impotence. Death struts about the house while Life cowers in the corner. 17 *Jules Henry*

[T]he reality of death has taken on a much more terrifying dimension as the intimate continuity of human beings with nature has diminished. 18 *Eugene Fontinell*

Out of the cosmos would come only chaos ... but death steps in. And death chooses.... Death is the evaluator.... We should all be lost in the wilderness of chance had not death, through a billion choosings, created the values of the world.... Chance proposes. Death disposes. 19
Robert Ardrey

Death, having been augmented by human strength, has lost its appointed place in the natural order and become a counter-evolutionary force, capable of destroying in a few years, or even in a few hours, what evolution has built up over billions of years. In doing so, death threatens even itself, since death, after all, is a part of life.... The question now before the human species, therefore, is whether life or death will prevail on the earth. 20
Jonathan Schell

[You] haven't got long before you are all going to kill yourselves.... I am only what lives inside each and every one of you. I am what you made me. I am only a reflection of you.... I say to myself, You want to kill *me*? Ha! I'm already dead, have been all my life. I've spent 23 years in tombs that you built.... 21 *Charles Manson*

The wages of sin is death. 22 *Saint Paul*

[D]eath can be accepted only through a state of confidence in which death has ceased to be the "wages of sin." 23 *Paul Tillich*

[N]o longer conceived as a circle, time in these modern philosophies ... presents itself as a precarious and evanescent duration, leading irremediably to death. 24 *Mircea Eliade*

Death is not a period that ends the great sentence of life, but a comma that punctuates it to more lofty significance. Death is not a blind alley that leads the human race into a state of nothingness, but an open door which leads man into life eternal. 25 *Martin Luther King Jr.*

Unconfronted, death is dreadful. It generates vague fears and anxieties that drive us away from authenticity and toward immersion in conventionality and everyday pleasures.... If, however, we confront death ... we are pressured to unify our lives, to relate our past experiences to our aspirations for the future, and to accept the ultimate transitoriness and insignificance of our lives. 26 *Mike W. Martin*

[T]he capacity to confront death [is] a capacity which is a prerequisite to growth, a prerequisite to self-consciousness.... This is a daring to leap into non-being with the prospect of achieving new being. 27 *Rollo May*

The confrontation with death—and the reprieve from it—makes everything look so precious, so sacred, so beautiful.... Death, and its ever present possibility makes love, passionate love, more possible. I wonder if we could love passionately, if ecstacy would be possible at all, if we knew we'd never die. 28
Abraham Maslow

What we think about death only matters for what death makes us think about life. 29
Charles de Gaulle

Death

If to philosophize is to learn how to die, then we must learn how to die in order to lead a good life. To learn to live and to learn how to die are one and the same thing. 30 *Karl Jaspers*

[T]hat there are things to which Man has, or may have, a stronger aversion than he has to Death, is evident from *Suicide.* 31
Bernard Mandeville

Survival is not the highest human value.... It is by the willingness to risk death that both men and animals gain life. 32 *Kenneth Boulding*

If you want to endure life, prepare yourself for death. 33 *Sigmund Freud*

Death ... challenges us to that isolation without which we cannot be ourselves. 34
Merold Westphal

[D]eath is anticipated to some important degree as a severance of the self's connections.... To die well one must feel a measure of self-completion—imagery of a life with connection, integrity, and movement, and of dying as part of some immortalizing current in the vast human flow. 35 *Robert Jay Lifton*

[O]ne of the conditions for the maintenance of a cohesive self as one faces death is the actual or at least vividly imagined presence of empathetically responsive selfobjects. 36
Heinz Kohut

Men can die without anxiety if they know what they love is protected from misery and oblivion. 37 *Herbert Marcuse*

[T]he basic question of death ... is how the meaning of life can survive its termination. 38
Charles Hartshorne

As a physician I am convinced that it is hygienic ... to discover in death a goal towards which one can strive; and that shrinking away from it is something unhealthy and abnormal which robs the second half of life of its purpose. 39 *Carl Jung*

Man always dies before he is fully born. 40
Erich Fromm

The question of the meaning of human existence in the totality of Being ... gains its true and practical importance through man's total discovery of death. 41 *Jacques Choron*

[E]verything that dies is deprived of meaning. To fight against death amounts to claiming that life has a meaning.... 42 *Albert Camus*

[D]eath is never that which gives life its meanings; it is, on the contrary, that which on principle removes all meaning from life. If we must die, then our life has no meaning because its problems receive no solution and because the very meaning of the problems remains undetermined. 43 *Jean-Paul Sartre*

[T]o die is to exist only through the Other, and to owe to him one's meaning.... 44
Jean-Paul Sartre

If life is an illusion, then so is death—the greatest of all illusions. 45 *Samuel Butler*

Where death is, Being in its wholeness is not. 46
Josiah Royce

Death is Dasein's *ownmost* possibility. Being towards this possibility discloses to Dasein its *ownmost* potentiality-for-Being, in which its very Being is the issue.... With death, Dasein stands before itself in its ownmost potentiality-for-Being. 47 *Martin Heidegger*

Authentic "thinking about death" is a wanting-to-have-a-conscience, which has become transparent to itself in an existential manner. 48
Martin Heidegger

One of the striking qualities of the American character is the unwillingness to face either the fact or meaning of death.... Because the great values of American culture are all associated with the power and pulsing of life, there is felt to be no point in dwelling on the values that transcend life.... The recoil from death betrays in itself a lack of sensitivity towards its implications for the spirit. 49 *Max Lerner*

One wonders how much of the radical casualness toward where things *lead* is derived from a worldview created by movies.... Where

everything is reversible and can be undone. Where heroes are killed in one movie only to rise in the next.... It is hard to sustain a traditional logic—an awareness of any sort of rational consequences—when a movie sensibly blurs even the terminal fact of mortality. 50
Renata Adler

Human horror of death is perhaps something exceptional in the universe, arising only when spirit is called back from its natural flights too often.... Simpler better-knit souls might normally die ... without making a fuss about it. 51
George Santayana

[H]ealthy children will not fear life if their elders have integrity enough not to fear death. 52
Erik Erikson

Tragic Man does not fear death as a symbolic punishment for forbidden pleasure aims (as does Guilty Man); he fears premature death, a death which prevents the realization of the aims of his nuclear self. And, unlike Guilty Man, he accepts death as part of the curve of his fulfilled and fulfilling life. 53 *Heinz Kohut*

Do not seek death. Death will find you. But seek the road which makes death a fulfillment. 54
Dag Hammarskjöld

If man hasn't discovered something that he will die for, he isn't fit to live. 55
Martin Luther King, Jr.

Deception
Self-deception

WERE A PORTRAIT OF MAN to be drawn, one in which there would be highlighted whatever is most human ... we should surely place well in the foreground man's enormous capacity for self-deception. 1 *Herbert Fingarette*

The will to appearance, to illusion, to deception ... is deeper, more "metaphysical," than the will to truth. 2 *Friedrich Nietzsche*

Nothing is so easy as to deceive one's self; for what we wish, we readily believe. 3 *Demosthenes*

Nothing is so difficult as not deceiving oneself. 4
Ludwig Wittgenstein

[H]uman life is nothing but a perpetual illusion; we do nothing but flatter and deceive one another.... The union which exists between men is based entirely on mutual deception.... Man is therefore nothing but disguise, deceit and hypocrisy. 5 *Blaise Pascal*

[W]e must expect lies and deceit ... whenever the interests of the genes of different individuals diverge. This will include individuals of the same species.... [W]e must even expect that children will deceive their parents, that husbands will cheat on wives, and that brother will lie to brother. 6 *Richard Dawkins*

Much of human interaction ... [and] social order on the large scale ... is ironically made possible by ruse, chicanery, fraud, stratagem, pretense, deception.... In short, deception works ... by facilitating reciprocal helpful behavior.... 7 *Joseph Lopreato*

Human beings seem to have an almost unlimited capacity to deceive themselves.... By such mystification, we achieve and sustain our adjustment, adaptation, socialization. But the result of such adjustment to our society is that ... [having] lost our *selves* ... we are expected to comply by inner consent with external constraints, to an almost unbelievable extent. 8
R. D. Laing

Deceit may also be a cause of consciousness.... Long-term deceit requires the invention of an analog self that can "do" or "be" something quite different from what the person actually does or is, as seen by his associates. 9 *Julian Jaynes*

In fostering self-esteem, self-deception may provide the confidence necessary for coping effectively.... And in fostering our faith in other people, it can support friendship, love, and community. 10 *Mike W. Martin*

Those incapable of self-deception are probably also incapable of romantic love, certain sorts of loyalty, and dedication to causes. 11
Amélie Rorty

Deception / Self-deception

[T]he objects of "strong" self-deception are precisely those commitments that constitute a person's sense of self-identity. These core commitments ... shape the meaningfulness of our lives. The attempt to abandon such commitments instantaneously would result in acute pain and disintegration. 12 *Bela Szabados*

If the self is essentially unified or at least strongly integrated, capable of critical, truth-oriented reflection ... it cannot deceive itself.... A true self cannot deceive itself. 13 *A. O. Rorty*

You can deceive others, you can deceive your brain-self, but you can't deceive your mind-self—for mind deals only in the discovery of truth and the interrelationship of all the truths. The cosmic laws with which mind deals are noncorruptible. 14 *R. Buckminster Fuller*

[M]uch self-deception can itself be viewed as a form of weakness of will insofar as it constitutes a failure to exercise one's rationality in implementing one's values. 15 *Mike W. Martin*

The ultimate goal of self-deception is ... to engage in conduct incompatible with one's values. 16 *Mike W. Martin*

[O]ne freely chooses to be ignorant so that he may sin more freely. 17 *Saint Thomas Aquinas*

Hitler's dictatorship seemed to thrive on the essential weakness and passive submission of his chief supporters.... [B]etween knowledge and ignorance there is a limbo of arrested perceptions and inhibited insights. Between calculated hypocrisy and hysterical dissociation there is a semi-conscious self-deception. It is possible to look at things without fully perceiving them, to divert one's attention from the unpleasant to the pleasant, from the ego-threatening to the ego-gratifying; to suspend the process of rational inference in mid-air, and to distort one's insights just enough to suppress anxiety. 18 *G. M. Gilbert*

Power, once attained, places the individual or the group in a position of perilous eminence so that security is possible only by the extension of power.... So inextricably are the two intertwined, that the one may always be used to justify the other in conscious and unconscious deception. 19 *Reinhold Niebuhr*

Truth threatens power, and power threatens truth. Power, in order to be effective, must appear as something other than what it actually is. Deception—deception of others and of self—is inseparable from the exercise of power. 20 *Hans Morgenthau*

It is this concealment of intent from one's self, this process of self-deception, that is particularly characteristic of American leaders.... [A] conflict arises between the desire to be open and sincere with others and the desire to climb above others in the hierarchy. One can fulfill both desires only by deceiving one's self ... in which the only plans and actions available for recall are those that are well intentioned and relatively harmless to others. 21 *William Blanchard*

Presidential deception is one of the prime characteristics of the modern presidency.... 22 *John Orman*

Indeed, self-deception is perhaps the rule for the political personality.... 23 *Harold D. Lasswell*

A dictator ... must fool all the people all the time and there's only one way to do that, he must also fool himself. 24 *W. Somerset Maugham*

Deception seems to be a universal method of control.... 25 *Alice Miller*

It is significant that in the traditional listing of the "Deadly Sins," Deception is not usually named. This nonnaming is an indicator of the pervasive deceptiveness of male-constructed "morality," which does not name its own primary Deadly Sin. Deception is in fact all-pervasive.... The basic sin of Phallocracy is *deception....* 26 *Mary Daly*

Those who deceive themselves are obliged to deceive others. 27 *R. D. Laing*

The urgent need to circumvent the lying and the self-deception was, for me, one of the "lessons of Vietnam." ... [T]he U.S. government,

Deception / Self-deception

starting ignorant, did not, would not, *learn*. There was a whole set of what amounted to institutional "anti-learning" mechanisms.... 28
Daniel Ellsberg

National security provides the acceptable ... rationale for official deception.... It is the rationale that permits decent men to make indecent decisions. 29 *David Wise*

The cult of intelligence is a secret fraternity of the American political aristocracy.... The purpose of the cult is to further the foreign policies of the U.S. government by covert and usually illegal means.... It does whatever is required to achieve its goals, without any consideration of the ethics involved or the moral consequences.... For adherents to the cult of intelligence, hypocrisy and deception, like secrecy, have become standard techniques. 30
Victor Marchetti & John D. Marks

[D]eceiving the Communist countries passed insensibly into the added objective of deceiving the American people.... More and more it appears that the art of governing is the art of deceiving on a large scale. 31 *Robert Nisbet*

The military policy of the U.S.A. deceiving its own public first became manifest during World War II.... The adoption of the policy of self-deception was never announced by the U.S.A., but it was assumed tacitly to have been instituted to bolster U.S.A. morale. That the U.S.A. fighting forces and their supporting public were assumed by the U.S.A. leaders to be so stupid as not to realize what was happening ... was the beginning of the end of U.S.A. populace credit for the operational integrity of its representative government. 32
R. Buckminster Fuller

In the eyes of posterity it will inevitably seem that, in safeguarding our freedom, we destroyed it; that the vast clandestine apparatus we built up ... only served in the end to confuse our own purposes; that the practice of deceiving others for the good of the state led infallibly to our deceiving ourselves ... with disastrous consequences to them and to us. 33
Malcolm Muggeridge

Self-deception ... tends to expand to other realms.... And the apocalyptic prospect of similarly spreading self-deception in the Faustian area of nuclear weapons systems ... could mean the extinction of virtually everyone. 34
Robert Jay Lifton

[T]o deceive by glutting the public with more expertly engineered information than it can digest is a [technique of deception] to which the computer makes an indispensable contribution. 35 *Theodore Roszak*

In the First Amendment ... [the] press was to serve the governed, not the governors.... Only a free and unrestrained press can effectively expose deception in government. 36
Justice Hugo Black

Supported by the Gutenberg technology, the power of the dunces to shape and befog the human intellect is unlimited. 37
Marshall McLuhan

To widen the market and to narrow the competition, is always the interest of the dealers.... The proposal of any new law or regulation of commerce which comes from this order, ought always to be listened to with great precaution.... It comes from an order of men, whose interest is never exactly the same with that of the public, who have generally an interest to deceive and even to oppress the public, and who accordingly have, upon many occasions, both deceived and oppressed it. 38
Adam Smith

It is sophistry to pretend that in a free country a man has some sort of inalienable or constitutional right to deceive his fellow men. There is no more right to deceive than to swindle, to cheat, or to pick pockets. 39
Walter Lippman

It is only at the highest stage of civilization that deceit is regarded with contempt, and is thought not to pay. That honesty is the best policy is current doctrine, but not established practice now. 40 *William Graham Sumner*

Contrary to popular belief, [P. T.] Barnum's great discovery was not how easy it was to

deceive the public, but rather, how much the public enjoyed being deceived. 41
Daniel J. Boorstin

For men are so simple, and yield so readily to immediate necessity, that the deceiver will never lack dupes. 42 *Niccolò Machiavelli*

[H]appiness ... is a perpetual possession of being well deceived. 43 *Jonathan Swift*

Rob the average man of his life-illusion and you rob him of his happiness. 44 *Henrik Ibsen*

Only the exceptional other who, for some reason, cares for one and is willing to risk ostracism or alienation, will dare to run counter to one's self-deceptive project. 45 *Bruce Wilshire*

While we have given others great power to deceive us, to create pseudo-events, celebrities, and images, they could not have done so without our collaboration. If there is a crime of deception being committed in America today, each of us is the principal, and all others are only accessories.... The hardest, most discomfiting discovery is that each of us must emancipate himself. 46 *Daniel J. Boorstin*

[B]ad faith is a lie to oneself.... [I]n bad faith it is from myself that I am hiding the truth. 47
Jean-Paul Sartre

Above all, don't lie to yourself. The man who lies to himself ... loses all respect for himself and for others. And having no respect he ceases to love. 48 *Feodor Dostoevsky*

The truth that is requisite for the honour and peace of spirit is not omniscience but the absence of delusions.... 49 *George Santayana*

[W]e cannot grow and develop unless we learn to face and overcome our own self-deception. 50
William Blanchard

For there is nothing worse than self-deception—when the deceiver is always at home and always with you. 51 *Socrates*

The self-deceiver undermines her own moral character and integrity by corrupting the very capacity for independent moral judgment that ... makes integrity possible. 52
Stephen Darwell

On personal integrity hangs humanity's fate. 53
R. Buckminster Fuller

Dehumanization

I think that the highly industrialized Western world has neglected to the utmost degree to leave room for man. The infernal production-consumption cycle has completely dehumanized life. The individual has become a tool. He hardly has any contact with nature anymore. That is, with himself. He has lost his soul and is not even trying to find it again. 1
Indira Gandhi

Ours is a progressively technical civilization ... committed to the quest for continually improved means to carelessly examined ends. Technique ... converts spontaneous and unreflective behavior into behavior that is deliberate and rationalized.... Purposes drop out of sight and efficiency becomes the central concern.... Progress then consists in progressive dehumanization.... 2 *Robert Merton*

[A] new God had appeared and a new religion had taken possession of the mind: and out of this conjunction arose the new mechanical world picture which, with every fresh scientific discovery, every successful new invention, displaced both the natural world and the diverse symbols of human culture with an environment cut solely to the measure of the machine. This ideology gave primacy to the denatured and dehumanized environment in which the new technological complex could flourish without being limited by any human interests and values.... 3 *Lewis Mumford*

[T]he rule of the capitalist over the worker is the rule of things over man, of dead labor over the living, of the product over the producer ... namely the inversion of subject into object.... Viewed *historically* this inversion is the indispensable transition without which wealth as such ... could not possibly be created by force at the expense of the majority. 4 *Karl Marx*

Dehumanization

The ongoing military-industrial drive toward rationalizing, disciplining, and ultimately dehumanizing the workplace is among the foundation stones of information technology. 5
Theodore Roszak

An individual is dehumanized whenever he is treated as less than a whole person. 6
Joseph Weizenbaum

The enemy, if he is to be tortured or killed, must first be dehumanized. 7 *Ralph White*

The [concentration] camps are meant not only to exterminate people and degrade human beings, but also serve the ghastly experiment of eliminating, under scientifically controlled conditions, spontaneity itself as an expression of human nature and of transforming the human personality into a mere thing, into something that even animals are not.… 8
Hannah Arendt

We have emerged from a war in which we had to accept the degradingly low ethical standards of the enemy. But instead of feeling liberated from his standards, and set free to restore the sanctity of life … we are in effect making the low standards of the enemy in the last war our own for the present. Thus we are starting toward another war degraded by our own choice. 9
Albert Einstein

A lot of [our] people wouldn't think of killing a man, I mean, a white man—a human being so to speak. 10 *Sgt. M. Bernhardt (Vietnam)*

The aim of dehumanizing the victim is not necessarily a conscious one. The denunciation has to be rationalized. 11 *Malise Ruthven*

A human being has the ability to convince himself that others are not fellow humans.… Communication barriers are raised to prevent individuals from becoming acquainted and discovering the truth. 12 *Irenäus Eibl-Eibesfeldt*

Whenever persons are present, questions of morality arise. Rulers of nations and leaders of parties find morality embarrassing. That is why they take such pains to depersonalize their opponents. All propaganda directed against an opposing group has but one aim: to substitute diabolical abstractions for concrete persons. The propagandist's purpose is to make one set of people forget that certain other sets of people are human. By robbing them of their personality, he puts them outside the pale of moral obligation. 13 *Aldous Huxley*

Of the factors … that enable man to overcome his innate inhibitions, I consider his capacity for mentally dehumanizing his fellow-men to be the most dangerous. In the last analysis it is this capacity to switch off pity that makes him into a cold-blooded murderer. 14
Irenäus Eibl-Eibesfeldt

In areas of scarcity … cannibalism … became literally a form of intraspecific predation. The "dehumanization" of the opponent, so important a factor in the history of human cruelty and prejudice, presumably played a role here. Once the enemy was seen as prey the whole range of hunting skills became available in warfare. 15 *John H. Crook*

[O]rganized predatory violence has always been a male monopoly, whether practiced against game animals or those enemy humans defined as "not-men" (and hence also a kind of prey animal). This is the important step in the move toward human warfare. 16
Lionel Tiger & Robin Fox

The dehumanization of the enemy is a characteristic of all wars. 17 *J. William Fulbright*

Every person, as well as every nation, seeks to dehumanize the adversary. We kill the nameless foe and discover later, as Oedipus did, that we are members of the same family. 18
Katherine Paterson

Today's wars are dreadful because man can exterminate his fellows as easily as vermin.… Aerial warfare and, *a fortiori*, long distance missiles have depersonalized the activity of killing and maiming … [to the extent that we] "may yet render the principle of humanity as archaic as the principle of chivalry may already have become." 19 *Guenter Lewy*

Whenever there is lost the consciousness that

every man is an object of concern for us just because he is a man, civilization and morals are shaken, and the advance to fully developed inhumanity is only a question of time. 20
Albert Schweitzer

[I]t is impossible for a human being to commit the sin of denying the humanity of others without incurring in the act the penalty of dehumanizing himself. 21 *Arnold Toynbee*

The dehumanization of man ... [requires] the unconditional surrender of the self. 22
Ashley Montagu & Floyd W. Matson

The surest way to dehumanize a person or group is to gain their cooperation in self-debasement. 23 *J. Howard & R. Somers*

In a case of rape ... the intent is not merely to "take," but to humiliate and degrade.... Pornography, like rape, is a male invention, designed to dehumanize women. 24
Susan Brownmiller

When man substituted God for the Great Goddess he at the same time substituted authoritarian for humanistic values.... When the goddess of justice gave way to the god of vengeance, man became harsh and inhuman and authoritarianism replaced compassion as the law of life. The dehumanization of modern society ... is the natural and predictable outgrowth of advanced patriarchalism. 25 *Elizabeth Gould Davis*

A corrupt society is one where the forces of death are stronger than the forces of life.... To corrupt is to dehumanize.... In our age we have seen more corruption than in any previous age. 26
Robert Payne

We conceive of dehumanization as a particular type of psychic defense mechanism and consider its increasing prevalence to be a social consequence of the nuclear age. By this growth it contributes, we believe, to heightening the risk of nuclear extermination. 27
V. Bernard et al.

If the decision process is mechanical and the self is not involved ... there is no guilt, only a lack of knowledge.... We are experiencing a dehumanization of man through a glorification of his analytical faculties and a separation of his emotions from his intellect. It is this process that makes possible the blind and unreflective use of the intellect in the development of instruments of repression and control, destruction and "pacification." 28
William Blanchard

[T]he capacity for man to abandon his humanity, indeed, the inevitability that he does so, as he merges his unique personality into larger institutional structures ... is a fatal flaw nature has designed into us, and which in the long run gives our species only a modest chance of survival. 29 *Stanley Milgram*

Any real hope for victory over the dehumanized society of the megamachine and for the building up of a humanist industrial society rests upon the condition that ... a society emerges in which love and integrity are possible. 30
Erich Fromm

Twentieth-century man has lost a meaningful world and a self which lives in meanings out of a spiritual center. The man-created world of objects has drawn into itself him who created it and who now loses his subjectivity in it. He has sacrificed himself to his own productions. But man is still aware of what he has lost or is continuously losing. He is still man enough to experience his dehumanization as despair. 31
Paul Tillich

In our "normal" alienation from being ... [any] attempt to recapture personal meaning in personal time and space from out of the sights and sounds of a depersonalized, dehumanized world ... are bridgeheads into alien territory. They are acts of insurrection. Their source is from the Silence at the centre of each of us. 32
R. D. Laing

Unlike the primitives who gave a face to every moving thing ... modern man is obsessed by the need to depersonalise.... There are two reasons for this tendency. The first is *analysis*, that marvellous instrument of scientific research ... which, breaking down synthesis after synthesis, allows one soul after another to escape, leaving us confronted with a pile of dismantled

machinery, and evanescent particles. The second reason lies in the discovery of the sidereal world, so vast that it seems to do away with all proportion between our own being and the dimensions of the cosmos.... So at the world's Omega, as at its Alpha, lies the Impersonal. Under the influence of such impressions as these, it looks as though we have lost both respect for the person and understanding of his true nature.... The only universe capable of containing the human person is an irreversibly "personalising" universe. 33
Pierre Teilhard de Chardin

The time has come for remaking. *Homo sapiens* has had his day on earth—and has failed. The great lesson ... is that sapience is not enough to save us. Mind divorced from feeling, rationality without mercy, is not a divine gift but a devil's bargain. The enveloping culture of nihilism, and the new dark age of dehumanization, reflect a fatal disorder of the modern world.... The coming of the Fifth Horseman of the Apocalypse coincides with the triumph of the computer and the disinheritance of the senses. No, mind alone cannot save us in this extremity; what is needed now is *minding*—the marriage of thought and feeling. 34
Ashley Montagu & Floyd W. Matson

[T]he immediate decision that now confronts man [is] ... namely, whether he shall devote himself to the development of his own deepest humanity, or whether he shall surrender himself to the now almost automatic forces he himself has set in motion and yield place to his dehumanized alter ego. 35 *Lewis Mumford*

DEMOCRACY

[D]EMOCRACY IS A MEANS, the best means so far found, of realizing ends that lie in the wide domain of human relationships and the development of human personality.... The foundation of democracy is faith in the capacities of human nature, faith in human intelligence and in the power of pooled cooperative experience.... 1 *John Dewey*

The democrat identifies himself with mankind as a whole and with all subordinate groups whose demands are in harmony with the larger loyalty.... The stability of a democratic community undoubtedly depends upon the formation of characters capable of respecting the basic humanity of all men. 2 *Harold D. Lasswell*

[T]he outstanding characteristic of democratic character [is] *the maintenance of an open as against a closed ego*.... We are speaking of an underlying personality structure which is capable of "friendship" ... and which is unalienated from humanity. 3 *Harold D. Lasswell*

The perpetuation of democracy depends upon the practice of the brotherhood of man. 4
Franklin D. Roosevelt

[D]emocracy is maturity, and maturity is health.... 5 *D. W. Winnicott*

[S]elf-esteem is the basis of any real democracy. 6 *Gloria Steinem*

The true democracy, living and growing and inspiring, puts its faith in people—faith that the people will not simply elect men who will represent their views ably and faithfully, but also elect men who will exercise their conscientious judgment—faith that the people will not condemn those whose devotion to principle leads them to unpopular courses, but will reward courage, respect honor and ultimately recognize right. 7 *John F. Kennedy*

Jeffersonian democracy was not an enthronement of the people, but simply of leaders with profound respect for them. 8 *William Miller*

There are two major meanings ... of the idea of democracy. In one aspect it is free of constitutional government.... In its second aspect the democratic idea is egalitarian.... Throughout the history of the American experience there has been a planetary struggle between the two aspects of the democratic idea. 9 *Max Lerner*

Democracy arises out of the idea that those who are equal in any respect are equal in all respects; because men are equally free, they claim to be absolutely equal. 10 *Aristotle*

In a democracy the poor ought to have more

power than the rich, as being the greater numbers, and that which is decreed by the majority is supreme. 11 *Aristotle*

Democracy is not identical with majority rule. No, democracy is a *State* which recognises the subjection of the minority to the majority, that is, an organisation for the systematic use of *violence* by one class against the other, by one part of the population against another.... [T]he destruction of the State involves also the destruction of democracy.... 12 *V. I. Lenin*

Marx splendidly grasped the *essence* of capitalist democracy, when ... he said that the oppressed are allowed, once every few years to decide which particular representatives of the opposing class are to represent and repress them in Parliament! 13 *V. I. Lenin*

[T]he regimes in many "democratic" countries might be defined as a sort of feudalism that is primarily economic and in which the principal instrument of governing is the manipulation of political followings. 14 *Vilfredo Pareto*

Democracy is not a limit one may not overstep; it is merely one of the stages in the course of development from Feudalism to Capitalism, and from Capitalism to Communism. 15
V. I. Lenin

Democracy is a poison which disintegrates the body of the nation, and its action is the more deadly the more naturally strong and healthy the nation it infects.... The era of democracy is over, inexorably finished. 16 *Adolf Hitler*

Woodrow Wilson spoke of making the world safe for democracy. Our task today is to make the world safe for liberty.... Liberty can survive and even flourish in other systems besides democracies.... Making the world safe for liberty, then, does not mean establishing democracies everywhere on earth. 17
Richard M. Nixon

Some of the problems of governance in the U.S. today stem from an excess of democracy.... [It creates] the danger of overloading the political system with demands which extend its functions and undermine its authority.... [A] pervasive spirit of democracy may pose an intrinsic threat and undermine all forms of association, weakening the social bonds which hold together family, enterprise, and community. Every social organization requires, in some measure, inequalities in authority and distinctions in function. To the extent that the spread of the democratic temper corrodes all of these ... [it] creates obstacles to collaboration for any common purpose.... The effective operation of a democratic political system requires some measure of apathy and noninvolvement on the part of some individuals or groups. 18
Michel Crozier et al.

The transformation of the theory of democracy into theology has created a desire for progress in the direction of more democracy among numbers of people whose material interests are in no way harmed, are even actively advanced, by the existing form of government which they desire to change. 19
Aldous Huxley

The share of infamy that is likely to fall to the lot of each individual in public acts is small indeed.... Their own approbation of their own acts has to them the appearance of a public judgement in their favor. A perfect democracy is therefore the most shameless thing in the world. 20 *Edmund Burke*

[I]nstitutions purely democratic must, sooner or later, destroy liberty or civilization, or both. 21
Thomas Macaulay

[A] pure democracy ... can admit of no cure for the mischiefs of faction.... Hence it is that such democracies have ever been spectacles of turbulence and contention; have ever been found incompatible with personal security or the rights of property; and have in general been as short in their lives as they have been violent in their deaths.... A republic, by which I mean a government in which the scheme of representation takes place, opens a different prospect and promises the cure for which we are seeking. 22 *James Madison*

Politically, we are currently in the process of a massive shift from a representative to a participatory democracy. 23 *John Naisbitt*

Democracy

Democracy is a failure because it is based upon a political unit which is not organic—the individual mind. 24 *Timothy Leary*

The premise of democracy is that each man is the best judge of his own interests, and that all whose interests are affected should be consulted in the determination of policy.... The findings of personality research show that the individual is a poor judge of his own best interests.... In a sense politics proceeds by the creation of fictitious values.... 25 *Harold D. Lasswell*

[M]odern democracy is a product of the capitalist process.... [T]here exists no more democratic institution than a market.... 26
Joseph Schumpeter

Political democracy requires economic growth ... [and] a gradual but relatively constant increase in the economic well-being of society. 27
Michel Crozier et al.

[O]n the soil of a democracy constitutional rights signify nothing without money and everything with it. 28 *Oswald Spengler*

[O]ften the more democratic the country, the more hostile it is to foreign investment. 29
David Rockefeller

The primary business of a democracy is not the making of dollars but the making of human beings.... 30 *Ashley Montagu*

[B]ecause the global corporation derives its great economic advantages through centralization, information control, and hierarchical organization, it is inherently antidemocratic.... An antidemocratic structure cannot plan democratic growth, either for the society or for its own employees. 31 *R. J. Barnet & R. E. Muller*

A world of unseen dictatorship is conceivable, still using the forms of democratic government. 32
Kenneth Boulding

Democracy would appear to be the most efficient system of domination. 33
Herbert Marcuse

Democracy is difficult, and it is made more difficult because many who call themselves democrats are totalitarians in disguise. The moral is not to call off the struggle but to struggle all the more. 34 *Sidney Hook*

The merits of democracy are negative: it does not insure good government, but it prevents certain evils. 35 *Bertrand Russell*

I distrust Great Men. They produce a desert of conformity around them and often a pool of blood too.... [O]ne of the minor merits of a democracy is that it does not encourage ... or produce that unmanageable type of citizen known as the Great Man. 36 *E. M. Forster*

[O]nly democratic institutions appear to stand between the human race and periodic plunges into barbarism. 37 *Charles Hampden-Turner*

[T]he prospect of an explicit renunciation of democratic principles poses the task for the rest of society, in addition to challenging the corporation, of moving intellectually beyond "organized individualism" and a scientific view of social reason. It requires that we develop a political theory which helps us to understand power in our society, [and] helps us see that freedom is a product of cooperation. 38 *R. Jeffrey Lustig*

[D]emocracy, the right of the people to judge and to dismiss their government, is the only known device by which we can try to protect ourselves against the misuse of political power.... And since political power can control economic power, political democracy is also the only means for the control of economic power. 39 *Karl Popper*

Democracy implies permanent insecurity for those in governing positions—the more truly democratic the governing system, the greater the insecurity. 40 *Seymour Lipset*

There is always a tendency in government to confuse secrecy with security.... [Disclosure] may be uncomfortable, but it is not the purpose of democracy to ensure the comfort of its leaders. 41 *Robert F. Kennedy*

Even if no formal secrecy is invoked by the government an issue might as well be classified as "secret" if the people in a democracy are incapable of carrying on an intelligent discussion of it.... [W]e face the real danger of a layered society in which a scientific elite fraction floats on top and dominates our policy-making. The danger is that a new priesthood of scientists may usurp the traditional roles of democratic decision-making. 42 *Ralph E. Lapp*

Democracy is the worst form of government.... Yet democracy is the only form of social order admissible, because it is the only one consistent with justice. 43 *Robert Briffault*

Man's capacity for justice makes democracy possible, but man's inclination to injustice makes democracy necessary. 44 *Reinhold Niebuhr*

[D]emocracy is a means of preserving liberty.... 45 *Friedrich von Hayek*

Democracy is the form of government which combines for its citizens as much freedom and as much equality as possible. 46 *Leslie Lipson*

The spinal principle of democracy is the perception that the traits and needs and interests that all men share have a superior claim to those put forward by any special organization, institution, or group. 47 *Lewis Mumford*

Democracy ... is not simply a means to the end of a good society, it is the only society in which the social tendencies that press man to exploit man may be restrained. 48 *Seymour Lipset*

The foundation of democracy is the sense of spiritual independence, which nerves the individual to stand alone against the powers of this world.... 49 *R. H. Tawney*

In a democracy the controller is found among the controlled.... 50 *B. F. Skinner*

As a practical system for controlling and making use of the competitive aggression which is so evident in political controversy, democracy seems the best system yet devised. 51 *Anthony Storr*

[T]he democratic method is that institutional arrangement for arriving at political decisions in which individuals acquire the power to decide by means of a competitive struggle for the people's vote. 52 *Joseph Schumpeter*

Representative democracy is a better system than any other chiefly because it evokes the experimental competition of elites. 53 *George Gilder*

Democracy means that the people rule by selecting the wisest, most intelligent and most human to tell them what to do to be happy. Thus Democracy is a method for arriving at a truly benevolent aristocracy. 54 *H. H. Goddard*

The way of the democratic idea is an incessant common struggle for truth. 55 *Karl Jaspers*

[T]he university has been the chief nurturer of the values of disciplined freedom, of language and culture, and of other intellectual and moral elements vital to a liberal democracy. 56 *Robert Nisbet*

By [the] democratic process of open discussion there is started a tendency which constantly forces a larger and larger part of the valuation sphere into conscious attention.... [D]emocracy itself provides a moral education of the people. 57 *Gunnar Myrdal*

Democracy is a long-range strategy, but because it diffuses decision-making and thereby maximizes small changes ... [it] feels chaotic, and tends to breed short-run thinking in its constituents. And because its constituents think in short-run terms, they can't appreciate the value of the long-range strategy.... Authoritarianism is the exact opposite—a short-run strategy that fosters long-range thinking. 58 *Philip Slater*

It becomes particularly difficult for people in democratic societies to take questions with real moral content seriously in public life. Morality involves a distinction between better and worse, good and bad, which seems to violate the democratic principle of tolerance. 59 *Francis Fukuyama*

[D]emocracy ... is a method that in its looseness and disorder permits conflicting urges to work

Democracy

themselves out, and the ends of paradox to be held in tolerable but changing resolution. It does not prefigure the ends or final results. It awaits the arrival of the new occasions before supplying the new duties. 60 *Elting E. Morison*

From a leader, from all of us, what is required is a tolerance for the untidiness of democracy.... 61 *Hedrick Smith*

The less democratic feedback (and feedforward), the more decisions become divorced from reality, and the greater the danger that errors will go uncorrected until they escalate into crisis. Democracy, in this sense ... is highly "efficient." 62 *Alvin Toffler*

[S]ystems of goal formation based on elitist premises are simply no longer "efficient." ... Political democracy, by incorporating larger and larger numbers in social decision-making, facilitates feedback. And it is precisely this feedback that is essential.... 63 *Alvin Toffler*

The essence of democratic machinery is the free vote (secret ballot). The point of this is that it ensures the freedom of the people to express deep feelings, *apart from conscious thoughts.* 64 *D. W. Winnicott*

Of all forms of government, democracy is the most likely to lead to wise policy in the long run. 65 *Carl Cohen*

Democracy as a sentiment has two sides. When it says "I am as good as you," it is wholesome, but when it says "you are no better than I am," it becomes oppressive and an obstacle to the development of exceptional merit. 66 *Bertrand Russell*

The difficulty for democracy is, how to find and keep high ideals. 67 *Matthew Arnold*

The young American has no respect for anything or anybody, for tradition or for public office—unless it is for the personal achievement of individual men. This is what the American calls "democracy." ... 68 *Max Weber*

The members of a democracy cannot be truly said to possess their power until they have been deliberately trained to use it. We are still far from such a time. 69 *Harold Laski*

Democracy is better understood as a habit of mind than as a system of government.... 70 *Lewis Lapham*

The United States is still in the process of being democratized. 71 *Philip Slater*

[D]emocratic citizens are made, not born. 72 *R. Jeffrey Lustig*

Without the democratic *family*, democracy would be a self-extinguishing mechanism. 73 *Philip Slater*

[T]o achieve full democracy in the public sphere, freedom and reciprocity are required in the personal relations of the private sphere.... For the cultivation of free choice in personal life contributes to an active character, which is required for participation in public life. 74 *Carol Gould*

[I]t remains true that democratic freedom is good for those who enjoy it and that practice in self-government is an almost indispensable element in the curriculum of man's moral and psychological education. 75 *Aldous Huxley*

Democracy is not so much a form of government as a set of principles. 76 *Woodrow Wilson*

[T]he most important thing for the world today is spiritual regeneration.... We must present democracy as a force holding within itself the seeds of unlimited progress for the human race. 77 *Gen. George C. Marshall*

[D]emocracy alone has constructed an unlimited civilization capable of infinite progress in the improvement of human life. 78 *Franklin D. Roosevelt*

As mankind approaches the end of the millennium, the twin crises of authoritarianism and socialist central planning have left only one competitor standing in the ring as an ideology of potentially universal validity: liberal democracy.... 79 *Francis Fukuyama*

No one pretends that democracy is perfect or all-wise. Indeed, it has been said that democracy is the worst form of government except all those other forms that have been tried from time to time. 80 *Winston Churchill*

DEPENDENCY / AUTONOMY

MAN'S CHILDHOOD LEARNING ... is contingent on prolonged dependence. Only thus does man develop conscience, that dependence on himself which will make him, in turn, dependable; and only when thoroughly dependable in a number of fundamental values (truth, justice, etc.) can he become independent and teach and develop tradition. 1 *Erik Erikson*

The basis for moral self-respect lies in viewing oneself as morally autonomous.... 2
Mike W. Martin

[M]uch human unhappiness springs from the conflict between the yearning for love and the striving for individuality and autonomy. 3
Althea Horner

In the covenant of marriage, [woman] is compelled to promise obedience to her husband, he becoming to all intents and purposes her master.... He has endeavored in every way that he could to destroy her confidence in her own powers, to lessen her self-respect, and to make her willing to lead a dependent and abject life. 4
Seneca Falls Declaration of Women's Rights (1848)

The fact is that men need women more than women need men; and ... man has sought to keep woman dependent upon him economically as the only method open to him of making himself necessary to her. 5
Elizabeth Gould Davis

Female fear of an open season of rape ... was probably the single causative factor in the original subjugation of woman by man, the most important key to her historic dependence, her domestication by protective mating. 6
Susan Brownmiller

Why, when we have the chance to move ahead, do we tend to retreat? Because women are not used to confronting fear and going beyond it. We've been encouraged to avoid anything that scares us, taught from the time we were very young to do only those things which allow us to feel comfortable and secure—In fact we were not trained for freedom at all, but for its categorical opposite—*dependency.* 7 *Colette Dowling*

[G]irls, from the time they are quite young, are trained *into* dependency, while boys are trained *out* of it. 8 *Colette Dowling*

Dependency, by its very nature, creates self-doubt, and self-doubt can lead all too quickly to self-hatred. 9 *Colette Dowling*

The dependence on irrational authority results in a weakening of the will in the dependent person and, at the same time, whatever tends to paralyze the will makes for an increase in dependence. Thus a vicious circle is formed. 10
Erich Fromm

Dependency and a feeling of incompetence, of being unable to cope, are closely connected. Helplessness marches hand in hand with hopelessness.... 11 *Anthony Storr*

Dependency feelings are terribly painful for a woman because they ... reinforce her feelings of unworthiness and emptiness. 12
Luise Eichenbaum & Susie Orbach

Although this is not usually made explicit within the relationship, men's dependency needs are most often met within marriage and their emotional worries are processed by their wives. No such equivalent place exists for women. 13
Luise Eichenbaum & Susie Orbach

The male is said to be emotionally shallow and unable to maintain a deeply intimate emotional relationship with a woman.... [T]his "shallowness" is simply a self-protective device used by the male to avoid revealing his vulnerability. That is, the male resists closeness and dependency on the female because once the unconscious defense is penetrated by a woman he becomes profoundly attached to the point of deep and almost total dependency. 14
Herb Goldberg

Dependency / Autonomy

If there is no true recognition of the mother's part, then there must remain a vague fear of dependence. This fear will sometimes take the form of a fear of WOMAN, or fear of a woman.... Traced to its root in the history of each individual, this fear of WOMAN turns out to be a fear of recognizing the fact of dependence. 15 *D. W. Winnicott*

The sexual dependency of the male on the female ... is distressing to the male psyche.... Patriarchy is the product of the male reaction to sexual dependency.... Aggression can then be viewed as one kind of response to need and dependency. 16 *J. C. Smith*

There are thousands of Himmlers living among us.... He was bound to his mother who encouraged his dependency.... 17 *Erich Fromm*

The psychology of giving is intimately feminine; the psychology of possession and taking is masculine. "Taking" is a denial of dependence.... 18 *Norman O. Brown*

It is known that the need of love is a mechanism for establishing security in a cultural situation producing dependency.... One sees that woman's alleged narcissism and greater need to be loved may be entirely the result of economic necessity. 19 *Clara Thompson*

All social dependence and oppression is rooted in the economic dependence of the oppressed upon the oppressor. 20 *August Bebel*

People may become dependent on us for food. I know that is not supposed to be good news. To me that is good news, because before people can do anything, they've got to eat. And if you are looking for a way to get people to lean on you and be dependent on you, it seems that food dependence would be terrific. 21
Hubert H. Humphrey

The way capitalism has exploited the alienated human needs for love and dignity, and has, above all, exploited the resulting sexual obsession for profit or power, has diverted people from paths toward true autonomy. 22
Betty Friedan

The market system of the last century ... made the concepts of community and individual ambivalent.... Shame about being dependent is the legacy of 19th century industrial society.... 23 *Richard Sennett*

Conservatives ... have long known and warned that real poverty is less a state of income than a state of mind and that the government dole blights most of the people who come to depend on it.... In the time since the war on poverty was launched, the moral blight of dependency has been compounded and extended to future generations by a virtual plague of family dissolution.... But no one can view that wreckage of broken homes and lives and call it victory over poverty without depriving the word of all meaning. 24 *George Gilder*

American fears of dependency and myths of independence contribute to less effective organizational functioning.... While Westerners seek to repress or disparage this common experience of ... dependence, the Japanese openly embrace it. Indeed, they build a great many aspects of organizational life around it.... The Japanese accomplish this through the concept of *wa*. Technically, *wa* means group harmony.... [This] secret weapon that Japanese culture permits and encourages managers to use ... gives them significant organizational advantages. 25 *R. T. Pascale & A. G. Athos*

Instead of resisting increased economic interdependence, we should be embracing it wholeheartedly.... If we get sufficiently interlaced economically, we will most probably *not* bomb each other off the face of the planet. 26
John Naisbitt

The sense of dependence that is bred by recognition that the intent and effort of man are never final but are subject to the uncertainties of an indeterminate future, would render dependence universal and shared by all. It would terminate the most corroding form of spiritual pride and isolation, that which divides man from man.... A sense of common participation in the inevitable uncertainties of existence would be coeval with a sense of common effort and shared destiny. 27 *John Dewey*

No one can truly extricate himself from dependency on others, from the need for recognition. 28 *Jessica Benjamin*

Dependency is the basic survival mechanism of the human organism. 29 *Willard Gaylin*

~ DEVIL ~

[T]HE DEVIL IS certainly nothing else than the personification of the repressed unconscious instinctual life. 1 *Sigmund Freud*

[I]n conceiving the image of the Devil there were no laws to be kept, and the creative imagination could run riot, emptying all its repressed and sensuous contents. Hence the persistent allure of Satanism and the fascination of evil. 2 *Alan Watts*

For the devil is wont, in affliction and in the conflict of conscience, by the law to make us afraid, and to lay against us the guilt of sin, our wicked life past, the wrath and judgment of God, hell and eternal death, that by this means he may drive us to desperation, make us bondslaves to himself, and pluck us from Christ. 3
Martin Luther

The Devil is the lineal descendent of the Trickster ... [who] is a projection of the psychological forces sustaining the economic activity of primitive peoples.... Through the archetype of the Devil mankind has said something about the psychological forces, inside man himself, sustaining the economic activity which ultimately flowered into capitalism. 4
Norman O. Brown

[T]ribal shamans ... play upon, and eventually help to allay the worst fears of the common people. They make real the threat of unseen demons, which they then exorcise. In the political world of Washington, shamans ... [invoke] the dreaded forces of world communism, the Mafia, monopoly cabals, the moral majority, or immoral minority. 5 *J. McIver Weatherford*

The militarization of American life is rooted in ... a demonological conception of the world. 6
Hans Morgenthau

[T]he central preconception of the paranoid style [is] the existence of a vast, insidious, preternaturally effective international conspiratorial network designed to perpetrate acts of the most fiendish character.... [The enemy] is a free, active, demonic agent.... This enemy seems to be on many counts a projection of the self. 7 *Richard Hofstadter*

If the devil doesn't exist, but man has created him, he has created him in his own image and likeness. 8 *Feodor Dostoevsky*

Each society is a hero system which promises victory over evil and death.... The Devil is the one who prevents the heroic victory of immortality in each culture. 9 *Ernest Becker*

Mass movements can rise and spread without belief in a God, but never without belief in a devil. 10 *Eric Hoffer*

A religion can no more afford to degrade its Devil than to degrade its God. 11
Havelock Ellis

Satan's real intention is not to have a godless political situation, he wants a religious situation. Satan loves religion.... Religion is the great blinder of the minds of men. 12
Hal Lindsey

In Eden, Satan is the embodiment of the daimonic of lust and the desire for power by means of knowledge which will make man immortal, "like god." 13 *Rollo May*

"Egotism," which is the extreme separation of the conscious ego from the rest of being, is characteristically attributed to Satan.... Satan is a projection in which the agentic in the human psyche is personified.... The psychological problem of the Satanic image is agency unmitigated by communion. 14 *David Bakan*

The devil, or some other personification of evil, tempts a person ... with the offer of unlimited powers.... Man in reaching out for the Infinite and the Absolute also starts destroying himself. When he makes a pact with the devil, who promises him glory, he has to go to hell—to the hell within himself. 15 *Karen Horney*

Devil

The daimonic is any natural function which has the power to take over the whole person.... The daimonic is the urge in every being to affirm itself, assert itself, perpetuate and increase itself. The daimonic becomes evil when it usurps the total self without regard to the integration of that self, or to the unique forms and desires of others and their need for integration. 16
Rollo May

The nerve of bedevilment is that it renders *any* harmony impossible either within a man or between man and nature. 17
George Santayana

In Western antiquity and especially in Eastern cultures the opposites often remain united in the same figure.... As the distance between conscious and unconscious increases ... the opposites contained in this image split apart.... The clearest expression of this is the Christian reformation of the Jewish concept of the Deity: the morally ambiguous Yahweh became an exclusively good God, while everything evil was united in the devil. 18 *Carl Jung*

A god outgrown becomes immediately a life-destroying demon. The form has to be broken and the energies released. 19
Joseph Campbell

The daimonic is present in all nature as blind, ambiguous power. But only in man does it become allied with the tragic. For tragedy is the self-conscious, personal realization of being in the power of one element.... 20 *Rollo May*

So long as the passions hide or excuse themselves in terms of some conventional morality, spirit seems to have only the flesh and the world for its enemies; but when each passion begins to assert its primary right to life and to liberty, spirit has come upon an enemy in the spiritual sphere. The devil has entered the stage; for by this personage I understand any enemy of spirit that is internal to spirit. 21
George Santayana

[T]he devil needs indeed to be exorcised, but cannot be destroyed so long as spirit endures, because in their substance the two are one. 22
George Santayana

The culture ... we now call modernism—took over, in effect, the relation with the demonic. But instead of taming it, as religion sought to do, the modernist culture began to accept the demonic, to explore it, to revel in it, and to see it (correctly) as the source of a certain kind of creativity. 23 *Daniel Bell*

[O]ne will find a devil in every narcissistic or psychopathic individual. 24 *Alexander Lowen*

Those who seek God in isolation from their fellowmen, unless trebly armed for the perils of the quest, are apt to find, not God, but a devil, whose countenance bears an embarrassing resemblance to their own. 25 *R. H. Tawney*

[A]s all the wise men of history have told us...[:] He who seeks to understand himself seeks the devil in himself as well as his God. 26
C. W. Churchman

The nameless powers of Nothingness are, in our world whence the gods have been driven forth, the analogy of the demons that confronted primitive man. 27 *Karl Jaspers*

The mere act of enlightenment may have destroyed the spirits of nature, but not the psychic factors that correspond to them.... [T]he psychic conditions which breed demons are as actively at work as ever. The demons have not really disappeared but have merely taken on another form: they have become unconscious psychic forces. 28 *Carl Jung*

❧ Dominance / Hierarchy

The basic features of all human society and political organizations can be discerned in the social organization of non-human primates. In humans, as in monkeys, the maintenance of peace within a given group is achieved through a dominance hierarchy. 1
Robert Bigelow

Domination in the most general sense is one of the most important elements of social action.... Without exception every sphere of social action is profoundly influenced by structures of dominancy. 2 *Max Weber*

Dominance / Hierarchy

Human political systems are based on hierarchy and competition for status.... [C]ompetition for status is to social process as sexual attraction is to reproduction.... [This is a] "primative" reflex.... We refine this reflex endlessly.... We create a god to whom we can be subordinate. So committed are we to the notion of hierarchy that even our mightiest leaders must subserve something or someone. 3
Lionel Tiger & Robin Fox

Hierarchism is a vital need of the human soul.... The effect of true hierarchism is to bring each one to fit himself morally into the place he occupies. 4 *Simone Weil*

Order is Heaven's first law; and this confessed / Some are, and must be, greater than the rest. 5
Alexander Pope

Appeals to reason or to the nature of the universe have been used throughout history to enshrine existing hierarchies as proper and inevitable. The hierarchies rarely endure for more than a few generations, but the arguments, refurbished for the next round of social institutions, cycle endlessly. 6 *Stephen Jay Gould*

Hierarchies try to convince us that all power and well-being come from the outside, that our self-esteem depends on obedience.... 7
Gloria Steinem

[T]he male is by nature superior, and the female inferior; and the one rules, and the other is ruled; this principle, of necessity, extends to all mankind. 8 *Aristotle*

The theory of aggressive male domination over women as a natural right is so deeply embedded in our cultural value system that all recent attempts to expose it ... have barely managed to scratch the surface. 9 *Susan Brownmiller*

Hierarchy incarnates superiority.... [M]ale structures are hierarchical.... [T]he true end of male institutions is to maintain at any cost the appearance of male control. 10 *Marilyn French*

Male supremist institutions rose as a by-product of warfare, of the male monopoly over weapons, and of the use of sex for the nurturance of aggressive male personalities.... Therefore, male supremacy is no more natural than warfare. 11 *Marvin Harris*

It seems that dominance seeking is ... a veritable obsession for the male of the species, whereas power for power's sake is more likely viewed with nonchalance, disdain, and puzzlement by the human female. 12 *Kent G. Bailey*

The first class antagonism appearing in history coincides with the development of the antagonism of man and wife in monogamy, and the first class oppression with that of the female by the male sex.... [Thus] develops the welfare and advancement of the one by the woe and submission of the other. 13 *Friedrich Engels*

If the human consciousness had not included the original category of the Other and an original aspiration to dominate the Other, the invention of the bronze tool could not have caused the oppression of woman. 14
Simone de Beauvoir

[T]he social dominance of males over females ... can be seen as a direct result of the division of labor between hunting and gathering. 15
Richard E. Leakey

The development of a hierarchical system of social labor not only rationalizes domination but also "contains" the rebellion against domination. 16 *Herbert Marcuse*

Because the relation between the sexes is not one of equality but of domination, men cannot trust women.... The threat of insurrection always accompanies domination; one of the reasons control is so unsatisfying is that it begets ... a sense of fear.... Thus the dominators hate those they oppress. 17 *Marilyn French*

The pathological desire of males to dominate females has not diminished: it has merely become more difficult to justify. But we still try. 18
J. C. Smith

[M]ale domination is rooted in a struggle for recognition between men in which women are mere objects or tokens: the prize. 19
Jessica Benjamin

Dominance / Hierarchy

In the final analysis the greatest danger to the future of humanity may be that ... males of today will rather sacrifice freedom than give up the domination of females. 20 *J. C. Smith*

[S]ocieties which ... give women authority in ... familial areas, will place an unusually strong emphasis on some suprafamilial area.... This would explain the fact that the relatively low degree of familial male dominance in the American family is correlated with a moderately high degree of patriarchy in the political and economic areas. 21 *Steven Goldberg*

[B]oth men and women use the unresolved early threat of female dominion to justify keeping the infantilism in themselves alive under male dominion. 22 *Dorothy Dinnerstein*

Domination begins with the attempt to deny dependency. 23 *Jessica Benjamin*

Unfortunately, the fear of domination does not lead groups of people to avoid being dominated; on the contrary, it draws them towards a specific or chosen domination. 24 *D. W. Winnicott*

We do not willingly submit to domination, except through our desire to dominate others. 25 *William Blanchard*

To some degree or other, every neurotic ... confines himself to circumstances in which he feels able to dominate.... Whether he dominates by bullying or by whining will depend on his training.... 26 *Alfred Adler*

[T]error is the essence of totalitarian domination.... Those who aspire to total domination must liquidate all spontaneity, such as the mere existence of individuality.... As long as all men have not been made equally superfluous—and this has been accomplished only in the concentration camps—the ideal of totalitarian domination has not been achieved. 27 *Hannah Arendt*

What prepares men for totalitarian domination in the non-totalitarian world is the fact that loneliness, once a borderline experience usually suffered in certain marginal social conditions like old age, has become an everyday experience of the evergrowing masses of our century. 28 *Hannah Arendt*

The traits of dominance and submission and loneliness "chase" each other around the vicious circle. 29 *Charles Hampden-Turner*

Behind everyone who behaves as if he were superior to others, we can suspect a feeling of inferiority which calls for very special efforts of concealment. 30 *Alfred Adler*

Indeed, it seems to me that all our human culture is based upon feelings of inferiority. 31 *Alfred Adler*

Where potency is lacking, man's relatedness to the world is perverted into a desire to dominate, to exert power over others as if they were things. Domination is coupled with death, potency with life. 32 *Erich Fromm*

Whosoever, without possessing that desire of glory which makes one fear to displease those who judge his conduct, desires domination and power, very often seeks to obtain what he loves by most open crimes.... [He] exceeds the beasts in the vices of cruelty.... 33 *Saint Augustine*

[D]ominance hierarchies are connected primarily with ... anger and fear. 34 *Robert Plutchik*

American society is increasingly organized in terms of hierarchy.... A hierarchy in a land that bills itself as a land of equality and opportunity is an inherently unstable structure. 35 *Charles A. Reich*

The rationality of domination has progressed to the point where it threatens to invalidate its foundations; therefore it must be reaffirmed more effectively than ever before.... The ideology of today lies in that production and consumption reproduce and justify domination. 36 *Herbert Marcuse*

The scientific method ... came to provide the pure concepts as well as the instrumentalities for the ever-more effective domination of man by man.... Today, domination extends and perpetuates itself not only through technology but *as* technology.... 37 *Herbert Marcuse*

Dominance / Hierarchy

Once we bring ourselves to abandon the pleasure principle, it is easy to accept the idea that the achievement of dominance, the overcoming of obstacles, and the mastery of the external world ... are as much innate human needs as sexuality or hunger. 38 *Anthony Storr*

Dominance—beyond any comprehension—is related to the mystery of the fundamental life force. 39 *Robert Ardrey*

[D]iscontent with one's status is a scarce commodity in a state of nature. Hierarchy is a force too valuable for natural selection to have favored the discontented. 40 *Robert Ardrey*

Nature, on the other hand, will conspire to preserve a substantial degree of *megalothymia*.... A civilization devoid of anyone who wanted to be recognized as better than others ... would have little art.... It would be incompetently governed.... It would not have much in the way of economic dynamism.... And perhaps most critically, it would be unable to defend itself from civilizations that were infused with a greater spirit of *megalothymia*, whose citizens were ready to forsake comfort ... for the sake of dominion. 41 *Francis Fukuyama*

It is the striving for superiority which is behind every human creation and it is the source of all contributions which are made to our culture. 42 *Alfred Adler*

[T]he continued exercise of every domination ... always has the strongest need of self-justification. Of such ultimate principles, there are only three: ... *Rationally regulated* association within a structure of domination finds its typical expression in *bureaucracy*. *Traditionally* prescribed social action is typically represented by *patriarchalism*. The *charismatic* structure of domination rests upon individual authority.... 43 *Max Weber*

The neoconservative attitude toward inequality and "merit" is ... a justification for an order of things they feel will always be unequal and hierarchical. 44 *Peter Steinfels*

Authority systems must be based on people arranged in a hierarchy. Thus the critical question in determining control is, Who is over whom? How much over is far less important than the visible presence of a ranked ordering.... For it is in the nature of hierarchical control that the response is linked in all-or-nothing fashion to the person of highest status. It need not be a great deal more status; a smidgen will do. 45
Stanley Milgram

We are not utopians, we do not indulge in "dreams" of how best to do away *immediately* with all management, with all subordination.... No, we want the Socialist revolution with human nature as it is now; human nature itself cannot do without subordination.... [T]here must be submission to the armed vanguard.... 46
V. I. Lenin

But, striving for Socialism, we are convinced that it will develop further into Communism, and, side by side with this, there will vanish all need for force, for the *subjection* of one man to another, of one section of society to another. ... 47 *V. I. Lenin*

The march of bureaucracy has destroyed structures of domination which had no rational character. 48 *Max Weber*

[I]n most hierarchies, *super-competence is more objectionable than incompetence ... because it disrupts the hierarchy*, and thereby violates *the first commandment* of hierarchical life: *the hierarchy must be preserved*. 49
Laurence J. Peter & Raymond Hull

The Peter Principle: IN A HIERARCHY EVERY EMPLOYEE TENDS TO RISE TO HIS LEVEL OF INCOMPETENCE. 50
Laurence J. Peter & Raymond Hull

Those who reach the top level of hierarchies are, increasingly, those who have successfully shed their rough edges of individualism. 51
Vance Packard

It would seem appropriate for the leaders of our big organization structures in all fields, with their neatly ordered hierarchies, to cast a searching eye on the human cost.... 52
Vance Packard

Dominance / Hierarchy

The failure of hierarchies to solve human problems has forced people to begin talking with one another outside their organizations, and that is the first step to forming a network.... In the future, institutions will be organized ... on the networking model. 53 *John Naisbitt*

The basic organizational principle on which the entire set of civilizational enterprises of the past 8,000 years, at least, have been founded, that of hierarchical organization, has played itself out. 54 *Elise Boulding*

The authoritarian hierarchic pyramid is only one of the most obvious systems for organizing cooperative effort—and may not be the most logical or desirable for the affluent, enlightened society we have today.... When power of decision is restricted to the top alone, the organization can never become any better than the men at the top. But conversely, an organization that surges with vitality and creativity all the way down can become better than the sum total of all the people. 55 *Vance Packard*

What sectors of society are best equipped to replace hierarchy with decentralist structures based on nonhierarchical communication? Women. Their underlife experience ideally equips them for this, and promotes fresh approaches to situations where present system designs do not work. 56 *Elise Boulding*

It may be that for *Homo sapiens* in the future, extreme manifestations of the behavior patterns of dominance and aggression will be evolutionarily at a discount.... [The male] may feel a little odd for the first few millennia because he is less accustomed to living without them then we are.... All we need to do is hold out loving arms to him and say: Come on in. The water's lovely. 57 *Elaine Morgan*

The first thing that spirit must renounce, if it would begin to be free, is any claim to domination. 58 *George Santayana*

Most in need of study ... [are] the ways whereby the very existence of a hierarchy encourages undue acquiescence.... The hierarchical psychosis (interweaving the social order with the motives of guilt, wonder, adventure, catharsis, and victimage) arises so spontaneously ... that a free society should ... make the building of hierarchical magic most difficult.... [But] in a world wholly "unmasked," no social cohesion would be possible. 59 *Kenneth Burke*

~ Duty ~

[I]n order to discern what I have to do in order that my volition may be morally good ... I ask myself only: Can I will that my maxim becomes a universal law? If not, it must be rejected.... [A]ctions from pure respect for the practical law constitutes duty. To duty every other motive must give place, because duty is the condition of a will good in itself, whose worth transcends everything. 1 *Immanuel Kant*

All aspects of our lives must be interpreted in light of duty, for only this enables ethical agency to unify the personality. Other overriding passions, such as desires for fame or wealth, fragment us in many directions rather than provide continuity and consistency in our lives. 2 *Mike W. Martin*

The first duty of men is ... to do nothing without a clear and individual conviction that it is right to be done. 3 *William Godwin*

In short, our first duty is to make a moral code for ourselves. 4 *Émile Durkheim*

Our first duty is to be true to our conscience. ... 5 *Harold Laski*

This is the conclusion of the whole matter: Fear God and keep his commandments: for this is the whole duty of man. 6 *Holy Bible*

I owe a duty, where I cannot love. 7 *Aphra Behn*

[The] difference between duty and responsibility corresponds to the distinction between the authoritarian and humanistic conscience. The authoritarian conscience ... is glorified obedience. The humanistic conscience is the readiness to listen to the voice of one's own humanity and is independent of orders given by anyone else. 8 *Erich Fromm*

Duty

The strongest is never strong enough to be always master, unless he transforms strength into right, and obedience into duty. 9
Jean-Jacques Rousseau

As soon as the devotion of the followers turns into a sense of duty, leadership becomes charismatic authority. Devotion creates the inner urge to obey the leader's wishes.... 10
Arthur Schweitzer

Sacrifice on behalf of the individuality of the State is the substantial tie between the State and all its members and so is a universal duty. 11
G. W. F. Hegel

[Fascism] builds up a higher life based on duty ... in which the individual by self-sacrifice, the renunciation of self-interest, by death itself can achieve that purely spiritual existence in which his value as a man consists.... 12
Benito Mussolini

Consciousness of duty, fulfillment of duty, and obedience are not ends in themselves, any more than the state is an end in itself; they should all be means for making possible and safeguarding on this earth the existence of a community of spiritually and physically homogeneous beings. 13 *Adolf Hitler*

It is usually crucial to collective ideologies that personal relations should be secondary to the individual's duty to the collective. Hence altruism on behalf of the collective can easily go with indifference to the fate of individuals. 14
Derek Wright

A person can be entirely dominated by his sadistic strivings and consciously believe that he is motivated only by his sense of duty. 15
Erich Fromm

Eichmann's opportunities for feeling like Pontius Pilate were many, and as the months and years went by, he lost the need to feel anything at all. This was the way things were, this was the new law of the land, based on the Führer's order; whatever he did he did, as far as he could see, as a law-abiding citizen. He did his *duty*.... 16 *Hannah Arendt*

[I]n an allegiance to a manifestly imperfect society ... our duty lies in the service of ideals which we cannot possibly achieve. 17
Michael Polanyi

For men an unnamed god of duty holds down the surface of the earth; and all stock markets, all football fields, all corporation parking lots, all suburban tracts, all offices, all firing ranges, belong to him. There a man makes a stand, makes a farm, makes an impression, makes an empire, but sooner or later, if he is lucky, the time comes to go inward, and live in "the garden." 18 *Robert Bly*

What's a man's first duty? The answer is brief: to be himself. 19 *Henrik Ibsen*

Our first duties are to ourselves.... 20
Jean-Jacques Rousseau

Men, be humane. This is your first duty. 21
Jean-Jacques Rousseau

Duty towards the human being as such—that alone is eternal. This obligation is an unconditional one.... And it is in relation to it that we measure our progress. 22 *Simone Weil*

The scout's motto is ... BE PREPARED, which means, you are always to be in a state of readiness in mind and body to do your DUTY. 23
Lord Baden-Powell

[M]an is so constituted that he can only attain a proper use of his faculties by exercising them, and will not exercise them unless necessity of some kind first set the wheels in motion. Virtue likewise can only be acquired by the discharge of relative duties.... 24
Mary Wollstonecraft

The duties of universal obligation are five ... [:] those between sovereign and minister, between father and son, between husband and wife, between elder brother and younger, and those belonging to the intercourse of friends. 25
Confucius

The being who discharges the duties of its station is independent; and, speaking of women at large, their first duty is to themselves as rational creatures, and the next in point of importance, as citizens, is that which includes so many, of a mother. 26 *Mary Wollstonecraft*

Duty is essential to marriage. The moral, social and legal evil of ERA is that it proclaims as a constitutional mandate that the husband no longer has the primary duty to support his wife and children. 27 *Phyllis Schlafly*

To the extent that American culture is ... obsessed with the individual and his rights, averse to the claims of social duties, it is a wonder that it holds together at all. 28 *Max Lerner*

It is our first duty to serve society, and, after we have done that, we may attend wholly to the salvation of our own souls. 29 *Samuel Johnson*

I fully agree with those who believe that men can reasonably define their rights only in terms of their duties.... I have a right to get some chance to do my duty. This is, in fact, my sole inalienable right. 30 *Josiah Royce*

A right is not effectual by itself, but only in relation to the obligation to which it corresponds. 31 *Simone Weil*

According to the Anglo-Saxon version of liberal theory ... men have perfect rights but no perfect duties to their communities. Their duties are imperfect because they are derived from their rights; the community exists only to protect those rights. Moral obligation is therefore entirely contractual. 32 *Francis Fukuyama*

Duty, indeed, seems at first to be of political consideration; but if thoroughly weighed, it truly relates to the rule and government of one's self, not others. 33 *Francis Bacon*

There is no growth except in the fulfillment of obligations. 34 *Antoine de Saint-Exupéry*

The obligation is something infinite.... All the devices men have thought that they had discovered for avoiding it have turned out to be lies.... [One] device consists in denying any sort of obligation.... Actually, such a negation is impossible. It amounts to spiritual suicide. 35 *Simone Weil*

Economics

[T]he ideas of economists ... are more powerful than is commonly understood. Indeed, the world is ruled by little else. Practical men, who believe themselves to be quite exempt from any intellectual influences, are usually the slaves of some defunct economist. Madmen in authority, who hear voices in the air, are distilling their frenzy from some academic scribbler of a few years back. 1 *John Maynard Keynes*

[E]conomists have become the clergy of the twentieth century. 2 *Philip Wylie*

The laws of commerce are the laws of nature, and therefore the laws of God. 3 *Edmund Burke*

All economic life is the expression of a soul-life. 4 *Oswald Spengler*

From a spiritual being, who, in order to survive, must devote a reasonable attention to economic interests, man seems sometimes to have become an economic animal, who will be prudent, nevertheless, if he takes due precautions to assure his spiritual well-being. 5 *R. H. Tawney*

Man feels himself to be responsible, but he is not. He does not feel himself an object, but he is. He has been so well assimilated to the economic world, so well adjusted to it by being reduced to the *homo economicus* ... that the appearance of personal life becomes for him the reality of personal life. 6 *Jacques Ellul*

Human beings in consequence of their material production and material intercourse transform their existence and therewith also their thinking and the products of their thinking. It is not consciousness which determines life but life which determines consciousness. 7 *Karl Marx & Friedrich Engels*

The danger to liberty lies in the subordination of belief to the needs of the industrial system.... [F]or if economic goals are the only goals of the society it is natural that the industrial system should dominate the state and the state should serve its ends. 8 *John K. Galbraith*

Economics

[T]he basic thrust of economic activity has moved subtly from the manipulation of *things* to the manipulation of *minds*—from the engineering of goods to the engineering of consent. 9 *Ashley Montagu & Floyd W. Matson*

Economists assume that jobs must be created for things that don't need to be done so people can have money to spend on things they don't need. And to get people to buy things they don't need, we create a huge industry to get them to want them. 10 *Philip Slater*

Advertising is an expression of an irrational economy.... If we were all logicians the economy could not survive, and herein lies a terrifying paradox, for *in order to exist economically as we are we must try by might and main to remain stupid*. 11 *Jules Henry*

The economy for its success requires organized public bamboozlement ... [and] the management of demand for particular products—[thus] requiring well-considered mendacity. 12 *John K. Galbraith*

[The market] depends on the assumption that people tell the truth.... [E]conomic man may be destroying moral man, and ... without moral man, economic man may cease to exist. 13 *Barry Schwartz*

Economic relations are *impersonal*.... The relation is neither one of cooperation nor one of mutual exploitation, but is completely non-moral, non-human. 14 *F. H. Knight*

Market behavior is influenced by rational, purposeful pursuit of interests. The partner to a transaction is expected to behave according to rational legality and, quite particularly, to respect the formal inviolability of a promise once given. These are the qualities which form the content of market ethics.... In sharp contrast to all other groups which always presuppose some measure of personal fraternalization ... the market is fundamentally alien to any type of fraternal relationship. 15 *Max Weber*

Rational economic association always brings about depersonalization, and it is impossible to control a universe of instrumentally rational activities by charitable appeals to particular individuals. 16 *Max Weber*

One cultural element after another has been absorbed into the ever-widening economy, subjected to the test of economic rationality, rationalized, and turned into a commodity.... [I]t now seems that anything can be thought of as a commodity and its value measured by a price ... [e.g.] art objects, ideas, experiences, enjoyment itself, and even social relations. As these become commodities they are all subject to a process of moral neutralization. 17 *Paul Diesing*

Freedom from scruple, from sympathy, honesty and regard for life, may, within fairly wide limits, be said to further the success of the individual in the pecuniary life. 18 *Thorstein Veblen*

The will to economic power, if it is sufficiently single-minded, brings riches. But if it is single-minded it destroys the moral restraints which ought to condition the pursuit of riches, and therefore also makes the pursuit of riches meaningful. 19 *R. H. Tawney*

Observe what happened to the seven deadly sins of Christian theology. All but one of these sins, sloth, was transformed into a positive virtue. Greed, avarice, envy, gluttony, luxury, and pride were the driving forces of the new economy: if once they were mainly the vices of the rich, they now under the doctrine of expanding wants embraced every class in society. 20 *Lewis Mumford*

[E]conomics has often seemed like a science of Greed in which all mention of Greed is banned. 21 *D. W. Winnicott*

Unsound economics ... pretends that Greed is only to be found in certain pathological individuals or gangs.... The assumption being a false one, a great deal of clever economics is only clever; that is to say, it is great fun to read, but it is dangerous as a foundation for planning. 22 *D. W. Winnicott*

For a whole century, economic progress has mainly consisted in freeing industrial relations

Economics

from all regulation. Until very recently, it was the function of a whole system of moral forces to exert this discipline.... [But] religion has lost most of its power. And government, instead of regulating economic life, has become its tool and servant.... Thereupon the appetites thus excited have become freed of any limiting authority. By sanctifying them, so to speak, this apotheosis of well-being has placed them above all human law. Their restraint seems like a sort of sacrilege. 23 *Émile Durkheim*

The modern economic principle that private vice makes public virtue has penetrated all aspects of daily life in such a way that there seems to be no reason to be a conscious part of civic existence. 24 *Allan Bloom*

[W]e have been expressly evolved by nature ... for the purpose of solving the economic problem. If the economic problem is solved, mankind will be deprived of its traditional purpose.... To use the language of today—must we not expect a general "nervous breakdown?" ... But beware! the time for all this is not yet. For at least another hundred years we must pretend to ourselves and to every one that fair is foul and foul is fair; for foul is useful and fair is not. Avarice and usury ... must be our gods for a little longer still. 25

John Maynard Keynes

It is scarcely necessary to remark that a stationary condition of capital and population implies no stationary state of human improvement. There would be as much scope as ever for all kinds of mental culture, and moral and social progress; as much room for improving the Art of Living and much more likelihood for its being improved. 26 *John Stuart Mill*

Wealth and luxury exert their evil effects through amusement. Poverty cuts down these products of wealth and brings societies back to simplicity and virtue. Men renounce what they cannot get. The periods of economic and social decay have cut off the development of forms of amusement, arrested vice, and forced new beginnings. 27 *William Graham Sumner*

In place of "progress" a similar abstraction, "the economy," is used today to justify sacrifices by working people. Through a peculiar inverse anthropomorphism, "the economy" can somehow be doing well while the majority of people are doing poorly. 28 *Barbara Garson*

Must we produce sick people in order to have a healthy economy? 29 *Erich Fromm*

[E]conomists ... take for granted that all of us are alienated from ourselves and must look at the world from a schizoid perspective. 30

Philip Slater

Call a thing immoral or ugly, soul-destroying or a degradation of man, a peril to the peace of the world or to the well-being of future generations; as long as you have not shown it to be "uneconomic" you have not really questioned its right to exist, grow, and prosper. 31

E. F. Schumacher

No doubt industrial activities have a reason for existing. They respond to needs, but these needs are not moral. 32 *Émile Durkheim*

[T]he economy *relies* on fear. Take away fear of competition, of failure, of loss of markets, of humiliation, of becoming obsolete, and the culture would stop.... 33 *Jules Henry*

The truth is we are all caught up in a great economic system, which is heartless. 34

Woodrow Wilson

Reaganomics offer up the worst of both worlds: a soft head and a hard heart.... To achieve this happy blend [of hard head and soft heart], we must join the rational economic calculation of the conservative Republican to the compassion of the liberal Democrat. 35 *Alan Blinder*

One of the two fundamental oppositions underlying social life is the contradiction between necessity and freedom.... This contradiction has been recognized in theory as the struggle between the strong and the weak.... It becomes impossible for those who are socialized into this structure to think of the economic problem of taking care of necessity except in terms of relations of dominance and submission. Then, to be prosperous means to be dominant, and to be poor means to submit. 36 *M. Gear et al.*

Economics

Even if the state protects its citizens from being bullied by physical violence (as it does, in principle, under the system of unrestrained capitalism), it may defeat our aims by its failure to protect them from the misuse of economic power. In such a state, the economically strong is still free to bully one who is economically weak, and to rob him of his freedom.... This, of course, means that the principle of nonintervention, of an unrestrained economic system has to be given up; if we wish freedom to be safeguarded, then we must demand that the policy of unlimited economic freedom be replaced by the planned economic intervention of the state.... And this is precisely what has happened. 37 *Karl Popper*

The belief that the fiscal state can effectively redistribute income, and thereby reform society through taxation and subsidies, has been decisively disproven. The least egalitarian countries are those that have tried hardest to redistribute income: the Soviet Union; the United States; Great Britain. All they accomplished was to give us the "pork-barrel state"—the most dangerous degenerative disease that the body politic is suffering from. 38 *Peter F. Drucker*

Political competition ... tends toward conflict, whereas economic competition tends toward co-operation. 39 *Quincy Wright*

All the evils, abuses, and iniquities, popularly ascribed to businessmen and to capitalism, were not caused by an unregulated economy or by a free market, but by government intervention into the economy. 40 *Ayn Rand*

The problem, in fact, is not whether government intervention is desirable. The truth is that government intervention is essential, and the problem is simply of methods whereby it can bear its maximum fruit. For to leave to the unfettered play of economic forces the supply of those needs by the satisfaction of which we live is to maintain a society empty of all moral principles; and such a society more surely moves to disaster than at any period in history. 41
Harold Laski

The reputable accommodation of economics to contentment begins with the broad commitment to the doctrine, more often called the principle, of laissez faire.... It supports the powerful commitment to the short run and to the rejection of longer-run concerns. 42
John K. Galbraith

Laissez-faire ... is demonstrably the offspring of that conception of universal laws that phenomena must observe which was a heritage of the Newtonian philosophy. But if man in knowing is a participator in the natural scene, a factor in things known, the fact that man participates as a factor in social affairs is no barrier to knowledge of them. On the contrary, a certain method of directed participation is a precondition of his having any genuine understanding. Human intervention for the sake of effecting ends is no interference, and it is a means of knowledge. 43 *John Dewey*

Economics is the art of allocating scarce goods among competing demands. 44 *Daniel Bell*

[T]he basic problem of social organization is how to co-ordinate the economic activities of large numbers of people.... Fundamentally, there are only two ways.... One is central direction involving the use of coercion.... The other is voluntary co-operation of individuals—the technique of the market place. 45
Milton Friedman

Wealth, in a free market, is achieved by a free, general, "democratic" vote—by the sales and the purchases of every individual who takes part in the economic life of the country.... And, in this type of voting, every man votes only on those matters which he is qualified to judge: on his own preferences, interests, and needs. 46 *Ayn Rand*

Underlying most arguments against the free market is a lack of belief in freedom itself. 47
Milton Friedman

Few tricks of the unsophisticated intellect are more curious than the naive psychology of the business man, who ascribes his achievements to his own unaided efforts, in bland unconsciousness of a social order without whose continuous support and vigilant protection he would be as a lamb bleating in the desert. 48
R. H. Tawney

Economics

Because a modern economy, like an ecosystem, is a single, interdependent whole, in which each part requires many other parts to keep functioning, its wholesale breakdown will leave people unable to perform the simplest, most essential tasks. 49 *Jonathan Schell*

A market economy "can only exist in a market society." But to exist, a market society requires centuries of transformation by Gutenberg technology.... [T]o create a market economy that can handle what comes off the assembly lines presupposes a long period of psychic transformation, which is to say, a period of altering perception and sense ratios. 50
Marshall McLuhan

[E]conomic prosperity is excessively dependent on a political and social atmosphere which is congenial to the average business man. 51
John Maynard Keynes

[T]here is an intimate connection between economics and politics.... The kind of economic organization that provides economic freedom directly, namely, competitive capitalism, also promotes political freedom because it separates economic power from political power and in this way enables the one to offset the other. 52
Milton Friedman

[E]conomic, rather than political and military, power has become the significant coercive force of modern society.... Political power has been made responsible, but economic power has become irresponsible in society. The net result is that political power has been made more responsible to economic power. 53 *Reinhold Niebuhr*

Economic power must not be permitted to dominate political power; if necessary, it must be fought and brought under control by political power. 54 *Karl Popper*

There are a great many things changing in our society.... But there's a roof that always blocks further healthy growth—a ceiling of concentrated economic power that holds us back, frustrates change, locks in flexibility. It has long since used up whatever potential it had for doing anything creative—all its energies are devoted to preserving its special advantaged position.... So long as that roof exists, all healthy social growths will be stunted. 55 *Philip Slater*

The millionaires ... may fairly be regarded as the naturally selected agents of society for certain work. They get high wages and live in luxury, but the bargain is a good one for society. 56
William Graham Sumner

Profits are the lifeblood of the economic system, the magic elixer upon which progress and all good things depend ultimately. 57
Paul A. Samuelson

The propensity for achievement and the repugnance to futility remain the underlying economic motive. 58 *Thorstein Veblen*

The entrepreneur is the economist's greatest hero.... An entrepreneur can, indeed, fail, but he can do no wrong. 59 *John K. Galbraith*

Politics and economics are concerned with power and wealth, neither of which should be the primary, still less the exclusive, concern of full-grown men. 60 *Arthur C. Clarke*

To the commies, as to capitalists, goods, if good, *must* be good for mankind. Both suffer the identical catastrophic blindness. 61
Philip Wylie

The fundamental delusion of our time, in my opinion, is the excessive emphasis upon the economic aspects of life, and I do not expect the strife between Capitalism and Communism as philosophies to cease until it is recognized that both are inadequate through their failure to recognize biological needs. 62
Bertrand Russell

The economy is geared to the least urgent set of human wants. It would be far more secure if it were based on the whole range of need. 63
John K. Galbraith

[M]an has changed from the giving animal ... to the wholly taking and keeping one ... giving expression to only one side of his nature.... And so we see how modern man, in his one-dimensional economics, is driven by the lie of his life, by his denial of limitation. 64 *Ernest Becker*

Economics

[M]odern economics ... tells us how to achieve economic growth but it cannot tell us whether economic growth is desirable.... There is a need for a new science of economics, one that can relate economic means to human objectives.... [It] will require us to recognize human values as the primary criterion for economic policy. 65
George E. Pugh

Rational economic man as a reflection of human nature is a fiction. It is a modern invention, a new path. But it is a powerful fiction ... [especially] as more and more of our institutions get pervaded by its assumptions and other paths are closed.... We must keep the other paths open. 66 *Barry Schwartz*

We must say harshly of the "science" of economics that it is generally the skilled, exact, technological application of a totally false theory of human needs and values, a theory which recognizes only the existence of lower needs or material needs.... Man has a higher and transcendent nature, and this is part of his essence.... 67 *Abraham Maslow*

The Church acknowledges the legitimate role of profits as an indication that a business is functioning well ... [and] on the level of individual nations and international relations [that] the free market is the most efficient instrument for utilizing resources and effectively responding to needs.... It is not wrong to want to live better; what is wrong is a style of life which is presumed to be better when it is directed towards "having" rather than "being," and which wants to have more, not in order to be more but in order to spend life in enjoyment as an end in itself. 68 *Pope John Paul II*

The stock exchange is a poor substitute for the Holy Grail. 69 *Joseph Schumpeter*

If there is one notion that virtually every successful politician on earth ... agrees on, it is that "economic growth" is good.... But where does economic growth end? It ends—or, at least, it runs straight through—the genetically engineered dead world that the optimists envision. 70 *Bill McKibben*

Beyond the question of specific practices of the persuaders and their associated scientists is the larger question of where our economy is taking us under the pressure of consumerism. That, too, is a moral question. In fact I suspect it is destined to become one of the great moral issues of our times. 71 *Vance Packard*

Economics today is in a profound conceptual crisis.... The current economic crisis will be overcome only if economists are willing to participate in the paradigm shift that is now occurring in all fields. 72 *Fritjof Capra*

The unexamined assumption of the old paradigm—dominant since the days of John Locke—is that human beings are most deeply motivated by economic concerns.... The real world [however] turns on different principles than those imposed by our partial economic philosophies.... And even if Locke were right about our economic motives, we would have to change: Our civilization cannot go on escalating its manufacture and consumption of non-renewable resources. 73 *Marilyn Ferguson*

A mature person gives up the personal fable of immortality on Earth; a mature society gives up the economic fable of infinite resources. 74
James Garbarino

A great problem of contemporary life is how to control the power of economic interests which ignore the harmful effects of their applied science and technology. 75 *Ralph Nader*

We are on the horns of a dilemma. In every country large numbers of people are suffering privations owing to defects in the economic machine. These people must be helped, and if they are to be helped effectively and permanently, the economic machine must be replanned. But economic planning undertaken by a national government for the benefit of its own people inevitably disturbs that international economic harmony which is the result of national planlessness. 76 *Aldous Huxley*

People who are forced by economic inequality to inhabit dissimilar universes will be unable to co-operate intelligently. 77 *Aldous Huxley*

Where the inequality of economic conditions

Economics

is too marked ... it becomes necessary for the rich to pretend that the poor are a separate and wicked race, who would certainly be damned if they were not given the opportunity for purification through misery. 78 *Rebecca West*

No nation can hope to survive, no civilisation has ever survived, in which there is a permanent division of its people into rich and poor. 79
Harold Laski

[Goods] add little real ease to life and the total worship of goods, in the end, takes away all peace and security.... In a world that is engaged in the reckless rush for mass-produced material objects there is neither room nor time for honesty, consideration, integrity of thought, introspection, or the operation of conscience. In such a world ... there will be no security because security comes from man's trust of man—man's confidence in man—and the mills cannot manufacture it.... But we are in a goods-mad world. 80 *Philip Wylie*

With increased prosperity desires increase.... Nothing gives satisfaction.... [There] is no reason why humanity should not improve its material condition. But though the moral danger involved in every growth of prosperity is not irremediable, it should not be forgotten. 81 *Émile Durkheim*

Industry is a means and not an end.... If the wealth resulting from prosperous industry is to be spent upon the gratification of unworthy desires, if the increasing perfection of manufacturing processes is to be accompanied by an increasing debasement of those who carry them on, I do not see the good of industry and prosperity. 82 *T. H. Huxley*

Homo oeconomicus is not the human being who represents his own needs to himself, and the objects capable of satisfying them; he is the human being who spends, wears out, and wastes his life in evading the imminence of death.... The positivity of economics is situated in that anthropological hollow. 83
Michel Foucault

A reasonable estimate of economic organization must allow for the fact that, unless industry is to be paralysed by recurrent revolts on the part of outraged human nature, it must satisfy criteria which are not purely economic. 84
R. H. Tawney

There seems to be a widespread sense that we are living in a period of historic exhaustion.... The malaise, I have come more and more to believe, lies in the industrial basis on which our civilization is based. Economic growth and technical achievement, the greatest triumphs of our epoch of history, have shown themselves to be inadequate sources for collective contentment and hope. Material advance, the most profoundly distinguishing attribute of industrial capitalism and socialism alike, has proved unable to satisfy the human spirit. Not only the quest for profit but the cult of efficiency have shown themselves ultimately corrosive for human well-being. 85 *Robert Heilbroner*

[U]pon the whole, economics has been treated as on a lower level than either morals or politics. Yet the life which men, women and children actually lead, the opportunities open to them ... are mainly determined by economic conditions. 86 *John Dewey*

[W]herever the truth may lie, this much is crystal clear: our bigger-and-better society is now like a hypochondriac, so obsessed with its own economic health as to have lost the capacity to remain healthy. 87
Aldo Leopold

Education

[E]ducation is the instruction of the intellect in the laws of Nature ... and the fashioning of the affections and of the will into an earnest and loving desire to move in harmony with these laws. 1 *T. H. Huxley*

One does not come naturally to the realisation of eternal truths and values. One is brought there by education in the widest sense. 2
J. B. S. Haldane

The aim of education is the knowledge not of facts but of values. 3 *William R. Inge*

Education

If you ask what is the good of education in general, the answer is easy: that education makes good men, and that good men act nobly. 4
Plato

Education has for its object the formation of character. 5 *Herbert Spencer*

[T]he aims of education may be identified with development, both intellectually and morally.... The democratic educational end for all humans must be "the development of a free and powerful character." Nothing less than democratic education will prepare free people for factual and moral choices that they will inevitably confront in society. 6 *Lawrence Kohlberg*

[T]he end product of ... liberal education ... is simply the self-educating, self-cultivating man or woman. 7 *C. Wright Mills*

[T]oday ... the development of broad and powerful thinking is desperately needed.... Instead we find ... an almost reptilian ritualization of the educational process. 8 *Carl Sagan*

What passes for education in the Western world today is more accurately described as instruction.... For the most part modern education prepares men to live better with machines than with themselves.... 9 *Ashley Montagu*

The concentration of public education on the purely mechanical and scientific aspects of life leads quite naturally to a cynical materialistic world view. 10 *George E. Pugh*

[S]cience and technology are fast becoming the basic determinants of education and ... of every major social institution.... We call this *bureautechnocracy*.... The world has enough scientists ... [and] technicians.... A bureautechnocratic culture stands against ... the development of personhood.... The new education will require a massive dosage of Socratic dialogue ... [and] the exchange of introspections.... It is this "personal growth" theme to which education must now turn. 11
Charles A. Tesconi & Van Cleve Morris

[T]he influence of unexamined assumptions derived from technology leads quite unnecessarily to maximal determinism in human life. Emancipation from that trap is the goal of all education. 12 *Marshall McLuhan*

[T]he central obsession in education is fear of failure. In order not to fail most students are willing to believe anything and to care not whether what they are told is true or false. 13
Jules Henry

A certain percentage of children have the habit of thinking; one of the aims of education is to cure them of this habit.... Capitalists, militarists, and ecclesiastics co-operate in education, because all depend for their power upon the prevalence of ... the rarity of critical judgment. 14
Bertrand Russell

Every educated person is a future enemy. 15
Martin Bormann (Nazi)

Unless an individual is free to obtain the fullest education with which his society can provide him, he is being injured by society. 16
W. H. Auden

A State which fails to offer an equal level of educational opportunity for its citizens is penalising the poor for the benefit of the rich. There cannot be a responsible State until there is an educated electorate. 17 *Harold Laski*

The "education" of the masses ... emancipates women and children from patriarchal authority, however, only to subject them to the new paternalism of the advertising industry, the industrial corporation, and the state. 18
Christopher Lasch

In a society where competition for the basic cultural goods is a pivot of action, people cannot be taught to love another. It thus becomes necessary for the school to teach children how to hate, and without appearing to do so, for our culture cannot tolerate the idea that babes should hate each other. 19 *Jules Henry*

What education does is to put a series of filters over your awareness so that year by year, step by step, you experience less and less and less. 20
Timothy Leary

Education

Education, I fear, is learning to see one thing by going blind to another. 21 *Aldo Leopold*

The function of education has never been to free the mind and the spirit of man, but to bind them.... It stands to reason that were young people truly creative the culture would fall apart, for originality, by definition, is different from what is given, and what is given is the culture itself. 22 *Jules Henry*

It cannot be doubted that, at any time, all ethical judgments are made through the atmosphere of the mores of the time.... It is only through high mental discipline that we can be trained to rise above that atmosphere and form rational judgments on current cases. This mental independence and ethical power are the highest products of education. 23
William Graham Sumner

Education, at heart, is a *discipline*.... Education itself cannot teach virtue, but the discipline which accompanies true education is like the discipline which virtue, too, requires. 24
Russell Kirk

The ideal aim of education is creation of power of self-control. 25 *John Dewey*

Since educational systems at present concern themselves mainly with fact and knowledge, they usually do little directly to help the individual to establish control of his thinking. 26
Elton Mayo

The intelligent fool ... has no knowledge of, or control over, himself.... Under the present dispensation, the educational system is designed to produce the greatest possible number of intelligent fools. 27 *Aldous Huxley*

[S]pecialist learning in higher education proceeds by ignoring interrelationships; for such complex awareness slows down the achieving of expertness.... For the specialist is one who never makes small mistakes while moving toward the grand fallacy. 28 *Marshall McLuhan*

Higher education and university degrees do not make a scrap of difference in confronting the evils of society. A learned neurotic is not any different than an uneducated neurotic. 29
A. S. Neill

Education is healthy when peoples themselves are in a healthy state; but it becomes corrupt with them, being unable to modify itself. 30
Émile Durkheim

I believe that education is a regulation of the process of coming to share in the social consciousness.... 31 *John Dewey*

Education, therefore, can be reformed only if society itself is reformed. 32 *Émile Durkheim*

But if education is once more to become what it was in its best days, namely the possibility, through historical continuity, of developing into a human being possessed of full selfhood, that can only ensue through a faith which, amid all necessary strictness in learning and practice, indirectly conveys a spiritual value. 33
Karl Jaspers

[T]he starting point of education ... [is to] recognize the difference between pure impulse, and the spontaneous energies which spring to life in a tranquilized spirit.... 34
Maria Montessori

Anxious as we rightly are in this age of technology to sustain the great tradition of liberal culture, we should ... not in the process muddy with erudition and vain learning those crystal fountains from which flow our most essential creative energies. Those fountains ... are the unpolluted rivers of perception and imagination. Education should therefore be conceived as primarily a cultivation of these sensuous activities, as *aesthetic* education. Such a concept of education has often been proposed ... and if we find it difficult to accept, it is no doubt because our sensibilities are no longer responsive to the original sources of human vitality and vision. 35 *Herbert Read*

Education, considered as a process of forming our mental habits and our outlook on the world, is to be judged successful in proportion ... as it gives us a true view of our place in society, of the relation of the whole human society to its non-human environment, and of the nature

of the non-human world as it is in itself apart from our desires and interests. 36
Bertrand Russell

What happens in the mind affects the body; what happens in the body affects the mind. Education must therefore be a process of physical as well as mental training. 37
Aldous Huxley

The great thing … in all education, is to make our nervous system our ally instead of our enemy. It is to fund and capitalize our acquisitions, and live at ease upon the interest of the fund. For this we must make automatic and habitual, as early as possible, as many useful actions as we can.… 38 *William James*

Education is what survives when what has been learned has been forgotten. 39 *B. F. Skinner*

[E]ducation can be considered as bringing to consciousness some of the limited-access programs, the "cognitive unconscious," already in the head. 40 *Paul Rozin*

All knowledge cannot be expressed in words, yet our education is based almost exclusively on the written or spoken word. 41
Robert E. Ornstein & Richard F. Thompson

In education we should be occupied in increasing the courage and interest of a child and in removing the limits which, through his interpretation of life, he has set to his own powers. 42
Alfred Adler

In the psychological relationship between teacher and child, the teacher's part and its techniques are analogous to those of the valet; they are to serve, and to serve well: to serve the spirit. 43 *Maria Montessori*

No one can know the minds of children so well as a teacher who lives with them and works with them.… Like the mother, he is the guardian of the future of mankind, and the service he can render is incalculable. 44 *Alfred Adler*

A teacher affects eternity; he can never tell where his influence stops. 45
Henry Brooks Adams

Teachers are more than any other class the guardians of civilization. 46 *Bertrand Russell*

Our current education system evolved to produce workers for the Industrial Revolution's factory-based economy, for work that requires patience, docility and the ability to endure boredom.… Artificial intelligence … will dominate the education system of 2019. 47
Arthur C. Clarke

In the school of tomorrow the students will be their own instructors, with a computer program as their own tool. 48 *Peter F. Drucker*

Tomorrow science will have moved forward yet one more step, and there will be no appeal from the judgment which will then be pronounced upon the uneducated. 49 *Alfred N. Whitehead*

[We may be developing] the profoundest revolution mankind has ever contemplated—the development of a society in which there will be no place for the illiterate or the ignorant. 50
Elton Mayo

[S]chooling can no longer be a monopoly of the schools. Education in the post-capitalist society has to permeate the entire society. 51
Peter F. Drucker

Education is not a function of any church … or a state; it is a function of all mankind. 52
Philip Wylie

I am certain that none of the world's problems … have any hope of solution except through total democratic society's becoming thoroughly and comprehensively self-educated. Only thereby will society be able to identify and intercommunicate the vital problems of total world society. 53 *R. Buckminster Fuller*

Each generation is inclined to educate its young so as to get along in the present world instead of with a view to the proper end of education: the promotion of the best possible realization of humanity as humanity. 54 *John Dewey*

A person is "great" because through him "relatively more" people are treated as ends.… [E]ducation is a way of making people "greater."

Education

An individual may be called educated inasmuch as it is relatively easy to ascertain his relevance for "relatively more" people. 55 *Alfred Adler*

Without the belief in man, the university is a contradiction in terms. The business of the university is education at its highest possible level, and the business of education at its highest possible level is the relation of men to their lives. 56 *Archibald MacLeish*

The philosophy of the schools was justified insofar as it rendered a philosophical life possible. To-day, however, it is incomplete, discursive, disintegrated and disintegrating. 57
Karl Jaspers

[A]ll the educational advances have not brought mankind one step further toward solving the basic needs of love, security, and true happiness; on the contrary, civilization seems more removed from these concepts than ever. 58
Hal Lindsey

Sometimes one sees in the school simply the instrument for transferring a certain maximum quantity of knowledge to the growing generation. But this is not right. Knowledge is dead; the school, however, serves the living.... It should develop in the young individuals those qualities and capabilities which are of value for the welfare of the commonwealth. 59
Albert Einstein

Our progress as a nation can be no swifter than our progress in education. 60 *John F. Kennedy*

If a nation expects to be ignorant and free, in a state of civilization, it expects what never was and never will be. 61 *Thomas Jefferson*

[T]he age of blind sacrifice and instinctive virtues is already long past, and I see a time approaching in which freedom, public peace, and social stability will not be able to last without education. 62 *Alexis de Tocqueville*

Human history becomes more and more a race between education and catastrophe. 63
H. G. Wells

Egoism / Selfishness

Let us not become egotistical, stirring up competition with one another, envying one another. 1 *Holy Bible*

In Adam all men were to be ... united to one another in their one vision and love of the One Truth.... All mankind fell from God in Adam. And just as Adam's soul was divided against itself by sin, so all men were divided against one another by selfishness. 2 *Thomas Merton*

[O]riginally the ego includes everything, later it separates off an external world from itself. A tendency arises to separate from the ego everything that can become a source of ... unpleasure, to throw it outside and to create a pure pleasure-ego which is confronted by a strange and threatening "outside." 3 *Sigmund Freud*

[E]very individual ... has regard for his own existence and well-being before everything else.... This disposition is *egoism*, which is essential to everything in Nature. 4
Arthur Schopenhauer

Every living being looks out for itself first of all.... Only through effort, often aggressive egoistic effort, can [man] maintain his fitness and assure his homeostatic equilibrium with the surrounding society and the inanimate world. 5
Hans Selye

[T]he development of the individual seems to us to be a product of the interaction between two urges, the urge towards happiness, which we usually call "egoistic," and the urge towards union with others in the community, which we call "altruistic." ... [T]he main accent falls on the egoistic urge. 6 *Sigmund Freud*

[E]gotism suits the age, and Freud's is only one of the most successful, and ... subtler, of contemporary ideologies of self-salvation. 7
Philip Rieff

Psychology has distinctions only between good and bad forms of selfishness. 8
Allan Bloom

Egoism / Selfishness

[I]t is absurd to say that the egoistic elements of experience should be suppressed. The axis of reality runs solely through the egoistic places—they are strung upon it like so many beads. 9 *William James*

That which we call egoism is the principle of psychic gravity, the necessary postulate. 10 *Miguel de Unamuno*

"One furthers one's ego always at the expense of others"; "Life always lives at the expense of other life"—he who does not grasp this has not taken even the first step toward honesty with himself. 11 *Friedrich Nietzsche*

Each mind, to begin with, must have a certain minimum of selfishness in the shape of instincts of bodily self-seeking in order to exist. The minimum must be there as a basis for all farther conscious acts, whether of self-negation or of a selfishness more subtle still. 12 *William James*

[A]t the gene level, altruism must be bad and selfishness good.... The gene is the basic unit of selfishness. 13 *Richard Dawkins*

The Objectivist ethics holds man's life as the *standard* of value—and *his own life* as the ethical purpose of every individual man.... [M]an must live for his own sake.... To live for his own sake means that *the achievement of his own happiness is man's highest moral purpose....* Since selfishness is "concern with one's own interests" ... [an] attack on "selfishness" is an attack on man's self-esteem. 14 *Ayn Rand*

She [Ayn Rand] will be remembered as this century's chief defender of the human ego. 15 *James T. Baker*

Each person's concern is and must be first and foremost a selfish one—one whose goal is the continued existence and well-being of himself and his family.... Capitalism is a selfish system in the sense that it is the one socio-economic system that recognizes each individual's right to pursue his own self-interest. 16 *John Hospers*

True selfishness, if obedient to the other constraints of mammalian biology, is the key to a more nearly perfect social contract. 17 *E. O. Wilson*

What I chiefly desire for you is a genuine, full-blooded egoism.... There is no way you can benefit society more than by coining the metal that you know is yourself. 18 *Henrik Ibsen*

It is not from the benevolence of the butcher, the brewer, the baker that we expect our dinner, but from their regard to their own interest. We address ourselves not to their humanity but to their self-love.... Nobody but a beggar chooses to depend chiefly on the benevolence of his fellow citizens. 19 *Adam Smith*

Thought requires *selfishness*, the fundamental selfishness of a rational faculty that places nothing above the integrity of its own function.... Man's mind requires selfishness, and so does his life in every respect: a living being has to be the beneficiary of its own actions.... The ethics of rational self-interest upholds the exercise of one's mind in the service of one's life.... 20 *Leonard Peikoff*

The essence of *selflessness* is the suspension of one's consciousness. When and to the extent that a man chooses to evade the effort and responsibility of thinking, of seeking knowledge, of passing judgment, his action is one of *self-abdication.* To relinquish thought, is to relinquish one's ego and to pronounce oneself unfit for existence, incompetent to deal with the facts of reality. 21 *Nathaniel Branden*

Looking out for Number One is the conscious, rational effort to spend as much time as possible doing those things which bring you the greatest amount of pleasure.... *All* people act in their own self-interest *all* the time.... [S]elfishness is neither bad nor good; it's simply a reality.... What you can choose is whether you will be *rationally* selfish or *irrationally* selfish. 22 *Robert Ringer*

In proportion as a person is in touch with his actual self, with his real needs ... he experiences a sense of inner strength ... that frees him of that fear of others which underlies all hostility and destructiveness. To achieve that state is the highest form of *selfishness.* It is man's

Egoism / Selfishness

greatest challenge. It is his greatest reward. 23
Nathaniel Branden

The glorious joy of self-assertion in the face of an uncontrollable world is indeed so deep and entire, that it furnishes just that transcendent element of worth for which we were looking when we tried to understand how the expression of pain could sometimes please. 24
George Santayana

Egoism is the very essence of the noble soul. 25
Friedrich Nietzsche

In our own generation extreme forms of ego-gratification are culturally supported.... Arrogant and unbridled egoists ... are entrusted with positions of great influence and importance.... They are not described in our manuals of psychiatry because they are supported by every tenet of our civilization. They are sure of themselves in real life in a way that is possible only to those who are oriented to the points of the compass laid down in their own culture. 26
Ruth Benedict

Spirituality has become egotism; and the ego, full of natural pride and jealousy, begins to assert itself defiantly, arguing the absolute freedom of some natural impulse in the self, not because this impulse is natural (as all impulses must be) nor because it is rational (as probably it is not) but because this impulse is *mine*, because it *exists*, because nothing else can abolish its *right to be as it is*. 27 *George Santayana*

The widely held expectation that a maximal consideration of self-interest would provide solutions most satisfactory from all points of view ... is not borne out by psychoanalytic experience.... Actually analysis has contributed much to shattering the widely held opinion that the only decisive motivating power in man is self-interest. 28 *Heinz Hartmann*

We seldom think of what we have, but always of what we lack. This maxim of egoism, which has, indeed, its advantages in procuring the means to the end in view, itself concurrently destroys the ultimate end, namely contentment. 29 *Arthur Schopenhauer*

Unless the personality is drawn out of itself and can be of value to someone, it may sicken and die. 30 *Norman Vincent Peale*

The world is a monster of selfishness that in tormenting and devouring its children asks them to be tormented and devoured willingly. 31
George Santayana

Ego is unsound, and so insane—but most men live largely by it; most, indeed, know nothing else. 32 *Philip Wylie*

Ego needs, particularly if they are neurotic, almost inevitably are irrational, obsessional, compulsive, gained at the expense of others, and make excessive use of material resources. 33
Edward T. Hall

It turns out that the pursuit of self-interest has much in common with heroin. Both are human inventions.... Both are addictive.... Both slowly destroy the fabric of whatever social institutions they invade.... Just as the unbridled pursuit of self-interest will cause the market economic system to erode, it will cause the democratic political system to explode. 34
Barry Schwartz

Loyalty to the nation is a high form of altruism.... Thus the unselfishness of individuals makes for the selfishness of nations.... Patriotism ... is simply another form of selfishness. 35
Reinhold Niebuhr

Our very egoism is in large part a product of society. 36 *Émile Durkheim*

Under *r* conditions of resource availability ... entrepreneurial "warfare" against neighbours might be expected with a stress on a high birthrate and an egocentric life-style without much emphasis on the wisdom of the elderly. The Vikings may provide an example. By contrast, under *K* selective circumstances with a large population living under conditions of finite plenty, there will be in the ethics of the people an emphasis on collectivity.... 37 *John H. Crook*

[A] natural and healthy philosophy of life must be based on what we have called "altruistic egoism," which maximizes eustress and minimizes distress in our lives.... The "philosophy of altruistic egoism" advocates the creation of feelings of accomplishment and security through the inspiration in others of love, goodwill and gratitude for what we have done or are likely to do in the future. 38 *Hans Selye*

What we seek is not the best of all conceivable worlds but the best of all possible worlds. In the intimacy of small groups altruism may be substantial and important; in large groups enlightened egoism is the most powerful motive ... [and] in fact the best motive that we can rely on. 39 *Garrett Hardin*

The Americans enjoy explaining almost every act of their lives on the principle of self-interest.... [But] there it is enlightened.... Self-interest properly understood is not at all a sublime doctrine.... If the doctrine of self-interest properly understood ever came to dominate all thought about morality, no doubt extraordinary virtues would be rarer. But I think that gross depravity would also be less common. 40
Alexis de Tocqueville

The gratifications which, merged together, make [for] selfishness are each of them ingenuous, and no more selfish than the most altruistic, impersonal emotion. The content of selfishness is a mass of unselfishness. 41
George Santayana

It is the inordinately selfish ... who are likely to be the most persuasive champions of selflessness. 42 *Eric Hoffer*

The pursuit of self-interest, formerly identified with the rational pursuit of gain and the accumulation of wealth, has become a search for pleasure and psychic survival.... Self-preservation has replaced self-improvement as the goal of earthly existence. 43 *Christopher Lasch*

The authority of the ego over our psychic life is itself the symptom of our problem and the basis of our unreal relations with ourselves.... It emerges as an either/or relationship, a construct founded on the opposition ... between Self and Other, and as such is paranoid. 44
Morris Berman

[S]elfishness is the setting up of a narrow self over against a larger self. 45 *George H. Mead*

Egos appear by setting themselves apart from other egos.... By setting itself apart from others, the ego moves away from being. 46
Martin Buber

[T]he true ethical principle is the reconciliation with one's own being ... from which we are estranged and in this sense separated.... Sin means the power that separates.... What overcomes this separation and brings us into communion with the ultimate ground of being, and into awareness of the meaning of our life, is love.... [S]elfishness and disgust toward oneself are one and the same thing. 47
D. MacKenzie Brown

The love for my own self is inseparably connected with the love for any other being.... The selfish person does not love himself ... in fact he hates himself. 48 *Erich Fromm*

Love aims at unity, egotism at solitude. Love is the citizen ruler of a flourishing republic, egotism is a despot in a devastated creation. 49
Friedrich von Schiller

It is only man and the devil who in everything seek their own. So far from self-love being a natural ordinance of God in nature, it is a devilish perversion. That which in all things only seeks its own, is thereby closed against God. 50
Anders Nygren

As soon as egoism becomes the ruler of a people, the bands of order are loosened and in the chase after their own happiness men fall from heaven into a real hell. 51 *Adolf Hitler*

Dante placed at the bottom of Hell ... a frozen lake. The silence of the eternal ice expressed the passion of hatred congealed into the rigidity of a cold and cruel egotism. 52 *Lewis Lapham*

Inside of man there is a selfish, self-centered nature. This is the source of what God calls sin. Sin is basically self-centered seeking and striving—going our own way, with our backs turned on God. It is because of this selfish nature ... that we cannot have consistent peace

Egoism / Selfishness

with ourselves, our family, our neighbor, or, on a broader scale, with other nations. 53

Hal Lindsey

[W]hereas formerly it was enough for a man to have freed himself to some extent from personal egotism to make him a valuable member of society, today he must also be required to overcome national and class egotism. Only if he reaches those heights can he contribute toward improving the lot of humanity. 54

Albert Einstein

[T]he shift from selfishness to responsibility ... is a move toward social participation. 55

Carol Gilligan

Egoism sterilizes the seeds of every virtue; individualism at first only dams the springs of public virtues, but in the long run it attacks and destroys all the others too and finally merges in egoism. 56 *Alexis de Tocqueville*

Each of us sees the Universe divided between himself and all the rest of it; and each of us seeks to make himself the centre.... A human soul's—even a saint's soul's—fight with self-centredness is unceasing. 57 *Arnold Toynbee*

[Each religion] speaks in its own language of man's irrepressible concern with Ultimate Meaning, and each one points to the overcoming of ego as the precondition for the perception of this Meaning. 58 *Frederick Franck*

The subjective sense of being at one with oneself, of possessing that inner serenity which stands at the opposite pole to neurosis, is, in fact, often accompanied by a feeling that there is something superior to the ego. 59 *Anthony Storr*

The LSD panic is the terror that ego is lost forever. The LSD ecstasy is the joyful discovery that ego, with its pitiful shams and strivings, is only a fraction of my identity. 60 *Timothy Leary*

[M]an's ego—the importance he puts upon his limited awareness of who and what he is—has become all of man to man, so far as man himself is concerned. This unholy, starveling error is responsible for the trouble he has with himself. 61 *Philip Wylie*

The egocentric ideal of a future reserved for those who have managed to attain egoistically the extremity of "everyone for himself" is false and against nature. No element could move forward and grow except with and by all the others with itself. 62 *Pierre Teilhard de Chardin*

In fact the whole antithesis between self and the rest of the world ... disappears as soon as we have any genuine interest in persons or things outside ourselves. Through such interests a man comes to feel himself part of the stream of life, not a hard separate entity like a billiard ball, which can have no relation with other such entities except that of collision. 63

Bertrand Russell

In order to keep Universe regenerative nature has placed human beings on this planet for their syntropic functioning.... The generous, compassionate propensity of humans is primarily syntropic. The selfish are "entropic." 64

R. Buckminster Fuller

If I decide to walk alone inside my own existence, egoistically, I make no progress. I arrive nowhere. I keep turning around and around in one spot. That is the labyrinth, the road that leads nowhere.... Life is lost at finding itself alone. Mere egoism is a labyrinth. 65 *José Ortega y Gasset*

We may want to curb egoism, but we had better not try to destroy it entirely. It is still needed for the survival of the human species. 66

Garrett Hardin

Emotion

Every human reality is a passion in that it projects losing itself so as to found being.... [M]an loses himself as man in order that God may be born. But the idea of God is contradictory and we lose ourselves in vain. Man is a useless passion. 1 *Jean-Paul Sartre*

Emotions are the life force of the soul. 2

Robert C. Solomon

The only valuable things in psychic life are ... the emotions. All psychic forces are significant only through their aptitude to arouse emotions. Ideas are represented only because they are bound up with releases of emotions. 3 *Sigmund Freud*

It is only momentarily that the particular individual is able to realize existentially a unity of the infinite and the finite which transcends existence. This unity is realized in the moment of passion. Modern philosophy has tried anything and everything in the effort to help the individual to transcend himself objectively, which is a wholly impossible feat.... [M]odern philosophy holds passion in contempt; and yet passion is the culmination of existence. 4
Søren Kierkegaard

The emotions ... give meaning and significance to human existence. 5 *Carroll Izard*

Decisions of the conscious mind are ultimately evaluated in terms of an innate "value scale" that is defined by the emotions. 6 *George E. Pugh*

The emotions constitute the principal motivation system for human beings.... 7
Carroll Izard

[E]motions are answers without words to the questions put to us by special situations of life; emotions are a language without speech.... [I]t is the remnant of an original speech which, once upon a time, unified all mankind.... The remnants of this language still live in our soul. 8
Karl König

Emotions are the lowest form of consciousness.... The emotional person is turned off sensually. His body is a churning robot; he has lost all connection with cellular wisdom or atomic revelation.... Check your emotions at the door to paradise. 9 *Timothy Leary*

Abstain from fleshly lusts, which war against the soul. 10 *Saint Peter*

Men's collective passions are mainly evil.... 11
Bertrand Russell

All the familiar deadly sins are the product of separate emotions. 12 *Aldous Huxley*

All passions are good when one remains their master; all are bad when one lets oneself be subjected to them.... It is not within our control to have or not to have passions. But it is within our control to reign over them. 13
Jean-Jacques Rousseau

The irrational emotions seem to be as truly human as reason itself, and therefore we are as truly responsible for our emotions as for our reasoning. 14 *Aristotle*

It is my firm conviction that irrational emphasis upon emotion and passion leads ultimately to what I can only describe as crime.... I insist that no emotion, not even love, can replace the rule of institutions controlled by reason. 15
Karl Popper

The truth is that mere sensation or mere emotion is an indignity to a mature human being. 16
George Santayana

If the intellectual has any function in society, it is to preserve a cool and unbiased judgment in the face of all solicitations to passion. 17
Bertrand Russell

In a system ... governed by rationality, emotions are traitors from within and must be checked by unswerving control. Peace may be attained but it is the peace of the grave. 18 *Karen Horney*

[There exists] the conviction that if man is not a wholly rational animal, he ought to be; and since he ought to be motivated solely by rational considerations, we might as well proceed as if he were. But the well being of man depends much more on his emotional life than this view is willing to accept. 19 *Bruno Bettelheim*

Your reason and your passion are the rudder and the sails of your seafaring soul. If either your sails or your rudder be broken, you can but toss and drift.... 20 *Kahlil Gibran*

[F]or the existence of good in any form it is not merely consciousness but emotional consciousness that is needed. Observation will not do, appreciation is needed. 21 *George Santayana*

Great passions are for the great of soul, and great events can be seen only by those who are on a level with them. 22 *Oscar Wilde*

Emotion

Individuality is founded in feeling; and the recesses of feeling, the darker, blinder strata of character, are the only places in the world in which we catch real fact in the making, and directly perceive how events happen, and how work is actually done. Compared with this world of living individualized feelings, the world of generalized objects which the intellect contemplates is without solidity or life. 23

William James

Conceive yourself, if possible, suddenly stripped of all the emotion with which your world now inspires you.... No one portion of the universe would then have importance beyond another; and the whole collection of its things and series of events would be without significance, character, expression, or perspective. 24

William James

Emotion is not the apprehension of an exciting object in an unchanged world; rather since it corresponds to a global modification of consciousness and of its relations to the world, emotion expresses itself by means of a radical alteration of the world. 25 *Jean-Paul Sartre*

There is no change from darkness to light or from inertia to movement without emotion. 26

Carl Jung

"Emotions are inherent in your nature, but their content is dictated by your mind. Your emotional capacity is an empty motor, and your values are the fuel with which your mind fills it." 27 *Ayn Rand*

A man's emotions are the product of his premises and values, of the thinking he has done or has failed to do. But the man who is run by his emotions, attempting to make them a substitute for rational judgment, experiences them as alien forces. The paradox of his problem is this: his emotions become his only source of personal identity, but his experience of identity becomes: *a being ruled by demons.* 28

Nathaniel Branden

Each emotion obeys a logic of its own, and makes deductions which no other logic can draw. 29 *William James*

The natural man has only two primal passions, to get and beget. 30 *Sir William Osler*

There are no "basic" emotions ... outside of the relationships a person has within one or other social context.... [E]ach emotion is always found in one or another inflection according to the group mode it occurs in. 31 *R. D. Laing*

Men do not act, as members of a group, in accordance with what each feels as an individual; each man feels as a function of the way in which he is permitted or obliged to act.... Actually, impulses or emotions explain nothing; they ... are consequences, never causes. 32

Claude Lévi-Strauss

If we fancy some strong emotion, and then try to abstract from our consciousness of it all the feelings of its bodily symptoms, we find we have nothing left behind, no "mind-stuff" out of which the emotion can be constituted.... A disembodied human emotion is a sheer nonentity. 33 *William James*

The democratization of genius is made possible by the fact that while one can argue with judgments, one cannot argue with feelings. The emotions generated by a work either appeal to you or they don't, and no man's feelings have more authority than another man's. 34 *Daniel Bell*

The emphasis is on the subjective: how we feel about things, rather than what we think or can know.... [Thus] we create an infantilized culture of complaint, in which Big Daddy is always to blame and the expansion of rights goes on without the other half of citizenship—attachment to duties and obligations.... Complaint gives you power—even if it's only the power of emotional bribery, of creating previously unnoticed levels of social guilt. 35 *Robert Hughes*

Emotions that have desirable social consequences are not so easily generated as hate and rage and fear.... Something, however, can be done, in the course of ordinary education, to provide the nourishment upon which the better emotions can grow, and to bring about the realization of what may give value to human life. 36

Bertrand Russell

[An] unfree education results in life that cannot be lived fully. Such an education almost entirely ignores the *emotions* of life; and because these emotions are dynamic, their lack of opportunity for expression must and does result in cheapness and ugliness and hatefulness. Only the head is educated. If the emotions are permitted to be really free, the intellect will look after itself. 37 *A. S. Neill*

A woman's whole life is a history of the affections. 38 *Washington Irving*

Though women *are* more emotional than men, men are emotionally weaker than women.... Women tend to make their emotions perform the functions they exist to serve, and hence remain mentally much healthier than men. 39 *Ashley Montagu*

To cherish secrets and to restrain emotions are psychic misdemeanors for which nature finally visits us with sickness.... 40 *Carl Jung*

The very efficiency of ... the satisfaction of ... external needs has resulted in the slighting of ... complex psychic needs.... [F]or the most part human society has been a place where, though man has survived physically, he has died emotionally. 41 *Jules Henry*

Enemy

[A]n enemy: a person who must die, so that one may oneself transcend death. 1 *Robert Jay Lifton*

I must kill my visible enemy.... Killing him gives me a feeling of relief because ... I have killed death. My enemy's death cannot be held against me ... if I killed him with the approval of society: that is the purpose of war. 2 *Eugene Ionesco*

We can kill thousands, because we have all first learned to call them the enemy. Wars commence in our cultures because we kill each other in euphemisms and abstractions long before the first missiles are ever launched. 3 *Petra Kelly*

No shots had been fired at the soldiers, no enemy troops were in the village [of My Lai], nobody was armed.... We operate on the principle that any action is permissible against an "enemy" ... even, when we come to strategic bombing, against anyone whose death might inconvenience a foe. 4 *Daniel Ellsberg*

Well, I was ordered to go in there and destroy the enemy.... I did not sit down and think in terms of men, women, and children. They were all classified the same and ... we dealt with them [as] enemy soldiers. 5 *Lt. William Calley (on My Lai)*

[A]s we wound and kill our enemy in the field and slaughter his women and children in their homes, our love for each other deepens.... [O]ur hatred of each other is being purged in the sufferings of our enemy. 6 *Hugh D. Duncan*

[G]uilt must be cancelled in society, and it is absolved by "victimage." ... [T]he enemy has a ritual role to play, by means of which evil is redeemed. 7 *Ernest Becker*

The Church should be a disciplined, charging army ... equipped for battle, ready to charge the enemy. 8 *Rev. Jerry Falwell*

[I]f the [Communist] Party acts on the belief that its enemies are annihilative, it is apt to render that belief less unrealistic by the very reactions which its conduct evokes. If imaginary enemies are treated as enemies, they are apt finally to become real enemies. 9 *Nathan Leites*

Groups which define themselves as enemies should be treated as enemies. 10 *Jeanne Kirkpatrick*

It is essential to have a tangible enemy, not merely an abstract one.... [Otherwise] we should have to invent him. 11 *Adolf Hitler*

Where there are various enemies ... it will be necessary to block them all together as forming one solid block, so that the mass of followers in a popular movement may only see one common enemy against whom they have to fight. Such uniformity intensifies their belief in their own cause and strengthens their feeling of hostility towards the opponents. 12 *Adolf Hitler*

Enemy

All of German history is nothing but a continuous chain of battles against its enemies. 13
Joseph Goebbels

[T]he real or symbolic existence of an enemy or out-group strengthens the existing dominance hierarchy.... One wonders if politicians who know that to wage war tends to solidify their regime are acting out an ancient pattern through which dominant early hominids maintained their places in political (and possibly reproductive) hierarchies. 14 *Lionel Tiger*

As long as enemies exist, terror will exist. 15
Albert Camus

[O]ur purpose is simple and direct: to ANNIHILATE the enemy—to smash him, beat him down and exterminate him. 16 *Ku Klux Klan*

A fundamental paradox of the paranoid style is the imitation of the enemy.... The KKK imitated Catholicism to the point of donning priestly vestments.... The John Birch Society emulates Communist cells.... This enemy seems to be on many counts a projection of the self. 17 *Richard Hofstadter*

Better face the enemy than the eternal Void. 18
William James

During the fifties ... an American character appeared with some consistency that became a model of manhood adopted by many men: the Fifties male.... Unless he has an enemy, he isn't sure that he is alive. 19 *Robert Bly*

Free institutions compete with authoritarian ones in making the Enemy a deadly force *within* the system.... [Thus] the Enemy is permanent.... He threatens in peace as much as in war (and perhaps more than in war); he is thus being built into the system as a cohesive power. 20
Herbert Marcuse

[T]he social and political needs for an enemy are so deeply entrenched in the real world of technology (as we know it today) that new enemies will quickly appear, to assure that the infrastructures can be maintained.... [T]he enemy does not have to be the government or the citizenry of a foreign state. There is lots of scope—as well as historical precedent—for seeking the enemy within. 21
Ursula Franklin

If we accept the notion that basically in our natures we are like our enemies, our task is immensely simplified. We can then fearlessly look at our own natures, at our greed, and at our ability to deceive ourselves, and if on top of this we find that we do stand for something valuable to the world, we are in a position to see this in proportion. 22 *D. W. Winnicott*

If the stranger has become fully human to you, there is also no longer an enemy.... 23
Erich Fromm

You have heard that it was said: "You must love your neighbor and hate your enemy." However I say to you: Love your enemies, bless them that curse you, do good to them that hate you ... for God makes his sun rise on the wicked and good alike. 24 *Jesus Christ*

Equality

We hold these truths to be self-evident: that all men are created equal. 1
American Declaration of Independence (1776)

We hold these truths to be self-evident: that all men and women are created equal. 2
Seneca Falls Declaration of Women's Rights (1848)

We know that men's passionate desire to see themselves as the equals of other human beings without distinctions of class or sex or race or nationhood is one of the driving forces of our day. 3 *Barbara Ward*

It is natural to suppose that not the particular prosperity of the few, but the greater well-being of all, is most pleasing in the sight of the Creator.... Equality may be less elevated, but it is more just, and in its justice lies its greatness and beauty. 4 *Alexis de Tocqueville*

The demand for equality is the root of social conscience and the sense of duty. 5
Sigmund Freud

Equality

There can only be a proper moral basis for relations between people when they are genuinely equal. 6 *Novosti Press Agency (USSR)*

The sense of human dignity ... is the cement of a society of equal men, for it expresses their knowledge that respect for others must be founded in self-respect. 7 *Jacob Bronowski*

[T]he Left would maintain that ... economic inequality brought about by capitalism *ipso facto* implies unequal recognition. The attack from the Right would argue ... [against] the goal of equal recognition itself ... because human beings are inherently *unequal*: to treat them as equal is not to affirm but to deny their humanity. 8 *Francis Fukuyama*

Equality of outcome is in clear conflict with liberty.... A society that puts equality—in the sense of equality of outcome—ahead of freedom will end up with neither equality nor freedom.... On the other hand, a society that puts freedom first will, as a happy by-product, end up with both greater freedom and greater equality. 9 *Milton & Rose Friedman*

The fact is that government cannot produce equality, and any serious attempt to do so can destroy liberty and other social goods. Equality is easy to conceive, literally impossible to realize. 10 *Jeanne Kirkpatrick*

[I]t is equality that is closest to the theoretical heart of democracy ... [and] the denial of it threatens not only the operation of democracy but its very foundation.... Only with liberty will democracy work, but only with equality is there reason to believe it ought to work.... 11
Carl Cohen

If I am freer than any other, then he will become my slave. Therefore, equality is an absolutely necessary condition of freedom. 12
Mikhail Bakunin

Equality without freedom creates a more stable social pattern than freedom without equality. 13
Eric Hoffer

The underdog demands "equality" and the upperdog demands "liberty" and neither can see that unless these two concepts are held in a just equilibrium, both are capable of wrecking the social fabric. 14 *Sydney Harris*

Nature has made men [essentially] equal in the faculties of the body and mind.... From this equality of ability arises equality of hope in the attaining of our ends. And therefore if any two men desire the same thing, which nevertheless they cannot both enjoy, they become enemies.... 15 *Thomas Hobbes*

[M]ost of the strictly egalitarian demands are based on nothing better than envy. 16
Friedrich von Hayek

Democratic institutions awaken and foster a passion for equality which they can never satisfy. 17 *Alexis de Tocqueville*

The evident contrast of equality is inequality. Perhaps it is not so evident that inequality means practically inferiority and superiority. And that this relation works out practically in support of a régime of authority or feudal hierarchy.... 18 *John Dewey*

The principle of equality, which makes men independent of each other ... tends to make them look upon all authority with a jealous eye, and speedily suggests to them the notion and the love of political freedom. 19
Alexis de Tocqueville

The pursuit of the democratic virtues of equality and individualism has led to the delegitimization of authority generally and the loss of trust in leadership. 20 *Michel Crozier et al.*

Today, equality has become equivalent to *interchangeability*.... Equality, instead of being the condition for the development of each man's peculiarity, means the extinction of individuality ... the very negation of individuality. 21 *Erich Fromm*

Equality is the very essence of Rousseau's political community; but it is the kind of equality that exists when every form of association and every social value that could possibly rival the General Will have been exterminated. 22
Robert Nisbet

Equality

Those who attempt to level never equalize. 23
Edmund Burke

"All animals are equal. But some animals are more equal than others." 24 *George Orwell*

[O]ne has to distinguish between *treating people equally* and *making them equal.* The effort to make people equal must lead to some determination by an administrative body of the degree of differences, and the degree of redress. It therefore means treating people *unequally.* The logic is inescapable. 25 *Daniel Bell*

Equality does not mean identity of treatment.... It means that no man shall be so placed in society that he can overreach his neighbour to the extent which constitutes a denial of the latter's citizenship.... Equality, therefore, means first of all the absence of special privilege. 26 *Harold Laski*

By equality, we should understand ... in respect of riches, no citizen shall ever be wealthy enough to buy another, and none poor enough to be forced to sell himself. 27 *Jean-Jacques Rousseau*

[A] striking fact, contrary to popular conception, is that capitalism leads to less inequality than alternative systems of organization and that the development of capitalism has greatly lessened the extent of inequality. 28
Milton Friedman

Equality in action—in other words, reciprocal good behaviour—is the only kind of equality that possesses a real existence. 29 *Aldous Huxley*

[T]o love one's neighbour means equality.... He is your neighbour on the basis of equality with you before God. 30 *Søren Kierkegaard*

Only a peace between equals can last. 31
Woodrow Wilson

If [men] would be willing to love an equal instead of a slave ... women would not be as haunted as they are by concern for their femininity.... 32 *Simone de Beauvoir*

Resolved, That woman is man's equal—was intended to be so by the Creator, and the highest good of the race demands that she should be recognized as such. 33
Seneca Falls Declaration of Women's Rights (1848)

[T]he most radical goal of the [feminist] movement is egalitarianism. 34 *Gloria Steinem*

[T]he equality of the sexes, of which so much is said, is incompatible with all social existence ... [for] each sex has special and permanent functions that it must fulfill in the natural economy of the human family. 35 *Auguste Comte*

Political equality for women, desirable and necessary as it is, is not going to remedy the radical disjunction between the sexes that begins and ends in the body. 36 *Camille Paglia*

[I]f gender is understood to be a hierarchy, perhaps the sexes are unequal so that men can be sexually aroused.... Maybe feminists are considered castrating because equality is not sexy. 37 *Catherine MacKinnon*

Once she is man's equal, woman cannot be "man's goal." ... It is but the sign and evidence of the victory of Agape over Eros. For a truly mutual love exacts and creates the equality of those loving one another. 38 *Denis de Rougemont*

[T]here can be no liberation of mankind without ... equality of the sexes. 39 *August Bebel*

As long as women are engaged in housework their position is still a restricted one. In order to achieve the complete emancipation of women and to make them really co-equal with men, we must have ... the participation of women in general productive labour. 40 *V. I. Lenin*

Genuine equality between the sexes can only be realized in the process of the socialist transformation of society as a whole. 41
Mao Tse-tung

Equality and an equal participation of men and women in the political arena are things that must be energetically striven for. Ultimately, they must be imposed. In both cases we must say "no" to nature—our own human nature. 42
Lionel Tiger & Robin Fox

Equality is the product of art, not of nature.... 43
Russell Kirk

The major inequalities in society are in the main social products, created and maintained by the institutions of property and inheritance, of political and military power, and supported by particular beliefs and doctrines.... 44
T. B. Bottomore

Equality is a principle necessary only in societies dominated by rule and law rather than by affection and bonding. 45 *Marilyn French*

Equality requires that everyone has the same chance, and by ignoring basic character traits, we can ignore the needs of a large part of society. 46 *James A. Corrick*

It seems that most of the primitive human societies are at the same time egalitarian. This must be related to the fact that because of rudimentary technology this kind of society depends on cooperation more fully. 47 *E. R. Service*

There is a physical difference between the white and the black races which I believe will forever forbid the two races living together on terms of social and political equality. And inasmuch as they cannot so live ... I as much as any other man am in favor of having the superior position assigned to the white race. 48
Abraham Lincoln

Now the adoption of an antiegalitarian attitude in political life, i.e. in the field of problems concerned with the power of man over man, is just what I should call criminal. For it offers a justification of the attitude that different categories of people have different rights; that the master has the right to enslave the slave; that some men have the right to use others as their tools. Ultimately, it will be used ... to justify murder. 49 *Karl Popper*

He who treats as equals those who are far below him in strength really makes them a gift of the quality of human beings, of which fate has deprived them. 50 *Simone Weil*

The true virtue of human beings is fitness to live together as equals.... 51 *John Stuart Mill*

Equality ... is the result of human organization insofar as it is guided by the principle of justice. We are not born equal; we become equal as members of a group on the strength of our decision to guarantee ourselves mutually equal rights. 52 *Hannah Arendt*

The principle of the equality of human beings is not a description of an alleged actual equality among humans: it is a prescription of how we should treat human beings.... Equality is a moral idea, not an assertion of fact. 53 *Peter Singer*

Equality is ... an ethical and not a biological concept. 54 *Theodosius Dobzhansky*

[T]he taking into account of the interests of the being, whatever those interests may be—must, according to the principle of equality, be extended to all beings, black or white, masculine or feminine, human or nonhuman. 55
Peter Singer

Animals, whom we have made our slaves, we do not like to consider our equal. 56
Charles Darwin

Animals can feel pain.... If a being suffers there can be no moral justification for refusing to take that suffering into consideration. No matter what the nature of the being, the principle of equality requires that its suffering be counted equally with the like suffering ... of any other being. 57 *Peter Singer*

Eros

Eros is the first, the creator, the principle from which all things proceed. 1
Arthur Schopenhauer

The right way of Eros ... is to begin with the beautiful things that are here and ascend ever upwards aiming at the beauty that is above, climbing, as it were, on a ladder from one beautiful body to two, and from two to all others, and from beautiful bodies to beautiful actions and from beauty of actions to beautiful forms of knowledge, till at length from these one reaches that knowledge which is the knowledge of nothing other than Beauty itself. 2 *Socrates*

Eros

The idea of Agape can be compared to a small stream which ... flows along an extremely narrow channel.... [B]ut Eros is a broad river that overflows its banks, carrying everything away with it.... For Eros, chief weight is undoubtedly given to self-love. Eros demands satisfaction for its own desires and longing.... When Eros-love is directed toward a fellow-man, it is because he is regarded, not as a "neighbour," but as an object which participates in the Idea of the Beautiful, or in the higher world generally, and which can therefore be used as a means of ascent to the world. 3 *Anders Nygren*

Agape is love descending from God to man; Eros is love ascending from man to God.... Agape ... shines upon the sinful.... Eros is given only to those who deserve it.... 4 *Pitirim Sorokin*

Agape is a love that loves to give, freely, selflessly; Eros is a love that loves to get, a highly refined form of self-interest and self-seeking. 5 *Philip Watson*

In the creative genius we see the need to combine the most intensive Eros of self-expression with the most complete Agape of self-surrender. 6 *Ernest Becker*

Eros and agape stand as direct opposites. Eros begins with self-love, and lays great stress on love to God as the final satisfaction of the needs of the self.... Agape is the precise opposite: ... Agape-Love for God lacks entirely the egocentric note, and is identical with the complete abandonment of self. 7 *Anders Nygren*

[The] primary tendency, I shall be loved always, everywhere, in every way, my whole body, my whole being—without any criticism, without the slightest effort on my part—is the final aim of all erotic striving. 8 *Michael Balint*

The erotic process introduces into life ... a desire that never relapses, that nothing can satisfy, that even rejects and flees the temptation to obtain its fulfilment in the world, because its demand is to embrace no less than the All. It is *infinite transcendence*, man's rise into his god. And this rise is *without return*. 9 *Denis de Rougemont*

When I speak of the erotic ... I speak of it as an assertion of the life force of women; of ... those physical, emotional, and psychic expressions of what is deepest and strongest and richest within each of us, being shared.... 10 *Audre Lorde*

Eroticism is a movement toward the *Other*, this is its essential character. 11 *Simone de Beauvoir*

Eros desires contact because it strives to make the ego and the loved object one, to abolish all spatial barriers between them. 12 *Sigmund Freud*

Eros is a biological urge. It's the zeal of the organs for each other. The personal factor doesn't matter. 13 *Joseph Campbell*

[W]hen [Freud] spoke of libido he was designating the agentic feature of sexuality, and when he spoke of Eros he was designating the communion feature. 14 *David Bakan*

Most men are erotically blinded—they commit the unpardonable mistake of confusing Eros with sex. 15 *Carl Jung*

If we are to escape from the treadmill of sexual fantasy, voracious need of love, and obsessiveness in all its forms we will have to reinstate our libido in its rightful function.... Eternal Eros is imprisoned now in the toils of the sado-masochistic symbiosis, and if we are to rescue him and save the world we must break the chain.... If half the world is to remain hostage to Death, then Eros must lose the battle.... 16 *Germaine Greer*

Eros is the instinct that makes for union, or unification, and Thanatos, the death instinct, is the instinct that makes for separation or division. 17 *Norman O. Brown*

It is the *failure* of Eros, lack of fulfillment in life, which enhances the instinctual value of death. 18 *Herbert Marcuse*

The god Eros is the slave of death because he wishes to elevate life above our finite and limited creature state.... *In ceasing to be god, he ceases to be a demon.* And he finds his proper place in the provisional economy of Creation and of what is human. 19

Denis de Rougemont

[I]t is only so long as destruction works in the service of Eros that it serves civilization and the individual; if aggression becomes stronger than its erotic counterpart, the trend is reversed. 20

Herbert Marcuse

If willingness to engage in war is an effect of the destructive instinct, the most obvious plan will be to bring Eros, its antagonist, into play against it. 21 *Sigmund Freud*

Men have gained control over the forces of nature to such an extent that ... they would have no difficulty in exterminating one another.... And now it is to be expected that the other of the two "Heavenly Powers," eternal Eros, will make an effort to assert himself in the struggle with his equally immortal adversary [Thanatos]. But who can foresee with what success and with what result? 22 *Sigmund Freud*

[E]roticism implies a claim of the instant against time, of the individual against the group.... [I]t is a rebellion against all regulation; it contains a principle hostile to society. 23

Simone de Beauvoir

Young people, and not only young people, have studied and practiced a crippled *eros* that can no longer take wing, and does not contain within it the longing for eternity and the divination of one's relatedness to being. 24 *Allan Bloom*

It is in our day that Jesus is, in the fullest and most radical sense, being put to death, since none of his words or actions or miracles have any relevance for Eros-inspired man.... Eros has triumphed through technical and political advances. God has fallen silent. 25 *Jacques Ellul*

The great tragedy of Eros is its blindness: remove the blindness produced by a too narrow and intense light, remove the bandage that turned vision into dreams, and Eros is charity itself: the pursuit of all Good, guided by all knowledge. 26 *George Santayana*

Eros is the drive toward union ... with significant other persons in our world in relation to whom we discover our own self-fulfillment. Eros is the yearning in man which leads him to dedicate himself to seeking *arete*, the noble and good life.... [T]he function of eros ... is to draw us toward the ideal forms. 27 *Rollo May*

Eros ... belongs on one side to man's primordial animal nature which will endure as long as man has an animal body. On the other side he is related to the highest forms of the spirit. But he only thrives when spirit and instinct are in right harmony. 28 *Carl Jung*

Human nature, in search of life's beauty, will not easily find a helper better than eros. 29

Socrates

Evil

Whatever seeks to separate itself from the Divine Principle ... is EVIL. 1

Samuel Taylor Coleridge

Good is all that serves life, evil is all that serves death. Good is reverence for life.... Evil is all that stifles life, narrows it down, cuts it to pieces. 2 *Erich Fromm*

Sin and evil are the separation of man from man, man from his environment, man's own ego from the other parts of his personality.... Evil, then, is best seen as the inability or unwillingness to overcome separation. 3

Charles Drekmeier

Evil is that which makes for separateness; and that which makes for separateness is self-destructive. 4 *Aldous Huxley*

It may seem melodramatic to treat the twin poles of human experience represented by the U.S. and the Soviet Union as the equivalent of Good and Evil, Light and Darkness, God and the Devil; yet if we allow ourselves to think of them that way ... it can help clarify our perspectives on the world struggle. 5 *Richard M. Nixon*

The view that good and evil are spiritual forces outside us, and that man is caught in the conflict

Evil

between them, is more bearable by far than the insight that the opposites are the ineradicable and indispensable preconditions of all psychic life, so much so that life itself is guilt. 6
Carl Jung

[The Vietnam] war seemed to sum up the evils of our society: destruction of people, destruction of environment, depersonalized use of technology, war by the rich and powerful against the poor and helpless, justification based on abstract rationality, hypocrisy and lies, and a demand that the individual, regardless of his conscience ... make himself into a part of the war machine, an impersonal projectile bringing death to the people. 7 *Charles A. Reich*

[M]an's natural and inevitable urge to deny mortality and achieve a heroic self-image are the root causes of human evil.... Evil is caused by ... man's hunger for righteous self-expansion and perpetuation.... [A]ll the intolerable sufferings of mankind result from man's attempt to make the whole world of nature reflect *his* reality, his heroic victory; he thus tries to achieve a perfection on earth, a visible testimonial to his cosmic importance.... 8
Ernest Becker

Most of the large-scale destructiveness is done by people who feel they have received some kind of permission for what they do—as we call it, a sanction for evil. 9 *Nevitt Sanford*

The American tradition is to locate the source of evil deeds in evil men. We have yet to learn that the greatest evils occur when social systems give average men the task of routinizing evil. 10
Edward M. Opton Jr.

It is indeed probable that more harm and misery have been caused by men determined to use coercion to stamp out a moral evil than by men intent on doing evil. 11 *Friedrich von Hayek*

There is no idea which has produced more evil, none more inimical to Christ's teachings, than the idea of a Church. 12 *Leo Tolstoy*

A very ridiculous thing it is, that any man should ignore vice and wickedness in himself, which is in his power to restrain, and should go about to suppress it in others, which is altogether impossible. 13 *Marcus Aurelius*

[T]he evils ... we know of ... may be roughly divided into three classes. There are, first, those due to physical nature.... Second, we may put those that spring from defects in character.... Third come those that depend upon the power of one individual or group over another.... A social system may be judged by its bearing upon these three kinds of evils. 14 *Bertrand Russell*

What we call Evil in this World ... is the grand Principle that makes us sociable creatures.... [T]he Moment Evil ceases, the Society must be spoiled if not totally dissolved. 15
Bernard Mandeville

[T]he decisive seat of evil in this world is not in social and political institutions ... but simply in the weakness and imperfection of the human soul itself.... For this reason, the success of a society may be said, like charity, to begin at home. 16 *George F. Kennan*

[T]he stronghold of evil is found in chaos, in the realm of anarchy and madness in each human being.... The evil spirits and monsters of human belief are personifications of different types and categories of this anarchic evil. 17
Richard Cavendish

From the ... beginning, the Judeo-Christian tradition has linked women with evil. Illicit sex and the powerful allure of women's bodies lie at the heart of the cosmology of heaven and hell, God and Satan. 18 *Mark Gerzon*

Evil, in the widest sense we can give it, is precisely the dark, disordered material out of which man's Freewill has to create an edifice of order and Good. 19 *Thomas Carlyle*

[T]he distinction between good and evil first comes about with the actuality of freedom. 20
Søren Kierkegaard

Man awakens only when he distinguishes between good and evil. 21 *Karl Jaspers*

Evil is nothing but the incompatibility between what is and what ought to be. 22 *G. W. F. Hegel*

Evil

Evil for you lies not in any self external to your own; nor yet in any phase or alteration of your material shell. Where is it then? In that part of you which forms your views of what is evil. Refuse the view, and all is well. 23 *Marcus Aurelius*

[W]hatsoever is the object of any man's appetite or desire, that is it which he for his part calls *good*; and the object of his hate and aversion, *evil*.... For these words ... are ever used with relation to the person that uses them, there being nothing simply and absolutely so, nor any common rule of good and evil to be taken from the nature of the objects themselves.... 24
Thomas Hobbes

[E]ither that is evil which we fear or the act of fearing is itself evil. 25 *Saint Augustine*

We call good, or evil, what is useful to, or harmful to, preserving our being. 26
Baruch Spinoza

All organisms have an inherent tendency to actualize their specific potentialities. The aim of man's life ... [is] the unfolding of his powers according to the laws of his nature.... Evil constitutes the crippling of man's powers.... 27
Erich Fromm

[M]an is not necessarily evil but becomes evil only if the proper conditions for his growth and development are lacking. 28 *Erich Fromm*

Evil and good are phases in the process of growth; and who shall say which is the better teacher? 29 *Lewis Mumford*

It seems highly probable that moral evil is absolutely necessary to the production of moral excellence. 30 *Thomas Malthus*

[E]vil is only the will to evil—the will to destruction as such.... 31 *Karl Jaspers*

[D]efection from that which supremely is, to that which has less of being—that is to begin to have an evil will.... For when the will abandons what is above itself, and turns to what is lower, it becomes evil—not because that is evil to which it turns, but because the turning itself is wicked. 32 *Saint Augustine*

The sinner does evil, the wicked man is evil. 33
Martin Buber

Evil-doing does not hurt the universe at large.... It is hurtful to the evil-doer only. 34
Marcus Aurelius

The ultimate evil in the temporal world is deeper than any specific evil. It lies in the fact that the past fades, that time is a "perpetual perishing." 35 *Alfred N. Whitehead*

Yes, everything deserves to be eternalized, absolutely everything, even evil itself, for that which we call evil would lose its evilness in being eternalized, because it would lose its temporal nature. For the essence of evil consists in its temporal nature, in its not applying itself to any ultimate and permanent end. 36
Miguel de Unamuno

Evil is a form of the unlimited, and good of the limited. 37 *Aristotle*

Evil blurs the conscience, and not only the moral conscience but the general, psychical consciousness. And everything that exalts and expands consciousness is good, while that which depresses and diminishes it is evil. 38
Miguel de Unamuno

Evil flourishes far more in the shadows than in the light of day. 39 *Jawaharlal Nehru*

In keeping silent about evil, in burying it so deep within us that no sign of it appears on the surface, we are *implanting* it, and it will rise up a thousandfold in the future. 40
Alexander Solzhenitsyn

The spread of evil is the symptom of a vacuum. Whenever evil wins, it is only by default: by the moral failure of those who evade the fact that there can be no compromise on basic principles. 41 *Ayn Rand*

There are two sides to every issue: one side is right and the other is wrong, but the middle is always evil. 42 *Ayn Rand*

Nourished for hundreds of years on a literature in which Right invariably triumphs in the

Evil

last chapter, we believe half-instinctively that evil always defeats itself in the long run. Pacifism, for instance, is founded largely on this belief. Don't resist evil, and it will somehow destroy itself. But why should it? What evidence is there that it does? 43 *George Orwell*

You heard that it was said: "An eye for an eye and a tooth for a tooth." However, I say to you: Do not resist evil: but whosoever strikes you on your right cheek, turn the left cheek also to him. 44 *Jesus Christ*

It is never right ... when we suffer evil to defend ourselves by doing evil in return. 45
Socrates

It has always been recognized that if you split Being down the middle ... if you cling to the good without the bad, denying the one for the other, what happens is that the dissociated evil impulse, now evil in a double sense, returns to permeate and possess the good and turn it into itself. 46 *R. D. Laing*

Out of evil, much good has come to me.... So now I intend to play the game of life, being receptive to whatever comes to me, good and bad, sun and shadow forever alternating, and, in this way, also accepting my own nature with its positive and negative sides. 47 *Carl Jung*

[T]he evil facts are as genuine parts of nature as the good ones, [and thus] the philosophic presumption should be that they have some rational significance.... 48 *William James*

If all evil were prevented, much good would be absent from the universe. 49
Saint Thomas Aquinas

There is ... nothing in all nature, perhaps, which is not an evil; nothing which is not unfavourable to some interest, and does not involve some infinitesimal or ultimate suffering in the universe of life. 50 *George Santayana*

It is evil, and more precisely the evil of human suffering, that entitles man to revolt against whatever power planned and organized this universe. 51 *Colin Connellan*

To say that God permits evil in this world may not be pleasing to the ear.... I know that He has no evil in Him, and yet if there is evil, He is the author of it and yet untouched by it. 52
Mohandes Gandhi

The nature of evil is that the characters of things are mutually obstructive. Thus the depths of life require a process of selection.... Selection is at once the measure of evil, and the process of its evasion. It means discarding the element of obstructiveness.... [T]hus the struggle with evil is a process of building up a mode of utilization by the provision of intermediate elements introducing a complex structure of harmony. 53 *Alfred N. Whitehead*

Evil is the brute motive force of fragmentary purpose, disregarding the eternal vision. 54
Alfred N. Whitehead

Good stands for the knowledge of His laws; and evil, for the ignorance of His ultimate laws. 55
Itzhak Bentov

He that doeth evil hath not seen God. 56
Saint John

Evil does not exist; once you have crossed the threshold, all is good. 57 *Franz Kafka*

Nothing is evil which is according to nature. 58
Marcus Aurelius

If only there were evil people somewhere ... and it were necessary only to separate them from the rest of us and destroy them. But the line dividing good and evil cuts through the heart of every human being. And who is willing to destroy a piece of his own heart? 59
Alexander Solzhenitsyn

Man, seek the author of evil no longer. It is yourself.... 60 *Jean-Jacques Rousseau*

Therefore the individual who wishes to have an answer to the problem of evil ... has need, first and foremost, of *self-knowledge*, that is, the utmost possible knowledge of his own wholeness. 61 *Carl Jung*

Evil is man's loss of himself in the tragic attempt

to escape the burden of his humanity. 62
Erich Fromm

[H]uman evil is largely human weakness, forgivable, understandable and also, in principle, curable. 63 *Abraham Maslow*

The real problem of evil ... is to reduce it to amounts that can be spiritually assimilated. 64
Lewis Mumford

There are few things wholly evil or wholly good. Almost everything ... is an inseparable compound of the two, so that our best judgment of the preponderance between them is continually demanded. 65 *Abraham Lincoln*

EXPLOITATION

IN WESTERN CULTURE, there are no nonexploitative relationships. 1 *Camille Paglia*

The only thing that matters technically is yield, production. This is the law of technique; this yield can only be obtained by the total mobilization of human beings, body and soul, and this implies the exploitation of all human psychic forces. 2 *Jacques Ellul*

Science is the product of our vital need to exploit the world.... 3 *Ilya Prigogine*

[T]he fundamental social cause of excesses which violate the rules of social life is the exploitation of the masses. 4 *V. I. Lenin*

Every exploitation of man by man is founded on class rule. 5 *August Bebel*

The exploiting classes need political supremacy in order to maintain exploitation, i.e., in the selfish interests of a tiny minority, and against the vast majority of the community. The exploited classes need political supremacy in order completely to abolish all exploitation. 6
V. I. Lenin

Exploitation must not be seen as such. It must be seen as benevolence. 7 *R. D. Laing*

[T]he Communist states have seen, in the final analysis, the origin of ... a new ruling and exploiting class. 8 *Milovan Djilas*

The Left has carried the exploitation of man to the extreme.... The Left, like capitalism, identifies freedom with its own dictatorship.... From the moment when the Left thus permanently betrayed the poor, it also betrayed the West. 9 *Jacques Ellul*

Property is the exploitation of the weak by the strong. Communism is the exploitation of the strong by the weak. 10 *Pierre Proudhon*

"The man at the top of the intellectual pyramid contributes the most to all those below him, but gets nothing except his material payment, receiving no intellectual bonus from others to add to the value of his time. The man at the bottom who, left to himself, would starve in his hopeless ineptitude, contributes nothing to those above him, but receives the bonus of all of their brains. Such is the nature of the ... 'exploitation' for which you have damned the strong." 11 *Ayn Rand*

Through the history of the world there have always been exploiters and exploited. There always will be ... because the great mass of men are ... unfit to control themselves, and for their own good need masters. 12
W. Somerset Maugham

There has never yet existed a wealthy and civilized society in which one portion of the community did not, in point of fact, live on the labour of the other. 13 *John C. Calhoun*

It is just as important to the capitalist mass producer as to the Soviet functionary to condition people into uniform, unresisting subjects.... We ostensibly free, Western civilized people are no longer conscious of the extent to which we are being manipulated by the commercial decisions of the mass producers. 14 *Konrad Lorenz*

The more a ruling group can make psychic cripples of those they dominate, the easier it is for them to exploit their underlings, using them to promote their own purposes. 15
Erich Fromm

Exploitation

As seen from the economic point of view, leisure ... is closely allied in kind with the life of exploit; and the achievements which characterize a life of leisure, and which remain as its decorous criteria, have much in common with the trophies of exploit. 16 *Thorstein Veblen*

Narcissists ... deny feelings that contradict the image they seek. Acting without feeling, they tend to be seductive and manipulative, striving for power and control.... [E]xploitiveness is common to all narcissistic personalities. 17 *Alexander Lowen*

If a person wants to live a parasitic existence, in which he can enjoy the possessions and the labor of his fellows, he risks the possibility of having to resort to violence.... The less socially adept and perceptive the exploiter, the greater the likelihood that he will have to invoke violence, or that he will meet unexpected violence which he must counter. 18 *Hans Toch*

Once ... an exploitative social system has developed ... warfare becomes a necessity for the maintenance of power to exploit. 19 *Helen B. Lewis*

It is only in an economy in which the exploitation of the many by the few is possible that war is beneficial. 20 *Donald A. Wells*

The dominion of man over the labor of other men is a shaky basis for civilization.... Any civilization based mainly upon ability to exploit the energies of men is precarious. 21 *John Dewey*

No one in the hunting band can afford to exploit or expropriate anyone else too consistently.... Such behavior carried to its logical conclusion would put an end to social relationships, since it would deny the fundamental importance of exchange and reciprocity.... Thus, in the ideal economy, accumulation and generosity are two sides of the same coin; getting and sharing are virtually one and the same activity. 22 *Lionel Tiger & Robin Fox*

Marx's condemnation of capitalism is fundamentally a moral condemnation.... The system is condemned, because by forcing the exploiter to enslave the exploited it robs both of their freedom. 23 *Karl Popper*

When I exploit and manipulate others, I'm also exploiting and manipulating myself. 24 *Philip Slater*

Faith

Faith is the assured expectation of things hoped for, the evident demonstration of realities though not beheld. 1 *Holy Bible*

The road that leads us to the living God, the God of the heart ... is the road of faith, not of rational or mathematical conviction. And what is faith?... [It] is a movement of the soul towards a practical truth, towards a person, towards something that makes us not merely comprehend life, but that makes us live. 2 *Miguel de Unamuno*

Faith organizes and equips man's soul for action. 3 *Eric Hoffer*

The path of human development begins with innocence.... From there it leads to guilt, to the knowledge of good and evil.... For everyone who passes through this stage seriously and as a differentiated individual it ends ... with the insight that ... consistent goodness is unattainable. Now this despair leads either to defeat or to a third realm of the spirit ... beyond morality and law ... to faith. 4 *Hermann Hesse*

He is ennobled who is tinged by the sincerity of a faith. 5 *Karl Jaspers*

Eternity ... is essential continuity and requires this of man, or requires that he shall be conscious of himself as spirit and shall have faith.... [F]aith is man's relation to the divine. 6 *Søren Kierkegaard*

That which in all things only seeks its own, is thereby closed against God. But when through faith man becomes open to God, the love from on high obtains a free course to and through him. He becomes a "tube," which by faith receives everything from God's love and then allows the Divine love to stream out over the world. 7 *Anders Nygren*

Faith

Faith is the experience that the intelligence is enlightened by love. 8 *Simone Weil*

It is the heart which experiences God, and not reason. This, then, is faith: God felt by the heart, not reason. 9 *Blaise Pascal*

I have found it necessary to deny *knowledge*, in order to make room for *faith*. 10 *Immanuel Kant*

Faith and "knowledge" are only two species of inner certitude, but of the two faith is the older and it dominates all the conditions of knowing.... 11 *Oswald Spengler*

What typifies the neurotic is that he "knows" his situation *vis-a-vis* reality.... [F]aith asks that man expand himself trustingly into the nonlogical. 12 *Ernest Becker*

Faith is in its essence simply a matter of will, not of reason.... 13 *Miguel de Unamuno*

[I]t is faith that moves mountains, not reason. Reason is a tool, but it can never be the motive force of the crowd.... The capacity of the modern man for faith is illimitable. 14 *Benito Mussolini*

Of all the forces at disposal of humanity, faith has always been one of the most tremendous, and the Gospel rightly attributes to it the power of moving mountains. To endow a man with faith is to multiply his strength tenfold. 15 *Gustave Le Bon*

Faith is the creative power in man. 16 *Miguel de Unamuno*

[I]f we did not have faith but could solve every puzzle in life by an application of the human reason what an unbearable burden life would be. We should have no art and no music and no wonderment. And we should have no science.... 17 *Max Planck*

All science is based upon an act of faith—faith in the validity of the mind's logical processes, faith in the ultimate explicability of the world, faith that the laws of thought are laws of things. 18 *Aldous Huxley*

Faith feels itself secure neither with universal consent, nor with tradition, nor with authority. It seeks the support of its enemy, reason. 19 *Miguel de Unamuno*

[F]aith is the state of being grasped by an ultimate concern. 20 *Paul Tillich*

[O]ne may ... be justified in defining religion as man's search for *ultimate* meaning. It was Albert Einstein who once contended that to be religious is to have found an answer to the question, What is the meaning of life? If we subscribe to this statement we may then define belief and faith as *trust* in ultimate meaning. 21 *Viktor Frankl*

Trust, then, becomes the capacity for *faith*—a vital need for which man must find some institutional confirmation.... For a reasonably coherent world provides the faith which is transmitted by the mothers to the infants in a way conducive to the vital strength of *hope*.... 22 *Erik Erikson*

Faiths are the genes of society.... Where life is disorganized ... there is search for change. Where a faith is discovered that has this organizing power, it is likely to grow and to prosper.... From the abyss of reason we turn again to clutch at the slender rope of faith. 23 *Kenneth Boulding*

In every culture, there stands a censor, governing the opportunity of recognizing and responding to novel stimuli. That governor ... we may call "faith." Faith is the compulsive dynamic of culture, channeling obedience to, trust in, and dependence upon authority ... from which they cannot detach themselves except at the terrible cost of guilt.... 24 *Philip Rieff*

Enforced faith is nothing but spiritual cramp. 25 *Carl Jung*

"Faith" means not *wanting* to know what is true. 26 *Friedrich Nietzsche*

Faith in a holy cause is to a considerable extent a substitute for the lost faith in ourselves. 27 *Eric Hoffer*

Psychologically, faith has two entirely different meanings. It can be the expression of an inner relatedness to mankind and affirmation of life;

Faith

or it can be a reaction formation against a fundamental feeling of doubt, rooted in isolation of the individual and his negative attitude toward life. 28 *Erich Fromm*

No man has faith—not in himself, not in another man, certainly not in God—who has no capacity to doubt. Without doubt there is no faith.... 29 *Lloyd J. Averill*

Faith embraces itself and the doubt about itself. 30 *Paul Tillich*

Final conviction can only come to those who make an act of faith. 31 *Aldous Huxley*

Faith may be defined as fidelity to our own being—so far as such being is not and cannot become an object of the senses.... 32
Samuel Taylor Coleridge

The power of ... self-affirmation is the power of being which is effective in every act of courage. Faith is the experience of this power.... [F]aith is the basis of the courage to be. 33
Paul Tillich

Through the vigour and conflict of faith ... is the fear of death overcome.... God has granted to faith this grace, that death, which is the admitted opposite to life, should become the instrument by which life is reached. 34
Saint Augustine

Faith leads to immortal life. But faith presumes the acceptance of ... evil, and resignation to injustice. The man who is prevented by the suffering of children from accepting faith will certainly not accept eternal life. 35
Albert Camus

Dialectics rather than dualism is the metaphysics of hope rather than despair. There is no way of eliminating questions of faith from human life as long as human life is subject to general conditions of repression. Or rather, since—as Freud said, faith is a derivative of love—dialectics is the metaphysics of Eros, hoping all things according to St. Paul and seeking reunification according to Freud. 36
Norman O. Brown

Once skepticism and rationalism were progressive forces for the development of thought.... Today the lack of faith is the expression of profound confusion and despair. 37 *Erich Fromm*

Once [man] has rejected faith, he abandons himself to the intellect as such, and from it falsely expects certainty in the decisive questions of life. But since thought cannot provide such certainty, his expectations can be fulfilled only by deceptions.... 38 *Karl Jaspers*

Faith ... means absolute emancipation from any kind of natural "law" and hence the highest freedom that man can imagine: freedom to intervene even in the ontological constitution of the universe. It is, consequently, a pre-eminently creative freedom. In other words, it constitutes a new formula for man's collaboration with the creation.... Only such a freedom ... is able to defend modern man from the terror of history.... 39 *Mircea Eliade*

Man cannot live without faith. The crucial question ... is whether this faith will be an irrational faith in leaders, machines, success, or the rational faith in man.... 40 *Erich Fromm*

By helping to raise man above the level of bestial vegetation, faith contributes in reality to the securing and safeguarding of his existence. 41
Adolf Hitler

Now this is specially the misery which has fallen on man in our Era. Belief, Faith has well-nigh vanished from the world.... Faith strengthens us, enlightens us, for all endeavours and endurances.... The true wretchedness lies here: that the Difficulty remain and the Strength be lost.... 42 *Thomas Carlyle*

Without Faith ... mankind succumbs first to the death of the spirit and then to the death of the body. 43 *Russell Kirk*

Absolute faith ... is the situation on the boundary of man's possibilities. It *is* this boundary. 44
Paul Tillich

[T]here can be no direct knowledge of God and existence. There can only be faith. 45
Karl Jaspers

~ FAMILY ~

THE FAMILY IS ONE of nature's masterpieces. It would be hard to conceive a system of instincts more nicely adjusted, where the constituents should represent or support one another better. The husband has an interest in protecting the wife, she in serving the husband.... Parents lend children their experience and a vicarious memory; children endow their parents with a vicarious immortality. 1 *George Santayana*

[W]e hold our present form of humanity on trust.... [T]he family, a patterned arrangement of the two sexes in which men play a role in the nurturing of women and children, has been a primary condition of this humanity.... 2 *Margaret Mead*

It should be obvious that family, not the individual, is the real molecule of society, the key link of the social chain of being. 3 *Robert Nisbet*

Families create children gendered, heterosexual, and ready to marry. 4 *Nancy Chodorow*

Patriarchy's chief institution is the family. It is ... a patriarchal unit within a patriarchal whole.... Serving as an agent of the larger society, the family not only encourages its own members to adjust and conform, but acts as a unit in the government of the patriarchal state which rules its citizens through its family heads. 5 *Kate Millet*

[T]he family has a dual political function: 1. It reproduces itself by crippling people sexually.... 2. It produces the authority-fearing, life-fearing vassal, and thus constantly creates new possibilities whereby a handful of men in power can rule the masses.... In this way, the family assumes, in the eyes of the conservatives, its special importance as a bulwark of the social order they affirm. 6 *Wilhelm Reich*

[T]he authoritarian family ... becomes the factory in which the state's structure and ideology are molded.... [Its] aim is to produce acquiescent subjects, who, despite distress and humiliation, are adjusted to the authoritarian order. Thus, the family is the authoritarian state in miniature.... 7 *Wilhelm Reich*

The Family's function is to repress Eros: to induce a false consciousness of security: to deny death by avoiding life: to cut off transcendence: to believe in God, not to experience the Void: to create, in short, one-dimensional man: to promote respect, conformity, obedience: to con children out of play: to induce fear of failure: to promote a respect for work: to promote a respect for "respectability." 8 *R. D. Laing*

To make both women and children totally independent would be to eliminate not just the patriarchal nuclear family, but the biological family itself.... [T]o assure the elimination of sexual classes requires ... feminine control of human fertility, including both the new technology and all the social institutions of childbearing and childrearing.... The tyranny of the biological family would be broken. And with it the psychology of power. 9 *Shulamith Firestone*

Civilization is sick and unhappy, and I claim that the root of it all is the unfree family.... The tragedy is that man, who holds his family in bondage, is, and must be, a slave himself.... 10 *A. S. Neill*

The family at present is a school of despotism ... [which] seeks out and evokes the latent germs of selfishness in the remotest corners of [the husband's] nature ... [and] offers him a licence for the indulgence of those points of his original character which in all other relations he would have found it necessary to repress and conceal. 11 *John Stuart Mill*

Everyone needs to be needed. The male satisfies his sense of need through his role as provider for the family. If he is deprived of this role, he tends to drop out of the family and revert to the primitive masculine role of hunter and fighter.... [T]he family is the institution that has civilized the male. 12 *Phyllis Schlafly*

[T]he disintegration of the bourgeois family ... is wholly attributable to the rationalization of everything in life, which we have seen is one of the effects of capitalist evolution. 13 *Joseph Schumpeter*

FAMILY

[L]arge-scale industry, in overturning the economic foundation on which the traditional family and the family labour corresponding to it was based, had also dissolved all traditional family ties. 14 *Karl Marx*

The bourgeois clap-trap about the family and ... about the hallowed co-relation of parent and child, become all the more disgusting, the more, by the action of modern industry, all family ties among the proletariat are torn asunder, and their children transformed into simple articles of commerce and instruments of labor. 15 *Karl Marx*

It is ironic that the form of community most praised and cherished by American society, the family, has probably suffered the greatest destruction at the hands of the Corporate State.... The State wants its consuming units as small as possible ... [but a] nuclear family is, quite evidently, not a large enough unit to supply the warmth, security, and familiarity of a communal circle of affection. 16 *Charles A. Reich*

For most of the time, at present, the family may be said to be reduced to the married couple alone, and we know that this union acts feebly against suicide. Consequently, since it plays a smaller role in life, it no longer suffices as an object of life. 17 *Émile Durkheim*

Were it not that love of offspring is the vital principle of the family, which hitherto has been the solid base and cement of society—the real social unit—it would be positively antisocial, almost ferocious sometimes, in its exclusive selfishness. 18 *Henry Maudsley*

The Family always has its own enrichment and aggrandizement in mind; it constitutes a pressure group in conflict with other pressure groups.... If we whittle Family down to nuclear families ... the quotient of self-interest will be reduced to a manageable level. If we concentrate on the copulating couple, and convince it that frequent and prolonged copulation is its chief good, then we have little or nothing to fear from its self-interest.... 19 *Germaine Greer*

The term *couples* itself implies the locked-off unit of male-female: ... This is virtually what the nuclear family has become.... What a notion—a family that is threatened by its children! 20 *Germaine Greer*

It often happens today that both partners face toward the outer world and neither is aware of the unconscious or inner world. The family is left unguarded at this point. 21 *Robert A. Johnson*

A pattern of historical forces has been at work in modern society which arouses the belief that personality development occurs only through the stabilization of personal interactions; nuclear family life has seemed well suited as a medium for people to attempt to put the belief into practice.... In other words, the nuclear family permits orderly human appearances to resolve into a matter of simplified human relationships. The less complex, the more stable; the less one has to cope with, the more one's personality can develop. 22 *Richard Sennett*

With the decline of the driving power supplied by the family motive, [one's] time-horizon shrinks, roughly, to his life expectation. 23 *Joseph Schumpeter*

In order to survive for any considerable period, the members of any society must possess a minimum of solidarity, altruism, and good will.... Until recently the family was such an agency.... As it has become more and more contractual, the family ... has grown ever more unstable, until it has reached the point of actual disintegration. 24 *Pitirim Sorokin*

Many of the problems of the contemporary American family ... arise precisely from the fact that it is approached by its members on strictly liberal grounds. That is, when the obligations of family become more than what the contractor bargained for, he or she seeks to abrogate the terms of the contract. 25 *Francis Fukuyama*

The important point is that it is not either women's or youth's revolt that is the primary cause of a weakening of the authority of the family; it is, rather, the weakening of the family's authority over the past century or two that is the cause of the contemporary revolts. 26 *Robert Nisbet*

As one would expect, a disruption of the family, whatever its causes, fosters automatically a collective spirit and creates a responsiveness to the appeal of mass movements. 27
Eric Hoffer

The fact that bad families lead to moral arrest and moral pathology does not imply, however, that a good family is necessary for moral development. 28 *Lawrence Kohlberg*

The family, both as the primary source of love and the primary source of socialization, is the primary source of "humanization." ... [C]ontemporary "dehumanization" ... is perhaps ... attributable to weakening of the family. 29 *Steven Goldberg*

As suicides diminish, family density regularly increases.... [J]ust as the family is a powerful safeguard against suicide, so the more strongly it is constituted the greater its protection. 30
Émile Durkheim

The family has been called the "giant shock absorber" of society. 31 *Alvin Toffler*

To children, the voluntary separation of parents seems worse than their death.... Of course, many families are unhappy. But that is irrelevant. The important lesson that the family taught was the existence of the only unbreakable bond, for better or for worse, between human beings. 32 *Allan Bloom*

The women's movement did not fail in the battle for equality. Our failure was our blind spot about the family.... The new frontier where the issues of the second stage will be joined is, I believe, the family.... For the family is the nutrient matrix of our personhood. 33
Betty Friedan

Today, family is actually becoming more important to most people. But it is also becoming a voluntary bond, as a bond of affection, of attachment, of mutual respect, rather than one of necessity. 34 *Peter F. Drucker*

Love has changed from a peripheral concern of the family into its primary justification. Indeed, the pursuit of love through family life has become, for many, the very purpose of life itself. 35 *Alvin Toffler*

If families do not foster the growth of individuals with coherent selves ... nothing else will. 36
C. Fred Alford

[F]uture planning [should] take place primarily in the individual home and family. If they do not plan for the future, no State organization can. It is only on their motive power that the larger progress can be made. 37
Winston Churchill

Only in the family are man's positive social tendencies aroused and with them the capacity for social responsibility and identification. 38
Irenäus Eibl-Eibesfeldt

Man has a sense of family, and is in a position by way of symbolic identification to regard humanity as a family. The child as unifying symbol would well express a major concern of us all.... 39 *Irenäus Eibl-Eibesfeldt*

The ethos of loving one's neighbor is the family ethos. It first springs to life within the extended family, but it is capable of extension until it embraces the whole of humanity. 40
Arnold Gehlen

Father

It may well be believed that the change from the mother family to the father family is the greatest and most revolutionary in the history of civilization.... All the folkways followed the change. 1 *William Graham Sumner*

Human fatherhood is a social invention. 2
Margaret Mead

As soon as the physiological fact of paternity is recognized, a quite new element enters into paternal feeling, an element which has led almost everywhere to the creation of patriarchal societies. As soon as a father recognizes that the child is ... his "seed," his sentiment towards the child is reinforced by two factors, the love of power and the desire to survive death.... A legitimate child is a continuation of a man's

Father

ego, and his affection for the child is a form of egoism. 3 *Bertrand Russell*

[M]any a father's sentiment for his children is very little, or not at all, tender, is not properly love, but is a mere extension of his self-regarding sentiment. He is gratified—i.e., his positive self-feeling attains satisfaction—when they are admired or when they achieve success.... 4 *William McDougall*

[Once] fatherhood became ... the universal way of assuring personal immortality ... fathers imitated the kings so as to reenact the divine plan in their own homes.... 5 *Ernest Becker*

Within the patriarchal family the will of the father is law.... The patriarchal family, in fact, is the archetypal paradigm for nearly all social hierarchy. God is conceived of as the Heavenly Father, and His subjects as His children.... The state is often called the "Fatherland," and the term "sovereign" is used to describe the power of the father over his children and wife or wives.... 6 *J. C. Smith*

If a father misuses his power by suppressing his children's critical faculties, then his weaknesses will stay hidden.... And so, when a man comes along and talks like one's own father and acts like him, even adults ... will submit to this man, will acclaim him, allow themselves to be manipulated by him, and put their trust in him, finally surrendering totally to him without even being aware of their enslavement.... A child cannot run away, and the citizen of a totalitarian regime cannot free himself or herself. 7 *Alice Miller*

Fatherly love is conditional love.... In the nature of fatherly love lies the fact that obedience becomes the main virtue, that disobedience is the main sin—and its punishment the withdrawal of fatherly love. 8 *Erich Fromm*

Unconditional ... [and] undemanding love is typically and in its essence, maternal. Fathers ... love "more dangerously": they set standards, demand performance, and condition respect (not love) on achievement; and it is necessary for the good of the next generation that they should do so. The indiscriminate "love" of the "flower children" of the 1960's demonstrated disastrously to what extent lack of standards leads to nonperformance and abdication. 9 *Wolfgang Lederer*

The first love of a mother for her child is ... of a purely *instinctive* character, and so it ceases when the child is no longer in a physically helpless condition.... The love of a father for his child is of a different order, and more likely to last, because it has its foundation in the fact that in the child he recognizes his own inner self; that is say, his love for it is metaphysical in origin. 10 *Arthur Schopenhauer*

[The] early love of the father is an "ideal love": the child idealizes the father because the father is the magical mirror that reflects the self as it wants to be—the ideal in which the child wants to recognize himself. 11 *Jessica Benjamin*

The identification with the father functions as a denial of dependency. 12 *Jessica Benjamin*

Freud had noted the high proportion of homosexuals with dominant mothers.... Where the mother hates the father it will be virtually impossible for the son to love or admire him.... [T]he son needs a father who is authoritative rather than authoritarian. 13 *John Carroll*

[F]athers of males with strong moral standards are not typified by strictness.... On the contrary, punitive behavior on father's part is more frequently linked with the son manifesting weak moral standards. 14 *Seymore Fisher & Roger P. Greenburg*

By rejecting the false premise of paternal authority as the only road to freedom, we may recover the promise on which oedipal theory has defaulted: coming to terms with difference. 15 *Jessica Benjamin*

Fathering before he is ready is one of the more self-destructive ways the average man aborts his own growth and development. 16 *Herb Goldberg*

He who cannot fulfill the duties of a father has no right to become one. 17 *Jean-Jacques Rousseau*

The function that every one expects most definitely of a father is a solution of the problem of occupation.... It does not so much matter, however, that he should consider his work useful; what is important is that it should *be useful.* 18 *Alfred Adler*

I think that a father ... will do best by his children, his wife and himself if he takes on half or more of the management of the children (and also participates in the housework).... This is what sons and daughters need to see in action if they are to grow up without sexist attitudes. 19 *Dr. Benjamin Spock*

[T]he token nature of fatherhood ... gives a man rights and privileges over children toward whom he assumes minimal responsibilities. 20 *Adrienne Rich*

Important for girls' development is the fact that *father is constantly leaving....* Thus girls grow up with a preconscious knowledge of the limited contact they will have with men.... The father-daughter relationship illustrates one of the tragedies of patriarchy. 21 *Luise Eichenbaum & Susie Orbach*

We have to recognize, at this moment of history, as through centuries past, that most of our sons are—in the most profound sense—virtually fatherless. 22 *Adrienne Rich*

[There] is a sense in which fathers no longer exercise ethical authority over their sons.... Its large-scale occurrence reflects the historical absence of a meaningful set of inner images of what one should value, how one should live ... experienced by the individual as a profound sense of fatherlessness.... Thus there emerges an *unencumbered generation....* 23 *Robert Jay Lifton*

No doubt the ideal father is better than none, but many fathers are so far from ideal that their non-existence might be a positive advantage to the children.... The case for fathers, from the point of view of children's psychology, is not ... a good one. 24 *Bertrand Russell*

There is no good father, that's the rule. Don't lay the blame on men but on the bond of paternity, which is rotten. 25 *Jean-Paul Sartre*

The father's birth gift cannot be quantified. His gift contributes to the love of knowledge, love of action, and ways to honor the world of things. It seems particularly important these days to name some of the father's gifts. 26 *Robert Bly*

Every generation revolts against its fathers and makes friends with its grandfathers. 27 *Lewis Mumford*

FEMALE / FEMININITY

WE SHOULD REGARD the female nature as afflicted with a natural defectiveness. 1 *Aristotle*

The central paradox in the theory of the castration complex is that confrontation with the fact of sexual differentiation produces in the child and bequeaths to the adult the image of the female as the castrated sex. 2 *Norman O. Brown*

[N]ature has far more difficulty in differentiating the gender identity of the male than the female. Nature makes more errors in the male. 3 *John Money & A. Ehrhardt*

Males appear to have "gone beyond" the basic mammalian model more than females in some respects; e.g., the more neotenous female is analogous to the young male.... 4 *Kent G. Bailey*

While woman remains nearer the infantile type, man approaches more to the senile. The extreme variational tendency of man expresses itself in a larger percentage of genius, insanity and idiocy; woman remains more nearly normal. 5 *W. I. Thomas*

Females should be taken as the norm because males have a stronger need to satisfy their sexual dependency and hence are less "complete" in themselves than females are. This results in the male need to control females, which results in much pathology. 6 *J. C. Smith*

The male brain appears to be more clearly laterally asymmetrical in terms of function, while

Female / Femininity

the female is characterized by greater bilateral symmetry. Recent findings indicate that females have a larger corpus callosum, presumably to allow for greater transmission of information between the hemispheres. 7 *Kent G. Bailey*

Further, their more unified … mind may be able to assemble information more quickly than men, which may be … the source of … female intuition. 8 *James A. Corrick*

"Feminine" thinking is reflective, associative and circular. "Masculine" thought is … logical, linear, and highly exclusionary. 9 *Marilyn French*

I realized that … girls and boys used space differently.… [T]he girls emphasized *inner* and the boys *outer* space … which correspond to the male and female principles in body construction … [and] are relevant throughout life to the elaboration of sex-roles in cultural space-times.… [W]omen have found their identities in the care suggested in their bodies … and seem to have taken it for granted that the outer world space belongs to the men. 10
Erik Erikson

[The] *fear of being left empty*, and, more simply, that of *being left*, seems to be the most basic feminine fear, extending over the whole of a woman's existence.… No wonder, then, that the anxiety aroused by these fears can express itself either in complete subjection to male thought, in desperate competition with it, or in efforts to catch the male and make him a possession. 11 *Erik Erikson*

Females tend to see death as a force which threatens to rob them of love or … to put them out of communion with the objects of their love. 12 *R. J. Lowery*

The feminine principle is associated with … the pole of sexual and bodily pleasure, of nutritiveness, compassion, sensitivity to others, mercy, supportiveness, and all giving qualities.… Love is "feminine." 13 *Marilyn French*

The essence of femaleness as presently conceived is communion [and] the concern for others at the expense of self-development.… 14
J. Boles & C. Tatro

[W]omen are becoming aware of an identity crisis in their own lives.… [T]his is the crisis of women growing up—a turning point from an immaturity that has been called femininity to full human identity. 15 *Betty Friedan*

[R]especting the first dawn of the female character, I will venture to affirm that a girl, whose spirits have not been damped by inactivity, or innocence tainted by false shame, will always be a romp, and the doll will never excite attention unless confinement allows her no alternative. 16 *Mary Wollstonecraft*

To the "feminist" of both sexes, femininity is synonymous with … strength, integrity, wisdom, justice, dependability.… 17
Elizabeth Gould Davis

Socially, femaleness means femininity, which means attractiveness to men, which means sexual attractiveness, which means sexual availability on male terms. 18 *Catherine MacKinnon*

The stereotype is the Eternal Feminine. She is the sexual object sought by all men, and by all women. She is of neither sex, for she has herself no sex at all. Her value is solely attested by the demand she excites in others.… [S]he is morally neuter.… This is the condition which is meant by the term *female eunuch.* 19 *Germaine Greer*

The female has lost her *shame functions* in our culture; impulse has broken through the wall of shame and advertising has been quick to see the pecuniary value.… How many points the GNP has risen on the feminine buttock is an interesting question.… The recesses of the feminine soul have become ransom for the gross national product. 20 *Jules Henry*

You can now see the Female Eunuch the world over … spreading herself wherever blue jeans and Coca-Cola may go. Wherever you see nail varnish, lipstick, brassieres, and high heels, the Eunuch has set up her camp. 21 *Germaine Greer*

The female sex is exploited, and the fundamental evolutionary basis for the exploitation is the fact that eggs are larger than sperms. 22
Richard Dawkins

There is no parity between the two sexes in regard to the consequences of sex. The male is male only at certain moments. The female is female her whole life.... 23
Jean-Jacques Rousseau

It's a curious fact that the all-male religions have produced no religious imagery.... The great religious art of the world is deeply involved with the female principle. 24
Kenneth Clark

Because female sexuality, as it evolved over the millennia, is psychologically rooted in the bearing and nurturing of children, women have long horizons within their bodies, glimpses of eternity within their wombs. 25
George Gilder

Biologically, males have one sex drive—to mate. But in female physiology there is a closely woven connection between sexuality and maternalism. 26 *Alice Rossi*

The female body is a chthonian machine, indifferent to the spirit who inhabits it. Organically, it has one mission, pregnancy, which we may spend a lifetime staving off. Nature cares only for species, never individuals: the humiliating dimensions of this biologic fact are most directly felt by women, who probably have a greater realism and wisdom than men because of it. Woman's body is a sea acted upon by the month's lunar wave-motion. Sluggish and dormant, her fatty tissues are gorged with water, then suddenly cleansed at high tide. 27
Camille Paglia

She who faces Death by torture for each life beneath her breast / May not deal in doubt or pity—must not swerve for fact or jest ... / And to serve that single issue, lest the generations fail / The female of the species must be deadlier than the male. 28 *Rudyard Kipling*

The male livingly experiences Destiny, and he *comprehends* Causality, the causal logic of the Become. The female, on the contrary, *is herself* Destiny and Time and the organic logic of the Becoming. 29 *Oswald Spengler*

FREEDOM / LIBERTY

ONE OF THE indispensable foods of the human soul is liberty. 1 *Simone Weil*

[A]ll the qualities of Spirit exist only through Freedom [and] all are but means for attaining Freedom.... The History of the world is none other than the progress of the consciousness of Freedom. 2 *G. W. F. Hegel*

The history of mankind is one of continuous development from the realm of necessity to the realm of freedom. This process is never-ending. 3 *Mao Tse-tung*

Liberty—not Communism—is the most contagious force in the world. It will permeate the Iron Curtain. it will eventually abide everywhere. 4 *Earl Warren*

You can only protect your liberties in this world by protecting the other man's freedom. 5
Clarence Darrow

I am only truly free when the other is also free and is recognized by me as free. 6
G. W. F. Hegel

Freedom is indivisible, and when one man is enslaved, all are not free. 7 *John F. Kennedy*

Freedom is not an idol, or an end, but a prerequisite condition of human worth. 8
Daniel Halévy

Freedom alone ... supplies ambition with greater objectives than the acquisition of riches, and creates the light that makes it possible to see and to judge the vices and virtues of mankind. 9 *Alexis de Tocqueville*

[F]reedom is the necessary condition of happiness as well as of virtue; freedom, not in the sense of the ability to make arbitrary choices and not freedom from necessity, but freedom to realize that which one potentially is, to fulfill the true nature of man according to the laws of his nature. 10 *Erich Fromm*

Surely, freedom consists in the right to discover

Freedom / Liberty

what we *ought* to be and in the liberty to be able to do it ... [i.e.] freedom to realize what one potentially is, to fulfill the true nature of man according to the laws of his existence. 11
Ashley Montagu

Freedom is an inherent part of the development of personality. Wherever freedom is diminished for anyone, the personality ... is thereby diminished. 12 *Max Lerner*

I think that the preeminent value that ought to underlie the feminist movement is freedom, that is, self-development. This arises through the exercise of agency ... [and] free choice ... to realize one's purposes and to satisfy one's needs.... [F]reedom from domination constitutes a social condition for self-development. 13
Carol Gould

By liberty I mean the eager maintenance of that atmosphere in which men have the opportunity to be their best selves. Liberty, therefore, is a product of rights.... Without rights there cannot be liberty, because, without rights, men are the subjects of law unrelated to the needs of personality. 14 *Harold Laski*

The word "need" should be eliminated from the vocabulary of political discourse.... The idea of "need" is dangerous because it strikes at the heart of the practical argument for freedom. That argument depends on recognizing that each person is best qualified to choose for himself which among a multitude of possible lives is best for him. 15 *David Friedman*

The only freedom which deserves the name, is that of pursuing our own good in our own way, so long as we do not attempt to deprive others of theirs.... [T]he sole end for which mankind are warranted, individually or collectively, in interfering with the liberty of action of any of their number, is self-protection. 16 *John Stuart Mill*

There can be no compromise between freedom and government controls; to accept "just a few controls" is to surrender the principle of inalienable individual rights and to substitute for it the principle of the government's unlimited, arbitrary power, thus delivering oneself into gradual enslavement. 17 *Ayn Rand*

[I see] freedom ... as absence of coercion, not as the power to do something. 18
John Hospers

[F]reedom is the basic acknowledgement that the individual is more important than his society. 19 *Jacob Bronowski*

We have gone on preaching the liberty of men. But having forgotten Man, we have defined our liberty as a sort of vague license limited only at the point where one man does injury to another. This seeming ideal is devoid of meaning, for in fact no man can act without involving other men. 20 *Antoine de Saint-Exupéry*

[T]he case for individual freedom rests chiefly on the recognition of the inevitable ignorance of all of us.... If there were omniscient men ... there would be little case for liberty.... Liberty is essential in order to leave room for the unforeseeable and unpredictable.... [W]hat is important is not what freedom I would personally like to exercise but what freedom some person may need in order to do things beneficial to society.... The benefits I derive from freedom are thus largely the result of the uses of freedom by others. 21 *Friedrich von Hayek*

The condition of freedom in any state is always a widespread and consistent skepticism of the canons upon which power insists. 22
Harold Laski

The main weapons in the arsenal of freedom ... are the gigantic vital forces in each new generation. 23 *Wilhelm Reich*

The history of liberty is the history of resistance. 24 *Woodrow Wilson*

Freedom, then, is not a positive value with religious significance, but a negative check that prevents the entities in the social structure from invading each other's spheres of authority and upsetting the natural and organic function of society. 25 *Craig Schiller*

It is this—the "positive" conception of liberty: not freedom from, but freedom to—which the adherents of the "negative" notion represent as being, at times, no better than a specious disguise for brutal tyranny. 26 *Isaiah Berlin*

We all declare for liberty; but in using the same word we do not all mean the same thing. With some the word liberty may mean for each man to do as he pleases with himself, and the product of his labor; while with others the same word may mean for some men to do as they please with other men, and the product of other men's labor.... Plainly, the sheep and the wolf are not agreed upon a definition of the word liberty. 27 *Abraham Lincoln*

How is it that we hear the loudest yelps for liberty among the drivers of negroes? 28
Samuel Johnson

Freedom in capitalist society always remains more or less the same as it was in the ancient Greek republics, that is, freedom for the slave owners. 29 *V. I. Lenin*

Liberty is, to the lowest rank of every nation, little more than the choice of working or starving. 30 *Samuel Johnson*

Freedom: invariably celebrated as the supreme good and almost always confused with the licence to exploit. The candidates never mention the use of freedom to create a higher order of responsibility or love. 31 *Lewis Lapham*

Liberty, next to religion, has been the motive of good deeds and the common pretext of crime.... 32 *Lord Acton*

Freedom [has] led not only to crimes but to the very opposite of itself. That is why no one could any longer take that freedom seriously, but only regard it as a lie, an illusion, a hypocritical declaration. 33 *Jacques Ellul*

The United States appears to be destined by Providence to plague America with misery in the name of Liberty. 34 *Simon Bolivar*

O Freedom, what liberties are taken in thy name! 35 *Daniel George*

O liberty! O liberty! what crimes are committed in thy name! 36 *Madame Roland*

I would remind you that extremism in the defence of liberty is no vice! 37 *Barry Goldwater*

"No price is too high for individual freedom" is a good slogan for those who do not have to pay it. 38 *Cosmas Desmond*

I hope women will not copy the vices of men.... I hope they will not regard their freedom as a licence to do wrong. 39 *Elizabeth Jones*

To American conservatives, *freedom* probably means lack of restraint on individual initiative and the *freedom* to achieve superior status, wealth, and power; to socialists, *freedom* probably means sufficient restraint on individual initiative to ensure greater *equality* for all. 40
Milton Rokeach

The democratic idea of freedom is not the right of each individual to *do* as he pleases, even if it is qualified by adding "provided he does not interfere with the same freedom on the part of others." ... [T]he basic freedom is that of freedom of *mind*.... The modes of freedom guaranteed by the Bill of Rights are all of this nature: Freedom of belief and conscience, of expression of opinion, of assembly for discussion and conference, of the press as an organ of communication. They are all guaranteed because without them individuals are not free to develop and society is deprived of what they might contribute. 41 *John Dewey*

We Americans know that if freedom means anything, it means the right to think. 42
Harry Truman & Herbert Hoover

I know no country in which, speaking generally, there is less independence of mind and true freedom of expression than in America. 43
Alexis de Tocqueville

[T]he organizations in which Americans find themselves prevent an understanding that freedom may exist in participation (indeed, Tocqueville said, *only* in participation), and that strength may be nurtured by particular forms of membership. 44 *R. Jeffrey Lustig*

Freedom ... has spread itself to cover the isolation of the individual from all connection with

Freedom / Liberty

others, therefore, from most of what gives life meaning.... 45 *Mary Midgley*

[S]uper-industrialism will not restrict man, will not crush him into bleak and painful uniformity. In contrast, it will radiate new opportunities for personal growth, adventure and delight. The problem is not whether man can survive regimentation and standardization ... [but] whether he can survive freedom. 46
Alvin Toffler

Unless a man has the talents to make something of himself, freedom is an irksome burden. 47
Eric Hoffer

Liberty means responsibility. That is why most men dread it. 48 *George Bernard Shaw*

Freedom puts a strain on the individual's whole personality; the free man is left with no relief from any ideas he may have of being persecuted. He is left with no logical excuse for angry or aggressive feelings except the insatiability of his own greed. And he has no one to give or withhold permission to do what he wants to do—in other words, to save him from the tyranny of a strict conscience. No wonder people fear not only freedom, but also the idea of freedom and the giving of freedom. 49 *D. W. Winnicott*

To be free is not simply to follow our ever-changing wants wherever they might lead. To be free is to choose what we shall want, what we shall value, and therefore what we shall be.... [It is] to choose in terms of commitments we have made to bodies of principle which we perceive as external to our choices.... 50
Laurence H. Tribe

[T]hrowing the individual into an unbounded and empty sea of free choice does not in itself give freedom, but is more apt to increase inner conflict. 51 *Rollo May*

[F]reedom is as great as one's tolerance for ambiguity and anxiety. 52
Charles Hampden-Turner

I can assure you that the feeling of *freedom* can plunge the soul into a sort of anguish. 53
André Gide

[T]he question remains: how can civilization freely generate freedom, when unfreedom has become part and parcel of the mental apparatus? 54 *Herbert Marcuse*

[F]reedom in its foundation coincides with the nothingness which is at the heart of man.... I am condemned to be free. 55 *Jean-Paul Sartre*

I am free when my existence depends upon myself. This self-contained existence of Spirit is none other than self-consciousness—consciousness of one's own being. 56
G. W. F. Hegel

Our freedom extends only as far as our consciousness reaches. 57 *Carl Jung*

[M]an, the more he gains freedom in the sense of emerging from the original oneness with man and nature and the more he becomes an "individual," has no choice but to unite himself with the world in the spontaneity of love and productive work or else to seek a kind of security by such ties with the world as destroy his freedom and the integrity of his individual self. 58 *Erich Fromm*

[L]ove is the loftiest form of freedom. 59
Pitirim Sorokin

True freedom ... is a breath of fresh air blowing through the soul to cleanse it of self-hatred and hatred of others. 60 *A. S. Neill*

The "from what" of man's freedom is his being driven; and the "to what" is his being responsible, his having conscience. 61 *Viktor Frankl*

Liberty consists in nothing so much as the encouragement of the will based on the instructed conscience.... 62 *Harold Laski*

Freedom of conscience is the basis of all personal freedom. 63 *Susanne Langer*

Liberty lives by morality alone.... 64
Philip Wylie

[T]he greatest and most precious freedom of man is identical with the moral laws within him. 65 *Konrad Lorenz*

Freedom / Liberty

Without freedom there can be no morality. 66
Carl Jung

Men are qualified for civil liberty in exact proportion to their disposition to put moral chains upon their appetites. 67 *Edmund Burke*

Sensate man has abdicated his sense of rationality and moral responsibility. In the frenzy of his ever-expanding appetites, he has lost all inner restraint and forfeited his own liberty.... [L]iberty is not so much external as internal; ... it demands self-control and the punctilious fulfillment of one's obligations. 68
Pitirim Sorokin

[A] man becomes free only when he has attained self-mastery.... 69 *Denis de Rougemont*

Freedom is a tenable objective only for responsible individuals. 70 *Milton Friedman*

The condition upon which God has given liberty to man is eternal vigilance.... 71
John Curran

The price of liberty *is* eternal vigilance, not only in observing public measures ... but in observing oneself.... 72 *Kathleen Nott*

In [the] insistence that freedom and moral self-realization are interdependent, that one cannot live without the other, lies the ultimate lesson of true anarchism. 73 *George Woodcock*

Liberty must be under law; there is no satisfactory alternative; liberty without law endures so long as a lamb among wolves. 74 *Russell Kirk*

Without law there is no freedom. 75
Albert Camus

Liberty is governed by the necessary conditions for liberty itself.... The limitation of liberty is justified only when it is necessary for liberty itself.... 76 *John Rawls*

Finite freedom has a definite structure, and if the self tries to trespass on this structure it ends in the loss of itself. 77 *Paul Tillich*

Freedom can consist only in the power of doing what we ought to will, and not in being constrained to do what we ought not to will. 78
Charles de Montesquieu

Man's struggle for freedom is not due to a will to be free, but to ... the avoidance of or escape from so-called "aversive" features of the environment. 79 *B. F. Skinner*

The hunting primate was free. He was free of the forest prison; wherever game roamed the world was his.... Ahead of him lay freedom of choice and invention as a new imperative.... Freedom—as the human being means freedom—was the first gift of the predatory way. 80 *Robert Ardrey*

Absolute freedom is the right of the strongest to dominate. 81 *Albert Camus*

Peace bores what Robert Ardrey calls "alpha-types"—leaders whose climate is war and domination. Individual and personal freedom needs peace. 82 *Kathleen Nott*

We must plan for freedom, and not only for security, if for no other reason than that only freedom can make security secure. 83
Karl Popper

Now that we *know* how positive reinforcement works and why negative doesn't, we can be more deliberate, and hence more successful, in our cultural design. We can achieve a sort of control under which the controlled ... nevertheless *feel free*. They are doing what they want to do.... By skillful planning, by a wise choice of techniques we *increase* the feeling of freedom. It's not planning which infringes upon freedom, but planning which uses force. 84
B. F. Skinner

There is no subjugation so perfect as that which keeps the appearance of freedom. Thus the will itself is made captive. 85
Jean-Jacques Rousseau

[T]he illusion of freedom can be created by strategic relaxation of regulations and law on obscenity, pornography, individual thought—provided it is *only* individual ... while all the time fundamental economic and political liberties are being circumscribed. 86 *Robert Nisbet*

Freedom / Liberty

The first significant discovery we shall make as we racket along our female road to freedom is that men are not free, and they will seek to make this an argument why nobody should be free. 87 *Germaine Greer*

Freedom is the most overrated modern idea, originating in the Romantic rebellion against bourgeois society. But only *in* society can one *be* an individual. 88 *Camille Paglia*

The liberty of the individual is no gift of civilization.... The development of civilization imposes restrictions on it, and justice demands that no one shall escape those restrictions.... The urge for freedom, therefore, is directed against particular forms and demands of civilization or against civilization altogether.... A good part of the struggles of mankind centre round the single task of finding an expedient accommodation ... between the claim of the individual and the cultural claims of the group; and one of the problems that touches the fate of humanity is whether such an accommodation can be reached by means of a particular form of civilization or whether this conflict is irreconcilable. 89 *Sigmund Freud*

They who clamor loudest for freedom are often the ones least likely to be happy in a free society. 90 *Eric Hoffer*

Let a man say he is free, and he will instantly feel constrained; but let him acknowledge limitations, and he will feel free. 91 *Goethe*

Freedom is ... the slogan of despotism itself. ... 92 *Goethe*

How strange that the consciousness of freedom and the will to give it concrete expression should always end in producing the opposite of what was sought!... The consequence of all this is that the whole human enterprise is in danger unless freedom itself is subjected to control. 93 *Jacques Ellul*

[F]reedom, pressed to its ultimate, negates itself. 94 *Alvin Toffler*

[F]or you can only be free when even the desire of seeking freedom becomes a harness to you, and when you cease to speak of freedom as a goal and fulfilment. 95 *Kahlil Gibran*

Freedom comes only to those who no longer ask of life that it shall yield them any of those personal goods that are subject to the mutations of Time. 96 *Bertrand Russell*

Perhaps freedom has only existed for a real but passing moment between two immeasurably long periods of sleep, of which the first period was that of the life of nature, and the second period was that of the life of technique. If so, human existence must die out, must come to an end in a more radical sense than ever before. Freedom would be nothing more than a transition, a brief period of awareness that Transcendence is the true human existence.... 97 *Karl Jaspers*

Only in the service of truth is perfect freedom.... 98 *E. F. Schumacher*

Freedom is the recognition of necessity. 99 *Baruch Spinoza*

Fate is encountered only by him that actualizes freedom. 100 *Martin Buber*

Such a spirit who *has become free* stands amid the cosmos with a joyous and trusting fatalism, in the *faith* that ... in the whole all is redeemed and affirmed—*he does not negate any more.* 101 *Friedrich Nietzsche*

Free Will

What is to be feared in the foreknowledge of future events? Doubtless it is that such foreknowledge ... implies that all that happens must happen by fate. But if this is to be so, then there is ... no such thing as free will; but if we grant this then the whole economy of human life is subverted. 1 *Saint Augustine*

[T]he denial of Free Will ultimately tends ... to the sacrifice of human dignity for the purposes of a supposed collective temporal and merely material good. 2 *Hilaire Belloc*

The fact is that no person can live, no ego remain

intact without hope and free will. 3
Erik Erikson

[E]very rational individual who possesses a will must necessarily also be endowed with the Idea of freedom.... 4 *Immanuel Kant*

[M]an must act, and his acts must be judged, *as if* he were free.... 5 *Hans Vaihinger*

Freedom is nothing other than the capacity to follow the voice of reason ... [and] conscience, against the voices of irrational passions. 6
Erich Fromm

The accepted rule ... is that the accused must be capable, not only of distinguishing between right and wrong, but that he was not impelled to do the act by an irrational impulse ... [such] as to deprive him of the will power to resist the insane impulse to perpetuate the deed, though knowing it to be wrong. 7
Smith v. United States (1929)

The human mind stands free, in the sense that it is the servant of no given instinct.... The mind may act as a witness, at times impartial. It may act as a brilliant investigative agency, at times uncorrupted. But on every occasion it will ride with the winner, whatever be the winner's cause, and devote to the cause in full, splendid measure its loyalty, honour, and devotion. 8 *Robert Ardrey*

A man can surely do what he wills to do, but he cannot determine what he wills. 9
Arthur Schopenhauer

The doctrine of "free-will" is a desperate attempt to escape from the consequences of the doctrine of fixed and immutable objective Being. With the dissipation of that dogma, the need for such a measure of desperation vanishes. Preferential activities characterize every individual as individual or unique.... They become true choices under the direction of insight. Knowledge ... puts in our possession the instrumentality by means of which preference may be an intelligent or intentional factor in constructing a future by wary and prepared action.... To be capable of such action is to be free. 10 *John Dewey*

The question of fact in the freewill controversy is thus extremely simple. It relates solely to the amount of effort of attention which we can at any time put forth. 11 *William James*

The will is called free ... where it is illuminated by knowledge, and when therefore motives, hence representations, are the causes that move it. 12 *Arthur Schopenhauer*

Freedom ... in any valuable sense, demands only that our volitions shall be, as they are, the result of our own desires, not of an outside force compelling us to will what we would rather not will. Everything else is confusion of thought, due to the feeling that knowledge *compels* the happening of what it knows when this is future, though it is at once obvious that knowledge has no such power in regard to the past. Free will, therefore, is true in the only form which is important; and the desire for other forms is a mere effect of insufficient analysis. 13
Bertrand Russell

What we really mean by free will, of course, is the visualizing of alternatives and making a choice between them. 14 *Jacob Bronowski*

Therefore the freedom of the will was primarily invented to account for wickedness. 15
Arthur Schopenhauer

"Free Will" after the fall is nothing but a word, and as long as it is doing what is within it, it is committing deadly sin. 16 *Martin Luther*

[T]he concept of "free will" ... has been invented essentially for the purpose of punishment.... Men were considered "free" so that they might be judged and punished—so that they might become *guilty*.... 17 *Friedrich Nietzsche*

I conclude that free will is not essential to any rational ethic, but only to the vindictive ethic that justifies hell and holds that "sin" should be punished regardless of any good that punishment may do.... 18 *Bertrand Russell*

That which is termed "freedom of the will" is essentially the emotion of supremacy in respect of him who must obey: "I am free, 'he' must obey"—this consciousness is inherent in every

Free Will

will.... The desire for "freedom of will" ... involves nothing less than to be precisely [the] *causa sui*, and ... to pull oneself up into existence by the hair, out of the slough of nothingness. 19 *Friedrich Nietzsche*

I am freeing man from ... the demands of a freedom and personal independence which only a few can bear.... To the Christian doctrine of the infinite significance of the individual soul and of personal responsibility, I oppose with icy clarity the saving doctrine of the nothingness and insignificance of the individual human being.... [The Fuehrerprinzip] liberates the masses of the faithful from the burden of free will. 20 *Adolf Hitler*

Once the [computer] programs are so complex that their inventors cannot quickly predict all possible responses, the machines will have the appearance of, if not intelligence, at least free will. 21 *Carl Sagan*

In the mind there is no absolute or free will, but the mind is determined to this or that volition by a cause, which is also determined by another cause, and this again by another, and so on *ad infinitum*. 22 *Baruch Spinoza*

But the whole feeling of reality, the whole sting and excitement of our voluntary life, depends on our sense that in it things are *really being decided* from one moment to another, and that it is not the dull rattling off of a chain that was forged innumerable ages ago. This appearance *may* not be an illusion. Effort may be an original force and not a mere effect, and it may be indeterminate in amount.... Psychology, however, as a would-be "Science," must, like every other Science, *postulate* complete determinism in its facts, and abstract consequently from the effects of free will, even if such a force exists. 23
William James

The hypothesis that man is not free is essential to the application of scientific method to the study of human behavior. 24 *B. F. Skinner*

Thus the basic problem of our time is whether an independent human being in his self-comprehended destiny is still possible. Indeed, it has become a general problem whether man can be free—and this is a problem which, as clearly formulated and understood, tends to annul itself; for only he who is capable of being free can sincerely and comprehendingly moot the problem of freedom. 25 *Karl Jaspers*

To be actively free, and at the same time entirely dominated by law, is the eternal paradox of human life.... 26 *Oscar Wilde*

A free will and a will subject to moral laws are one and the same. 27 *Immanuel Kant*

The fully functioning person ... not only experiences, but utilizes, the most absolute freedom when he spontaneously, freely, and voluntarily chooses and wills that which is also absolutely determined. 28 *Carl Rogers*

[W]hat I will is fate. 29 *John Milton*

That it is true that God ... also wills in me, is indeed the unquestionable result of the unity of the divine consciousness.... When I thus consciously and uniquely will, it is I then who just here *am* God's will, or who just here consciously act for the whole. I then am so far free. 30
Josiah Royce

Living is precisely the inexorable necessity to make oneself determinate, *to enter into an exclusive destiny*, to accept it—that is, to resolve to *be* it. 31 *José Ortega y Gasset*

Future

[N]othing has a sense for man except in so far as it is directed towards the future. 1
José Ortega y Gasset

The present is never our goal; the past and the present are our means; the future alone is our goal. 2 *Blaise Pascal*

This is the very lesson I learned in three years spent in Auschwitz and Dachau ... : Only those who are oriented toward the future, toward a goal in the future, toward a meaning to fulfill in the future, were likely to survive.... And I think that this ... also holds for the survival of mankind. 3 *Viktor Frankl*

FUTURE

The individual or the nation which has no sense of direction in time, no sense of a clear future ahead is likely ... to have a poor chance of surviving.... The person or the nation that has a date with destiny goes somewhere.... 4
Kenneth Boulding

The fact of being able to occupy himself with the future is ... an indication of man's nobility; the conflict with it is most ennobling.... He who fights with the future ... can never remain ignorant about himself; for he fights with himself. 5 *Søren Kierkegaard*

Personality can be understood only as we see it on a trajectory toward its future; a man can understand himself only as he projects himself forward ... always becoming, always emerging into the future. 6 *Rollo May*

The future ... appears on the horizon to announce to me what I am from the standpoint of what I shall be. 7 *Jean-Paul Sartre*

Only a being which has to be its being instead of simply being it can have a future. 8
Jean-Paul Sartre

To understand what a person is, it is necessary to refer to what he may be in the future, for every state of the person is pointed in the direction of future possibilities. 9
Gordon W. Allport

All love of humanity is bound up with the future.... 10 *Thomas Mann*

[I]n human beings the ... future ... becomes an "ideal." ... But the *theoretical* idea of the future—that idea which is a prerequisite of all man's higher cultural activities ... is more than a mere expectation; it becomes an imperative of human life.... This is man's *symbolic future*.... [Here] man's symbolic power ventures beyond all the limits of his finite existence.... [I]t marks a decisive phase in man's ethical and religious life. 11 *Ernst Cassirer*

[A]s society increased ... [p]ower became divorced from the control of the genetic future of the population, and fastened instead on the control of material goods and the symbolic future. The leaders could not ensure that they controlled the future merely by peopling it with their own offspring; they had to ensure that their offspring controlled the future by having the monopoly on wealth and power. 12
Lionel Tiger & Robin Fox

The Socialist feels the Future as his task and aim, and accounts the happiness of the moment as worthless in comparison.... And here Socialism becomes tragic ... for, from Rousseau onwards, Faustian man has nothing more to hope for in anything pertaining to the grand style of Life.... [Of] the dynamic force and insistence that had expressed itself in world-historical visions of the future ... nothing remains but the mere pressure ... the form without content. 13
Oswald Spengler

Utopia replaces God by the future.... The future is the only transcendental value for men without God. 14 *Albert Camus*

[In] the future, it seems to me that we have to worry less about old-fashioned dictatorships than about domination by corporate systems that nobody seems able to control. 15 *Nevitt Sanford*

[T]he corporate ideology [has] established the corporation as the workplace of the future, the managers as the men of the future, and transience as the way of the future. 16 *Diane Margolis*

Rather than being afraid of the powerless, let us be afraid of the powerful, the rich and sterile nations, who ... have no stake in the future. 17
Germaine Greer

Men flatter themselves on being realists, on living in the present.... [Women] see not alone the present but the coming into being of the future. They do so because they are creators of the future—through their children. 18
Ashley Montagu

For in every act of love and will ... we mold ourselves and our world simultaneously. This is what it means to embrace the future. 19
Rollo May

We are told that our youth are our future. Yet, unless we can create a world which offers the

FUTURE

possibility of aging with grace, honor, and meaningfulness, no one—young or old—can look forward to the future. 20
Seymour L. Halleck

Like all other innate human values, this concern for future generations cannot be rationally explained. 21 *George E. Pugh*

Real generosity toward the future lies in giving all to the present. 22 *Albert Camus*

The future belongs to those who know how to make the best use of the present. 23
Hugh Farrell

The most effective way to ensure the value of the future ... is to confront the present courageously and constructively. For the future is born out of and made by the present. 24
Rollo May

In a ... fundamental sense, the future does not exist—it cannot be reached in any unitary way from within the present.... [But] in tomorrow's "now," we hold a memory of what we once believed that tomorrow to be! 25 *F. David Peat*

The future is merely real, without being actual; whereas the past is a nexus of actualities.... The present is the immediacy of teleological process whereby reality becomes actual. 26
Alfred N. Whitehead

The opposition of future to past or past to future is absurd. The future brings us nothing, gives us nothing; it is we who in order to build it have to give it everything, our very life. But to be able to give, one has to possess; and we possess no other life, no other living sap, than the treasures stored up from the past and digested, assimilated and created afresh by us. Of all the human soul's needs, none is more vital than this one of the past. 27 *Simone Weil*

[T]he past refuses to be dismissed for it is the voice of all human wisdom. Derided, the Past exacts its vengeance. 28 *Russell Kirk*

A man's destiny stands not in the future but in the past. 29 *Havelock Ellis*

The gee-whiz futurists are always wrong because they believe technological innovation travels in a straight line. It doesn't. It weaves and bobs and lurches and sputters. 30 *John Naisbitt*

All in all, the prospects for the industrialized minority of mankind are, in the short run, remarkably bright. 31 *Aldous Huxley*

In the long run we are all dead. 32
John Maynard Keynes

Of all the crimes against the future, extinction is the greatest. It is the murder of the future. 33
Jonathan Schell

The consequence of a rising standard of living will be that the birth rate will rise and the death rate will fall and there will be a massive increase in population.... Thus, although societies may progress for a time, the ultimate future is dismal. 34 *Thomas Malthus*

No great improvements in the lot of mankind are possible, until a great change takes place in the fundamental constitution of their modes of thought. 35 *John Stuart Mill*

The unleashed power of the atom has changed everything save our modes of thinking and we thus drift toward unparalleled catastrophe. 36
Albert Einstein

[I]ncreasing entropy corresponds to the *spontaneous evolution* of the system. Entropy thus becomes an "indicator of evolution," or an "arrow of time." ... For all isolated systems, the future is the direction of increasing entropy. 37
Ilya Prigogine

We must expect ... that the future will disclose dangers. It is the business of the future to be dangerous; and it is among the merits of science that it equips the future for its duties. 38
Alfred N. Whitehead

The most real change we could achieve would be one that would give us a holiday from our frantic and desperate pursuit of the future.... Thus we're confronted with the paradox of trying to build a future that doesn't always look to the future. 39 *Philip Slater*

Future

[T]here are discoverable limits to the amount of change that the human organism can absorb.... [U]nless man quickly learns to control the rate of change in his personal affairs as well as in society at large, we are doomed to a massive adaptational breakdown.... Future shock is the response to [such] overstimulation. 40
Alvin Toffler

The world to-day is suffering from a grave demoralization.... No one knows towards what centre human things are going to gravitate in the near future, and hence the life of the world has become scandalously provisional. 41
José Ortega y Gasset

The central feature of anxiety, as distinguished from fear, is a dread of the future, for the future is the most ambiguous and unknowable medium in man's cognitive world. It follows that attempts to cope with anxiety should involve a de-emphasis of the present and a preoccupation with the future. It also follows that persons characterized as having relatively closed [belief] systems should manifest not only more anxiety but also more future-orientation than those with relatively open systems. 42
Milton Rokeach

[W]orship of the future, which is a different aspect of the worship of "progress" ... is precisely the alienation of hope. 43 *Erich Fromm*

The narcissist has no interest in the future because, in part, he has no interest in the past.... A denial of the past, superficially progressive and optimistic, proves on closer analysis to embody the despair of a society that cannot face the future.... Narcissism emerges as the typical form of character structure in a society that has lost interest in the future. 44 *Christopher Lasch*

Our age has shifted all emphasis to the here and now, and thus brought about a daemonization of man and his world.... [M]an has been robbed of transcendence.... 45 *Carl Jung*

We need faith in a future that will redeem the past. 46 *Gloria Steinem*

Who controls the past controls the future.... 47
George Orwell

The empires of the future are empires of the mind. 48 *Winston Churchill*

Within the very near future ... we shall have acquired an extensive and empirically tested theory of human cognitive processes and their interaction with human emotions, attitudes, and values.... [W]e shall have the technical capability of substituting machines for any and all human functions.... 49 *Herbert Simon*

It is a world in which the human race has been swept away by the tide of cultural change, usurped by its own artificial progeny.... Concepts of life, death, and identity will lose their present meaning.... Our speculation ends in a super-civilization ... converting nonlife into mind. 50 *Hans Moravec*

One can imagine a time when men who still inhabit organic bodies are regarded with pity by those who have passed on to an infinitely richer mode of existence.... In adolescence we leave childhood behind; one day there may be a second and more portentous adolescence, when we bid farewell to the flesh. 51
Arthur C. Clarke

The era of carbon-chemistry life is drawing to a close on the earth and a new era of silicon-based life ... is beginning. 52 *Robert Jastrow*

I have ... faith that despite power structure, soulless technologies, and the mechanization of life, we will prevail because we can remain the architects of our future. 53 *René Dubos*

We now see the future not as a world that is forced upon us, but as a world that we ourselves create. 54 *Edward Cornish*

[T]he ultimate objective of social futurism ... [is] the subjection of the process of evolution itself to conscious human guidance. For this is the ... turning point in [man's] history at which ... from being the unconscious puppet of evolution he becomes either its victim or its master. 55
Alvin Toffler

Creating a desirable future demands more than foresight; it requires vision. 56 *René Dubos*

Future

[A]ny guarantees for the human future can be sought nowhere else but within ourselves. 57
Aurelio Peccei

We must become the agriculturalists of time. If we do not plant and cultivate the future years of human life, we will never reap them. 58
Jonathan Schell

The future is the most daunting human invention.... [I]t can only be a cultural invention, for the future will either be the inspired product of a great cultural revival, or there will be no future. 59 *Aurelio Peccei*

The future brings us nothing, gives us nothing; it is we who in order to build it have to give it everything, our very life. 60 *Ruth N. Anshen*

Gender

Gender is a term that has psychological or cultural rather than biological connotations. 1
Robert J. Stoller

In the absence of androgen, the genetic male differentiates genitally as a female.... [But] gender identity is not dependent on prenatal hormones.... Establishment of core gender identity is obviously a process of learning, insofar as it takes place in social interaction. 2
John Money & A. Ehrhardt

Sex/Gender is the fundamental categorical distinction of culture as it defines our identity as individuals, and thus underlies our entire psychological development. 3 *J. C. Smith*

[N]o social characteristic is more basic to individual self-identity than sense of gender.... [It] is the earliest to be solidified in the individual, the hardest to change, and the most inextricably connected with how we conceptualize and relate to ourselves, to others, and to nature. 4
Sandra Harding

In life ... no new thing has ever arisen, or can arise, save out of the impulse of the male upon the female, the female upon the male. The interaction of the male and female spirit begot the wheel, the plough, and the first utterance that was made on the face of the earth. 5
D. H. Lawrence

[T]he feminine element in man is only something in the background, as is the masculine element in woman. If one lives out the opposite sex in oneself one is living in one's own background, and one's real individuality suffers. A man should live as a man and a woman as a woman. 6 *Carl Jung*

[To] fully appreciate being a woman one has to be a man, and to fully appreciate being a man one has to be a woman. 7 *D. W. Winnicott*

In all cultures one of the primary laws is that of sexual categories of masculine and feminine. People are not seen to be simply human.... 8
Luise Eichenbaum & Susie Orbach

The human race ... is organized like the bees: the masculine soul is a worker, sexually atrophied, and essentially dedicated to impersonal and universal arts; the feminine is a queen, infinitely fertile ... but passive and abounding in intuitions without method and passions without justice. 9 *George Santayana*

The basic feminine sense of self is connected to the world, the basic masculine sense of self is separate. 10 *Nancy Chodorow*

Since masculinity is defined through separation while femininity is defined through attachment, male gender identity is threatened by intimacy while female gender identity is threatened by separation. 11 *Carol Gilligan*

The feminine principle is the pole of life ... [and] life is the highest value for "feminine" people.... "Masculine" experience is rooted in power-in-the-world, with its epitomizing act: to kill. "Feminine" experience is rooted in nature, with its epitomizing act: to give birth. 12
Marilyn French

When animus and anima meet, the animus draws his sword of power and the anima ejects her poison of illusion and seduction. 13 *Carl Jung*

The masculine character can be defined as having the qualities of penetration, guidance, activity, discipline and adventurousness; the feminine character by the qualities of productive receptiveness, protection, realism, endurance, motherliness. 14 *Erich Fromm*

Perfection is a masculine desideratum, while woman inclines by nature to *completeness*.... 15 *Carl Jung*

[I]n the psyche it is only the conscious mind, in a man, that has the masculine sign, while the unconscious is by nature feminine. The reverse is true in the case of a woman. 16 *Carl Jung*

Gender continues, consciously and unconsciously, to represent only one part of a polarized whole, one aspect of the self-other relationship.... Each gender is able to represent one aspect of the self-other relationship, either merging or separation. Each gender plays a part in a polarized whole. But neither attains true independence. 17 *Jessica Benjamin*

[W]ith low self-esteem, both males and females are likely to seek refuge and approval in exaggerated versions of their gender roles, and thus to become even less complete as they grow up. 18 *Gloria Steinem*

The child learns ... to choose among the many possible dimensions of human personality only that subset defined as applicable ... [and thus the] child's self-concepts become sex-typed.... Simultaneously, the child also learns to evaluate his or her adequacy as a person according to the gender schema.... The gender schema becomes a prescriptive standard or guide, and self-esteem becomes its hostage. 19 *Sandra Bem*

In women gender identity and personal fulfillment often seem to work in opposite directions. 20 *John H. Crook*

The exhaustion women are expressing now, in relation to their "double burden," is the result of conflict—the clash between wanting to hang on to the domestic security housebound women have always enjoyed and the desire to be free and self-fulfilling. This unresolved, and thus paralyzing, conflict breeds Gender Panic.... 21 *Colette Dowling*

[T]he male gender role, we believe may be a major cause of men's health disadvantage.... [But] both male and female roles are dangerous to health—the prohibition against vulnerability in men; the barriers to gaining power and control in women. 22 *R. Barnett et al.*

Gender is a social system that divides power. It is therefore a political system. 23 *Catherine MacKinnon*

The castration of women has been carried out in terms of a masculine-feminine polarity, in which men have commandeered all the energy and streamlined it into an aggressive conquistatorial power, reducing all heterosexual contact to a sado-masochistic pattern. 24 *Germaine Greer*

Women have very little idea of how much men hate them.... Men do not themselves know the depth of their hatred. 25 *Germaine Greer*

An unconscious misogyny and gynophobia is a part of the psyche of the male of the species. A similar phenomenon is not to be found in the female. In fact the English language doesn't even contain a term which would be the antonym of "misogyny." It is not the case that women do not often hate men, but rather that the hatred of women for men, where it exists, tends to be conscious rather than unconscious. 26 *J. C. Smith*

It seems possible that now, for the first time in history, women in substantial numbers hate, fear, and loathe men as profoundly as men have all along hated, feared, and loathed women. 27 *Dorothy Dinnerstein*

I should say without reservation that men fear and hate women more than women fear and hate men. I think it is this rather than the male's superior strength that makes it possible for our civilization to be called "a man's world." It is not a contest of strength; it is a contest of hate. 28 *Karl Menninger*

In truth women have never set up female values in opposition to male values; it is man who, desirous of maintaining masculine prerogatives, has invented that divergence. 29 *Simone de Beauvoir*

Gender

In human beings there is no such thing as pure masculinity or femininity, either in the psychological or the biological sense. 30
Sigmund Freud

[T]he integrity of the personality is violated when it is identified with either the masculine or the feminine side. 31 *Erich Neumann*

The great mind must be androgynous. 32
Samuel Taylor Coleridge

[T]he union of the sexes offers us the greatest possibilities for happiness. 33 *Karen Horney*

It is the men and women united that make the complete human being. Separate, she wants his force of body and strength of reason; he, her softness, sensibility, and acute discernment. Together they are more likely to succeed in the world. 34 *Benjamin Franklin*

[D]eeper than the problem of the relation between the sexes is the problem of the reunification of the sexes in the self. 35
Norman O. Brown

A perfect spirit cannot be conceived as sexually differentiated. 36 *Søren Kierkegaard*

We can build a whole society only by using both the gifts special to each sex and those shared by both sexes—by using the gifts of the whole of humanity. 37 *Margaret Mead*

The hope of our future civilization lies in the development in equal freedom of both the masculine and the feminine elements in life. 38
Havelock Ellis

God

[T]he principle of life is inherent in God; for the energy or active exercise of mind constitutes life and God is this act and this essential act belongs to God.... 1 *Aristotle*

God ... has nothing of the already made; He is unceasing life, action, freedom. 2
Henri Bergson

God is a spirit: and they that worship him must worship him in spirit and in truth. 3
Jesus Christ

To believe in God is to long for His existence and, further, it is to act as if He existed; it is to live by this longing and to make it the inner spring of our action. This longing or hunger for divinity begets hope, hope begets faith, and faith and hope beget charity. Of this divine longing is born our sense of beauty, of finality, of goodness. 4 *Miguel de Unamuno*

The belief in God is nothing but the belief in human dignity. 5 *Ludwig Feuerbach*

You are God, not in your ego, but in your deepest being, where you are at one with the nondual transcendent. 6 *Joseph Campbell*

[T]he power of transcendence places [man] so much outside of everything else that he can find a home only in God. 7 *Reinhold Niebuhr*

Our personhood is assured by our simultaneous contact with universal aspirations which place us in a transcendent perspective.... We undertake the task of attaining the universal in spite of our admitted infirmity, which should render the task hopeless, because we hope to be visited by powers for which we cannot account in terms of our specifiable capabilities. This hope is a clue to God.... 8
Michael Polanyi

By *God* I mean a being absolutely infinite—that is, a substance consisting in infinite attributes, of which each expresses eternal and infinite essentiality. 9 *Baruch Spinoza*

We know then the existence and nature of the finite, because we are also finite and have extension.... But we know neither the existence nor the nature of God, because He has neither extension nor limits.... If there is a God, He is infinitely incomprehensible, since, having neither parts nor limits, He has no affinity to us. We are then incapable of knowing either what He is or if He is.... But by faith we know His existence; in glory we shall know His nature. 10
Blaise Pascal

God

One does not find God if one remains in the world; one does not find God if one leaves the world. Whoever goes forth to his You with his whole being and carries to it all the being of the world, finds Him whom one cannot seek. 11
Martin Buber

[T]he psychology of giving takes us beyond egoism, beyond the desire for individual happiness—in Freud's phrase, beyond the pleasure principle.... [This] psychology is not egoist but self-sacrificial. Hence the intrinsic connection with the sacred. The gods exist ... in order to structure the human need for self-sacrifice. 12 *Norman O. Brown*

[S]urrender to God ... represents ... the furthest reach of the self, the highest idealization man can achieve. 13 *Ernest Becker*

The self is sound in health and free from despair only when, precisely by having been in despair, it is grounded transparently in God.... The decisive thing is, that for God all things are possible. 14 *Søren Kierkegaard*

"God" [is] ... the presence of "promise" in the world. 15 *William James*

[B]elief in God and symbolic resurrection directs and energizes us toward personal transformation and self-realization ... and toward a new community in which love would be the determining and controlling quality.... [O]nly a self which has as one of its constituent relations the relation to God has the *possibility* for immortality. 16 *Eugene Fontinell*

[If] people lose the idea of God nothing happens—not immediately and personally at least. But socially the masses begin to breed mental epidemics, of which we have now a fair number. 17 *Carl Jung*

Eros-love is acquisitive desire, appetite, which as such strives to obtain advantages. Since God is the Highest Good ... man reaches up toward God and seeks to secure participation in His riches and blessedness.... [When] "God is Agape" ... God transcends everything that can be made an object of human desire and longing. He is not the "Highest Good." ... Man loves God [as Agape] ... because God's unmotivated love has overwhelmed him and taken control of him, so that he cannot do other than love God. 18 *Anders Nygren*

No one can hate God. 19 *Baruch Spinoza*

[I]f there exists in a man faith in God joined to a life of purity and moral elevation, it is not so much the believing in God that makes him good, as the being good, thanks to God, that makes him believe in Him. 20 *Miguel de Unamuno*

God is not a substance existing outside of me but merely a moral relation within me. 21
Immanuel Kant

God does not speak through the commands and revelations of other men but in man's selfhood and through his freedom, not from without but from within. 22 *Karl Jaspers*

The concept of God is certainly one essential element in religious feeling. But the converse is not true; the concept of religious feeling is not an essential element in the concept of God's function in the universe. 23
Alfred N. Whitehead

The idea of a universal and beneficent Creator does not seem to arise in the mind of man, until he has been elevated by long-continued culture. 24 *Charles Darwin*

[T]he concept of *God* must be viewed as originally generated and maintained for the purpose ... of furthering the interests of one group of humans at the expense of [another].... Gods are inventions originally developed to extend the notion that some have greater rights than others to design and enforce rules, and that some are more destined to be leaders, others to be followers. 25 *Richard Alexander*

The optimistic conception ... in the all-renewing bosom of the Great Goddess seems ... to have given way to a gloomy pessimistic view of the hereafter. With the retreat of the maternal world and the appearance of the new male gods, the world grew uglier, the ideas of destruction more dominant, and the hope of salvation dimmed. 26 *Sibylle von Cles-Redin*

God

The notion of a high god is more likely to be found in more complex societies, those which have fully accepted control over nature as a high value. 27 *Marilyn French*

[C]ontrol is a degree of inhibition, and a system which is perfectly inhibited is perfectly frozen.... We should rather think of God as the one whose spontaneity is so perfect that it needs no control, whose inside is so harmonious that it requires no conscious scrutiny. 28 *Alan Watts*

God is intelligent, but in what way?... [T]he supreme intelligence does not need to reason. For it there are neither premises nor conclusions; there are not even propositions. It is purely intuitive; it sees equally everything which is and everything which can be. 29

Jean-Jacques Rousseau

[T]he question [arises] of why it is that we and the universe exist. If we find the answer to that, it would be the ultimate triumph of human reason—for then we would know the mind of God. 30 *Stephen Hawking*

God and the World introduce the note of interpretation. They embody the interpretation of the cosmological problem in terms of a fundamental metaphysical doctrine.... 31

Alfred N. Whitehead

God is the ultimate limitation, and His existence is the ultimate irrationality. For no reason can be given for just that limitation which it stands in His nature to impose.... No reason can be given for the nature of God, because that nature is the ground of rationality. 32

Alfred N. Whitehead

As long as there will be an unknown there will be a God.... 33 *Samuel Butler*

Sects and parties have claimed God's favor and power. They have boldly declared that they would accept success or failure as proof of his approval on their doctrines and programme. No one of them ever stood by the test. 34

William Graham Sumner

It is as atheistic to affirm the existence of God as to deny it. 35 *Paul Tillich*

Atheism, rightly understood, is the necessary expression of a spirituality that has accomplished itself and exhausted its religious possibilities, and is declining into the inorganic.... The atheist is unable to experience any difference between the Nature-picture of physics and that of religion.... But *dead* space and *dead* things are the "facts" of physics. 36 *Oswald Spengler*

When ... a man turns away from God, he simply gives himself up to the law of gravity. Then he thinks he can decide and choose, but he is only a thing, a stone that falls. 37

Simone Weil

Accounts of spontaneous ecstacy and conversion characteristically include a preceding period of depression.... [A]ll may be manifestations of the drive-arrest-release sequence in biogenic amine inhibitory systems, releasing temporal lobe limbic, hippocampal-septal hypersynchrony that lasts for long periods of after-discharge. They may all reflect the neurobiological mechanisms underlying transcendence, God in the brain. 38

Arnold Mandell

The Trojan War was directed by hallucinations. And the soldiers ... were noble automatons.... The gods are what we now call hallucinations.... Iliadic man did not have subjectivity as we do; he had no awareness of the world, no internal mind-space to introspect upon.... In fact, the gods take the place of consciousness. 39

Julian Jaynes

That psychological fact which is the greatest power in your system is the god, since it is always the overwhelming psychic factor which is called god. 40 *Carl Jung*

[I]f we decide, under the pressure of facts, in favour of an optimism of unification, we run into the technical necessity of discovering—in addition to the impetus required to push us forward and in addition to the particular objective which should determine our route—the special binder or cement which will associate our lives together, vitally, without diminishing or distorting them. Hence, belief in a supremely attractive centre which has personality. 41

Pierre Teilhard de Chardin

God

If God did not exist, it would be necessary to invent him. 42 *Voltaire*

God is dead. God remains dead. And we have killed him.... Must not we ourselves become gods simply to seem worthy of it? 43
Friedrich Nietzsche

The tragedy of [Nietzsche] is that, because his God died, Nietzsche himself became a god. ... 44 *Carl Jung*

Wherever the spirit of God is extruded from our human calculations, an unconscious substitute takes its place.... They induced that *hubris* of reason which led to Nietzsche's superman and hence to the catastrophe that bears the name of [Nazi] Germany. 45 *Carl Jung*

Rather than the death of God—or, rather, in the wake of that death and in profound correlation with it—what Nietzsche's thought heralds is the end of his murderer.... [N]ew gods, the same gods, are already swelling the future Ocean; man will disappear. 46 *Michel Foucault*

Theologians and philosophers have been saying for a century that God is dead, but what we confront is the possibility that man is dead. 47
Erich Fromm

God, if there is a God, is not dead. He will come back ... when man comes back. 48
Michael Novak

[T]he silence of god entails the disappearance of the very meaning of Western History.... From now on, all that is left is a drab, insipid unfolding of implications, an interplay of forces and mechanisms.... Man is now seeing the very purpose of his struggling being removed from him, as well as every opportunity for a more intense life.... God's absence means the abandonment of the world, but in this world man will discover that he himself is likewise absent. 49 *Jacques Ellul*

They that deny a God destroy man's nobility; for certainly man is of kin to the beasts by his body; and, if he be not of kin to God by his spirit, he is a base and ignoble creature. 50
Francis Bacon

From the moment that man submits God to moral judgment, he kills Him in his own heart. And then what is the basis of morality? 51
Albert Camus

The Existentialist ... thinks it very distressing that God does not exist.... [I]f God does not exist, we find no values or commands to turn to which legitimize our conduct. So, in the bright realm of values, we have no excuse behind us, nor justification before us. We are alone, with no excuses.... 52 *Jean-Paul Sartre*

The courage to be is rooted in the god who appears when God has disappeared in the anxiety of doubt. 53 *Paul Tillich*

In the horizon of archetypes and repetition, the terror of history, when it appeared, could be supported. Since the "invention" of faith, in the Judeo-Christian sense of the word (= for God all is possible), the man who has left the horizon of archetypes and repetition can no longer defend himself against that terror except through the idea of God.... Any other situation of modern man leads, in the end, to despair. 54
Mircea Eliade

God's existence is the guarantee of an ideal order that shall be permanently preserved. 55
William James

[W]e need God in order to save consciousness; not in order to think existence, but in order to live it; not in order to know the why and how of it, but in order to feel the wherefore of it. 56
Miguel de Unamuno

God's life ... sees the one plan fulfilled through all the manifold lives, the single consciousness winning its purpose by virtue of all the ideas, of all the individual selves, and of all the lives.... We have no other dwelling-place but the single unity of the divine consciousness. 57
Josiah Royce

It is God who is the ultimate reason of things, and the knowledge of God is no less the beginning of science than his essence and will are the beginning of beings. 58
Gottfried Wilhelm von Leibniz

God

God is not to be treated as an exception to all metaphysical principles.... He is their chief exemplification.... Viewed as primordial, he is the unlimited conceptual realization of the absolute wealth of potentiality. In this respect, he is not *before* all creation, but *with* all creation. 59 *Alfred N. Whitehead*

God is the goal of evolution. It is God who is the source of the evolutionary force and God who is the destination.... We are growing toward godhood. 60 *M. Scott Peck*

The whole of existence ... presents the spectacle of a ceaseless ascent, an incessant pursuit of that which is higher. Only in God can the desire of created beings ... come to rest. 61 *Anders Nygren*

Man was created to see God. 62 *Saint Anselm*

My secret is that I need God—that I am sick and can no longer make it alone. I need God to help me give, because I no longer seem to be capable of giving; to help me be kind, as I no longer seem capable of kindness; to help me love, as I seem beyond being able to love. 63 *Douglas Coupland*

We do not need God in order that he may teach us the truth of things, or the beauty of them, or in order that He may safeguard morality by a system of penalties and punishments, but in order that He may save us, in order that He may not let us die utterly. 64 *Miguel de Unamuno*

That you need God more than anything, you know at times in your heart. But don't you know that god also needs you.... You need God in order to be, and God needs you for that which is the meaning of your life.... That there are world, man, the human person, you and I, has divine meaning. 65 *Martin Buber*

We and God have business with each other; and in opening ourselves to his influence our deepest destiny is fulfilled. 66 *William James*

Guilt

[T]HE SENSE OF GUILT [is] the most important problem in the development of civilization and ... the price we pay for our advance in civilization is a loss of happiness through the heightening of the sense of guilt. 1 *Sigmund Freud*

Selection ... clearly favored those creatures with a propensity to obey rules, to feel guilty about breaking them, and generally, to control their sexual and aggressive tendencies ... [required] for a successful and cultural animal. 2 *Lionel Tiger & Robin Fox*

Social organization ... is a structure of shared guilt.... Guilt is mitigated by being shared. 3 *Norman O. Brown*

[A]cts that are illegal for the individual ... can be justified if the whole group shares responsibility for them.... If one murders without guilt, and in imitation of the hero ... then it is no longer murder.... [This] allows us to understand more subtly the dynamics of group sadism, the utter equanimity with which groups kill.... The leader takes responsibility for the destructive act, and those who destroy on his command are no longer murderers, but "holy heroes." ... [He] can use their guilt against them, binding them closer to himself ... [keeping] them docile and obedient for further atrocities. 4 *Ernest Becker*

[Sexual] repression ... leads to feelings of guilt.... Feelings of guilt make men easily led. 5 *Irenäus Eibl-Eibesfeldt*

When we control the alleviation of guilt in guilt-prone people we have considerable power over them. 6 *Derek Wright*

Cruelty is especially common among those who have felt guilty and inferior. 7 *Harold D. Lasswell*

Guilt is perhaps the most painful companion of death. 8 *Elizabeth Kübler-Ross*

[T]he sense of guilt is an expression of the conflict due to ambivalence, of the eternal struggle between Eros and the instinct of destruction or death. 9 *Sigmund Freud*

Aggression against those simultaneously loved is guilt. 10 *Norman O. Brown*

[G]uilt is very little more than ... anxiety felt because of the conflict between love and hate. Guilt-sense implies tolerance of ambivalence.... But ambivalence and the tolerance of it ... implies a considerable degree of growth and health. 11 *D. W. Winnicott*

I contend that giving anyone a sense of sin, guilt, or self-blame is the worst possible way to help him be an emotionally sound and adequately socialized individual.... For the toll, in terms of the immense amounts and intense degrees of anxiety and hostility that ensue, is so great as to call into question almost any amount of morality which is thereby achieved. 12 *Albert Ellis*

[M]an's will to find himself guilty and ... his *will* to infect and to poison the fundamental basis of the universe with the problem of punishment and guilt.... [:] Here is *disease*, indubitably the most ghastly disease that has as yet played havoc among men.... 13
Friedrich Nietzsche

The more sinful and guilty a person tends to feel, the less chance there is that he will be a happy, healthy or law-abiding citizen. His sense of sin will literally drive him away from not doing wrong and toward doing it.... Blaming, in all its insidious ramifications, is the essence of virtually all emotional disturbances. 14
Albert Ellis

[N]eoconservatives have set themselves against ... sentimental humanitarianism and guilt.... Guilt is assumed to be bad.... More important, whatever responses the neoconservative critic judges to be self-abnegating or excessive are interpreted as "guilt." Oddly enough, such a strategy appears to be aimed at making people feel guilty about feeling guilty. 15 *Peter Steinfels*

The savage ... at least performed penance after murder to allay his sense of guilt. But the modern civilized killer does not share this sense of guilt with his savage predecessor—not because he has shed all moral scruples, but because his public morality is too sharply divided from his private. 16 *Philip Rieff*

[N]othing is gained by using the word *guilt*.... For the time being, we do not know of any better solution. But this does not alter the fact that the need to commit murder is the outcome of a tragic childhood.... 17 *Alice Miller*

All true guilt ... is aroused by ... conflict with the inner representation of an integrated parental figure.... [It implies] an injury to, a betrayal of, or a failure to protect, the peoples or values that symbolize their good internal objects. 18
R. E. Money-Kyrle

The humanistic-flexible and conventional-rigid groups appear to be two variants of an internalized conscience.... [T]he humanistic-flexible subjects ... experience guilt primarily as a direct result of harmful consequences of their behavior for others.... The conventional-rigid subjects, on the other hand, are more likely to give a religious or legal basis for their moral judgments.... [Their] guilt stems less from the amount of harm actually done to others than from an awareness of unacceptable impulses.... 19 *M. L. Hoffman*

[S]elf-righteousness ... so often hides guilt feelings. 20 *Anna Freud*

Females were much more likely than males to report guilt following transgression.... In contrast, moral transgressions were associated to a greater degree with fear of detection and punishment in males than in females. 21 *Ervin Staub*

Men ... are more strongly inclined to deny and repress their guilt feelings ... for which aggression is often the source.... 22
Margarete Mitscherlich

[A] great part of the sense of guilt must normally remain unconscious, because the origin of conscience is closely connected with the Oedipus complex which belongs to the unconscious. 23 *Sigmund Freud*

Only pure narcissistic megalomania can banish guilt. 24 *Ernest Becker*

Guilt

As a type, the "guiltless man" seems to have one common attribute: He is without empathy.... His spirit is not extended to others. 25
Joseph A. Amato

Guilt ... resides in the perennial human tasks of weighing one's interests against those of others; of assessing one's loyalties to parents, spouse, children; and of forever being forced to choose between the practical way and the honorable way. 26 *Joseph A. Amato*

Guilt is a chain that binds one person to another out of the impossibility of separateness. 27
Luise Eichenbaum & Susie Orbach

I am guilty when ... I look at the Other, because by the very fact of my own self-assertion I constitute him as an object and as an instrument, and I cause him to experience that same alienation which he must now assume. 28
Jean-Paul Sartre

The basic idea involved in guilt ... is that of the boundary, or limit, which is *transgressed*.... The focus of guilt ... is on the creation, maintenance, and repair of boundaries, within society and within ourselves. 29 *Roger W. Smith*

Existential guilt occurs when someone injures an order of the human world whose foundations he knows and recognizes as those of his own existence and of all common human existence. 30 *Martin Buber*

The atom bomb sets us into conflict with the symbolic mother ... *mother* nature.... No wonder Western man shows signs of bearing—in some buried depth—a great quantity of guilt! 31
Rollo May

Guilt ... is our richest and most hidden resource, the essence of humanness.... What happens once culture fails to connect the individual to his fellowmen in a way that will allow his guilt expression, to be worked through, and out, in the social arena? Is it simply that guilt turns inward and overwhelms its victims with depression? Are we to be members of an ever-more indifferent and listless population? 32
John Carroll

Guilt is a reflection of [man's] ... not being able to securely place himself in an eternal meaning system. 33 *Ernest Becker*

Being-guilty ... becomes possible only "on the basis" of a primordial Being-guilty.... This means that *Dasein as such is guilty*.... Wanting-to-have-a-conscience resolves upon this Being-guilty.... By "resoluteness" we mean "letting oneself be called forth to one's ownmost *Being*-guilty." 34 *Martin Heidegger*

Metaphysical guilt is the lack of absolute solidarity with the human being as such.... 35
Karl Jaspers

The punishment for inauthenticity are feelings of guilt. 36 *C. Hall & G. Lindzey*

Guilt can teach ... how utterly a man can be alienated from the very sources of his being. But the recognition may point the way to a reunion and a reconciliation. 37 *J. Glenn Gray*

Guilt threatens either when it predominates in its disintegrating potential or when its absence permits inwardly unchallenged destructiveness. In its relationship to vitality no less than to death imagery, the experience of guilt is central to ... the balancing functions of the human mind. 38 *Robert Jay Lifton*

[G]uilt ... is necessary in order to actualize the potentialities which are in man. 39
D. MacKenzie Brown

True guilt is guilt at the obligation one owes to oneself to be oneself, to actualize oneself. False guilt is guilt at not being what other people feel one ought to be.... 40 *R. D. Laing*

[F]inding the true self is intimately tied up with the overcoming of guilt and death. 41
Merold Westphal

Our conscience is the call to ourselves.... Having the courage to be as ourselves we become guilty, and we are asked to take this existential guilt upon ourselves. Meaninglessness in all its aspects can be faced only by those who resolutely take the anxiety of finitude and guilt upon themselves. 42 *Paul Tillich*

The courage to take the anxiety of the demonic upon oneself in spite of its destructive and often despairing character was the form in which the anxiety of guilt was conquered. But this was only possible because the personal quality of evil had been ... replaced by cosmic evil, which is structural and not a matter of personal responsibility. The courage to take the anxiety of guilt upon oneself has become the courage to affirm the demonic trends within oneself. This could happen because the demonic was not considered unambiguously negative but was thought to be part of the creative power of being. 43 *Paul Tillich*

And the fact that guilt is collective must not actuate me to throw mine upon the shoulders of others, but rather to take upon myself the burden of the guilt of others, the guilt of all men; not to merge and sink my guilt in the total mass of guilt, but to make this total guilt my own; not to dismiss and banish my own guilt, but to open the doors of my heart to the guilt of all men, to centre it within myself and appropriate it to myself. 44 *Miguel de Unamuno*

The root of the guilt problem lies in human nature itself, in our failure as human beings to live in accordance with our potentialities and our vision of the good.... If guilt is not experienced deeply enough to cut into us, our future may well be lost. 45 *J. Glenn Gray*

HAPPINESS

HAPPINESS IS THE ONLY sanction of life; where happiness fails, existence remains a mad and lamentable experiment. 1 *George Santayana*

The notion that human beings have a right to be happy is a peculiarly modern, Western idea. In societies of great poverty, rigid hierarchy, or strong religious passions, psychic gratification can have little meaning as an end in itself. 2 *Richard Sennett*

America is a happiness society even more than it is a freedom society or a power society. The underlying strivings may be toward success, acquisitiveness, or power, toward prestige or security. But what validates these strivings for the American is the idea that he has a natural right to happiness. 3 *Max Lerner*

No one has a right to happiness. 4 *Eric Hoffer*

We have no more right to consume happiness without producing it than to consume wealth without producing it. 5 *George Bernard Shaw*

Happiness is that state of consciousness which proceeds from the achievement of one's values.... The Objectivist ethics holds man's life as the *standard* of value—and *his own life* as the ethical purpose of every individual man.... To live for his own sake means that *the achievement of his own happiness is man's highest moral purpose.* 6 *Ayn Rand*

Man, from the very constitution of his nature, prefers his own happiness to that of all other sentient beings put together. 7 *Jeremy Bentham*

A happiness that is sought for ourselves alone can never be found: for a happiness that is diminished by being shared is not big enough to make us happy. 8 *Thomas Merton*

An exclusive desire for happiness is the surest way to prevent happiness from coming into being. Happiness has a way of "sneaking up" on persons when they are preoccupied with other things; but when persons deliberately and single-mindedly set off in pursuit of happiness, it vanishes utterly from sight and cannot be captured. This is the famous "paradox of hedonism." ... 9 *Joel Feinberg*

Happiness ... can exist only in *acceptance*, and succumbs as soon as it is laid claim to. For it appertains to being, not to having.... 10 *Denis de Rougemont*

[H]appiness consists in man's being able to preserve his being. 11 *Baruch Spinoza*

Whoever supposes that ... the superior being, in anything like equal circumstances, is not happier than the inferior—confounds the two very different ideas of happiness.... [A] highly endowed being will always feel that any happiness which he can look for, as the world is

HAPPINESS

constituted, is imperfect.... It is better to be a human being dissatisfied than a pig satisfied; better to be Socrates dissatisfied than a fool satisfied. 12 *John Stuart Mill*

A life without much happiness can be a meaningful one.... 13 *Irving Singer*

There is in man a Higher [goal] than Love of Happiness: he can do without happiness, and instead thereof find Blessedness. Was it not to preach forth this same Higher that sages and martyrs, the Poet and the Priest, in all times, have spoken and suffered, bearing testimony ... of the Godlike that is in Man, and in the Godlike only has he Strength and Freedom.... Love not Pleasure, love God. 14 *Thomas Carlyle*

Happiness ... is a problem of the economics of the individual libido. 15 *Sigmund Freud*

No matter how acute the happiness they give, the pleasures of the flesh are ephemeral; they cannot be accumulated in the form of any kind of capital. 16 *Hans Selye*

As pleasure accompanies the normal exercise of intermittent functions, it is indeed an element of happiness.... But it is not happiness.... In short, what happiness expresses is not the momentary state of a particular function, but the health of physical and moral life in its entirety.... [H]appiness resides in permanent dispositions. 17 *Émile Durkheim*

Happiness arises from the harmonious operation of all the sentiments of a well-organized and unified personality.... Hence the richer, the more highly developed, the more completely unified or integrated is the personality, the more capable it is of sustained happiness.... [T]hat the proper end of moral effort is the development of personalities ... [or] the increase of happiness ... we now see to be identical ends. 18 *William McDougall*

The pragmatic ground of impulse to live is happiness. Can I then take my own life because I cannot live happily? No! It is not necessary that whilst I live I should live happily; but it is necessary that so long as I live I should live honourably. 19 *Immanuel Kant*

True happiness for human beings is possible only to those who develop their godlike potentialities to the utmost. 20 *Bertrand Russell*

All sober inquiries after truth, ancient and modern, pagan and Christian, have declared that the happiness of man, as well as his dignity, consists in virtue. 21 *John Adams*

[H]appiness is some kind of activity of the soul in conformity with virtue. 22 *Aristotle*

He is a happy man who in his lifetime deals himself a happy lot. A happy lot is, good inclinations of the soul, good desires, good actions. 23 *Marcus Aurelius*

Happiness is contagious. For this reason its expression is a social service and almost a duty. 24 *René Dubos*

The right and proper end of government in every political community is the greatest happiness of all the individuals of which it is composed, say, in other words, the greatest happiness of the greatest number. 25 *Jeremy Bentham*

[T]he happiness of the human species is the most desirable object for human science to pursue.... 26 *William Godwin*

[I]f we choose as our goal the state of happiness for human beings ... and if we involved all of society in a successful scientific program by which people became happy, we would be locked in a colossal rigidity in which no one would be free to question this goal [and] our scientific operations could not transcend themselves to question their guiding purposes. 27 *Carl Rogers*

[O]f all political ideals, that of making the people happy is perhaps the most dangerous one. It leads invariably to the attempt to impose our scale of "higher" values upon others, in order to make them realize what seems to us of greatest importance for their happiness; in order, as it were, to save their souls. It leads to Utopianism.... [But] the attempt to make heaven on earth invariably produces hell. 28 *Karl Popper*

Happiness

"God isn't compatible with machinery and scientific medicine and universal happiness. You must make your choice." 29 *Aldous Huxley*

The ideals which have always shone before me and filled me with the joy of living are goodness, beauty, and truth. To make a goal of comfort and happiness has never appealed to me; a system of ethics built on this basis would be sufficient only for a herd of cattle. 30
Albert Einstein

The happy man inevitably confines himself within ancient limits.... The world owes all its onward impulses to men ill at ease. 31
Nathaniel Hawthorne

"Happiness is possible only to a rational man, the man who desires nothing but rational goals, seeking nothing but rational values and finds his joy in nothing but rational actions." 32 *Ayn Rand*

Happiness is hidden from a free and casual will; it belongs rather to one chastened by a long education and unfolded in an atmosphere of sacred and perfected institutions. It is discipline that renders men rational and capable of happiness, by suppressing without hatred what needs to be suppressed to attain a beautiful naturalness. 33 *George Santayana*

To the man actively happy, from whatever cause, evil simply cannot there and then be believed in. 34 *William James*

The matricentric world was one of sharing, of community bound by friendship and love, of emotional centeredness in home and people, all of which led to happiness. The patriarchal world gave higher regard to the individual than to the community, to ownership of property than to sharing, to competition and rivalry than to friendship, to wandering and isolation than to the centrality of home; and it held power rather than love to be its greatest good. But property, competition, homelessness, and isolation cannot lead to happiness. Patriarchal myths almost forbid happiness to men. 35
Marilyn French

[T]he common disappointments of capitalism and socialism with regard to the achievement of "happiness" can ... be traced to the presence of scientific technology and the industrial civilization that is built upon it.... [Both overvalue] efficiency, with its tendency to subordinate the optimum human scale of things to the optimum technical scale. 36
Robert Heilbroner

Happiness ... *still* has no cultural value. 37
Theodore Roszak

Money and power interests are substitutes for happiness.... 38 *Wilhelm Reich*

Happiness means that the consciousness of power and triumph has begun to prevail. 39
Friedrich Nietzsche

It is the total *pattern* of responses that is adaptive.... The lesson for man is that personal happiness has very little to do with all this. It is possible to be unhappy and very adaptive. 40
E. O. Wilson

Inner happiness and serviceability do not always agree. What immediately feels most "good" is not always most "true," when measured by the verdict of the rest of experience. 41
William James

The problem of happiness becomes important only when attention is shifted from the purely biological aspects of life to the far different problems of human values. 42 *René Dubos*

Everybody in the world is seeking happiness—and there is one sure way to find it. That is by controlling your thoughts. Happiness doesn't depend on outward conditions. It depends on inner conditions. 43 *Dale Carnegie*

Obviously, in the realm of the Happy Consciousness, guilt feeling has no place. 44
Herbert Marcuse

Happiness is the indication that man has found the answer to the problem of human existence: the productive realization of his potentialities and thus, simultaneously, being one with the world and preserving the integrity of his self. 45 *Erich Fromm*

Happiness

The happiest man is he who is able to integrate the end of his life with its beginning. 46
Goethe

Happiness is the glow that attends the integration of the person while pursuing or contemplating the attainment of goals. 47
Gordon W. Allport

The happiest excitement in life is to be convinced that one is fighting for all one is worth on behalf of some clearly seen and deeply felt good.... 48 *Ruth Benedict*

Happiness, if it is to have any depth and solidity, demands a life built round some central purpose of a kind demanding continuous activity and permitting of progressively increasing success. 49 *Bertrand Russell*

The secret of happiness is this: let your interests be as wide as possible, and let your reactions to the things and persons that interest you be as far as possible friendly rather than hostile. 50 *Bertrand Russell*

Remember this, that very little is needed to make a happy life. 51 *Marcus Aurelius*

I doubt that Western men can be persuaded again to the Greek opinion that the secret of happiness is to have as few needs as possible. The philosophers of therapeutic deprivation are disposed to eat well when they are not preaching. 52 *Philip Rieff*

Perfect happiness, the oceanic feeling of complete harmony between inner and outer worlds, is only transiently possible. Man is constantly in search of happiness but, by his very nature, is precluded from finally or permanently achieving it.... 53 *Anthony Storr*

[I]s it true that the happiness of the individual increases as man advances? Nothing is more doubtful. 54 *Émile Durkheim*

The goal towards which the pleasure-principle impels us—of becoming happy—is not attainable; yet we may not—indeed, we cannot—give up the effort.... 55 *Sigmund Freud*

Harmony

[I]t is only when a certain harmony has been achieved in the psyche that spirit can awake.... 1
George Santayana

Accepting that which ... spirit cannot help doing, it may distinguish the direction in which its Good lies. It lies in the direction of harmony; harmony between the Will and its fortunes, and harmony within the subject-matter open to its apprehension. 2
George Santayana

The aim of reaching some kind of harmony with the universe is part of the aim of living in harmony with ourselves. 3 *Thomas Nagel*

The sense of perfect harmony with the universe, of perfect harmony with another person, and of perfect harmony within the self are intimately connected; indeed, I believe them to be essentially the same phenomena. 4
Anthony Storr

[C]ivilization is nothing other than the unremitting aim at the major perfections of harmony. 5 *Alfred N. Whitehead*

[T]he image of the world clock produced the impression of "most sublime harmony." It was the first intimation of a possible solution of the devastating conflict between matter and spirit, between the desires of the flesh and the love of God. 6 *Carl Jung*

[T]here are always two methods of securing harmony: one is to unify all the given elements, and another is to reject and expunge all the elements that refuse to be unified. Unity by inclusion gives us the beautiful; unity by exclusion ... gives us the sublime.... The one identifies us with the world, the other raises us above it. 7 *George Santayana*

If a man's life is to be satisfactory ... it requires two kinds of harmony; an internal harmony of intelligence, emotion, and will, and an external harmony with the wills of others. In both these respects, existing education is defective. 8 *Bertrand Russell*

Harmony

Sustainable development requires changes in values and attitudes ... that would stress individual and joint responsibility towards the environment and towards nurturing harmony between humanity and environment. 9

World Commission on Environment & Development

Achieving a sustainable society will not be possible without a massive reordering of priorities.... [T]he value changes that lead to a more harmonious relationship with nature may also lead to a more harmonious relationship with each other. 10 *Lester Brown*

[M]en tend either to attempt to gain an advantage over others (e.g. they are exploitative ...) or to distribute rewards as a function of quality of performance. Women favor equality, perhaps because they seek "harmonious relations." 11 *Ervin Staub*

The concept of harmony is one of the keys to the feminine universe.... 12 *Simone de Beauvoir*

We could say that New Age people in general are addicted to harmony. The alchemical woodcut says that a child will not become an adult until it breaks the addiction to harmony ... and enters into a joyful participation in the tensions of the world. 13 *Robert Bly*

If ... the unity of life is to be found solely in the impulse that pushes it along the road of time, the harmony is not in front, but behind.... So the discord between species will go on increasing. 14 *Henri Bergson*

Harmony, or rather "complementarity," is revealed only in the mass, in tendencies rather than in states.... I mean that the original impetus is a *common* impetus, and the higher we ascend the stream of life the more do diverse tendencies appear.... Harmony, therefore, does not exist in fact; it exists rather in principle.... 15

Henri Bergson

The whole self is an ideal, an imaginative projection. Hence the ideal of a thoroughgoing and deep-seated harmonizing of the self with the universe operates only through imagination. 16

John Dewey

How at once the objective world conforms itself to ideas in us, and ideas in us conform themselves to the objective world, it is impossible to conceive, unless there exists, between the two worlds—the ideal and the real—a preestablished harmony. But this preestablished harmony itself is not conceivable, unless the activity, whereby the objective world is produced, is originally identical with that which displays itself in volition, and *vice versa*.... [If] the two activities are only one in principle ... [then] this preestablished harmony is a reality, and the contradiction is solved. 17 *F. W. Schelling*

All nature is but art, unknown to thee;
All chance, direction, which thou canst not see;
All discord, harmony, not understood.... 18

Alexander Pope

A man's nature is in harmony with itself when he desires to be nothing but what he is.... 19

Arthur Schopenhauer

[T]he satisfaction of an impulse can be called good only if it can be related in terms of inner consistency with a total harmony of impulses. 20

Reinhold Niebuhr

[The] reasonable harmony of being ... is the primary article of metaphysical doctrine. It means that for things to be together involves that they are reasonably together. 21

Alfred N. Whitehead

[T]he meaning of life for a person can reside only in his attainment of the greatest possible harmony with his human environment and with the universe. 22 *Josef Rattner*

[A]gape, unlike justice, arises out of a ... notion of the ideal unity of people with each other and with God or Nature ... in which the interests of the self and the other are no longer seen as antagonistic but as being in profound harmony. 23 *Lawrence Kohlberg*

We feel ourselves urged by duty to strive after a universal highest end ... [and] it is only in so far as we strive after this end that we can judge ourselves to be in harmony with the final purpose of an intelligent cosmic cause—if such there be. 24 *Immanuel Kant*

Harmony

Perhaps the human species is just a ghastly biological blunder, having evolved beyond a point at which it can thrive in harmony with itself and the world around it. That must be a possibility. 25 *Richard E. Leakey*

~ Hate ~

Hate is a Sadness, accompanied by the idea of an external cause. 1 *Baruch Spinoza*

Hate, as a relation to objects, is older than love. It derives from the narcissistic ego's primordial repudiation of the external world.... [It] always remains in an intimate relation with the self-preservative instincts ... [reflecting] the ego's struggle to preserve and maintain itself. 2
Sigmund Freud

In time we hate that which we often fear. 3
William Shakespeare

It is normal to hate what we fear, and it happens frequently that we fear what we hate.... 4
Bertrand Russell

One cannot defeat the enemy without learning to hate him with every fiber of one's soul. 5
Joseph Stalin

God willing, the warrior Iranian people will maintain their revolutionary sacred rancor and anger in their hearts and use their oppressor-burning flames against the criminal Soviet Union and the world-devouring U.S. and their surrogates. 6 *Ayatollah Khomeini*

If a people is to become free, it needs pride and will power, defiance, and hate, hate, and once again hate. 7 *Adolf Hitler*

The will to eliminate despised groups is stronger when a population is pervaded with a sense of self-hatred.... 8 *Marilyn French*

The steps are not big from the feeling of worthlessness of one's self to self-hatred to hatred for others. 9 *Rollo May*

Among the frustrated, insecure, inadequate, unsuccessful, hate is deepest and most violent.... Frustrated people require scapegoats. 10
Samuel Tenenbaum

If you hate a person, you hate something in him that is part of yourself. What isn't a part of ourselves doesn't disturb us. 11 *Hermann Hesse*

All hate is self-hate. 12 *A. S. Neill*

The *power and tenacity of self-hate* is astonishing, even for the analyst who is familiar with the way it operates. 13 *Karen Horney*

That hatred springs more from self-contempt than from legitimate grievance is seen in the intimate connection between hatred and a guilty conscience. 14 *Eric Hoffer*

[H]ate is the hate of ... the general principle of the existence of others. The Other whom I hate actually represents all Others. 15
Jean-Paul Sartre

If the world hates you, you know that it hated me before it hated you. 16 *Jesus Christ*

The occasion which arouses hate is simply an act by the Other which puts me in the state of *being subject to* his freedom. This act ... is humiliating as the concrete revelation of my instrumental object-ness in the face of the Other's freedom. 17 *Jean-Paul Sartre*

Hate that is sheer antagonism ... is not an emotion, but is an energy devoted to ruthless destruction. 18 *John Dewey*

The rage and hate of our culture flames across pages and screens, as its artifacts, so dearly bought ... explode one after the other in a great triumphal rite of destruction. 19 *Marilyn French*

Instead of investing in building and developing the region, the arms race, military buildups, wars, destruction and devastation bleed the region of its main resources. The tremendous arms budget swallows all profits. The desert is spreading and the water sources are dwindling. A vicious cycle is created.... The solution to breaking this vicious cycle is clear: Crush the barriers of hatred. 20
Shimon Peres

Hate

The stockpiling of nuclear weapons is only a symbol of bottled-up feelings of hatred and of the accompanying inability to perceive and articulate genuine human needs. 21 *Alice Miller*

Man's slavery is his slavery to hate.... The fight is an unequal one, for the haters control education, religion, the law, the armies, and the vile prisons. 22 *A. S. Neill*

Whoever cannot hate is not a man, and history is made by men. 23 *Oswald Spengler*

All men naturally hate each other. 24
Blaise Pascal

Sons who grow up ... watching their fathers beat their mothers ... learn early to hate. 25
Marilyn French

[H]atred ... grows up in many lives as a consequence of blocked self-esteem and blocked affiliation.... Unless one first loves, one cannot hate, for hatred is an emotion of protest.... 26
Gordon W. Allport

Hate is love that has been changed to the other side of the coin—by thwarting. 27 *A. S. Neill*

Although no one ever dies of lack of sex, thwarted or unrequited love turns into hate. 28
Helen B. Lewis

[N]ot only [is] it that in human relationships hate is frequently a forerunner of love, but also that in many circumstances hate changes into love and love into hate. 29 *Sigmund Freud*

Poet and psychoanalyst alike have long known how close love and hate are.... [I]n every case of genuine love there is such a high measure of latent aggression, normally obscured by the bond, that on the rupturing of this bond the horrible phenomenon known as hate makes its appearance. There is no love without aggression, but there is no hate without love! 30
Konrad Lorenz

[T]here is need in every society for hate satisfaction. But unless there are some forms of hating which are socially approved and justified, everyone will remain in an intolerable conflict situation, and neuroticism will be endemic in the population. 31 *Clyde Kluckhohm*

Hating or resenting is often the person's only way to keep from committing psychological or spiritual suicide. It has the function of preserving some dignity, some ... identity. 32
Rollo May

Hate ... is a perfect, if temporary, antidote for panic. The more destructive ... the more useful hate is for plugging up the gaping emptiness and the better it harnesses panic and dread.... When rational thinking, self-examination, and moral considerations are present, hate never is. 33 *Reuven Bar-Levav*

Hatred remains blind by its very nature; one can hate only part of a being. Whoever sees a whole being and must reject it, is no longer in the dominion of hatred. 34 *Martin Buber*

Hate can never be good. We strive to destroy the man we hate, i.e., we strive for something that is evil. 35 *Baruch Spinoza*

Love impels to being, hate to nonbeing. Love grows in bond with transcendence; hate, severed from transcendence, dwindles into the abstract punctuality of the ego. 36
Karl Jaspers

Nothing corrupts our soul more surely and more subtly than the consciousness of others who fear and hate us. 37 *J. Glenn Gray*

When you hate you generate a reciprocal hate.... The only thing that will redeem mankind is co-operation, and the first step toward co-operation lies in the hearts of individuals. 38
Bertrand Russell

[H]ate is of all qualities the most cancer-like to its possessor. It leads us to develop in ourselves the character we condemn in others. 39
Harold Laski

Love makes a man better, hate makes him worse.... 40 *Carl Jung*

Don't hate other people because hatred destroys yourself. 41 *Richard M. Nixon*

HUMANITY

HUMANITY

MAN IS A SYNTHESIS of the infinite and the finite, of the temporal and the eternal, of freedom and necessity.... 1 *Søren Kierkegaard*

[W]hat is man in nature? A Nothing in comparison with the Infinite, an All in comparison with the Nothing, a mean between nothing and everything. Since he is infinitely removed from comprehending the extremes, the end of things and their beginning are hopelessly hidden from him in an impenetrable secret; he is equally incapable of seeing the Nothing from which he was made, and the Infinite in which he is swallowed up. 2 *Blaise Pascal*

The significance of man is that he is that part of the universe that asks the question, What is the significance of Man?... The significance of man is that he is insignificant and is aware of it. 3
Carl Becker

Pitiful, indeed may seem the lot of Man whose little days end in a black night of nothingness; yet though humanity may mean so little in the scheme of things, it is weak, human hands ... that draw forth images whose aloofness or communion alike bear witness to the dignity of Man.... 4 *André Malraux*

[M]an is the only creature in the world to whom we owe respect.... [His] noble actions, works of art or science, serve no material need, but demand, on the contrary, material sacrifices.... And it is because man is capable of such sacrifice that he himself demands to be respected.... 5 *Michael Polanyi*

Respect for man, as man, is the foundation of every noble sentiment. 6 *Mary Wollstonecraft*

Man is the measure of all things. 7 *Protagoras*

Mankind is to be thought of not as something that possesses a certain worth ... but as the inexhaustible source of all the possible forms of worth, which has no existence or meaning without human life. Mankind is not, in the ancient phrase, the measure of all things; he is the measurer, and is himself measureless. 8 *Jonathan Schell*

So act as to treat humanity, whether in your own person or in that of any other, in every case as an end, and never as a means only. 9
Immanuel Kant

Man is an end, not a means. 10
Miguel de Unamuno

[T]here is no human nature.... Man simply is.... Man is nothing else but that which he makes of himself. That is the first principle of existentialism. 11 *Jean-Paul Sartre*

Men have made themselves to no less an extent than they have made the races of their domestic animals, the only difference being that the process has been less conscious or voluntary. 12 *Claude Lévi-Strauss*

[T]he animal merely *uses* its environment.... [M]an by his changes makes it serve his ends, *masters* it. This is the final, essential distinction between man and other animals, and once again it is labour that brings about this distinction. 13 *Friedrich Engels*

Man is a tool-making animal.... Without tools he is nothing; with tools he is all. 14
Thomas Carlyle

Mankind has wandered from the trees to the plains, from the plains to the seacoast, from climate to climate.... When man ceases to wander, he will cease to ascend in the scale of being. Physical wandering is still important, but greater still is the power of man's spiritual adventures—adventures of thought, adventures of passionate feeling, adventures of aesthetic experience. 15 *Alfred N. Whitehead*

The manner in which the spirit is united to the body cannot be understood by man, and yet it is the essence of man. 16 *Saint Augustine*

[T]he spiritual life is part of our biological life. It is the "highest" part of it, but yet part of it.... But this higher, spiritual "animality" ... can become widely actualized *only* in a culture which approves of human nature, and therefore actively fosters its fullest growth. 17
Abraham Maslow

Humanity

The basis of man's life with man is twofold ... [:] the wish of every man to be confirmed as what he is, even as what he can become, by men; and the innate capacity in man to confirm his fellow-men in this way. That this capacity lies so immeasurably fallow constitutes the real weakness and questionableness of the human race: actual humanity exists only where this capacity unfolds. 18 *Martin Buber*

[T]he individual human being ... is defined by the problems he confronts ... problems that arise from his unique biological and emotional needs. The human individual is in a constant state of becoming. The maintenance of that state, of his humanity, indeed, of his survival, depends crucially on his seeing himself, and on his being seen by other human beings, as a human being. No computer can be made to confront genuine human problems in human terms. 19 *Joseph Weizenbaum*

"[M]an" is a panhuman enterprise, in a continual process of becoming.... Man *is* society, and history. 20 *Ernest Becker*

To be a man is to have a history: this means, then, that the human is a vast brotherhood, and that it is both perilous and pretentious when a man sets himself against it or apart from it. 21 *Lloyd J. Averill*

The humanistic view of rational man ... proceeds on the fundamental premise that reason and intellect have the inherent power to control destiny.... [But] we are, by nature, rather selfish, xenophobic, regressive, and pleasure loving creatures who possess the potential for the most wicked and vile acts, and the most lofty and inspiring ones.... And to channel and mold this unpredictability into full personhood is a task too great for any single individual. 22 *Kent G. Bailey*

It is the humanity, not the individuality, of the person which is at stake. 23 *Cosmas Desmond*

[T]he course of human development ... consists in educing, more and more, the characteristic features of humanity ... [which] can come into play only in that advanced state of social life for which they are exclusively destined. 24 *Auguste Comte*

Humanism cannot only mean destroying God; its chief job is to understand and save man. But man can neither be understood nor saved alone. 25 *Mary Midgley*

We are now in the middle of a long process of transition in the nature of the image which man has of himself.... 26 *Kenneth Boulding*

At the heart of everything is what we shall call a change of consciousness.... America is dealing death.... [T]oday's emerging consciousness seeks a new knowledge of what it means to be human ... in order that man once more can become a creative force ... giving life back to his society. 27 *Charles A. Reich*

Man ... is constitutionally an open system, reacting to another open system, that of nature.... For its effective salvation mankind will need to undergo something like a spontaneous religious conversion: one that will replace the mechanical world picture with an organic world picture, and give to the human personality, as the highest known manifestation of life, the precedence that it now gives to its machines and computers. 28 *Lewis Mumford*

In the nineteenth century the problem was that *God is dead*; in the twentieth century the problem is that *man is dead*. In the nineteenth century inhumanity meant cruelty; in the twentieth century it means schizoid self-alienation. The danger of the past was that men became slaves. The danger of the future is that men may become robots. 29 *Erich Fromm*

Women love the human race; men behave as if they were, on the whole, hostile to it. 30 *Ashley Montagu*

Every man has hated mankind when he was less than a man. 31 *G. K. Chesterton*

Man is a machine.... 32 *B. F. Skinner*

Man is not a machine. 33 *Joseph Weizenbaum*

[T]he best way to conceive of the fundamental project of human reality is to say that man is the being whose project is to be God.... To be

Humanity

man means to reach toward being God. 34
Jean-Paul Sartre

Man is a failed attempt to become God. 35
Jean-Paul Sartre

Far from seeing in man the irrevocable and unsurpassable image of God, I assert … that the long-sought missing link between animals and the really humane being is ourselves! 36
Konrad Lorenz

Man is a rope stretched between the animal and the Superman—a rope over an abyss. 37
Friedrich Nietzsche

I teach you the superman. Man is something to be surpassed. 38 *Friedrich Nietzsche*

Unfortunately, there is no impartial arbiter to decide on the merits of the human race; but for my part, when I consider their poison gases, their researches into bacteriological warfare, their meannesses, cruelties and oppressions, I find them, considered as the crowning gem of creation, somewhat lacking in lustre. 39
Bertrand Russell

Even within the life of our planet man is only a brief interlude.… It is difficult to believe that Omnipotence needed so vast a setting for so small and transitory a result. 40
Bertrand Russell

I cannot think of the present state of humanity as that in which it is destined to remain.… Only insofar as I can regard this state as the means toward a … higher and more perfect state, has it any value in my eyes. 41
Johann Fichte

[W]e have … lost the hope in man, yea, the will to be man. The sight of man now fatigues—what is present-day Nihilism if it is not *that*? We are tired of man. 42 *Friedrich Nietzsche*

The human being may well be beyond redemption. 43 *Peter F. Drucker*

It is comforting … to think that man is only a recent invention, a figure not yet two centuries old, a new wrinkle in our knowledge, and that he will disappear again as soon as that knowledge has discovered a new form. 44
Michel Foucault

It is no longer possible to think in our day other than in the void left by man's disappearance.… To all those who still wish to talk about man, about his reign or his liberation, to all those who still ask themselves questions about what man is in his essence, to all those who wish to take him as their starting point in their attempts to reach the truth … we can only answer with a philosophical laugh—which means, to a certain extent, a silent one. 45 *Michel Foucault*

The disappearance of Man at the end of History … is not a cosmic catastrophe: the natural World remains what it has been from all eternity. And therefore, it is not a biological catastrophe either: Man remains alive as animal in *harmony* with Nature or given Being. What disappears is Man properly so-called—that is, Action negating the given, and Error, or in general, the Subject *opposed* to the Object.… 46
Alexandre Kojève

Man, most fundamentally, is not engaged in the discovery of what is there, nor in production, nor even in communication, nor in invention. He is enabling being to emerge from nonbeing. 47
R. D. Laing

[T]he substance of man is *existence*. 48
Martin Heidegger

Man is the being through whom nothingness comes into the world. 49 *Jean-Paul Sartre*

As far as we can discern, the sole purpose of human existence is to kindle a light in the darkness of mere being. 50 *Carl Jung*

Western man will light his path only by the torch he carries, even if it burns his hands, and what that torch is seeking to throw light on is everything that can enhance the power of Man. 51
André Malraux

The world is human.… Knowledge puts us in the presence of the absolute, and there is a truth of knowledge. But this truth, although releasing to us nothing more and nothing less than

the absolute, remains strictly human. 52
Jean-Paul Sartre

The end of man is to create science, to catalogue the Universe, so that it may be handed back to God in order.... 53
Pierre Teilhard de Chardin

Man is still in his childhood; for he cannot respect an ideal which is not imposed on him against his will, nor can he find satisfaction in a good created by his own action. He is afraid of a universe that leaves him alone. 54
George Santayana

[I]f we banish man ... the universe becomes quiet; silence and might take over.... It is the presence of man that renders natural existence interesting.... Man is the unique end form from which we must begin and to which everything must return. 55 *Denis Diderot*

Man is not adorable, but he adores, and the object of his adoration may be discovered within him and elicited from his own soul. In this sense the religion of humanity is the only religion, all others being sparks and abstracts of the same. 56 *George Santayana*

In no other period of human knowledge has man ever become more problematic to himself than in our own days. We have a scientific, a philosophical, and a theological anthropology that know nothing of each other. Therefore we no longer possess any clear and consistent idea of man. 57 *Max Scheler*

In addition to the science of material things we must develop a science of humanity. 58
René Dubos

The main historical mission of mankind consists in an unbounded creation, accumulation, refinement, and actualization of Truth, Beauty, and Goodness in the nature of man himself, in man's mind, and behavior, in man's sociocultural universe and beyond it, and in man's relationships to all human beings, to all living creatures, and to the total cosmos. By discharching this task man is fulfilling in the best and most faithful way his duty of master creator toward the Supreme Cosmic Creator. 59 *Pitirim Sorokin*

[N]ot only does consciousness appear as the motive principle of evolution, but also, among conscious beings themselves, man comes to occupy a privileged place.... So that, in the last analysis, man might be considered the reason for the existence of the entire organization of life on our planet. 60 *Henri Bergson*

Man is not the centre of the universe as once we thought in our simplicity, but something much more wonderful—the arrow pointing the way to the final unification of the world in terms of life. Man alone constitutes the last-born, the freshest, the most complicated, the most subtle of all the successive layers of life. 61
Pierre Teilhard de Chardin

For man ... is himself a representative sample of the cosmos and embodies its emergent characteristics at their highest point of organization and self-awareness. 62 *Lewis Mumford*

Man, the centre of perspective, is at the same time the *centre of construction* of the universe. And by expediency no less than by necessity, all science must be referred back to him. If to see more is really to become more, if deeper vision is really fuller being, then we should look closely at man in order to increase our capacity to live. 63 *Pierre Teilhard de Chardin*

[O]f probable future inventions that those who have surrendered to the myth of the machine are now so busily propagating ... from lunar landings to weather control, from suspended animation to artificial life, no one of them has the slightest relation to man's central historic task, more imperative today than ever—the task of becoming human. 64
Lewis Mumford

The crucial problems of our civilization are human problems. 65 *Carl Rogers*

My civilization is founded upon the reverence for Man present in all men, in each individual. My civilization has sought through the ages to reveal Man to men.... It is Man that is the essence of our culture.... It is Man who must be restored to his place among men. 66
Antoine de Saint-Exupéry

Humanity

The [primary] obstacle to the achievement of well-being, deeply rooted in the spirit of modern society, is the fact of man's dethronement from his supreme place.... The achievement of well-being is possible only under one condition: *if we put man back into the saddle.* 67
Erich Fromm

This diminishment of the idea of man has been a long time in progress.... The arts with us became aware of a flatness in human life, a loss of depth as though a dimension had somehow dropped from the world—as though our human shadows had deserted us.... And yet we cannot help but wonder why—why the belief in man has foundered; why it has foundered *now*—now at the moment of our greatest intellectual triumphs, our never equalled technological mastery, our electronic miracles. Why was man a wonder to the Greeks ... while now that he knows the whole of modern science he is a wonder to no one. 68 *Archibald MacLeish*

What is demanded of us now ... is a second humanism that will free us from our new paralysis of soul.... [A] belief in man—a return to a belief in man—is the reality on which a new age can be built. 69 *Archibald MacLeish*

The wise man believes in the future because he has put his faith in humanity. 70
Ashley Montagu

The only alternative to despair is faith in *man....* 71 *Karl Jaspers*

Hypocrisy

The most fearful evil in the world is hypocrisy. 1
Leo Tolstoy

For neither man nor angel can discern Hypocrisy, the only evil that walks Invisible, except to God alone. 2 *John Milton*

Take good care not to practice your righteousness in front of men in order to be observed by them.... Hence when you go making gifts of mercy, do not blow a trumpet ahead of you, just as the hypocrites do ... that they may be glorified by men.... Also when you pray, you must not be as the hypocrites; because they like to pray standing in the synagogues and on the corners of the broad ways to be visible to men.... You, however, when you pray, go into your private room and, after shutting your door, pray to your Father who is in secret; then your Father who looks on in secret will repay you. 3 *Jesus Christ*

[H]e is guilty of "an inner lie" to whom the moral law is an inconvenient chain but who yet pretends to himself and to his God that he loves the moral law.... But the man who has the name of God always on his lips, when God is to him not the sacred author of an ethical code which embraces the whole spirit-world, but an arbitrary and capricious tyrant whose favour he attempts to gain by flattery—this man is guilty of an "external lie" ... [and he] insults the dignity of man in his own person. 4
Immanuel Kant

Great hypocrites are the true atheists. 5
Francis Bacon

[The word] "hypocrite" is a morally loaded term.... [T]he peculiarity of hypocrisy lies in the fact that the hypocrite is condemned by reference to his own avowed standards of proper conduct.... [T]he hypocrite is, as it were, self-condemned either from his own mouth or from his own heart. 6
Bela Szabados

[O]nly the hypocrite is really rotten to the core. 7
Hannah Arendt

The true hypocrite is the one who ceases to perceive his deception, the one who lies with sincerity. 8 *André Gide*

[S]elf-aware hypocrites may be unusually morally sensitive ... [whereas] self-deceiving hypocrites may be diabolical. 9 *Mike W. Martin*

[H]ypocrisy is an unvarying element in the moral life of all human beings. It is ... the device by which the lesser self gains the consent of the larger self to indulge in impulses and ventures which the rational self can approve only when disguised.... [H]ypocrisy is both a tribute to the growing rationality of man and a proof of the ease with which rational demands may be circumvented. 10 *Reinhold Niebuhr*

Hypocrisy is a tribute that vice pays to virtue. 11
François de la Rochefoucauld

The choice is not really between a society of vice or virtue—we will never have the latter. The choice is between a society of hypocrisy or cynicism. The cynic does not admit to doing wrong. The hypocrite has the saving grace of paying homage to virtue by at least publicly acknowledging its sovereignty. 12
Charles Krauthammer

[B]efore we condemn political hypocrisy, let us remember that ... the acting of the part of someone better than oneself may actually commit one to a course of behavior perceptibly less evil than what would be normal and natural in an avowed cynic. 13 *Aldous Huxley*

Idealists ... abominate what they call hypocrisy. But hypocrisy—the insincere profession of unfulfilled ideals—is the means by which the influence of ideals is extended beyond the small circles of true believers. Hypocrisy is indeed the tribute paid by vice to virtue.... Hypocrisy might also be described as manners or exalted as civilization ... : the means by which we at once protect one another from the rough edges of a perennial social struggle and indicate our hopes for something else. Hypocrisy can make us better than we are. 14 *George Gilder*

In all Civil Societies Men are taught insensibly to be Hypocrites from their Cradle.... [I]t is impossible we could be sociable Creatures without Hypocrisy. 15 *Bernard Mandeville*

[It is] a debateable point whether a certain degree of cultural hypocrisy is not indispensable for the maintenance of civilization. 16
Sigmund Freud

A wise ruler ... cannot and should not keep his word when such an observance of faith would be to his disadvantage.... But it is necessary to know how to disguise this nature well and to be a great hypocrite and a liar ... for in order to maintain the state he is often obliged to act against his promise, against charity, against humanity.... [H]e should know how to enter into evil when necessity commands. 17
Niccolò Machiavelli

Perhaps the most significant moral characteristic of a nation is its hypocrisy. 18
Reinhold Niebuhr

My own experience tells me that most nations make decisions in the name of self-interest, and then explain their decisions in terms of morality. 19 *Abba Eban*

A censored press only serves to demoralize. That greatest of vices, hypocrisy, is inseparable from it.... The government only hears its own voice while all the time deceiving itself.... 20
Karl Marx

One of the most ominous developments in recent American history has been the decline in the U.S. government's respect for the institutions of international law.... [The] present [Reagan] administration came into power on a wave of promises to restore respect for law and order.... [We] are faced with a form of hypocrisy bordering on schizophrenia. 21 *Harvey Cox*

If you are extraordinarily high-minded in your political pronouncements, you are bound in the nature of things to be more than ordinarily hypocritical. But it is only in the last half century or so that high-minded hypocrisy has completely driven statesmanlike reasonableness out of the American political forum. 22
Irving Kristol

American moral standards have had to fight a difficult battle against the mounting hypocrisy of institutions. If the knowledge of this hypocrisy spreads it may produce a feeling of hopelessness about enforcing the codes in the case of the top power elite. Where this hopelessness exists, morality is hard to inculcate. 23 *Max Lerner*

[O]ne of the chief sources of cultural paranoia is the everwidening rift between the beliefs of the people and their actual behavior, and the tacit assumption among these same people that this duplicity ... is a normal state of affairs.... Hypocrisy is accepted as a normal property of life.... 24 *Lionel Rubinoff*

Hypocrisy

Our collective sense of guilt comes from a general awareness that our praise of human and natural values is hypocrisy as long as we practice social indifference and convert our land into a gigantic dump. 25 *René Dubos*

The very accusation of hypocrisy is a direct product of the freedom that western man alone has achieved. But there has been a sea change.… At the present time, the same accusation is nothing but an attempt at self-justification, an excuse for abandoning principles. 26 *Jacques Ellul*

Hypocrisy is a condition of the ego brought about by the use of the brain for the subjective repression of truth instead of its recognition.… Hypocrisy is the most vicious mechanism of which the brain is capable.… The chief hypocrites of A.D. 30 were the businessmen and they are still tops. 27 *Philip Wylie*

The moral attitudes of dominant and privileged groups are characterized by universal self-deception and hypocrisy.… The most common form of hypocrisy among the privileged classes is to assume that their privileges are the just payments with which society rewards specially useful or meritorious functions. 28 *Reinhold Niebuhr*

Every man alone is sincere. At the entrance of a second person, hypocrisy begins. 29 *Ralph Waldo Emerson*

The best defence against hypocrisy is love.… 30 *Søren Kierkegaard*

Ideals

A man becomes truly Man only when in quest of what is most exalted in him. 1 *André Malraux*

How necessary it is to keep realizing that idealism does not represent a superfluous expression of emotion, but that in truth it has been, is, and will be, the premise for what we designate as human culture, yes, that it alone created the concept of "man." 2 *Adolf Hitler*

All men are "idealists." … Indeed, there is no more powerful source of energy in man. 3 *Erich Fromm*

Our ultimate allegiance is always to the ideal. … 4 *Harold Laski*

[T]here can be no moral allegiance except to the ideal. 5 *George Santayana*

We need to clarify our ideals, and enliven our vision of perfection. No atheism is so terrible as the absence of an ultimate ideal … or more incompatible with healthy life. 6 *George Santayana*

For most there is virtually no experience—not even a highly pleasurable one—that will seem meaningful unless it can be justified in terms of an ideal one has chosen. 7 *Irving Singer*

[T]he essence of the psychoanalytic cure resides in a patient's newly acquired ability to identify and seek out appropriate selfobjects—both mirroring and idealizable … and to be sustained by them.… [W]e must be in possession of … core ideals and goals … in order to seek out idealizable selfobjects and be enlivened by the enthusiasm we feel for them. 8 *Heinz Kohut*

Growth motives … maintain tension in the interest of distant and often unattainable goals. As such they distinguish human from animal becoming.… By growth motives we refer to the hold that ideals gain upon the process of development. 9 *Gordon W. Allport*

[I]t is a biologic law that—like all lower animals—man has to fight and work for some goal that he considers worthwhile. He must use his innate capacities to enjoy the eustress of fulfilment.… [Thus] the greatest problem of our time is not atmospheric pollution, nor overpopulation, nor even the atomic bomb, but the lack of motivation by generally acceptable and respected ideals. 10 *Hans Selye*

The death of a culture begins when its normative institutions fail to communicate ideals in ways that remain inwardly compelling, first of all to the cultural elites themselves. 11 *Philip Rieff*

Ideals

Our world is being drained of its ideal content.... 12 *Irving Kristol*

The shock and uncertainty so characteristic of the present marks the discovery that ... ideals themselves are undermined.... The result is disillusionment about all comprehensive and positive ideas. The possession of constructive ideals is taken to be an admission that one is living in a realm of fantasy. 13 *John Dewey*

Modern nihilism in philosophy and art is the violent outcry of a disillusioned idealism. 14 *Herbert Read*

Tempted, like no generation before us, to believe we can fabricate our experience ... we finally believe ... we can make our very ideals.... Images now displace ideals. 15 *Daniel J. Boorstin*

Narcissists do not function in terms of the actual self-image, because it is unacceptable to them.... [Instead] the narcissist identifies with the idealized image. 16 *Alexander Lowen*

Among the upper classes of society every striving after higher aims has been smothered; they are devoid of ideals. Owing to the lack of ideals and loftier aspirations, the unbounded love of enjoyment and the inclination to excesses are disseminated, with the resulting physical and moral deterioration. How can young persons, growing up in such an atmosphere, be different? 17 *August Bebel*

[M]oral and spiritual idealisms with all their efforts and disciplines aimed at the future are forms of the very mode of awareness which is giving us the trouble. For they perceive good and bad, ideal and real ... and fail to see that "goodness" is necessarily a "bad" man's ideal. 18 *Alan Watts*

One is deceived every time one expects "progress" from an ideal; every time so far the victory of the ideal has meant a retrograde movement. 19 *Friedrich Nietzsche*

[T]he twentieth century is the century of the idealists.... The unprecedented dehumanization our century has seen was conceived and engineered by idealists.... Man must be dehumanized, must be turned into an object, before he can be processed into something wholly different from what he is. 20 *Eric Hoffer*

[T]here is no crime, no murder, no massacre that cannot be justified, provided it be committed in the name of some ideal. 21 *Stanley Loomis*

Every form of addiction is bad, no matter whether the narcotic be alcohol or morphine or idealism. 22 *Carl Jung*

Teaching high ideals to men will not in itself produce better men and women. It may merely provide the taught with new ways of justifying their devotion to their own security. 23 *Langdon Gilkey*

"Ideals" are thought to be remote and inaccessible of attainment.... They hover in an indefinite way over the actual scene; they are expiring ghosts of a once significant kingdom of divine reality whose rule penetrated to every detail of life.... The very meaning of the word "ideals" is significant of the divorce which has obtained between means and ends.... It is impossible to form a just estimate of the paralysis of effort that has been produced by indifference to means. 24 *John Dewey*

A successful experience with the real vitiates the need for the ideal.... 25 *Jessica Benjamin*

There is nothing cheaper than idealism. It can be had by merely not observing the ineptitude of our chance prejudices, and by declaring that the first rhymes that have struck our ear are the eternal and necessary harmonies of the world. 26 *George Santayana*

We must understand every ideal ... as expressions of the same human need and we must judge them ... [as] to the extent to which they are conducive to the unfolding of man's powers and to the degree to which they are a real answer to man's need for equilibrium and harmony in his world. 27 *Erich Fromm*

A particular ideal may be an illusion, but having ideals is no illusion. It embodies features of existence. 28 *John Dewey*

Ideals

The purest idealism is unconsciously equivalent to the deepest knowledge. 29 *Adolf Hitler*

What we perceive and understand depends upon what we are; and what we are depends ... profoundly on the nature of the efforts we have made to realize our ideal and the nature of the ideal we have tried to realize. 30 *Aldous Huxley*

From an ideal I draw conclusions about those who need it! 31 *Friedrich Nietzsche*

Objectively, of course, each one of us is as determinate as a rat in a Skinner box.... Subjectively, I am always a projection into the future, a set of hopes and ideals.... I am an ideal to be lived through.... Self-consciousness ultimately amounts to this existential realization: "We are never merely what we are." 32 *Robert Solomon*

The human being is simultaneously that which he is and that which he yearns to be. 33 *Abraham Maslow*

[I]deals awaken the spirit to burgeoning possibilities for self-realization. 34 *Irving Singer*

[T]he ego-ideal answers ... to what is expected of the higher nature of man. In so far as it is a substitute for the longing for a father, it contains the germ from which all religions have evolved. The self-judgement which declares that the ego falls short of its ideal produces the sense of worthlessness with which the religious believer attests his longing.... Social feelings rest on the foundation of identifications with others, on the basis of an ego-ideal in common with them. 35 *Sigmund Freud*

In order not to become cynically or apathetically lost, young people in search of an identity must somewhere be able to convince themselves that those who succeed thereby shoulder the obligation of being the best, that is, of personifying the nation's ideals. 36 *Erik Erikson*

Just as the water of the streams we see is small compared to that which flows underground, so the idealism which becomes visible is small compared with what men and women bear locked in their hearts, unreleased or scarcely released. To unbind what is bound, to bring the underground waters to the surface: mankind is waiting and longing for such as can do that. 37 *Albert Schweitzer*

The ideal determines the standards to which a person holds himself responsible.... 38 *Michael Polanyi*

Social science ... does not deal in ideals. It accepts the dependence of culture on economic development as a fact. 39 *William Graham Sumner*

It seems probable that, in spite of all that "science" may do to the contrary, men will continue to pray to the end of time.... The impulse to pray is a necessary consequence of the fact that whilst the innermost of the empirical selves of a man is a Self of the *social* sort, it yet can find its only adequate *Socius* in an ideal world. All progress in the social Self is the substitution of higher tribunals for lower; this ideal tribunal is the highest; and most men, either continually or occasionally, carry a reference to it in their breast. The humblest outcast on this earth can feel himself to be real and valid by means of this higher recognition. And, on the other hand, for most of us, a world with no such inner refuge when the outer social self failed and dropped from us would be the abyss of horror. 40 *William James*

[W]e belong in the most intimate sense wherever our ideals belong. 41 *William James*

Man is not free to choose between having or not having "ideals," but he is free to choose between different kinds of ideals.... 42 *Erich Fromm*

An ideal cannot wait for its realisation to prove its validity. To deserve loyalty it needs only to be adequate as an ideal, that is, to express completely what the soul at present demands, and to do justice to all extant interests. 43 *George Santayana*

[Human existence] contributes to meaning in life only by virtue of an intervening variable—our propensity to formulate ideals.... To pursue ideals as human beings do is to direct one's striving toward remote achievements that are often subsumed under some imagined perfection. 44 *Irving Singer*

Mystical states indeed wield no authority due simply to their being mystical states. But the higher ones among them point in directions to which the religious sentiments even of non-mystical men incline. They tell of the supremacy of the ideal, of vastness, of union, of safety, and of rest. 45 *William James*

He who lives in the ideal and leaves it expressed in society or in art enjoys a double immortality. The eternal has absorbed him while he lived, and when he is dead his influence brings others to the same absorption. 46 *George Santayana*

The main task of human life is [for man to achieve] ... a congruent proximity to his ideals. He must find the means of sublimation ... through which to maintain contact with the sacred order.... There is no alternative fulfilment. Serenity is the coming into the presence of an ideal, and thereby rejoining the sacred. 47 *John Carroll*

[T]he root of our human nature ... leads us, in the exercise of our highest creative and synthetic powers, to fashion a world of the ideal ... in which to find again the true Home of our Spirit.... [By means of an] architecture of ideals ... a temple is erected for the worship of the Eternal and the Divine. 48 *F. A. Lange*

An ideal is not more elevated because more transcendent, but because it leads us to vaster perspectives. What is important is not that it tower high above us, until it becomes a stranger to our lives, but that it open to our activity a large enough field. 49 *Émile Durkheim*

IDENTITY

[M]AN NEEDS to have a *sense of identity*. Man can be defined as the animal that can say "I," that can be aware of himself as a separate entity.... [T]his need for a sense of identity is so vital and imperative that man could not remain sane if he did not find some way of satisfying it. 1 *Erich Fromm*

The word "I" is the true shibboleth of humanity. 2 *Martin Buber*

The Me, like every other aggregate, changes as it grows.... The identity which we recognize as we survey the long procession can only be the relative identity of a slow shifting in which there is always some common ingredient retained. The commonest element of all, the most uniform, is the possession of some common memories. However different the man may be from the youth, both look back on the same childhood and call it their own. 3 *William James*

Human memory ... is the invisible psychic adhesive that holds our identity together from moment to moment. 4 *Theodore Roszak*

The conviction which every man has of his identity, as far back as his memory reaches, needs no aid of philosophy to strengthen it; and no philosophy can weaken it, without first producing some degree of insanity. 5 *Thomas Reid*

The consciousness of identity is really ... the consciousness of the one and original self. 6 *Mary W. Calkins*

We must go forward ... but we cannot kill the past in doing so, for the past is part of our identity and without our identity we are nothing. 7 *Carlos Fuentes*

[In] the social jungle of human existence, there is no feeling of being alive without a sense of ego identity. Deprivation of identity can lead to murder. 8 *Erik Erikson*

[Y]outh often prefers to find and to adopt a negative identity rather than none at all. 9 *Erik Erikson*

No wonder, then, that some of our troubled children constantly break out of their play into some damaging activity in which they seem to us to "interfere" with our world; while analysis reveals that they only wish to demonstrate their right to find an identity in it. 10 *Erik Erikson*

Identity

The problem of alienation and the problem of personal identity are inseparable. The man who lacks a firm sense of personal identity feels alienated; the man who feels alienated lacks a firm sense of personal identity. 11

Nathaniel Branden

The widespread preoccupation with identity ... may be seen not only as a symptom of "alienation" but also as a corrective trend in historical evolution.... For each *positive identity* is also defined by *negative* images ... and we must now discuss the simple fact that our God-given identities often live off the degradation of others. 12 *Erik Erikson*

[T]he two basic emotions connected with identity are acceptance and rejection. 13

Robert Plutchik

In narcissism, as in any form of personality structure, it is only through the other that one can have an identity confirmed. 14 *M. Gear et al.*

Man is a social being and, as such, needs the company and support of other humans to sustain him.... [H]e also needs to preserve his own identity.... And the more insecure we are, the more do we look for ... affirmation of our own identities. 15 *Anthony Storr*

A person's "own" identity cannot be completely abstracted from his identity-for-others.... All "identities" require an other.... Intense *frustration* arises from failure to find that other required to establish a satisfactory "identity." 16

R. D. Laing

To the classic question of identity "Who are you?" a traditional man would say, "I am the son of my father." A person today says, "I am I, I come out of myself, and in choice and action I make myself." This change of identity is the hallmark of our own modernity.... But this change is, also, the source of an "identity crisis." 17 *Daniel Bell*

As the traditional social class structure dissolves, more and more individuals want to be identified not by their occupational base ... but by their cultural tastes and life-styles. 18

Daniel Bell

The breakdown of social structure ... leads to the denial of feeling and the loss of a sense of self. In place of the self, one creates an image to provide some identity. In today's culture, that image is described as a life-style. We are told that we are free to create our own life-styles, in effect creating our own identities.... [But] a life-style without a self is not a person. 19

Alexander Lowen

[In contemporary society man's] powers and what they create become estranged, something different from himself, something for others to judge and to use; thus his feeling of identity becomes as shaky as his self-esteem; it is constituted by the sum total of roles he can play: "I am as you desire me." 20 *Erich Fromm*

Identity is inseparable from the role one is assigned.... The child derives his identity from a social environment. The social environment remains to his death the only source for validating that identity. 21 *Ernest Becker*

The more individualized people are, the more difficult it is to attain identification. 22

Karl Mannheim

Culture, for a society, a group, or person, is a continual process of sustaining an identity.... 23 *Daniel Bell*

[G]overnments, in order to succeed in a democratic era, must provide their people with a public identity.... National identities are ethical identities. 24 *Joseph A. Amato*

The individual's political identity, far from waxing with the enlargement of popular and public opinion as a force in democracy, has decayed. So ... has the individual's identity in the social order and in culture. 25

Robert Nisbet

Industrial revolution, world-wide communication, standardization, centralization, and mechanization threaten the identities which man has inherited from primitive, agrarian, feudal, and patrician cultures. What inner equilibrium these cultures had to offer is now endangered on a gigantic scale. As the fear of loss of identity dominates much of our irrational

motivation, it calls upon the whole arsenal of anxiety which is left in each individual.... In this emergency masses of people become ready to seek salvation in pseudo identities. 26
Erik Erikson

In a world where technological change is radically transforming traditional occupational subcultures, where geographical communities no longer root people in time and place, and where traditional authorities and conventional wisdoms are constantly questioned, the texture of personal identity grows thin, its outlines blurred. And the task of building a coherent self becomes a compelling project—indeed a necessity.... And the self becomes a strategy, a tool ... to be deployed in the service of "personal growth." ... The answer is for the corporation to embrace this search for a self and harness the new social character to its own ends.... [W]orkers can be made to see the corporation as the pathway ... to personal growth and psychological identity.... 27 *Robert Howard*

The west insists on the discrete identity of objects. To name is to know; to know is to control.... Identity is power. 28 *Camille Paglia*

Sex is the single most decisive determinant of personal identity. 29 *Steven Goldberg*

Because our culture privileges sex-identity as the truest part of our beings, we are secured voluntarily in a social unit which subordinates women. 30 *Rosalind Coward*

It is my thesis that the core of the problem for women today is not sexual but a problem of identity ... perpetuated by the feminine mystique.... The feminine mystique permits, even encourages, women to ignore the question of their identity. 31 *Betty Friedan*

During the early years when the child forms his crucial image of himself and of his future role, he may miss the firm model of a self-respecting adult.... Parents who have lost their identity ... cannot expect thus to help him find his. 32 *Max Lerner*

A strong sense of personal identity is the product of two things: a policy of independent thinking and, as a consequence, the possession of an integrated set of values. Since it is his values that determine a man's emotions and goals, and give direction and meaning to his life, a man experiences his values as an extension of himself, as an integral part of his identity, as crucial to that which makes him himself. 33
Nathaniel Branden

The principle of identity is the negation of every species of relation at the heart of being-in-itself. Presence to self, on the contrary, supposes that an impalpable fissure has slipped into being. If being is present to itself, it is because it is not wholly itself.... Thus in order for a *self* to exist, it is necessary that the unity of this being include its own nothingness as the nihilation of identity. 34 *Jean-Paul Sartre*

The Second Law [of Thermodynamics] states unequivocally that the entropy of an open system must increase.... The death sentence of the Second Law applies only to identities, and could be rephrased: "Mortality is the price of identity." 35 *J. E. Lovelock*

Knowledge of men sometimes seems easier to those who allow themselves to be caught up in the snare of personal identity. But they thus shut the door on knowledge of man.... 36
Claude Lévi-Strauss

~ IDEOLOGY ~

IN A SENSE, ideology is the most distinctively human of the conventional divisions of culture, for if culture issues from a mental ability peculiar to man among all animals, and since ideology is that aspect of culture most purely mental, then it is the most basic and direct indicator of our humanness. 1 *E. R. Service*

Ideology influences perception, perception shapes expectation, and expectation shapes behavior, making for what is called the self-fulfilling prophesy. 2 *J. William Fulbright*

Ideological thinking orders facts into an absolutely logical procedure which starts from an axiomatically accepted premise, deducing everything else from it.... Hence ideological

Ideology

thinking becomes emancipated from the reality that we perceive with our five senses, and insists on a "truer" reality concealed behind all perceptible things ... requiring a sixth sense that enables us to become aware of it. The sixth sense is provided by precisely the ideology.... 3
Hannah Arendt

[I]deology ... reduces the reality of human existence to fit certain fanciful theories and then seeks to remedy the situation by forcing changes in the makeup of humanity. 4
Craig Schiller

Ideology—that is what gives evildoing its long-sought justification and gives the evildoer the necessary steadfastness and determination.... Thanks to *ideology*, the twentieth century was fated to experience evildoing on a scale calculated in the millions. 5 *Alexander Solzhenitsyn*

[T]he clash of ideologies ... has all but done away with any sense of common humanity in relation to the "enemy." 6 *Guenter Lewy*

[T]o have any ideology requires the *possibility* of enemies. 7 *Robert C. Solomon*

[E]very ideology provides a scapegoat outside the confines of its own splendid group.... 8
Alice Miller

At the present point of history ... it was discovered that if either side used that new greatest weapon [the H bomb], both sides and the rest of humanity would perish.... Both sides then discovered that killing of the enemy's people was not their objective. Killing the enemy's ideology *is* the objective. 9 *R. Buckminster Fuller*

Ideological conflicts brook no compromises.... 10 *William G. Hyland*

At a time when the world is torn by a profound *ideological* conflict, do not join those who have no ideology—no ideas, no philosophy—to offer you. Do not go into battle armed with nothing but stale slogans, pious platitudes, and meaningless generalities.... Those who do not realize that the battle is ideological, had better give up, because they have no chance. 11
Ayn Rand

It is the very nature of politics to compel the actor on the political stage to use ideologies in order to disguise the immediate goal of his action.... The nation that dispensed with ideologies and frankly stated that it wanted power ... would at once find itself at a great and perhaps decisive disadvantage in the struggle for power. 12 *Hans Morgenthau*

The ideology represents, so to speak, a "shared solution," a means whereby members of the culture may, collectively, project their phantasies into social reality. 13 *Richard Koenigsberg*

[A]ll ideology ... is about one's qualifications for eternity; and so are all disputes about who really is dirty.... And the highest heroism is the stamping out of those who are tainted.... All human ideologies, then, are affairs that deal directly with *the sacredness of the individual or the group life*. 14 *Ernest Becker*

Our blight is ideologies—they are the long-expected Antichrist! 15 *Carl Jung*

Ideologies are likely to appear and gather momentum during periods ... characterized by a widespread sense of stagnation and unmanageable death imagery. Central to their function is their invocation of the classical mythological theme of death and rebirth ... together with their revitalizing promise of a "new life." 16
Robert Jay Lifton

A truly powerful ideology opens up a new vision of life to the imagination; once formulated, it remains part of the moral repertoire to be drawn upon by intellectuals, theologians, or moralists as part of the range of possibilities open to mankind. 17 *Daniel Bell*

Ideology is the conversion of ideas into social levers.... One might say, in fact, that the most important, latent, function of ideology is to tap emotion.... Ideology fuses these energies and channels them into politics. 18 *Daniel Bell*

Control the manner in which a man interprets his world, and you have gone a long way toward controlling his behavior.... Ideological justification is vital in obtaining *willing* obedience, for it permits the person to see his

behavior as serving a desirable end. Only [then] is compliance easily exacted. 19
Stanley Milgram

Ideological education is the key link to be grasped in uniting the whole Party for great political struggles. Unless this is done, the Party cannot accomplish any of its political tasks. 20
Mao Tse-tung

We find a tendency toward ideological unity in other parties ... [but] in Communist parties it has become obligatory.... Communists are educated in the idea that ideological unity, or the prescription of ideas from above, is the holy of holies.... 21 *Milovan Djilas*

The communist and fascist doctrine is a device, and an effective one, for enlisting the support of the masses of the new élite through an apparent identification of those interests with the interests of the masses themselves.... Through this notion of an élite or vanguard, these ideologies thus serve at once the twofold need of justifying the existence of a ruling class and at the same time providing the masses with an attitude making easy the acceptance of its rule. 22 *James Burnham*

An *ideology* is an organization of beliefs and attitudes ... shared with others, deriving from external authority. 23 *Milton Rokeach*

Ideologies ... are guardians of identity. 24
Martha Crenshaw

An ideology may be defined as that part of his image of the world which a person defines as essential to his identity.... His ideology, therefore, is a part of a man's image of the world which is particularly valuable to him and which he is concerned to defend and propagate. 25
Kenneth Boulding

By an *ideologue*, I shall mean someone who ... has a sense of mystical inevitability about herself.... For the ideologue, a conceptual anomaly is intolerable.... [It threatens] the rational intelligibility of the universe and her predestined place in it.... To undermine the theory, then, is to undermine everything at once. 26
Adrian Piper

Ideologies by their very nature have been Utopian in design, and in order to be effective have to fill a gap or need in social psychology traditionally served by myth ... resting the entire ideological structure on an idealized perspective of human nature totally out of touch with psychological reality. 27 *J. C. Smith*

A day comes when ideology conflicts with psychology. Then there is no more legitimate power. 28 *Albert Camus*

A central conflict is a set of memories and concepts in which an individual expresses painfully contradictory themes.... [It] can be said to delineate an *existential problem* in the subject's life.... Ideology is the system of general beliefs that supplies the framework for a solution to the central conflict at the conceptual level. 29
Michael R. Jackson

Ideology ... means thought that is socially determined without being conscious of its determinations. 30 *Catherine MacKinnon*

[Sexist] ideology has now become unconscious.... We are very much like the fish who is unaware of the fact that his environment is wet. After all, what else could it be? Such is the nature of all unconscious ideologies in a society. Such, in particular, is the nature of America's ideology about women.... It has simply been obscured by an equalitarian veneer.... 31
Sandra Bem & Daryl Bem

Ideology today is concerned only with the denial of other human beings.... 32
Albert Camus

Ideology and passion may no longer be necessary to sustain the class struggle within stable and affluent democracies, but they are clearly needed ... to develop free political and economic institutions in the rest of the world. It is only the ideological class struggle within the West which is ending. 33 *Seymour Lipset*

The danger of ideology is that it suppresses the learning process. If a man has an ideology which explains everything that happens to him, it relieves him of the necessity for learning. He knows everything already! The great dilemma

Ideology

of ideology therefore is that while it is capable of resolving internal conflict both in the individual and in the society and therefore of generating substantial power and motive force, in the course of generating this powerful engine it is likely to destroy the steering wheel and the compass. 34 *Kenneth Boulding*

Anything which therefore can mitigate or moderate ideological conflict in the present circumstances is so much gain, and anything which intensifies it is a threat to man's future. 35
Kenneth Boulding

Immortality

A *SENSE* OF IMMORTALITY ... reflects a compelling and universal inner quest for continuous symbolic relationship to what has gone before and what will continue after our finite individual lives.... That quest is central to the human project.... [We may] view the struggle for symbolic immortality as neither rational nor irrational but as a psychic expression of man's existential and organismic state. 1
Robert Jay Lifton

[I]mmortality is one of the great spiritual needs of man. 2 *William James*

[B]elief in immortality ... gives us our fundamental goal and meaning, as well as our basic moral criterion: whatever contributes to the saving of my soul is good; whatever obstructs this salvation is bad. 3 *Eugene Fontinell*

God would be dead if there were no immortality. 4 *James B. Pratt*

[A]rchaic man recovers the possibility of definitely transcending time and living in eternity. Insofar as he fails to do so, insofar as he "sins," [he] falls into historical existence, into time.... 5
Mircea Eliade

[O]nly with faith in his immortality does man comprehend the full meaning of his rational destination on earth.... In a word, the idea of immortality is life itself—"live life" its ultimate formula.... 6 *Feodor Dostoevsky*

Since man is Nature itself, and indeed Nature at the highest grade of its self-consciousness ... the man who has contemplated this point of view may well console himself, when contemplating his own death and that of his friends, by turning his eyes to the immortal life of Nature, which he himself is. 7 *Arthur Schopenhauer*

[I]mmortality is not a privilege reserved for a part only of existence, but rather a relation pervading every part. 8 *George Santayana*

Immortality, if we could believe in it, would enable us to ... hold that although our souls, during their sojourn here on earth are in bondage to matter and physical laws, they pass from earth into an eternal world.... Unfortunately all the evidence is against this. 9
Bertrand Russell

[A] world of immortals would soon stagnate. 10
Arthur C. Clarke

The research for *physical* immortality proceeds from a misunderstanding.... [T]he basic problem is: to enlarge the pupil of the eye, so the *body* with its attendant personality will no longer obstruct the view. Immortality is then experienced as a present fact.... 11
Joseph Campbell

[I]mmortality is a present quality of the spirit, not a future fact or event. 12 *Walter T. Stace*

If we take eternity to mean not infinite temporal duration but timelessness, than eternal life belongs to those who live in the present. 13
Ludwig Wittgenstein

And immortality is not a question of time, of everlasting life. It is a question of consummate being. 14 *D. H. Lawrence*

[W]hen immortality is misunderstood as being an everlasting body, it turns into a clown act, really. On the other hand, when immortality is understood to be identification with that which is of eternity in your own life now, it's something else again. 15 *Joseph Campbell*

We are mortal persons responding to the advance of perhaps immortal ideas. We are not ourselves only; we are also part of human experience and thought.... The thoughts existed before we were born and will go on after we are finished. 16 *H. G. Wells*

Man is immortal, but not men. 17
H. G. Wells

When we have served our purpose we are cast aside. But genes are denizens of geological time.... The genes are the immortals.... 18
Richard Dawkins

The question of immortality is of its nature not a scholarly question. It is a question welling up from the interior which the subject must put to itself as it becomes conscious of itself. 19
Søren Kierkegaard

[I]n the unconscious every one of us is convinced of his own immortality. 20
Sigmund Freud

[I]t is the immortality motive and not the sexual one that must bear the larger burden of our explanation of human passion. 21
Ernest Becker

The finiteness of personal life is ... a challenge to property.... By transcending the limits of human life in planning for an automatic continuous growth of wealth ... individual property is ... taken out of the sphere of mere private life. Private interests which by their very nature are temporary, limited by man's natural life span, can now escape into the sphere of public affairs and borrow from that infinite length of time which is needed for continuous accumulation. 22 *Hannah Arendt*

[M]an aggressively builds immortal cultures and makes history in order to fight death.... [H]istory-making is always the quest for group immortality. 23 *Norman O. Brown*

We can understand much of human history as the struggle to achieve, maintain, and reaffirm a collective sense of immortality under constantly changing psychic and material conditions. 24 *Robert Jay Lifton*

[Movements are] valuable only if they create values for eternity, for the higher development of all of mankind. 25 *Alfred Adler*

Every conflict over truth is in the last analysis just the same old struggle over ... immortality. 26
Otto Rank

[E]very doctrine of immortality implies a tragic preoccupation with death. 27
Denis de Rougemont

The decisive question for man is: Is he related to something infinite or not. That is the telling question of his life. Only if we know that the thing which truly matters is the infinite can we avoid fixing our interest upon futilities. 28
Carl Jung

The weightiest questions of metaphysics arise practically out of our desire to arrive at an understanding of the possibility of our immortality—from this fact they derive their value and cease to be merely the idle discussions of fruitless curiosity. For the truth is that metaphysics has no value save in so far as it attempts to explain in what way our vital longing can or cannot be realized. 29 *Miguel de Unamuno*

The stamen of immortality, if I may be allowed the phrase, is the perfectibility of human reason.... 30 *Mary Wollstonecraft*

[T]here is little in American philosophical speculation that deals with the theme of immortality. American culture cuts away the sensitivity to death and grief, to suicide and immortality, emphasizing the here-and-now as it emphasizes youth and action. 31 *Max Lerner*

[In the modern world] we are dealing with breakdowns in man's sense of symbolic unity and impairment of his sense of immortality.... This is characterized by an inability to believe in larger connections, by pervasive expressions of psychic numbing. These states can be directly manifested in various kinds of apathy, unrelatedness, and general absence of trust or faith.... 32 *Robert Jay Lifton*

The major problem of our time is the decay of the belief in personal immortality.... 33
George Orwell

Immortality

For we must not lose sight of the fact that the problem of the personal immortality of the soul involves the future of the whole human species. 34 *Miguel de Unamuno*

Since the aim of love is the permanent possession of goodness, it necessarily follows that we desire immortality along with goodness, and consequently the aim of love is immortality as well. 35 *Diotima*

If you were to destroy in mankind the belief in immortality, not only love but every living force maintaining the life of the world would at once be dried up. 36 *Feodor Dostoevsky*

Individuality

The [Eden] myth speaks of other consequences of the first act of freedom. The original harmony between man and nature is broken.... Man has become separate from nature, he has taken the first step toward becoming human by becoming an "individual." ... To transcend nature, to be alienated from nature and from another human being, finds man naked, ashamed. He is alone and free, yet powerless and afraid. 1 *Erich Fromm*

What now confronts man in an external way has been drawn down into the sphere of the independent human being, and it is no longer in full harmony with the divine-spiritual cosmos.... And this is the true meaning of "original sin." ... This is the moment when the possibility of illness first occurred in human evolution, for it is bound up with the individualisation of man. When man was still connected with the divine-spiritual world the possibility of illness did not exist. 2 *Rudolf Steiner*

The individual, in so far as he is a created being, can oppose himself only to the Creator. He has need of God, with whom he carries on a kind of gloomy flirtation. 3 *Albert Camus*

The emancipation of the individual was indeed the great spiritual revolution which led to the breakdown of tribalism and to the rise of democracy.... [I]ndividualism, united with altruism, has become the basis of our western civilization. It is the central doctrine of Christianity ("love your neighbour," not "love your tribe").... There is no other thought which has been so powerful in the moral development of man. 4 *Karl Popper*

Individualism is of democratic origin and threatens to grow as conditions get more equal.... [Americans] form the habit of thinking of themselves in isolation and imagine that their whole destiny is in their own hands. Each man is forever thrown back on himself alone, and there is a danger that he may be shut up in the solitude of his own heart. 5 *Alexis de Tocqueville*

Not conformity but differentiation is the end of the ways of God.... But the danger is obvious. The romantic irony elevated the individual beyond all content and made him empty: he was no longer obliged to participate in anything seriously. 6 *Paul Tillich*

[T]he emergence of social humanity out of animality would have been impossible had the members of primitive social groups been actuated by the individualism which governs the behaviour of modern man. Humanity could never have come into being had its earliest representatives been hordes of jealous and suspicious individualists, in which every member sought his personal advantage only. 7 *Robert Briffault*

[A] man wholly solitary would either be a God or a brute. 8 *Aristotle*

The mere pursuit of individual ends is harmful to the ends and peace of the whole ... and hence in the end to the individual. 9 *Marcel Mauss*

The individual *is the social being*. His life ... is therefore an expression and confirmation of *social life*. 10 *Karl Marx*

The more self-sufficient an individual appears to be, the more sure it is that ... he carries a whole society in his bosom. 11 *Lewis Mumford*

Man cannot find himself, he cannot become aware of his individuality, save through the medium of social life. 12 *Ernst Cassirer*

Individuality

Human individuality—the ability each of us has to mark himself off as different from the ... world around him—is socially conferred. 13
Lloyd J. Averill

Individuality is something which the society possesses. 14 *Émile Durkheim*

The individual is the product of social life; without it, he could be no more than a bundle of unconditioned reflexes. 15 *W. H. Auden*

The detached individual is an essentially lost being. 16 *Josiah Royce*

Excessive individualism not only results in favoring the action of suicidogenic causes, but it is itself such a cause. 17 *Émile Durkheim*

The neurotic loses every kind of collective spirituality ... placing himself entirely within the immortality of his own ego, as the observations and cosmic fantasies of psychotics so clearly show. 18 *Otto Rank*

Civilized man asserts his individuality.... But the individuality he asserts is not life-affirming or life-enjoying, but the life-negating (ascetic) individuality of (Faustian) discontent and guilt. 19 *Norman O. Brown*

[We may ask] to what extent it is necessary to develop ritual solutions of types of guilt which are engendered by ... the extreme individualism of the economic arrangements of each household in modern North America [such as] ritual giving to the Community Chest, the Red Cross, the Hundred Neediest Cases etc.... 20
Margaret Mead

Everyone strives to keep his individuality as apart as possible, wishes to secure the greatest possible fullness of life for himself; but meantime all his efforts result not in attaining fullness of life but self-destruction, for instead of self-realization he ends by arriving at complete solitude.... [M]en have, in their mockery, ceased to understand that true security is to be found in social solidarity rather than in isolated individual effort. 21
Feodor Dostoevsky

Human solidarity is the necessary condition for the unfolding of any one individual. 22
Erich Fromm

An ideal of individualism which denies the obligations of man to others is manifestly impossible in a society such as ours, and it is a credit to our wisdom that while we preached it, we never fully practiced it. 23
William H. Whyte

The individual is foolish ... but the species is wise.... 24 *Edmund Burke*

[T]he individual does not exist—he is worth nothing.... Rational life consists in each person forgetting himself in the species.... 25
Johann Fichte

[T]o desire that individuality should be immortal really means to wish to perpetuate an error infinitely. For at bottom every individual is really only a special error, a false step ... nay, something which it is the real end of life to bring us back from. 26 *Arthur Schopenhauer*

The more we know of Nature the more we realize how profligate she is of lives.... Obviously the survival of the individual is not the *summum bonum*, the "greatest good," in Nature's eyes. 27 *Garrett Hardin*

Making great and spectacular efforts to save the life of an individual makes sense only when there is a shortage of people. I have not lately heard that there is a shortage of people. 28
Garrett Hardin

[I]t may be said of individuality that, while the tendency to individuate is everywhere present in the organized world, it is everywhere opposed by the tendency toward reproduction. For the individuality to be perfect, it would be necessary that no detached part of the organism could live separately. But then reproduction would be impossible.... Individuality therefore harbors its enemy at home. 29 *Henri Bergson*

The problem with individualism is not that it is immoral but that it is incorrect. The universe does not consist of a lot of unrelated particles but is an interconnected whole. Pretending that

INDIVIDUALITY

our fortunes are independent of each other may be perfectly ethical, but it is also perfectly stupid. 30 *Philip Slater*

[L]ife nevertheless manifests a search for individuality, as if it strove to constitute systems naturally isolated, naturally closed. 31
Henri Bergson

Life is individual. 32 *Philip Rieff*

It is only to the individual that a soul is given. 33
Albert Einstein

"Society" is nothing more than a term, a concept for the symbiosis of a group of human beings. A concept is not a carrier of life. The sole and natural carrier of life is the individual, and that is so throughout nature. 34
Carl Jung

What we fear in death is the *end of the individual* ... and since the individual is a particular objectification of the will to live itself, its whole nature struggles against death. 35
Arthur Schopenhauer

[T]he world of Being is the world of individually expressed meanings—an individual life, consisting of the individual embodiments of the wills represented by all finite ideas.... Individual determination itself remains ... the principal character of the Real; and is ... the Limit towards which we endlessly aim.... [T]he Individual [is] the only ultimate form of Being. 36
Josiah Royce

In the last analysis, the essential thing is the life of the individual. This alone makes history, here alone do the great transformations first take place, and the whole future, the whole history of the world, ultimately spring as a gigantic summation from these hidden sources in individuals. 37 *Carl Jung*

The individual is the end of the Universe. 38
Miguel de Unamuno

The individual is the only reality. The further we move away from the individual toward abstract ideas about *Homo sapiens*, the more likely we are to fall into error. 39 *Carl Jung*

Each person is an idiom unto himself, an apparent violation of the syntax of the species.... Unlike plants and lower animals ... incapable of becoming ... man is not merely a creature of cell structure, tropism, and instinct ... repeating, with trivial variation, the pattern of his species. Nature's heavy investment in individuality stands forth chiefly in *homo sapiens*. 40
Gordon W. Allport

Individualisation happens by way of the effect of the male sex on the female.... If there were only the female element, human individuality would be extinguished, and men would all become alike.... That is the significance of the interworking of the two sexes.... If it had been possible for human beings to propagate without the two sexes, this individualising would not have taken place. 41 *Rudolf Steiner*

[E]very individual is, as it were, a sort of experiment made by nature to test this or that group of qualities. 42 *H. G. Wells*

Personality, individuality, is a biological device which has served its end in evolution and will decline. 43 *H. G. Wells*

The killing of man's individuality, of the uniqueness shaped in equal parts by nature, will, and destiny ... creates a horror that ... gives rise to the nihilistic generalizations which maintain plausibly enough that essentially all men alike are beasts. 44 *Hannah Arendt*

The [Nazi] concentration camps ... affected the autonomy of civilians only step by step. In the first years ... they were meant to punish and deter ... in the old sense—as individuals. But then came an important innovation: the systematic attempt to do away with individuals as such.... [S]imilar tendencies are present in any mass society.... 45 *Bruno Bettelheim*

The very notion of morality is impossible apart from the ideal of the individual as an autonomous agent, who assumes responsibility for his own conduct, his own principles, his own comportment. In fact, apart from such a view of man, free, personal relations among men, including above all the relations of contract and personal loyalty and love, can scarcely exist. 46 *Henry D. Aiken*

Individualism grows along with power and with wealth. But it also grows together with the responsibility which the single individual has towards himself and towards others.... 47
Ferdinand Tonnies

[T]he morality of rights differs from the morality of responsibility in its emphasis on separation rather than attachment, in its consideration of the individual rather than the relation as primary.... 48 *Carol Gilligan*

The basic building block of the society is shifting from the family to the individual. 49
John Naisbitt

The movement of the progressive societies has been uniform in one respect.... The Individual is steadily substituted for the Family, as the unit of which civil laws take account.... Nor is it difficult to see what is the tie between man and man which replaces ... the Family. It is Contract. 50 *Sir Henry Maine*

Individualism has brought about its own demise; it has undermined the very family that gave birth to the stable individual. 51
Jessica Benjamin

[W]e can afford to become individualized just to the extent that we can replace the natural ties which used to hold us to our kind by symbolic ones.... 52 *Susanne Langer*

Every man that comes near me threatens my very existence: nay, more, my very being. This is the ugly fact which underlies our civilization.... Individualism has triumphed. If I am a sheer individual, then every other being ... is over against me as a menace to me.... The sense of isolation, followed by the sense of menace and of fear, is bound to arise as the feeling of oneness and community with our fellow-men declines, and the feeling of individualism and personality, which is existence in isolation, increases. 53 *D. H. Lawrence*

The problem of mankind today ... [is that] no meaning is in the group—none in the world: all is in the individual. But there the meaning is absolutely unconscious.... The lines of communication between the conscious and the unconscious zones of the human psyche have all been cut, and we have been split in two. 54
Joseph Campbell

Individualism means deliberately stressing and giving prominence to some supposed peculiarity, rather than to collective considerations and obligations. But individuation means precisely the better and more complete fulfillment of the collective qualities of the human being ... [and] aims at a living cooperation of all factors.... The aim of individuation is nothing less than to divest the self of the false wrappings of the persona.... 55 *Carl Jung*

The fact is that self-actualizing people are simultaneously the most individualistic and the most altruistic ... of all human beings. The fact that we have in our culture put these qualities at opposite ends of a single continuum is apparently a mistake.... These qualities go together and the dichotomy is resolved in self-actualizing people. 56 *Abraham Maslow*

INSTITUTION

AN INSTITUTION consists of a concept (idea, notion, doctrine, interest) and a structure. 1
William Graham Sumner

Institutions ... must be produced which will hold the activities of society in channels of order, deliberation, peace, regulated antagonism of interests, and justice, according to the mores of the time. These institutions put an end to exploitation and bring interests into harmony under civil liberty. 2
William Graham Sumner

An institution can be considered as an anticipating device designed to pay off its members now for behavior which will benefit and stabilize society later. 3 *George Berg*

[I]nstitutions [are] the vehicles of the impersonal relations in which all societies have their existence.... 4 *Arnold Toynbee*

[I]nstitutions [are] ... systems of defined complementary role expectations. 5
Lawrence Kohlberg

Institution

Now by an institution I shall understand a public system of rules.... The primary subject of the principles of social justice is the basic structure of society, the arrangement of major institutions into one scheme of co-operation. These principles govern the assignment of rights and duties and they determine the appropriate benefits and burdens of social life. 6
John Rawls

The formation of a mature sense of justice requires participation in just institutions. 7
Lawrence Kohlberg

The Cold War years were grim, bleak times for American liberty.... Curiously, only the more sober, more restrained spirit that is reflected in our institutions rather than in ourselves established limits and ended the American Inquisition. 8 *Stanley Kutler*

[S]uch freedom of the mind as can be possessed by man is due to the services of social institutions.... 9 *Michael Polanyi*

Under severe conditions morality disappears.... In a desperate community long-term interests can be protected only by institutional means.... Only institutions can then take actions that would be called altruistic.... Moralists try to achieve desired ends by exhorting people to be moral.... [I]nstitution-designers count on people acting egoistically. 10
Garrett Hardin

[I]nstitutions delineate a symbolic area which [men] call *reality*, and define and regulate relations and actions within that area.... Only in institutional life can men pass power directly to other men without the intervention of a woman. Institutional life, therefore, has great meaning to men, and is often perceived as a truer home than the familial home. 11
Marilyn French

[I]nstitutions arise and survive because they meet certain physical or psychological social needs. Since for both ancient and tribal law, "almost every known legal concept began and ended with the family" and since the family structures of almost all cultures and people are patriarchal, we must inevitably conclude that the need that law evolved to meet was the legitimization and maintenance of patriarchal social structures. 12 *J. C. Smith*

[I]n our society loyalty is expected to be tendered to the institution; the institution is not expected to be loyal to the men and women in its domain. 13 *R. Jeffrey Lustig*

The morally autonomous person is a threat to any institution since he will not be psychologically dependent upon it. 14 *Derek Wright*

If threat leads to dogmatism in individuals, by the same token it should also lead to dogma in institutions. Dogma serves the purpose of ensuring the continued existence of the institution and the belief-disbelief system for which it stands. 15 *Milton Rokeach*

[A] culture survives principally, I think, by the power of its institutions to bind and loose men in the conduct of their affairs with reasons which sink so deep into the self that they become commonly and implicitly understood.... 16 *Philip Rieff*

[I]nstitutions are, in substance, prevalent habits of thought with respect to particular relations.... [They] may, on the psychological side, be broadly characterised as a prevalent spiritual attitude or a prevalent theory of life. 17
Thorstein Veblen

In their institutions [citizens] have invested more than their everyday ideas which parallel their actual behavior. They have placed in them their ideals of how the world rightly ought to be. 18 *Gunnar Myrdal*

Each society and each age must find the institutionalized form of reverence which derives vitality from its world-image—from predestination to indeterminacy. 19 *Erik Erikson*

Although men sometimes shape institutions, institutions always select and form men. 20
C. Wright Mills

Marx was quite right when he insisted that "history" cannot be planned on paper. But *institutions* can be planned; and they are being planned. Only by planning, step by step, for institutions to safeguard freedom, especially freedom from exploitation, can we hope to achieve a better world. 21 *Karl Popper*

[T]he belief ... that we owe all beneficial institutions to design, and that only such design has made or can make them useful for our purposes, is largely false.... Many of the institutions of society which are indispensable ... are in fact the result of customs, habits, or practices ... whose purpose or origin we often do not know and of whose very existence we are often not aware. 22 *Friedrich von Hayek*

A nation does not choose its institutions at will.... They are not the creators of an epoch, but are created by it. 23 *Gustave Le Bon*

In our time the institutions built upon the foundations of the public philosophy still stand. But they are used by a public who are not being taught, and no longer adhere to, the philosophy. Increasingly, the people are alienated from the inner principles of their institutions. 24 *Walter Lippmann*

[W]e have lost the *institution* of government in terms of responsibility and accountability to the people. We now have nothing but a bunch of managers, who run the country to make it safe for technology. 25 *Ursula Franklin*

Institutional structures are designed to accomplish specific purposes, and in the process are designed to screen out information the people in control perceive as unwanted or irrelevant.... Thus institutions have built-in capacities for selecting, distorting, concealing, and impounding information.... Since most of our institutions are limited in purpose, and hence ignore aspects of reality ... social problems which do not correspond to existing institutions are often not perceived, much less researched. 26

Hazel Henderson

Institutions—government, churches, industries, and the like have properly no other function than to contribute to human freedom; and in so far as they fail, on the whole, to perform this function, they are wrong and need reconstruction. 27 *Charles Horton Cooley*

[W]e are approaching one of those historical watersheds that separate worlds in time.... It involves the slow draining away of legitimacy of existing institutions and prevailing traditions. 28 *Irving Kristol*

That institutions yield no public life is felt by more and more human beings, to their sorrow: this is the source of the distress and search of our age. 29 *Martin Buber*

The great error of our times has been the belief in structural or institutional solutions. The enemy is within each of us.... Once a new way of life is established, structural and institutional questions may again become worthy of discussion. 30 *Charles A. Reich*

Of course institutions distort and corrupt, and when they do, they require reformation or replacement—*by other institutions*; for it is precisely by the institutionalization of experience that humanness is nurtured.... [P]rotest against the institutionalization of experience is simply protest against being human. 31

Lloyd J. Averill

The first task of a system is to maintain itself, and every institution must therefore reactivate continually the motivational eccentricities that gave rise to it in the first place.... Change can take place only when institutions have been discredited and disassembled, and the motivations that gave rise to them redirected onto new pathways.... 32 *Philip Slater*

If there are realistic possibilities for institutional change ... on a global plane, then pursuing them would seem to be of the utmost urgency, because this holds out the greatest hope that combined moral efforts will accumulate into lasting progress.... Moral efforts are likely to be of enduring historical significance only when they become cumulative in this way. 33

Thomas Pogge

[T]he prospects of civilization depend, in large degree, upon our ability to work its institutions. Our awareness of their nature will be, also, the degree in which we perceive their fragility. 34

Harold Laski

Institution

[E]ven in the darkest ages, it was institutions that made society work, and if civilization is to survive society must somehow be made to work. 35 *Kenneth Clark*

~ Intelligence ~

[I]F NATURE has added intelligence to animal life it is because they belong together. Intelligence is a natural emanation of vitality. 1
George Santayana

Intelligence is a property of living systems and is concerned with ... those responses to the environment which affect the system's survival, and the survival of the association of systems to which it belongs. 2 *J. E. Lovelock*

When an interaction intervenes which directs the course of change, the scene of natural interaction has a new quality and dimension. This added type of interaction *is* intelligence. 3
John Dewey

Intelligence and choice can only arise when more than one stimulus is presented at the same time in the same place. 4 *W. H. Auden*

[A]ll concrete instinct is mingled with intelligence, as all real intelligence is penetrated by instinct.... [T]he advantage of intelligence over instinct only appears ... when intelligence, having raised construction to a higher degree, proceeds to construct constructive machinery. 5
Henri Bergson

Basically, any animal that can modify its behavior by making use of information it receives from its environment may be thought of as intelligent.... [I]n human evolution ... creative intelligence [was] the ability to predict an outcome when confronted by a novel combination of events. 6 *Richard E. Leakey*

Intelligence is essentially the ability to solve the problems of present behavior in terms of its possible future consequences as implicated on the basis of past experience.... 7
George H. Mead

[T]he evolutionary use of intelligence is that it enables the individual to profit by error without being slaughtered by it. 8
Alfred N. Whitehead

The true test of intelligence is not how much we know how to do, but how we behave when we don't know what to do. 9 *John Holt*

In an act of intelligence ... the end is established from the outset and pursued after a search for the appropriate means. 10
Jean Piaget & Bärbel Inhelder

[I]t is intelligence that apprehends the fundamental principles. 11 *Aristotle*

Every intelligent action is characterized by an *understanding* of the relations between the given elements and by the *invention* of an appropriate solution on the basis of that understanding. 12 *Gaston Viaud*

[T]he intellect, by its native strength, makes for itself intellectual instruments, whereby it acquires strength for performing other intellectual operations, and from these operations gets again fresh instruments, or the power of pushing its investigations further, and thus gradually proceeds till it reaches the summit of wisdom. 13 *Baruch Spinoza*

[T]he function of the intellect is essentially unification, [and thus] the common object of all its operations is to introduce a certain unity into the diversity of phenomena.... 14
Henri Bergson

[I]ntelligence essentially requires postulates, and moves in the sphere of belief; and intelligence rather than idle intuition was what the psyche required when she gave birth to spirit. It was in learning to behave intelligently that she stretched those threads of telepathic communication which when duly connected struck the first spark of intuition. 15 *George Santayana*

Wherever intelligence operates, things are judged in their capacity of signs of other things. 16
John Dewey

[I]ntelligence is a slippery customer; if one door is closed to it, it finds, or even breaks, another entrance to the world. If one symbolization is inadequate, it seizes another; there is no eternal decree over its means and methods. 17 *Susanne Langer*

[A] mind consists of a number of fairly specific and fairly independent computational mechanisms ... or "multiple intelligences" ... [and] each ... works pretty much under its own steam, using its own peculiar perceptual and mnemonic capacities.... [But] it is evident that the intelligences cannot be viewed merely as a group of raw computational capacities. The world is enwrapped in meanings, and intelligences can be implemented only to the extent that they partake of these meanings, that they enable the individual to develop into a functioning, symbol-using member of his community. 18 *Howard Gardner*

Intelligence isn't a single trait ... but a single name applied ... to a cluster of aptitudes. 19 *Beryl Benderly*

The test of a first-rate intelligence is the ability to hold two opposed ideas in the mind at the same time, and still retain the ability to function. 20 *F. Scott Fitzgerald*

[A] salient feature of human intelligence is the ability to operate with many ways of knowing, often in parallel, so that something can be understood on many levels. 21 *Seymour Papert*

[T]here is intelligence in relation to the not-self and there is intelligence in relation to the self. The completely intelligent person is intelligent both in regard to himself and to the outer world. But completely intelligent people are unhappily rare. 22 *Aldous Huxley*

Delayed reaction is necessary to intelligent conduct.... Indeed, it is this process which constitutes intelligence.... The process is made possible by the mechanism ... which permits the individual's taking of the attitude of the other toward himself, and thus becoming an object to himself. 23 *George H. Mead*

We can assume that the genetic code constitutes at least some part of the ingredients of genius ... [but] to reproduce an intelligence like that of Einstein or Bertrand Russell, however, a nation would need to reproduce the cultural and educational environment that enabled their genius to flourish in the first place. 24 *Peter Singer & Deane Wells*

The heritability of intelligence generally works out at about 60%.... The percentages attributed to genetic influences tell us little about the heritability of a trait in a particular individual.... If the heritability of intelligence were low, more effective applications of current educational techniques should enable everyone to achieve better; if it were high, it would be necessary to search for novel approaches ... that would be better adapted to children with different gene patterns. 25 *Philip Vernon*

What craniology was for the nineteenth century, intelligence testing has become for the twentieth.... 26 *Stephen Jay Gould*

An individual can lose his entire frontal lobes, in the process becoming a radically different person, unable to display any initiative or to solve new problems—and yet may continue to exhibit an I.Q. close to genius level. 27 *Howard Gardner*

It is in our I.Q. testing that we have produced the greatest flood of misbegotten standards. Unaware of our typographic cultural bias, our testers assume that uniform and continuous habits are a sign of intelligence, thus eliminating the ear man and the tactile man. 28 *Marshall McLuhan*

"Intelligence" tests measure your ability to achieve personal success in our society at all costs. They tap your willingness to ignore your body, your physical surroundings, your human relationships.... This may *be* a kind of smartness, but it hardly seems like wisdom. The fact that we value it so highly helps explain the trouble we're in. 29 *Philip Slater*

[T]he age-old myth that women are of inferior intelligence to men has, so far as the scientific evidence goes, not a leg to stand upon. Indeed ... with the exception of the tests for arithmetic, mathematics, mechanics, and mazes, females achieve significantly and con-

Intelligence

sistently higher scores on the intelligence tests than males. 30 *Ashley Montagu*

An intelligent being bears within himself the means to transcend his own nature. 31
Henri Bergson

Intelligence has been used ... to control impulse in the interests of conscious desire. 32
Bertrand Russell

Optimism is expressed by some who feel that since we have evolved a high level of intelligence ... we shall be able to twist any situation to our advantage ... that our intelligence can dominate all our basic biological urges. I submit that this is rubbish. Our raw animal nature will never permit it. 33 *Desmond Morris*

Even in democratic countries, intelligence is generally used only to create ... improved means to unimproved ends—to ends that are dictated by socially sanctioned prejudices and the lowest passions. 34 *Aldous Huxley*

When men act on the principle of intelligence they go out to find the facts and make their wisdom. When they ignore it, they go inside themselves and find only what is there. They elaborate their prejudice, instead of increasing their knowledge. 35 *Walter Lippmann*

Reason is man's instrument for arriving at the truth, intelligence is man's instrument for manipulating the world more successfully; the former is essentially human, the latter belongs also to the animal part of man. 36
Erich Fromm

At a certain level of development intelligence becomes aware of its own role as one function among others, sees its own activity in correct perspective among the other mental tendencies.... Only after this broadening of awareness has been put at the disposal of action does intelligence serve the highest synthetic and differentiating functions of the ego. 37
Heinz Hartmann

Intelligence is mankind's only true capital. 38
Arnold Toynbee

The hope of the world certainly lies in intelligence. Certainly there is no hope anywhere else. 39 *Irwin Edman*

In the conditions of modern life the rule is absolute: the race which does not value trained intelligence is doomed. 40
Alfred N. Whitehead

It may well be that only in space ... will intelligence be able to reach its fullest stature.... The dullards may remain on placid Earth, and real genius will flourish only in space—the realm of the machine, not of flesh and blood. 41
Arthur C. Clarke

[A]rtificial intelligence is good at doing what humans find difficult ... but inept at doing what humans find easy.... 42
William H. Calvin

If we come to believe that it is possible to capture intelligence within artificial devices, then we shall come to believe that human beings can make their own history, a profoundly totalitarian idea—indeed, perhaps the essence of the totalitarian. If we are capable of making history then we have nothing to learn from it. 43
Anthony Smith

[T]he grim fact about human destiny is that intelligence has very little to do with it. 44
Germaine Greer

Pure intelligence is a product of dying, or at least of becoming mentally insensitive, and is therefore in principle madness. 45
Sandor Ferenczi

There is, unfortunately, no necessary correlation between intelligence and decency; the genius and the moron are equally susceptible to corruption. 46 *Albert Speer*

Intelligence is valid only as it serves love. 47
Antoine de Saint-Exupéry

Intelligence and love have evolved in feedback relation with one another—the dissociation of one from the other always spelling danger.... Indeed, Satan represents the symbol of the evil that cleverness unregulated by love can become.... This is the situation which man faces today, and unless he learns in time to understand what the consequences are of the rise in intelligence at the cost of a declining humanity, he may yet perish from this earth. 48 *Ashley Montagu*

[T]he intellect, so skilful in dealing with the inert, is awkward the moment it touches the living. Whether it wants to treat the life of the body or the life of the mind, it proceeds with the rigor, the stiffness and the brutality of an instrument not designed for such use.... *The intellect is characterized by a natural inability to comprehend life.* 49 *Henri Bergson*

[This is] the question we now must ask: Is the intelligence alone, however purified and decontaminated, an adequate agent for doing justice to the needs and purposes of life? 50
Lewis Mumford

Joy

Man is more himself, man is more manlike, when joy is the fundamental thing in him.... 1
G. K. Chesterton

Joy, rather than happiness, is the goal of life, for joy is the emotion which accompanies our fulfilling our natures as human beings. 2
Rollo May

Happiness arises from the harmonious operation of all the sentiments of a well-organized and unified personality.... Joy arises from the harmonious operation of an organized system or sentiment that constitutes a considerable feature or part of one's whole being.... 3
William McDougall

We call "happiness" a certain set of circumstances that makes joy possible. But we call joy that state of mind and emotions that need nothing to feel happy. 4 *André Gide*

Joy is the emotional expression of the courageous Yes to one's own true being. 5
Paul Tillich

Joy is a man's passing from a lesser to a greater perfection. 6 *Baruch Spinoza*

What has become perfect, all that is ripe—wants to die.... All that is unripe wants to live. All that suffers wants to live, that it may become ripe and joyous and longing—longing for what is farther, higher, brighter.... Joys want the eternity of all things, they want deep, profound eternity. 7 *Friedrich Nietzsche*

Anticipatory resoluteness is ... that understanding which follows the call of conscience and which frees for death the possibility of acquiring *power* over Dasein's *existence* and of basically dispersing all fugitive Self-concealments.... Along with the sober anxiety which brings us face to face with our individualized potentiality-for-Being, there goes an unshakable joy in this possibility. 8 *Martin Heidegger*

All the joy and pain we experience ... work creatively in our being. 9 *Rudolf Steiner*

Your joy is your sorrow unmasked.... The deeper that sorrow carves into your being, the more joy you can contain. 10 *Kahlil Gibran*

Everything human must have in it both joy and sorrow; the only matter of interest is the manner in which the two things are balanced.... 11
G. K. Chesterton

[I]t is wrong to believe that unmixed joy is the normal state of sensibility. Man could not live if he were entirely impervious to sadness. 12
Émile Durkheim

Man was made for joy and woe / Joy and woe are ... clothing for the soul divine. 13
William Blake

People ... can transform their emotional lives ... simply by viewing their present misery as serving a higher, perhaps other-worldly goal. They need only believe that they will later benefit in some significant way, such as eternal tranquility, merging with godhead, or Nirvana.... [T]heir suffering ... will now evoke ... tranquility and joy. 14 *Eric Klinger*

The emotion that deals with loss is sadness.... Joy is the experience of rejoining or of possession and is thus the opposite of sadness. 15
Robert Plutchik

Joy

[J]oy ... renders our world ... "wonderful." 16
Robert C. Solomon

If there were no joy in life, it would not be worth living. 17 *Abraham Maslow*

Dante ... described the song of the angels in heaven as "the laughter of the universe." ... For there is really no other reason for creation than pure joy. 18 *Alan Watts*

[T]here is nothing more conducive to goodness in the humanistic sense than the experience of joy.... Every increase in joy a culture can provide for will do more for the ethical education of its members than all the warnings of punishment or preachings of virtue could do. 19 *Erich Fromm*

Joy, beautiful radiance of the gods ... : all men become brothers under your tender wing. 20
Friedrich von Schiller

There is no joy in the world so true and warm as to witness a great soul opening toward one. 21
Goethe

Nothing in America is so painful to the traveller as the lack of joy. Pleasure is frantic and bacchanalian, a matter of momentary oblivion, not of delightful self-expression. 22
Bertrand Russell

[S]cientific culture makes no allowance for "joy," since that is an experience of intense personal involvement. Joy is something that ... does not submit to objectification. 23
Theodore Roszak

[W]hat the modern youth are seeking ... [is] communion in joy.... It is a replay of the basic Dionysian expansiveness, the submergence and loss of identity in the transcending power of the pulsating "now" and the frenzied group of like-minded believers ... an expression that modern, secular, mechanistic society has denied them. 24 *Ernest Becker*

[T]he conquest of the immense joylessness which technology brings into the world is the common task of all men in this age. 25
Karl Jaspers

It is a woman's supreme privilege and development to be a bringer of joy.... A man values a woman so highly because she has just this capacity or power. Men cannot find this ecstasy alone without the aid of the feminine element, so they find it either in an outer woman or in their own inner woman. Joy is a gift from the heart of woman. 26 *Robert A. Johnson*

Follow your joy—it's your truest compass. 27
Candice Bergen

Justice

[The] replacement of the power of the individual by the power of a community constitutes the decisive step of civilization.... The first requisite of civilization, therefore, is that of justice—that is, the assurance that a law once made will not be broken in favour of an individual. 1 *Sigmund Freud*

Justice and injustice ... are qualities that relate to men in society.... Where there is no common power, there is no law; where no law, no injustice. 2 *Thomas Hobbes*

[W]here no covenant has preceded there has no right been transferred, and every man has right to every thing; and consequently no action can be unjust. But when a covenant is made, then to break it is *unjust*, and the definition of INJUSTICE is no other than *the not performance of covenant.* 3 *Thomas Hobbes*

Justice is the first virtue of social institutions.... Each person possesses an inviolability founded on justice that even the welfare of society as a whole cannot override.... [A]n injustice is tolerable only when it is necessary to avoid an even greater injustice. 4 *John Rawls*

Injustice anywhere is a threat to justice everywhere. 5 *Martin Luther King Jr.*

Men condemn injustice because they fear being a victim of it, not because they are opposed to committing it themselves. 6 *Plato*

[T]he principles of justice for the basic structure of society are ... the principles that free and rational persons concerned to further their own interests would accept in an original position of equality.... This way of regarding the principles of justice I shall call justice as fairness. 7 *John Rawls*

I hold that the core structure of stages of moral reasoning consists of the set of operations or ideas that define justice or fairness. The two principal justice operations are the operation of equality and of reciprocity.... [One can then] identify justice with equilibration in valuing. 8
Lawrence Kohlberg

The foundation of justice is that the weakest shall have the same rights as the strongest. 9
Woodrow Wilson

[T]he justice of a society is well defined in terms of how it treats the weak. And there is nothing human which is weaker than the foetus. 10
George Grant

Justice is essentially human, i.e. it affects the mutual relations of men as men. 11 *Aristotle*

Women have less sense of justice than men ... [and] they are more often influenced in their judgments by feelings of affection and hostility. 12 *Sigmund Freud*

[T]he logic underlying an ethic of care is a psychological logic of relationships, which contrasts with the formal logic of fairness that informs the justice approach.... [A] morality of rights and noninterference may appear frightening to women in its potential justification of indifference and unconcern. 13 *Carol Gilligan*

FIAT JUSTITIA, RUAT COELUM.... That something called justice is to be done even though it bring down the heavens in ruin, is the final word of an ethics which is resolutely irrelevant to the circumstances of action and conditions of life. 14 *John Dewey*

The male system brings justice, the female system compassion.... In true moral maturity, both perspectives must converge. 15
Carol Tavris & Carole Wade

Harmonious social relations depend upon the sense of justice as much as ... of benevolence. This sense of justice is a product of the mind and not of the heart.... [But] it must be observed that reason may provide the law but does not, of itself, furnish the reverence.... Love meets the needs of the neighbour, without carefully weighing and comparing his needs with those of the self. It is therefore ethically purer than the justice which is prompted by reason. 16
Reinhold Niebuhr

It is creative justice which transforms by accepting the unacceptable. And creative justice *is* love. 17 *Paul Tillich*

Justice ... partitions and divides; it determines what each one has the right to call his own; it judges and punishes if anyone does not make the distinction between mine and yours.... [I]n love there is no mine and yours. 18
Søren Kierkegaard

Where there is no conflict of interests, there is no need for justice. 19 *Hans Kelsen*

Social justice means that we deny ourselves many things so that others may have to do without them as well.... This demand for equality is the root of social conscience and the sense of duty. 20 *Sigmund Freud*

As early as seven or eight and increasingly thereafter, justice prevails over obedience ... [and] is often acquired at the expense of the parents.... 21 *Jean Piaget & Bärbel Inhelder*

[B]eneficence and punishment alike have their firmest and most essential root in the parental instinct.... This intimate alliance between tender emotion and anger is of great importance for the social life of man, and ... the germ of all moral indignation; and on moral indignation justice and the greater part of public law are in the main founded. 22 *William McDougall*

The emotion of anger is probably the ultimate source of the legal concept of "natural law." ... Because justice avoids anger, it follows that justice is intrinsically "good." ... Thus the basic concept of justice seems to be an almost inevitable social response to the emotion of anger. 23
George E. Pugh

JUSTICE

The first essential step on the road to total domination is to kill the juridical person in man. 24 *Hannah Arendt*

Fellow Germans, my measures will not be crippled by any judicial thinking.... I don't have to worry about justice; my mission is only to destroy and exterminate, nothing more! 25
Hermann Goering

Justice ... will not be a powerful spring of action unless it extend to the whole of creation; nay, I believe that it may be delivered as an axiom, that those who can see pain, unmoved, will soon learn to inflict it. 26 *Mary Wollstonecraft*

Justice being taken away, what are kingdoms but great robberies? 27 *Saint Augustine*

The men who today snatch the worst criminals from justice will murder the most innocent persons tomorrow. 28 *Edmund Burke*

If I came upon a community in which no sort of violence was ever resisted and it was claimed in that community that the non-resistance was a matter of conscience we should have to conclude ... not that this was a community of saints, but rather that this community lacked the concept of justice.... 29
Jan Narveson

Human life ... involves a curious paradox: it seems to require injustice, for the struggle against injustice is what calls forth what is highest in man. 30 *Francis Fukuyama*

Justice is the first virtue of law and of political action, so it is the first virtue of a person. 31
Lawrence Kohlberg

Justice is the basis of all other virtues. 32
Marcus Aurelius

Justice is inseparable from goodness. 33
Jean-Jacques Rousseau

Any law that uplifts human personality is just. Any law that degrades human personality is unjust. 34 *Martin Luther King Jr.*

A society in which men are given an equal opportunity of self-realisation is, also, a society in which there is justice. For by justice we mean ... the rendering to each man of his own. 35
Harold Laski

The greatest possible amount of free development of individuals is, to my mind, the goal at which a social system ought to aim. To secure this end, we need a compromise between justice and freedom.... Justice and freedom have different spheres: the sphere of justice is the external conditions of a good life; the sphere of freedom is the personal pursuit of happiness.... 36 *Bertrand Russell*

Absolute justice is achieved by the suppression of all contradiction: therefore it destroys freedom.... Absolute freedom mocks at justice. Absolute justice denies freedom. To be fruitful, the two ideas must find their limits in each other. 37 *Albert Camus*

Freedom ... is the motivating principle of all revolutions. Without it, justice seems inconceivable to the rebel's mind. There comes a time, however, when justice demands the suspension of freedom. Then terror, on a grand or small scale, makes its appearance to consummate the revolution. 38 *Albert Camus*

[W]hoever succeeds in making a more successful and more enduring revolution is from that moment on graced with the bright robes of Justice.... 39 *Alexander Solzhenitsyn*

The demand for justice ends in injustice if it is not primarily based on an ethical justification of justice; without this, crime itself one day becomes a duty. 40 *Albert Camus*

The overemphasis on justice may be ... a camouflage for vindictiveness. 41 *Karen Horney*

Punishment can never be dealt out with justice, for no man can be just. Justice implies complete understanding. 42 *A. S. Neill*

But mercy is ... an attribute to God himself,
And earthly power then doth show likest God's
When mercy seasons justice. 43
William Shakespeare

[T]he sense of justice is continuous with the love of mankind. 44 *John Rawls*

[T]he criterion of justice ... is the influence my conduct will have upon the stock of general good. 45 *William Godwin*

Justice is the constant and perpetual wish to render every one his due. 46 *Justinian*

Truth is the summit of being; justice is the application of it to affairs. 47
Ralph Waldo Emerson

Justice is truth in action. 48 *Benjamin Disraeli*

[It] is of fundamental importance that justice should not only be done, but should manifestly and undoubtedly be seen to be done. 49
Viscount Hewart

Men must learn that the actions of the State are their own. They must learn that they will realise justice only to the degree that they bend their efforts to the making of justice. 50 *Harold Laski*

Certainly no man can over-estimate the importance of the mechanisms of justice. 51
Harold Laski

[T]he arm of the moral universe is long, but it bends toward justice. 52
Martin Luther King Jr.

The tragic wisdom is rather religious; it is the resignation of the demand for justice in order to accept life in a cosmos that is just in no humanly understandable sense. 53
Lawrence Kohlberg

KILLING

MAN IS THE ONLY SPECIES that is a mass murderer.... 1 *Nino Tinbergen*

Man's destructive hand spares nothing that lives; he kills to feed himself, he kills to clothe himself, he kills to adorn himself, he kills to attack, he kills to defend himself, he kills to instruct himself, he kills to amuse himself, he kills for the sake of killing. 2 *Josef de Maistre*

And now kill every male among the little ones, and kill every woman who has had intercourse with man by lying with a male.... Everyone who has killed a soul and everyone who has touched someone slain, you should purify yourselves on the third day.... 3 *Moses*

[I]n accepting Abel's offering of meat ... and rejecting Cain's offering of the "fruits of the ground," the new male God was announcing his law: that henceforth harmony among men and beasts was out, and killing and violence were in. 4 *Elizabeth Gould Davis*

Man is a predator whose natural instinct is to kill with a weapon.... [This] created not only the human being but also the human predicament.... We are Cain's children. 5
Robert Ardrey

Civilization develops not from Abel, but from Cain the murderer. 6 *Carl Sagan*

[T]he rate of civilization's rise has corresponded ... closely with man's ascendant capacity to kill. Civilization is a compensatory consequence of our killing imperative; the one could not exist without the other. 7
Robert Ardrey

For it is not in giving life but in risking life that man is raised above the animal; that is why superiority has been accorded in humanity not to the sex that brings forth but to that which kills. 8 *Simone de Beauvoir*

During the Roman Empire, gladiatorial contests involving human sacrifice were dedicated to the gods. Such sacrifices are rooted in a value structure that was created by breaking the matricentric bond: display of power through killing is a greater good than life. 9 *Marilyn French*

[C]eremoniously killing captives is a way of affirming power over life, and therefore over death.... [I]f you kill your enemy, your life is affirmed because it proves that the gods favor you. 10 *Ernest Becker*

[S]oldiers fight in terms of the sanctions and patterns of their immediate social group.... [T]he phenomena of ... killing and abuse are

Killing

directly related to the sense of personal manly validation individual men feel in terms of their male groups.... 11 *Lionel Tiger*

When you want to create a solidary group of male killers ... you kill the women in them. That is the lesson of the Marines. And it works. 12 *George Gilder*

The process of killing ... is the prime sexual act for men in reality and/or imagination. 13 *Andrea Dworkin*

It is forbidden to kill; therefore all murderers are punished unless they kill in large numbers and to the sound of trumpets. 14 *Voltaire*

[T]he rule in our society [is] that while those who kill ... a single person are severely punished, those (heads of state, inventors, manufacturers) who are responsible for the death, mutilation, or general wretchedness of thousands or millions are rewarded with fame, riches, and prizes. The old culture's rules speak very clearly on this: ... if you're going to kill, kill big. 15 *Philip Slater*

Kill a man, and you are an assassin. Kill millions of men, and you are a conqueror. Kill everyone, and you are a god. 16 *Jean Rostand*

The influence of men like Hitler and Stalin lies precisely in their unlimited capacity and willingness to kill.... 17 *Philip Slater*

When defense of the group is involved, killing is regarded as a noble deed. 18 *Irenäus Eibl-Eibesfeldt*

The hero is he who kills or makes it possible to kill the greatest number of the enemy. Virtually all our institutions, traditions, and public media conspire to elevate and sanctify the uninhibited killing of the enemy as the most noble of moral obligations in the service of one's country. Those who refuse to participate in such killing ... are condemned, jailed, or otherwise penalized. 19 *Ashley Montagu*

Kings and Emperors are surprised and horrified when one of themselves is murdered, and yet the whole of their activity consists in managing murder and preparing for murder. 20 *Leo Tolstoy*

There is a limit to the number of people you can kill out of hatred or lust for slaughter, but there is no limit to the number you can kill in the cool, systematic manner of the military "categorical imperative." 21 *Arthur Seyss-Inquart*

[J]ust as the law in civilized countries assumes that the voice of conscience tells everybody "Thou shalt not kill," even though man's natural desires and inclinations may at times be murderous, so the law of Hitler's land demanded that the voice of conscience tell everybody: "Thou shalt kill." ... 22 *Hannah Arendt*

I had no feeling in carrying out these things because I had received an order to kill.... That, by the way, was the way I was trained. 23 *S.S. Capt. Josef Kramer* ("Beast of Belsen")

I was furious with myself ... because I hadn't been able to kill without emotion.... I had to do something to free myself from this disabling emotionalism.... [F]inally, I could kill efficiently and without emotion or thought. 24 *G. Gordon Liddy*

[M]en are most apt to kill or wish to kill when they feel themselves symbolically dying—that is, overcome by ... meaninglessness, and the separation from the larger currents of human life. 25 *Robert Jay Lifton*

Killing is one way of experiencing that one *is*. ... 26 *Erich Fromm*

This is the final realization of freedom: the power to kill ... saves the soul from utter emptiness. 27 *Albert Camus*

[M]urder is sometimes committed to avert suicide. 28 *Karl Menninger*

It is ... a general rule that where homicide is very common it confers a sort of immunity against suicide. 29 *Émile Durkheim*

Killing is a way of ... warding off one's own death. 30 *Eugene Ionesco*

The death fear of the ego is lessened by the killing, the sacrifice, of the other. 31 *Otto Rank*

[O]ur society needs killers from time to time—it doesn't need lovers. It depends heavily on its population being angry and discontented; and the renunciation of violence would endanger our society as we now know it. 32
Philip Slater

War is the last socially acceptable outlet for a barbarian species which is not yet willing to be civilized.... Now the killing is encapsulated in myths of dominoes, communist tyranny, freedom, and democratic doctrines.... The issues are so confounded by sophistry that the military enterprise is carried out on the assumption that soldiers have a right to kill anyone whose innocence has not been demonstrated. 33
Donald A. Wells

The distance at which all shooting weapons take effect screens the killer against the stimulus situation which would otherwise activate his killing inhibitions.... No sane man would ever go rabbit hunting for pleasure if the necessity of killing his prey with natural weapons brought home to him the full, emotional realization of what he is actually doing. 34
Konrad Lorenz

The dogma of "Thou shalt not kill" is not a possible dogma.... [T]hat particular dogma must be set aside as pretentious and silly until the time when men have cleaned out their private urges to kill on a subjective plane.... The ingrained vanity of one class, grinding against another, murders millions.... Intolerance of race and creed and nation, of rich for poor and the organized poor for the embattled rich—all these and a myriad other social processes collectively engaged in—make murder on the plane of subjective crowd behaviour an everyday affair and we are all parties to these murders. 35 *Philip Wylie*

And so, to the end of history, murder shall breed murder, always in the name of right and honour and peace, until the gods are tired of blood and create a race that shall understand. 36
George Bernard Shaw

We shall know nothing until we know whether we have the right to kill our fellow men, or the right to let them be killed. In that every action today leads to murder, direct or indirect, we cannot act until we know whether or why we have the right to kill. 37 *Albert Camus*

Thou shalt not kill. 38 *Holy Bible*

[M]an became man, not when he asserted his superiority ... but when he formulated the rule, "You shall not kill." That moment marked the beginning of humanness, the beginning of reason, the beginning of self-control. 39
Jacques Ellul

KNOWLEDGE

IT IS IN THE NATURE of man to desire to know. 1
Aristotle

Today we still yearn to know why we are here and where we came from. Humanity's deepest desire for knowledge is justification enough for our continuing quest. And our goal is nothing less than a complete description of the universe we live in. 2 *Stephen Hawking*

[T]he trend of modern philosophy has been to arrive at theories regarding the nature of the universe by means of theories regarding the nature of knowledge.... 3 *John Dewey*

Taken in the full modern sense of the word, knowledge is the twin sister of mankind. Born together, the two ideas (or two dreams) grew up together to attain an almost religious valuation in the course of the last century. 4
Pierre Teilhard de Chardin

In the highest sense, the soul is permeated by the spirit of the higher self and this spirit ... bears within itself the element of "knowing." ... "To know" is to understand, to recognize, to identify; it is the kingly power of man.... It is the spirit of the "true" light which gives to the soul the quality of knowing itself and of recognizing man, earth and universe. 5 *Karl König*

Since survival requires increasing amounts of intelligence and learning, then intelligence and

Knowledge

learning are "good" for us as a species, and are rewarded by pleasure. Endorphins act as filters and determiners of "reality," and as rewards for survival-oriented—i.e. intelligent—behavior seem to be favoring and guiding us toward ... "perfect knowledge." 6 *Michael Hutchinson*

The correct apprehension of facts and events by the mind, and the correct inferences as to the relations between them, constitute knowledge, and it is chiefly by knowledge that men have become better able to live well on earth. 7
William Graham Sumner

The only genuine wealth, for which we ought to give away all others, is true knowledge. 8
Socrates

For also knowledge itself is power. 9
Francis Bacon

Knowledge is the most democratic source of power. 10 *Alvin Toffler*

It is the conquest of knowledge that is the real source of our hopes, its conquest and its extension to the common man. 11 *Harold Laski*

If the knowledge industry is large enough to create a surplus of production of knowledge over and above what is constantly lost by death and old age, then the society cannot avoid development. 12 *Kenneth Boulding*

[T]he increase of knowledge itself is anti-entropic. It builds structure out of what previously was chaos. 13 *Kenneth Boulding*

For archaic man ... knowing is magical power. For him all particular knowledge is sacred knowledge—esoteric and wonder-working wisdom, because any knowing is directly related to the cosmic order itself. 14
Johan Huizinga

The greatest crisis facing modern civilization is going to be how to transform information into structured knowledge. 15 *Carlos Fuentes*

We are drowning in information but starved for knowledge. 16 *John Naisbitt*

From now on there is only *one* important type of information: *knowledge.* 17
Paul Feyerabend

It is probably fundamental to all knowledge processes that we gain knowledge by the orderly loss of information. 18
Kenneth Boulding

Information is not knowledge.... You cannot mass-produce knowledge, which is created by individual minds, drawing on individual experience, separating the significant from the irrelevant, making value judgments. 19
Theodore Roszak

The control of knowledge is the crux of tomorrow's worldwide struggle for power in every human institution.... [Thus] knowledge *about* knowledge becomes the prime source of power. 20 *Alvin Toffler*

Knowledge works as a tool of power. 21
Friedrich Nietzsche

Knowledge and power are not truly united inside the ruling circles; and when men of knowledge do come to a point of contact with the circles of powerful men, they come not as peers but as hired men. 22 *C. Wright Mills*

If knowledge is power, then the love of knowledge is the love of power. 23
Bertrand Russell

Omnipotence once exploded, the devil may tempt us with omniscience. This is an aspiration far more deeply rooted in the spirit than the childish illusion of power. 24
George Santayana

Our dream of heaven cannot be realized on earth.... For those who have eaten from the tree of knowledge, paradise is lost. 25
Karl Popper

And the Lord God commanded ... : Of every tree of the garden thou mayest freely eat.... But of the tree of knowledge of good and evil, thou shalt not eat of it: for in the day that thou eatest thereof thou shalt surely die. 26 *Holy Bible*

Knowledge

[W]hen Adam and Eve ate the fruit of the tree of knowledge God punished them by withdrawing from them the privilege of immortality and dooming them ... to die. Now our species has eaten more deeply of the fruit of the tree of knowledge, and has brought itself face to face with a second death—the death of mankind. 27 *Jonathan Schell*

We are sinful not merely because we have eaten from the Tree of Knowledge, but also because we have not yet eaten of the tree of Life. 28 *Franz Kafka*

Adam in being tempted by the tree of knowledge lost touch with the tree of life. He abandoned faith for reason. 29 *John Carroll*

To maintain the species indefinitely we are compelled to drive toward total knowledge, right down to the levels of the neuron and gene. When we have progressed enough to explain ourselves in these mechanistic terms ... the result might be hard to accept. 30 *E. O. Wilson*

The Western paradigm of knowledge ... is given in the conception of "machine." 31 *George Grant*

[H]ow we think about knowledge affects how we think about ourselves. 32 *Seymour Papert*

The great movement for independent thought instilled in the modern mind a desperate refusal of all knowledge that is not absolutely impersonal, and this implied in its turn a mechanical conception of man. 33 *Michael Polanyi*

The more the fruits of knowledge become accessible to men, the more widespread is the decline of religious belief. 34 *Sigmund Freud*

Without knowledge there can be no morality! 35 *Mary Wollstonecraft*

Integrity without knowledge is weak and useless, and knowledge without integrity is dangerous and dreadful. 36 *Samuel Johnson*

[E]pistemology is always and inevitably *personal*.... It is surely so that all outside knowledge whatsoever must derive in part from what is called *self-knowledge*. 37 *Gregory Bateson*

Knowledge is a form of union of Self and not-Self. 38 *Bertrand Russell*

There is, in fact, no more perfect dominion than knowledge; he who knows something, possesses it. Knowledge unites the knower with the known. 39 *Miguel de Unamuno*

Knowing ... is a form of appropriation.... The truth discovered, like a work of art, is *my* knowledge.... It is through me that a facet of the world is revealed; it is to me that it reveals itself. In this sense I am creator and possessor.... 40 *Jean-Paul Sartre*

[I]nto every act of knowing there enters a tacit and passionate contribution of the person knowing what is being known, and ... this coefficient is no mere imperfection, but a necessary component of all knowledge. 41 *Michael Polanyi*

Whoever speaks of man therefore will have to speak at some stage of human knowledge.... [But] every time we acquire knowledge we enlarge the world, the world of man ... and in this sense a comprehensive knowledge of man must appear impossible. 42 *Michael Polanyi*

The further we reach into the depths of our own being, or someone else's being, the more the goal of knowledge eludes us. 43 *Erich Fromm*

[N]o form of knowledge ... constitutes a simple copy of reality, because it always includes a process of assimilation to previous structures ... and this is true from elementary sensorimotor behavior right up to the higher logico-mathematical operations. 44 *Jean Piaget*

[T]he criterion of knowledge lies in the method used to secure consequences and not in metaphysical conceptions of the nature of the real. 45 *John Dewey*

Knowledge is a matter of degree.... 46 *Abraham Maslow*

Knowledge advances by steps, and not by leaps. 47 *Thomas Macaulay*

Knowledge

The first of these [rules of knowledge] was to accept nothing as true which I did not clearly recognize to be so.... The second was to divide up each of the difficulties which I examined into as many parts as possible.... The third was to carry on my reflections in due order, beginning with objects that were the most simple and easy to understand, in order to rise little by little, or by degrees, to knowledge of the most complex.... 48 *René Descartes*

Often, correct knowledge can be arrived at only after many repetitions of the process leading from matter to consciousness and then back to matter, that is, leading from practice to knowledge and then back to practice. Such is the Marxist theory of knowledge, the dialectical materialist theory of knowledge. 49
Mao Tse-tung

All knowledge—and this naturally includes philosophy—is polemical by nature.... Competition is an outstanding feature of the whole development of Scholasticism and the Universities. 50 *Johan Huizinga*

There is only intuitive knowledge. Deduction and discursive argument, incorrectly called examples of knowing, are only instruments which lead to intuition. 51 *Jean-Paul Sartre*

[T]here are as many kinds of valid knowledge as there are conclusions wherein distinctive operations have been employed to solve the problems set by antecedently experienced situations. 52 *John Dewey*

[A]ll knowledge is the result of imposing some kind of order upon the reactions of the psychic system as they flow into our consciousness—an order which reflects the behavior of a *metaphysical* reality, of that which is in itself real. 53 *Carl Jung*

All advances in knowledge consist of making one's mental representations of the world more accurate pictures of the world as it really is. 54
Calvin S. Hall

If you want knowledge, you must take part in the practice of changing reality. 55
Mao Tse-tung

The function proper to knowledge is not seeing or demonstrating; it is interpreting. 56
Michel Foucault

Human knowledge is by its very nature symbolic knowledge. 57 *Ernst Cassirer*

In brief, the function of knowledge is to make one experience freely available in other experiences.... In other words, knowledge is a perception of those connections of an object which determine its applicability in a given situation. 58
John Dewey

What is it that the common people take for knowledge?... Nothing more than this: Something strange is to be reduced to something *familiar*. 59 *Friedrich Nietzsche*

Knowledge is a status conferred upon an idea. ... 60 *Theodore Roszak*

Knowledge is only a late form of belief. 61
Oswald Spengler

[A]ll our knowledge, has been built up communally: there would be no astrophysics, there would be no history, there would not even be language, if man were a solitary animal. 62
Jacob Bronowski

Just as a single human being, restricted wholly to the fruits of his own labor, could never amass a fortune ... so, also, no knowledge worthy of the name can be gathered up in a single human mind limited to the span of a human life.... 63 *Ernst Mach*

All knowledge is rooted in a life, a society, and a language that have a history; and it is in that very history that knowledge finds the element enabling it to communicate with other forms of life, other types of society, other significations.... 64
Michel Foucault

Knowledge and language are rigorously interwoven.... To know is to speak correctly.... But language is knowledge only in an unreflecting form.... The sciences are well-made languages, just as languages are sciences lying fallow. All languages must therefore be renewed ... and readjusted if necessary so that the chain of knowledge may be made visible in all its clarity.... 65 *Michel Foucault*

The tree of knowledge may grow from within, but it is also constrained from without.... Values are the food of knowledge, and knowledge like any other organism moves toward that part of a possible field of growth where the values are highest. 66 *Kenneth Boulding*

It is the vitality, not the particular direction of the tree of knowledge which makes for hope in the whole course of time. 67
Kenneth Boulding

All knowledge has an ultimate object. Knowledge for the sake of knowledge is, say what you will, nothing but a dismal begging of the question. 68 *Miguel de Unamuno*

The acquisition of knowledge for which no use can be found is a sure method of driving a man to revolt. 69 *Gustave Le Bon*

If I accept utility as the ultimate standard of knowledge, I surrender my own selfhood therein. But if knowledge be pursued for its own sake, in the pursuit I achieve self-awareness. 70 *Karl Jaspers*

Perhaps the most important advantage of "useless" knowledge is that it promotes a contemplative habit of mind. There is in the world much too much readiness, not only for action without adequate previous reflection, but also for some sort of action on occasions on which wisdom would counsel inaction. 71
Bertrand Russell

The great end of life is not knowledge but action. 72 *T. H. Huxley*

The knowledge which comes first to persons, and that remains the most deeply ingrained, is knowledge of *how to do*.... 73 *John Dewey*

Knowledge is always a function of being. 74
Aldous Huxley

In both West and East, knowledge had always been seen as applying to *being*. Then, almost overnight, it came to be applied to *doing*. It became a resource and a utility. Knowledge had always been a private good. Almost overnight it became a public good. 75 *Peter F. Drucker*

Upon the whole, a proof of a person's having knowledge is the ability to teach. 76 *Aristotle*

[E]xpert knowledge alone is never adequate for it only becomes significant in virtue of him who possesses it. 77 *Karl Jaspers*

[A]s knowledge grows, is enriched, and becomes specialized, the student will move farther and farther away from feeling any immediate and genuine need for it.... And so the terrible gap which began at least a century ago continues to grow, the gap between living culture, genuine knowledge, and the ordinary man.... This culture [of knowledge], which does not have any root structure in man ... lacks any native and indigenous values.... Underneath this culture ... man will remain ... uncultured, a barbarian. 78 *José Ortega y Gasset*

Today ... we witness an increasing channelling of energies into a limited range of knowing patterns. The result is the increasing institutionalization of knowing and knowledge which in turn directly contributes to an interesting paradox: the rapid enlargement of our fund of knowledge, and more difficulty for greater numbers of people to have access to and act upon the increasing store of knowledge. 79
Charles A. Tesconi & Van Cleve Morris

Happiness involves knowledge: it is the prerogative of the *animal rationale*. With the decline in consciousness, with the control of information, with the absorption of the individual into mass communication, knowledge is administered and confined. The individual does not really know what is going on; the overpowering machine of education and entertainment unites him with all the others in a state of anaesthesia from which all detrimental ideas tend to be excluded. And since knowledge of the whole truth is hardly conducive to happiness, such general anaesthesia makes individuals happy. 80
Herbert Marcuse

[T]he growth of knowledge in the social sciences contains within itself a powerful tendency

Knowledge

toward social control, toward control of the many by the few. An equally strong tendency is toward the weakening or destruction of the existential person. When all are regarded as objects, the subjective individual, the inner self, the person in the process of becoming ... is weakened, devalued, or destroyed. 81 *Carl Rogers*

[T]he very process of augmenting human knowledge ... diminishes man. For man, as the whole of science as well as the whole of poetry will demonstrate, is not what he thinks he knows, but what he thinks he *can* know, can become. 82 *Archibald MacLeish*

Almost by definition a cultured man is one who is dissatisfied with the state of his knowledge and is aware of his limitations.... All that he knows is that human nature is infinitely perfectible and that ultimately all human knowledge—and all knowledge is human—must be brought into the service of that end, the perfection of human nature. 83 *Ashley Montagu*

However far knowledge pushes its discovery of the "essential fire" and however capable it becomes some day of remodeling and perfecting the human element, it will always find itself in the end facing the same problem—how to give to each and every element its final value by grouping them in the unity of an organised whole. 84 *Pierre Teilhard de Chardin*

The first pre-condition for establishing an adequate epistemology of life is the recognition that *the life process is a knowledge process*, that the knowledge of the brain cannot be separated from the knowledge contained in our elementary cells, that abstract knowledge is only one end of the spectrum of which the other end is ... biological knowledge. 85 *Henryk Skolimowski*

[M]y knowing is a small part of a wider integrated knowing that knits the entire biosphere or creation. 86 *Gregory Bateson*

Man is no longer satisfied merely to acquire knowledge; while accumulating more of this, he regards himself as the "knower" and his research is daily brought a little more to bear on the two inseparable factors presented by a humanity that transforms the world and a humanity that, while it acts, is transforming itself. 87 *Claude Lévi-Strauss*

The growth of knowledge is one of the most irreversible forces known to mankind.... Hence there is no hope for ignorance or for a morality based on it. Once we have tasted the fruit of the tree of knowledge ... Eden is closed to us.... Therefore either we must wander hopelessly in the world or we must press forward to Zion. We must learn to master ourselves as we are learning to master nature. 88 *Kenneth Boulding*

Man's destiny is to know, if only because societies with knowledge culturally dominate societies that lack it. 89 *E. O. Wilson*

The further the spiritual evolution of mankind advances, the more certain it seems to me that the path to genuine religiosity does not lie through ... blind faith, but through striving after rational knowledge. 90 *Albert Einstein*

Actively to participate in the making of knowledge is the highest prerogative of man and the only warrant of his freedom. 91 *John Dewey*

Quest for complete certainty can be fulfilled in pure knowing alone. Such is the verdict of our most enduring philosophic tradition. 92 *John Dewey*

Knowledge is based on perceptions of what is fixed, yet if the present is always born anew, this process can never be completed.... A society dominated by the authority of knowledge will never allow more subtle and creative human functions to flower, for our whole desire for certainty and control implies that we are clinging to the past and seeking security in the realm of the known. 93 *F. David Peat*

Man has never had such a varied body of knowledge in his possession before, and probably never before has he been so uncertain.... 94 *John Dewey*

Man does not want to know. When he knows very little he plays with the possibility of knowledge, but when he finds that the pieces he has been putting together are going to spell out the answer to the riddle he is frightened and he throws them in every direction; and another civilization falls. 95 *Rebecca West*

He that increaseth knowledge increaseth sorrow. 96 *Holy Bible*

Human life is limited, but knowledge is limitless. To drive the limited in pursuit of the limitless is fatal; and to presume that one really knows is fatal indeed! 97 *Chuang-Tzu*

So knowledge doth itself far more extend / Than all the minds of men can comprehend. 98
Fulke Greville

Women accepted limited knowledge as their natural condition, a great human truth that a man may take a lifetime to reach. 99
Camille Paglia

The more we know, the more we know that we don't know. 100 *Kenneth Boulding*

It is the supreme striving of knowledge to reach the point where cognition fails. For our consciousness of being finds an indispensable source in nonknowledge, but only in fulfilled, conquered nonknowledge. 101 *Karl Jaspers*

Knowledge shrinks as wisdom grows. 102
Alfred N. Whitehead

~ LANGUAGE ~

LANGUAGE IS, without a doubt, the most momentous and at the same time the most mysterious product of the human mind. Between the clearest animal call of love or warning or danger, and a man's least, trivial *word*, there lies a whole day of Creation—or in modern phrase, a whole chapter of evolution. 1 *Susanne Langer*

Speech is the means by which the raw material of *Homo* is transformed into the finished article *sapiens*. 2 *Ashley Montagu*

The intelligibility of Being-in-the-world ... expresses itself as discourse.... As an existential state in which Dasein is disclosed, discourse is constitutive for Dasein's existence.... The way in which discourse gets expressed is language. 3
Martin Heidegger

The study of man is the study of talk. Human society is an edifice spun out of the tenuous webs of conversation. 4 *Kenneth Boulding*

[I]t is language [which] reveals to man that world which is closer to him than any world of natural objects and touches his weal and woe more directly than physical nature. For it is language that makes his existence in a *community* possible.... 5 *Ernst Cassirer*

Language is a social phenomenon.... 6
Claude Lévi-Strauss

In speaking their own language, people also speak the language of their masters, benefactors, advertisers.... Thus they do not only express *themselves* ... but also something other than themselves.... This must necessarily be so, for language ... is societal material. 7
Herbert Marcuse

Language is an instrument of *collective thought*. 8
Maria Montessori

Language is the great container of culture. 9
Lewis Mumford

[O]ur selves must be accounted for in terms of the social process, and in terms of communication.... We are, especially through the use of the vocal gestures, continually arousing in ourselves those responses which we call out in other persons, so that we are taking the attitudes of the other persons into our own conduct. The critical importance of language in the development of human experience lies in this fact.... [I]t is of very fundamental importance in the development of what we call self-consciousness and the appearance of the self.... 10
George H. Mead

[L]anguage must have been prior to the development of mind or thought. 11
George H. Mead

Language, an unreflecting totalization, is human reason which has its reasons of which man

Language

knows nothing.... Linguistics thus presents us with a dialectical and totalizing entity outside (or beneath) consciousness and will. 12

Claude Lévi-Strauss

In order for ideas or memories to become conscious, it is necessary for them to be associated with language. 13 *Calvin S. Hall*

Language is like money, without which specific relative values may well exist and be felt, but cannot be reduced to a common denominator. 14 *George Santayana*

Language does not simply symbolize a situation or object which is already there in advance; it makes possible the existence or the appearance of that situation or object, for it is a part of the mechanism whereby that situation or object is created. 15 *George H. Mead*

Language and myth are near of kin.... They are two different shoots from one and the same root.... Both are based on a very general and a very early experience of mankind, an experience of a social rather than of a physical nature.... Language is [thus], by its very nature and essence, metaphorical. 16

Ernst Cassirer

The development of language brought about the emancipation of understanding from sensation.... Only when understanding has become, through language, detached from visual awareness and pure, does death appear to man as the great enigma.... 17 *Oswald Spengler*

Pre-verbal knowledge appears as a small lighted area surrounded by immense darkness, a small patch illuminated by accepting a-critically the unreasoned conclusions of our senses.... Even adults show no distinctly greater intelligence than animals so long as their minds work unaided by language. 18 *Michael Polanyi*

Language is the cause of learning. 19 *Aristotle*

Language enables the logic of a strategy to be stated, examined, and developed.... [It] is the software of the cerebral computer. 20

John H. Crook

What distinguishes language from all other signs and enables it to play a decisive role in representation is ... that it analyses representations according to a necessarily successive order.... [L]anguage cannot represent thought, instantly, in its totality; it is bound to arrange it, part by part, in a linear order. 21

Michel Foucault

Language does for intelligence what the wheel does for the feet and the body. It enables them to move from thing to thing with greater ease and speed and ever less involvement. Language extends and amplifies man but it also divides his faculties. His collective consciousness or intuitive awareness is diminished by his technical extension of consciousness that is speech. 22

Marshall McLuhan

In modern times the apparatus of suggestion is in language, not in pictures.... [W]ords have been called "symbols." They might better be called "tokens." They are like token coins. They "pass"; that is their most noteworthy characteristic. They are familiar, unquestioned.... They always reveal the invincible tendency of the masses to mythologize.... They carry a coercion with them and overwhelm people who are not trained to verify assertions and dissect fallacies. 23 *William Graham Sumner*

Whoever controls the language, the images, controls the race. 24 *Allen Ginsberg*

Tyranny thrives only on deception.... By calling "autonomous" that which is powerless ... "democratic" that which is autocratic ... "popular" that which is imposed by terror ... in brief, by systematically corrupting language to obscure reality—the Communists ... made inroads into our sense of reality. Language is, after all, the only medium in which we can think. 25

Jeanne Kirkpatrick

"Don't you see that the whole aim of Newspeak is to narrow the range of thought? In the end we shall make thoughtcrime literally impossible, because there will be no words in which to express it.... Every year fewer and fewer words, and the range of consciousness always a little smaller." 26 *George Orwell*

Language

The fact is that our primary world of reality *is* a verbal one. Without words our imagination cannot retain distinct objects and their relations, but out of sight is out of mind. 27
Susanne Langer

A [world] picture held us captive. And we could not get outside it, for it lay in our language and language seemed to repeat it to us inexorably. 28
Ludwig Wittgenstein

[P]rint culture confers on man a language of thought which leaves him quite unready to face the language of his own electro-magnetic technology. 29 *Marshall McLuhan*

Machines are already becoming better at communicating with each other than human beings are with human beings. The situation is ironical. More and more concern about communication, less and less to communicate. 30
R. D. Laing

The great enemy of clear language is insincerity.... But if thought corrupts language, language can also corrupt thought. 31
George Orwell

Corrupt language is very deeply imbedded in the rhetoric of the technological elite.... Language, hence reason too, has been transformed into nothing more than an instrument for affecting the things and events in the world.... [N]ow that language has become merely another tool, all concepts, ideas, images that artists and writers cannot paraphrase into computer-comprehensible language have lost their function and their potency.... In the process of adapting ourselves to these systems, we ... have castrated not only ourselves (that is, resigned ourselves to our impotence), but our very language as well. 32 *Joseph Weizenbaum*

Error is never so difficult to be destroyed, as when it has its roots in language. Every improper term ... conceals the nature of the thing, and presents a frequently invincible obstacle to the discovery of the truth. 33 *Jeremy Bentham*

Philosophy is a battle against the bewitchment of our intelligence by means of language. 34
Ludwig Wittgenstein

Language disguises thought. So much so, that from the outward form of the clothing it is impossible to infer the form of the thought beneath it, because the outward form of the clothing is not designed to reveal the form of the body, but for entirely different purposes. 35
Ludwig Wittgenstein

If language is to grow into a vehicle of thought, an expression of concepts and judgments, this evolution can be achieved only at the price of forgoing the wealth and fullness of immediate experience. In the end, what is left of the concrete sense and feeling content it once possessed is little more than a bare skeleton. 36
Ernst Cassirer

Language not merely opened the doors of the mind to consciousness, but partly closed the cellar door to the unconscious and restricted the access of the ghosts and demons of that underworld to the increasingly well-ventilated and lighted chambers of the upper stories. 37
Lewis Mumford

Speech ... is often used less to express genuine feelings and thoughts than to hide, veil, or deny them, and thus to express the false self. 38
Alice Miller

I ... solved the great mystery of why so many millions of human beings not only originally became emotionally disturbed, but why they persistently ... remained so. The very facility with language which enabled them to be essentially human—to talk to others ... also enabled them to abuse this facility by talking utter nonsense to themselves.... 39 *Albert Ellis*

The popular faith in words is a veritable disease of the mind. 40 *Carl Jung*

The intellectual is so hung up on the disease of words that nothing exists unless he writes it down. 41 *Timothy Leary*

[W]ords are wise men's counters, they do but reckon by them; but they are the money of fools.... 42 *Thomas Hobbes*

To-day no attempt is made to use language as a means of contemplating being, language be-

Language

ing substituted for being.... The fundamental significance of language for human existence has been transformed into a phantom by turning away the attention. 43 *Karl Jaspers*

[O]ur vocabulary reinforces the emergence of an abstract, if not mystical, world conception. And this is the penultimate disjunction between the everyday world of fact and experience, and the world of concepts and matter. 44
Daniel Bell

What civilizations and peoples leave us as the monuments of their thought is not so much their texts as their vocabularies, their syntaxes, the sounds of their languages rather than the words they spoke; not so much their discourse as the element that made it possible, the discursivity of their language. 45
Michel Foucault

Just as the living organism manifests, by its inner coherence, the functions that keep it alive, so language, in the whole architecture of its grammar, makes visible the fundamental will that keeps a whole people alive.... 46
Michel Foucault

[F]or language is neither an instrument nor a product ... but a ceaseless activity—an *energeïa*. 47 *Michel Foucault*

There is a deeper source of anxiety, below the level of ... explicit thought: that is the growing inadequacy of words, and especially certain key words which have always functioned in our moral and political discourse, to express exactly what we mean.... The world image has collapsed. 48 *Susanne Langer*

[W]hen, as in our time, a reawakening of the love of beauty has prompted a refinement of our poetical language, we pass so soon into extravagance, obscurity, and affectation. Our modern languages are not susceptible of great formal beauty. 49 *George Santayana*

To the extent to which human language falls short of divine beauty, to that extent Man's sentient and intellectual faculties fall short of truth, and the necessities of social life fall short of justice. 50 *Simone Weil*

[A]s a result of the importance of linguistics and of its applications to the knowledge of man, the question of the being of language, which ... is so intimately linked with the fundamental problems of our culture, reappears in all its enigmatic insistence. With the continually extended use of linguistic categories ... we must henceforth ask ourselves what language must be in order to structure in this way what is nevertheless not in itself either word or discourse, and in order to articulate itself on the pure forms of knowledge.... The question as to what language is in its being is once more of the greatest urgency. 51 *Michel Foucault*

As to be a tool, or to be used as a means for consequences, is to have and to endow with meaning, language, being the tool of tools, is the cherishing mother of all significance. 52
John Dewey

Language is that which gives us reality, and not as a mere vehicle of reality, but as its true flesh, of which all the rest, dumb or inarticulate representation, is merely the skeleton. 53
Miguel de Unamuno

The limits of my language mean the limits of my world. 54 *Ludwig Wittgenstein*

Without language there are no universals; without universals no transcending of nature and no relation to it as nature. 55 *Paul Tillich*

Only in communication is all other truth revealed, only in communication am I myself not merely living but fulfilling life. 56 *Karl Jaspers*

For man is that being on earth who does not have language. Man *is* language. 57
Ruth N. Anshen

Leadership

In the endless wars of [ancient] times, leaders were absolutely needed for the tribe's survival. If there were any tribes who owned no leaders, they can have left no issue to narrate their doom. The leaders always had good conscience, for conscience in them coalesced with will.... 1 *William James*

Leadership

[L]eaders ... govern through overt threat, potential threat, controlled aggression, and a variety of implicit cues.... [S]ocial organization is premised, in large measure, on inhibition of aggressive tendencies, and the leader serves as a prime-inhibitor of aggression. 2
Kent G. Bailey

The uncanny powers of a leader manifest themselves not so much in the hold he has on the masses as in his ability to dominate and almost bewitch a small group of able men. These men must be fearless, proud, intelligent and capable of organizing and running large-scale undertakings, and yet they must submit wholly to the will of the leader.... 3 *Eric Hoffer*

The first qualification of the true leader ... is that he remain uninvolved with those he leads, and at the same time destroy his followers' wills to remain separate. 4 *Philip Rieff*

Human structure is determined by the conflict between longing for freedom and fear of freedom.... Any variety of social leadership is nothing but the social expression of one or the other side of this human mass structure.... 5
Wilhelm Reich

[T]he good leader can activate ideology and mobilize ... the prevailing order against its enemies, or reimpose order out of chaos, or shatter the prevailing order to create a new order. 6
David Loye

An agitator who demonstrates the ability to transmit an idea to the broad masses must always be a psychologist, even if he were only a demagogue.... *For leading means: being able to move masses.* 7 *Adolf Hitler*

Naturally, the common people don't want war.... That is understood. But after all it is the leaders of the country who determine the policy, and it is always a simple matter to drag the people along, whether it is a democracy, or a fascist dictatorship.... Voice or no voice, the people can always be brought to the bidding of the leaders. That is easy. 8 *Hermann Goering*

The crowd that obeys a leader is under the influence of his prestige.... The influence of the leaders is due in very small measure to the arguments they employ, but in a large degree to their prestige. 9 *Gustave Le Bon*

The chief qualification of a mass leader has become unending infallibility; he can never admit an error. 10 *Hannah Arendt*

The great leaders of crowds of all ages ... have been of lamentably narrow intellect.... [I]t is precisely those whose intelligence has been the most restricted who have exercised the greatest influence. 11 *Gustave Le Bon*

[N]arcissistically fixated persons, bordering on the paranoid ... possess an unshakable self-confidence with enormous, if brittle, self-esteem.... Their absolute certainty risks total failure but also makes possible confident leadership. They possess an all-or-nothing character. 12
Charles Strozier

We cannot trust in the sanity and stability of world leaders. In fact, great power tends to attract disturbed individuals. 13 *Helen Caldicott*

Mustn't every true leader refuse to be ... degraded to the level of a political gangster? 14
Adolf Hitler

A political leader, as a minister of God, is a revenger to execute wrath upon those who do evil. 15 *Rev. Jerry Falwell*

The modern charismatic leader destroys any distance between his own sentiments and impulses and those of his audience, and so, focusing his followers on his motivations, deflects them from measuring him in terms of his acts.... The electronic media play a crucial role in this deflection.... Leadership on these terms is a form of seduction. 16 *Richard Sennett*

Charlatanism of some degree is indispensable to effective leadership. There can be no mass movement without some deliberate misrepresentation of facts. 17 *Eric Hoffer*

[M]any of us are being influenced and manipulated, far more than we realize.... What happens, actually, to public confidence when the public becomes aware (as it gradually must)

Leadership

that the leaders of industry and government are resolutely committed to a confidence-inspiring viewpoint?... What is the morality of manipulating small children.... What is the morality of subordinating truth...? 18

Vance Packard

The masses look to the leaders to give them just the untruth that they need. 19 *Ernest Becker*

[L]eaders lead people where they are willing to be led. 20 *Lewis Richardson*

When conditions are not ripe, the potential leader, no matter how gifted, and his holy cause, no matter how potent, remain without a following.... He cannot conjure a movement out of a void. 21 *Eric Hoffer*

The male bias is reflected in the false conception of leadership as mere command or control. As leadership comes properly to be seen as a process of leaders engaging and mobilizing the human needs and aspirations of followers, women will be more readily recognized as leaders and men will change their own leadership styles. 22 *James MacGregor Burns*

To resolve our problems, we may need to balance the dominant Alpha, or masculine leadership style, with the Beta, a more feminine leadership style.... The Beta style is able to deal with change, while the Alpha style focuses on the short range, perceiving change as chaotic and disruptive and relying on "order" to control it. 23 *Betty Friedan*

[M]ore women ought to rise to high office. Unfortunately, the first to do so will, inevitably, rise via the virtual *absence* of the useful feminine logic so much needed in high places. It is very much in the interests of men ... to ensure that those who are permitted to rise will provide us with a chilling example of all the most disagreeable male traits. 24 *Alistair Mant*

[W]omen leaders do not inspire "followership" chiefly because they are women and ... because males are strongly predisposed to form and maintain all-male groups, particularly when matters of moment for the community are involved. 25 *Lionel Tiger*

The true mark of leadership is not simply to support what is popular but to make what is unpopular popular, if that serves [the] national interest. 26 *Richard M. Nixon*

A real leader, a leader of real moment, will make his tactics dependent, not on the temporary spirit of the masses, but on the inexorable laws of historical development. He will steer his course by these laws in defiance of all disappointments and he will rely on history to bring about the gradual maturing of his actions. 27

Rosa Luxemburg

Effectiveness is the leader's capacity to bring consciousness into line with the unconscious.... 28

Graham Little

Essentially the leader's task is consciousness-raising on a wide plane.... The most lasting tangible act of leadership is the creation of an institution ... that continues to exert moral leadership and foster needed social change. 29

James MacGregor Burns

The most effective leader is one who can create the conditions by which he will actually lose the leadership. 30 *Carl Rogers*

The honor of the political leader, of the leading statesman ... lies precisely in an exclusive *personal* responsibility for what he does, a responsibility he cannot and must not reject or transfer. It is in the nature of officials of high moral standing to be poor politicians, and above all, in the political sense of the word, to be irresponsible politically. 31 *Max Weber*

[S]trong leadership is anathema to a democracy.... We don't need strong leaders.... The new leader is a facilitator, not an order giver. 32

John Naisbitt

[M]en who, at an earlier historical period, were political leaders are now busy with the other-directed occupation of studying the feedback from all the others.... Indeed, mood leadership in the topmost social and political groups in America is becoming increasingly self-conscious; it is part of the same development that has taken us from morality to morale. 33

David Riesman

The preservation of democratic forms can only come about as a result of intellectually farsighted and politically gifted leadership. Paradoxically, it is only through leadership that authoritarian rule can be minimized, if not wholly avoided. Unhappily, we know nothing about how such leadership evolves, much less how it can be cultivated. 34
Robert Heilbroner

Mankind has real need of leaders, but only of men who lead in the interests of all others; and such leadership we do not often find. 35
Alfred Adler

One may guess that America will lead the world in technology and power for at least several generations to come. But it is one thing to fill a power vacuum in the world with a transitional leadership, and quite another to offer to the world the qualities of leadership which it requires, attuned at once to the life of nature and the life of the spirit. Unfortunately American leadership in world affairs has not displayed this capacity.... 36 *Max Lerner*

[T]he influence of [the] major political elite has been disappearing, and no comparable elite has arisen to temper policy and to provide a source of judgment.... Without such an elite there is a problem of authoritative leadership. Given the divisions in the society, the question of whether an elite can emerge is moot. 37 *Daniel Bell*

Leadership is in disrepute in democratic societies.... The pursuit of the democratic virtues of equality and individualism has led to the delegitimization of authority generally and the loss of trust in leadership.... A pervasive suspicion of the motives and power of political leaders ... has given rise to the imposition of legal and institutional barriers which serve to prevent them from achieving goals.... Without confidence in its leadership, no group functions effectively. 38 *Michel Crozier et al.*

In times of stress the mask of civilization is torn away from the primitive countenance of raw humanity in the rank-and-file; but the moral responsibility for the breakdown of civilizations lies upon the heads of the leaders. 39
Arnold Toynbee

The greater the need for economic and social change, the greater the need for leadership to guide the process.... Leadership was never needed more than it will be in the years immediately ahead. 40 *Lester Brown*

It is not the lack of leadership that creates ruin ... but a failure, at last, of common men to heed their leaders or, at the least, to elect to follow wise ones. 41 *Philip Wylie*

We, the people, are the boss, and we will get the kind of political leadership, be it good or bad, that we demand and deserve. 42 *John F. Kennedy*

LEARNING

HUMANS ARE LEARNING ANIMALS.... [I]ntelligence sets us apart among organisms ... [because] natural selection acted to maximize the ... selection for learning rules. 1
Stephen Jay Gould

[G]enes ... create a predisposition that enhances the probability that certain kinds of learning will take place.... 2 *Ervin Staub*

[B]ehavioral or cultural changes are stored not in genes, but in the man-made, the learned, part of the environment, in the culture, in the tools, customs, institutions, laws.... Human nature is what one learns from the man-made environment; it is not something with which one is born. What one is born with are the potentialities for learning.... 3 *Ashley Montagu*

[T]he development of a high intelligence was conditioned upon the ability to learn.... [L]earning must take place if the capacity is to become an ability. 4 *Ashley Montagu*

To the degree that learning is paramount ... behavior cannot evolve.... What evolves is the directedness of learning—the relative ease with which certain associations are made and acts are learned.... 5 *E. O. Wilson*

What, then, is learning theory? In its simplest form, it is the study of the circumstances under which a response and a cue stimulus become connected. 6 *N. E. Miller & J. Dollard*

Learning

[To] direct attention and so isolate the particular response that answers to it ... makes learning possible.... [It] is essential to what we call human intelligence, and it is made possible by language. 7 *George H. Mead*

Learning is becoming capable of doing some correct or suitable thing in *any* situations of certain general sorts. It is becoming prepared for *variable* calls within certain ranges. 8
Gilbert Ryle

All real learning is learning of a mastery. It begins with dependence and ends in freedom. 9
Paul Kecskemeti

The hypothesis of formative causation provides an alternative interpretation [of memory], in the light of which the persistence of learned habits in spite of damage to the brain is far less puzzling: the habits depend on motor fields which are not stored within the brain at all, but are given directly from its past states by morphic resonance. 10 *Rupert Sheldrake*

[W]hatever else learning may be it is clearly *a disposition to form structures*.... Learning, as it operates on instinct and inheritance, thus leads to the formation of more or less stable structures, among which we have listed the moral conscience, a self-concept, and a hierarchical organization of personality. 11 *Gordon W. Allport*

A person learns significantly only those things which he perceives as being involved in the maintenance of, or enhancement of, the structure of self. 12 *Carl Rogers*

Example is the school of mankind, and they will learn at no other. 13 *Edmund Burke*

Above all else, we human beings are social animals.... The reason the higher primates tend to be social animals is that group living offers the opportunity for prolonged learning during childhood ... [which] implies dependency on an adult.... 14 *Richard Leakey*

[A] child living in a positive social climate will be more willing to learn.... 15
Lawrence Kohlberg

There is, I think, no point in the philosophy of progressive education which is sounder than its emphasis upon the importance of the participation of the learner in the formation of the purposes which direct his activities in the learning process.... 16 *John Dewey*

I have come to feel that the only learning which significantly influences behavior is self-discovered, self-appropriated learning. 17
Carl Rogers

The spontaneous wish to learn ... should be the driving-force of education. The substitution of this driving-force for the rod is one of the great advances of our time. 18
Bertrand Russell

Post-capitalist society requires lifelong learning. For this, we need a discipline of learning. But lifelong learning also requires that learning be alluring; indeed, that it become a high satisfaction in itself, if not something the individual craves. 19 *Peter F. Drucker*

Under electric technology the entire business of man becomes learning and knowing.... [T]his means that all forms of employment become "paid learning," and all forms of wealth result from the movement of information. 20
Marshall McLuhan

In a postcivilized society the amount of learning which must be performed by the average individual is so great that the task of education ... has to be an increasing proportion of resources.... This deliberate investment in the human resource is the main key to the transition from civilized to postcivilized society. 21
Kenneth Boulding

[L]earning to learn has been and continues to be *Homo sapiens*' most formidable evolutionary task. 22 *Jules Henry*

A little learning is a dangerous thing;
Drink deep, or taste not the Pierian spring. 23
Alexander Pope

LIBERALISM

IT IS IN THE LIBERAL intellectual tradition that American belief has characteristically expressed itself. 1 *Max Lerner*

Liberalism implies particularly freedom of thought, freedom from orthodox dogma, the right of others to think differently from one's self. It implies a free mind, open to new ideas and willing to give attentive consideration.... 2 *Robert A. Taft*

One can hardly call oneself a liberal if one does not believe in criticism, in the sense of keeping one's mind open as long as possible and taking all authority, even the most scientific, with a grain of salt. 3 *Kathleen Nott*

The liberal differs from the conservative in his willingness to face [his] ignorance and to admit how little we know, without claiming the authority of supernatural sources of knowledge where his reason fails him. 4 *Friedrich von Hayek*

The essence of the Liberal outlook lies not in *what* opinions are held, but in *how* they are held: instead of being held dogmatically, they are held tentatively, and with a consciousness that new evidence may at any moment lead to their abandonment.... The scientific outlook, accordingly, is the intellectual counterpart of what is, in the practical sphere, the outlook of Liberalism. 5 *Bertrand Russell*

[L]iberalism [is] a philosophy of toleration and compromise.... 6 *R. Jeffrey Lustig*

Liberal means confidence in a process of compromise and consensus as the best means of approximating that very complex human arrangement we call social justice. 7 *Lloyd J. Averill*

The heart of the liberal tradition is ... rule of law, rather than an arbitrary rule of men ... [and] that within a framework of settled law the pursuit of self-interest does not lead to disorder. On the contrary, the mutual adjustment of one interest to another often promotes relative harmony. 8 *David Green*

Liberalism ... derives from the discovery of a self-generating or spontaneous order in social affairs ... an order [which] makes it possible to utilize the knowledge and skill of all members of society to a much greater extent than would be possible in any order created by central direction ... and the consequent desire to make as full use of these powerful spontaneous ordering forces as possible. 9 *Friedrich von Hayek*

The "liberal" position holds that there is a tendency for both individuals and society to move in a positive direction under normal circumstances. 10 *Lawrence Kohlberg*

This is the essential difference between the Liberal outlook and that of the totalitarian State, that the former regards the welfare of the State as residing ultimately in the welfare of the individual, while the latter regards the State as the end and individuals merely as [means].... Liberalism, in valuing the individual, is carrying on the Christian tradition; its opponents are reviving certain pre-Christian doctrines. 11 *Bertrand Russell*

The liberal conceives of the individual person as the source and the instrument of authentic morality. 12 *Kathleen Nott*

[T]he sorry decline of the liberal ideal in the West [is] from one originally rooted in desire to be free to follow the precepts of morality to the kind of escape from morality in any form that highlights contemporary liberalism. 13 *Robert Nisbet*

[Formerly] conservatives wanted economic freedom but moral regulation. Today ... liberals want economic regulation and moral freedom. 14 *Daniel Bell*

Liberals aren't saying that we should have ... freedom for its own sake, because freedom is the most valuable thing in the world. Rather, it is our projects and tasks that are the most important things in our lives, and it's because *they* are so important that we should be free to revise and reject them.... 15 *Will Kymlicka*

When the liberal tries to make concrete the ideal of freedom which he proposes, he finds himself always constrained to endorse ... the

Liberalism

habits and predilections of a particular way of life—the way of life of the emancipated urban intellectual.... Such a philosophy presents no idea of the self, over and above the desires which constitute it: it therefore has no idea of self-fulfillment other than the free satisfaction of desire. 16 *Roger Scruton*

On the level of the largest association, the country itself, liberal principles can be destructive of the highest forms of patriotism which are necessary for the very survival of the community. 17 *Francis Fukuyama*

Liberalism will be seen historically as *the* great destructive force of our time.... "Down With Us!" Such is the everlasting slogan of the liberal through the ages.... [It] is really just a death wish. 18 *Malcolm Muggeridge*

Liberalism is extremely harmful in a revolutionary collective.... It is an extremely bad tendency. 19 *Mao Tse-tung*

To the political Liberals, personal freedom actually meant the personal power of the man of property.... [T]he unrepentant Liberal refuses to recognise—cannot even be made to understand—that, in the modern industrial state, a man who is divorced from the instruments of production cannot ... even live his own life, let alone do what he likes with his own personality. 20 *Sidney & Beatrice Webb*

In the name of welfare and equality, the twentieth century liberal has come to favor a revival of the very policies of state intervention and paternalism against which classical liberalism fought. 21 *Milton Friedman*

[L]iberals tend to view social problems as symptoms of the underlying social structure, while conservatives view them as results of individual incompetence or immorality. 22 *Adorno et al.*

Liberal democracy replaces the irrational desire to be recognized as greater than others with a rational desire to be recognized as equal. A world made up of liberal democracies, then, should have much less incentive for war, since all nations would reciprocally recognize one another's legitimacy. 23 *Francis Fukuyama*

World peace ... [:] Liberals tend to associate it with justice and conservatives with freedom. Liberals tend to seek it through nuclear disarmament, conservatives in "peace through strength." 24 *Richard Hutcheson Jr.*

Liberalism ... is the supreme form of generosity; it is the right which the majority concedes to minorities and hence it is the noblest cry that has ever resounded in this planet. It announced the determination to share existence with the enemy; more than that, with an enemy which is weak. 25 *José Ortega y Gasset*

[L]iberalism ... [is] democracy and individualism. 26 *W. M. McGovern*

The *genuine liberal* is close to the psychoanalytic ideal, representing a balance of superego, ego and id. Perhaps the outstanding features of this pattern are moral courage and a sense of personal autonomy. 27 *Nevitt Sanford*

[T]he growth of liberal democracy, together with its companion, economic liberalism, has been the most remarkable macropolitical phenomenon of the last 400 years.... [I]t constitutes further evidence that there is a fundamental process at work that dictates a common evolutionary pattern for *all* human societies—in short, something like a Universal History of mankind in the direction of liberal democracy. 28 *Francis Fukuyama*

Life

Life exists in the universe only because the carbon atom possesses certain exceptional properties. 1 *Sir James Jeans*

Almost all aspects of life are engineered at the molecular level.... 2 *Francis Crick*

The truth is that life is possible wherever energy descends the incline indicated by Carnot's law and where a cause of inverse direction can retard the descent—that is to say, probably, in all the worlds suspended from all the stars. 3 *Henri Bergson*

The impetus of life ... consists in a need of creation. It cannot create absolutely, because it

is confronted with matter.... But it seizes upon this matter, which is necessity itself, and strives to introduce into it the largest possible amount of indetermination and liberty. 4
Henri Bergson

[L]ife, far from being outside the natural order [is] the supreme expression of the self-organizing processes that occur [in nature]. 5
Ilya Prigogine

Active communication is an essential feature of all life.... Life is the physical manifestation of this creative flow of coherent information. 6
F. David Peat

[T]he living being is above all a thoroughfare, and ... the essence of life is in the movement by which life is transmitted. 7 *Henri Bergson*

Life is the progressive realization of potential acts; and as every realized act changes the pattern and range of what is possible, the living body is an ever-new constellation of possibilities. 8 *Susanne Langer*

[L]ife is a characteristic of "empty space" and not of space "occupied." ... Life lurks in the interstices of each living cell, and in the interstices of the brain. 9 *Alfred N. Whitehead*

The solution of the riddle of life in space and time lies *outside* space and time. 10
Ludwig Wittgenstein

[T]he story of life is no more than a movement of consciousness veiled by morphology.... 11
Pierre Teilhard de Chardin

Life is an illusion. 12 *Timothy Leary*

Are we ourselves—living creatures capable of observing and manipulating—mere fictions produced by our imperfect senses? Is the distinction between life and death an illusion? 13
Ilya Prigogine

For life and death are one, even as the river and the sea are one. 14 *Kahlil Gibran*

The normal process of life contains moments as bad as any of those which insane melancholy is filled with, moments in which radical evil gets its innings and takes its solid turn. 15
William James

[W]hether or not it be for the general good, life is robbery. 16 *Alfred N. Whitehead*

Life is a battleground. It always has been, and always will be; and if it were not so, existence would come to an end. 17 *Carl Jung*

Some races increase, others are reduced, and ... like runners relay the torch of life. 18 *Lucretius*

In itself, an act of injury, violation, exploitation or annihilation cannot be wrong, for life operates, essentially and fundamentally, by injuring, violating, exploiting and annihilating and cannot even be conceived of outside of this character. 19 *Friedrich Nietzsche*

The philosophy of any one person is comprehended and expressed in the habit of his being.... This habit has its deepest shape in the primary attitude of the person toward life. 20
Pearl S. Buck

I have been shocked at the materials that come to us. I have been shocked at the clear attempts to slip something by us. I am deeply disturbed at the constant, direct, personal pressure some industry representatives have placed on our people.... At the end of the long line is a human life. Some of you have forgotten that basic fact. 21 *Dr. James Goddard*
(ex-head of [U.S.] F.D.A.)

Taken as a whole, the record shows that in manufacturing and marketing the Corvair, GM acted in reckless disregard of human life. 22
U.S. Rep. John Burton

Here I find myself in rare agreement with Ralph Nader: the Corvair really was unsafe ... but GM is so big and powerful that it can withstand a disaster or two. 23 *Lee Iacocca*

Once a human life is made cheap every life becomes cheap. 24 *Samuel Tenenbaum*

[T]here is a subject nowadays which is taboo in the way that sexuality was once taboo, which

Life

is to talk about life as if it had any meaning. 25
Nicholas Mosley

[W]e fulfill our basic humanity whenever we live a life that has significance in terms of life itself. 26 *Irving Singer*

[The] font of life is the core of the individual, and within himself he will find it—if he can tear the coverings away. 27 *Joseph Campbell*

Love of life is the uninhibited expression of interest, or curiosity—the "cosmological urge" ... a response rooted in trust. 28 *Morris Berman*

The more the mother and her breast are cathected ... the more securely will the internalized good breast, the prototype of good internal objects, be established in the infant's mind. This in turn influences both the strength and the nature of projections; in particular it determines whether feelings of love or destructive impulses predominate ... [and thus] whether ... the Life instinct prevails. 29
Melanie Klein

[M]uch of woman's psychic potential stems from her close identification with organic life and its perpetuation; from this potential she derives a special capacity to mediate between biology and history.... [G]iven the precarious nature of our psychic and physical existence, we have no choice but to return to organic principles.... [W]oman as knower, closest to those principles, can ... bring her wisdom to bear where it is most needed. 30 *Robert Jay Lifton*

Women value life more than men do.... Woman is the creator and fosterer of life; man has been the mechanizer and destroyer of life. 31
Ashley Montagu

The rulers of patriarchy—males with power—wage an unceasing war against life itself. Since female energy is essentially biophilic, the female spirit/body is the primary target. 32
Mary Daly

[T]he fantasies of automation and absolute power have historically gone together.... *The desired reward of this magic is not just abundance but absolute control....* Once complete and universal, total automation means total renunciation of life.... 33 *Lewis Mumford*

The proposal ... that an animal's visual system and brain [could] be coupled to computers ... represents an attack on life itself. One must wonder what must have happened to the proposers' perception of life, hence to their perceptions of themselves as part of the continuum of life, that they can even think of such a thing. 34
Joseph Weizenbaum

My life no more belongs to me than to the wall. In this, it differs from the supposed reality called thought. Thought is mine, is I. My life is not mine, but I belong to it. This is the broad, immense reality of my coexistence with things. 35
José Ortega y Gasset

For him that is joined to all the living there is hope. 36 *Holy Bible*

Hope is a psychic commitment to life and growth. 37 *Erich Fromm*

The great fault of all ethics hitherto has been that they believed themselves to have to deal only with the relations of man to man. In reality, however, the question is what is his attitude to the world and all life that comes within his reach. A man is ethical only when life, as such, is sacred to him, that of plants and animals as that of his fellow-men.... 38 *Albert Schweitzer*

Human beings have broken out of the circle of life, driven not by biological need, but by the social organization which they have devised to "conquer" nature.... Once more, to survive, we must close the circle. We must learn how to restore to nature the wealth that we borrow from it. 39 *Barry Commoner*

By restoring our severed links with life, we will restore our own lives. Instead of stopping the course of time and cutting off the human future, we would make it possible for the future generations to be born.... Two paths lie before us. One leads to death, the other to life. 40
Jonathan Schell

Human beings may ... be divided into ... those who choose life and those who choose death.

And when an individual chooses between these two he chooses between two parts of himself. 41
Pearl S. Buck

There is no more fundamental distinction between men, psychologically and morally, than the one between those who love death and those who love life, between the *necrophilous* and the *biophilous*. 42 *Erich Fromm*

It is a race between the believers in deadness and the believers in life. And no man dare remain neutral: that will mean death. 43
A. S. Neill

Life is stronger, more enduring, more cunning, more extraordinary than the cunning and extraordinariness of one of its species. I believe that life will prevail in spite of us, in spite of the death wish of our civilization. 44
Henryk Skolimowski

[A]n eschatology for the 20th century is the way to serve the life instinct and bring hope to distracted humanity. 45 *Norman O. Brown*

"New Romanticism" is the thesis that it is the passions that give our lives meaning.... The key to Romanticism ... was a renewed awareness of *life*.... Against the dehumanizing and lifeless mechanism of Isaac Newton's universe, the Romantics urged an organic conception of a living universe.... Today, when the universe has once again become dehumanized ... a "new Romanticism" is in order. 46 *Robert Solomon*

~ Logic ~

The content of Logic is the representation of God as he is in his eternal essence. 1
G. W. F. Hegel

Logic is not a body of doctrine, but a mirror-image of the world. Logic is transcendental. 2
Ludwig Wittgenstein

Logical order is not a form imposed upon what is known; it is the proper form of knowledge as perfected. 3 *John Dewey*

The exploration of logic means the exploration of *everything that is subject to law*. And outside logic everything is accidental. 4
Ludwig Wittgenstein

What makes logic *a priori* is the *impossibility* of illogical thought. 5 *Ludwig Wittgenstein*

"Logic is the art of *non-contradictory identification*. A contradiction cannot exist." 6
Ayn Rand

The logical infallibility of thought is adhered to by the logical optimist as though it were Gospel in which he blindly believed; and with the same intolerance that accompanies religious superstitions.... But if a thinker at a higher stage of civilization does not question this objectivity, he becomes a primitive man again.... Whatever objective reality may be, one thing can be stated with certainty—it does *not* consist of logical functions ... [though] logical functions, working according to their own laws, do constantly coincide in the end with reality. 7 *Hans Vaihinger*

By becoming capable of logical thinking, of developing thought in accordance with its necessity, the possibility of error has been created. 8
Rudolf Steiner

Empirical verification, the positivist test of science, can apply only to that which is fully in consciousness.... Negation is the primal act of repression.... [F]ormal logic and the law of contradiction are the rules whereby the mind submits to operate under general conditions of repression.... Kant's categories of rationality would then turn out to be the categories of repression. 9 *Norman O. Brown*

One of the problems in examining any decision after the fact is that the decision-maker has a strong tendency to explain his behavior in a cause-and-effect context ... as though he made a series of logical decisions.... It is also a means of concealing one's intentions. If every decision is merely a matter of the person making a logical deduction from present facts in the light of his memory of past events, like the operation of a computer, it is devoid of moral implications. If everything is a matter of logic, one can avoid altogether the problem of good and evil. Wrong

Logic

decisions are merely "mistakes," based on an incomplete knowledge of the facts.... [O]ne's intention is irrelevant. 10 *William Blanchard*

Every narcissist is afraid of going crazy.... Denying one's emotions becomes a habit, engraved in the personality. Action is taken solely on the basis of reason and logic.... Indeed, the world of feeling is seen as unreal and, therefore, allied to insanity.... As long as one sticks to logic, one is safe. 11 *Alexander Lowen*

[L]ogic, the conceptual understandability of existence ... calms and gives confidence—in short, a certain warm narrowness that keeps away fear and encloses one in optimistic horizons. 12 *Friedrich Nietzsche*

The only capacity of the human mind which needs neither the self nor the other nor the world in order to function safely ... is the ability of logical reasoning whose premise is the self-evident. 13 *Hannah Arendt*

Logicality in regard to practical matters is the most useful quality an animal can possess ... but outside of these it is probably of more advantage to the animal to have his mind filled with pleasing and encouraging visions, independently of their truth.... 14 *Charles S. Peirce*

[L]ogic cannot penetrate the loneliness of the human soul. 15 *Gail Sheehy*

[L]ogic excludes love. 16 *Margaret Atwood*

Have rarely listened to such a logical and fanatical man. 17
Capt. Truman Smith (on Adolf Hitler)

[A]dvanced moral reasoning depends upon advanced logical reasoning. There is a parallel between an individual's logical stage and his or her moral stage.... Many individuals are at a higher logical stage than the parallel moral stage, but essentially none are at a higher moral stage than their logical stage. 18
Lawrence Kohlberg

[A] statement can be logical and have no connection with reality. 19 *Marilyn French*

[N]atural forms must never be confused with their mechanical representations. Once again, because the order of thought is a linear, bit-by-bit series, it can approximate but never comprehend a system of relations in which everything is happening simultaneously.... [N]ature is not strung out in a line. Nature is, at the very least, a volume, and at most an infinitely dimensioned field. We need, then, another conception of natural order than the logical ... based on bit-by-bit awareness. 20 *Alan Watts*

[T]he human intellect feels at home among inanimate objects.... [O]ur logic is, pre-eminently, the logic of solids.... But from this it must follow that our thought, in its purely logical form, is incapable of presenting the true nature of life.... 21 *Henri Bergson*

[I]n the history of civilization, reasoning becomes more and more logical, not because each individual carries out his thought in a more logical manner, but because the traditional material which is handed down to each individual has been thought out and worked out more thoroughly and more carefully. 22
Franz Boas

The world seems logical to us because we have made it logical. 23 *Friedrich Nietzsche*

There is always a background of presupposition which defies analysis.... Logic, conceived as an adequate analysis of the advance of thought, is a fake. It is a superb instrument, but it requires the background of common sense.... 24 *Alfred N. Whitehead*

Logic is one thing, and thinking is another; thought may be logical, but logic itself is not a way of thinking.... 25 *Susanne Langer*

Logic in its purest form, which is mathematics, only co-ordinates and articulates one truth with another. It gives harmony to the superstructure of science; but it cannot provide the foundation or the building stones. 26 *Max Planck*

Logic was intended to be a method of *facilitating* thought: a *means of expression*—not truth.... Later on it got to *act* like truth.... 27
Friedrich Nietzsche

Logic alone ... is a poor prophet. Intuition is necessary to complete the picture. 28
Marilyn Ferguson

[O]ur faith in logic is misplaced.... Logical thinking is but one of the special methods of using the mind, and cannot itself achieve an adequate inspection of reality because it is unable to achieve self-knowledge without the other forms of thinking. The ultimate paradox of logical thinking is that it is self-destroying when it is too sedulously cultivated.... It becomes intolerant of the immediate, unanalyzed, primitive abundance of the mind, and by so doing destroys its own source. 29 *Harold D. Lasswell*

[T]he basic assumption underlying the belief that man has achieved mastery over his surroundings mainly through his capacity for logical deduction from explicit premises is factually false, and any attempt to confine his actions to what could thus be justified would deprive him of many of the most effective means to success that have been available to him. 30 *Friedrich von Hayek*

The genius of a man's logical method should be loved and reverenced as his bride, whom he has chosen from all the world. He need not condemn the others; on the contrary, he may honor them deeply, and in so doing he only honors her the more. 31 *Charles S. Peirce*

LOVE

IT IS LOVE that reveals to us the eternal in us and in our neighbours. 1 *Miguel de Unamuno*

Love cannot save life from death; but it can fulfill life's purpose. 2 *Arnold Toynbee*

Only love can bring individual beings to their perfect completion, as individuals, by uniting them one with another, because only love takes possession of them and unites them by what lies deepest within them. 3
Pierre Teilhard de Chardin

Love is the drive to bring together that which has been separated.... What overcomes this separation and brings us into communion with the ultimate ground of being, and into awareness of the meaning of our life, is love.... [T]he only real moral imperative [is] the principle of love. 4 *D. MacKenzie Brown*

[N]o obedience to moral rules can take the place of love, and ... where love is genuine, it will, if combined with intelligence, suffice to generate whatever moral rules are necessary. 5
Bertrand Russell

What is done from love is always beyond good and evil. 6 *Friedrich Nietzsche*

When we love, we give up the center of ourselves.... To love completely carries with it the threat of the annihilation of everything.... Love is the cross-fertilization of mortality and immortality.... To love means to open ourselves to the negative as well as the positive. 7
Rollo May

When one loves another there is always the sense that, should the relationship be destroyed, one's life would end.... The possibility of withdrawing love can be perceived by the other as total separation and disintegration, as death itself. 8 *Robert Jay Lifton*

The forms and structures in which love embodies itself are the forms and structures in which life overcomes its self-destructive forces. 9
Paul Tillich

[O]ur real aim in life is to be loved, and ... any other observable activity is really a detour, an indirect path toward that goal. All of this follows from the emptiness at the core. 10
Morris Berman

The conviction of being unlovable is closely akin to the incapacity for love; it is, in fact, a conscious reflection of that incapacity. 11
Karen Horney

We receive love ... roughly in proportion to our own capacity to love. 12 *Rollo May*

[I]t seems that to love is in essence the project of making oneself be loved. 13 *Jean-Paul Sartre*

[T]o be loved without loving is not a blessing but a curse in disguise. 14 *Theodore Reik*

Love

The only way one learns to love is by being loved. 15 *Ashley Montagu*

The love for my own self is inseparably connected with the love for every other being. 16 *Erich Fromm*

We cannot love ourselves unless we love others, and we cannot love others unless we love ourselves.... Love, therefore, is its own reward. 17 *Thomas Merton*

To love one's self in the right way and to love one's neighbor correspond perfectly to one another, fundamentally they are one and the same thing. 18 *Søren Kierkegaard*

To command that we love our neighbors as ourselves ... is impossible to fulfill; such an enormous inflation of love can only lower its value.... 19 *Sigmund Freud*

It is easier to love humanity than to love your neighbor. 20 *Eric Hoffer*

We cannot really love "in the abstract"; we can only love those whom we know.... Thus we might say: help your enemies; assist those in distress, even if they hate you; but love only your friends. 21 *Karl Popper*

It is strange but true that he who preaches brotherly love also preaches against love of mother, father, brother, sister, wife and children. 22 *Eric Hoffer*

Feelings accompany the metaphysical and metapsychical fact of love, but they do not constitute it.... Love is responsibility of an *I* for a *Thou*. In this lies the likeness—impossible in any feeling whatsoever—of all who love, from the smallest to the greatest and from the blessedly protected man ... to him who is all his life nailed to the cross of the world, and who ventures to bring himself to the dreadful point—to love *all men*. 23 *Martin Buber*

Anyone who loves only one person really loves none. 24 *Erich Fromm*

A universal love is not only psychologically possible; it is the only complete and final way in which we are able to love. 25 *Pierre Teilhard de Chardin*

Much as we might wish to believe otherwise, universal love and the welfare of the species as a whole are concepts which simply do not make evolutionary sense. 26 *Richard Dawkins*

[W]hether it be natural to be loving and cooperative or not, as far as the human species is concerned, its evolutionary destiny, its very survival, are more closely tied to the capacity for love and cooperation than to any other. 27 *Ashley Montagu*

Given our drive dispositions and our environment, the love for fellow men must be considered just as indispensable for the survival of mankind as is technology. 28 *Sigmund Freud*

[L]ove is not altruistic. The initial attraction is based on curious admiration ... for the self-possession, the integrated unity, of the other and a wish to become part of this Self in some way.... Love is the final opening up (or, surrender to the dominion of) the other.... Thus, love is the height of selfishness: the self attempts to enrich itself through the absorption of another being. 29 *Shulamith Firestone*

The desire for possession is only another form of the desire to endure; it is this that comprises the impotent delirium of love. 30 *Albert Camus*

[Man could] to feel heroic merge himself with some higher, self-absorbing meaning.... One of the first ways [is that] ... the love partner becomes the divine ideal within which to fulfil one's life. All spiritual and moral needs now become focussed in one individual. 31 *Ernest Becker*

Few people love others for what they are. Rather do they love them for what they project into them. 32 *Goethe*

If I love someone, he must deserve it in some way.... He deserves it if he is so like me in important ways that I can love myself in him; and he deserves it if he is so much more perfect than myself that I can love my ideal of my own self in him. 33 *Sigmund Freud*

Love, friendship, respect, admiration are the emotional responses of one man to the virtues of another, the spiritual *payment* given in exchange for the personal, selfish pleasure which one man derives from the virtues of another man's character.... To love is to value. Only a rationally selfish man, a man of *self-esteem*, is capable of love.... 34 *Ayn Rand*

Love is an emotion of strength.... Ultimately, love requires more ... self-confidence and preexisting self-esteem than any other emotion. 35 *Robert C. Solomon*

A strong egoism is a protection against disease, but in the last resort we must begin to love in order that we may not fall ill, and must fall ill if, in consequence of frustration, we cannot love. 36 *Sigmund Freud*

Deficiency of "the vitamin of love" is ... responsible for many mental disorders. 37 *Pitirim Sorokin*

The reiteration in this conference of the basic need for love ... is indeed noteworthy. It comes not as a sentimental exhortation or a pious repetition of the familiar injunction to love our neighbours, but as a psychological truth that is irrefutable. 38 *Conclusion from 1948 International Congress on Mental Health*

Mental health, indeed, is the ability to love, for love is the essential human relationship. 39 *Ashley Montagu*

[T]he real problem for people in our day is ... to become *able* to love. To be capable of giving and receiving mature love is as sound a criterion as we have for the fulfilled personality. 40 *Rollo May*

[A]dulthood begins with the ability to receive and give love and care. 41 *Erik Erikson*

Love for equals is difficult. We love what is weak and suffers. It appeals to our strength without challenging it. 42 *Reinhold Niebuhr*

To love with the spirit is to pity.... Pity, then, is the essence of human spiritual love, of the love that is conscious of being love, of the love that is not purely animal, of the love, in a word, of a rational person. 43 *Miguel de Unamuno*

[I]rrational love is love which enhances the person's dependency, hence anxiety and hostility. Rational love is a love which relates a person intimately to another, at the same time preserving his independence and integrity. 44 *Erich Fromm*

Love is the recognition of dignity, the discernment of worth. 45 *Lloyd J. Averill*

Love recognizes the full otherness of the other. 46 *Lloyd J. Averill*

The capacity to love presupposes self-awareness, because love requires the ability to have empathy with the other person, to appreciate and affirm his potentialities. 47 *Rollo May*

The key to life ... would seem to be "love." Essential to any love worthy of the name would seem to be a care, concern, and desire that the one loved realize to the fullest his or her aims and ideals insofar as this realization brings enrichment and enhancement of life. 48 *Eugene Fontinell*

Love is the demonstratively active involvement in the welfare of another in such manner that one not only contributes to the survival of the other, but does so in a creatively enlarging manner, in a manner calculated to stimulate the potentialities of the other so that they may develop to their optimum capacity. 49 *Ashley Montagu*

Genuine love ought to be founded on the mutual recognition of two liberties; the lovers would then experience themselves both as self and as other.... 50 *Simone de Beauvoir*

Love may be viewed as a sharing of the self with another person. 51 *Alexander Lowen*

[T]he fact can never be ignored that we have our greatest delight when we realize ourselves in others, and this is the definition of love. 52 *Rabindranath Tagore*

Love

Real love is a permanently self-enlarging experience. Falling in love is not. 53 *M. Scott Peck*

[M]any who have been attracted by love's bright promise … may think themselves ready for love's physical nakedness, when it is moral nakedness love requires.… 54 *Lloyd J. Averill*

Love is more a question of friendship than intercourse. 55 *Aristotle*

Desire arises from the death of love.… 56
Jean-Paul Sartre

[W]here love is lacking, power fills the vacuum. 57 *Carl Jung*

Doubtless the personal bond, love, arose in many cases from intra-specific aggression, by way of ritualization of a redirected attack or threatening.… Thus intra-specific aggression can certainly exist without its counterpart, love, but conversely there is no love without aggression. 58 *Konrad Lorenz*

The roots of love are not in sexuality, although love makes use of it for the secondary strengthening of the bond.… [Love] has arisen with the evolution of parental care. 59
Irenäus Eibl-Eibesfeldt

[T]he tender protectiveness and dependency of the mother-infant relationship in mammals may provide some of the basic emotional raw material drawn upon in the evolution of love between men and women. 60 *Sidney Mellen*

Love, which was once believed to be the Answer, we now know to be nothing more than an inherited behaviour pattern. 61
James Thurber

[H]uman love can be seen going out beyond itself and finding its first object in the world, the mother.… [T]his early experience of love stays with us as the immortal dream of love … as the source of our restless discontent. 62
Norman O. Brown

The most tragic thing in the world and in life … is love. Love is the child of illusion and the parent of disillusion; love is consolation in desolation; it is the sole medicine against death, for it is death's brother. 63
Miguel de Unamuno

[T]he idealized eroticism that pervades our culture … glorifies passion.… The cult of passionate love has been *democratized* so far as to have lost its aesthetic virtues together with its spiritual and tragic values; and we are left with a dull and diluted pain, something unclean and gloomy. 64 *Denis de Rougemont*

One procedure … by which men strive to gain happiness and keep suffering away … aims of course at making the subject independent of Fate.… But it does not turn away from the external world; on the contrary, it clings to the objects belonging to that world and obtains happiness from an emotional relation to them.… I am, of course, speaking of the way of life which makes love the centre of everything.… The weak side of this technique of living is … that we are never so defenceless against suffering as when we love, never so helplessly unhappy as when we have lost our loved object or its love. 65 *Sigmund Freud*

Love suffers and hopes; it is attached in its aspirations to something not spiritual; it clothes this something as best it may in spiritual guise, but constantly with the sense or the fear of a misfit, of a disappointment. 66
George Santayana

Love is the burning point of life, and since all life is sorrowful, so is love. The stronger the love, the more the pain.… Love itself is a pain, you might say—the pain of being truly alive. 67
Joseph Campbell

To fear love is to fear life, and those who fear life are already three parts dead. 68
Bertrand Russell

There is no fear in love; but perfect love casteth out fear.… Indeed he that is under fear has not been made perfect in love. 69 *Saint John*

The moment love becomes happy and satisfied, it no longer desires and is no longer love. 70
Miguel de Unamuno

[T]he loneliness of the human soul is unendurable; nothing can penetrate it except the highest intensity of the sort of love that religious teachers have preached; whatever does not spring from this motive is harmful, or at best useless; it follows that ... in human relations one should penetrate to the core of loneliness in each person and speak to that. 71
Bertrand Russell

Is it not ... the fundamental function of love, unifying what is separate, integrating what is disintegrated, making "lovable" what is "ugly," and "pure" what is "sick" and "sinful"?... Any society that wants to be animated by an abundant energy of love must have, must produce, and must cultivate ... heroes of love. 72
Pitirim Sorokin

Love is ... an *orientation* of *character* which determines the relatedness of a person to the world as a whole. 73 *Erich Fromm*

Love is simply the name for the desire and pursuit of wholeness. 74 *Aristophanes*

When I speak of love ... I am speaking of that force which all of the great religions have seen as the supreme unifying principle of life. Love is somehow the key that unlocks the door which leads to ultimate reality. 75
Martin Luther King Jr.

[T]he highest test of a value is whether it performs an entropic or anti-entropic function in society. On this principle, love, in the sense of the Greek *agape*, emerges as the most anti-entropic of all human relationships. It always builds up, it never tears down.... 76
Kenneth Boulding

I hold that he who teaches that not reason but love should rule opens the way for those who would rule by hate. 77 *Karl Popper*

Without the fire of love, the dangerous fissures in Mankind's social solidarity cannot be annealed.... A cold-blooded calculation of expediency will not inspire us with the spiritual power to save ourselves. This power can ... be given to men by nothing but love. 78
Arnold Toynbee

[T]his nomadic civilization ... throws upon personal relations stress greater than ever borne before. Under cosmopolitanism, if it comes, we shall receive no help from the earth. Trees and meadows and mountains will only be a spectacle, and the binding force they once exercised on character must be entrusted to Love alone. May Love be equal to the task. 79 *E. M. Forster*

Love should be a tree whose roots are deep in the earth, but whose branches extend into heaven. 80 *Bertrand Russell*

God manifests Himself only indirectly, and only through man's love of man.... 81
Karl Jaspers

Love in all its subtleties is nothing more, and nothing less, than the more or less direct trace marked on the heart of the element by the psychical convergence of the universe upon itself.... Driven by forces of love, the fragments of the world seek each other so that the world may come to being. 82 *Pierre Teilhard de Chardin*

What is Love? It is that powerful attraction towards all that we conceive, or fear, or hope beyond ourselves. 83 *Percy Bysshe Shelly*

Why is the search for love so universal? Because it is the search for the self that could never be.... The search seems endless because few people really know what they are looking for. 84
Arthur Janov

We really know very little about love. 85
Sigmund Freud

Love is the destiny for which men are made. 86
Lloyd J. Averill

Ultimately love is everything. 87
M. Scott Peck

~ MACHINES / MECHANICS

THE MODERN AGE is the Machine Age.... The machine is our way of life and our world view rolled up in one. We view the universe as a grand machine set in motion eons ago by the supreme technician, God. 1 *Jeremy Rifkin*

Machines / Mechanics

From Descartes time on until the present … a "mechanistic" explanation of organic behavior was accepted as a sufficient one.… Hidden within this whole movement of thought … were two guiding aims whose magical nature has only now become apparent, and whose undeclared ultimate goals are now at last visible.… First: he who creates a perfect automaton is in fact creating life, since, according to mechanistic doctrine, there is no essential difference between living organisms and machines.… But, second, beneath this magic wish was a more insidiously flattering idea: *he who creates life is a God.* 2 *Lewis Mumford*

A man created in God's image, or a god created in man's image, no less than a devil created in man's image, tells us much about the fears and aspirations of man. A machine god thus tells us about the fears and aspirations of man in a machine age. 3 *Bruno Bettelheim*

The Faustian inventor and discoverer … created the *idea of the machine* as a small cosmos obeying the will of man alone.… But for that very reason Faustian man has become *the slave of his creation.* The machine has forcibly increased his numbers and changed his habits in a direction from which there is no return. 4
Oswald Spengler

If we … [are] unable to banish the impression that [the cosmos] is a realm of final purposes … we place intelligence at the heart of it and have a religion. If, on the contrary … we can think of the present only as so much mere mechanical sprouting from the past, occurring with no reference to the future, we are atheists and materialists. 5 *William James*

The machine was the true symbol for the Calvinist's unrelenting God and his predestined order: its very austerities and abnegations and self-denials, the driving discipline of the factory, with no time for idleness, and therefore no opportunity for sin—all this gave the machine a foundation in protestant culture that it long lacked in [other] countries.… The bourgeoisie became the new Elect; and the proletariat were obviously those predestined to damnation. 6 *Lewis Mumford*

The "mechanized" nature of modern science, created and ruled according to a plan that totally dominates it, but of which it is unaware, glorifies its creator, and was thus admirably suited to the needs of both theologians and the physicists. 7 *Ilya Prigogine*

[T]he machine which is a creature of the human being becomes … its maker's ideal. The machine … embodies the myth of objective consciousness as Jesus incarnated the Christian conception of divinity. Under its spell, a grand reductive process begins in which culture is redesigned to meet the needs of mechanization. 8
Theodore Roszak

Men are grown mechanical in head and heart, as well as in hand.… Not for internal perfection, but for external combinations and arrangements … for Mechanism of one sort or another, do they hope and struggle. 9 *Thomas Carlyle*

[I]mbued with an almost blind faith in the power and efficiency of machines, the revolutionary founders of Second Wave societies … invented political institutions that shared many of the characteristics of early industrial machines. 10 *Alvin Toffler*

The sway of the machine is less disputed in America than that of any other institution, including the science which made it possible, the capitalism which has organized its use, and the democracy governing the distribution of the power that flows from it.… The American has been a machine-intoxicated man. 11
Max Lerner

Americans love their machines more than life itself.… 12 *Philip Slater*

[I]n the U.S. … the desire for a sense of innocence and personal goodness and … the development of a mechanical system for gathering information and reaching a decision—tend to work together to suppress awareness of our intentions. If the decision process is mechanical and the self is not involved, it is possible to remain innocent of the consequences.… Self-reflection is not necessary; there is no guilt, only a lack of knowledge. 13 *William Blanchard*

Machines / Mechanics

The perfecting of machinery is making human labor superfluous.... Thus it comes about, to quote Marx, that machinery becomes the most powerful weapon in the war of capital against the working class; that ... the very product of the worker is turned into an instrument for his subjugation. 14 *Friedrich Engels*

The machine accommodates itself to the *weakness* of the human being in order to make the *weak* human being into a machine. 15
Karl Marx

It is the sin of greed that has delivered us over into the power of the machine. If greed were not the master of modern man ... [h]ow could we explain the almost universal refusal on the part of the rulers of the rich societies ... to work towards *the humanization of work*? 16
E. F. Schumacher

The mere standardization of ideas made possible by modern machinery is in itself [an] obstacle to culture.... [M]achinery makes it possible for the capitalists who control it to impose whatever ideas and art-forms they please on the mass of humanity.... Their tendency, therefore, is to disseminate ideas and art of the lowest quality.... Mass production is an admirable thing when applied to material objects: but applied to the things of the spirit, it is not so good. 17 *Aldous Huxley*

[M]achines deprive us of two things which are certainly important ingredients of human happiness, namely, spontaneity and variety. 18
Bertrand Russell

[H]uman thought is being replaced by the thinking of machines. 19 *Erich Fromm*

When man allows machines and the machine-state to master his consciousness, he imperils not only his inner being but ... permits himself to be forced to exist in a universe that is, in the most profound sense, at war with human life. 20 *Charles A. Reich*

It may very well be that in our conscious inner lives ... *touch* is not just skin contact with *things*, but the very life of things in the *mind*.... Our mechanical technologies for extending and separating the functions of our physical beings have brought us near to a state of disintegration by putting us out of touch with ourselves. 21
Marshall McLuhan

The machine tends not only to create a new human environment, but also to modify man's very essence.... He must adapt himself ... to a universe for which he was not created.... He was made to have contact with living things, and he lives in a world of stone. 22
Jacques Ellul

In building machines, man followed the laws of mechanics, of non-living energy. 23
Wilhelm Reich

[N]ecrophilia ... is increasing throughout our cybernetic industrial society ... [in which] the machine constitutes the very meaning of progress, and where the living person becomes an appendix to the machine. 24 *Erich Fromm*

Can the synthesis of Man and Machine ever be stable, or will the purely organic component become such a hindrance that it has to be discarded? If this eventually happens—and ... it must—we have nothing to regret.... Man, said Nietzsche, is a rope stretched between the animal and the superman—a rope across the abyss. That will be a noble purpose to have served. 25 *Arthur C. Clarke*

The mechanical man may scorn and fear living things, but I think it is precisely because he feels that they do not have the power over life and death that machines have.... [T]he Machine is a tribute to the expansion of an implacable, efficient force with which modern men can identify—it would not be an attraction to the stillness of death itself. 26 *Ernest Becker*

"The machine, the frozen form of a living intelligence, is the power that expands the potential of your life by raising the productivity of your time." 27 *Ayn Rand*

Machine production cannot be abolished; it is here to stay. The question is whether it is here to stay as an instrument of slavery or as a way to freedom. 28 *Aldous Huxley*

Machines / Mechanics

[W]e are becoming the servants in thought, as in action, of the machine we have created to serve us. 29 *John K. Galbraith*

Men may use what mechanical instruments they please and be none the worse for their use. What kills their souls is when they allow their instruments to use *them.* 30 *R. H. Tawney*

The product of his mechanistic technic … is an expansion of man himself. The machines are, in fact, an enormous expansion of his biological organization.… Thus, the machine has become a part of man himself, a beloved and highly esteemed part. He has the perennial *dream* that the machines will … give him an increased enjoyment of life. And in *reality*? In reality, the machine has become man's worst enemy. *It will remain his worst enemy unless he differentiates himself from the machine.* 31
Wilhelm Reich

If our Machine Age has any promise for culture, it is not in the actual multiplication of motor cars and vacuum cleaners, but in the potential creation of leisure. But so long as "comfort" and not life is our standard, the Machine Age will remain impotent. 32
Lewis Mumford

The machine age begets its own triumphs … for with the ability to conquer the world and keep it conquered, it creates the will to conquer it. Yet it may also beget its own destruction. 33 *Hans Morgenthau*

If the mechanical rhythm by which 90% of an organism is made subservient to the rest, in order that the remaining 10% of energy may be concentrated on creative evolution, is extended to the whole, then "a marvel of mechanical ingenuity" is degraded into a monstrosity.… The difference between 90% and 100% of mechanization is … [the] difference between a society that is in growth and a society that has become arrested. 34 *Arnold Toynbee*

[A] machine does not represent a sum of means employed, but a sum of obstacles avoided: it is a negation rather than a positive reality. 35
Henri Bergson

Undue cultivation of the outward … must, in the long-run, by destroying Moral Force, which is the parent of all other Force, prove … pernicious. This, we take it, is the grand characteristic of our age. By our skill in Mechanism, it has come to pass, that in the management of external things we excel all other ages; while … in true dignity of soul and character, we are perhaps inferior to most civilised ages. 36
Thomas Carlyle

The mathematical and mechanical order that runs through the material world renders it amenable to industry, but leaves us in a moral wilderness, piling the earth with ruins of civilizations whose souls had perished long before their works. 37 *George Santayana*

It may be that civilisation will never recover from the bad climate which enveloped the introduction of machinery. 38
Alfred N. Whitehead

Biological evolution has given way to a far more rapid process—technological evolution. To put it bluntly and brutally, the machine is going to take over. 39 *Arthur C. Clarke*

A man's world. But finished. They themselves have sold it to the machines. 40
Adrienne Rich

But the sum of man's misery is even this, that he feels himself crushed under the Juggernaut wheels, and knows that Juggernaut is no divinity, but a dead mechanical idol. 41
Thomas Carlyle

Our true Deity is Mechanism.… This faith in Mechanism, in the all-importance of physical things, is in every age the common refuge of Weakness and blind Discontent; of all who believe, as many will ever do, that man's true god lies without him, not within. 42
Thomas Carlyle

Male / Masculinity

We know that our society produces a plentiful supply of boys, but seems to produce fewer and fewer men. 1 *Robert Bly*

Male / Masculinity

Masculinity is not something given to you, something you're born with, but something you gain. And you gain it by winning small battles with honor. 2 *Norman Mailer*

Femininity is a function of the female body.... But masculinity must be learned, earned, and constantly rewon. It is thus more fragile than femininity.... [O]ne *is* a woman; one *learns* to *be* a man.... Further, femininity is the given and masculinity is deduced from it. That is, in order to have a secure sexual identity, men must define themselves and their proper spheres of behavior as the opposite of what women do. 3 *Carol Tavris & Carole Wade*

[B]ecause of a primary oneness and identification with his mother, a primary femaleness, a boy's and a man's core gender identity—the ... sense of being male—is an issue. A boy must learn his gender identity as being not-female, or not-mother.... The male's self, as a result, becomes based on a more fixed "me"—"not-me" distinction.... It gives men a psychological investment in difference that women do not have. 4 *Nancy Chodorow*

[M]asculinity requires eternal vigilance on the boundaries of the self. 5 *Beryl Benderly*

Masculinity becomes an issue as a direct result of a boy's experience of himself in his family—as a result of his being parented by a woman.... Thus, boys define and attempt to construct their sense of masculinity largely in negative terms. 6 *Nancy Chodorow*

Is it not really remarkable ... that so little recognition and attention are paid to the fact of men's secret dread of women? 7 *Karen Horney*

Masculinity must fight off effeminacy day by day. Woman and nature stand ever ready to reduce the male to boy and infant. 8 *Camille Paglia*

The female of the human species is not only often identified with evil, childishness, the body and bodily functions, but with nature itself. All of these all viewed as negative identifications, so that the male, in preserving his "masculinity," must suppress not only the female but children.... Males fear that which threatens their masculinity ... [which] entails an admission that we are not what we claim but have within us that which we fear. 9 *J. C. Smith*

The goal of being on top, of being male, is contained in every neurotic mentality, usually in hidden form; it becomes apparent in thousands of variants but always as an ideal which the person involved hopes will help him overcome his often exaggerated feeling of inferiority.... [This is] the so-called *masculine protest*. 10 *Josef Rattner*

The masculine ideal in our culture ... has traditionally been one of almost complete emotional constipation. 11 *Philip Slater*

Men are men because they don't cry, don't feel, don't need. Like Henry Moore's sculptures, much of their greatness consists of a hole. 12 *Marilyn French*

Psychiatrists ... have stressed the "masculine" virtues, the virtues necessary for exploiters, e.g., aggressiveness, independence, objectivity and emotional control. 13 *Mary Anne Warren*

Male power is a myth that makes itself true. 14 *Catherine MacKinnon*

Masculinity is conceived as something purely egoistic, something which satisfies self-love, gives a feeling of superiority and domination over others ... [requiring] the winning of all manner of victories, especially those over women. 15 *Alfred Adler*

The fear of being considered a woman ... [i.e.] fear of our feminine side, the "anima" in Jungian terms, seems inextricably involved in triggering our capacity for destructiveness. 16 *Mark Gerzon*

[M]asculinity plus aggression equals "machismo." 17 *Helen B. Lewis*

Put a bunch of males together long enough, and once they establish some hierarchy and etiquette they will begin to seek some external focus for their interest—something to change, to

Male / Masculinity

master, to construct, to destroy.... 18
Lionel Tiger & Robin Fox

The National Socialist Movement is in its nature a masculine movement. 19 *Joseph Goebbels*

The chain of command from chancellery to crematorium remained entirely within men's domain.... In following orders, they cast aside the last vestiges of their humanity, but clung to a prefabricated and socially acceptable vision of masculinity. 20 *Claudia Koonz*

Manhood was very much in the minds of the architects of [the Vietnam war].... They wanted to show who had bigger balls. 21
David Halberstam

Whether, as some psychologists believe, some women suffer from penis envy, I am not sure. I am quite certain, however, that all males without exception suffer from penis rivalry, and that this trait has now become a threat to the future existence of the human race. 22 *W. H. Auden*

The special dangers of the nuclear age clearly have brought male leadership close to the limit of its adaptive imagination. The dominant male identity is based on a fondness for "what works" ... whether it helps to build or to destroy. For this very reason the all too obvious necessity to sacrifice some of the possible climaxes of technological triumph and of political hegemony for the sake of the mere preservation of mankind is not itself an endeavor enhancing the male sense of identity. 23 *Erik Erikson*

[M]en, who have dominated world history, carry within them an unalterable, evolutionarily developed death drive, an apparatus of destruction that forces them to undo with one hand everything that they have built up with the other, with the aim of finally destroying themselves and the entire globe. 24 *Margarete Mitscherlich*

[A] commitment to masculinity is a double-edged commitment to both suicide and genocide. 25 *Andrea Dworkin*

The history and future of masculinity is interwoven with the history and future of war.... The "masculine" traits that formerly assured survival will now, if not balanced by the "feminine," assure destruction. 26 *Mark Gerzon*

[Over] 100 million people have been killed by war since 1900. Responsibility for this mass slaughter rests directly upon the male members of the species.... This is true in developed civilizations and primitive cultures.... The human male, alone among animals, slaughters masses of his own species without the direct motivation of hunger or individual personal danger to his life.... [However] one-half of the species is constructed so that the species should survive. 27 *Helen B. Lewis*

If women understand by emancipation the adoption of the masculine role then we are lost indeed. If women can supply no counterbalance to the blindness of male drive the aggressive society will run to its lunatic extremes at ever-escalating speed. 28 *Germaine Greer*

[C]omplete masculinity is hardly distinguishable from stupidity. 29 *H. L. Mencken*

The male hormonal system gives men a head start (in terms of probabilities) that enables them to better deal with those elements of the societal environment for which aggression leads to success.... 30 *Steven Goldberg*

The male mind ... is assumed to function primarily like a penis. Its fundamental character is seen to be aggression, and this quality is held essential to the highest or best working of the intellect. 31 *Mary Ellman*

[T]he hemispheres in males are more specialized than those in females. The representation of analytic and sequential thinking is more clearly present in the left hemispheres of males than in females.... 32
Robert E. Ornstein & Richard F. Thompson

In every known human society, the male's need for achievement can be recognized.... When the same occupations are performed by women, they are regarded as less important. 33
Margaret Mead

The man's world is the nation, the state, business concerns, etc. His family is simply a means to an end.... The general means more to him than the personal. 34 *Carl Jung*

Nature records the male but a secondary and comparatively humble place in the home, the breeding-place of the race; he may compensate himself if he will, by seeking adventure or renown in the outside world. 35 *Havelock Ellis*

The masculine component in personality, in man and in woman, deals primarily with the outer world, while the feminine component deals primarily with the inner world. 36 *Robert A. Johnson*

If a man were given total freedom to act, he could theoretically inseminate thousands of women in his lifetime.... It pays males to be aggressive, hasty, fickle, and undiscriminating. 37 *E. O. Wilson*

Because of a fundamental difference between the size and numbers of sperms and eggs, males are in general likely to be biased towards promiscuity and lack of parental care. 38 *Richard Dawkins*

The little respect paid to chastity in the male world is, I am persuaded, the grand source of many of the physical and moral evils that torment mankind, as well as of the vices and follies that degrade and destroy women.... The little attention paid to the cultivation of modesty amongst men, produces great depravity in all the relationships of society; for, not only love—love that ought to purify the heart, and first call forth all the youthful powers, to prepare the man to discharge the benevolent duties of life, is sacrificed to premature lust; but, all the social affections are deadened by the selfish gratifications, which very early pollute the mind, and dry up the generous juices of the heart. 39 *Mary Wollstonecraft*

A man is unable to feel both sex and affection for the same object.... The question that remains for every normal male is ... how do I get someone to love me without her demanding an equal commitment in return? 40 *Shulamith Firestone*

If objectivity is the epistemological stance of which women's sexual objectification is the social process, its imposition the paradigm of power in the male form, then the state will appear most relentless in imposing the male point of view when it comes closest to achieving its highest formal criterion of aperspectivity. When it is most ruthlessly neutral, it will be most male.... Abstract rights will authorize the male experience of the world.... Once masculinity appears as a specific position, not just the way things are, its judgments will be revealed.... 41 *Catherine MacKinnon*

The male perspective is systemic and hegemic. Male is a social and political concept, not a biological attribute. 42 *Catherine MacKinnon*

The masculine principle is associated with linear time, time that has a beginning and end; linearity coupled with rivalry leads to a vision of life as a struggle, a competition.... Victory itself is more important than the content.... [W]inning is what matters.... We can hypothesize that the extremities of "masculine" values do lead to the extinction of the people and cultures that entertain them. 43 *Marilyn French*

[T]he extreme competitiveness of the masculine world teaches all men to fear and mistrust each other. 44 *Marilyn French*

It is undeniably true that men, in their dealings with other men, are often competitive.... But it is not true that, because men compete, they are therefore "noncooperative," "nonaffiliative," or "emotionally isolated." Competition among men, as among boys playing baseball, soccer, or any other competitive sport, has always had also the function of mutual training, of mutual exploration and appreciation of positive qualities, in fact: of mutual bonding. He who fights me best will be my best comrade-in-arms, my best friend. 45 *Wolfgang Lederer*

If there was nothing else to do but love ... woman would be supreme.... But we have above everything else to think and to act, in order to carry on the struggle against a rigorous destiny; therefore man takes the command. 46 *Auguste Comte*

For thousands of generations men have been asked to do something more than be good lovers

Male / Masculinity

and husbands and fathers.... They have been asked to develop and elaborate, each in terms of his own ability, the structure within which the children are reared ... to dream new dreams and see new visions ... to learn new ways of making life more human and more rewarding. 47

Margaret Mead

The development in an individual of character depends ... [on] an innately undemocratic process in which the weak and dependent learn by identification with the strong.... [T]he swing of the family into mother domination caused enough of a shift in disposition to crack the pillars of authority.... The masculine virtues of strength, courage, work, discipline, striving, industry, technology, mastery and conquest are in disrepute.... The most difficult task of all for us is ... to arm ourselves against the humanist values deeply embedded in our hearts; the values of compassion, nurture and tenderness.... Humanism is a seductive monster with ... the head of a woman. 48 *John Carroll*

The myth of the temptation of Adam and Eve in Paradise continues to influence our conceptions ... that "woman is the great seducer, the source of sin." Men ought to be ashamed of the pitiable and unworthy part they are playing, but it is pleasing to them to be regarded as "weak" and as "victims of seduction" for the more they are protected the more they may sin. 49

August Bebel

[T]here are no truly or directly demasculinizing women. There are many males, unfortunately, who *think* they can be castrated psychologically by their wives or sweethearts and who, because they think they can be, actually are. But these males, in a very real sense, are always *self*-castrated rather than demasculinized by any woman. 50 *Albert Ellis*

The male is an attachment of the female in our civilization.... He does most of what he does—eighty per cent, statistically—to supply whatever women have defined as their necessities, comforts, and luxuries. 51 *Philip Wylie*

Men climb mountains for the hell of it, to test their mind and muscle and to conquer the universal enemy, fear, and to come in touch, at the outer boundaries of experience, with the mystery of being, with the spirit, with God. And for all that they must be, they *want* to be, *hard*, not soft, male, all male.... [But] men have always defended and supplied the "nest" and have seen in this their most *meaningful* activity. All other manly activities are extensions, elaborations—or perversions—of this basic function which is essentially *to serve* ... the biologic function of woman, to serve her needs, well-being, and happiness.... 52 *Wolfgang Lederer*

The true index of a man's character is the health of his wife. 53 *Cyril Connolly*

A woman has the capacity to show the value of her man with the lamp of her consciousness. At his best, a man knows who he is; and he knows he has a god, a magnificent being, somewhere within him. But when a woman lights the lamp and sees the god in him, he feels called upon to live up to that, to be strong in his consciousness.... [H]e seems to require this feminine acknowledgement of his worth. 54

Robert A. Johnson

Most men expect women in general to keep male secrets, cherish male frailty, forgive male cruelty ... to assuage male insecurity and loneliness ... to provide them with some comfort, some immediate validation of themselves.... Men, more than women, seem thwarted by exile from Paradise and Innocence. 55 *Phyllis Chesler*

(Male) culture was (and is) parasitical, feeding on the emotional strength of women without reciprocity. 56 *Shulamith Firestone*

Men know they are sexual exiles. They wander the earth seeking satisfaction, craving and despising, never content. There is nothing in that anguished motion for women to envy. 57

Camille Paglia

The souls of men—their ambitious, warlike, protective character—must be dismantled in order to liberate women from their domination.... With machismo discredited, the positive task is to make men caring.... And indeed it is possible to soften men. But to make them "care" is another thing, and the project must inevitably fail. 58 *Allan Bloom*

If [a man] can make peace with his female inside, he can make peace with the females outside. 59 *Abraham Maslow*

[The] sovereignty of the male is a real usurpation, and destroys that ... which nature established between the sexes. We are, by nature, their lovers, their friends, their patrons: would we willingly exchange such endearing appellations for the barbarous title of master and tyrant? 60 *David Hume*

That your sex are naturally tyrannical is a truth so thoroughly established as to admit of no dispute; but such of you as wish to be happy willingly give up the harsh title of master for the more tender and endearing one of friend. 61

Abigail Adams

~ Marxism / Communism Socialism ~

COMMUNISM IS THE positive abolition of private property, of human self-alienation, and thus, the real appropriation of human nature. It is therefore the return of man himself as a *social*, that is, really human, being.... Communism is the phase of negation of the negation, and is consequently ... the necessary form and the active principle of the immediate future, but communism is not itself the aim of human development or the final form of human society. 1 *Karl Marx*

The distinctively Jewish ... inspiration of Marxism is the apocalyptic vision of violent revolution which is inevitable ... [and] which is to carry the Chosen People, at one bound, from the lowest to the highest place in the Kingdom of This World. 2 *Arnold Toynbee*

Marxism is readily seen as a secular form of the Judeo-Christian mythic structure of the Old and New Testament. The state of nature of primitive man before the development of private property is the analogue of the Garden of Eden. Humans fall from innocence with the rise of private property. The struggle between good and evil becomes the class conflict. Communism becomes the gospel, or true path of redemption. After an apocalyptic struggle between the forces of capitalism and the proletariat, the millennium of communism is ushered in by a withering away of the state. 3 *J. C. Smith*

[I]n order that Socialism ... might assume so quickly that religious form which constitutes the secret of its power, it was necessary that it should appear at one of those rare moments of history when the old religions lose their might and exist only on sufferance while awaiting the new faith that is to succeed them. 4 *Gustave Le Bon*

Heretics have been more despised by the leadership throughout Soviet history than "fascist," "capitalist," and "imperialist" enemies. 5

Seweryn Bialer

Bolshevik doctrine required a uni-directional effort towards the total destruction of all enemies. Lenin demanded the suppression of mercy in action; as the scale of Bolshevik violence mounted, and as more of it came to be directed against the masses and the Party, Stalin came to require ... the repression of pity and its replacement by hate. 6 *Nathan Leites*

Marx pretended that he wanted the happiness of the proletariat. What he really wanted was the unhappiness of the bourgeois, and it was because of ... that hate element that his philosophy produced disaster. 7 *Bertrand Russell*

Communism is not love. Communism is a hammer that we use to crush our enemies. 8

Mao Tse-tung

[W]e must destroy whatever is superfluous ... but we do not find any of this immoral. You see, all acts that further history and socialism are moral acts. It is so written. 9

Lazar Kaganovich (the "wolf of the Kremlin")

As for us, we were never concerned with the Kantian priestly and vegetarian Quaker prattle about the "sacredness of human life." 10

Leon Trotsky

We stand for organized terror. The Cheka is obliged to defend the revolution and conquer the enemy even if its sword does by chance sometimes fall upon the heads of the innocent. 11

Felix Dzerzhinsky (founder of "Cheka")

Marxism / Communism / Socialism

Communist regimes are a form of latent civil war between the government and the people. 12
Milovan Djilas

Marx ... showed with indomitable energy the weakness of a State built upon the sandy foundation of a division into rich and poor. But the reconstruction he suggested was largely a prophesy of inevitable conflict, and the prospect he envisaged was less a remedy than an unexplored formula. 13 *Harold Laski*

The Marxian reading of Hegel in its monism, its absolutism and its conviction that movement comes by internal strife, is embodied in Bolshevik Russia.... The one law of history is strife, internal conflict, civil war of classes. 14
John Dewey

Once Lenin had decided that all means were permissible to bring about the dictatorship of the proletariat, with himself ruling in the name of the proletariat, he ... made Stalin inevitable. 15 *Robert Payne*

[Lenin's] methods lead to this, that the party organization takes the place of the party itself, the central committee takes the place of the party organization, and finally a "dictator" takes the place of the central committee ... while the "people keep silent." 16 *Leon Trotsky*

In relation to Stalin they [his lieutenants] learned only to acquiesce and to be prepared to carry out their leader's every order, even if it was criminal. Anyone who was unable to commit a criminal act was not merely removed from power but physically eliminated. 17 *Roy Medvedev*

Stalinism and Fascism ... are symmetrical phenomena. In many of their features they show a deadly similarity. 18 *Leon Trotsky*

The sin of nearly all left wingers from 1933 onward is that they have wanted to be anti-fascist without being anti-totalitarian. 19
George Orwell

In the last instance, the Party is always right, because it is the only historic instrument which the working class possesses for the solution of its fundamental task. 20 *Leon Trotsky*

Comrades, we are building not a land of idlers where rivers flow with milk and honey, but the most organized and most industrious society in human history. 21 *Leonid Brezhnev*

Socialism is science applied to all realms of human activity. 22 *August Bebel*

Our Revolution is a rebellion in the name of the conscious ... [and] purposeful ... principle of life against the elemental, senseless, biological automatism of life. 23 *Boris Pilnyak*

The communists are no doubt right in thinking that all moral problems will be resolved when all men have become technicians. 24
Jacques Ellul

We believe that there can be no real individual freedom without a rational organization of society. The ultimate ideal of communism is the free and comprehensive development of the personality of each individual. This goal can be achieved only in a society organized for the common good.... 25
Georgi Arbatov & Willem Oltmans

Beginning with the premise that they alone know the laws which govern society, Communists arrive at the oversimplified and unscientific conclusion that this alleged knowledge gives them the power and the exclusive right to change society and to control its activities. This is the major error of their system. 26
Milovan Djilas

The ultimate source of the whole train of evils lies in the Bolshevik outlook on life: in its dogmatism of hatred and its belief that human nature can be completely transformed by force. 27 *Bertrand Russell*

The fundamental principle of our legislation ... is: everything is prohibited which is not specially permitted. 28
A. L. Malitzki (Soviet theorist)

All socialism is slavery. 29 *Herbert Spencer*

Communism is anti-humanity. 30
Alexander Solzhenitsyn

Marxism / Communism / Socialism

Communism is the most favorable social condition for women. 31 *August Bebel*

Communism has made its way by its idealism and not its realism, by its spiritual promise, not its materialistic prospects. 32 *Harold Laski*

The supreme principle of socialism is that man takes precedence over things, life over property, and hence, work over capital; that power follows creation, and not possession; that man must not be governed by circumstances, but circumstances must be governed by man. 33 *Erich Fromm*

Marx did not combat wealth, nor did he praise poverty.... Marx's condemnation of capitalism is fundamentally a moral condemnation. The *system is condemned*, for the cruel injustice inherent in it.... By laying such stress on the moral aspect of social institutions, Marx emphasized our responsibility for the more remote social repercussions of our actions.... 34 *Karl Popper*

Communism is not a reaction against the failure of the 19th century to organize optimal economic output. It is a reaction against its comparative success. It is a protest against the emptiness of economic welfare, an appeal to the ascetic in all of us.... 35 *John Maynard Keynes*

There are not a few people who are irresponsible in their work, preferring the light to the heavy.... At every turn they think of themselves before others.... They feel no warmth towards comrades.... In fact such people are not Communists, or at least cannot be counted as true Communists. 36 *Mao Tse-tung*

Socialism ... is drifting toward truth which the Christian tradition has always supported. 37 *Pope Pius XI*

Marxian socialism represents the most stunning and cataclysmic triumph of the romantic fallacy ... [that] man is naturally peaceable and good.... [T]he true competition between males is for territory or status.... With the abolition of private territories the new societies unwittingly installed competition for dominance as the sole ... permanent feature of socialism's internal relations. 38 *Robert Ardrey*

Marxism is still regarded by purists as a form of scientific materialism, but it is not.... Marxism is sociobiology without biology.... In fact, it is equally based on an inaccurate interpretation of human nature. 39 *E. O. Wilson*

Communism is completely opposed to the natural law itself, and its establishment would entail the complete destruction of all property and even human society. 40 *Pope Pius IX*

The Jewish doctrine of Marxism rejects the aristocratic principle of Nature and replaces the eternal privilege of power and strength by the mass of numbers and their dead weight. 41 *Adolf Hitler*

Collective ownership of the means of production certainly delivers the workers from their servitude to many petty dictators.... [But] then the result will be, not responsible freedom for the workers, but another form of passive and irresponsible bondage. Delivered from servitude to many small dictators, they will find themselves under the control of the agents of a single centralized dictatorship, more effective than the old.... 42 *Aldous Huxley*

All history shows that government is always conducted in the interests of the governing class, except in so far as it is influenced by fear of losing its power. This is the teaching, not only of history, but of Marx. 43 *Bertrand Russell*

[T]he history of Russian Communism gives the lie to every one of its principles. 44 *Albert Camus*

The Left has now become as much of a liar and hypocrite as the bourgeoisie.... It has chosen the path of the total lie.... 45 *Jacques Ellul*

[T]he stifling of every divergent thought, the exclusive monopoly over thinking ... will nail the Communists to a cross of shame in history. 46 *Milovan Djilas*

Our paramount duty is to rehabilitate the untarnished and honest image of a Communist leader, an image somewhat degraded.... 47 *Mikhail Gorbachev*

Marxism / Communism / Socialism

I am not a Marxist. 48 *Karl Marx*

Up to a certain point ... it may be said that Marxism ... represents a defense against the terror of history. 49 *Mircea Eliade*

Here for the militant Marxist, lies the secret of the remedy for the terror of history: just as the contemporaries of a "dark age" consoled themselves for their increasing sufferings by the thought that the aggravation of evil hastens final deliverance, so the militant Marxist of our day reads, in the drama provoked by the pressure of history, a necessary evil, the premonitory symptom of the approaching victory that will put an end forever to all historical "evil." 50 *Mircea Eliade*

The left has all too often served as a refuge from the terrors of inner life. 51 *Christopher Lasch*

Socialism is an insurance policy bought by all the members of a national economy to shield them from risk. But the result is to shield them from knowledge of the real dangers and opportunities ubiquitous in any society. 52 *George Gilder*

Marxism is the opium of the intellectuals. 53 *Raymond Aron*

An understanding of the importance of the desire for recognition as the motor of history allows us to reinterpret many phenomena.... Communism is being superseded by liberal democracy in our time because of the realization that the former provides a gravely defective form of recognition. 54 *Francis Fukuyama*

Communism *humiliated* ordinary people by forcing them to make a myriad of petty, and sometimes not so petty, moral compromises with their better natures. 55 *Francis Fukuyama*

I have only *one* objection to the concept of comprehensive socialism: So far it has made no provision for effective development of the individual initiative of humans. 56 *R. Buckminster Fuller*

Communism may be the quickest possible way out of underdevelopment.... [W]hat is crucial is that communism, as an ideology and as a practical political movement, is prepared to undertake the revolutionary reorganization of society—a task before which the noncommunist governments shrink. 57 *Robert Heilbroner*

The new wealth-creation methods require so much knowledge, so much information and communication, that they are totally out of the reach of centrally planned economies. 58 *Alvin Toffler*

Marxist leaders knew better than to waste their time on such matters as technology. "Workers of all countries, unite!"—that exhausted their practical program. When the workers of their countries were united ... they left the workers high and dry. The leaders did not know what to do. They waited for the promised suicide of capitalism.... Slowly the leaders began to realize the terrible consequences of a policy of waiting and hoping for the great political miracle. But it was too late. Their opportunity was gone.... The suffering masses needed more than that. 59 *Karl Popper*

For the fact is that Marxism lost its main bet at the outset. It wagered its entire claim to historical inevitability on the idea that humankind would divide along the lines of class, not nationality. In this it was wrong. 60 *Robert Hughes*

The collapse of Marxism and Communism brought to a close two hundred and fifty years that were dominated by a secular religion—I have called it *the belief in salvation by society.* 61 *Peter F. Drucker*

[T]he Right, in any of its forms from capitalism to fascism, really represents ... the diametrical opposite of all the great values the West had discovered.... The Left alone, with its grand and generous vision, its gaze turned toward the future ... truly embodied the West that had been forged in the fires of the last 2000 years. 62 *Jacques Ellul*

The ideal of Socialism is grand and noble ... but such a state of society cannot be manufactured—it must grow. Society is an organism, not a machine. 63 *Henry George*

Communism is like prohibition; it's a good idea, but it won't work. 64 *Will Rogers*

Whenever it ceases to be true that mankind, as a rule, prefer themselves to others, and those nearest to them to those more remote, from that moment Communism is not only practicable, but the only defensible form of society. ... 65 *John Stuart Mill*

The victory of Socialism was never more certain then when it was thought to be destroyed. 66 *August Bebel*

Meaning

THE CHARACTERISTIC HUMAN need is for possession and appreciation of the meaning of things. ... 1 *John Dewey*

The least of things with a meaning is worth more in life than the greatest of things without. 2 *Carl Jung*

The field of meaning is the reality in which the individual lives.... 3 *Michael R. Jackson*

Human beings live in the realm of *meanings*.... We experience reality always through the meanings we give it. 4 *Alfred Adler*

If there are no meanings, no values ... then man, as creator, must invent, conjure up meanings and values ... out of nothing. 5 *R. D. Laing*

It appears to be necessary for man to ask the question of the meaning of their own existence—that is one of the universal characteristics of men.... 6 *Lloyd J. Averill*

The average man of today seems to be haunted by a feeling of the meaninglessness of life. 7 *Viktor Frankl*

The problem of extreme meaninglessness—"existential vacuum" or *void*—seems to afflict a significant part of the population. 8 *Eric Klinger*

We live in a world *without* a goal, purpose, or meaning, but we cannot *live* without a goal, purpose, or meaning. 9 *Eugene Fontinell*

Meaninglessness inhibits fullness of life and is therefore equivalent to illness. Meaning makes a great many things endurable—perhaps everything. 10 *Carl Jung*

The man who regards his own life and that of his fellow creatures as meaningless is not merely unhappy but hardly fit for life. 11 *Albert Einstein*

If man finds no meaning in life, he dies. 12 *Leo Tolstoy*

The problem of meaninglessness may be based on the unadmitted domination of certain *degrading* passions, dragging us down and constituting our world in self-demeaning shades of distance and defensiveness.... [T]he meaninglessness of life is in fact a projection of our own sense of worthlessness onto the world. 13 *Robert C. Solomon*

[O]ur sense of self-worth undergirds whatever personal meaning we find in life. 14 *Mike W. Martin*

[M]an is originally characterized by his "search for meaning" ... [or by] "the will to meaning." ... [T]he will to power and ... a will to pleasure are substitutes for a frustrated will to meaning. 15 *Viktor Frankl*

What people seek in addictive experience is ... a sense of meaningfulness. The capacity of drugs and alcohol to induce transient illusions ... of life being filled with meaning is probably underestimated.... 16 *Dr. J. Satinover*

Ours is a postmaterialistic [culture] ... in which the world of objects has lost much of its meaning.... Meaning comes to be equated with satisfaction. 17 *Charles Drekmeier*

Man transcends death not only by continuing to feed his appetites, but especially by finding a meaning for his life, some kind of larger scheme into which he fits.... This is how man assures the expansive meaning of his life in the face of the real limitations of his body; the "immortal

MEANING

self" can take very spiritual forms, and spirituality ... is an expression of the will to live ... to make a difference. 18 *Ernest Becker*

[A] meaningful world is one that holds a future that extends beyond the incomplete personal life of the individual; so that a life sacrificed at the right moment is a life well spent, while a life too carefully hoarded, too ignominiously preserved, is a life utterly wasted. 19 *Lewis Mumford*

When people say their life is meaningful, they generally mean they are involved emotionally with personal relationships, gratifying experiences, or important undertakings.... 20
Eric Klinger

When the personal distinctions are destroyed, the innate human value system does not function ... [and] the individual experiences a "meaningless" existence. 21 *George E. Pugh*

The mark of all true "meanings of life" is that they are common meanings—they are meanings in which others can share.... The meaning expressed in such a life will always be, "Life means—to contribute to the whole." 22
Alfred Adler

Parents must not only have certain ways of guiding by prohibition and permission; they must also be able to represent to the child a deep, an almost somatic conviction that there is a meaning to what they are doing. Ultimately, children become neurotic not from frustrations, but from the lack or loss of societal meaning in these frustrations. 23 *Erik Erikson*

[T]he nature of meaning is intimately associated with the social process.... It is that which constitutes ... the common response in one's self as well in the other person.... 24
George H. Mead

Meanings do not come into being without language, and language implies two selves involved in a conjoint or shared undertaking. 25
John Dewey

Meaning is only possible in communication.... 26 *Alfred Adler*

Meaning as such, i.e., the object of thought, arises in experience through the individual stimulating himself to take the attitude of the other in his reaction toward the object. 27
George H. Mead

[T]hough the structure of an input may access consciousness, its meaning may be at least temporarily blocked ... through a pre-conscious appraisal of the emotional significance of the stimuli in relation to feelings about the self.... 28 *Norman F. Dixon*

[T]he structural relation [between] ... perceptions and interpretations *is* the meaning of the world in which we live. These meanings are constructed, which implies ... that no two individuals find exactly the same meaning in the identical objective world. 29 *George Mandler*

Paradigms ... provide maps of what the world is believed to be like.... Above all, paradigms provide the framework of meaning within which "facts" and experiences acquire significance and can be interpreted. 30
Steven F. Cotgrove

Sociobiologists ... read motives and meaning directly from action.... [But] to forget that the relation between motive and action is mediated by the meaning given to the action by the culture, is to make a serious error. 31
Barry Schwartz

For man, the whole purpose, the whole meaning of life, lies in life itself, in the process of living.... To comprehend the purpose and meaning of life, one must above all love life. 32
Kostya Ryabtsev

Life cannot be meaningless to anyone who loves. 33 *Irving Singer*

[M]eaninglessness is no threat so long as enthusiasm for the universe and for man as its center is alive. 34 *Paul Tillich*

The anxiety of meaninglessness is anxiety about the loss of an ultimate concern, of a meaning which gives meaning to all meanings. 35
Paul Tillich

MEANING

The moment a man questions the meaning and value of life, he is sick, since objectively neither has any existence; by asking this question one is merely admitting to a store of unsatisfied libido to which something else must have happened, a kind of fermentation leading to sadness and depression. 36 *Sigmund Freud*

The premises of the behaviorist contain no propositions about meaning.... It has no scientific connotation.... Meaning is just one way of telling what the individual is doing. 37
John B. Watson

[I]ntensive specialization tends to reduce each branch of science to a condition almost approaching meaninglessness.... Specialized meaninglessness has come to be regarded, in certain circles, as a kind of hall-mark of true science. 38 *Aldous Huxley*

It was all a machine yesterday. It is something like a hologram today. Who knows what intellectual rattle we shall be shaking tomorrow to calm the dread of the emptiness of our understanding of the explanations of our meaningless correlations? 39 *R. D. Laing*

In the human mind, an original idea has a living meaning.... To sweep these orders of experience under the rubric *information* can only contribute to cheapening the quality of life. 40
Theodore Roszak

[R]eason ... has always pretended to provide our lives with the meanings we demand but has never succeeded.... In short, the answer lies in our passions.... Our passions constitute our lives.... It is our passions, and our passions alone, that provide our lives with meaning. 41
Robert C. Solomon

The only reference that can constitute the meaning of an idea is one which involves the complete expression of the will of the idea. 42
Josiah Royce

Intentionality ... refers to ... the *totality* of the person's orientation to the world.... [I]ntentionality gives meaningful contents to consciousness.... [E]very meaning has within it a commitment. 43 *Rollo May*

[T]here is no meaning to life except the meaning man gives his life by the unfolding of his powers, by living productively.... 44
Erich Fromm

[T]he whole universe, precisely in so far as it is, is the expression of a meaning, is the conscious fulfilment of significance in life.... 45
Josiah Royce

First and foremost meaning must be explained in terms of being; for being ... is the most universal category which links and binds together truth and reality. 46 *Ernst Cassirer*

There exists ... something in "my" world other than a plurality of possible meanings; there exist objective meanings which are given to me.... I, by whom meanings come to things, I find myself engaged in an *already meaningful* world which reflects to me meanings which I have not put into it. 47 *Jean-Paul Sartre*

Meaning is objective as well as universal.... The ownership of meanings or mind vests in nature.... 48 *John Dewey*

[I]s evolution the intelligent and continued development of [a] symphony of meaning? Indeed, if the individual organism is viewed as the manifestation of coherence and information, then the whole history and pattern of life's unfolding on earth must be seen in the same way. Synchronicities now become just one more aspect of this greater dance of meaning. 49
F. David Peat

Meaning can actually modify the structure of the human brain. 50 *F. David Peat*

Concern with *effect* rather than *meaning* is a basic change of our electric time.... The effect of electric technology had at first been anxiety. Now it appears to create boredom.... The principle of numbness comes into play with electric technology, as with any other. We have to numb our central nervous system when it is extended and exposed, or we will die. Thus the age of anxiety and of electric media is also the age of the unconscious and of apathy. 51
Marshall McLuhan

Meaning

By the meaningless sign linked to the meaningless sound we have built the shape and meaning of Western man. 52
Marshall McLuhan

Moments of meaning and wholeness have become so rare within our culture that we have had to invent special words to describe them, such as ... *epiphany*. 53 *F. David Peat*

Nihilism represents a pathological transitional phase.... 54 *Friedrich Nietzsche*

Life is—or has—meaning and meaninglessness. I cherish the anxious hope that meaning will preponderate and win the battle. 55
Carl Jung

Military

In whichever way I might like to relate my life to the rest of the world, my way takes me always across a great battlefield; unless I enter upon it, no permanent happiness can be mine.... [O]nly war can bring me to the happy goal. 1 *Carl von Clausewitz*

It is in the nature of peacetime to attract to the military those authoritarian personalities ... most needing a container for aggressive instincts. Because such people ... need war to give coherence to their tunnel-like perspective on the world, it is easy for them to believe in the absolute Satanic evil of the adversary, whoever it happens to be. Because such people are very energetic, they usually succeed collectively in shifting the national consciousness towards the likelihood, the inevitability, and finally, the desirability of war. The war, when it comes, releases their own internal tensions and, ironically, reveals their absolute incompetence. After a while ... countervailing anti-war forces emerge. By this time, inevitably, a new and more competent breed of military leaders has emerged, most of them destined to get out of the peacetime military as soon as they possibly can. Thus peacetime tends to tug us into war, and war, after awhile, pulls us back to peace again, like the ebb and flow of the tides. 2
Alistair Mant

The indispensability of play-acting in the grim business of dying and killing is particularly evident in the case of armies. Their uniforms, flags, emblems, parades, music, and elaborate etiquette and ritual are designed to separate the soldier from his flesh-and-blood self and mask the overwhelming reality of life and death. We speak of the theater of war and of battle scenes. In their battle orders army leaders invariably remind their soldiers that the eyes of the world are on them, that their ancestors are watching them and that posterity shall hear of them. The great general knows how to conjure an audience out of the sands of the desert and the waves of the ocean. 3 *Eric Hoffer*

The man who enjoys marching in line and file to the strains of music falls below my contempt; he received his great brain by mistake—the spinal cord would have been amply sufficient. This heroism at command, this senseless violence, this accursed bombast of patriotism—how intensely I despise them! 4
Albert Einstein

War is too serious a matter to entrust to military men. 5 *Georges Clemenceau*

One of the surest indicators of twilight ages in history is the pervasiveness and intensity of war, and also of military types of mind in high political places. 6 *Robert Nisbet*

The military mind also indicates the sharing of a common outlook, the basis of which is the metaphysical definition of reality as essentially military reality.... [T]he political role of the high military ... has become greatly enlarged.... [I]ts fundamental purpose: to define the reality of international relations in a military way.... 7 *C. Wright Mills*

In and out of uniform, generals and admirals ... are now more powerful than they have ever been in the history of the American elite.... [T]hey are now operating in a nation whose elite and whose underlying population have accepted what can only be called a military definition of reality. 8 *C. Wright Mills*

[W]e have been compelled to create a permanent armaments industry of vast proportions....

Yet we must not fail to comprehend its grave implications.... In the councils of government we must guard against the acquisition of unwarranted influence, whether sought or unsought, by the military-industrial complex. The potential for the disastrous rise of misplaced power exists and will persist. We must never let the weight of this combination endanger our liberties or democratic processes. 9
Dwight D. Eisenhower

The U.S. has been running an arms race with itself ... and in the process became a military culture.... 10 *Jerome Wiesner*

Despite charges of "war-mongering" and the impulses toward military muscle-flexing, America can scarcely be described as a warlike civilization or a military society.... [T]o be pugnacious as individuals is different from being aggressive as a nation or militarist as a society. 11 *Max Lerner*

The effects of army education are more violent the more it conforms with the ideas and sentiments of the civilian population itself; for then, this education is not restrained at all. 12
Émile Durkheim

To understand this world you must know that the military establishments of the U.S. and the Soviet Union have united against the civilians of both countries. 13 *U.S. Dept. of State official*

The autonomous power of the military establishment is substantially independent of the existence of an enemy; its power is self-sustaining. 14 *John K. Galbraith*

I was amazed how many American civilian soldiers appeared to put great weight on taking the oath of the soldier. Frequently, I heard the remark: "When I raised my right hand and took that oath, I freed myself of the consequences for what I do. I'll do what they tell me and nobody can blame me...." The satisfaction in this sloughing off responsibility was often plainly visible. Becoming a soldier was like escaping from one's own shadow. 15 *J. Glenn Gray*

If the soldier is to be good for anything as a soldier, he must be exactly the opposite of a reasoning and thinking man. The measure of the goodness in him is his possible use in war. War, and even peace, require of the soldier absolutely peculiar standards of morality. The recruit brings with him common moral notions, of which he must seek immediately to get rid. For him victory, success, must be *everything.* 16
William James

The military virtues are subordination, hierarchy, loyalty, clan honor, physical prowess, and above all the habit of mind that regards all questions as settled by authority.... What makes militarism suicidal is ... their effect on cultural growth. 17 *Max Lerner*

An army without culture is a dull-witted army, and a dull-witted army cannot defeat the enemy. 18 *Mao Tse-tung*

[M]ilitary tradition is to train men not to think. It is past time to reverse that. 19 *Philip Wylie*

The informed soldier fights best. 20
U.S. Army orientation booklet

The military mind is ... not a mind but a habit.... 21 *Philip Wylie*

[M]ilitary training unfits a person for democratic living. The military trains for obedience, for unquestioning acting on orders from superiors, and for non-participation in decision-making. 22 *Donald A. Wells*

Military discipline gives birth to all discipline. 23
Max Weber

The principle of uniformity and repeatability was to find ever fuller expression as print raised visual quantification to eminence.... The modern soldier is especially the instance of the movable type, the replaceable part, the classic Gutenberg phenomenon.... Here the uniform and the homogeneous are *most* visibly at one. 24
Marshall McLuhan

Soldiers were made on purpose to be killed. 25
Napoleon Bonaparte

The exemption of women from military service is founded not on any inaptitude that men

Military

do not share, but on the fact that communities cannot reproduce themselves without plenty of women. Men are more largely dispensable, and are sacrificed accordingly. 26

George Bernard Shaw

The entire aim of military training is to … break down any residues of individuality and selfhood.… [Military] formations consist not of individuals, but automatons. 27

Stanley Milgram

Military law punishes disobedience by death, and its honor is servitude. When all the world has become military, then crime consists in not killing if orders insist on it. 28 *Albert Camus*

It would repel me less to be a hangman than a soldier, because the one is obliged to put to death only criminals sentenced by the law, but the other kills honest men who like himself bathe in innocent blood at the bidding of some superior. 29 *George Santayana*

[T]he dropping of atomic bombs on Hiroshima and Nagasaki clearly constituted war crimes in the sense of the Hague Convention.… [But] the truth of the matter was that by the end of the Second World War everybody knew that technical developments in the instruments of violence had made the adoption of "criminal" warfare inevitable. It was precisely the distinction between soldier and civilian, between army and home population, between military targets and open cities, upon which the Hague Convention's definition of war crimes rested, that had become obsolete. Hence, it was felt that under these new conditions war crimes were only those outside all military necessities.… 30

Hannah Arendt

In practice, however, the line between necessary and unnecessary suffering has been drawn in a way hardly suggested by the humanitarian spirit of the Hague Convention. The criterion has normally been whether a weapon inflicts suffering disproportionate to the military advantage to be gained by its use, and this has meant that no military decisive weapon has ever been regarded as causing superfluous injury, no matter how painful the suffering resulting from its use. 31 *Guenter Lewy*

It is characteristic of the military mentality that non-human factors … are considered essential, while the human being … is degraded to a mere instrument; he becomes "human matériel." The normal ends of human aspiration vanish with such a viewpoint. Instead, the military mentality raises "naked power" as a goal in itself—one of the strangest illusions to which man can succumb. 32 *Albert Einstein*

One of the most useful defenses of the self is denial … [of] emotion.… The B-52 may be the maximum technological expression to date of the militaristic man's continuing refusal to be human. 33 *Gail Sheehy*

No President ever escalated enough to satisfy the military, who always complained about civilian restrictions on military action and kept insisting that they be allowed to bomb, shoot, and drown more and more Vietnamese. 34

Arthur M. Schlesinger Jr.

[In] the account I've given of the decline from warrior to soldier to murderer … it is important to notice the result. The disciplined warrior, made irrelevant by mechanized war, disdained and abandoned by the high-tech culture, is fading in American men. The fading of the warrior contributes to the collapse of civilized society. A man who cannot defend his own space cannot defend women and children.… The inner warriors I speak of do not cross the boundary aggressively; they exist to defend the boundary. 35 *Robert Bly*

Every male brought into existence should be taught from infancy that the military service of the Republic carries with it honor and distinction, and his very life should be permeated with the ideal that even death itself may become a boon when a man dies that a nation may live and fulfill its destiny. 36

Gen. Douglas MacArthur

He who will not bear arms injures the community. 37 *Aristotle*

We only recently reviled our generals and our admirals and advertised them in our periodicals as the stooges of businessmen.… We despised war and we broke our weapons. Now, suddenly, we are bidding our soldiers to save us, for the love of God, quickly, and with little sacrifice. 38 *Philip Wylie*

The political objective of military preparations of any kind is to deter other nations from using military force.... [I]n other words, to make the actual application of military force unnecessary.... 39 *Hans Morgenthau*

As long as armies exist they are necessary ... in order to maintain by force what has been obtained by force. 40 *Leo Tolstoy*

Abandoning compulsory military service is not so much a sign of peaceful intentions as it is a sign of galloping automation.... *Military* service from citizens is no longer a prerequisite for war. What is a prerequisite is the compulsory *financial* service of all citizens, well before any military exchange begins. 41 *Ursula Franklin*

The enormous expenditure of energy, scientific sophistication and wealth on the military is the main cause of poverty, inflation and despair in the world. 42 *Petra Kelly*

Every gun that is made, every warship launched, every rocket fired signifies, in the final sense, a theft from those who hunger and are not fed, those who are cold and are not clothed. This world in arms ... is spending the sweat of its labourers, the genius of its scientists, the hopes of its children. 43 *Dwight D. Eisenhower*

Military pursuits are the most entropic activity of humans. 44 *Marilyn French*

Dead battles, like dead generals, hold the military mind in their dead grip.... 45 *Barbara Tuchman*

Militarism ... is fetish worship. It is the prostration of men's souls and the laceration of their bodies to appease an idol. 46 *R. H. Tawney*

Militarism and warfare are childish things.... They must become things of the past. They must die. 47 *H. G. Wells*

Modern

[M]odernism as a cultural movement trespassed religion and moved the center of authority from the sacred to the profane. 1 *Daniel Bell*

Modern man is profoundly religious, but his religion is no longer centered upon the propitiation of heavenly or infernal powers; rather it concentrates on his propitiation of himself. 2 *Germaine Greer*

The fundamental assumption of modernity ... is that the social unit of society is not the group, the guild, the tribe, or the city, but the person. 3 *Daniel Bell*

For the threshold of our modernity is situated not by the attempt to apply objective methods to the study of man, but rather by the constitution of an empirico-transcendental doublet which was called *man*. 4 *Michel Foucault*

[M]odern industrial society has generally done a very good job of providing for ... basic "selfish" human needs.... In the process, however, it has interfered with the individual's ability to find appropriate psychological satisfaction in socially beneficial activities connected with the "higher" values. Thus modern society may be inadvertently frustrating the higher motivations that it overtly seeks to encourage. 5 *George E. Pugh*

The particularly modern self, the emotist self, in acquiring sovereignty in its own realm lost its traditional boundaries provided by a social identity and a view of human life ordered to a given end. 6 *Alasdair MacIntyre*

[T]he same commentators who celebrate "modernization" as an ever-increasing abundance of personal choices rob choice of its meaning by denying that its exercise leads to any important consequences.... These assumptions obviously preclude any public discussion of values at all. They make choice the test of moral and political freedom and then reduce it to nonsense. 7 *Christopher Lasch*

Modern

Our modern society ... produces not only goods but also needs.... [D]esires are awakened and cultivated from without.... This situation promotes passivity as well as envy and greed and, ultimately, a sense of inner weakness, of powerlessness, of inferiority. A person's sense of self comes to be based solely on what he *has*, not on what he *is*. 8 *Erich Fromm*

Modern civilization has brought us a huge assortment of goods but very little else. For every disease it has wiped out, it has created another through chronic stress.... No one can claim that people are happier under modern conditions, or more refined, or less bloodthirsty; for every stress indicator—crime, mental illness, suicide, chronic disease, and so forth—increases with the spread of civilization. 9 *Philip Slater*

How is it possible to think that the modern paradigm is sufficient to the needs of human beings? 10 *George Grant*

[T]he modern temper—first under capitalism, then under state socialism—has ignored [the] longings of humanity.... The behavior of modern society now exhibits the symptoms of a consummate hideous frustration. 11 *Russell Kirk*

Modern man is drinking and drugging himself out of awareness, or he spends his time shopping, which is the same thing. 12 *Ernest Becker*

[C]ontemporary artists and writers ... convey the contemporary feeling of helplessness, victimization and paralyzing self-consciousness but without connecting it to any larger social life outside the self. The only experience they convey with any conviction, in short, is the experience of unreality. 13 *Christopher Lasch*

The psyche of modern man ... is enfeebled, multifragmented, and disharmonious. 14 *Heinz Kohut*

When one's customary ways of orienting oneself are threatened, and one is without other selves around one, one is thrown back on inner resources and inner strength, and this is what modern people have neglected to develop. 15 *Rollo May*

The danger to modern man arises not so much from his power of mastering natural phenomena as from his powerlessness to control sensibly what is happening today in his own society. 16 *Konrad Lorenz*

He alone is modern who is fully conscious of the present ... [and] has become "unhistorical" in the deepest sense.... Indeed, he is completely modern only when he has come to the very edge of the world ... acknowledging that he stands before a void out of which all things may grow. 17 *Carl Jung*

[O]ur modern attitude looks back proudly upon the mists of superstition and of medieval or primitive credulity and entirely forgets that it carries the whole living past in the lower stories of the skyscraper of rational consciousness. Without the lower stories our mind is suspended in mid-air. 18 *Carl Jung*

[T]he modern man can be creative only insofar as he is historical; in other words, all creation is forbidden him except that which has its source in his own freedom; and, consequently, everything is denied him except the freedom to make history by making himself.... [But it] is becoming more and more doubtful ... if modern man can make history. On the contrary, the more modern he becomes—that is, without defenses against the terror of history—the less chance he has of himself making history. 19 *Mircea Eliade*

Primitive man lives in a world which has a spatial unknown, a dread frontier populated by the heated imagination. For modern man the world is a closed and completely explored surface. This is a radical change in spatial viewpoint. It produces effects in all other spheres of life. 20 *Kenneth Boulding*

Modern culture is defined by [an] extraordinary freedom to ransack the world storehouse and to engorge any and every style it comes upon.... And in its search, there is a denial of any limits or boundaries to experience. It is a reaching out for all experience; nothing is forbidden, all is to explored. 21 *Daniel Bell*

No doubt, on the level of appearances, modernity

begins when the human being begins to exist within his organism, inside the shell of his head ... when he begins to exist at the centre of a labour by whose principles he is governed and whose product eludes him; when he lodges his thought in the folds of a language so much older than himself that he cannot master its significations. 22 *Michel Foucault*

Modern times have been made what they are by industry on rational lines of effort, with faith in the direct relation of effort to result.... That change accounts for a great deal of the modern change of feeling about religion. 23 *William Graham Sumner*

[This will] sum up the attitude of that mighty and rather terrible person, the Modern Man, toward the world: the complete submission to what he conceives as "hard, cold fact." To exchange fictions, faiths, and "constructed systems" for facts is his supreme value.... 24 *Susanne Langer*

I believe that if a hundred of the men of the seventeenth century had been killed in infancy, the modern world would not exist. And of these hundred, Galileo is the chief. 25 *Bertrand Russell*

The myth of science, the myth of the heroic knower, whether we call that consciousness Darwin or Einstein or Freud or Newton, a whole myth of the modern age is the myth of heroic consciousness. 26 *John Beebe*

Modern societies have substituted utopia for religion—utopia not as a transcendental ideal, but one to be realized through history (progress, rationality, science) with the nutrients of technology and the midwifery of revolution. 27 *Daniel Bell*

Modern man no longer seeks his nirvana, his escape from the unsolvable problems of life, in heaven, but in outer space. 28 *Bruno Bettelheim*

What makes the world in which we live specifically modern is our discovery in it and around it of evolution. And I can now add that what disconcerts the modern world at its very roots is not being sure, and not seeing how it could ever be sure, that there is an outcome—*a suitable outcome*—to that evolution. 29 *Pierre Teilhard de Chardin*

[T]he great problem of modern times [is] the discovery that to rescue man from destiny is to deliver him to chance. 30 *Albert Camus*

Modern man no longer knows what to do with the time and the potentialities he has unleashed. 31 *Pierre Teilhard de Chardin*

Modern man has learned that acquisitions are fundamentally unsatisfying; that freedom without the knowledge of real choice is a contradiction; that living for one's own pursuits, surrounded by others doing likewise, is not community.... Worst of all is the gradual disengagement from the sense of community, from shared dedication to larger spiritual goods and common worthwhile goals, from real social challenges, and from the possibilities of continuing interhuman dignity. 32 *Ernest Becker*

Strange and contradictory as it may seem, modern men hate the very order of things which they themselves support. 33 *Leo Tolstoy*

The most poignant problem of modern life is probably man's feeling that life has lost significance. 34 *René Dubos*

[I]ndifference is what characterizes modern man's relationship to himself and to others. 35 *Erich Fromm*

The man of modern times is more and more a prey to indifference. 36 *Gustave Le Bon*

So we find the modern man too dubious, too indifferent, to call a rival out to a duel. He feels constantly challenged within himself; courage has lost all charm and all finality. At the moment of his most confident thrust he perceives that he, too, is wounded, and the sense of moral disaster all round embitters every practical effort. 37 *George Santayana*

Tragic heroes overvalue justice and their own honor connected with it, and this leads them to destroy those they love.... [M]odern consciousness, resting on autonomous human principles of justice and a scientific view of

Modern

human mortality, implies a tragic view of life. 38
Lawrence Kohlberg

The real problem of *modernity* is … nihilism; lacking a past or a future, there is only a void. 39
Daniel Bell

The atrocities and "incidents" of Vietnam … [were] more or less a product of modern culture, which has increasingly grown godless. 40
J. Glenn Gray

Modern thought has never, in fact, been able to produce a morality.… For modern thought, no morality is possible. 41 *Michel Foucault*

The modern world debases. It debases the state; it debases man. It debases love; it debases woman … it debases the child … it debases the family. It even … debases death. 42 *Charles Péguy*

It is true that modern man is a culmination … of an age-old development, but he is at the same time the worst conceivable disappointment of the hopes of humankind. 43 *Carl Jung*

The crisis of modern man is to have lost his soul, or become rootless; but at the same time to have become godlike in the ability to manipulate birth, death, and the potential destruction of all known life. We understand almost all the technical causes—but not the meaning. 44
S. Segaller & M. Berger

Traditional societies were centered upon human needs and instincts.… Modern societies, on the other hand, are centered on technical necessity.… Cats and dogs disappear little by little from the city, going the way of the horse. Only rats and men remain to populate a dead world. 45 *Jacques Ellul*

Money / Wealth

In our day money is the chief asset, and people bow far more readily before the man with a great fortune than before the man of knowledge and great intellectual abilities, especially if it is his ill fortune to be poor. The worship of Mammon was never greater than it is in our day. 1
August Bebel

Mammon. The god of the world's leading religion. His chief temple is the holy city of New York. 2 *Ambrose Bierce*

In every well-governed state, wealth is a sacred thing; in democracies it is the only sacred thing. 3 *Anatole France*

[T]he first banks were temples and the first ones to issue money were the priests.… The thing that connects money with the domain of the sacred is its *power*. 4 *Ernest Becker*

What else but money, radiant and godlike, can ward off the pursuing shadows of death and time? 5 *Lewis Lapham*

[M]oney represents an illegitimate immortality system … devoid of moral vision. The reliance upon it is part of the emptiness—the absence of larger meaning.… And as Luther made explicit, there is always a devil lurking underneath the monetary mode of immortalization—or, in Marxist-secular terms, a life-destroying fetish.… Money as "immortal stuff," as an indestructible material-symbolic form of transcendence is always at the same time the "evil excrescence" or "filthy lucre." 6 *Robert Jay Lifton*

In reality, whenever archaic modes of thought have predominated or persist in unconscious thinking, in dreams and in neuroses—money is brought into the most intimate relationship with dirt. 7 *Sigmund Freud*

Money is condensed wealth; condensed wealth is condensed guilt.… Money is organic dead matter which has been made alive by inheriting the magic power which infantile narcissism attributes to the excremental product. 8
Norman O. Brown

Money bears no taint. It serves the murderer and the saint with equal indifference.… The effect of money is exhausted when … it makes wealth mobile and lets forces work out their full result by removing friction.… It is … an entire mistake to regard a money-system as in itself a mischief-working system. 9
William Graham Sumner

Money is the symbol of duty, it is the sacrament

of having done for mankind that which mankind wanted. 10 *Samuel Butler*

In the domestic societies of Western civilization the possession of money has become the outstanding symbol of the possession of power. Through the competition for the acquisition of money the power aspirations of the individual find a civilized outlet in harmony with the rules of conduct laid down by society. 11
Hans Morgenthau

Money creates a group by virtue of material interest relations between actual and potential participants in the market.... Furthermore, any act of exchange involving the use of money (sale) is a social action simply because the money used derives its value from its relation to the potential action of others. 12 *Max Weber*

Money is a formal token of delayed reciprocal altruism. 13 *Richard Dawkins*

Money ... is the oil which renders the motion of the wheels [of trade] more smooth and easy. 14
David Hume

Money is information in motion. 15
John Naisbitt

Like words and language, money is a storehouse of communally achieved work, skill, and experience. 16 *Marshall McLuhan*

Money is a material memory, a self-duplicating representation, a deferred exchange. 17
Michel Foucault

Money in its significant attributes is, above all, a subtle device for linking the present to the future.... 18 *John Maynard Keynes*

Wealth is itself expressive of reason for it arises whenever men, instead of doing nothing or beating about casually in the world, take to gathering fruits of nature which they may have for uses in the future, or fostering their growth.... 19
George Santayana

Money is simply a way of making it possible for us all not to have to work at the same tasks. 20
Philip Slater

The chief difference between money and other liabilities is its indefiniteness. Money bears a presumption of faith and a grant of freedom. Without money all exchanges must be partly determined. It is the willingness of man to give—or work—without a specific reward that allows liberty. 21 *George Gilder*

Money represents my strength; it ... represents the effectiveness of my desire as such ... and renders the desire immediately operative, like the magic wishes of fairy tales.... But *to me* it appears as a creative force: to buy an object is a symbolic act which amounts to creating the object.... To have is first to create. And the bond of ownership which is established then is a bond of continuous creation.... The bond of possession is an internal bond of *being*. 22
Jean-Paul Sartre

The nature of money is ... that the mediating activity of the human social action ... is alienated and becomes the characteristic of a material thing.... Through this alien intermediary—whereas man himself should be the intermediary between men—man sees his ... relation to others as a power which is independent of him and of them.... When man exteriorizes this mediating activity he is active only as an exiled and dehumanized being.... 23 *Karl Marx*

Money is the alienated *ability of mankind*. 24
Karl Marx

One of the little probed mysteries of social history is society's hostility to its greatest benefactors, the producers of wealth.... [This] is the function of the rich: fostering opportunities for the classes below them in the continuing drama of the creation of wealth and progress.... How the rich are regarded and how they see themselves—whether they are merely rich or also bearers of wealth—is a crucial measure of the health of a capitalist economy. 25 *George Gilder*

[Wealth] is God's way of blessing people who put Him first. 26 *Rev. Jerry Falwell*

The Bible ... is the undisputed book on financial success. There are some 500 verses in the Bible on prayer, but there are over 2,000 on money and possessions. 27 *William C. Wagner*

Money / Wealth

The most important thing is to have a spiritual environment in this country that will mean we can keep the money we make. 28

Nelson B. Hunt

Money, not morality, is the principle of commercial nations. 29 *Thomas Jefferson*

Money speaks sense in a language all nations understand. 30 *Aphra Behn*

"[A] *country of money*—and I have no higher, more reverent tribute to pay to America, for this means: a country of reason, justice, freedom, production, achievement.... Until and unless you discover that money is the root of all good, you ask for your own destruction." 31

Ayn Rand

However, those who are determined to be rich fall into temptation and a snare and many senseless and hurtful desires, which plunge men into destruction and ruin. For the love of money is the root of all evil.... 32 *Saint Paul*

Love of money is the mother of all evils. 33

Diogenes

Money does motivate people but mainly for the wrong things. That is to say, *money motivates people to do what they wouldn't otherwise want to do.* 34 *Philip Slater*

Whatever else it may mean, freedom means that you have the power to do what you want.... And in American society, the power to do what you want ... requires money. Money provides power and power provides freedom. 35

C. Wright Mills

The gold-plated lobbying, high-priced foreign contracts, and big PAC war chests all underscore the blatant influence of money in the new power game. 36 *Hedrick Smith*

[T]he pressures to gather large amounts of money are so great that the legislative process is inherently distorted, even corrupted.... What is at stake is the idea of representative government, the soul of this country. 37

Elizabeth Drew

The problem isn't corruption; it is more serious than that.... America is becoming a special-interest nation where money is displacing votes. Congress commands less and less support among the electorate as it panders increasingly to groups with money.... 38

Brooks Jackson

Plutocrats in a democracy work by corrupting public life.... [A]s the money goes, so goes the legislation. 39 *Amitai Etzioni*

Through money, democracy becomes its own destroyer, after money has destroyed intellect. 40

Oswald Spengler

Plutocracy, or rule by the rich ... directs the energies of the nation toward inhuman goals.... Worst of all, a plutocracy deadens the healthy aspirations of the young. 41 *Robert Payne*

Money, as the nexus in all human relations and as the main motivation in all social effort, replaced the reciprocal obligations and duties of families, neighbors, citizens, friends. And as other moral and esthetic considerations diminished, the dynamics of money power increased. Money was the only form of power which ... knew no limits.... 42 *Lewis Mumford*

If *money* is the bond binding me to human life, binding society to me, binding me and nature and man, is not money the bond of all *bonds*? Can it not dissolve and bind all ties? Is it not the universal *agent of separation*? 43 *Karl Marx*

Money encourages ego-centered social relations, loosens group and moral allegiances, [and] invites the person to be an individual.... 44

Keneln Burridge

Money became the great equalizer of man and proved to be more powerful than birth and caste. 45 *Erich Fromm*

It is this rapid redistribution of money that limits the personal value of the old focus on the lineage, the extended family, and instead increases the value of purely personal initiatives and the maintenance of less expensive and more independent monogamous nuclear families. 46 *John H. Crook*

Money / Wealth

Money destroys human roots wherever it is able to penetrate, by turning desire for gain into the sole motive. 47 *Simone Weil*

The desire for limitless quantities of money has as little relevance to the welfare of the human organism as the stimulation of the "pleasure center." ... When capitalists become aware of the nature of such pecuniary over-stimulation, once called the curse of Midas, they either commit suicide or turn repentantly to public service and philanthropy. 48 *Lewis Mumford*

Apparently the stimulation of [the] pleasure center is so rewarding that [an] animal will continue to press the current regulator ... even to the point of starvation. The intensity of this abstract stimulus produces something like a total neurotic insensibility to life needs. The power complex seems to operate on the same principle. The magical electronic stimulus is money.... Money has proved the most dangerous of modern man's hallucinogens. 49
Lewis Mumford

When the accumulation of wealth is no longer of high social importance ... love of money as a possession—as distinct from the love of money as a means to the enjoyments and realities of life—will be recognized for what it is, a somewhat disgusting morbidity, one of those semi-criminal, semi-pathological propensities which one hands on with a shudder to the specialists in mental disease. 50
John Maynard Keynes

Money is the natural preoccupation of so many neurotics because the neurotic, by definition, must feel worthless; he was not valued for what he was. Not being able to feel his true needs, he will always want more than he needs. 51
Arthur Janov

Money as such is not particularly dangerous. It becomes dangerous only if it can buy power, either directly, or by enslaving the economically weak who must sell themselves in order to live. 52 *Karl Popper*

A society which reverences the attainment of riches as the supreme felicity will naturally be disposed to regard the poor as damned in the next world, if only to justify itself for making their life a hell in this. 53 *R. H. Tawney*

[I]f the power of money has conquered completely, then mercifulness is altogether abolished. 54 *Søren Kierkegaard*

Money, besides, saves me the trouble of being dishonest: I am therefore presumed honest. 55
Karl Marx

[T]he principle element in a man's well-being—indeed, in the whole tenor of his existence—is what he is made of, his inner constitution.... And still men are a thousand times more intent on becoming rich than on acquiring culture, though it is quite certain that what a man *is* contributes much more to his happiness than what he *has*. 56 *Arthur Schopenhauer*

Wealth is excessive when it reduces a man to a middleman and a jobber, when it prevents him, in his preoccupation with material things, from making his spirit the measure of them. 57
George Santayana

When triumphant robbery is found among the rich, subversive doctrine will grow among the poor. 58 *William Lecky*

If one's acts are motivated by profit, he will have many enemies. 59 *Confucius*

Money is coined liberty. 60 *Feodor Dostoevsky*

But in reality the rich, unless they are more than rich, are slaves to the world, and captives of their successes and their possessions. They must keep earning their money, or defending it, spending it as the world demands, trembling at losing it or finding it insufficient, and countering the endless claims, obligations, and jealousies that it brings. 61 *George Santayana*

The money which a man possesses is the instrument of freedom; that which we eagerly pursue is the instrument of slavery. 62
Jean-Jacques Rousseau

Of all forms of tyranny the least attractive and the most vulgar is the tyranny of wealth; the tyranny of plutocracy. 63 *J. P. Morgan*

Money / Wealth

The man who dies ... rich dies disgraced. 64
Andrew Carnegie

The rich are like ravening wolves, who, having once tasted human flesh, henceforth desire and devour only men. 65 *Jean-Jacques Rousseau*

I cannot concede that a rich man is truly happy unless he is also a good man, and must state that to be at once exceedingly wealthy and good is impossible.... 66 *Plato*

The general tendency of a uniform course of prosperity is rather to degradation than to exalt the character. 67 *Thomas Malthus*

The pursuit of riches is obviously one of the great regressors.... Indeed, it takes a person of great character to receive a great financial windfall, and then use his or her good fortune to rise to higher planes of humanity. 68 *Kent G. Bailey*

Money is human happiness *in abstracto*, consequently he who is no longer capable of happiness *in concreto* sets his whole heart in money. 69 *Arthur Schopenhauer*

Happiness is the deferred fulfillment of a prehistoric wish. That is why wealth brings so little happiness; money is not an infantile wish. 70
Sigmund Freud

It is better to give a child too little than too much.... Too much money handicaps a child's fantasy life. 71 *A. S. Neill*

[T]oo much money has killed men and left them dead years before burial.... 72 *Carl Sandburg*

Man becomes ever poorer as man [as] his need for *money* becomes ever greater.... 73
Karl Marx

I make it my sole business to persuade you, both young and old, not to care for riches nor anything else so earnestly as for your souls. I remind you that riches do not produce virtue, but virtue brings riches and all other goods, private and public. 74 *Socrates*

I am absolutely convinced that no wealth in the world can help humanity forward, even in the hands of the most devoted worker in the cause. 75 *Albert Einstein*

The substitution of money for all other systems of value facilitates the attack on self, on culture, on country, on time past and time future.... The emptiness of the faith in money reveals itself in the monthly best-seller lists, which, together with the instruction manuals for the making of new fortunes, contain so many tracts promising spiritual remedies for the despair associated with rapid consumerism. 76
Lewis Lapham

[One may] clarify the nature of money by two processes that are almost endemic to the heights of a money culture—cynicism and a blasé attitude—both of which are the results of the reduction of the concrete values of life to the mediating value of money. 77 *Georg Simmel*

When there are no values, money counts. 78
E. Digby Baltzell

The money changers have fled from their high seats in the temple of our civilization. We may now restore that temple to the ancient truths. The measure of the restoration lies in the extent to which we apply social values more noble than mere monetary profit. 79
Franklin D. Roosevelt

No man can serve two masters.... You cannot serve both God and Mammon. 80 *Jesus Christ*

Morality / Ethics

Two things fill the mind with ever new and increasing wonder and awe, the more often and the more seriously reflection concentrates upon them: the starry heaven above me and the moral law within me. 1 *Immanuel Kant*

Man first puts himself in relation with Nature and her Powers, wonders and worships over those; not till a later epoch does he discern that all Power is Moral, that the grand point is the distinction for him of Good and Evil.... 2
Thomas Carlyle

Man is the "ethical animal." ... 3 *Rollo May*

Morality / Ethics

There is an imperative which commands a certain conduct immediately, without having as its condition any other purpose to be attained by it. This imperative is Categorical.... This imperative may be called that of Morality. 4
Immanuel Kant

The moral imperatives are not arbitrary ordinances of a transcendent tyrant.... The moral law is man's own essential nature appearing as commanding authority. If man were united with himself and his essential being there would be no command. 5 *Paul Tillich*

With maturity comes the recognition that the authorized precepts of morality were essentially not arbitrary; that they expressed the genuine aims and interests of a practised will; that their alleged alien and supernatural basis ... was but a mythical cover for their forgotten natural springs. 6 *George Santayana*

No form of life can be inherently wrong.... But when life is firmly organized in a special way, as it must before spirit can appear, some impulses will be indispensable for it, and others disruptive. Hence human morality is quite safely and efficiently established by human nature, and maintained by swift natural sanctions. 7
George Santayana

Ethics and morality exist even without religion. Only fools or hypocrites would assert the contrary. 8 *August Bebel*

[L]ife is a moral problem.... 9 *Ernest Becker*

Every condition of life as it moves toward coherent organization develops its own *ethos*, its own standards and codes. 10 *John Dewey*

[T]he task of ethics or moral philosophy is to determine what the real and pressing needs of human beings are and then to determine how these needs can be fairly and justly met. 11
Joseph P. Fell

To plunge down below our moral rules is ... not to abolish their restraints; it is to yield to an insanity from which wild animals would recoil. 12 *Denis de Rougemont*

"It is for the purpose of self-preservation that man needs a code of morality." 13 *Ayn Rand*

Ethics is an objective, metaphysical necessity of man's survival.... The first step is to assert man's right to a moral existence, that is: to recognize his need of a moral code to guide the course and the fulfillment of his own life.... [C]oncern with his own interests is the essence of a moral existence.... 14 *Ayn Rand*

[E]very healthy morality—is dominated by an instinct of life.... *Anti-natural* morality—that is, almost every morality which has so far been taught, revered, and preached—turns, conversely, *against* the instincts of life.... Life has come to an end where the "kingdom of God" begins. 15 *Friedrich Nietzsche*

Morality is ... essentially the expression of hostility to life, in so far as it would overcome vital types. 16 *Friedrich Nietzsche*

The existence of strict moral principles has invariably signified that the biological, and specifically the sexual, needs of man were not being satisfied. Every moral regulation is itself sex-negating, and all compulsory morality is life-negating. 17 *Wilhelm Reich*

Morality, when it is formal, devours.... Absolute virtue is impossible, and the republic of forgiveness leads, with implacable logic, to the republic of the guillotine. 18 *Albert Camus*

[To Freud] moral ideas are named as the *problem* of life rather than as the basis for a solution to the problem. The Freudian dislike of social idealism, as a way of symbolizing and masking power, emerges in a powerful suspicion of self-sacrifice as sickness.... "Morality," the sadism of the superego, appears as a stupid alternative to the "will to power," the sadism of the ego. 19 *Philip Rieff*

From the point of view of morality, the control and restriction of instinct, it may be said of the id that it is totally non-moral, of the ego that it strives to be moral, and of the superego that it can be hyper-moral and then becomes as ruthless as only the id can be. 20
Sigmund Freud

Morality / Ethics

[P]assions, such as desires for fame or wealth, fragment us in many directions rather than provide continuity and consistency to our lives. Only moral commitment generates sufficient unifying power and discipline by imparting a sense that it matters unconditionally whether we choose the good or the bad. 21 *Mike W. Martin*

Ethics and moral codes are necessary to man because of the conflict between intelligence and impulse.... [W]e have need of ethics to suggest purposes, and of moral codes to inculcate rules of action.... [E]thics considered as a matter of give-and-take is scarcely distinguishable from politics. 22 *Bertrand Russell*

In the area of ethical choice ultimate world views clash. 23 *Max Weber*

We have ... the precise location of the barricades between contending primary ethics: between, namely that which favours the restriction of material enablements (the right), and that which favours the extension of material enablements (the left).... [T]hese concepts represent the basic, opposing ways of moral life on earth.... 24 *John McMurtry*

Once a morality of principles is accepted ... moral attitudes are no longer connected solely to the well-being and approval of particular individuals and groups, but are shaped by a conception of right chosen irrespective of these contingencies. 25 *John Rawls*

Whereas the rights conception of morality ... is geared to arriving at an objectively fair or just resolution to the moral dilemmas ... a morality of rights and noninterference may appear to women as frightening in its potential justification of indifference and unconcern.... Given the differences in women's conception of self and morality, women bring to the life cycle a different point of view and order human experience in terms of different priorities. 26 *Carol Gilligan*

Nothing is intrinsically immoral except ill-will and nothing intrinsically good except goodwill.... The moral will expresses itself unconsciously in terms of consideration for the life, the interests and the rights of others.... 27 *Reinhold Niebuhr*

"Teacher, which is the greatest commandment in the moral law?" Jesus said to him: "You must love God with your whole heart and your whole soul and your whole mind.... And like it is this: You must love your neighbour as yourself. On these two commandments rests the whole moral law."... 28 *Holy Bible*

What is hateful to thyself do not do to another. This is the whole Law, the rest is commentary. 29 *Hillel*

[T]he most radical injunction is still the Golden Rule.... It turns healthy self-interest into equally healthy altruism.... Ethics are their own reward. 30 *Gloria Steinem*

Gratitude ... points backward in time toward first gifts. It forms exclusive attachments involving ... trust, affection, obedience, and subservience. Almost inevitably, gratitude serves the authorities of established tradition.... Gratitude is at the ethical-moral core of ourselves. 31 *Joseph Amato*

Ethics is in origin the art of recommending to others the sacrifices required for co-operation with oneself. Hence, by reflexion, it comes, through the operation of social justice, to recommend sacrifices by oneself.... 32 *Bertrand Russell*

I am never to act otherwise than so that I could also will that my maxim should become a universal law. 33 *Immanuel Kant*

A truly rational morality, or social regimen, has never existed in the world.... In lieu of a rational morality, however, we have rational ethics.... It sets forth the method of judgment and estimation which a rational morality would apply universally and express in practice. 34 *George Santayana*

Morality of outlook is inseparably conjoined with generality of outlook. The antithesis between the general good and the individual interest can be abolished only when the individual is such that its interest is the general good.... 35 *Alfred N. Whitehead*

Ethics at large may be defined, the art of

directing men's actions to the production of the greatest possible quantity of happiness.... 36
Jeremy Bentham

Morality is that system of conduct which is determined by a consideration of the greatest general good ... and made subservient to public utility. 37 *William Godwin*

The function of the ethical system in any given society is to sustain the life of that particular society. 38 *Erich Fromm*

What is moral becomes and remains self-evident only within a powerful and deeply compelling system of culture. 39 *Philip Rieff*

Morality is neither the internalization of established cultural values nor the unfolding of spontaneous impulses and emotions; it is justice, the reciprocity between the individual and others in the social environment. 40
Lawrence Kohlberg

Moral systems are systems of indirect reciprocity. They exist because of conflicts of interest.... The function or *raison d'etre* of moral systems is evidently to provide the unity required to enable the group to compete successfully with other human groups. 41 *Richard Alexander*

Human behavior ... is the circuitous technique by which human genetic material has been and will be kept intact. Morality has no other demonstrable ultimate function. 42
E. O. Wilson

[A]lthough a high standard of morality gives but a slight or no advantage to each individual man and his children ... [an] advancement in the standard of morality will certainly give an immense advantage to one tribe over another. 43
Charles Darwin

Morality is the herd-instinct in the individual. 44
Friedrich Nietzsche

[M]orality ... rests entirely on the moral sense of the individual and the freedom necessary for this. Hence every man is, in a certain sense, unconsciously a worse man when he is in society than when acting alone; for he is carried by society and to that extent relieved of his individual responsibility. Any large company composed of wholly admirable persons has the morality and intelligence of an unwieldy, stupid, and violent animal. 45 *Carl Jung*

Morality is inversely proportional to the number of individuals involved. 46
Aldous Huxley

[W]hen it is the question of the interests of the nation ... morality stops. 47
Hermann Goering

[I]t is evident, that the first Rudiments of Morality, broach'd by skilfull Politicians, to render Men useful to each other as tractable, were chiefly contrived; that the Ambitious might reap the more Benefit from, and govern vast Numbers of them with the greater Ease and Security. 48 *Bernard Mandeville*

The word "moral" means what belongs or appertains to the mores.... Goodness or badness of the mores is always relative only. Their purpose is to serve needs, and their quality is to be defined by the degree to which they do it. 49
William Graham Sumner

Morality seems to be a gift like intelligence. You cannot pump it into a system where it is not indigenous, though you may spoil it. 50
Carl Jung

Morality is an artifice most fragile. 51
Russell Kirk

[In the] system as it is today ... something ought to be done because it is technically possible.... [A]ll other values are dethroned and technological development becomes the foundation of ethics. 52 *Erich Fromm*

[A] principle characteristic of technique ... is its refusal to tolerate moral judgments. It is absolutely independent of them and eliminates them from its domain.... [E]verything which is technique is necessarily used as soon as it is available, without distinction of good or evil. This is the principle law of our age. 53
Jacques Ellul

Morality / Ethics

What reconciles science and ethics is the science of ethics, for at the same time that it teaches us to respect the moral reality, it furnishes us the means to improve it. 54
Émile Durkheim

The antagonism between a virtue policy and a success policy is a constant ethical problem.... The mores aim always to arrive at correct notions of virtue. In so far as they reach correct results the virtue policy proves to be the only success policy. 55 *William Graham Sumner*

The primary determinant of a morality is the way in which a society conceives of humanness.... [W]hat we value depends on our sense of what it means to be a human, our way of seeing ourselves. 56 *Marilyn French*

[T]he application of *intrinsic* value to persons produces ethics. 57 *Robert Hartman*

The end of morality is to give personal, human finality to the universe.... 58
Miguel de Unamuno

[T]he initial helplessness of human beings is the primal source of all moral motives. 59
Sigmund Freud

Of all moral principles, the one that comes closest to being universally accepted is this: one should not inflict suffering on a helpless person who is neither harmful nor threatening to oneself. 60 *Stanley Milgram*

The truth is that morality is not mainly concerned with the attainment of pleasure; it is rather concerned, in all its deeper and more authoritative maxims, with the prevention of suffering. 61 *George Santayana*

The day *may* come when the rest of the animal creation may acquire those rights which never could have been withholden from them but by the hand of tyranny.... [A] full-grown horse or dog is beyond comparison a more rational ... animal, than an infant.... But suppose they were otherwise, what would it avail? The question is not, Can they *reason*? nor Can they *talk*? but, Can they *suffer*? 62
Jeremy Bentham

The land ethic simply enlarges the boundaries of the [moral] community.... In short, a land ethic changes the role of *Homo sapiens* from conqueror of the land-community to plain member and citizen of it.... A land ethic, then, reflects the existence of an ecological conscience.... A thing is right when it tends to preserve the integrity, stability, and beauty of the biotic community. It is wrong when it tends otherwise. 63 *Aldo Leopold*

For humanistic ethics all evil strivings are directed against life and all good serves the preservation and unfolding of life. 64 *Erich Fromm*

The ultimate reality of the world is not moral.... God is not good; but if I want to have even the smallest knowledge of God, I must be good at least in some slight measure; and if I want as full a knowledge of God as it is possible for human beings to have, I must be as good as it is for human beings to be. Virtue is the essential preliminary to the mystical experience. 65 *Aldous Huxley*

For me ... the true ethical principle is the reconciliation with one's own being. It is not the acceptance of a strange command from outside, whether conventional or human or divine, but the command of our true being, from which we are estranged and in this sense separated. And in every morally positive act there is a reunion. 66 *D. MacKenzie Brown*

The failure to achieve maturity and integration of the whole personality is a moral failure.... 67
Erich Fromm

Integrity alone can be morally free, being alone compatible with a radical self-knowledge and the perception of an ultimate good. 68
George Santayana

Morals concern nothing less than the whole character.... The moral and the social quality of conduct are, in the last analysis, identical with each other. 69 *John Dewey*

It is better to sacrifice one's life than one's morality. To live is not a necessity; but to live honourably while life lasts is a necessity. 70
Immanuel Kant

MORALITY / ETHICS

Morality has perished through the poverty of great men.... 71 *Saint Augustine*

Moral codes are always obstructive, relative, and man-made. Yet they have been of enormous profit to civilization. They *are* civilization. 72 *Camille Paglia*

When man loses sight of moral ends, his degradation commences. 73 *Russell Kirk*

[A] decisive step in the preparation of living corpses is the murder of the moral person in man. 74 *Hannah Arendt*

Our greatest challenge today is the "morality gap" between our cumulative accelerating advance in science and technology and our appalling failure in our relations with each other. 75 *Arnold Toynbee*

It is evident that we are at a primitive stage of moral development. Even the most civilized human beings have only a haphazard understanding of how to live, how to treat others, how to organize their societies. 76 *Thomas Nagel*

The deterioration of international morality which has occurred in recent years with regard to the protection of life is only a special instance of a general and ... much more far-reaching dissolution of an ethical system that in the past imposed its restraints upon the day-by-day operations of foreign policy but does so no longer. 77 *Hans Morgenthau*

The maladjustment from which we suffer does not exist because the objective causes of suffering have increased in number or intensity; it bears witness not to greater economic poverty, but to an alarming poverty of morality. 78 *Émile Durkheim*

Our moral problem is man's *indifference* to himself. 79 *Erich Fromm*

The organization of indifference may well succeed the organization of love, producing a culture at lower cost to individual energies. 80 *Philip Rieff*

[T]he modern cultural revolution ... is deliberately not in the name of any new order of communal purpose.... On the contrary, this revolution is being fought for a permanent disestablishment of any deeply internalized moral demands. 81 *Philip Rieff*

The western world is now suffering from the limited moral outlook of the three previous generations. 82 *Alfred N. Whitehead*

In America the cultural life goals—success, competition, power, prestige, security, happiness—speak more loudly than the moral codes.... When the moral middle classes in America bemoan the "moral breakdown," they are bemoaning something which they and their life values have largely brought about, corroding the old moral code without bringing a new one into being. 83 *Max Lerner*

What Americans are suffering is not so much a moral breakdown as ... a moral interregnum. 84 *Max Lerner*

The world crisis of today is a *moral* crisis—and nothing less than a moral revolution can resolve it.... 85 *Ayn Rand*

All reform except a moral one will prove unavailing. 86 *Thomas Carlyle*

The process of moral learning is a long uphill climb, and the hill seems to get steeper and slipperier as we climb it. 87 *Kenneth Boulding*

The fate of humanity hangs on the question whether or not responsible morality will be able to cope with its rapidly growing burden. 88 *Konrad Lorenz*

The destiny of civilized humanity depends more than ever on the moral forces it is capable of generating. 89 *Albert Einstein*

Ethics ... may be termed the art of discharging one's duty to one's neighbour. 90 *Jeremy Bentham*

Without "ethical culture" there is no salvation for humanity. 91 *Albert Einstein*

Mother

~ Mother ~

The most elementary of the natural ties is the tie of the child to the mother.… Mother is food; she is love; she is warmth; she is earth. To be loved by her means to be alive, to be rooted, to be at home. 1 *Erich Fromm*

It seems to me that there is something missing in human society. Children grow up and become in their turn fathers and mothers, but, on the whole, they do not grow up to know and acknowledge just what their mothers did for them at the start. 2 *D. W. Winnicott*

Is not this contribution of the devoted mother unrecognized precisely because it is immense? If this contribution is accepted, it follows that every man or woman who is sane, every man or woman who has the feeling of being a person in the world, and for whom the world means something, every happy person, is in infinite debt to a woman. 3 *D. W. Winnicott*

All our mothers have faced death in giving us life.… 4 *August Bebel*

The relationship which stands at the origin of all culture, of every virtue, of every nobler aspect of existence, is that between mother and child; it operates in a world of violence as the divine principle of love, of union, of peace. 5 *J. J. Bachofen*

The mother is at the threshold of the development of social interest … and with it the essential existence of human civilization. 6 *Alfred Adler*

[T]he mother-infant bond precedes all others.… It is not only emotional maturity that is affected by the bond, but the capacity to learn in general. Bold exploration and mischievous curiosity, the desire to manipulate and investigate the environment—none of these will successfully mature if the young animal lacks a sense of security. 7 *Lionel Tiger & Robin Fox*

Maternal love was not only the first kind of love. For many millennia it was the only kind. When women, after she had tamed man, extended her love for her children to include their father, then perhaps man began to learn for the first time what love was. 8 *Elizabeth Gould Davis*

"Everyone should be able to look back in their memory and be sure that he had a mother who loved him, all of him; even his shit and piss. If he can't fall back on this, he can be broken." 9 "Joan," in *The Divided Self*

The mother's yearning, that completest type of the life in another life which is the essence of real human love, feels the presence of the cherished child even in the debased, degraded man. 10 *George Eliot*

Motherly love by its very nature is unconditional.… Unconditional love corresponds to one of the deepest longings, not only of the child, but of every human being.… Mother has the function of making [the child] secure in life, father has the function of teaching him, guiding him to cope [in society]. 11 *Erich Fromm*

[A] drastic loss of accustomed mother love without proper substitution … can lead to acute infantile depression or to a mild but chronic state of mourning which may give a depressive undertone to the whole remainder of life … [leaving] a residue of a primary sense of evil and doom.… 12 *Erik Erikson*

The competent mother can take in and feel the panic and dread and feed it back, modified and softened, like a psychic shock-absorber. 13 *Alistair Mant*

Just as the child's *primary empathy* with the mother is the precursor of the adult's ability to be empathetic, so his *primary identification* with her must be considered the precursor of an expansion of the self, late in life, when the finiteness of individual existence is acknowledged. 14 *Heinz Kohut*

Deprived of maternal care in the first year and a half, the child cannot develop the capacity to form human bonds. Qualities of self-observation and self-criticism, the conscience itself, all fail to develop.… 15 *Charles Drekmeier*

No relationship has been found between the moral level of fathers and their children.…

Mother

[But] a clear relationship between mother's level and the level of her children ... has been found. 16 *Lawrence Kohlberg*

[B]eyond a certain basic minimum, differences in maternal affection are not important in producing differences in moral behaviour.... [But] when there is no maternal affection the consequences for moral growth are serious. 17 *Derek Wright*

Without a mother, no strong love focused on a personal object; without such love, no conflict of unreconcilable influences, no guilt; and without such guilt, no effective moral sense. 18 *Julian Huxley*

[A]ll feelings of a sympathetic, compassionate, altruistic character, which are in direct contrast to biological impulses ... and are specific characters of human psychology, are extensions of the maternal reaction.... Those determining factors in the origin of the human race and of society are dependent upon the operation of the maternal impulses. 19 *Robert Briffault*

Disturbances of attachment behaviour are of many kinds. In the Western world much of the commonest ... are the results of too little mothering, or of mothering coming from a succession of different people. Disturbances arising from too much mothering are much less common.... 20 *John Bowlby*

Maturity and the capacity to be alone implies that the individual has had a chance through good enough mothering to build up a belief in a benign environment. 21 *D. W. Winnicott*

The first task of a mother is to give her child the experience of a trustworthy other person: later she must widen and enlarge this feeling of trust until it includes the rest of the child's environment.... [Otherwise] he will expect [society] always to be cold.... He will thus be suspicious of others and unable to trust himself. 22 *Alfred Adler*

[I]n a young child an experience of separation from, or loss of, mother-figure is especially apt to evoke psychological processes of a kind that are ... crucial for psychopathology.... 23 *John Bowlby*

Motherhood is neither a duty nor a privilege, but simply the way that humanity can satisfy the desire for physical immortality and triumph over the fear of death. 24 *Rebecca West*

[T]he image of mother in each person's internal world is extremely powerful. Mother is embedded psychically in almost magical terms. 25 *Luise Eichenbaum & Susie Orbach*

The early mother's apparent omnipotence, [and] her ambivalent role as ultimate source of good and evil, is a central source of human malaise: our species' uneasy, unstable stance toward nature, and its uneasy, unstable sexual arrangements, are inseparable aspects of this malaise. 26 *Dorothy Dinnerstein*

The sentimental ideal of motherhood is the product of the historic separation of public and private spheres that gave gender polarity its present form.... To accept the old ideal of motherhood—even as an ideal—is to remain inside the revolving door of gender polarity. 27 *Jessica Benjamin*

There does not seem to be evidence to demonstrate that exclusive mothering is necessarily better for infants. However, such mothering is "good for society." 28 *Nancy Chodorow*

What matters is the quality of a mother's relationship with her children, not the time of day it happens to be administered. This conclusion should come as no surprise; successful fathers have been demonstrating it for years. Some fathers are great, some fathers stink, and they're all at work at least eight hours a day.... 29 *Sandra Bem & Daryl Bem*

There is no mystical power in the skill of motherhood. 30 *Alfred Adler*

The mother-child relationship is the essential human relationship. In the creation of the patriarchal family, violence is done to this fundamental human unit.... The mother's battle for her child ... needs to become a common human battle, waged in love.... But for this to happen, the institution of motherhood must be destroyed. 31 *Adrienne Rich*

Mother

Institutionalized features of family structure and the social relations of reproduction reproduce themselves.... Women mother daughters who, when they become women, mother.... Women's mothering also reproduces the family as it is constituted in male-dominant society. 32 *Nancy Chodorow*

If there is no true recognition of the mother's part, then there must remain a vague fear of dependence. 33 *D. W. Winnicott*

[A]ttachment to mother is one of the ... main causes of neurosis or psychosis.... [T]here is a close correlation between persons with a strong fixation to their mothers and those with exceptionally strong ties to nation and race, soil and blood.... Inasmuch as a person remains caught in this dependency, his own independence, freedom, and responsibility are weakened. 34 *Erich Fromm*

[T]he anima, in the form of the mother image, is transferred to the wife; and the man as soon as he marries, becomes childlike, sentimental, dependent, and subservient, or else truculent, tyrannical, hypersensitive, always thinking of his superior masculinity.... [H]e is really seeking his mother's protection. 35 *Carl Jung*

If there is any female who truly might be called castrating it is a man's mother: for she often gives him the original attitudes, prejudices, and interpretations which, later on in life, he employs ... to make himself give over-serious heed to ... the so-called demasculinizing wife. 36 *Albert Ellis*

Never marry a man who hates his mother, because he'll end up hating you. 37 *Jill Bennett*

If a mother cannot love herself enough truly to love another, and her son suffers too much the pain of needing and being denied that loving touch—he has to turn his own sex, and its object, into a machine.... Psychiatrists ... do not ask why, in such families, the mothers have so little sense of self, why they are forced to act out that inauthentic love. 38 *Betty Friedan*

Each mother can only react empathetically to the extent that she has become free of her own childhood, and she is forced to react without empathy to the extent that, by denying the vicissitudes of her early life, she wears invisible chains. 39 *Alice Miller*

Mothers of the future should ... be far less driven to flood their male children with frustrated longings and resentments. Living fuller, less constricted lives themselves, they will have less need to invest their sons with Oedipally-tinged ambition. 40 *Philip Slater*

To be a good mother—a woman must have sense, and that independence of mind which few women possess who are taught to depend entirely on their husbands.... I now only mean to insist, that unless the understanding of women be enlarged, and her character rendered more firm, by being allowed to govern her own conduct, she will never have sufficient sense or command of temper to manage her children properly. 41 *Mary Wollstonecraft*

The weakness of the mother will be visited on the children! 42 *Mary Wollstonecraft*

In the wife who has lived through a happy marriage, for whom the bonds of passionate love have been fully cemented, maternal desire is intensified and matured. Motherhood becomes for such a woman ... the road by which she travels onward toward completely rounded self-development.... When motherhood is a mere accident, as so often it is in the early years of careless or reckless marriages ... marriage is thus converted into a tragedy. Motherhood becomes for her a horror instead of a joyfully fulfilled function. 43 *Margaret Sanger*

No woman can call herself free until she can choose consciously whether she will or will not be a mother. 44 *Margaret Sanger*

The change in woman's historical, political reality is that motherhood—which was once her necessity and passive destiny, and which confined, defined, used up her whole life—is now no longer necessity, but choice, and even when chosen, no longer can define or even use up most of her life. 45 *Betty Friedan*

The heart of woman's oppression is her childbearing and childrearing roles.... *Pregnancy is barbaric.* 46 *Shulamith Firestone*

How come ... some liberationists groan and growl when they hear people croon about the joys of motherhood?... Having more or less exploded the myth that some women are frigid to the delights of sex, are we now to discover that some are frigid to the pleasures of maternity? Why is it that they are ready to hire other women to bring up their children, whereas even the most *spirituelle* have seldom contemplated hiring other women to relieve them of the equally earthy chore of sleeping with their husbands? 47 *Elaine Morgan*

These two technologies—artificial insemination and in vitro fertilization—enable women to sell their wombs.... Motherhood is becoming a new branch of female prostitution.... 48 *Andrea Dworkin*

The subordination of all aspects of life to the instrumental principles of the public world also subverts the very values of private life, and thus threatens [its] maternal aspects.... The destruction of maternal values is not the result of women's liberation; it is the consequence of the ascendance of male rationality. 49 *Jessica Benjamin*

The ideal of autonomous individuality with its stress on rationality, self-sufficiency, performance, and competition threatens to negate the mother so completely that there may be no one to come home to. 50 *Jessica Benjamin*

The [maternal] instinct ... works directly in the service of the species, while the other instincts work primarily in the service of the individual life.... [T]he human species is dependent on this instinct for its continued existence and welfare. 51 *William McDougall*

Women are the carriers of the true spirit of humanity—the love of the mother for her child.... [I]t is the evolutionary destiny of human beings so to love each other.... What mothers are to their children, so will man be to man. 52 *Ashley Montagu*

Endless Becoming is comprehended in the idea of Motherhood, Woman as Mother *is* Time and *is* Destiny.... *Care* is the root-feeling of future, and all care is motherly. 53 *Oswald Spengler*

[B]eing human depends upon what has developed and become self-conscious and aware during millions of years and on the miraculous processes of primary nurture by innumerable creative processes—and innumerable mothers.... The human soul is the product of aeons of love. 54 *David Holbrook*

~ MYTH ~

MYTH NARRATES A SACRED HISTORY; it relates an event that took place in primordial Time, the fabled time of the "beginnings." In other words, myth tells how, through the deeds of Supernatural Beings, a reality came into existence.... In short, myths describe the various and sometimes dramatic breakthroughs of the sacred (or the "supernatural") into the World. It is this sudden breakthrough of the sacred that really *establishes* the World and makes it what it is today. 1 *Mircea Eliade*

To tell a myth is to proclaim what happened *ab origine*. Once told, that is, revealed, the myth becomes apodictic truth; it establishes a truth that is absolute.... It is for this reason that myth is bound up with ontology; it speaks only of *realities*.... Obviously these realities are sacred realities. 2 *Mircea Eliade*

Myth is a directing of the mind and heart, by means of profoundly informed figurations, to that ultimate mystery which fills and surrounds all existences. 3 *Joseph Campbell*

Myths ... are pictures of the deepest secrets of human existence. 4 *Rudolf Steiner*

[A] myth always refers to events alleged to have taken place long ago. But what gives the myth an operational value is that the specific pattern described is timeless; it explains the present and the past as well as the future. 5 *Claude Lévi-Strauss*

Myths are things which never happened but always are. 6 *Salustius*

The origin of myth is dynamic, but its purpose is philosophical. It is the primitive phase of metaphysical thought, the first embodiment of *general ideas*. 7 *Susanne Langer*

Myth

The elements of mythical thought … lie halfway between percepts and concepts. 8
Claude Lévi-Strauss

Myth is the natural and indispensable stage between unconscious and conscious cognition. 9
Carl Jung

Myth is an intermediary entity between a statistical aggregate of molecules and the molecular structure itself.… [I]t closely corresponds, in the realm of the spoken word, to a crystal in the realm of physical matter.… Its *growth* is a continuous process, whereas its *structure* remains discontinuous. 10 *Claude Lévi-Strauss*

Mythology … is an inherent necessity of language, if we recognize in language the outward form and manifestation of thought; it is in fact the dark shadow which language throws upon thought, and which can never disappear till language becomes entirely commensurate with thought, which it never will. 11 *Max Muller*

Myth is language, functioning on an especially high level where meaning succeeds practically at "taking off" from the linguistic ground on which it keeps on rolling. 12
Claude Lévi-Strauss

Myth casts an image rather than denoting an object and thus is able to catch truths no merely literal language can contain. 13
Lloyd J. Averill

Mythical thought for its part is imprisoned in the events and experiences which it never tires of ordering and re-ordering in its search to find them a meaning. But it also acts as a liberator by its protest against the idea that anything can be meaningless.… 14 *Claude Lévi-Strauss*

Myths create, sustain, and reinforce meaning in human cultures.… They tell a people what is right and wrong, sacred and profane.… If old myths are destroyed, new ones will rush in to fill the vacuum. 15 *J. K. Hadden & A. Shupe*

Mythical thinking has its roots in reality, but, like a plant, touches the ground only at one end. It stands unmoved and flowers wantonly into the air, transmuting into unexpected and richer forms the substances it sucks from the soil. It is therefore a fruit of experience, an ornament, a proof of organic vitality.… 16
George Santayana

[T]he myth at its deepest level is that collectively created thing which crystallizes the great, central values of a culture. 17 *Theodore Roszak*

[I]t seems extremely probable that myths … are distorted vestiges of the wish-phantasies of whole nations—the age-long dreams of young humanity. 18 *Sigmund Freud*

We have created our myth. The myth is a faith, it is passion. It is not necessary that it shall be a reality.… Our myth is the Nation; our myth is the greatness of the Nation. 19
Benito Mussolini

[T]he transcendent Idea was deliberately used by patriarchal society for purposes of self-justification; through the myths this society imposed its laws and customs.… [I]t is under a mythical form that the group-imperative is indoctrinated into each conscience. 20
Simone de Beauvoir

The myth structure from which legal authority is derived must justify the existence of a social hierarchy in terms of power relationships.… The refusal of males in Western society to recognize women as equal, to forego their domination of the female sex … has meant that mythical systems of thought still had to be retained to justify a status relationship.… Political theories can thus be seen as mythic structures which attempt to legitimize domination of some human beings by other human beings. 21
J. C. Smith

The breakdown of the political system can be the result [when] … legitimation collapses … [and] the political myth becomes impossible. 22
M. Gear et al.

All civilizations rest on myths, but in America myths have exceptional meaning.… The true crime of Richard Nixon was simple: he destroyed the myth that binds America together, and for this he was driven from power. 23
Theodore White

Myth

The cult of the nation as social myth has run as a thread through the whole of American history. 24 *Max Lerner*

[M]yth is the dream of the people and a dream is the myth of an individual. 25 *Rosalind Coward*

[The] experience of participation in a divinely ordered cosmos extending beyond man can be expressed only by means of the myth; it cannot be transformed into processes of thought within consciousness.... When consciousness becomes noetically luminous, a new myth is required. 26 *Eric Voegelin*

Myth ... provides man with an "instantaneous" perception of the eternal, or with the one kind of immortality that is accessible to temporal beings. 27 *Stanley Rosen*

In a certain sense the whole of mythical thought may be interpreted as a constant and obstinate negation of the phenomenon of death. 28 *Ernst Cassirer*

The statement of a myth disarms all criticism ... [for] *a myth is needed to express the dark and unmentionable fact that passion is linked with death*, and it involves the destruction of any one yielding himself up to it with all his strength. 29 *Denis de Rougemont*

The true function of mythical ideas is to present and interpret events in terms relative to spirit. 30 *George Santayana*

Every myth of the great style stands at the beginning of an awakening spirituality. It is the first formative act of that spirituality. 31 *Oswald Spengler*

Myths are clues to the spiritual potentialities of the human life. 32 *Joseph Campbell*

It has always been the prime function of mythology ... to supply the symbols that carry the human spirit forward.... In fact, it may well be that the very high incidence of neuroticism among ourselves follows from the decline among us of such effective spiritual aids. 33 *Joseph Campbell*

Mythology helps to give weight to our private wounds. 34 *Robert Bly*

Myths basically serve four functions. The first is the mystical function ... [i.e.] realizing what a wonder the universe is.... The second is a cosmological dimension, the dimension with which science is concerned.... The third function is the sociological one—supporting and validating a certain social order.... But there is a fourth function of myth, and this is the one that I think everyone must try today to relate to—and that is the pedagogical function, of how to live a human lifetime under any circumstances. 35 *Joseph Campbell*

Myth ... at least at its best, is a recognition of natural conflicts, of human desire frustrated by nonhuman powers, hostile oppression, or contrary desires; it is a story of the birth, passion, and defeat by death which is man's common fate. Its ultimate end is not wishful distortion of the world, but serious envisagement of its fundamental truths; moral orientation, not escape. 36 *Susanne Langer*

The myths preserve and transmit the paradigms, the exemplary models, for all the responsible activities in which men engage. 37 *Mircea Eliade*

Einstein's discovery appealed to deep mythic themes. A new man appears abruptly.... He carries a message of new order in the universe.... His mathematical language is sacred.... He fulfills two profound needs in man, the need to know and the need not to know but to believe.... [H]e represents order and power. He became the divine man of the twentieth century. 38 *Abraham Pais*

Today it is the myths of death, and they alone, that speak to us in our madness. 39 *Jacques Ellul*

Our myth has become mute, and gives no answers. 40 *Carl Jung*

If we wish to change or improve the world, we must invent a new myth capable of inspiring mankind to heroic action. 41 *W. M. McGovern*

~ NARCISSISM ~

NARCISSISTS ARE more concerned with how they appear than what they feel. Indeed, they deny feelings that contradict the image they seek. Acting without feeling, they tend to be seductive and manipulative, striving for power and control.... Narcissists do show a lack of concern for others, but they are equally insensitive to their own true needs.... Without a solid sense of self, they experience life as empty and meaningless. 1 *Alexander Lowen*

The new narcissist is haunted not by anxiety. He seeks not to inflict his own certainties on others but to find a meaning in life.... The narcissist's pseudo-insight into his own condition, usually expressed in psychiatric clichés, serves him as a means of deflecting criticism and disclaiming responsibility.... The inner void, however, persists.... 2 *Christopher Lasch*

A narcissistic person considers only those things real and important that directly affect him. 3 *Erich Fromm*

Narcissism ... is self-absorption which prevents one from understanding what belongs within the domain of the self and self-gratification and what belongs outside it.... This absorption in self, oddly enough, prevents gratification of self needs; it makes the person at the moment of attaining an end or connecting with another person feel that "this isn't what I wanted." Narcissism thus has the double quality of being a voracious absorption in self needs and the block to their fulfillment.... There is a never-ending search for gratification, and at the same time the self cannot permit gratification to occur. 4
Richard Sennett

Narcissistic eros wants satisfaction now and forever. 5 *C. Fred Alford*

As a character disorder, narcissism is the very opposite of strong self-love. Self-absorption does not produce gratification, it produces injury to the self; erasing the line between self and other means that nothing new, nothing "other," ever enters the self; it is devoured and transformed until one thinks one can see oneself in the other—and then it becomes meaningless. 6 *Richard Sennett*

[N]arcissism is an expression not of self-love, but of alienation from the self.... A person clings to illusions about himself because and as far as he has lost himself. 7 *Karen Horney*

Narcissism depends on an elementary part of the psychic apparatus going into suspension. This is "enlightened self-interest".... 8 *Richard Sennett*

In narcissism the self-preserving function of the ego is, on the surface at least, retained, but, at the same time, split off from that of consciousness and thus lost to rationality. 9
Theodor W. Adorno

The narcissist is not hungry for experiences, he is hungry for Experience. Looking always for an expression or reflection of himself in Experience, he devalues each particular interaction or scene, because it is never enough to encompass who he is. The myth of Narcissus neatly captures this: one drowns in the self—it is an entropic state. 10 *Richard Sennett*

Severe narcissistic disturbances ... also entail an inability to experience others as more than manipulable or resistant objects in the self's world. 11 *Jessica Benjamin*

The conventional narcissist ... basically conforms to our concept of the sadist, who looks for his own satisfaction at the expense of the frustration of others.... In narcissism, as in any form of personality structure, it is only through the other that one can have an identity confirmed. 12 *M. Gear et al.*

Notwithstanding his occasional illusions of omnipotence, the narcissist depends on others to validate his self-esteem. 13 *Christopher Lasch*

Narcissistic personalities have a great need to be loved and admired by others. 14
Elizabeth Moberly

Narcissism is a defence, an evasion ... a denial of the reality of separation and the pain of losing the centrality that accompanies it. 15
Graham Little

Narcissism

Narcissism ensures that woman identifies with that image of herself that man holds up.... 16
Catherine MacKinnon

A woman's sense of self is wounded too often for her not to need narcissistic compensation.... 17 *Margarete Mitscherlich*

Achieving an irreversible cohesive self is concomitant with achieving freedom from the imperative intrusions of narcissistic tensions.... 18
Ernest S. Wolf

We know that love puts a check upon narcissism.... 19 *Sigmund Freud*

[N]arcissism is neither sick nor healthy. It is the human condition. What is sick or healthy, regressive or progressive, is how individuals come to terms with their narcissism, understood as a longing for perfection, wholeness, and control over self and world. 20
C. Fred Alford

Narcissistic thinking is by definition unable to decide and understand narcissistic thinking.... [The narcissist] has no "mirror of mirrors." ... In fact, he is not even aware that he is playing the game at all. 21 *M. Gear et al.*

[N]arcissism conflicts with reason and with love. 22 *Erich Fromm*

[I]n narcissistic personalities ... the reasoning capacity, while totally under the domination and in the service of the overriding emotion, is often not only intact but even sharpened.... Narcissistic rage enslaves the ego and allows it to function only as its tool and rationalizer. 23
Heinz Kohut

Narcissistic rage ... is characterized by the persistence of the goal of physical destruction of the object.... Such outrage and humiliation express the overt regression from an adult to an infantile level of relating. 24
Meyer Gunther

The heightened sadism, the adoption of a policy of preventive attack, the need for revenge ... [are all] characteristic of narcissistic rage. 25
Heinz Kohut

One can recognize the narcissistic person by his insensitivity to any kind of criticism. 26
Erich Fromm

Only pure narcissistic megalomania can banish guilt. 27 *Ernest Becker*

The narcissistic personality, like the psychotic, lives by its own rules. 28 *Camille Paglia*

Psychosis is a state of absolute narcissism, one in which the person has broken all connection with reality outside, and has made his own person the substitute for reality. 29 *Erich Fromm*

Narcissism sets up the illusion that once one has a feeling, it must be manifest—because, after all, "inside" is an absolute reality.... Thus there is reinforced the belief that one's own impulses are the only reality upon which one can rely. To find out what one feels becomes a search for oneself. 30 *Richard Sennett*

[The] narcissistic mode of relating and of desire gratification based on the pleasure principle precludes those very intersubjective relationships that should form the core of any social and political vision. 31 *Nancy Chodorow*

[T]he state of adult culture ... leads adults to invest a great deal of passion in uncovering their own motives for action and the motives of others with whom they come into contact. These discoveries of inner reasons and authentic impulses are seen to be freer, the less people are impeded by abstract rules, or forced to express themselves in terms of "clichés," "stereotyped feelings," or other conventional signs.... The psychic principle governing this adult culture is narcissism. 32 *Richard Sennett*

Narcissism has become one of the central themes of American culture.... 33
Christopher Lasch

We have fallen in love with our own image, with images of our making, which turn out to be images of ourselves.... As individuals and as a nation, we now suffer from social narcissism. 34
Daniel J. Boorstin

Narcissism describes both a psychological and

Narcissism

a cultural condition.... When wealth occupies a higher position than wisdom, when notoriety is admired more than dignity, when success is more important than self-respect, the culture itself overvalues "image" and must be regarded as narcissistic. 35 *Alexander Lowen*

It's the structured narcissism of the old culture that brings down on our heads the evils we detest, and we will only escape those evils when we have abandoned the narcissistic dreams that sustain them. 36 *Philip Slater*

Today, practically everyone is self-conscious and imprisoned in self-consciousness.... Vast numbers of people don't want to come out of the prison of their self-consciousness; they have so little left to come out with. But some people, surely, want to escape this doom of self-enclosure which is the doom of our civilization.... We have to be sufficiently conscious, and self-conscious, to know our own limits and to be aware of the greater urge within us and beyond us. Then we cease to be primarily interested in ourselves. 37 *D. H. Lawrence*

Nature

Man is above, outside and against nature. Man is part and product of nature. These two visions of man ... represent the two contrasting philosophies of our time. 1 *Mario Palmieri*

God created man in his own image.... And God blessed them, and God said unto them: Be fruitful, and multiply, and replenish the earth, and subdue it; and have dominion over the fish of the sea, and over the fowl of the air, and over every living thing that moveth upon the earth. 2 *Holy Bible*

Everything great in western culture has come from the quarrel with nature. 3 *Camille Paglia*

The only way that man can advance is to conquer nature—"to transform the face of the earth to satisfy his wants." ... Power over nature is the touchstone of human progress; on it civilizations are built. 4 *John Hospers*

Man became what he is, not with the aid of, but in spite of nature. Humanization meant breaking away from nature.... By the same token, dehumanization means the reclamation of man by nature.... Man's chief goal in life is still to become and stay human, and defend his achievements against the encroachment of nature. 5 *Eric Hoffer*

For the purpose of attaining freedom in the world of nature, man must use natural science to understand, conquer and change nature and thus attain freedom from nature. 6 *Mao Tse-tung*

It is we who create values and our desires which confer value. In this realm we are kings, and we debase our kingship if we bow down to Nature. It is for us to determine the good life, not for Nature—not even for Nature personified as God. 7 *Bertrand Russell*

Religious ideas have sprung from the same need as all the other achievements of culture: from the necessity for defending itself against the crushing supremacy of nature. 8 *Sigmund Freud*

Nature is a possession which is saturated through and through with the most personal connotations. *Nature is a function of the particular Culture.* 9 *Oswald Spengler*

[T]he absolute love of *nature* hardly exists among us. What we love is the stimulation of our own personal emotions and dreams.... 10 *George Santayana*

[T]he humanitarian's projection onto nature of illegal murder and the rights of civilized people to safety not only misses the point but is exactly contrary to fundamental ecological reality: the structure of nature is a sequence of killings. 11 *Paul Shepard*

There is no return to a harmonious state of nature. If we turn back, then we must go the whole way—we must return to the beasts. 12 *Karl Popper*

Let us not flatter ourselves overmuch on account of our human conquest of nature. For each conquest nature takes its revenge on us. Each of them … has quite different unforeseen effects which only too often cancel out the first.… [I]t is still more difficult in regard to the more remote social consequences of these actions. 13 *Friedrich Engels*

When man attempts to rebel against the iron logic of Nature, he comes into struggle with the principles to which he himself owes his existence as a man. And this attack must lead to his own doom. 14 *Adolf Hitler*

Modern society makes war on nature. 15
Charles A. Reich

As man proceeds toward his announced goal of the conquest of nature, he has written a depressing record of destruction, directed not only against the earth he inhabits but against the life that shares it with him. 16 *Rachel Carson*

[The] separation of man from nature as a consequence of our too-exclusive interest in power is in part responsible for the total wars of our century. 17 *J. Glenn Gray*

Seen as a planetary event, the rising tide of human mastery over nature has brought about a categorical increase in the power of death on earth.… The question now before the human species, therefore, is whether life or death will prevail on earth. 18 *Jonathan Schell*

It looks as if Man will not be able to save himself from the nemesis of his daemonic material power and greed unless he allows himself to undergo a change of heart.… Will mankind murder Mother Earth or will he redeem her?… This is the enigmatic question which now confronts Man. 19 *Arnold Toynbee*

However far Man may succeed in carrying his conquest of non-human Nature, he will remain at Nature's mercy in so far as he continues to fail to master his own human nature.… 20
Arnold Toynbee

The ancients … believed primarily in nature, in which they participated wholeheartedly. To rebel against nature amounted to rebelling against oneself. 21 *Albert Camus*

[T]he Western absorption in conquering and gaining power over nature has resulted not only in the estrangement of man from nature, but also indirectly in the estrangement of man from himself. 22 *Rollo May*

Men … seem to have observed that this newly-won power over space and time, this subjugation of the forces of nature, which is the fulfillment of a longing that goes back thousands of years, has not increased the amount of pleasurable satisfaction which they may expect from life and has not made them feel happier. 23
Sigmund Freud

The debasement of nature is parallel to the glorification of all that eludes it, God and man. 24
Ilya Prigogine

Between God and ourselves stands nature. 25
Pope Pius XII

Our dialogue with nature will be successful only if it is carried on from within nature. 26
Ilya Prigogine

Nature speaks with a thousand voices, and we have only begun to listen. 27 *Ilya Prigogine*

Nature is a dull affair, soundless, scentless, colourless; merely the hurrying of material, endlessly, meaninglessly. 28 *Alfred N. Whitehead*

Nature, so far as it is the object of scientific research, is a collection of facts governed by *laws*: our knowledge of nature is our knowledge of laws. 29 *William Whewell*

Nature … is a chaos just mitigated enough to keep breaking out, on the surface, into some image of achievement. 30 *George Santayana*

We can think of machines as we know them today as very crude simulators of the machinery of life. 31 *Kenneth Boulding*

The hearsay knowledge that everything in Nature is subject to mechanical laws often tempts people to say that Nature is either one big machine, or else a conglomeration of machines. But in fact there are very few machines in Nature. 32
Gilbert Ryle

Nature

[T]he science of mechanics has much more to do with our way of approaching and measuring facts than it has to do with nature. 33
John Dewey

Nature *has* a mechanism sufficiently constant to permit calculation, inference and foresight. But only a philosophy which hypostatizes isolated results and results obtained for a purpose, only a substantiation of the function of a tool, concludes that nature *is* a mechanism and only a mechanism. 34 *John Dewey*

[T]he scientist *as* scientist does not see nature at all.... More importantly, man as ego does not see nature at all. 35 *Alan Watts*

There is no future in loving nature.... We have deprived nature of its independence, and that is fatal to its meaning. Nature's independence *is* its meaning; without it there is nothing but us. 36 *Bill McKibben*

[T]echnology does allow us to design nature out of much of our lives.... Nature is then outside for "us" who are in an internal cocoon.... [Hence the] environment in which we live is much more structured for the well-being of technology [than people]. 37 *Ursula Franklin*

Nature, as man has always known it, he knows no more. Since he has learned ... to suppress his emotional reactions in favor of practical ones and *make use of nature* instead of holding so much of it sacred, he has altered the face, if not the heart, of reality. 38 *Susanne Langer*

Nature never became a toy to a wise spirit.... Neither does the wisest man extort her secret, and lose his curiosity by finding out all her perfection. 39 *Ralph Waldo Emerson*

Science cannot solve the ultimate mystery of nature. And that is because, in the last analysis, we ourselves are a part of nature and therefore part of the mystery we are trying to solve. 40
Max Planck

That man's physical and spiritual life is linked to nature means simply that nature is linked to itself, for man is part of nature. 41
Karl Marx

The first move toward a richer and more human philosophy of life should be to rediscover man's partnership with nature. 42 *René Dubos*

[W]e are not yet a truly collective species, corralled and tamed as an integral part of the biosphere.... It may be that the destiny of mankind is to become tamed, so that the fierce, destructive, and greedy forces of tribalism ... are fused into a compulsive urge to belong to the commonwealth of all creatures which constitute Gaia. It might seem to be surrender, but I suspect that the rewards, in the form of an increased sense of well-being and fulfilment, in knowing ourselves to be a dynamic part of a far greater entity, would be worth the loss.... 43
J. E. Lovelock

The notion of nature as an organic extensive community omits the equally essential point that nature is never complete. It is always passing beyond itself. 44 *Alfred N. Whitehead*

Nature is the seething excess of being. 45
Camille Paglia

[N]ature emerges from what lies beyond all attempts to be pinned down; from what is beyond anything that can be expressed in terms of order, form, language, or law; from what ... can never be reduced to something that is more elementary. The laws of nature are, in essence, the expression of unifying patterns within an ever-changing landscape and in themselves are never absolute. 46 *F. David Peat*

Nature consists of facts and of regularities, and is in itself neither moral nor immoral. It is we who impose our standards upon nature.... We are products of nature, but nature has made us together with our power of altering the world, of foreseeing and of planning for the future, and of making far-reaching decisions for which we are morally responsible. 47 *Karl Popper*

We must make a strenuous effort to preserve what we can of primeval Nature, lest we lose the opportunity to re-establish contact now and then with our biological origins. A sense of continuity with the past and with the rest of creation is a form of religious experience essential to sanity. 48 *René Dubos*

Nature is really an infinite Society.... And the work of man is to supernaturalize Nature—that is to say, to make it divine by making it human, to help it become conscious of itself, in short. 49 *Miguel de Unamuno*

As soon as the human turns away from the divine, nature becomes, like the devils, an instrument of the wrath of God.... [Thus] nature will always be the enemy to the man who has lost God. 50 *Alan Watts*

If ignorance of nature gave birth to the Gods, knowledge of nature is destined to destroy them. 51 *Paul Henri*

When one has become an individual, one stands alone and faces the world in all its perilous and overpowering aspects.... However, submission is not the only way of avoiding aloneness and anxiety. The other way, the only one which is productive and does not end in an insoluble conflict, is that of *spontaneous relationship to man and nature*, a relationship that connects the individual with the world without eliminating his individuality. This kind of relationship ... [is] rooted in the integration and strength of the total personality and ... therefore subject to the very limits that exist for the growth of the self. 52 *Erich Fromm*

It takes a strong self ... to relate fully to nature without being swallowed up.... This is the profound threat of "nothingness," or "non-being," which one experiences when he fully confronts his relation with inorganic being. 53 *Rollo May*

Nature can be tamed without being destroyed. Unfortunately, taming has come to imply subjugating animals and Nature to such an extent as to render them spiritless. Men tamed in this manner lose their real essence in the process of taming. 54 *René Dubos*

As scientific understanding has grown, so our world has become dehumanized. Man feels himself isolated in the cosmos, because he is no longer involved in nature and has lost his emotional "unconscious identity" with natural phenomena.... His contact with nature has gone, and with it has gone the profound emotional energy that this symbolic connection supplied. 55 *Carl Jung*

One day through telemetering devices ... we will know the way of an eagle in the sky, of a whale in the sea, or a tiger in the jungle. And so we will regain our kinship with the animal world, the loss of which is one of modern man's most grievous deprivations. 56 *Arthur C. Clarke*

It may be that a sense of continuing biological life is necessary to the viability of imagery transcending biological death.... Man's imagery of nature as the ultimate life source takes on special significance in the nuclear age as an antagonist to extinction. 57 *Robert Jay Lifton*

We do not live in the wilderness but we need it for our biological and psychological welfare.... Experiencing wildness in nature contributes to our self-discovery and ... the expression of aspects of our fundamental being that are still in resonance with cosmic forces.... [It] helps us to be aware of the cosmos from which we emerged, and to maintain some measure of harmonious relation to the rest of creation. 58 *René Dubos*

Obedience

Obedience is a vital need of the human soul. 1 *Simone Weil*

The genetic qualities that favored scientific activity or associative learning, "general intelligence" or the ability to inhibit present gratification ... [became] the propensity to obey rules.... Selection, then, clearly favored those creatures with a propensity to obey rules [and] to feel guilty about breaking them.... 2 *Lionel Tiger & Robin Fox*

The most obedient, the tamest tribes are, at the first stage in the real struggle for life, the strongest and the conquerors.... How you get the obedience of men is the hard problem; what you do with that obedience is less critical. 3 *Walter Bagehot*

In all hierarchically structured societies obedience is perhaps the most deeply ingrained

Obedience

trait. Obedience is equated with virtue, disobedience with sin.... The soldier who kills and maims, the bomber pilot who destroys thousands of lives in one moment, are not necessarily driven by a destructive or cruel impulse, but by the principle of unquestioning obedience. 4 *Erich Fromm*

Hitler's most drastic "contribution" to the development of social institutions was undoubtedly the creation of the SS-police and Gestapo system as the most formidable agency of human destruction in modern history.... Absolute, unthinking, unconditional obedience under all circumstances was the very basis of life in their microcosm. 5 *G. M. Gilbert*

The fact that the defendant acted pursuant to an order of his Government or of a superior shall not free him from responsibility, but may be considered in mitigation of punishment. 6
Charter of the Nuremberg Tribunal

It is not provided in any military law that a soldier in the case of a despicable crime is exempt from punishment because he blames his superior, especially if the orders of the latter are in evident contradiction to all human morality.... 7 *Joseph Goebbels*

[T]he prosecution could thank its own obedient soldiers for being in a position to prosecute. 8
General Alfred Jodl

The horrors which we have seen ... are not signs that rebels, insubordinate, untamable men, are increasing in constant numbers but rather that there is a stupendously rapid increase in the number of obedient, docile men. 9
Georges Bernanos

There are a number of signs showing that the men of our age have now for a long time been starved of obedience. But advantage has been taken of the fact to give them slavery. 10
Simone Weil

The true believer ... is basically an obedient and submissive person. People whose lives are barren and insecure seem to show a greater willingness to obey than people who are self-sufficient and self-confident. 11 *Eric Hoffer*

We obey our authority figures all our lives ... because of the anxiety of separation ... [from] their powers and approval.... This is part of the psychology of ancient ancestor worshippers.... Every time we try to do something other than what they wanted, we awaken the anxiety connected with them and their possible loss. 12
Ernest Becker

[D]isobedience amounts to a declaration of war against you. Your son is trying to usurp your authority, and you are justified in answering force with force in order to insure his respect, without which you will be unable to train him. The blows you administer should not be merely playful ones but should convince him that you are his master.... Obedience is so important that all education is actually nothing other than learning how to obey. 13 *J. G. Kruger*

Obedience should be social courtesy. Adults should have no right to the obedience of children. It must come from within—not be imposed from without. 14 *A. S. Neill*

The exercise of power by one human being over another is a necessary condition for government. Voluntariness is a necessary condition for the effective and efficient use of power. A belief in the legitimacy of a government is a sufficient condition for voluntary obedience. 15
J. C. Smith

The characteristic of social life is the unthinking obedience of the many to the will of the few. 16 *Harold Laski*

[T]he first rule of society is obedience—obedience to God and the dispensations of Providence.... 17 *Russell Kirk*

Obedience, submission to God, is the secret of justice in society and tranquility in life, quite as much as it is indispensable to eternal salvation. 18 *Russell Kirk*

Guilt sanctions the order of things.... [I]f culture is to recreate itself so as to restore our links to the sacred order, through sublimated guilt ... above all [it involves] the task of learning again to obey, so that those broken on the rack of guilt may be revived. 19 *John Carroll*

The function of commanding and obeying is the decisive one in every society. As long as there is any doubt as to who commands and who obeys, all the rest will be imperfect and ineffective. Even the very consciences of men ... will be disturbed and falsified. 20
José Ortega y Gasset

[T]he first lesson of civilization [is] that of obedience. 21 *John Stuart Mill*

[C]ivilization means, above all, an unwillingness to inflict unnecessary pain. Within the ambit of that definition, those of us who heedlessly accept the commands of authority cannot yet claim to be civilized men. 22 *Harold Laski*

If civil authorities legislate for or allow anything that is contrary to the will of God, neither the laws made or the authorizations granted can be binding on the consciences of the citizens, since God has more right to be obeyed than man. 23 *Pope John XXIII*

People committing acts in obedience to law or habit are not being moral. 24 *W. H. Auden*

In a country where the sole employer is the State ... the old principle, who does not work shall not eat, has been replaced by a new one: who does not obey shall not eat. 25 *Leon Trotsky*

[N]o reform which leaves the masses of the people wallowing in the slothful irresponsibility of passive obedience to authority can be counted as a genuine change for the better. 26
Aldous Huxley

Every actual State is corrupt. Good men must not obey the laws too well. 27
Ralph Waldo Emerson

In a democracy dissent is an act of faith. 28
J. William Fulbright

[T]he passage through the gauntlet ahead may be possible only under governments capable of rallying obedience far more effectively than would be possible in a democratic setting. If the issue for mankind is survival, such governments may be unavoidable, even necessary. 29
Robert Heilbroner

[O]bedience to authority, long praised as a virtue, takes on a new aspect when it serves a malevolent cause.... This is a fatal flaw nature has designed into us, and which in the long run gives our species only a modest chance of survival. 30 *Stanley Milgram*

Human history begins with man's act of disobedience which is at the same time the beginning of his freedom and development of his reason. 31 *Erich Fromm*

At this point in history the capacity to doubt, to criticize and to disobey may be all that stands between a future for mankind and the end of civilization. 32 *Erich Fromm*

Objectivity

Objective consciousness *is* alienated life promoted to its most honorific status as the scientific method. 1 *Theodore Roszak*

Objectivism requires a specifiably functioning mindless knower. 2 *Michael Polanyi*

[I]f we probe the technocracy in search of the peculiar power it holds over us, we arrive at the myth of objective consciousness. There is [the] one way of gaining access to reality—so the myth holds.... What flows from this state of consciousness qualifies as knowledge, and nothing else does. 3 *Theodore Roszak*

As long as the spell of the objective consciousness grips our society, the regime of experts can never be far off; the community is bound to remain beholden to the high priests of the citadel who control access to reality. 4
Theodore Roszak

Power to create the world from one's point of view is power in its male form. The male epistemological stance, which corresponds to the world it creates, is objectivity: the ostensibly non-involved stance.... It does not comprehend its own perspectivity.... The objectively knowable is object. Woman through male eyes is sex object.... 5
Catherine MacKinnon

Objectivity

From an I-Thou relationship based on the fact that "thou" is always unique, unclassifiable, and unpredictable, and has to be experienced intuitively in a reciprocal relationship, the human mind progressed slowly to a "subject-object" form of understanding based on the fact that, stripped of the "thou" personalism, the objectified "it" can be scientifically related to other objects, become part of a series, and be amenable to universal, impersonal laws—again, an essentially masculine approach. Man questions the external world, no longer in terms of "who" but of "what." 6 *Amaury de Riencourt*

Objectification, carried by the male not only as if it were his personal nature but as if it were nature itself, denotes who or what the male loves to hate; who or what he wants to possess, act on, conquer, define himself in opposition to; where he wants to spill his seed. 7 *Andrea Dworkin*

[T]he American style of revelation is one in which great emphasis is placed on the facts.... By concentrating attention on the external facts, the decision maker takes the position that he is being "objective." This helps to justify his neglect of the internal and subjective aspects of the decision process.... If the decision process is mechanical and the self is not involved, it is possible to remain innocent of the consequences. 8 *William Blanchard*

"Objectivity" in the philosopher: moral indifference toward oneself, blindness toward good or evil consequences: lack of scruples about using dangerous means; perversity and multiplicity of character considered and exploited as an advantage. 9 *Friedrich Nietzsche*

Objectivism has totally falsified our conception of truth, by exalting what we can know and prove, while covering up with ambiguous utterances all that we know and *cannot* prove, even though the latter knowledge underlies ... all that we *can* prove. In trying to restrict our minds to the few things that are demonstrable ... it has overlooked the a-critical choices which determine the whole being of our minds.... 10 *Michael Polanyi*

Psychological existence is subjective in so far as an idea occurs in only one individual. But it is objective in so far as it is established by a society—by a *consensus gentium*. 11 *Carl Jung*

[I]t takes a long evolutionary process to arrive at *objectivity*, that is, to acquire the faculty to see the world, nature, other persons, and oneself as they are and not distorted by desires and fears. The more man develops this objectivity, the more he is in touch with reality, the more he matures, the better can he create a human world in which he is at home. 12 *Erich Fromm*

All epochs that are regressive and in process of dissolution are subjective; all progressive epochs, on the other hand, bear the objective stamp. 13 *Goethe*

I am willing to believe that history is for the most part inaccurate and biased, but what is peculiar to our own age is the abandonment of the idea that history *could* be truthfully written.... This kind of thing is frightening to me, because it often gives me the feeling that the very concept of objective truth is fading out of the world. 14 *George Orwell*

We are Marxists, and Marxism teaches that in our approach to a problem we should start from objective facts.... If a man wants to succeed in his work, that is, to achieve the anticipated results, he must bring his ideas into correspondence with the laws of the objective external world.... 15 *Mao Tse-tung*

Each man tries to turn his own self-confidence into an objective truth. And so each aims at the destruction and death of the other. 16 *G. W. F. Hegel*

[T]he state of objective self-awareness will lead to a negative self-evaluation and negative affect whenever the person is aware of a self contradiction ... and at such point he will prefer to revert to the subjective state. 17 *S. Duval & R. A. Wicklund*

Objectivity is the central problem of ethics.... Ethical thought is the process of bringing objectivity to bear on the will. 18 *Thomas Nagel*

The concern of objectivity is Truth and "the facts"; the concern of subjectivity is living and self-esteem.... Subjectivity without objectivity is blind; objectivity without subjectivity is meaningless. 19 *Robert C. Solomon*

We have learned to identify ourselves with the narrow and superficial area of the consciousness and the voluntary.... This is perhaps what Western Man would himself like to be—a person in total control of himself, analyzed to the ultimate depths of his own unconscious, understood and explained to the last atom of his brain, and to this extent completely mechanized. When every last element of inwardness has become an object of knowledge, the person is ... reduced to a rattling shell. 20

Alan Watts

[In attempting] to accumulate objective knowledge about it ... American psychology seems to have lost its soul. 21 *Michael R. Jackson*

When we challenge the finality of objective consciousness as a basis for culture, what is at issue is the size of man's life. 22

Theodore Roszak

Objective knowledge provides us with powerful instruments for the achievements of certain ends, but the ultimate goal itself and the longing to reach it must come from another source. 23 *Albert Einstein*

A belief in objective reality ... is not an empirical conclusion; it is a philosophical position and a psychological stance. 24

Beryl Benderly

Objectivity of whatever kind is not the test of reality. It is just one way of understanding reality. 25 *Thomas Nagel*

The new physics, quantum mechanics, tells us clearly that it is not possible to observe reality without changing it.... According to quantum mechanics there is no such thing as objectivity. 26 *Gary Zukav*

The electron does not *have* objective properties independent of mind. 27 *Fritjof Capra*

There can never be an absolute and independent objective existence; indeed such an existence is unintelligible. For the objective, as such, always and essentially has its existence in the consciousness of a subject, is thus the idea of this subject, and consequently is conditioned by it.... 28 *Arthur Schopenhauer*

Objectivity needs subjective material to work on.... How far outside ourselves we can go without losing contact with this essential material—with the forms of life in which values and justifications are rooted—is not certain. 29

Thomas Nagel

Objectivity does not mean detachment, it means respect; that is, the ability not to distort and to falsify things, persons, and oneself. 30

Erich Fromm

Objectivity does not demand that we estimate man's significance in the universe by the minute size of his body ... [or] that we see ourselves as a mere grain of sand in a million Saharas. It inspires us, on the contrary, with the hope of overcoming the appalling disabilities of our bodily existence, even to the point of conceiving a rational idea of the universe which can authoritatively speak for itself. 31

Michael Polanyi

If we are to move toward a more holistic and healthy world, then we must discover a way of unifying the statements of objective science with our personal vision of the world, and we must do this without diluting the authenticity of either approach. 32 *F. David Peat*

Other

THE CATEGORY of the *Other* is as primordial as consciousness itself . 1 *Simone de Beauvoir*

All consciousness is, basically, the desire to be recognized and proclaimed as such by other consciousnesses. It is others who beget us. Only in association do we receive a human value, as distinct from an animal value. 2

Albert Camus

My original fall is the existence of the Other. Shame—like pride—is the apprehension of myself as a nature.... The Other as a look is ...

Other

my transcendence transcended. 3
Jean-Paul Sartre

[Y]ou have not empirically found your whole final object, the entire and individual fact of Being that you seek, so long as you seek still for an Other.... And in the presence of death you do thus seek for the Other, namely, for the meaning of this fact, for the solution of this mystery, for the beloved object that is gone, for the lost life, for something not here, for the unseen—yes, for the Eternal. 4 *Josiah Royce*

I need the Other in order to realize fully all the structures of my being.... [T]he Other is the indispensable mediator between myself and me. 5 *Jean-Paul Sartre*

The sympathy we extend to one another establishes our humanity. If we refuse to recognize the existence of others, we deny our own existence. 6 *Joseph A. Amato*

Only in a unity with the "other" is the self-realization of the individual guaranteed.... This is ultimately the value which guarantees human existence, i.e., its essential nature. 7
Kurt Goldstein

[Plato says that] the tyrant is mad because otherness has ceased to exist for him.... Human beings are in their essence needing beings, and when otherness has become completely absent for us, we are hardly human beings at all.... To exist is a gift. 8 *George Grant*

[D]uring the early childhood of most (if not all) of us, the person who was closest to us (usually our mother) failed to move in harmony with our needs ... and from that point on, relations between ourselves and the world, Self and Other, were disturbed. This surfaced in our psyche as the feeling that something was missing. A crevice, an abyss of sorts ... had irrevocably opened up in our soul, and we would spend the rest of our lives, usually in an unconscious and driven way, attempting to fill it up. 9 *Morris Berman*

Differentiation is not distinctness and separateness, but a particular way of being connected to others. This connection to others, based on early incorporations, in turn enables that empathy and confidence that is basic to the recognition of the other as a self. 10
Nancy Chodorow

The social and political arrangements that surround the adult ... are the history of our attempts to resolve the self/other dilemma—to be individual (a self) and at the same time to establish connection with other people.... There are only three possible responses ... [:] self versus other, self-in-other, self-and-other. 11
Graham Little

Dualistic ontologies based on the opposition of self and other generate two related views of the person and of ethics: the patriarchal view and that of individualism.... The self-other opposition is at the heart of ... "Western thought." 12 *Caroline Whitbeck*

[I]n well-established states it becomes possible to abolish capital punishment and send criminals to psychiatric hospitals instead of prisons. Yet even in the most beneficent state, force remains the ultimate authority ... because, politically conceived, people are *others* ... alien wills and isolated consciousnesses upon which order has to be imposed. 13 *Alan Watts*

Women inspire fear in men only insofar as they are seen as alien, as the Other; and they cease to be fearful only insofar as they are recognized as fellow human creatures, no more and no less. 14
Mary Anne Warren

Prosocial goals are one indication of a person's connectedness to other people.... [V]ariation in the connection between self and others may determine whether helping another is regarded as a self-sacrifice, so that it diminishes the self, or whether sufficient identification with the other person results for the goals of others to be perceived as interrelated, even identical, with one's own. 15 *Ervin Staub*

[M]odern thought is advancing towards that region where man's Other must become the Same as himself. 16 *Michel Foucault*

The organized community or social group which gives to the individual his unity of self

may be called "the generalized other." 17
George H. Mead

The common bond between Us may be the other. The Other may not be even as localized as a definable Them that one can point to.... [T]he Other is everywhere and nowhere.... The Other is everyone's experience. 18 *R. D. Laing*

[F]or the other-directed man ... [the] presence of the guiding and approving "others" is a vital element in his whole system of conformity and self-justification. Depriving him of the sociability his character has come to crave will not make him autonomous, but only anomic.... 19
David Riesman

[T]he fundamental intrapsychic "double bind" of the schizophrenic ... is his "deathly paradox": to remain totally unrelated to others is to pursue psychosis and psychic death; to attempt relationship is to court "the risk of annihilation." 20 *Robert Jay Lifton*

[T]he age-old problem of good and evil, originally designating eligibility for immortality, [is also found] in its emotional significance of being liked or disliked by the other person. On this plane ... personality is shaped and formed according to the vital need to please the other person.... 21 *Otto Rank*

We can bear everything except not to be borne by others. 22 *Kenneth Boulding*

Self-realization ... is firmly based on the fact that men need each other in order to be themselves, and that those people who succeed in achieving the greatest degree of independence and maturity are also those who have the most satisfactory relationships with others. 23 *Anthony Storr*

[T]hrough receiving love from external love-objects, the ego is formed and built up. The sense of self and of self-worth is received *from others....* 24 *Elizabeth Moberly*

The unresponsive or impervious other induces a sense of emptiness and impotence in self. Destruction in phantasy of the other sets off a vicious circle. Self receives and gives. Other is needed to give and to receive. The more self receives, the more self needs to give. The more other cannot *receive*, the more self needs to destroy. The more self destroys other, the more empty self becomes. The more empty the more envious, the more envious the more destructive. 25 *R. D. Laing*

In the sound and fury of the passing centuries, each separate consciousness, to ensure its own existence, must ... desire the death of others. 26 *Albert Camus*

[W]e cannot become humane until we understand our need to visit suffering and death on others.... The sociology of our times must begin in [such] anguished awareness.... 27
Hugh D. Duncan

[When we] destroy any vestige of wild, disorganized Other entirely, so that self now reigns supreme in a pure, dead, and totally predictable world ... [h]atred and destruction of life is the inevitable outcome. 28 *Morris Berman*

[N]o person taught by experience ever escapes the reflection that no matter how much he does for himself, what endures is only what is done for others.... 29 *John Dewey*

Only a life lived for others is a life worthwhile. 30 *Albert Einstein*

The faith in others has its culmination in faith in *mankind.* 31 *Erich Fromm*

It seems to be a universal desire to wish to occupy a place in the world of at least one other person. Perhaps the greatest solace in religion is the sense that one lives in the Presence of an Other. 32 *R. D. Laing*

[T]he gaze of the other is so deeply constitutive of the self that it is a mistake to try to strip it away. Authenticity consists in merging in the gazing of the all-compassionate and all-perceiving One: being lifted out of the delusory center of ego and being placed in full consciousness where one in fact already is, in the great circle of the community of all sentient beings. 33 *Bruce Wilshire*

I am only in conjunction with the Other, alone I am nothing. 34 *Karl Jaspers*

Other

You in others—this is what you are, this is what your consciousness has breathed, and lived on, and enjoyed throughout your life, your soul, your immortality—YOUR LIFE IN OTHERS. 35
Boris Pasternak

Parents

If survival depended solely on the triumph of the strong, then the species would perish. So the real reason for survival, the principal factor in the "struggle for existence," is the *love of adults* for their young. 1 *Maria Montessori*

Where the parent-child affectional system develops satisfactorily, children develop the affectional behavior of humans; they become "humanized." ... 2 *Irving Bieber*

Just as the father acts as a protection against the dangers of the external world and thus serves his son as a model persona, so the mother protects him against the dangers that threaten from the darkness of his psyche. 3
Carl Jung

Mother's love is unconditional.... Fatherly love is conditional love.... Mother has the function of making [the child] secure in life, father has the function of teaching him ... a sense of competence.... 4 *Erich Fromm*

It is the fusion of these sentiments, the altruistic and the egoistic, in the parental sentiment that gives it its incomparable hold upon our natures, and makes it a sentiment from which proceed our most intense joys and sorrows. 5
William McDougall

Parents must not only have certain ways of guiding by prohibition and permission, they must ... [project a] conviction that there is a meaning in what they are doing. In this sense a traditional system of child care can be said to be a factor making for trust.... 6
Erik Erikson

Basically, parents shape their children's behavior in three ways: by punishing them, by rewarding them, and by the example they set. 7
Derek Wright

[A] parent's most potent weapon is rejection, or the threat of it. 8 *Alexander Lowen*

The most effectively trained youngsters are those whose parents: (1) have consistently prescribed firm standards for the child's behavior; (2) have employed ... the use of reason rather than physical punishment and the deprivation of privileges; and (3) have been affectionate and nurturant to the child throughout childhood. 9
Leonard Berkowitz

[T]he disposition of parents to allow or encourage dialogue on value issues is one of the clearest determinants of moral stage advance in children. 10 *Lawrence Kohlberg*

Bringing up children in America is not the product of impulse followed by neglect. If anything, the approach is too rational.... [I]n no other culture has there been so pervasive a cultural anxiety about the rearing of children. 11
Max Lerner

Increasingly in doubt as to how to bring up their children, parents ... cannot help show their children, by their own anxiety, how little they depend on themselves and how much on others.... [T]hey are passing on to him their own contagious, diffuse anxiety. 12 *David Riesman*

Much of the anxiety directed toward the child had always sprung from the insecurity of the parents about themselves and their society. 13
Max Lerner

All the frustrated hopes of men and women who have come to adulthood without fulfilling their dreams and drives are poured into the child's upbringing, which becomes a means of vicarious living or reliving for the parents. They seek to fashion the child into their own cherished image, using him eagerly to fill the emotional void in their own lives.... If the parent tries to be the culture surrogate for the child, the child is often the emotion surrogate for the parent. 14 *Max Lerner*

Parental love which is so moving at bottom, so childish, is nothing but the parents' narcissism born again. 15 *Sigmund Freud*

Parents

Long before our birth, even before we are conceived, our parents have decided who we will be. 16 *Jean-Paul Sartre*

The more insight one gains into the unintentional and unconscious manipulation of children by their parents, the fewer illusions one has about the possibility of changing the world.... 17 *Alice Miller*

The orientation toward power and the contempt for the allegedly inferior and weak ... must likewise be considered as having been taken over from the parents' attitude toward the child. The fact that his helplessness as a child was exploited by the parents and that he was forced into submission must have reinforced any existing antiweakness attitude. 18
T. W. Adorno et al.

[M]orality ... is most profoundly rooted in the affectionate attachment between parents and child.... [F]ailure or frustration of their affectionate natures leads ... especially the men ... into the most bloodthirsty, sadistic aggression. 19
Helen B. Lewis

The evidence is for an association between the child's perception of himself and his perception of the parent's attitudes toward him.... [C]hildren who are not loved by their parents do not develop a capacity to love either themselves or others. 20 *Ruth Wylie*

Perhaps the most important precondition for a prosocial orientation ... is an affectionate relationship between parents and children. 21
Ervin Staub

One who has been brought up unwisely is not likely to bring up others wisely. 22
August Bebel

There is never a problem child, there are only problem parents. 23 *A. S. Neill*

When other members of the society assist the parent in the care of offspring, the potential for social evolution is enormously enlarged. 24
E. O. Wilson

The universal exploitation of women is rooted in our attitudes toward very early parental figures, and will go on until these figures are male as well as female. 25 *Dorothy Dinnerstein*

[P]arental care of the young eventually generalizes to other members of the species, a psychological development that amounts to an evolution of a sense of responsibility and what we call conscience.... We can divine in this situation the evolutionary roots of unity of the family, unity of the clan, [and] unity of the larger societies.... 26 *Paul MacLean*

The invasion of the family by industry, the mass media, and the agencies of socialized parenthood has ... created an ideal of perfect parenthood while destroying parents' confidence in their ability to perform the most elementary forms of childrearing. 27 *Christopher Lasch*

If advertising has invaded the judgment of children, it has also forced its way into the family, an insolent usurper of parental function, degrading parents to mere intermediaries between their children and the market. This indeed is a social revolution of our time! 28
Jules Henry

What good mothers and fathers instinctively feel like doing for their babies is usually best. 29
Dr. Benjamin Spock

Inhibited from presenting their children with sharply silhouetted images of self and society, parents in our era can only equip the child to do his best, whatever that may turn out to be. 30
David Riesman

Parents can help only a little; the best they can do is to *survive*, to survive intact, and without changing colour, without relinquishment of any important principle. 31 *D. W. Winnicott*

If parents are also able to give their child the same respect and tolerance that they had for their own parents, they will surely be providing him with the best possible foundation for his entire life. 32 *Alice Miller*

There could be no greater illusion than the belief that one can treat one's own parents unfeelingly and with contempt and yet expect that

Parents

one's own children will someday treat one otherwise; for such people break the golden chain of affection that binds the generations and gives continuity and meaning to life. 33

George F. Kennan

Honour thy father and thy mother. 34

Holy Bible

[W]e are in the process of substituting old-age and medical insurance programs for the preindustrial system in which children took care of their aged parents. When this process is completed, the last vestige of significant counterflow in the parent-child account will have disappeared. 35 *Marvin Harris*

It is already technically possible to make a machine that will interact with a child from the beginning of his life.... [But] fooling around with dependence of children on their mother, father and siblings is very dangerous.... [W]e could easily turn out a generation of psychotic children.... 36 *Seymour Papert*

[T]his long and exacting task, the parent's job of seeing their children through, is a job worth doing; and, in fact, we believe that it provides the only real basis for society, and the only factory for the democratic tendency in a country's social system. 37 *D. W. Winnicott*

I have found the happiness of parenthood greater than any other that I have experienced. I believe that when circumstances lead men or women to forego this happiness, a very deep need remains ungratified.... To be happy in this world, especially when youth is past, it is necessary to feel oneself not merely an isolated individual whose day will soon be over, but part of the stream of life.... 38 *Bertrand Russell*

Patriarchy

[M]illions of women in the 1960's and 1970's rebelled against an impossible social role.... Women examined their life experiences together and named the system that was oppressing them: patriarchy. 1

Luise Eichenbaum & Susie Orbach

[S]exual suppression forms the mass-psychological basis for a specific culture in all its forms, namely, the *patriarchal* culture.... 2

Wilhelm Reich

Ever since the Old Testament, the religion of the Western world has been patriarchy. 3

Erich Fromm

The Biblical story of Cain and Abel reflects the changeover from the previous age of peace and nonviolence to the barbarism of the patriarchal age.... [H]enceforth harmony among men and beasts was out, and killing and violence were in. 4 *Elizabeth Gould Davis*

[The] patriarchal image of reality: life is struggle, life is hell. Such a vision fosters the image of man in control, or, supremely heroic, failing or dying in the effort to control.... The ability to kill soon became the distinguishing mark of the heroic man. 5 *Marilyn French*

[P]atriarchy will [always] retain the ultimate power for itself: the power to destroy. 6

Mark Gerzon

In fact, patriarchy *requires* violence or the subliminal threat of violence in order to maintain itself. 7 *Gloria Steinem*

[O]ur society, like all other historical civilizations, is a patriarchy. The fact is evident at once if one recalls that ... every avenue of power within the society, including the coercive force of the police, is entirely in male hands. 8

Kate Millet

No anthropologist contests the fact that patriarchy is universal. There is not, nor has there ever been, any society that even remotely failed to associate authority and leadership in suprafamilial areas with the male. 9

Steven Goldberg

In all patriarchal myths ... the significance and function of the female was systematically downgraded.... But this revolution was also a major breakthrough, the birth of a new man endowed with Promethean drive to master the forces of nature and dominate the earth.... Detached and psychologically free of the powers of nature in whose psychological clutches he left woman, man at last became conscious of consciousness, able to reflect on himself and, simultaneously, to ask radical questions concerning his destiny. 10 *Amaury de Riencourt*

The process which has raised civilized humanity above savagery is fundamentally an intellectual process ... [and found only] in societies organized on patriarchal principles.... Women have very little direct share in them. 11

Robert Briffault

[E]very society tends to assume a patriarchal form when man's evolution brings him to the point of self-awareness and the imposition of the will. 12 *Simone de Beauvoir*

Male dominance ... [is] the product of the child's revolt against the primal mother.... And if the incest taboo involves a preference for masculinity so strong as to see femininity as castration, it would seem likely that a tendency toward patriarchy is intrinsic to the human condition. 13 *Norman O. Brown*

The matriarchate implied communism and equality of all. The rise of the patriarchate implied the rule of private property and the subjugation and enslavement of woman.... As a result of this subjugation, woman came to be regarded as an inferior being and to be despised. 14 *August Bebel*

[M]an's violent capture and rape of the female led first to the establishment of a rudimentary mate-protectorate and then sometime later to the full-blown male solidification of power, the patriarchy.... Concepts of hierarchy, slavery and private property flowed from, and could only be predicated upon, the initial subjugation of women. 15 *Susan Brownmiller*

Patriarchy is itself the prevailing religion of the entire planet, and its essential message is necrophilia.... The rulers of patriarchy—males with power—wage an unceasing war against life itself. Since female energy is essentially biophilic, the female spirit/body is the primary target.... [W]omen are the enemy against whom all patriarchal wars are waged.... 16

Mary Daly

In patriarchal history, one passion is necessarily fundamental and unchanging: the hatred of women. 17 *Andrea Dworkin*

The woman's body is the terrain on which patriarchy is erected. 18 *Adrienne Rich*

Under patriarchy, women's bodies are expropriated and "mined" for their resources.... 19

Mary Anne Warren

Biological technology is in the hands of men.... Ultimately the new technology will be used for the benefit of men and to the detriment of women.... What may be happening is the last battle in the long war of men against women.... Will we be fighting to retain or reclaim the right to bear children—has patriarchy conned us once again? 20 *Robyn Rowland*

[S]pecies preservation can be characterized as a female force in the world; males have historically been the authors and kingpins of destruction, enslavement, and war. Perhaps the final irony in patriarchal attempts to control reproduction would be if male cooptation of woman's power to reproduce worked to inhibit the pervasive patriarchal need to destroy. 21

Roberta Steinbacher

[S]ince patriarchy is universal and derives its legitimacy from mythic structure, we can infer the existence of a need on the part of males to dominate females. Since that need ... has produced institutions and human practices which are antilife, and violent, it is reasonable to view that state of mind as pathological. 22 *J. C. Smith*

[P]atriarchy can never, whatever its form, improve the human condition for the majority of humankind. And often it makes the elite the sickest and most unhappy class—like the Aztec priests or the faceless suits who rule much of today's world. 23 *Marilyn French*

It was Jung's view that masculine, patriarchal values have produced a Western culture ... which neglects the soul.... 24

S. Segaller & M. Berger

We live in a patriarchal society in which patriarchal principles have ceased to be valid....

Patriarchy

Power, energy, ambition, intellect, the interests of the combative male, no more achieve the fulfillment of his being than they can of themselves build up a human society. 25
Robert Briffault

[P]atriarchy ... may be a very large part of the problem, because it may be *the* system underlying all the other systems. 26 *Shere Hite*

[W]hat is the Third Wave bringing?... It's the revolt against patriarchy. 27 *Alvin Toffler*

When the mythological layer collapses, and the political kings fall, then the patriarchy, as a positive force, is over. 28 *Robert Bly*

Women are now becoming increasingly free to adopt masculine values and join with males in repressing those aspects of the human personality which males have historically and culturally defined as feminine and childlike. Should this become the path of women's liberation, patriarchy will have truly won out. 29
J. C. Smith

Philosophy

[P]hilosophy is the intellectual conception a man forms to himself of the universe. 1
Havelock Ellis

Apart from detail, and apart from systems, a philosophic outlook is the very foundation of thought and of life. The sort of ideas we attend to, and the sort of ideas which we push into the negligible background, govern our hopes, our fears, our control of behavior. As we think, we live. This is why the assemblage of philosophic ideas is more than a specialist study. It moulds our type of civilization. 2
Alfred N. Whitehead

Neither a man nor a nation can exist without some form of philosophy. 3 *Ayn Rand*

Philosophy is the factor that moves a nation, shaping every realm and aspect of men's existence, including their values, their psychology, and, in the end, the headlines of their daily newspapers. 4 *Leonard Peikoff*

Philosophy works slowly. Thoughts lie dormant for ages; and then, almost suddenly as it were, mankind finds that they have embodied themselves in institutions. 5 *Alfred N. Whitehead*

The philosophers, one might say stand at the crossroads. While they may not cause the traffic to move, they can stop it and start it, they can direct it one way or the other. 6
Walter Lippmann

The philosophers must become kings.... Until that happens, there can be no rest from troubles ... for the whole human race. 7 *Socrates*

Much depends upon the philosophers. For though they are not kings, they are, we may say, the teachers of the teachers. 8
Walter Lippmann

Those who have handled sciences have been either men of experiment or men of dogmas. The men of experiment are like the ant; they only collect and use; the reasoners resemble spiders, who make cobwebs out of their own substance. But the bee takes a middle course; it gathers its material from the flowers of the garden and the field, but transforms and digests it by a power of its own. Not unlike this is the true business of philosophy; for it neither relies solely or chiefly on the powers of the mind, nor does it take the matter which it gathers from natural history and mechanical experiments and lay it up in the memory whole, as it finds it; but lays it up in the understanding altered and digested. 9 *Francis Bacon*

[I]f a man finds himself in possession of great mental faculties, such as alone should venture on the solution of the hardest of all problems—those which concern nature as a whole and humanity in its widest range, he will do well to extend his view equally in all directions.... What a vast distinction there is between students of physics, chemistry, anatomy, mineralogy, zoology, philology, history, and the men who deal with the great facts of human life, the poet and the philosopher! 10
Arthur Schopenhauer

A given philosophy has ... no other standard of its value than that of truth. For the rest, philosophy is essentially *world-wisdom*: its problem is the world. 11 *Arthur Schopenhauer*

[T]he meaning of life is not a problem created by philosophy but rather that problem which gives rise to philosophy. And that problem is precisely the lack of harmony between the intellect and the passions.... The business of philosophy is not to transcend the human, but to illuminate it.... [It] is not to find or invent transcendent meanings, but to illuminate the meanings *in life*.... [It] is the art of living, the search for *wisdom*. 12 *Robert C. Solomon*

[A] first-rate test of the value of any philosophy which is offered to us: Does it end in conclusions which, when they are referred back to the ordinary life-experiences and their predicaments, render them more significant, more luminous to us, and make our dealings with them more fruitful? 13 *John Dewey*

In modern conceptions, philosophy is the clarification of concepts for the purpose of critically evaluating beliefs and standards.... These include standards of the right or good (ethics), of the true (epistemology), and of the beautiful (esthetics). 14 *Lawrence Kohlberg*

The traditional business of moral philosophy is attempting to understand ... and harmonize so far as possible the claims arising from the different sides of our nature. 15 *Mary Midgley*

Philosophy ... strips the human world of all authority and liberates the spirit intellectually; but it cannot strip the world of its power, or even of its ascendancy over the philosopher's soul. He remains an unhappy creature, divided against himself.... 16 *George Santayana*

Philosophy is born of estrangement. 17 *William E. Kaufmann*

To philosophize is to learn how to die. 18 *Montaigne*

[T]he existentialist philosophers have returned to the wisdom of Montaigne, that to learn philosophy is to learn how to die.... [I]n facing death they are serving the cause of life. 19 *Norman O. Brown*

[W]e commonly become philosophers only after despairing of instinctive happiness.... 20 *George Santayana*

And new philosophy calls all in doubt.... 21 *John Donne*

Philosophy lives upon the comprehension of the meaning of its own doubts. 22 *Josiah Royce*

The courage of truth, faith in the power of Spirit, is the first condition of philosophy. 23 *G. W. F. Hegel*

[O]ne might well conclude that something like the "philosophical" life, in which one attempts to pursue and to certify "truth" independent of the ... crowd, offers the only escape from a life of "existential" alienation within the crowd. 24 *David Kipp*

No praise ... is too great for philosophy!—which enables this period [of old age] ... to be lived without anxiety. 25 *Cicero*

Our life is a warfare and a mere pilgrimage. Fame after life is no better than oblivion. What is it then that will adhere and follow? Only one thing, philosophy. 26 *Marcus Aurelius*

Kant still represents the ideal of what the philosophical mind at its best can be: uncynically disillusioned, highly critical and self-conscious of its limitations, yet still loyal to the standards of reasonableness and humanity whose grounds it seeks; steadfastly devoted to the principles of human self-enlightenment, yet aware that self-enlightenment is compatible with respect for the principle that man is a social being responsible to and for others as well as himself. 27 *Henry D. Aiken*

Plato remains the truest philosopher, since he defines philosophy as sublimation and ... the elevation of Spirit above Matter.... And, like the doctrine of the soul ... sublimation, as an attempt to be more than man, aims at immortality. 28 *Norman O. Brown*

It has gradually become clear to me what every great philosophy up to now has consisted of—

Philosophy

namely, the confession of its originator, and a species of involuntary and unconscious autobiography: and moreover that the moral (or immoral) purpose in every philosophy has constituted the true vital germ out of which the entire plant has always grown.... Accordingly, I do not believe that an "impulse to knowledge" is the father of philosophy.... 29
Friedrich Nietzsche

The kind of philosophy a man chooses depends upon the kind of man he is.... It is animated with the spirit of the man who possesses it. 30
Johann Fichte

Philosophy is the thought with which or as which I am active as my own self. It is not to be regarded as the objective validity of any sort of knowledge, but as the consciousness of being in the world. 31 *Karl Jaspers*

Working in philosophy ... is really more a working on oneself. On one's own interpretation. On one's way of seeing things. 32
Ludwig Wittgenstein

I believe that the function of philosophic reflection consists in bringing to light, and affirming as my own, the beliefs implied in such of my thoughts and practices as I believe to be valid.... 33 *Michael Polanyi*

[T]he office of philosophy is to project by dialectic, resting supposedly upon self-evident premises, a realm in which the object of completest cognitive certitude is also one with the object of the heart's best aspiration. 34
John Dewey

[P]hilosophy is the effort of our human mind to know itself.... 35 *William Barrett*

Without philosophy thoughts are, as it were, cloudy and indistinct: its task is to make them clear and to give them sharp boundaries. 36
Ludwig Wittgenstein

Philosophy is the self-correction by consciousness of its own initial excess of subjectivity. 37
Alfred N. Whitehead

The continual pursuit of meanings—wider, clearer, more negotiable, more articulate meanings—is philosophy. 38 *Susanne Langer*

The currency of philosophy is ideas—their meaning and rational foundation.... 39
Tom Regan

It is the primary aim of philosophy to unify completely, bring into clear coherence, all departments of rational thought.... 40
Henry Sidgwick

The study of philosophy is a voyage towards the larger generalities. 41 *Alfred N. Whitehead*

Myth, religion, art, language, even science, are ... variations on a common theme—and it is the task of philosophy to make this theme audible and understandable. 42 *Ernst Cassirer*

Philosophy, in short, is man's quest for the unity of knowledge: it consists in a perpetual struggle to create the concepts in which the universe can be conceived as a *universe* and not a *multi*verse. 43 *William Halverson*

Philosophy sets limits to the much disputed sphere of natural science.... It must set limits to what can be thought; and, in doing so, to what cannot be thought. 44
Ludwig Wittgenstein

Most of the propositions and questions to be found in philosophical works are not false but nonsensical.... Most of the propositions and questions of philosophers arise from our failure to understand the logic of our language. 45
Ludwig Wittgenstein

Philosophy has been defined as "an unusually obstinate attempt to think clearly"; I should define it rather as "an unusually ingenious attempt to think fallaciously." 46
Bertrand Russell

Analytic philosophy is not a liberation of the mind (as its practitioners want to insist), but a confinement of the mind in the circus of technical virtuosity. 47 *Henryk Skolimowski*

Some philosophers have made a virtue of talking to themselves; perhaps because they felt

there was nobody else worth talking to. I fear that the practice of philosophizing on this somewhat exalted plane may be a symptom of the decline of rational discussion. 48
Karl Popper

The linguistic philosophy, which cares only about language, and not about the world, is like the boy who preferred the clock without the pendulum because, although it no longer told the time, it went more easily than before and at a more exhilarating pace. 49 *Bertrand Russell*

Minimal philosophy ... retreats to texts, narrowly framed analytic issues regarding language use, logical puzzles, and so forth, because the larger philosophical questions, the metaphysical questions with which philosophy has traditionally been concerned, now seem beyond human mastery. The cultural consensus that once allowed such mastery ... seems gone forever. 50 *C. Fred Alford*

The springs of philosophical thought have run dry once more.... If we would have new knowledge, we must get us a whole world of new questions. 51 *Susanne Langer*

[W]e have lost sight of the final significance of effective philosophy.... A doctrine that does not attack and affect the life of the period in its inmost depths is no doctrine and had better not be taught. 52 *Oswald Spengler*

The rise of philosophy itself can be interpreted, I think, as a reaction to the breakdown of the closed society and its magical beliefs. It is an attempt to replace the lost magical faith by a rational faith; it modifies the tradition of passing on a theory or a myth by founding a new tradition—the tradition of challenging theories and myths and of critically discussing them. 53 *Karl Popper*

[P]hilosophy ought to question the basic assumptions of the age.... 54 *John Rodman*

I submit that human beings have three "eyes." The scientific eye looks out. The religious eye looks in. The philosophical eye looks at the looking. 55 *Troy W. Organ*

Philosophers are as free as others to use any method in searching for truth. *There is no method peculiar to philosophy.* 56 *Karl Popper*

[A] philosophy is characterized more by the *formulation* of its problems than by its solution of them. 57 *Susanne Langer*

People seem to be more concerned with examining the correctness of their thoughts than with the validity of their values, to such an extent that modern Western philosophy has largely dedicated itself to this single task. 58
Eric Klinger

All the sciences have now to pave the way for the future task of the philosopher; the task being understood to mean, that he must solve the problem of *value*, that he has to fix the *hierarchy of values*. 59 *Friedrich Nietzsche*

[T]he problem of philosophy concerns the *interaction* of our judgments about ends to be sought with knowledge of the means for achieving them. 60 *John Dewey*

The philosophers have only *interpreted* the world in various ways; the point is to change it. 61 *Karl Marx*

The significance of philosophising to-day is our attempt to confirm ourselves in a faith that arises independently of revelation. 62
Karl Jaspers

Philosophy secularizes the ideal. 63
Albert Camus

Philosophy ... is something intermediate between theology and science. 64
Bertrand Russell

Philosophy and religion are enemies, and because they are enemies they have need of one another. There is no religion without some philosophic basis, no philosophy without roots in religion. Each lives by its contrary. The history of philosophy is, strictly speaking, a history of religion. 65 *Miguel de Unamuno*

[T]hrough the greatness of the universe which philosophy contemplates, the mind is also

Philosophy

rendered great, and becomes capable of that union with the universe which constitutes its highest good. 66 *Bertrand Russell*

[T]hat all the labours of the ages, all the devotion, all the inspiration, all the noonday brightness of human genius, are destined to extinction in the vast death of the solar system ... are yet so nearly certain, that no philosophy which rejects them can hope to stand. Only within the scaffolding of these truths, only on the firm foundation of unyielding despair, can the soul's habitation henceforth be safely built. 67
Bertrand Russell

[W]e may say that the most characteristic current philosophies have ... a touch of suicidal mania. The mere questioner has knocked his head against the limits of human thought; and cracked it. 68 *G. K. Chesterton*

Since modern philosophy, in essence, is a concerted attack against the conceptual level of man's consciousness—a sustained attempt to invalidate reason, abstractions, generalizations, and integration of knowledge—men have been emerging from universities, for many decades past, with the helplessness of epistemological savages, with no inkling of the nature, function, or practical application of principles. 69
Ayn Rand

For having wished to prevent all conflict between science and philosophy, we have sacrificed philosophy without any appreciable gain to science. 70 *Henri Bergson*

The enormous success of the scientific abstractions, yielding on the one hand matter with its simple location in space and time, on the other hand mind, perceiving, suffering, reasoning, but not interfering, has foisted on to philosophy the task of accepting them as the most concrete rendering of fact. Thereby, modern philosophy has been ruined. 71 *Alfred N. Whitehead*

In modern professional language a philosopher is one who discusses the problems of epistemology. It is not thought necessary that he should live like a wise man. The biographies of the great metaphysicians often make extremely depressing reading. 72 *Aldous Huxley*

If a philosopher is not a man, he is anything but a philosopher; he is above all a pedant, and a pedant is a caricature of a man.... [For] the most tragic problem of philosophy is to reconcile intellectual necessities with the necessities of the heart and the will. 73
Miguel de Unamuno

Vain is the word of a philosopher who does not heal any suffering of man. 74 *Epicurus*

By consulting only Man's reason and not his heart, the philosophy of detachment is arbitrarily putting asunder what God has chosen to join together.... In pressing its way to a conclusion that is logically inevitable and at the same time morally intolerable, the philosophy of detachment ultimately defeats itself.... [W]e are moved to revolt against their denial of man himself. 75 *Arnold Toynbee*

[M]ost of contemporary philosophy is spiritually dead.... The death wish of our civilization has pervaded its philosophical edifices. 76
Henryk Skolimowski

Philosophy ... scarcely exists today in any sense that would be recognizable by our ancestors.... Who at this moment would have the slightest interest in what a living philosopher had to say on any subject, cosmological, moral, political, or social? 77 *Robert Nisbet*

[I]n sum, the philosophical landscape is largely bleak. 78 *Allan Bloom*

The chief intellectual characteristic of the present age is its despair of any constructive philosophy ... in the sense of any integrated outlook and attitude. 79 *John Dewey*

The circuitous paths travelled by specialists in philosophy have meaning only if they lead man to an awareness of being and his place in it. 80
Karl Jaspers

For centuries philosophic thought had sustained a consciousness of the ultimate reason of human existence.... [But] from the opening of the second half of the 19th century the traditional philosophy became everywhere an enterprise carried on by university schools....

Philosophy was divorced from its origin, and had no longer any responsibility for the real life.… Philosophy, thus renouncing its task, multiplied its enterprises but reduced itself to chaos. The task it renounced was sublime. Only through philosophy could man, being no longer able to guide his life in accordance with the dictates of a revealed religion, become aware of his own true will. 81 *Karl Jaspers*

Philosophy in the old mold *demythologizes* and *demystifies*. It has no sense of the sacred; and by *disenchanting* the world and *uprooting* man, it leads into a void. The revelation that philosophy finds nothingness at the end of its quest informs the new philosopher that mythmaking must be his central concern in order to make a world. 82 *Allan Bloom*

The problem of restoring integration and coöperation between man's beliefs about the world in which he lives and his beliefs about the values and purposes that should direct his conduct is the deepest problem of modern life. It is the problem of any philosophy that is not isolated from that life. 83 *John Dewey*

The problem of restoring the mental balance which humanity has obviously lost in this age is not psychiatric, or religious, or pedagogical, but philosophical. 84 *Susanne Langer*

Philosophy always comes too late to teach the world what it should be.… The owl of Minerva takes its flight only when the shades of twilight have fallen. 85 *G. W. F. Hegel*

~ POLITICS ~

MAN IS BY NATURE a political animal. 1 *Aristotle*

[I]t is a grave error to assume that men in general are, at least actively and continuously, political creatures. The context of their lives which is, for the majority, the most important is a private context.… They obey the orders of government from inertia; and even their resistance is too often a blind resentment rather than a reasoned desire to secure an alternative. 2 *Harold Laski*

It is not too far fetched to say that everyone is born a politician, and most of us outgrow it. 3 *Harold D. Lasswell*

politician: … frequently used in a derogatory sense, with implications of seeking personal or partisan gain, scheming, opportunism, etc. 4 *Webster's New World Dictionary*

The fully developed political type works out his destiny in the world of public objects in the name of public good. He displaces private motives on public objects in the name of collective advantage. 5 *Harold D. Lasswell*

Most political leaders acquire their position by causing large numbers of people to believe that these leaders are actuated by altruistic desires. 6 *Bertrand Russell*

It is when the politician loves neither the public good nor himself, or when his love for himself is limited and is satisfied by the trappings of office, that the public interest is badly served. And it is when his regard for himself is so high that his own self-respect demands he follow the path of courage and conscience that all benefit. 7 *John F. Kennedy*

Private vices by the dextrous Management of a skilful Politician may be turn'd into Public Benefits. 8 *Bernard Mandeville*

The greatest art of a politician is to render vice serviceable to the cause of virtue. 9 *Henry St. John*

Patronage and pork amalgamate and stabilize thousands of special opinions, local discontents, private ambitions. There are but two alternatives. One is government by terror and obedience; the other is government based on … a highly developed sense of information, analysis, and self-consciousness.… The secret of great statebuilders … is that they know how to calculate these principles. 10 *Walter Lippmann*

The term "political community" shall apply to a community whose social action is aimed at subordinating to orderly domination by the participants a "territory" and the conduct of the persons within it, through readiness to resort

Politics

to physical force.... Owing to the drastic nature of its means of control, the political association is particularly capable of arrogating to itself all the possible values toward which associational conduct might be oriented; there is probably nothing in the world which at one time or another has not been an object of social action on the part of some political association. 11 *Max Weber*

In politics the nation and not humanity is the ultimate fact. 12 *Hans Morgenthau*

[T]he *history of mankind* ... is the *history of political power*.... [and] the history of power politics is nothing but the history of international crime and mass murder ... [in which] some of the greatest criminals are extolled as its heroes. 13 *Karl Popper*

The first political figure in history is not patriarch but *military leader*. 14 *Robert Nisbet*

Modern politics is, at bottom, a struggle not of men but of forces. 15 *Henry Brooks Adams*

Politics ... has always been the systematic organization of hatreds. 16 *Henry Brooks Adams*

Since political parties are mainly fighting machines for crushing their opponents and for acquiring power and control, they are instruments of conflict rather than of co-operation.... 17 *Pitirim Sorokin*

Anybody in politics must have great competitive instinct ... that's life itself. 18 *Richard M. Nixon*

Politics is war without bloodshed while war is politics with bloodshed. 19 *Mao Tse-tung*

Every Communist must grasp the truth, "Political power grows out of the barrel of a gun." 20 *Mao Tse-tung*

There are signs in our own society of a lack of self-confidence in our political images and a desire to maintain them by violence and coercion. 21 *Kenneth Boulding*

All politics is a struggle for power; the ultimate kind of power is violence.... And in America, too, into the political vacuum the warlords have marched. 22 *C. Wright Mills*

So it goes: hate politics and love power.... 23 *Robert Nisbet*

It is necessary to completely abolish ... everything which may be called political power. As long as political power exists there will always be rulers and ruled, masters and slaves, exploiters and exploited. 24 *Mikhail Bukunin*

International politics, like all politics, is a struggle for power. 25 *Hans Morgenthau*

[I]nternational politics today should be defined less as a struggle for power than as a contest for the shaping of perceptions. 26 *Stanley Hoffman*

The opinion of crowds tends ... more and more to become the supreme guiding principle in politics. 27 *Gustave Le Bon*

Your representative owes you, not his industry only, but his judgment; and he betrays instead of serving you if he sacrifices it to your opinion. 28 *Edmund Burke*

Twentieth century politics has come to consist more and more of the study and control of public opinion.... Political parties now specialize in marketing politicians for public consumption. 29 *Christopher Lasch*

At last there will be an election in which the public will vote for the poll that it thinks most accurately reflects the public's opinion. Politics in the Information Age. 30 *Theodore Roszak*

Our modern politicians know very well that great masses are much more easily moved by the force of imagination than by sheer physical force. And they have made ample use of this knowledge. The politician becomes a sort of public fortuneteller. Prophesy is an essential element in the new technique of rulership. 31 *Ernst Cassirer*

All issues are political issues, and politics itself is a mass of lies, evasions, folly, hatred and schizophrenia.... Political language is designed to make lies sound truthful and murder respectable, and to give an appearance of solidity to pure wind. 32 *George Orwell*

Our national politics has become a competition for images or between images, rather than between ideals. 33 *Daniel J. Boorstin*

[Currently] there is an atrophy of the political sense and political functioning of the individual.... To combat this danger of indifference and apathy ... there is one sovereign remedy: glamour. 34 *David Riesman*

Where there is apathy about politics, we expect to find an appeal to glamour. 35
David Riesman

Politically speaking, we are facing the exhaustion of male rationality and the resurgence of erotic fantasy. 36 *Jessica Benjamin*

Recognition is the central problem of politics because it is the origin of tyranny, imperialism, and the desire to dominate. But ... it is simultaneously the psychological ground for political virtues like courage, public-spiritedness, and justice. All political communities must make use of the desire for recognition, while at the same time protecting themselves from its destructive effects. 37
Francis Fukuyama

[T]he most potent sources of political motivation—the key elements of political ambition—are unfulfilled esteem needs. 38
James MacGregor Burns

Political candidacy ... is most likely to be taken by two kinds of people: Those who have such high self-esteem that they can manage relatively easily the threats and strains and anxieties involved ... and those who have such low self-esteem that they are ready to do this ... to raise it. 39 *James David Barber*

Our attitudes toward the world around us are to a very large extent shaped by our particular standing in the social structure. This is perhaps most conspicuously evident in our political predispositions. More and more, our voting habits are determined by status factors.... 40
Vance Packard

The business of politics ... requires skills and attitudes that are peculiarly male.... To females, political procedure must seem hopelessly bizarre and almost frighteningly irrelevant to the simple concerns of constituents, children, and anyone else who wants clean air and an agreeable sense of community. 41 *Lionel Tiger & Robin Fox*

Carefully avoiding the twin hazards of egalitarianism and delight, sexual politics ... began in bed; having established its doctrine of female subjection there, it confidently applied it to the rest of life. 42 *Kate Millet*

Few aspects of social life are more completely or universally male dominated than politics. 43
Jeanne Kirkpatrick

[I]t is unlikely that any important nation would develop a female-biased or feminized political system unless other competing nations develop them also.... To forego the exclusive or predominant use of men in international relations would involve considerable trust in the intentions and internal controls of other nations. 44
Lionel Tiger

The whole business of politics and government as conducted by males hinges around the process of identifying or inventing the kind of leopard that will unite the greatest possible number of men in the tightest possible bond.... Politically, the leopard must always be the quintessence of evil or the system breaks down. 45
Elaine Morgan

There must be more women in politics, but not merely as a new elite alongside the patriarchal elite and alienated from people in general ... but in order to bring about change.... [A] certain "critical number" of women politicians is required before a substantial difference is made. 46
Elina Haavio-Mannila

Today the fight for life, the fight for Eros, is the *political* fight. 47 *Herbert Marcuse*

As the feminist adage says, *The personal is political*.... It's time to turn the feminist adage around.

Politics

The political is personal. 48 *Gloria Steinem*

Political action in a given community presumes the desire and capacity of individuals to work together; the political function cannot operate in a community from which this capacity has disappeared. 49 *Elton Mayo*

[P]olitics is the process by which the irrational bases of society are brought into the open. 50 *Offia Seliktar*

Politics is the art of the possible. 51 *Otto von Bismarck*

Politics … is everyone looking for [an] absolute on behalf of all. But society and politics only have the responsibility of arranging everyone's affairs so that each will have the leisure and the freedom to pursue this common search. 52 *Albert Camus*

True politics is the art of apprehending and applying the Justice which ought to prevail in a community of souls. 53 *Russell Kirk*

[A]n ethical ideal no group ever has. If it pretended to have one it would be a humbug. That is why the introduction of "moral ideas" into politics serves the most immoral purposes and plays into the hands of the most immoral men. 54 *William Graham Sumner*

All nations are tempted—and few have been able to resist the temptation for long—to clothe their own particular aspirations and actions in the moral purposes of the universe.… [I]t is exactly the concept of interest defined in terms of power that saves us from both that moral excess and that political folly. 55 *Hans Morgenthau*

[P]olitical decisions must be, so far as is possible, independent of any particular conception of the good life, or of what gives value to life. Since the citizens of a society differ in their conceptions, the government does not treat them as equals if it prefers one conception to another. 56 *Ronald Dworkin*

The political world has lost its connection not only with religion or metaphysics but also with all the other forms of man's ethical and cultural life. It stands alone—in an empty space. 57 *Ernst Cassirer*

[P]olitics in our society … has become illusory; [for] the real problems cannot be solved by political means.… The only tensions that still exist are political tensions, but … they are false tensions, emptying into a void, dealing with nothing serious in the structure of our society, and incapable of producing any solution or basic innovation.… [W]e must therefore leave politics behind.… 58 *Jacques Ellul*

The most characteristic trait of the American political style [is] the belittling of politics.… This belittling of politics is partly responsible for the abandonment of politics to the professional politicians.… This has meant a break with the Jacksonian doctrine of rotation in office, which was based on the belief that there are no mysteries in governing, just common sense, integrity, and a devotion to the public good, and that any able citizen can therefore do it.… 59 *Max Lerner*

We differ from other states in regarding the man who holds aloof from public life not as "quiet" but as useless; we … [hold] that acts are foredoomed to failure when undertaken undiscussed. 60 *Pericles of Athens*

[T]he typical citizen drops down to a lower level of mental performance as soon as he enters the political field. He argues and analyzes in a way which he would readily recognize as infantile within the sphere of his real interests. He becomes a primitive again. 61 *Joseph Schumpeter*

The fact is, politicians can be a menace. 62 *David Stockman*

The withered emasculation of our democratic statesmenship is the withered emasculation of America. The witch-hunting savagery of pompous male sluts in our national halls is that quality of all the people. The petty greed and relentless solicitation of these quasi males is our own. The sacrifice of power, of dignity, of responsibility, of national security and interest to a little patronage or the achievement of a trivial local profit is the measure of our universal loss of aim, purpose, moral worth, view, vision, integrity, and common cause. The appalling stupidity of these men ... is the exact measure of the stupidity of the people.... 63 *Philip Wylie*

The condition ... of making a beginning in good politics is to find a set of men with well-knit character and cogent traditions, so that there may be a firm soil to cultivate and that labour may not be wasted in ploughing the quicksands. 64 *George Santayana*

I have found, sadly, that a global view of reality and a sense of moral responsibility for humanity's future are very rare among political figures. 65 *Helen Caldicott*

Politics and the fate of mankind are formed by men without ideals and without greatness. Those who have greatness within them do not go in for politics. 66 *Albert Camus*

Until philosophers become kings, or kings and princes acquire the spirit of philosophy and political power and wisdom join together ... there will be no rest from evils. 67 *Socrates*

The question of our age is whether a change radical enough to close the gap between traditional political behavior and the requirements of survival is possible *within the limits* imposed by human nature. 68 *J. William Fulbright*

POWER

A LIVING THING seeks above all to discharge its strength—life itself is Will to Power. 1 *Friedrich Nietzsche*

[Normally we] answer "Happiness" to the question: What do men want?... In fact, man does *not* want "happiness." Pleasure is a feeling of power.... [W]hat man wants, what every smallest part of a living organism wants, is an increase of power. 2 *Friedrich Nietzsche*

[T]he object of man's desire is not to enjoy once only and for one instant of time, but to assure forever the way of his future desire.... So that, in the first place, I put for a general inclination of all mankind a perpetual and restless desire of power after power that ceases only in death. 3 *Thomas Hobbes*

The love of liberty is the love of others; the love of power is the love of ourselves. 4 *William Hazlitt*

Power, like vanity, is insatiable.... Love of power is greatly increased by the experience of power. 5 *Bertrand Russell*

Those who have been once intoxicated with power ... can never willingly abandon it. 6 *Edmund Burke*

The effect of power ... is the aggravation of self, a sort of tumour that ends by killing the victim's sympathies. 7 *Henry Brooks Adams*

Where love rules, there is no will to power; and where power predominates, there love is lacking. The one is the shadow of the other. 8 *Carl Jung*

[T]he power seeker ... pursues power as a means of compensation against deprivation. Power is expected to overcome low estimates of the self.... [It] is compensation against estimations of the self as weak, contemptible, immoral, unloved. 9 *Harold D. Lasswell*

[I]n a psychological sense, the lust for power is not rooted in strength but in weakness.... Thus power can mean one of two things, *domination* and *potency* ... [which] are mutually exclusive.... [T]o the extent to which an individual is potent, that is, able to realize his potentialities on the basis of freedom and integrity of his self, he does not need to dominate and is lacking the lust for power. 10 *Erich Fromm*

In many ways, power is a denial of one's humanity.... To sell out the kingdom of heaven for power is a devil's bargain. It is the bargain that the narcissist makes. 11 *Alexander Lowen*

A striving for power and control characterizes all narcissistic individuals. 12 *Alexander Lowen*

To be subject to another person's power is a humiliating experience.... Every narcissist has

Power

his deep fear of humiliation.... Power is a way to protect oneself against humiliation.... Obviously there can be no love in a relationship when power plays an important role. 13
Alexander Lowen

[One] approach of the cult of self is through power.... [Its] leaders draw upon feelings of helplessness and offer the exhilaration of power in its stead. 14 *Althea Horner*

Power is the great aphrodisiac. 15
Henry Kissinger

As one of America's elder statesmen has said, power is the greatest aphrodisiac. But such a statement can only be made in a society that worships power and that sees sex as one more area for the exercise of power. 16
Marilyn French

[I]n the case of men, power equals sexual potency, whereas in the case of women, sexual appeal equals power. 17 *Alexander Lowen*

Beneath the sensationalism of power and powerlessness the yearning for recognition—to know and be known—lies numbed, not fulfilled. 18 *Jessica Benjamin*

"Power for power's sake" is psychologically based on prestige gratification. 19
C. Wright Mills

The hero always presses for greater powers. It is natural to his vocation that he should do so. He is as eager to accept new powers as he is reluctant to surrender them after they are granted. And it is true that, in a troubled world, no democratic community can survive for long unless it entrusts its leaders with great powers. At the same time, what it gives with reluctance, it must take back with eagerness. 20
Sidney Hook

Presidents must have a will to power or they will not be successful presidents. They must constantly search for power, building it, if necessary, out of every scrap of formal authority and personal influence they can locate. 21
James MacGregor Burns

For the active-negative Presidents, the central hypothesis is this: having experienced severe deprivations of self-esteem in childhood, the person developed a deep attachment to *achievement* as a way to wring from his environment a sense that he is worthy; progressively, this driving force is translated into a search for independent *power* over others ... justified idealistically. 22 *James David Barber*

What moves the world for good or ill is power.... [We must] stop feeling guilty about being powerful.... World peace is inseparable from national power.... If the American leadership class does not come to grips with that reality, the U.S. will lose its chance to act as a force for good in the world. 23
Richard M. Nixon

The American imperium is about power, but power in the service of certain values. These values we hold ... to be not only good but self-evidently good.... If Americans are going to intervene in the world, it has to be for something more than just interest defined as power. It is interest defined as values. 24
Charles Krauthammer

Power pursued by the individual for his own sake is considered an evil.... Power disguised by ideologies and pursued in the name and for the sake of the nation becomes a good for which all citizens must strive. 25 *Hans Morgenthau*

National destinies are firmly forged only by the prospect of a common success in the sense of gains, conquests; in short, of a mutual extension of power. 26 *Adolf Hitler*

Foreign investments ... became a permanent feature of all economic systems as soon as it was protected by export of power.... Only the unlimited accumulation of power could bring about the unlimited accumulation of capital.... The state-employed administrators of violence soon formed a new class within the nations.... They were the first who ... would claim that power is the essence of every political structure. 27 *Hannah Arendt*

Chief among the forces affecting political folly is lust for power.... Government remains the

paramount area of folly because it is there that men seek power over others.... 28
Barbara Tuchman

[We] are feverishly in pursuit of power, and we are not a bit afraid to say so. We are madly keen on it. We are fanatically pursuing it.... [T]he will to power is for us literally the whole meaning of this life. 29 *Adolf Hitler*

Power is the alpha and the omega ... an end in itself and the essence of contemporary Communism.... The thirst for power is insatiable and irresistible among Communists. Victory in the struggle for power is equal to being raised to a divinity; failure means the deepest mortification and disgrace. 30 *Milovan Djilas*

"The Party seeks power entirely for its own sake.... We know that no one ever seizes power with the intention of relinquishing it. Power is not a means, it is an end.... The object of power is power.... God is power." 31 *George Orwell*

The lust for power in particular has shown itself to be antihuman. We savor power not when we move mountains ... but when we can turn men into objects, robots, puppets, automata, or veritable animals. 32 *Eric Hoffer*

All power is in essence power to deny mortality. 33 *Ernest Becker*

[P]ower is in essence a psychological category. And to pursue the tracks of power, we will have to enter the domain of the sacred ... : all power is essentially sacred power. 34
Norman O. Brown

Great power announced itself by its power over order; it covers order, creates order, maintains it and destroys it. 35 *Edward Shils*

When a system of power is thoroughly in command, it has scarcely need to speak itself aloud; when its workings are exposed and questioned, it becomes not only subject to discussion, but even to change. 36 *Kate Millet*

Power, in fact, is ever true to its vital principle, for in every shape it would reign without control or inquiry. Its throne is built across a dark abyss, which no eye must dare to explore, less the baseless fabric should totter under investigation. 37 *Mary Wollstonecraft*

When power is robbed of its shining armor of political, moral and philosophical theories, by which it defends itself, it will fight on ... but it will be more vulnerable. 38 *Martin Buber*

[C]onstant experience shows us that every man invested with power is apt to abuse it, and to carry his authority as far as it will go.... To prevent this abuse it is necessary from the very nature of things that power should be checked by power. 39 *Charles de Montesquieu*

All history is the history of one power balanced against another.... 40 *Leo Tolstoy*

Actually ... the very threat of a world where power reigns not only supreme, but without rival, engenders that revolt against power which is as universal as the aspiration for power itself. 41 *Hans Morgenthau*

My question is whether America can overcome the fatal arrogance of power. 42
J. William Fulbright

Among precautions against ambition, it may not be amiss to take one precaution against our *own*. I must fairly say, I dread our *own* power.... [E]very other nation will think we shall abuse it. It is impossible but that, sooner or later, this state of things must produce a combination against us which may end in our ruin.... I dread our being too much dreaded. 43
Edmund Burke

Nothing but might has ever made right, and if we include in might (as we ought to) elections and the decisions of courts, nothing but might makes right now. 44 *William Graham Sumner*

[W]e stand at the edge of the deepest powershift in human history.... What has not yet been appreciated is the degree to which raw, elemental power ... will be transformed in the decades ahead as a result of the new role of "mind." 45
Alvin Toffler

The word *power* is freely sprinkled through the

Power

literature of computers.... It is a power of the mind. It is the greatest power of the mind—the power to process limitless information with absolute correctness. We live in an Information Age which needs that power. Getting a job, being successful, means acquiring that power. The machine has it; you don't. As time goes on, the machine will have more and more of it. It will deserve that power because it fits better with the world than human brains. 46 *Theodore Roszak*

[T]he government's capacity to distort information in order to preserve its own political power is almost limitless.... If information is power, the ability to distort and control information will be used more often than not to preserve and perpetuate that power. 47 *David Wise*

Power is not exercised in this country by force of arms.... Power rests on control of consciousness. 48 *Charles A. Reich*

Power and truth do not go together. 49 *Wilhelm Reich*

The truth is that all men having power ought to be distrusted. 50 *James Madison*

Power is purpose.... This is a human, not a gender-based need. 51 *Rosiland Miles*

The only purpose for which power can be rightfully exercised over any member of a civilized community ... is to prevent harm to others. 52 *John Stuart Mill*

[T]he exercise of power is not intrinsically evil: it becomes an ill only when it has no end beyond itself.... 53 *Marilyn French*

It is not the misuse of power that is the evil; the very *existence* of power is an evil. 54 *Charles A. Reich*

Power tends to corrupt and absolute power corrupts absolutely. 55 *Lord Acton*

Striving for personal power is a deleterious delusion and poisons the communal life of human beings. Anyone who desires human community must renounce the striving for power over others. 56 *Alfred Adler*

Nothing is poisonous if taken in small enough quantities, and the more power is diffused, the more the assumption of power looks like the assumption of responsibility. It's when power is concentrated that the pursuit of it takes on an unhealthy hue. 57 *Philip Slater*

Subjectivity is our source of self-esteem.... The constitution of our Selves ... is virtually always an *intersubjective* concern.... [P]ower draws us away from subjectivity and traps us in the defense of our objective relations. 58 *Robert C. Solomon*

Western man ... has sought for mastery of everything without exception.... By bringing power to its highest degree of importance, efficacy, and abstractness, the West thus created the means of its own negation and condemnation. 59 *Jacques Ellul*

There is no hope for the world unless power can be tamed, and brought into the service ... of the whole human race.... [F]or science has made it inevitable that all must live or all must die. 60 *Bertrand Russell*

I repeat ... that all power is a trust ... from the people and for the people.... 61 *Benjamin Disraeli*

The urgent task is to chasten and subordinate power to the service of respect. 62 *Harold D. Lasswell*

Science promised man power. But, as so often happens when people are seduced by promises of power, the price exacted ... is servitude and impotence. 63 *Joseph Weizenbaum*

[Soon man] will have not only conquered nature, but detached himself as far as possible from the organic habitat.... From the standpoint of human life, indeed of all organic existence, assertion of absolute power [is] a confession of psychological immaturity—a radical failure to understand the natural processes of birth and growth, of maturation and death. 64 *Lewis Mumford*

[P]ower seems to engender a kind of willed ignorance, a moral stupidity. 65 *Adrienne Rich*

The man who *needs* power, for whatever reason, is not the man of the future, but the man whose future is past. There is no room for him in this world. His vision is depraved and is not really suited for life, much less for leadership in our delicately balanced world. 66
D. Slusser & G. Slusser

PROGRESS

PROGRESS, man's distinctive mark alone, / Not God's, and not the beasts': God is, they are, / Man partly is and wholly hopes to be. 1
Robert Browning

[P]rogress is dominantly characteristic of modern society or civilization.... According to modern thought, there are no fixed or determined ends or goals toward which social progress necessarily moves; and such progress is hence genuinely creative and would not otherwise be progress.... For the world-view of modern culture is essentially a dynamic one—a world-view which allows for, and indeed emphasizes, the reality of genuine creative change and evolution in things.... That notion or conception was utterly foreign to ... the thought and civilization of the ancient world.... 2 *George H. Mead*

No single idea has been more important than ... the idea of progress in Western civilization for nearly 3000 years. 3 *Robert Nisbet*

The doctrine of the most ruthless and swift progress has become an article of faith. 4
Émile Durkheim

The idea of progress always precedes development. 5 *Kenneth Boulding*

Progress, then, is the amassing of greater and greater material abundance, which is assumed to result in an ever more ordered world. Science and technology are the tools for getting the job done. This, in a nutshell, is the chief operating assumption of the mechanical world paradigm. 6 *Jeremy Rifkin*

Progress ... to the present day, has consisted in gradually enlarging the stronghold where, according to his own rules, man without God brutally wields power ... to the point of making the entire universe into a fortress erected against the fallen and exiled deity. Man, at the culmination of his rebellion, incarcerated himself.... 7 *Albert Camus*

The shaft of Mephistopheles, which drops harmless from the armour of Reason, pierces the lazy caricature which masquerades beneath that sacred name, to flatter its followers with the smiling illusion of progress won from the mastery of the material environment by a race too selfish and superficial to determine the purpose to which its triumphs shall be applied. 8
R. H. Tawney

Material security even has gone by the board, for modern man begins to see that every step in material "progress" adds just so much force to the thrust of a more stupendous catastrophe. 9
Carl Jung

Technology is the only field of human activity in which there has been progression. 10
Arnold Toynbee

Has "progress" as such a recognizable meaning that goes beyond the technical, so that to serve it is a meaningful vocation? The question must be raised. 11 *Max Weber*

Progress has enabled us to know how everything works, while forgetting the importance of understanding what something means. 12
S. Segaller & M. Berger

Not blind opposition to progress, but opposition to blind progress. 13
Motto of Sierra Club

Progress can come only out of *individual surplus*, i.e., from the work, the energy, the creative over-abundance of those men whose ability produces more than their personal consumption requires.... In a capitalist society, where such men are free to function ... progress is not a matter of sacrificing to some distant future, it is a part of the living present, it is the normal and natural.... 14 *Ayn Rand*

All progress is based upon a universal innate

Progress

desire on the part of every organism to live beyond its income. 15 *Samuel Butler*

In every domain, the achievement of progress requires an excess of effort.… Every synthesis costs something. 16 *Pierre Teilhard de Chardin*

Progress, far from consisting in change, depends on retentiveness. When change is absolute there remains no being to improve and no direction is set for possible improvement: and when experience is not retained, as among savages, infancy is perpetual.… Retentiveness, we must repeat, is the condition of progress. 17 *George Santayana*

Only perfect freedom of thought makes uninterrupted progress possible. 18 *August Bebel*

[P]rogress can be made only if the distinction between the *ought* and the *is* is regarded as a temporary device rather than as a fundamental boundary line. 19 *Paul Feyerabend*

The only principle that does not inhibit progress is: *anything goes.* 20 *Paul Feyerabend*

The more man becomes man, the less he will be prepared to move except towards that which is interminably and indestructibly new. 21 *Pierre Teilhard de Chardin*

[W]e are rushing nowhere at an ever increasing speed. 22 *Jacques Ellul*

Economic progress, in capitalist society, means turmoil. 23 *Joseph Schumpeter*

Mankind today … seems to be making itself more unhappy and calling that unhappiness progress. 24 *Norman O. Brown*

We have made so much progress that we cannot even speak with confidence about the prospect of *human* survival.… If we continue feverishly planning and inventing and building and rebuilding for more of this progress, we will achieve the level of *Total-Life-Incompetence.* 25 *Laurence J. Peter & Raymond Hull*

The reasonable man adapts himself to the world. The unreasonable one persists in trying to adapt the world to himself. Therefore, all progress depends on the unreasonable man. 26 *George Bernard Shaw*

[I]n the past, professionals have formed unprogressive castes. The point is that professionalism has now been mated with progress. The world is now faced with a self-evolving system, which it cannot stop. 27 *Alfred N. Whitehead*

As soon as men are inoculated with the precept that their duty is to progress, it is harder to make them accept resignation; so the number of the malcontent and disquieted is bound to increase. The entire morality of progress and perfection is thus inseparable from a certain amount of anomy. 28 *Émile Durkheim*

[S]ocial, scientific or technological progress, in order to better, not worsen man's lot, requires a more elaborate consciousness and an integration of personality that reaches into deeper levels than heretofore.… At present external progress has far surpassed a matching [inner] integration. 29 *Bruno Bettelheim*

The magnitude of a "progress" is gauged by the greatness of the sacrifice that it requires: humanity as a mass sacrificed to the prosperity of the one *stronger* species of Man—that *would be* progress. 30 *Friedrich Nietzsche*

Progress of humanity consists in removing whatever keeps one human being, one class or one sex in slavery and dependence upon another. 31 *August Bebel*

It is through interest in our fellow men that all the progress of our race has been made. 32 *Alfred Adler*

I mean by wisdom a right conception of the ends of human life. This is something which science in itself does not provide. Increase of science by itself, therefore, is not enough to guarantee any genuine progress, though it provides one of the ingredients which progress requires. 33 *Bertrand Russell*

The experience of the twentieth century made highly problematic the claims of progress on the basis of science and technology. For the ability of technology to better human life is critically dependent on a parallel moral progress in man. 34 *Francis Fukuyama*

To maintain a moral universe is constantly to engage in acts of transcendence. Progress in the real sense signifies the process of perpetual transcendence. 35 *Henryk Skolimowski*

[T]he idea of the possibility of moral progress is an essential condition of moral progress. None of it is inevitable. 36 *Thomas Nagel*

Progress can be defined only in regard to the special ideal that we have in mind. There is no absolute progress. 37 *Franz Boas*

[T]here is nothing inherent in human affairs to ensure material and moral progress. 38
Marvin Harris

The fact of progress is written plain and large on the page of history; but progress is not a law of nature. The ground gained by one generation may be lost by the next. 39
H. A. L. Fisher

If we think that history progresses, or that we are bound to progress, then we commit the same mistake as those who believe that history has a meaning that can be discovered in it.... [O]nly we, the human individuals, can do it; we can do it by defending and strengthening those democratic institutions upon which freedom, and with it progress, depends. And we shall do it much better as we become more fully aware of the fact that progress rests with us, with our watchfulness, with our efforts, with the clarity of our conception of our ends, and with the realism of their choice. 40
Karl Popper

I am convinced that finally it is upon the idea of progress and faith in progress that Mankind, today so divided, must rely and reshape itself. 41
Pierre Teilhard de Chardin

All that is human must retrograde if it does not advance. 42 *Edward Gibbon*

The tragedy is that today there is a great deal more conviction of the reality of progress in some of the unfree nations of the world ... than there is in the free Western nations. 43
Robert Nisbet

There is a growing disenchantment with "progress" ... and even a feeling that, in many directions, we have already gone too far. 44
Arthur C. Clarke

The contemporary human crisis has led to a retreat from the hopes and ideas of the Enlightenment under the auspices of which our political and economic progress had begun. The very idea of progress is called a childish illusion, and "realism," a new word for the utter lack of faith in man, is preached instead. 45
Erich Fromm

Now here comes in the whole collapse and huge blunder of our age.... Progress should mean that we are always changing the world to suit the vision. Progress does mean (just now) that we are always changing the vision.... We are not altering the real to suit the ideal. We are altering the ideal: it is easier. 46 *G. K. Chesterton*

It is possible to speak of historical progress only if one knows where mankind is going. 47
Francis Fukuyama

Never was there a time when it was more necessary to search for the conditions upon which progress depends, until we can reaffirm our faith in its possibility upon grounds better than those upon which we have too blindly relied. 48 *John Dewey*

PROJECTION

[T]HE UNDERSTANDING has in itself the existential structure which we call "projection." ... In projection, Being is understood. 1
Martin Heidegger

A projective mechanism for interpreting an event felt but difficult to locate in space may be a fundamental feature of human brain function. 2 *Arnold Mandell*

[T]he unconscious can become conscious only through projection onto the external world....

PROJECTION

[H]uman culture is a set of projections of the repressed unconscious. 3 *Norman O. Brown*

Men project their unconscious wishes upon the screen of their society and make their institutions and their gods in the image of their desires.... How often do men mistake their prejudices for the laws of nature. 4 *Ashley Montagu*

Human imagination, by the invention of myths, has created a cosmos consonant to our preconceptions ... in which the whole gamut of human emotions is projected upon the outer world.... We love, and therefore the gods may be kind; we hate, therefore the gods may be cruel; we wish to obey unquestionable authority, and are therefore pious; we wish to exert unquestionable authority, and therefore believe ourselves mouthpieces of God.... 5
Bertrand Russell

If oxen, horses, and lions had hands and could paint pictures and carve statues, they would represent the gods under the guise of oxen, horses, and lions, in the manner of men who represent them in their own image. 6 *Xenophanes*

To-day we aim at projecting the mathematical and physical laws of the physical universe into man, with the object of explaining the phenomenon of life by physics and mathematics; whereas the Greeks sought to extrapolate man into the expanse of the cosmos and regarded the cosmos as a living organism. 7
Samuel Sambursky

My explanation for the male domination of art, science, and politics, an indisputable fact of history, is based on an analogy between sexual physiology and aesthetics. I ... argue that all cultural achievement is a projection, a swerve into Apollonian transcendence, and that men are anatomically destined to be projectors. 8
Camille Paglia

[The] tendency toward projection ... is particularly characteristic of the manner in which men deal with their aggressions—that is, by seeking and finding scapegoats.... Without projection and without displacement of guilt by both sides, the mentality of war and the arms race would be inconceivable. 9 *Margarete Mitscherlich*

The view of communism as an evil philosophy is a distorting prism through which we see projections of our own minds rather than what is actually there. 10 *J. William Fulbright*

In projection, we experience an inner harm as an outer one: we endow significant people with the evil which actually is in us. 11 *Erik Erikson*

Psychic projection is one of the commonest facts of psychology.... Everything that is unconscious in ourselves we discover in our neighbour, and we treat him accordingly.... What we combat in him is usually our own inferior side. 12 *Carl Jung*

We project the unbearable self onto others, so that we can hate it in others, and destroy it. 13
Anaïs Nin

[P]rojection is to transform neurotic or moral anxiety into objective anxiety.... [A] person who is afraid of his own conscience consoles himself with the thought that other people are responsible for bothering him.... [He] may use this belief as a justification for attacking his imaginary enemy ... [and] to gain satisfaction for his hostile impulses.... Of course, the whole affair is an elaborate subterfuge or rationalization for evading personal responsibility.... [It] serves the purpose of changing an internal danger from the id or the superego which is difficult for the ego to handle into an external danger which is easier for the ego to deal with. 14
Calvin S. Hall

The more severe the conscience ... [and] the greater the quantity of aggression channeled inwards through it, the higher the general level of tension within the system. The only way in which temporary relief from this tension can be achieved is by creating conditions under which this superego aggression can be turned outwards on to someone else. 15 *Derek Wright*

Projection of one's inner impulses, particularly of aggression, onto others will naturally lead to a conception of a dangerous and hostile world and consequently to a general suspiciousness of others ... [as well as] an oversimplified survival-of-the-fittest idea.... [I]n persons possessed by such fearfulness, the approach to people will tend to be manipulative and exploitive. 16 *T. W. Adorno et al.*

[E]verybody is blindly convinced that he is nothing more than his own extremely unassuming and insignificant conscious self.... As nobody is capable of recognizing where and how much he himself is possessed and unconscious, one simply projects one's own condition upon the neighbor, and thus it becomes a sacred duty to have the biggest guns and the most poisonous gas. 17 *Carl Jung*

Unable to tolerate the anxiety associated with the idea that separation from the mother is permanent, men invent and embrace a substitute for the mother ... the nation, in which they may find her once again.... The nation, that is to say, may be viewed as a projection of our narcissistic ego.... Through identification with the country, then, we attempt to ... restore our lost omnipotence. 18 *Richard Koenigsberg*

Narcissism splits the reality of an individual into accepted and rejected aspects, the latter being projected, then, upon others.... The need to project and maintain an image forces the person to prevent any feeling from reaching consciousness that would conflict with the image. 19 *Alexander Lowen*

[T]he mechanisms of splitting off and projection can help us to understand the phenomenon of the Holocaust.... From the start, it had been the aim of [the Nazis'] upbringing to stifle their childish, playful, and life-affirming side. The cruelty inflicted on them, the psychic murder of the child they once were, had to be passed on in the same way: each time they sent another Jewish child to the gas ovens, they were in essence murdering the child within themselves. 20 *Alice Miller*

British colonists in Kenya's Rift Valley flogged their servants for laziness or incompetence, yet themselves lived lives of incredible idleness.... [T]his kind of projection ... —the ability to look down at a set of human beings and to attribute to them all that one has been taught to despise in the self ... is identical to that of male supremacy. 21 *Marilyn French*

When aggression is projected outward and harnessed by civilization, it winds up doing *outside* what it would otherwise do *inside*: reducing the world, objectifying it, subjugating it. 22 *Jessica Benjamin*

[F]ear of death ... [is] the fear of a projected aggression originally evolved in the interests of self-preservation.... [A]n organism's capacity to "recognize" the danger from its potential enemies results from the evolution of a tendency to project into them the aggression felt within oneself. 23 *R. E. Money-Kyrle*

One thing about a healthy person is that he or she does not have to use in a big way the technique of projection in order to cope with his or her own destructive impulses and thoughts. 24 *D. W. Winnicott*

All gaps in actual knowledge are still filled with projections.... We must still be exceedingly careful in order not to project our own shadows too shamelessly; we are still swamped with projected illusions. 25 *Carl Jung*

Through the withdrawal of projections, conscious knowledge slowly developed.... This was the first stage in the despiritualization of the world. 26 *Carl Jung*

People create the reality they need.... Projection is necessary and desirable for self-fulfillment. Otherwise man is overwhelmed by his loneliness and separation.... 27 *Ernest Becker*

Reality

Nothing is real that is not eternal. 1 *Miguel de Unamuno*

The belief in permanence ... is the basis of all belief in "reality." 2 *Hans Vaihinger*

But the whole feeling of reality, the whole sting and excitement of our voluntary life, depends on our sense that in it things are *really being decided* from one moment to another, and that it is not the dull rattling off of a chain that was forged innumerable ages ago. 3 *William James*

Reality

We must assume that desire for a firmer grasp of reality is implicit in the nature of Being. 4
Herbert Read

[T]o feel real [is] to have a sense of *self* and of *being*. 5 *D. W. Winnicott*

The reality of the world cannot be evaded. Experience of the harshness of the real is the only way by which a man can come to his own self.... For selfhood is only possible in virtue of this tension.... 6 *Karl Jaspers*

When I find myself, I always find that self coexisting with something facing that self.... It is certain that this something does not exist by itself, apart from me. To believe the opposite was the realist error which we have forever overcome. But neither do I exist alone and within myself; my existing is coexisting with that which is not I. Reality, then, is this interdependence and coexistence. 7 *José Ortega y Gasset*

Psychosis is a state of absolute narcissism, one in which the person has broken all connection with reality outside, and has made his own person the substitute for reality. 8 *Erich Fromm*

In its extreme form ... fear of losing one's orientation is the fear of psychosis. When persons actually are on the brink of psychosis, they often have an urgent need to seek out some contact with other human beings ... [which] gives them a bridge to reality. 9 *Rollo May*

[F]or primitives as for the man of all pre-modern societies, the *sacred* is equivalent to a *power*, and, in the last analysis, to *reality*. The sacred is saturated with *being*.... [The] *sacred* and *profane* are two modes of being in the world, two existential situations assumed by man.... Sacred space makes it possible to obtain a fixed point and hence to acquire orientation in the chaos of homogeneity.... The profane experience, on the contrary, maintains the homogeneity and hence the relativity of space. 10 *Mircea Eliade*

A classic study on higher brain function is the work of the Canadian neurosurgeon, Wilder Penfield.... In one case of electric stimulation of the occipital lobe ... the patient reported seeing a fluttering butterfly of such compelling reality that he stretched his hand from the operating table to catch it. In an identical experiment performed on an ape, the animal peered intently, as if at an object before him, made a swift catching motion with his right hand, and then examined, in apparent bewilderment, his empty fist. 11 *Carl Sagan*

In Sir Charles Sherrington's splendid metaphor, the brain is an "enchanted loom where millions of flashing shuttles weave a dissolving pattern." Since the mind recreates reality from the abstractions of sense impressions, it can equally well simulate reality by recall and fantasy. The brain invents stories and runs imagined and remembered events back and forth through time ... travelling easily into the realms of myth and perfection. 12 *E. O. Wilson*

Instead of merely receiving our mental model of reality, we are now compelled to invent it and continually reinvent it. This places an enormous burden on us. But it also leads toward greater individuality.... Some of us crack under the new pressure or withdraw into apathy or rage. Others emerge as well formed, continually growing.... 13 *Alvin Toffler*

The new physics, quantum mechanics, tells us clearly that it is not possible to observe reality without changing it.... Not only do we influence our reality but, in some degree, we actually *create* it ... [i.e.] we *create* certain properties because we choose to measure those properties. 14 *Gary Zukav*

[Quantum mechanics entails] the necessity of a final renunciation of the classical ideal of causality and a radical revision of our attitude toward the problem of physical reality. 15 *Niels Bohr*

[A] scientific theory is just a mathematical model we make to describe our observations: it exists only in our minds. So it is meaningless to ask: Which is real, "real" or "imaginary" time? It is simply a matter of which is the more useful description. 16 *Stephen Hawking*

Ontologically there are an infinite number of realities, each one defined by the particular space-time dimension which you use. 17
Timothy Leary

Reality

Physicists have come to see that all their theories of natural phenomena ... are creations of the human mind; properties of our conceptual map of reality, rather than of reality itself. 18
Fritjof Capra

A theory of reality with pretensions to completeness would have to include a theory of the mind. 19 *Thomas Nagel*

Fortunately there a number of different ways in which our minds can reach reality. 20
Pierre Teilhard de Chardin

Reality is not just objective reality. 21
Thomas Nagel

And nobody can deny that there may not exist, and perhaps do exist, aspects of reality unknown to us, to-day at any rate, and perhaps unknowable, because they are in no way necessary to us for the preservation of our own actual existence. 22 *Miguel de Unamuno*

Reality is more fluid and elusive than reason, and has, as it were, more dimensions than are known even to the latest geometry. Hence the understanding, when not suffused with some glow of sympathetic emotion or some touch of mysticism, gives but a dry, crude image of the world. 23 *George Santayana*

There is nothing in the real world which is merely an inert fact. Every reality is there for feeling: it promotes feeling; and it is felt. 24
Alfred N. Whitehead

Emotions are said to distort our reality; I argue that they are responsible for it.... The passions are judgments, constitutive judgments according to which our reality is given its shape and structure. 25 *Robert C. Solomon*

Reality is a construct of our senses, a chart which slowly emerges as we take soundings of our feelings [and] trace the contours of our sensations.... The chart changes as our knowledge increases, as our recording instruments improve in precision. A new kind of instrument may result in a completely revised chart, and those of us who are skeptics will always regard the latest edition of the chart as provisional. 26 *Herbert Read*

Whatever we call reality, it is revealed to us only through the active construction in which we participate. 27 *Ilya Prigogine*

[I]f that elusive concept "reality" has any meaning, it must be that toward which the entire human being reaches out for satisfaction, and not simply some fact-and-theory-mongering fraction of the personality. 28 *Theodore Roszak*

The real is realization. 29 *Jean-Paul Sartre*

[A]n individual being is a Life of Experience fulfilling Ideas, in an absolutely final form.... The essence of the Real is to be Individual, or to permit no other of its own kind, and this character it possesses only as the unique fulfilment of its purpose. 30 *Josiah Royce*

[A]n existential system cannot be formulated.... Reality itself is a system—for God; but it cannot be a system for any existing spirit. 31
Søren Kierkegaard

The reality of the world as a whole is no object of knowledge. 32 *Karl Jaspers*

Reality ... is the world of phenomenal experience, perceived with a minimum of distortion and with a maximum of customary validation agreed upon in a given state of technology and culture. 33 *Erik Erikson*

Our perception of "reality" is the perfectly achieved accomplishment of our civilization. 34
R. D. Laing

The scientific establishment of the 20th Century is the real Church of the West ... because it is the ultimate (and official) arbiter of reality. 35 *Morris Berman*

It is whatever is lower that we take to be more real. The superstition of our time expresses itself in a mania for equating the sublime with the trivial and for quaintly mistaking a merely necessary condition for a sufficient cause. The mania usurps the name of "scientific integrity," and is defended on the ground that it emancipates the mind from delusions about "spirit." 36
Denis de Rougemont

Reality

Our mania for rational explanation obviously has its roots in our fear of metaphysics.... The idea that anything could be real or true which does *not* come from outside has hardly begun to dawn on contemporary man. 37 *Carl Jung*

"[R]ealism" [is] a new word for the utter lack of faith in man.... 38 *Erich Fromm*

The "realist" sees only the surface features of things; he sees the manifest world.... The insane person is incapable of seeing reality as it is.... Both are sick.... [T]he psychotic ... cannot function socially. The sickness of the "realist" impoverishes him as a human being. 39 *Erich Fromm*

The sublimations of civilized man desiccate the magic out of the human body and thus represent a victory for the reality-principle. But ... a victory for the reality-principle is also a victory for the death-instinct. 40 *Norman O. Brown*

Yet now, in the height of our power in this age of the Graphic Revolution, we are threatened by a new and a peculiarly American menace.... It is the menace of unreality.... We risk being the first people in history to have been able to make their illusions so vivid, so persuasive, so "realistic" that they can live in them.... We have come to believe in our own images, till we have projected ourselves out of this world.... Yet by doing, we may be defeating ourselves. 41 *Daniel Jay Boorstin*

Reason

Reason, like beauty, is its own excuse for being. 1 *George Santayana*

Reason is natural revelation.... 2 *John Locke*

The function of man is activity of soul in accordance with reason.... It follows that the good of man is activity of soul in accordance with virtue.... Virtue is a state of deliberate moral purpose consisting in a mean that is relative to ourselves, the mean being determined by reason.... Reason, more than anything else, *is* man. 3 *Aristotle*

Since the foundation of human thought lies in the rise into consciousness of the categories in which our experience is classified, the principal difference between the mental processes of primitives and ourselves lies in the fact that we have succeeded by reasoning to develop from the crude, automatically developed categories a better system of the whole field of knowledge, a step which the primitives have not found. 4 *Franz Boas*

"Reasoning" is the process of building up insight into relations which are too complex to be grasped by direct inspection.... Reasoning is the use of logic to make implicitly given conditions explicit.... 5 *Susanne Langer*

Man—that, namely, which should contra-distinguish him from the Animals—is to be taken from his reason rather than from his understanding: in that in other creatures there may be something of understanding, but there is nothing of reason. 6 *Samuel Taylor Coleridge*

Reason is the Power of Universal and necessary Convictions, the Source and Substance of Truths above Sense.... On the other hand, the Judgments of the Understanding are binding only in relation to the objects of our Senses.... Hence we ... speak of the *human* understanding.... But there is, in this sense, no *human* reason. There neither is nor can be but one reason.... 7 *Samuel Taylor Coleridge*

No matter how strongly the unity and integrity of the mind is asserted, this unity is nothing more than verbal if the mind is not in principle the expression of reason.... The power of reason is simply the power of the whole mind at its fullest stretch and compass. 8 *J. E. Creighton*

Reason ... is like love. Just as love is an orientation which refers to all objects and is incompatible with the restriction to one object, so is reason a human faculty which must embrace the whole of the world with which man is confronted. 9 *Erich Fromm*

The function of Reason is to promote the art of life. 10 *Alfred N. Whitehead*

Reason

Maturity lies in taking reason at its word and learning to believe and to do what it bids us. 11
George Santayana

Mortal life cannot offer you anything better than justice and truth; that is, peace of mind in the conformity of your actions to the laws of reason. 12 *Marcus Aurelius*

Only reason can convince us of those three fundamental truths without a recognition of which there can be no effective liberty: that what we believe is not necessarily true; that what we like is not necessarily good; and that all questions are open. 13 *Clive Bell*

Faith in reason is the trust that the ultimate natures of things lie together in a harmony which excludes mere arbitrariness. 14
Alfred N. Whitehead

Reason as such represents or rather constitutes a single formal interest, the interest in harmony. 15
George Santayana

[T]he friends of reason ... are the only true friends of humanity. 16 *Bertrand Russell*

[T]he dominant philosophy of our age is a virulent revolt against reason.... 17 *Ayn Rand*

Reason is to insure, through the ever more effective transformation and exploitation of nature, the fulfillment of the human potentialities. 18 *Herbert Marcuse*

[T]he real threat to democracy comes, not from overmanagement, but from undermanagement. To undermanage reality ... is simply to let some force other than reason shape reality.... But whatever it is, if it is not reason that rules man, than man falls short of his potential. 19
Robert McNamara

Life is very widely dominated still by the belief that rational solutions exist for all problems, and that problems which don't respond to reason cannot be real. 20 *S. Segaller & M. Berger*

The man who listens to Reason is lost: Reason enslaves all whose minds are not strong enough to master her. 21 *George Bernard Shaw*

[R]eason ... is enslaved to the reality-principle. 22 *Norman O. Brown*

[U]nconscious death wishes are cloaked with the conscious and sincere dedication to reason and science.... 23 *Louis J. Karmel*

[Behaviorists], while disclaiming normative content, advocate an authoritarianism based on expertise.... They have reduced reason itself to only its role in the domination of things, man, and, finally, nature. 24 *Joseph Weizenbaum*

The rationalist who desires to subject everything to human reason is faced with a real dilemma. The use of reason aims at control and predictability. But the process of the advance of reason rests on freedom and the unpredictability of human action. Those who extol the powers of human reason usually see only one side of that interaction.... They do not see that, for advance to take place, the social process from which the growth of reason emerges must remain free from its control.... We are not far from the point where the deliberately organized forces of society may destroy those spontaneous forces which have made advance possible. 25 *Friedrich von Hayek*

It is not by reason, but most often in spite of it, that are created those sentiments that are the mainsprings of all civilization.... 26
Gustave Le Bon

Reason, that ... distinguishing mark of man, is a social product. 27 *Miguel de Unamuno*

What we term "reason" arises when one of the organisms takes into its own response the attitude of the other organisms involved. It is possible for the organism so to assume the attitudes of the group that are involved in its own act within this whole co-operative process. When it does so, it is what we term "a rational being." 28
George H. Mead

The truth must be admitted that thought works under strange conditions. Pure "reason" is only one out of a thousand possibilities in the thinking of each of us. 29 *William James*

Pure reason is, in fact, occupied with itself, and

Reason

not with any object.... [It] is only the cognitions of the understanding that are presented to it, for the purpose of receiving the unity of a rational conception, that is, of being connected according to a principle. The unity of reason ... is not an objective principle extending its dominion over objects, but a subjective maxim.... But the real aim of reason has nothing in view except principles of systematic unity for the explanation of the phenomena of the soul. 30 *Immanuel Kant*

Reason's function is to embody the good, but the test of excellence is itself ideal; therefore before we can assure ourselves that reason has been manifested in any given case we must make out the reasonableness of the ideal that inspires us. And in general, before we can convince ourselves that a Life of Reason, or behaviour guided by science and directed toward spiritual goods, is at all worth having, we must make out the possibility and character of its ultimate end. 31 *George Santayana*

By itself, reason can only devise means to achieve otherwise determined ends; it cannot set up goals.... 32 *Konrad Lorenz*

"Reason" ... signifies the choice of the right means to an end that you wish to achieve. It has nothing whatever to do with the choice of ends.... Reason is not a cause of action but only a regulator. 33 *Bertrand Russell*

Reasoning power does not translate into moral power.... 34 *Craig Dykstra*

The ruling passion, be what it will,
The ruling passion conquers reason still. 35
Alexander Pope

Reason is, and ought only to be, the slave of the passions, and can never pretend to any other office than to serve and obey them.... Morals excite passions, and produce or prevent actions. Reason of itself is utterly impotent in this particular. The rules of morality, therefore, are not conclusions of our reason. 36 *David Hume*

[R]eason ... has always pretended to provide our lives with the meanings we demand but has never succeeded.... In short, the answer lies in our passions.... [W]isdom is a matter of living both thoughtfully and passionately.... The function of reason—whose result is wisdom—is ... the maximization of personal dignity and self-esteem. 37 *Robert C. Solomon*

Reason flows from the blending of rational thought and feeling. If the two functions are torn apart, thinking deteriorates into schizoid intellectual activity, and feeling deteriorates into neurotic life-damaging passions. 38
Erich Fromm

[H]eart and reason can no longer be kept in their separate places.... Our hearts must know the world of reason, and reason must be guided by an informed heart. 39 *Bruno Bettelheim*

Reason's last step is the recognition that there are an infinite number of things which are beyond it; it is merely feeble if it does not go so far as to grasp that.... The heart has its reasons which reason cannot understand. 40
Blaise Pascal

Reason ... cannot decide the value of things. 41
Blaise Pascal

Even the wisest of mankind cannot live by reason alone; pure arrogant reason, denying the claims of prejudice (which commonly are also the claims of conscience), leads to a wasteland of withered hopes and crying loneliness, empty of God and Man.... 42 *Russell Kirk*

[T]he highest purpose of human reason is to evolve a comprehensive understanding of mankind's place in the universe, not merely to serve as a detector of consistency and causality and thus as an instrument for morally blind desire. 43 *Laurence H. Tribe*

In a society that has reduced reason to mere calculation, reason can impose no limits on the pursuit of pleasure—on the immediate gratification of every desire no matter how perverse, insane, criminal, or merely immoral. 44
Christopher Lasch

The dream of reason produces monsters. 45
Francisco José de Goya

Reason

Reason perhaps teaches certain bourgeois virtues, but it does not make either heroes or saints. 46 *Miguel de Unamuno*

Reason ... manifests itself when it becomes one with the reality of our being.... [R]eason guides its meaning ... and recognizes its limits. 47
Karl Jaspers

Reason, man's blessing, is also his curse; it forces him to cope everlastingly with the task of solving an insoluble dichotomy.... [H]e is compelled to go forward and with everlasting effort to make the unknown known.... He must give account of himself, and of the meaning of his existence. He is driven to overcome this inner split, tormented by a craving for "absoluteness," for another kind of harmony which can lift the curse by which he was separated from nature, from his fellow men, and from himself. 48 *Erich Fromm*

The man of reason believes he possesses within himself the "meaning" of the world and of his life. He projects the semblance of order and efficiency of a well-organized individual into the world.... His most feared enemy is death ... and when he cannot avoid the idea of death he ... seeks refuge in acquisitive activity: for possessions, for knowledge, for laws, for a rational mastery of the world.... [B]ecause he is an active link in the eternal chain of progress he believes that he is fully protected against annihilation. 49 *Hermann Hesse*

With the death of God, mankind remains.... Man, on an earth that he knows is henceforth solitary, is going to add, to irrational crimes, the crimes of reason that are bent on the triumph of man. 50 *Albert Camus*

Reason has ... become a tool ... in the domination of man and nature. The cost-effectiveness calculus refuses to take into account such classic concerns of reason as the long-range consideration ... or the consequences of a policy for the spirit and character of those who execute it. 51 *Charles Drekmeier*

[R]eason by itself is little more than an instrument to justify man's defensive ways of thinking. Reason, devoid of the purifying power of faith, can never free itself from distortions and rationalizations. 52 *Martin Luther King Jr.*

No pattern of human reason but only the will of God can be the principle of the form and order to which human life must be conformed. 53
Reinhold Niebuhr

Reason is the greatest enemy that faith has; it never comes to the aid of spiritual things, but—more frequently than not—struggles against the divine Word, treating with contempt all that emanates from God. 54 *Martin Luther*

The faith in the categories of reason is the cause of nihilism. We have measured the value of the world according to categories that refer to a purely fictitious world. 55
Friedrich Nietzsche

Absolute relativism, which is neither more nor less than scepticism ... is the supreme triumph of the reasoning reason.... But reason going beyond truth itself, beyond the concept of reality itself, succeeds in plunging itself into the depths of scepticism. And in this abyss the scepticism of the reason encounters the despair of the heart.... 56 *Miguel de Unamuno*

It is quite natural that with the triumph of the Goddess of Reason a general neuroticizing of modern man should result.... 57 *Carl Jung*

The loss of supernatural moral guidance in the light of scientific reason has not made people more grown-up; it has only unleashed the amoral greed of infancy. 58
Dorothy Dinnerstein

The madman is not the man who has lost his reason. The madman is the man who has lost everything except his reason. 59
G. K. Chesterton

The more the critical reason dominates, the more impoverished life becomes; but the more of the unconscious, and the more of myth we are capable of making conscious, the more of life we integrate. Overvalued reason has this in common with political absolutism: under its dominion the individual is pauperized. 60
Carl Jung

Reason

[N]ow the greater danger to man [comes] not from rampant, uncontrolled instinct breaking down the restraining bonds of reason and self-control but from rampant reason oppressing and destroying instinct and nature.... Bestiality had been the cause of many horrors, but it had never threatened the species with extinction.... Now reason must sit at the knee of instinct and learn reverence for the miraculous instinctual capacity for creation. 61 *Jonathan Schell*

Man has been endowed with reason, with the power to create.... But up to now he hasn't been a creator, only a destroyer. Forests keep disappearing, rivers dry up, wild life's become extinct, the climate's ruined and the land grows poorer and uglier every day. 62 *Anton Chekhov*

The web of domination has become the web of Reason itself, and this society is fatally entangled in it. 63 *Herbert Marcuse*

Reason is unable to establish its unity.... It floats without compass or rudder. 64 *Allan Bloom*

Reason was meant to be ... the compass, chart, and sextant that would enable the captain to plot the right course for his ship, but it was not meant to deny the unpredictable wind that pushes the ship forward!... Yet, exalted by the discovery of this marvellous tool, man went to extremes and denied the very thing that gave him life! 65 *Jacques Ellul*

Reason is not an iron collar set on the neck of reality.... On the contrary, it relates man to reality so as to situate him within it.... The passage to utopia by way of rationalism shows quite clearly the process by which the West has betrayed reason.... Reason ceased to be itself and became simply the center of a vast machinery that ceased to obey it.... Reason has been betrayed, and now we have nothing more to fall back on that would enable us to resume our journey. 66 *Jacques Ellul*

Religion

We define religion as the assumption that life has meaning. 1 *Rollo May*

One may ... be justified in defining religion as man's search for *ultimate* meaning.... If we subscribe to this statement we may then define belief and faith as *trust* in ultimate meaning. 2 *Viktor Frankl*

[O]nly religion can answer the question of the purpose of life. One can hardly be wrong in concluding that the idea of life having a purpose stands and falls with the religious system. 3 *Sigmund Freud*

To make clear [our] fundamental ends and valuations, and to set them fast in the emotional life of the individual, seems to me precisely the most important function which religion has to perform in the social life of men. 4 *Albert Einstein*

[R]eligious man feels the need always to exist in a total and organized world, in a cosmos.... [I]t is by virtue of this eternal return to the sources of the sacred and the real that human existence appears to be saved from nothingness and death. 5 *Mircea Eliade*

Religious feeling is ... an absolute addition to the Subject's range of life. It gives him a new sphere of power. When the outward battle is lost ... it redeems and vivifies an interior world which otherwise would be an empty waste.... It ought to mean nothing short of this new reach of freedom for us, with the struggle over, the keynote of the universe sounding in our ears, and everlasting possession spread before our eyes. This sort of happiness in the absolute and everlasting is what we find nowhere but in religion. 6 *William James*

Religion is the vision of something which stands beyond, behind, and within, the passing flux of immediate things; something which is real, and yet waiting to be realised; something which is a remote possibility, and yet the greatest of present facts; something that gives meaning to all that passes, and yet eludes comprehension; something whose possession is the final good, and yet is beyond all reach; something which is the ultimate ideal, and the hopeless quest. 7 *Alfred N. Whitehead*

No power, either physical or psychical, has the

least moral prerogative nor any just place in religion at all unless it supports and advances the ideal native to the worshipper's soul. 8
George Santayana

The worship of God is not a rule of safety—it is an adventure of the spirit, a flight after the unattainable. The death of religion comes with the repression of the high hope of adventure. 9
Alfred N. Whitehead

[T]he only salutary powers visible in the world today are the great "psychotherapeutic" systems which we call the religions.... [They] express, almost perfectly, the nature of the psychic experience. They are the repositories of the secrets of the soul, and this matchless knowledge is set forth in grand symbolic images. 10
Carl Jung

Religion ... seems to make for an ultimate harmony within the soul and for an ultimate harmony between the soul and all the soul depends upon. So that religion, in its intent, is a more conscious and direct pursuit of the Life of Reason than is society, science, or art. 11
George Santayana

Every soul has religion, which is the only word for its existence. All living forms in which it expresses itself ... are ultimately religious, and *must* be so. 12 *Oswald Spengler*

The predisposition to religious belief is the most complex and powerful force in the human mind and in all probability an ineradicable part of human nature. 13 *E. O. Wilson*

Religion is one of the intrinsic faculties of human nature. 14 *Arnold Toynbee*

Man is by his constitution a religious animal; atheism is not only against our reason, but our instincts. 15 *Edmund Burke*

[H]uman beings who declare that they have no religion are deceiving themselves through failing to search their own hearts. 16
Arnold Toynbee

The general result of the modern form of thoroughly rationalizing the conception of the world ... has been that religion has been shifted into the realm of the irrational. 17
Max Weber

The experience of the irrationality of the world has been the driving force of all religious revolution. 18 *Max Weber*

The unconscious is the only source of religious experience. 19 *Carl Jung*

Religion flourishes because man will not, *cannot*, face his unconscious. Religion makes the unconscious the devil, and warns men to flee from its temptations. But make the unconscious, conscious, and religion will have no function. 20 *A. S. Neill*

[F]or all fideists, basic religious questions do not admit of rational answers. But this, no doubt, is because religious questions are not motivated by ... a desire for information. What they seek is not understanding, but something that passes understanding, namely, salvation. And for salvation there is no recourse save an act of faith. 21 *Henry D. Aiken*

The individual must strive to realize his life by losing and finding himself in something greater than himself.... Religion is always a citadel of hope, which is built on the edge of despair. 22
Reinhold Niebuhr

The essential task of the religious enterprise is to face the actual termination of individual existence ... and to create a transindividual ego identification.... [O]ne can avoid that other death by allowing communion to function together with agency.... [W]e can be spared the sense of ultimate despair by not separating ourselves from each other. 23 *David Bakan*

Religion is, first and foremost, a system of ideas by means of which individuals can envisage the society of which they are members, and the relations, obscure yet intimate, which they bear to it. That is the primordial task of a faith. 24
Émile Durkheim

All cultures of the past have crystallized and nucleated around their religion because it is the religion which supplies the manifest image of

Religion

their destiny toward which they feel themselves to be drawn.... The person or the nation that has a date with destiny goes somewhere.... [N]onreligious ideologies are incapable of providing the kind of manifest image of life, history, and purpose which are satisfying to the masses of mankind. 25 *Kenneth Boulding*

[T]he essential teachings of all the great humanist religions can be summarized [as:] It is the goal of man to overcome one's narcissism. 26 *Erich Fromm*

The universe is no longer a mere *It* to us, but a *Thou*, if we are religious.... 27 *William James*

Religion teaches that there is a tremendous power in the universe and that this power can dwell in personality. 28 *Norman Vincent Peale*

The distinctive feature of the higher religions ... is that the higher religions address themselves to human beings direct as individual persons, and not through the medium of the societies in which these persons are participants.... 29 *Arnold Toynbee*

[Religions] all seem to reject the total annihilation of whatever is understood as my "authentic" or "true" self. 30 *Eugene Fontinell*

I conceive the essential task of religion to be to develop the *consciences*, the *ideals*, and the *aspirations* of mankind. 31 *Robert A. Millikan*

[R]eligion, expressed generally, is consciousness of the infinite; thus it is and can be nothing else than the consciousness which man has of his own, not finite and limited, but infinite nature. 32 *Ludwig Feuerbach*

The problem of religion is to link finitude with infinitude. 33 *Alfred N. Whitehead*

Every known religion tends to *sublimate* man, and culminates in condemning his "finite" life. 34 *Denis de Rougemont*

The basic religious idea in all patriarchal religions *is the negation of the sexual needs.* 35 *Wilhelm Reich*

One of the attractions of religion is doubtless its power to reduce guilt.... 36 *Derek Wright*

[N]o religion is free from the accusation that it has sounded the war trumpet.... Religion has been a convenient weapon for a variety of causes. In its organizational and institutional manifestations it serves commonly as a holy medal to ward off twinges of conscience. 37 *Donald A. Wells*

It would seem ... that the three human impulses embodied in religion are fear, conceit, and hatred. The purpose of religion, one may say, is to give an air of respectability to these passions provided they run in certain channels. 38 *Bertrand Russell*

Men never do evil so completely and cheerfully as when they do it from religious conviction. 39 *Blaise Pascal*

Religion is a great force—the only real motive force in the world; but what you fellows don't understand is that you must get at a man through his own religion and not through yours. 40 *George Bernard Shaw*

[T]he one form of altruism that religions seldom display is tolerance of other religions. 41 *E. O. Wilson*

The baseness so commonly charged to religion's account are ... not chargeable at all to religion proper, but rather to religion's wicked practical partner, the spirit of corporate dominion. And the bigotries are ... chargeable to religion's wicked intellectual partner, the spirit of dogmatic dominion.... 42 *William James*

Intellectually, religious emotions are not *creative* but *conservative.* They attach themselves readily to the current view of the world and consecrate it. 43 *John Dewey*

Religion replaces doubt with certainty. 44 *D. W. Winnicott*

[E]mpirical results show that religious people are on the average less humane, more bigoted, more anxious.... [T]here exists simultaneously, within the organized religions of the West, psychologically conflicting forces for good *and* evil—teaching brotherhood with the right hand and bigotry with the left, facilitating mental health in some and mental conflict [in others].... 45 *Milton Rokeach*

We have just enough religion to make us hate, but not enough to make us love one another. 46 *Jonathan Swift*

Religion, pure source of comfort in this vale of tears! how has thy clear stream been muddied by the dabblers, who have presumptuously endeavoured to confine in one narrow channel the living waters that ever flow towards God—the sublime ocean of existence! 47 *Mary Wollstonecraft*

[Religion's] extreme potency is simply a measure of the strength of our fundamental biological tendency, inherited directly from our monkey and ape ancestors, to submit ourselves to an all-powerful, dominant member of the group. Because of this, religion has proved immensely valuable as a device for aiding social cohesion, and it is doubtful whether our species could have progressed far without it.... 48 *Desmond Morris*

The derivation of a need for religion from the child's feeling of helplessness and the longing it evokes for a father seems to me incontrovertible, especially since this feeling ... is kept alive perpetually by the fear of what the superior power of fate will bring. 49 *Sigmund Freud*

[T]he principle of performing all duties as divine commands, is religion. 50 *Immanuel Kant*

[T]he character of the love of God depends on the respective weight of the maternal and paternal aspects of religion. The paternal aspect makes us love God like a father; I assume he is just and strict, that he punishes and rewards.... In the maternal aspect of religion, I love God as an all-embracing mother. I have faith in her love, that no matter whether I am poor and powerless, no matter whether I have sinned, she will love me.... [In Western religion] the love of God is essentially the same as the belief in God.... The love of God is essentially a thought experience. In the Eastern religions and in mysticism, the love of God is an intense feeling experience of oneness.... 51 *Erich Fromm*

The [child's] experience of helplessness ... is preceded by the "oceanic" contentment of the womb, which we spend the rest of our lives trying to recapture. Religion, like art at its best, seeks precisely to restore the original sense of union with the world. 52 *Christopher Lasch*

[R]eligion maintains the basic love relation of the individual with some embracing principle.... 53 *Gordon W. Allport*

The essence of religion is the personal experience of a transcendent spiritual reality and the personal quest for harmony with this experienced reality. 54 *Arnold Toynbee*

Religion is an ultimate craving to infuse into the insistent particularity of emotion that non-temporal generality which primarily belongs to conceptual thought.... [I]t is directed to the end of stretching individual interest beyond its self-defeating particularity. 55 *Alfred N. Whitehead*

The developed religious sentiment is ... a comprehensive attitude whose function is to relate the individual meaningfully to the whole of Being. 56 *Gordon W. Allport*

You cannot understand the history of religion, without appreciating the mystical definition of Being. 57 *Josiah Royce*

[R]eligion solves the problem of death.... The two ontological motives are both met: the need to surrender oneself in full to the rest of nature, [and] to become a part of it by laying down one's whole existence to some higher meaning.... [I]t gives hope, because it holds open the dimension of the unknown and the unknowable. 58 *Ernest Becker*

The truth is, men have lost their belief in the Invisible, and believe, and hope, and work only in the Visible; or, to speak it in other words: This is not a Religious Age. 59 *Thomas Carlyle*

Religion

The most beautiful thing we can experience is the mysterious.… He to whom this emotion is a stranger, who can no longer pause to wonder and stand rapt in awe, is as good as dead: his eyes are closed.… In this sense, and in this sense only, I belong in the ranks of devoutly religious men. 60 *Albert Einstein*

One could define religious experience as that kind of experience which is accorded the highest value, no matter what its contents may be. 61

Carl Jung

Religion … is the opium of the people. 62

Karl Marx

The religions of mankind must be classified among the mass-delusions.… 63

Sigmund Freud

[S]omething about the [human brain] … inclines it to yield to a belief in a greater order than that perceived around it.… [R]eligious beliefs … all proposed a unified, orderly universe, governed by one superordinate, logical force.… [Similarly the] "temporal lobe syndrome" … causes a deepening of religious conviction. 64 *Michael Gazzaniga*

Even those who do not regret the disappearance of religious illusions from the civilized world of today will admit that so long as they were in force they offered those who were bound by them the most powerful protection against the danger of neurosis. 65

Sigmund Freud

Psychoanalysis is a technique to cure suffering individuals of … unreal terrors.… [T]he patient released from these finds himself able to participate with comparative satisfaction in the more realistic fears.… [T]he aim of the religious teaching is not to cure the individual back again to the general delusion, but to detach him from delusion altogether; and this not by readjusting the desire (*eros*) and hostility (*thanatos*) … but by *extinguishing* the impulses to the root.… 66 *Joseph Campbell*

It is essential to the understanding of the function of religion that it presents jointly and in fusion two analytically discernable alternatives: either a therapeutic control of everyday life or a therapeutic respite from that control. 67

Philip Rieff

The rate of return on hope invested in religion is … much higher than on hope invested in, say, rational work-a-day pursuits. Hence, those with small capitals of hope may do best by investing their "savings" in religion.… [I]nvesting hope in religious faith is perhaps one of the best psychological investments a person can make. 68 *Thomas Szasz*

The wise person devotes his life exclusively to the religious search—for therein is found the only ecstasy, the only meaning. 69

Timothy Leary

A little philosophy inclineth man's mind to atheism, but depth in philosophy bringeth men's minds about to religion. 70

Francis Bacon

Among all my patients in the second half of life—that is to say, over thirty-five—there has not been one whose problem in the last resort was not that of finding a religious outlook on life.… 71 *Carl Jung*

The folk religions are dead. They can no longer satisfy the wants of men. 72

William Graham Sumner

Any religion that professes to be concerned about the souls of men and is not concerned about the slums that damn them, the economic conditions that strangle them and the social conditions that cripple them is a spiritually moribund religion awaiting burial. 73

Martin Luther King Jr.

It may be that religion is dead, and if it is, we had better know it and set ourselves to try to discover other sources of moral strength before it is too late. 74 *Pearl S. Buck*

Religion is the reaction of human nature to its search for God. The presentation of God under the aspect of power awakens every modern instinct of critical reaction. This is fatal; for religion collapses unless its main positions command immediacy of assent. In this respect

the old phraseology is at variance with the psychology of modern civilisations. This change in psychology is largely due to science.... 75
Alfred N. Whitehead

Religion will not regain its old power until it can face change in the same spirit as does science. Its principle must be eternal, but the expression of those principles requires continual development. 76 *Alfred N. Whitehead*

[I]t can, in a sense, be said that religion consists in a *humanization of natural laws.* 77
Claude Lévi-Strauss

By and large, the naturalistic religions hold out for man no greater hope than a philosophical acceptance of the inevitable, a noble but sorrowful resignation to the truth that nature is beyond good and evil, and that death is the necessary counterpart of life, as pain of pleasure. But this sacrifices the most human thing about man—his eternal, child-like hope that somehow, someday, the deepest yearnings of his heart will come true. 78 *Alan Watts*

Religion must find a form in which the dignity of men cannot be destroyed by discoveries about Nature whose creatures men are. 79
Sidney Hook

In a world where events and ideas are analyzed to the point of lifelessness, where complexity grows by quantum leaps, where the information din is so high we must shriek to be heard above it, we are hungry for structure.... The revival of religion in America will continue, I think, for as long as we remain in a transitional era because of the need for structure during times of great change. 80 *John Naisbitt*

A "profane" universe ... is one dominated by the visual sense. The clock and the alphabet, by hacking the universe into visual segments, ended the music of interrelation. The visual desacralizes the universe and produces the "nonreligious man of modern societies." 81
Marshall McLuhan

[M]odern nonreligious man assumes a tragic existence.... After the first "fall," the religious sense descended to the level of the "divided consciousness"; now, after the second, it has fallen even further, into the depths of the unconscious; it has been "forgotten." 82
Mircea Eliade

The popular drift of psychological science aims at freeing the individual ... from the burden of opposition. On the other hand, religion, with its symbols of remembrance, may be that very submission to the past that will preserve in us some capacity for a radical criticism of the present. 83 *Philip Rieff*

What religion can restore is the continuity of generations, returning us to the existential predicaments which are the ground of humility and care for others. 84 *Daniel Bell*

By being religious we establish ourselves in possession of ultimate reality at the only points at which reality is given us to guard.... Religion, occupying herself with personal destinies and keeping us thus in contact with the only absolute realities which we know, must necessarily play an eternal part in human history. 85
William James

[E]very existential crisis once again puts in question both the reality of the world and man's presence in the world. This means that the existential crisis is, finally, "religious." ... For religion is the paradigmatic solution for every existential crisis. 86 *Mircea Eliade*

If religion perishes in the land, truth and justice will also. We have already strayed too far from the faith of our fathers. Let us return to it, for it is the only thing that can save us. 87
Alfred Lord Denning

RESPONSIBILITY

[T]HE STUDY OF MAN must start with an appreciation of man in the act of making responsible decisions. 1 *Michael Polanyi*

To be a man is, precisely, to be responsible. 2
Antoine de Saint-Exupéry

[O]ne's goal is to live each moment with freedom, honesty and responsibility. One is then

Responsibility

in each moment fulfilling so far as he can his own nature and his evolutionary task. 3
Rollo May

Liberty and responsibility are inseparable.... [The] denial of responsibility is ... commonly due to a fear of responsibility, a fear that necessarily becomes also a fear of freedom. It is doubtless because the opportunity to build one's own life also means an unceasing task, a discipline that man must impose upon himself. 4 *Friedrich von Hayek*

It is the extreme willingness of adults to go to almost any lengths on the command of authority that ... is the most common characteristic of socially organized evil in modern society.... The person who assumes full responsibility for the act has evaporated. 5 *Stanley Milgram*

The order, as such, even now I consider to have been wrong, but there is no question for me whether it was moral or immoral, because a leader who has to deal with such serious questions decides from his own responsibility.... I am not entitled to do so. 6
Otto Ohlendorf (Nazi executioner)

[B]eing in a position to know and nevertheless shunning knowledge creates direct responsibility for the consequences—from the very beginning. 7 *Albert Speer*

Individual acts of initiative and courage cannot, of course, bear the burden of preventing catastrophes like Vietnam. Institutional and political changes are essential.... [I]ndividuals within the Government [must] assume greater risks and a greater sense of responsibility than has been shown in the past.... [W]e as citizens [must] demand more of them and find a way to change these attitudes and ways of behaving. And that probably means first changing ourselves and our own sense of responsibility. 8
Daniel Ellsberg

[A]ccepting oneself is the condition for accepting responsibility.... 9 *Herbert Fingarette*

The attitude of self-acceptance is essential to the achieving of unobstructed self-awareness.... The more a person grows in self-awareness, the more he is prepared to acknowledge responsibility for his actions.... 10 *Nathaniel Branden*

Existentialism's first move is to make every man aware of what he is and to make the full responsibility of his existence rest on him. And when we say that a man is responsible for himself, we do not only mean that he is responsible for his own individuality, but that he is responsible for all men. 11
Jean-Paul Sartre

[M]an being condemned to be free carries the weight of the whole world on his shoulders; he is responsible for the world and for himself as a way of being.... I am responsible for everything, in fact, except for my own responsibility, for I am the foundation of my being. 12
Jean-Paul Sartre

From the fact that human beings do not ultimately shape their own character ... it *follows* that they are never morally responsible. 13
Paul Edwards

Blaming others, or outside conditions for one's own misbehavior may be the child's privilege; if an adult denies responsibility for his actions, it is another step toward personal disintegration. 14 *Bruno Bettelheim*

Men grow to their full stature only in the environment of responsibility. 15 *Harold Laski*

For men, moral problems arise from competing rights, moral development requires the increased capacity for fairness, and the resolution of moral problems requires absolute judgments arrived at through the formal, abstract thinking necessary for taking the role of the generalized other.... In contrast, women's moral problems arise from conflicting responsibilities to particular dependent others [and] moral development requires the increased capacity for understanding and care.... Is justice [based in rights] sufficient to maximize social welfare? 16 *Sandra Harding*

In [the woman's] conception, the moral problem is seen to arise from conflicting responsibilities rather than from competing rights.... [T]he morality of rights differs from the morality of responsibility in its emphasis on separation rather than attachment, in its consideration of the individual rather than the relation as primary. 17 *Carol Gilligan*

To abdicate one's own moral understanding, to tolerate crimes against humanity, to leave everything to someone else, the father-ruler-king-computer, is the only irresponsibility. 18 *Germaine Greer*

[T]he power elite of America has no ideology and feels the need of none.... [I]ts rule is naked of ideas, its manipulation without attempted justification.... [It] is not composed of representative men whose conduct and character constitute models for American imitation and aspiration.... [T]heir high position is not a result of moral virtue ... connected with meritorious ability.... Commanders of power unequalled in human history, they have succeeded within the American system of organized irresponsibility. 19 *C. Wright Mills*

As the twenty-first century approaches ... the peoples of the earth seem to be discovering that their lives are ever more affected by forces which are, in the full meaning of the word, irresponsible. 20 *Paul Kennedy*

The myth of technological and political and social inevitability is a powerful tranquilizer of the conscience. Its service is to remove responsibility from the shoulders of everyone who truly believes in it. 21 *Joseph Weizenbaum*

Responsibility, in a word, is gone. 22 *Ernest Becker*

From the point of view of profane existence, man feels no responsibility except to himself.... 23 *Mircea Eliade*

Consciousness II represents the values of an organizational society.... A prime characteristic of the Consciousness II person is his disclaimer of personal responsibility for what he or his organization does.... He pictures himself as a person without absolute or transcendental values ... [for] he must accept the premises of society. 24 *Charles A. Reich*

[T]o make a decision presupposes the willingness and capacity to assume responsibility for it. This would include the risk of making a wrong decision and the willingness to bear the consequences without blaming others for them. It ... presupposes more inner strength and independence than most people apparently have nowadays. 25 *Karen Horney*

[R]esponsibility must be the principle which informs and organizes the post-capitalist society.... Organizations have to take "social responsibility." There is no one else around in the society ... to take care of society itself. 26 *Peter F. Drucker*

In the view of the theologians, contemporary developments in molecular biology raise issues of responsibility rather than being matters to be prohibited because they usurp powers that human beings should not possess. The Biblical religions teach that human beings are, in some sense, co-creators with the Supreme Creator. Thus ... these major religious faiths respect and encourage the enhancement of knowledge about nature, as well as responsible use of that knowledge. 27 *Theological "General Secretaries"*

As electrically contracted, the globe is no more than a village. Electric speed in bringing all social and political functions together in a sudden implosion has heightened human awareness of responsibility to an intense degree. 28 *Marshall McLuhan*

While compulsion by force or by neurotic obsession excludes responsibility, compulsion by universal intent establishes responsibility.... The freedom of the subjective person to do as he pleases is overruled by the freedom of the responsible person to act as he must. 29 *Michael Polanyi*

We are still incapable of understanding that the only genuine backbone of our actions—if they are to be moral—is responsibility. Responsibility to something higher than my family, my country, my firm, my success. 30 *Václav Havel*

The end of the belief in salvation by society surely marks an inward turning.... It may even lead—at least we can so hope—to a return to individual responsibility. 31 *Peter F. Drucker*

SACRED

[T]HE SACRED ... [is] a connecting link between the seen and the unseen, the temporal and the eternal, [and] was one of the decisive steps in the transformation of man. 1 *Lewis Mumford*

During the past two centuries mankind has undergone the most traumatic social change it has experienced since the beginnings of settled culture in the Neolithic age. I refer to the decline of the local community, the dislocation of kinship, and the erosion of the sacred in human affairs. 2 *Robert Nisbet*

[T]he *completely* profane world, the wholly desacralized cosmos, is a recent discovery in the history of the human spirit. 3 *Mircea Eliade*

[F]or the archaic mentality ... the outstanding reality is the sacred; for only the sacred *is* in an absolute fashion, acts effectively, creates things and makes them endure. The innumerable acts of consecration ... reveal the primitive's obsession with the real, his thirst for being. 4
Mircea Eliade

Even by savages certain objects are held sacred, for whose sake they are ready to suffer rather than submit. But what is sacred for the man of the modern world?... Life has no significance for him except as it concerns his personal welfare.... 5 *Leo Tolstoy*

Modern nonreligious man ... regards himself solely as the subject and agent of history, and he refuses all appeal to transcendence. In other words, he ... *makes himself*, and he only makes himself completely in proportion as he desacralizes himself and the world. The sacred is the prime obstacle to his freedom.... He will not be totally free until he has killed the last god. 6 *Mircea Eliade*

The modern therapeutic idea is to empty those meanings that link the individual to dying worlds by assents of faith for which his analytic reason tells him he is not truly responsible. In this way, by acts of interpretation, the sacred becomes symptom. Sacred images are, then, the visible form not of grace but of sickness. The sacralist yields to the analyst as the therapeutic functionary of modern culture. 7
Philip Rieff

Capitalist rationality does not do away with sub- or super-rational impulses. It merely makes them get out of hand by removing the restraint of sacred or semi-sacred tradition. 8
Joseph Schumpeter

The sacred is what man decides unconsciously to respect.... To a great extent, mystery is desired by men.... [T]echnique desacralizes because it demonstrates ... that mystery does not exist. Science brings to the light of day everything man has believed sacred. Technique takes possession of it and enslaves it.... The individual who lives in the technical milieu knows ... that there is nothing spiritual anywhere. But man cannot live without the sacred. 9
Jacques Ellul

The sacred [is] the central phenomenon of the self.... The sacred turns out to be a need, like food or sex; and in a well-ordered community, it must get its satisfactions like the other needs. 10 *Allan Bloom*

Each man is born with the sacred somewhere within him.... Shame is the guardian of [the] sacred.... A man who moves too far away from the sacred becomes shameless. 11 *John Carroll*

To live the life of a human being is to entertain sacredness and participate in sacredness, both of which, however, are given to us only potentially. One has to strive and labor, sometimes in great pain, to actualize this potential. 12
Henryk Skolimowski

[M]an's passions that unify his energy in search of their goal belong to the realm of the ... sacred. 13 *Erich Fromm*

Transcendence refers to the very highest and most inclusive or holistic levels of human consciousness.... [The] sacredness of every person and even of every living thing, even of nonliving things that are beautiful ... is so easily and directly perceived in its reality by every transcender that he can hardly forget it for a moment. 14 *Abraham Maslow*

To understand the transcendent, man requires a sense of the sacred. To remake nature, man can invade the profane. But if there is no separation of realms, if the sacred is destroyed, then we are left with the shambles of appetite and self-interest and the destruction of the moral circle which engirds mankind. Can we—must we not—reestablish that which is sacred and that which is profane? 15 *Daniel Bell*

Only ... in the context of a true culture in which the core is a deep and wide sense of the *sacred* are we likely to regain the vital conditions of progress itself and of faith in progress.... 16
Robert Nisbet

Seeing holiness only in others—or only in ourselves—is the problem. Seeing the sacred in ourselves and in all living things is the solution. 17 *Gloria Steinem*

To the man who is truly ethical all life is sacred.... 18 *Albert Schweitzer*

[W]hen you dispute the life of things ... you wind up before the nothing; when you consecrate life you encounter the living god. 19
Martin Buber

Man needs ... the "sacred." 20 *Erich Fromm*

Sadism / Masochism

Man, aware of his separateness, needs to find new ties with his fellowman; his very sanity depends on it.... He can love others, which requires the presence of independence and productiveness, or if his sense of freedom is not developed, he can relate to others symbiotically.... In this symbiotic relationship he strives either to control others (sadism), or to be controlled by them (masochism). 1 *Erich Fromm*

To be a human being means to possess a feeling of inferiority which constantly presses towards its own conquest.... The greater the feeling of inferiority ... the more powerful is the urge for conquest.... 2 *Alfred Adler*

All the different forms of sadism ... go back to one essential impulse ... [:] to have complete mastery over another person.... [T]he aim of sadism is to transform a man into a thing. 3
Erich Fromm

Where domination and exploitation ... are not openly approved in a culture, the positions of the sadist and masochist are disguised behind the system of expectations normally imposed by authority. Thus, the sadist always claims to be the one who complies with those expectations and deserves his reward, while accusing the masochist of being a rebel who deserves to be punished.... Generally, the sadist is a victimizer who calls himself a victim, and the masochist is a victim who calls himself a victimizer. 4 *M. Gear et al.*

Facing "hard" facts, making "hard" decisions ... are a masochistic pleasure and a sadistic claim to superiority; one serves order, the other serves power. 5 *Graham Little*

Masochistic dependency is conceived as love or loyalty.... A person can be entirely dominated by his sadistic strivings and consciously believe that he is motivated only by his sense of duty.... [One type of sadism] is to make others dependent on oneself and to have absolute and unrestricted power over them, so as to make of them nothing but instruments.... Sadistic tendencies for obvious reasons are usually less conscious and more rationalized than ... masochistic trends. 6 *Erich Fromm*

[The sadist] is pathologically independent.... He tends to overqualify, to idealize himself as being "good," "clever" or "sensible." ... He disguises himself as the superego of others.... He punishes anybody who tries to be independent of him.... The sadistic agent fears the loss of his pleasure while the masochist [fears] that he won't survive. The sadist ... fears being overwhelmed by frustration, while the masochist ... fears complete loneliness. 7 *M. Gear et al.*

Masochism is the attempt ... to look for security by attaching oneself to another person. 8
Erich Fromm

Our modern society, culminating in the present alienation of labor, evolved first the *receiving* character, with a masochistic loyalty to outside directives. (This was evidenced in Calvinism,

Sadism / Masochism

Lutheranism and early Puritanism). Later came the *exploiting* character with sadistic authority over others; this also regards value as external but must achieve it and subordinate others in the process. 9 *Charles Hampden-Turner*

The [sadomasochistic] type has been jokingly described as the "bicyclist's character," because such individuals bow from the waist to those above them and kick with their feet at those below them. 10 *Erich Fromm*

The Nazi is either at your knees or at your throat. 11 *Winston Churchill*

Domination can only be maintained when it is based on concealed sadomasochistic foundations. In such cases, one person's pleasure in issuing orders is combined with another's pleasure in discharching them and enjoyment of obedience, order, and submission.... In the absence of such a sadomasochistic social structure, it would be difficult to conduct wars. 12
Margarete Mitscherlich

Sadomasochism is the style and basic content of patriarchal structures.... 13 *Mary Daly*

[T]he catalogue of human cruelty is so long and the practice of torture so ubiquitous that it is impossible to believe that sadism is confined to a few abnormals.... The sombre fact is that we are the cruellest and most ruthless species that has ever walked the earth.... 14 *Anthony Storr*

Woman, through the ages (at any rate, the patriarchal ones), has lent herself to a variety of roles conducive to an exploitation of masochistic potentials: she has let herself be confined and immobilized, enslaved and infantilized, prostituted and exploited.... That she must protect means that she must rely on protection—and she may demand overprotection. 15
Erik Erikson

A painful bodily injury—the breaking of the hymen and the forcible stretching and enlargement of the vagina by the penis—are the prelude to woman's first complete sexual enjoyment. This ... connection endows the sexual experience with a masochistic character. The whole psychology of woman suggests that this juncture between pleasure and pain was organized in the course of phylogenesis and that it created some measure of constitutional readiness in every woman, something we might call a masochistic reflex mechanism. 16 *Helene Deutsch*

A misogynist society has created a myriad of situations that make women unhappy. And then that same society uses the myth of women's masochism to blame the women themselves for their misery. These tendencies are the defining characteristics of scapegoating. 17
Paula Caplan

The facts appear to be that in our cultural areas, masochistic phenomena are more frequent in women than in men.... [In] our culture it is hard to see how any women can escape becoming masochistic to some degree. 18 *Karen Horney*

[M]asochism is a perpetual effort to *annihilate* the subject's subjectivity by causing it to be assimilated by the Other; this effort is accompanied by the exhausting and delicious consciousness of failure so that finally it is the failure itself which the subject ultimately seeks as his principal goal. 19 *Jean-Paul Sartre*

[M]asochism is *the* basic neurosis. 20
Edmund Bergler

[A] minor degree of the masochistic tendency may be said to be fairly common.... It very frequently affects persons of a sensitive, refined, and artistic temperament. It may even be said that this tendency is in the line of civilization. 21
Havelock Ellis

Masochism, like sadism, is the assumption of guilt. I am guilty due to the very fact that I am an object; I am guilty toward myself since I consent to my absolute alienation. 22
Jean-Paul Sartre

The underlying theme of sadism is the attempt to break through to the other. The desire to be discovered underlies its counterpart, namely, masochism. 23 *Jessica Benjamin*

[S]adism is a refusal to be incarnated.... But as the sadist neither can nor will realize the Other's incarnation by means of his own incarnation ...

he seeks to utilize the Other's body as a tool to make the Other realize an incarnated existence. Sadism is an effort to incarnate the Other through violence.... [T]he sadist refuses his own flesh at the same time that he uses instruments to reveal by force the Other's flesh to him.... Sadism is the failure of desire, and desire is the failure of sadism. 24 *Jean-Paul Sartre*

The sadistic person is ... suffering from an impotence of the heart. 25 *Erich Fromm*

Real sadism, the desire to inflict pain, only occurs after the child has experienced masochism—only after it has internalized, turned against itself, the original sadism. 26
Jessica Benjamin

Only when the child internalizes his aggression and moves into the masochistic position can he imagine the pain that might come to the other. Then "real" sadism, the desire to hurt and reduce the other as one has been hurt oneself, comes into being. In short, aggression, internalized as masochism, reappears as sadism. 27 *Jessica Benjamin*

Sadism and masochism may be regarded as complementary emotional states; they cannot be regarded as opposed states.... "Sadism" and "masochism" are simply convenient clinical terms for classes of manifestations which quite commonly occur in the same person. 28
Havelock Ellis

In brief, sadomasochism seems to be a universal and basic way of dealing with destructiveness in order to avoid the disorganization of the psychic apparatus. 29 *M. Gear et al.*

These sadomasochistic bonds, which go back to the equivocal and unpredictable nature of a parent, are stronger than a genuine love relationship; they are impossible to break, and signal permanent destruction of the self. 30
Alice Miller

We exist as self-aware beings only by virtue of (our awareness of) other conscious beings.... To be seen by another is to experience oneself as an object ... [which] poses the danger that one may be used.... One [response] is to turn back upon the other, so as to make of him an object, and in an attempt to eradicate his freedom. (This is the attitude of sadism). The other is to identify with the other's view of oneself as object, in an attempt to eradicate one's own freedom. (This is masochism). Both attitudes are futile.... 31 *Mary Anne Warren*

The truly great is he who would master no one, and who would be mastered by none. 32
Kahlil Gibran

Science

The eventual goal of science is to provide a single theory that describes the whole universe. 1
Stephen Hawking

All science is cosmology.... 2 *Karl Popper*

[T]he Scientific Revolution ... was the unremitting search for hidden divinity.... Without this religious motivation, science would have been mere technology, limping along on economic necessity. 3 *Julian Jaynes*

There is no science that is without unconscious presuppositions.... There is no Natural science without a precedent Religion. 4
Oswald Spengler

[S]cience can only be created by those who are thoroughly imbued with the aspiration toward truth and understanding. This source of feeling, however, springs from the sphere of religion. To this there also belongs the faith in the possibility that the regulations valid for the world of existence are rational, that is, comprehensible to reason.... The situation may be expressed by the image: science without religion is lame, religion without science is blind. 5
Albert Einstein

[I]n this materialistic age of ours the serious scientific workers are the only profoundly religious people. 6 *Albert Einstein*

Scientism is ... a special form of idealism, for it puts one type of human understanding in charge of the universe and what can be said about it. At its most myopic it assumes that everything there is must be understandable by

Science

the employment of scientific theories.... 7
Thomas Nagel

Science might almost be defined as the process of substituting unimportant questions which can be answered for important questions which cannot. 8 *Kenneth Boulding*

Science will be able to satisfy ... our increasing logical or intellectual needs, our desire to know and understand the truth; but science does not satisfy the needs of our heart and our will, and far from satisfying our hunger for immortality it contradicts it. 9 *Miguel de Unamuno*

Science is the infidel to all gods in behalf of none. 10 *Theodore Roszak*

[S]cience ... takes as its task precisely the disenchantment of the world. 11
Christopher Lasch

[S]cience and everything scientific can be and often is used as a tool in the service of a ... de-emotionalized, desacralized and desanctified *Weltanschauung*. 12 *Abraham Maslow*

Because of the prestige of science as a source of power, and because of the general neglect of philosophy, the popular *Weltanschauung* of our times contains a large element of what may be called "nothing-but" thinking. Human beings ... are nothing but bodies, animals, even machines.... [V]alues are nothing but illusions.... Spirituality is nothing but ... and so on. 13 *Aldous Huxley*

It seemed that science debased everything it touched. 14 *Ilya Prigogine*

As modern civilization ruthlessly eliminates Eros from culture, modern science ruthlessly demythologizes our view of the world and of ourselves. In getting rid of our old loves, modern science serves both the reality-principle and the death instinct. 15 *Norman O. Brown*

Science has shaken our blind faith in virtually every traditional value and "infallible authority." ... An attitude of pessimism and doubt seems to have settled upon mankind. 16 *Hans Selye*

Science without conscience is but the ruin of the soul. 17 *François Rabelais*

[T]his age ... is a period characterized by supreme and near miraculous achievements in science and technology combined with a profound sense of alienation, frustration, and despair.... [A]s our knowledge of the cosmos has increased, our knowledge of ourselves has not. 18 *Eugene Fontinell*

[I]nner integrity is obviously essential, if you are to do a whole job of thinking about anything.... [But] modern science has bashed inner integrity to bits and gone to work on the half-problem of objective integrity. 19
Philip Wylie

I believe in science: but up to now has science ever troubled to look at the world other than from *without*? 20 *Pierre Teilhard de Chardin*

[The sciences] relate to knowledge of the external object ... so that nowadays the backwardness of psychic development in general and of self-knowledge in particular has become one of the most pressing contemporary problems.... The marvellous development of science and technics is counterbalanced by an appalling lack of wisdom and introspection. 21
Carl Jung

Science is one thing, wisdom is another. 22
Sir Arthur Eddington

Today our science and method strive not towards a point of view but to discover how not to have a point of view.... Such is now the only viable method under electric conditions of simultaneous information movement and total human interdependence. 23
Marshall McLuhan

[The] ideal of a science which is completely independent of man is an illusion. 24
Werner Heisenberg

Science has its meaning as the objective pursuit of a purpose which has been subjectively chosen by a person or persons.... Consequently ... [the] sciences must first and most deeply concern itself with the subjectively chosen purposes which [any] application of science is intended to implement. 25 *Carl Rogers*

Scientists have until recently got away with the pronouncement that their work was "value free," perhaps the most innocent (or serpentine) opinion ever perpetuated by associations of grown persons. 26 *Charles Hampden-Turner*

Science is based on human values and is itself a value system. 27 *Abraham Maslow*

Science is a system of beliefs to which we are committed. 28 *Michael Polanyi*

[A] new scientific truth does not triumph by convincing its opponents and making them see the light, but rather because its opponents eventually die, and a new generation grows up that is familiar with it. 29 *Max Planck*

[M]odern science *overpowered* its opponents, it did not *convince* them. Science took over by *force*, not by argument.... 30 *Paul Feyerabend*

[S]cience still reigns supreme. It reigns supreme because its practitioners are unable to understand, and unwilling to condone, different ideologies, because they use this power just as their ancestors used their power to force Christianity on the peoples they encountered.... The separation between state and church must therefore be complimented by the separation between state and science. 31

Paul Feyerabend

[S]cientists, being only human, cannot always admit their errors, even when confronted with strict proof.... The source of resistance is the assurance that the older paradigm will ultimately solve all its problems, that nature can be shoved into the box the paradigm provides.... That same assurance is what makes normal or puzzle-solving science possible. 32

Thomas Kuhn

Science, however, buys its success at a price; indeed at a high price. The price is a severe limitation of its field of inquiry.... Messages which will not conform to the subculture are condemned as illusion. 33 *Kenneth Boulding*

Things have taken a strange turn in recent years; almost the full circle from Galileo's famous struggle with the theological establishment. It is the scientific establishment that now forbids heresy. 34 *J. E. Lovelock*

I foresee the time when all who care for the freedom of the human spirit will have to rebel against a scientific tyranny. Nevertheless, if there is to be a tyranny, it is better that it should be scientific. 35 *Bertrand Russell*

The wrong view of science betrays itself in the craving to be right; for it is not his *possession* of knowledge, of irrefutable truth, that makes the man of science, but his persistent and recklessly critical *quest* for truth. 36

Karl Popper

Science has organized this nervousness [about error] into a regular *technique*, her so-called method of verification; and she has fallen so deeply in love with the method that one may even say she has ceased to care for truth by itself at all. 37 *William James*

[S]cience is a *way of perceiving* and making what we may call "sense" of our percepts. But perception operates only upon difference.... [S]cience, like all other methods of perception, is limited in its ability to collect the outward and visible signs of whatever may be truth.... Science *probes*; it does not prove. 38 *Gregory Bateson*

Our whole progress in scientific theory ... depends on the use of suspended judgments. It is to be noted that a suspended judgment is not a judgment of probability. It is a judgment of compatibility. 39 *Alfred N. Whitehead*

Science has made its way by releasing, not by suppressing, the elements of variation, of invention and innovation, of novel creation in individuals. 40 *John Dewey*

There are never more than a hundred people who deserve the term *scientist* in any age. The rest of them are just engineers who are simply playing out one little aspect of a metaphor, of a visionary experience, that someone had in the past. 41 *Timothy Leary*

Science

Every great advance in science has advanced from a new audacity of imagination. 42
John Dewey

Science is rooted in creative interpretation. 43
Stephen Jay Gould

[T]he knowledge of the relations between changes which enable us to connect things as antecedents and consequences *is* science. 44 *John Dewey*

Science is organized knowledge. 45
Herbert Spencer

[T]he advance of scientific knowledge may be measured by the progress made in resolving complex facts into simpler ones. 46
John Stuart Mill

Much of today's public anxiety about science is the apprehension that we may be overlooking the whole by an endless, obsessive preoccupation with the parts. 47 *Lewis Thomas*

Science today aims more and more at reducing all processes to purely mathematical relations where ... all that is generally called "understanding" ceases. 48 *Hans Vaihinger*

[T]here is, even in our epoch, a general faith in science. But inasmuch as science only becomes accessible through methodical culture, and since astonishment at the achievements of science does not imply participation in its significance, this faith is no more than superstition.... Almost every one is under the spell of this superstition, men of learning not excepted. 49 *Karl Jaspers*

In pursuit of truth, the scientist sanctified his own discipline and what was more dangerous placed it above any other obligations of morality. The consequences of this dedication has only begun to appear in our age. Scientific truth achieved the status of an absolute.... Now, if the history of the human race teaches any plain lessons, this is one of them: *Man cannot be trusted with absolutes.* 50 *Lewis Mumford*

Science is still the prophetic announcement of a description of the world seen from a divine or demonic point of view. It is the science of Newton, the new Moses to whom the truth of the world was unveiled; it is *revealed* science that seems alien to any social and historical context identifying it as the result of the activity of human society. 51 *Ilya Prigogine*

Humbug is humbug, even though it bear the scientific name, and the total expression of human experience, as I view it objectively, invincibly urges me beyond the narrow "scientific" bounds. 52 *William James*

If we reject the scientific method as the supreme authority in judgment of both fact and value, what can we substitute in its stead? Every alternative involves at some point an institutional authority which, historical evidence shows, lends itself to abuse, which proclaims itself to be above all interests and becomes the expression of a particular interest invested with the symbols of public authority. 53 *Sidney Hook*

Our predilection [is] for premature acceptance and assertion, our aversion to suspended judgment.... Science represents the safeguard of the race against these natural propensities and the evils which flow from them. 54 *John Dewey*

The function which science has to perform ... [is] emancipating an idea from the particular context ... [so that] the results of the experience of any individual are put at the disposal of all men. Thus ultimately and philosophically science is the organ of general social progress. 55 *John Dewey*

America is a civilization founded on science and rooted in its achievements. Without science the whole ribbed frame of American technology, and with it American power, would have been impossible. 56 *Max Lerner*

Science is the last step in man's mental development and it may be regarded as the highest and most characteristic attainment of human culture.... [It is] the last chapter in the history of mankind.... 57 *Ernst Cassirer*

What science has done has been to set us free. It has delivered us from our material poverty and opened a great area of choice where vision and will can operate.... 58 *Barbara Ward*

SCIENCE

Science aspires to increase the freedom of choice, but science ends, as it must, in a technique of power. 59 *Philip Rieff*

The scientist, like the technologist, is a toy in the hands of the will to power disguised as the thirst for knowledge.... 60 *Ilya Prigogine*

[T]he issue is not the conscious structure of science, but the unconscious premises of science; the trouble is in the unconscious strata of the scientific ego, in the scientific character structure. 61 *Norman O. Brown*

A science which tries to create a province outside morality wherein to reason or experiment is self-confuted, because such regions exist only in the vainest imaginings of man's ego. 62 *Philip Wylie*

Science ... brings us to the threshold of the ego and there leaves us to ourselves. Here it resigns us to the care of other hands. In the conduct of our own lives the causal principle is of little help.... 63 *Max Planck*

We are living now, not in the delicious intoxication induced by the early successes of science, but in a rather grisly morning after, when it has become apparent that what triumphant science has done hitherto is to improve the means for achieving unimproved or actually deteriorated ends. 64 *Aldous Huxley*

As science grew, minds shrank in width of comprehension. 65 *Alfred N. Whitehead*

Classical science, the mythical science of a simple, passive world, belongs to the past, killed not by philosophical criticism or empiricist resignation but by the internal development of science itself. 66 *Ilya Prigogine*

[F]rom the time of Einstein ... science no longer existed to serve human needs, but in its own right. We have no idea where we are going. 67 *Kenneth Clark*

[W]e should be on our guard not to overestimate science and scientific methods when it is a question of human problems. 68 *Albert Einstein*

Science must be humanized, which means among other things that it must not be permitted to go on a rampage. It must be an integral part of our culture and must remain a part of it subservient to the rest. 69 *George Sarton*

In regard to the aesthetic needs of civilised society the reactions of science have so far been unfortunate. Its materialistic basis has directed attention to *things* as opposed to *values*. 70 *Alfred N. Whitehead*

Like most psychologists, I knew that science could teach me nothing as to what virtue is. Science could speak about causal relations, about the relations of means to ends, but [not] ... about ends or values themselves. 71 *Lawrence Kohlberg*

[T]he rationality-is-logicality equation, which the very success of science has drugged us into adopting as virtually an axiom, has led us to deny the very existence of ... the collision of genuinely incommensurable human interests, hence the existence of human values themselves. 72 *Joseph Weizenbaum*

It is often said that science has destroyed our values and put nothing in their place. What has really happened of course is that science has shown in harsh relief the division between our values and our world.... [Science] is the acceptance of what works and the rejection of what does not.... Science will create values, I believe, and discover virtues, when it looks into man; when it explores what makes him man and not an animal. 73 *Jacob Bronowski*

[S]cience has humanized our values. Men have asked for freedom, justice and respect precisely as the scientific spirit has spread among them. The dilemma of today is ... the scientific spirit is more human than the machinery of governments. 74 *Jacob Bronowski*

Science is nothing else than conscience carried to its highest point of clarity.... That is why intelligence guided by science must take a larger part in the course of collective life. 75 *Émile Durkheim*

Is modern science hostile to our humanity?...

Science

Our capacity for fulfillment can come only through faith and feelings. But our capacity for survival must come from reason and knowledge. 76 *Heinz Pagels*

[A]ntiscience could wipe out mankind just as easily as could value-free, amoral, technological science. 77 *Abraham Maslow*

One of the only two articles that remain in my creed of life is that the future of our civilization depends upon the widening spread and deepening hold of the scientific habit of mind.... It represents the only method of thinking that has proved fruitful in any subject—that is what we mean when we call it scientific. 78 *John Dewey*

Science enhances the moral values of life, because it furthers a love of truth and reverence ... [and] because every advance in knowledge brings us face to face with the mystery of our own being. 79 *Max Planck*

[T]here can be no integrity, reason, or human dignity without a true scientific attitude.... Where science is lost man falls into the twilight of vaguely edifying sentiments, of fanatical decisions arrived at in self-willed blindness. Barriers are erected, man is led into new prisons. 80 *Karl Jaspers*

Has any thought been given to the number of things that must remain active in men's souls in order that they may still continue to be "men of science" in real truth? Is it seriously thought that as long as there are dollars there will be science? 81 *José Ortega y Gasset*

Men sometimes speak as though the progress of science must necessarily be a boon to mankind, but that, I fear, is one of the comfortable 19th century delusions which our more disillusioned age must discard. 82 *Bertrand Russell*

We must no longer cherish the illusion that the scientific world view is still our salvation.... 83 *Henryk Skolimowski*

Scientific progress may yet deliver us from many evils, but there are at least two evils that it cannot deliver us from: its own findings and our own destructive and self-destructive bent. 84 *Jonathan Schell*

Science enables us to realize our purposes, and if our purposes are evil, the result is disaster. If the world remains filled with malevolence and hate, the more scientific it becomes the more horrible it will be. 85 *Bertrand Russell*

Our scientific power has outrun our spiritual power. We have guided missiles and misguided men. 86 *Martin Luther King Jr.*

Science may be a boon if war can be abolished and democracy and cultural liberty preserved. If this cannot be done, science will precipitate evils greater than any that mankind has ever experienced. 87 *Bertrand Russell*

[W]ith our present psychology and political organization, every increase in scientific knowledge brings the destruction of civilization nearer. 88 *Bertrand Russell*

Scientists are priests of patriarchy, performing the last rites. 89 *Mary Daly*

[I]t is necessary to understand that science is far too important an activity to leave to the scientists.... 90 *Ashley Montagu*

I can think of nothing more objectionable than the idea of science for the scientists. 91 *Albert Einstein*

[S]cience can be just as potent for good as for evil. It is not science, however, which will determine how science is used. Science, by itself, cannot supply us with an ethic.... [A]mong ends that can be achieved our choice must be decided by other than purely scientific considerations. 92 *Bertrand Russell*

Science can tell us what exists; but to compare the *worths*, both of what exists and what does not exist, we must consult not science, but what Pascal calls our heart.... 93 *William James*

Once Einstein said that the problem of the Now worried him seriously. He explained that the experience of the Now means something special for man, something essentially different from the past and the future, but that this important difference does not and cannot occur within physics.... Einstein thought that these scientific descriptions cannot possibly satisfy our human needs; that there is something essential about the Now which is just outside of the realm of science. 94

Rudolf Carnap

I have been saying that modern science broke down the barriers that separated the heavens and the earth, and that it united and unified the universe. And that is true. But ... it did this by substituting for our world of quality and sense perception, the world in which we live, and love, and die, another world—the world of quantity, of reified geometry, a world in which, though there is a place for everything, there is no place for man. 95 *Alexander Koyré*

Science cannot produce ideas by which we could live. 96 *E. F. Schumacher*

The maps of science are no longer satisfying to us. They do not bind us together and make us whole. Instead, they fragment our experience and reduce the landscape to an object. They are maps of alienation. 97 *F. David Peat*

Science means abstraction, and abstraction is always an impoverishment of reality. 98

Ernst Cassirer

Science will remain an effective method for acquiring knowledge meaningful to man only if orthodox techniques can be supplemented by others which come closer to the human experience of reality.... Science can become fully integrated in the socio-cultural body only if it achieves a more meaningful relationship to the living experience of man. 99 *René Dubos*

Science contributes moral as well as material blessings to the world. Its great moral contribution is objectivity, or the scientific point of view. This means doubting everything except facts.... One of the facts hewn to by science is that every river needs more people, and all people need more inventions, and hence more science; the good life depends on the infinite extension of this chain of logic. That the good life on any river may likewise depend on the perception of its music, and the preservation of some music to perceive, is a form of doubt not yet entertained by science. 100

Aldo Leopold

The spirit of truth can dwell in science on condition that the motive prompting the savant is the love of the object which forms the stuff of his investigations. That object is the universe in which we live. What can we find to love about it, if it isn't its beauty? The true definition of science is this: the study of the beauty of the world. 101 *Simone Weil*

[A]s soon as science outgrows the analytic investigations which constitute its lower and preliminary stages, and passes on to synthesis—synthesis which naturally culminates in the realisation of some superior state of humanity—it is at once led to foresee and place its stakes on the *future* and on the *all*. And with that it out-distances itself and emerges in terms of *option* and *adoration*. 102

Pierre Teilhard de Chardin

Science ... presupposes that what is yielded by scientific work is important in the sense that it is "worth being known." In this, obviously, are contained all our problems.... Redemption from the rationalization and intellectualization of science is the fundamental presupposition of living in union with the divine. 103

Max Weber

[S]cience has no greater authority than any other form of life. Its aims are certainly not more important than are the aims that guide the lives in a religious community or in a tribe that is united by a myth.... It is, therefore, necessary to re-examine our attitude towards myth, religion, magic, witchcraft and towards all those ideas which rationalists would like to see forever removed from the surface of the earth.... 104 *Paul Feyerabend*

Science must begin with myths, and with the criticism of myths. 105 *Karl Popper*

There is [a] silly conflict of religion and science, in which science must triumph, not because what it says about religion is just, but because religion rests on a young and provisional form of thought, to which philosophy of nature—profoundly called "science," or "knowledge"—must succeed if thinking is to go on.... Some day when the vision is totally rationalized, the ideas exploited and exhausted, there will be another vision, a new mythology. 106 *Susanne Langer*

SELF

[T]HE DISTINCTION between self and not-self is the basis of all distinctions, including the distinction between life and death.... [It] remains the source of our existential uneasiness, as well as the source of our intellectual mastery of the world around us. 1 *Christopher Lasch*

[I]t is the self and the survival of its nuclear program that is the basic force in everyone's personality. 2 *Heinz Kohut*

[T]he self becomes the principal value around which life revolves. 3 *Percival M. Symonds*

If the unconscious can be recognized as a co-determining factor along with consciousness, and if we can live in such a way that conscious and unconscious demands are taken into account as far as possible, then the centre of gravity of the total personality shifts its position. It is no longer in the ego, which is merely the centre of consciousness, but in the hypothetical point between conscious and unconscious. This new centre might be called the Self. 4 *Carl Jung*

The question of the "who" of Dasein has been answered with the expression "Self." Dasein's Selfhood has been defined formally as a *way of existing*, and therefore not as an entity present-at-hand. 5 *Martin Heidegger*

[T]he self ... does not actually exist; it is only that which it is to become. 6 *Søren Kierkegaard*

Intellectually the self is no more than a psychological concept, a construct that serves to express the unknowable essence which we cannot grasp as such.... It might equally well be called the "God within us." ... [A]ll our highest and ultimate purposes seem to be striving towards it. 7 *Carl Jung*

Self-existence or selfhood is the condition in default of which the world as the reality of human activity, a reality permeated by an ideal, is no longer possible. 8 *Karl Jaspers*

The world in which the self exists is no less fiction than is the self: both are created from symbolic stuff. 9 *Ernest Becker*

Self and world determine each other; subject and object cannot exist, do not exist, in isolation from each other. 10 *Walter Weisskopf*

Self is that conscious thinking thing (whatever substance made up of, whether spiritual or material ...) which is sensible or conscious of pleasure and pain, capable of happiness or misery, and so is concerned for *itself*, as far as that consciousness extends. 11 *John Locke*

Patients who have had prefrontal lobotomies have been described as losing a "continuing sense of self"—the feeling that I am a particular individual with some control over my life.... 12 *Carl Sagan*

Our memories are almost the same thing as our "selves." 13 *James W. Kalat*

Selfhood is the supreme instrument of knowledge.... 14 *Karl Jaspers*

"Your self is your *mind*." ... 15 *Ayn Rand*

[The] lower self which man has in the physical world is the sum total of all the experiences which consist of the sense-perceptions we receive in the physical world.... The higher self, on the other hand, "inspires our destiny." Our experience of joy and sorrow are inspired by our higher self out of the spiritual world. 16 *Rudolf Steiner*

[O]ur higher self guides our life through joy and sorrow from one stage of destiny to the next from beyond the gate of birth. This higher self is like a higher being which shows us our way through life on earth. 17 *Karl König*

Having destroyed his higher self, a man dooms his lower self too. 18 *Russell Kirk*

The self, whether in the sector of its ambitions or in the sector of its ideals, does not seek pleasure through stimulation and tension-discharge; it strives for fulfillment through the idealization of its nuclear ambitions and ideals. Its fulfillment does not bring *pleasure*, as does the satisfaction of a drive, but triumph and the glow of *joy*. And its blocking does not evoke the signal of *anxiety* ... but the anticipation of *despair*. 19 *Heinz Kohut*

While the biologically based ego apparatus can be thought of as the *source* of mental activity, the image or concept of self refers to the *content* of mental activity, part of the individual's field of meaning.... It is not meaning which is derived from the self, but the self which is derived from meaning. 20 *Michael R. Jackson*

[T]he self is the principle and archetype of orientation and meaning.... The self is our life's goal, for it is the completest expression of that fateful combination we call individuality. 21 *Carl Jung*

Eventually the self indicates all the meanings and evaluations that a person has about himself and his relations to the world around him. 22 *Percival M. Symonds*

[M]y selfhood is a gift which I may continue to receive only under the conditions of intimacy and communication with other selves.... So it is that only when I aim at the good of another man can I begin to find my own self fulfilled. 23 *Lloyd J. Averill*

Enter into every man's Inner Self: and let every other man enter into thine. 24 *Marcus Aurelius*

[W]e are *intersubjective* Selves, what Hegel called "spirit," a sense of *we* which is not reducible to any aggregation of I's. This is what defines us, providing the structures with which we *mutually* constitute our Selves and give our lives their meanings, through that sense of indispensability which comes only in our intersubjective relationships with other people. 25 *Robert C. Solomon*

[T]he core of the Self is held in common between oneself and all others.... 26 *Alan Watts*

The self, as that which can be an object to itself, is essentially a social structure, and it arises in social experience.... The organization of the self is simply the organization, by the individual organism, of the set of attitudes toward its social environment—and toward itself from the standpoint of that environment.... So far as he is a self, [one] must be an organic part of the life of the community.... 27 *George H. Mead*

The self, cut off from participation in its world, is an empty shell, a mere possibility. 28 *Paul Tillich*

The self is a field within larger fields. When the self joins the Self, there is power. Brotherhood overtakes the individual.... This discovery transforms strangers into kindred, and we know a new, friendly universe. 29 *Marilyn Ferguson*

[T]he ego crystallizes out of an amorphous and undifferentiated matrix.... Coming to consciousness means a rupture in that continuity, the emergence of a divide between Self and Other ... and Self vs Other remains the issue that we shall have to negotiate for the rest of our lives. 30 *Morris Berman*

[T]he basic [political] distinction is that with ... the "left" concept, the self is construed as *universal*, embracing the whole of the material universe ... whereas, with ... the "right" concept, the self is construed as radically *exclusive*, in life-and-death *contest with* the rest of humanity and nature.... [The left] conceives of the self as *internally directed* by virtue of "human-heartedness." ... [The right] conceives of the self as *externally directed*. 31 *John McMurtry*

The more secure the central self ... the less one has to define one's self through separateness from others. 32 *Nancy Chodorow*

The less justified a man is in claiming excellence for his own self, the more ready is he to claim all excellence for his nation, his religion, his race or his holy cause. 33 *Eric Hoffer*

Self

The Self is an ideology that tells us not only who we are but also who we believe we ought to be. 34 *Robert C. Solomon*

Self ... is most profoundly revealed (if not discovered) in the context of moral decision. 35
George McCall

In the experience of the self it is no longer the opposites "God" and "man" that are reconciled ... but rather the opposites within the God-image itself. That is the meaning of divine service ... that light may emerge from the darkness, that the Creator may become conscious of His creation, and man conscious of himself. 36 *Carl Jung*

To have a self, it is necessary to be aware of oneself having a self.... Human selfhood thus means self-distance, self-detachment, self-separation, self-in-conflict-with-self, self-negating self. In a word, selfhood means alienation from self. 37 *Lloyd J. Averill*

Psychological man lives by the ideal of insight—practical, experimental insight leading to the mastery of his own personality. Psychological man has withdrawn into a world always at war, where the ego is an armed force capable of achieving armistice but not peace.... The West ... now chooses to move against its last enemy, the self, in an attempt to conquer it and assimilate it to the world as it is. 38 *Philip Rieff*

[W]ith Western man the value of the self sinks to zero. Hence the universal depreciation of the soul in the West. 39 *Carl Jung*

Modern society, in spite of all the emphasis it puts upon happiness, individuality, self-interest, has taught man ... the illusion that his actions benefit his self-interest, though he actually serves everything else *but* the interests of his real self. 40 *Erich Fromm*

[H]omogeneous repetition *a la Gutenberg* still leaves something to be desired in the way of self. How is one to reason with the person who feeds himself into a buzz-saw because the teeth are invisible? Such was the fate of the unified "self" in the age of print segmentation. 41
Marshall McLuhan

In contemporary society the Self dies a little bit at a time. 42 *Jules Henry*

We have to face the fact that striving for a whole self means going against—and thus helping to change—most of current culture. 43
Gloria Steinem

Consciousness III starts with self.... When self is recovered, the power of the Corporate State will be ended, as miraculously as a kiss breaks a witch's evil enchantment. 44 *Charles A. Reich*

The failure of modern culture lies not in ... the fact that people are too much concerned with their self-interest, but that they are not concerned enough with the interest of their real self; not in the fact that they are too selfish, but that they do not love themselves. 45 *Erich Fromm*

The new religion will be based on knowledge of self and acceptance of self. A prerequisite for loving others is a true love of self. 46 *A. S. Neill*

This above all: to thine own self be true.... 47
William Shakespeare

[T]he axial principle of modern culture is the expression and remaking of the "self" in order to achieve self-realization and self-fulfillment. 48
Daniel Bell

Self-realization is the ultimate fact of facts. 49
Alfred N. Whitehead

The living self has one purpose only: to come into its own fullness of being.... 50
D. H. Lawrence

The supreme value toward which consciousness at every instant surpasses itself by its very being is the absolute being of the self with its characteristics of identity, of purity, of permanence, etc., and as its own foundation. 51
Jean-Paul Sartre

[T]he greatest attainment of identity, autonomy, or self-hood is itself simultaneously a transcending of itself, a going beyond and above self-hood. The person can then become egoless. 52 *Abraham Maslow*

Spirit

for the ascent of mankind, for mankind's real welfare and real progress. 48 *Rudolf Steiner*

[T]he human being is a great mystery. Whence does he come? He springs from nature.... It is a response to her own deepest desire. For it was to the end of her own spiritualization that she brought man forth. 49 *Thomas Mann*

State

[W]e have to say that a state is a human community that (successfully) claims the *monopoly of the legitimate use of physical force* within a given territory. 1 *Max Weber*

The State is the product of society at a certain stage of its development. The State is tantamount to an acknowledgment that the given Society has become entangled in an insoluble contradiction with itself, that it has broken up into irreconcilable antagonisms, of which it is powerless to rid itself. And in order that these antagonisms, these classes with their opposing economic interests may not devour one another and Society ... some force ... becomes necessary.... [T]his force is the State. 2 *Friedrich Engels*

[T]he State is a special organization of force: it is an organization of violence for the suppression of some class. 3 *V. I. Lenin*

The concept of the State implies the concept of war, for the essence of the State is power. 4 *Heinrich von Treitschke*

The word *state* is identical with the word *war*. 5 *Peter Kropotkin*

From the beginning the state was nothing more, basically, than an institutionalization of the war-making power. 6 *Robert Nisbet*

Protestantism ... legitimated the state as a divine institution and hence violence as a means. Protestantism, especially, legitimated the authoritarian state. Luther relieved the individual of the ethical responsibility for war and transferred it to the authorities. To obey the authorities in matters other than those of faith could never constitute guilt. 7 *Max Weber*

A single person, I need hardly say, is something subordinate, and as such he must dedicate himself to the ethical whole. Hence if the state claims life, the individual must surrender it. 8 *G. W. F. Hegel*

[Carl von] Clausewitz was a man of his age; he stood on the threshold of an era when the nation state seemed to embody the answer to man's quest for immortality. Unlike the great mystical or cosmic relations (Christianity, Buddhism), which demand a dissolution of the self into a Godhead or the cosmos, state worship allows the *assertion* of the *self* ... dissolved into the state, but ... differentiated from other selves (the enemy).... Thus state worship offers an outlet for boundless love and for boundless hate, both passions elevated to sacred duties. 9 *Anatol Rapoport*

[T]here is no way of eliminating egoism without destroying the state. 10 *Carl Slevin*

Civilization, the rise of the state, kingship, the universal religions—all are fed by the same psychological dynamic: guilt and the need for redemption.... Man still gropes for transcendence.... The stake is identical—immortality power.... 11 *Ernest Becker*

[A]ll the worth which the human being possesses, all spiritual reality, he possesses only through the State.... The State is the Divine Idea as it exists on Earth. 12 *G. W. F. Hegel*

Where there is no religion, no state can exist. 13 *Nikolai Bukharin*

Not what we were yesterday, but what we are going to be tomorrow, joins us together in the State. 14 *José Ortega y Gasset*

In the youth of a state arms do flourish; in the middle age of a state, learning; and then both of them together for a time; in the declining age of a state, mechanical arts and merchandise. 15 *Francis Bacon*

State power can only guarantee law and order when the content of the state coincides with the philosophy dominant at that particular time.... 16 *Adolf Hitler*

Unity / Wholeness

The making of a unified and meaningful whole is necessary if one hopes to have a good life. 14
Irving Singer

I have come to know happy individuals ... who are happy only because they are whole. Even the lowliest, provided he is whole, can be happy and in his own way perfect. 15 *Goethe*

That which determines a man, that which makes him one man, one and not another, the man he and the man he is not, is a principle of unity.... And in a sense a man is so much the more a man the more unitary his action. 16
Miguel de Unamuno

[T]he earth shall surely be complete to him or her who shall be complete ... and broken to him who remains jagged and broken. 17
Walt Whitman

Hidden antisocials are not "whole persons" any more than are manifest antisocials, since each needs to find and to control the conflicting force in the external world outside the self. By contrast, the healthy person, who is capable of becoming depressed, is able to find the whole conflict within the self as well as being able to see the whole conflict outside the self, in external (shared) reality. When healthy persons come together, they each contribute a whole world, because each brings a whole person. 18
D. W. Winnicott

I use the term "individuation" to denote the process by which a person becomes ... a separate, indivisible unity or "whole." ... Individuation does not shut one out from the world, but gathers the world to oneself ... [for] the self comprises infinitely more than a mere ego. 19
Carl Jung

The longing for unity within ourselves is no mystical desire but is prompted by the practical necessity of having to function in life—an impossibility when one is continually driven in opposite directions—and by what in consequence amounts to a supreme terror of being split apart. 20 *Karen Horney*

[T]he wholeness of personal integration brings with it ... the acceptance of death ... [and] relief from fear of ... disintegration. 21
D. W. Winnicott

To remove our distress, to overcome our weakness, and thus successfully to wage our life-battle in Germany the necessary pre-condition is unity.... You must fuse your will with mine. 22
Adolf Hitler

[The] desire for inter-personal fusion is the most powerful striving in man. It is the most fundamental passion, it is the force which keeps the human race together.... The failure to achieve it means insanity or destruction—self-destruction or destruction of others.... The full answer lies in the achievement of inter-personal union, of fusion with another person, in love. 23
Erich Fromm

Only a development of thought achieved through the self-education of the whole man can prevent any body of thought whatsoever from becoming a poison; can prevent enlightenment from becoming an agent of death. 24
Karl Jaspers

The unrelated human being lacks wholeness, for he can achieve wholeness only through the soul, and the soul cannot exist without its other side, which is always found in a "You." 25
Carl Jung

[I]n the spontaneous realization of the self man unites himself anew with the world—with man, nature, and himself. Love is the foremost component of such spontaneity ... as spontaneous affirmation of others, as the union of the individual with others. 26 *Erich Fromm*

Looking back on my own experiences, they all converge towards a kind of insight to which I cannot help ascribing some metaphysical significance. The keynote of it is invariably a reconciliation. It is as if the opposites of the world, whose contradictoriness and conflict make all our difficulties and troubles, were melted into unity. 27 *William James*

Unfortunately, our Western mind ... has never yet devised a concept, nor even a name, for the *union of opposites through the middle path*, that most fundamental item of inward experience,

meant moral power, then woman is immeasurably man's superior.... If non-violence is the law of our being, the future is with women. 68
Mohandes Gandhi

Women have accomplished as much as they could accomplish under *exceedingly unfavorable* circumstances, and that entitles us to great expectations for the future. 69 *August Bebel*

Perhaps ... the reign of woman is approaching, when the enigma of her anthropological superiority will be deciphered. 70
Maria Montessori

~ WORK / LABOUR ~

MAN'S OUTSTANDING CHARACTERISTIC, his distinguishing mark, is not his metaphysical nature but his work. It is this work, it is the system of human activities, which defines and determines the circle of "humanity." 1
Ernst Cassirer

[The] fall into selfhood, Adam's fall, is a fall from eternity into time, and therefore the beginning of human history; it is also the moment when Adam ceased to play and started to work. 2 *Norman O. Brown*

After primal man had discovered that it lay in his own hands, literally, to improve his lot on earth by working ... man acquired the value for him of a fellow-worker, with whom it was useful to live together. 3 *Sigmund Freud*

In determining the principal cause of the progress of the division of labor, we have at the same time determined the essential factor of what is called civilization. 4
Émile Durkheim

When nature is left to herself, energy is transformed along the line of its natural "gradient." In this way natural phenomena are produced, but not "work."... It is culture that provides the machinery whereby the natural gradient is exploited for the performance of work. 5
Carl Jung

It is probable that the work a man does represents his most important function in society; but unless there is some sort of integral social background to his life, he cannot even assign a value to his work. 6 *Elton Mayo*

It is the means by which we nourish a sense of mastery and achievement in the world. It is the major activity through which we shape our ambitions and our talents and, thus, come to know ourselves. Work also takes us beyond the self. It is our link to society. 7 *Robert Howard*

Work is the social process of shaping and transforming the material and social worlds, creating people as social beings as they create value. It is that activity by which people become who they are. 8 *Catherine MacKinnon*

Man's desire to be continuously associated in work with his fellows is a strong, if not the strongest, human characteristic. 9 *Elton Mayo*

What nature demands is work: few working aristocracies, however tyrannical, have fallen; few functionless aristocracies have survived. 10
R. H. Tawney

[T]o deny a human enjoyment of work is to a person's behavioral needs as the denial of a vitamin is to his blood, as movement is to his muscles. 11 *Lionel Tiger & Robin Fox*

The importance of work is underscored by the data that demonstrates that morbidity and mortality rates for men skyrocket one year after mandatory retirement. 12 *Kenneth Solomon*

A man has not only the right to work.... What is fundamental is the recognition that to be his best self a man must work.... 13 *Harold Laski*

The necessity to work is a neurotic symptom. 14
C. B. Chisholm

[T]he main male sublimation of guilt in modern society appears as obsessional neurosis in the form of the need for carefully timed and programmed work. 15 *John Carroll*

Having a powerful superior whom we can both praise and blame is one way of satisfying a strong need for avoiding uncertainty.... For

Pages 69–75

6 *Male and Female*, 1949, chap. 1.
7 *The Mind of Primitive Man*, [1911] 1938, 159.
8 *Human Paleopsychology*, 1987, 112.
9 *The Triumph of the Therapeutic*, 1966, 4.
10 *An Essay on Man*, [1944] 1970, 252.
11 *Democracy and Education*, [1916] 1963, 123.
12 *On Becoming a Person*, 1961, 347–48.
13 *The Image*, 1956, 75–76.
14 *A Study of War*, [1942] 1964, 112.
15 *The Making of a Counter Culture*, 1969, 85.
16 *Eros and Civilization*, [1955] 1966, 83.
17 [1927] *Works*, vol. 21, 97.
18 *Collected Papers*, [1912] 1959, vol. 4, 216.
19 *The Dialectic of Sex*, 1970, 213.
20 *Sexual Personae*, 1990, 9, 12.
21 *The Origin and Function of Culture*, 1943, 93.
22 *The Birth and Death of Meaning*, 1962, 81.
23 *The Triumph of the Therapeutic*, 1966, 4.
24 "On Psychic Energy" [1928] in *Collected Works*, vol. 8, par. 111.
25 *The Cultural Contradictions of Capitalism*, 1976, 12.
26 *Escape from Evil*, 1975, 64.
27 *Life Against Death*, 1966, 101.
28 *Eros and Civilization*, [1955] 1966, 108.
29 *Civilization and Its Discontents*, 1930, 103.
30 "Why War?," open letter to Albert Einstein, 1932.
31 *The Minimal Self*, 1984, 195.
32 quoted in *The Second Sex*, S. de Beauvoir, 1964, xviii.
33 *The Selfish Gene*, 1976, 177, 203.
34 *On Aggression*, 1966, 260.
35 in *Current Anthropology*, 1963, 4:138, 147.
36 *The Population Bomb*, 1971, 13.
37 *The Cult of Information*, 1986, 88–91.
38 *Tragic Sense of Life*, [1912] 1954, 308.
39 *The Dragons of Eden*, 1977, 185.
40 *Escape from Freedom*, 1941, 98.
41 *The Origin and Function of Culture*, 1943, 81.
42 *The International Journal of Psycho-Analysis*, vol. 22, 1941, 3.
43 *The Triumph of the Therapeutic*, 1966, 67.
44 *The Cultural Contradictions of Capitalism*, 1976, 33.
45 *Psychological Reflections*, [1953] 1970, 149.
46 *Eros and Civilization*, [1955] 1966, 104.
47 *The Cultural Contradictions of Capitalism*, 1976, 95.
48 *The Decline of the West*, [1932] 1965, 28–30.
49 *Culture and Value*, [1947] 1980, 64.
50 *Man in the Modern Age*, [1931] 1951, 117.
51 *The Greening of America*, 1970, 178.
52 *Media Sexploitation*, 1976, 206.
53 *Eco-Philosophy*, 1981, 93.
54 *Culture Against Man*, 1965, 452.
55 *The Life of Reason*, 1954, 138.
56 *In Bluebird's Castle*, 1971, 53–56.
57 *The Revolt of the Masses*, 1932, 72.
58 *Icon and Image*, [1954] 1965, 138.
59 "Science and Culture," 1880.
60 *Edinburgh Review*, 1827, No. XCI.
61 *Patterns of Culture*, [1934] 1960, 219.
62 *The Closing of the American Mind*, 1987, 188.
63 *The Cultured Man*, 1958, 41, 67.
64 *Personal Knowledge*, 1962, 174.
65 *Education and the Social Order*, 1932, 82.

Death

1 Birmingham [Alabama] funeral sermon, Sept. 15, 1963.
2 "Death," 1933.
3 *The Decline of the West*, vol. 1, 1926, 166.
4 *The Denial of Death*, 1973, 70, 96.
5 *The Sickness Unto Death*, [1849] 1944, 24.
6 in *New Directions in Psycho-Analysis*, M. Klein ed., 1955, 312.
7 *Mind and Nature*, 1979, 141.
8 *The Decline of the West*, [1926] 1965, 89.
9 *On Death and Dying*, 1969, 268.
10 *The Ego and the Id*, [1927] 1950, 86.
11 in *Moral Values and the Superego Concept in Psychoanalysis*, C. Seymour, 1968, 20.
12 *The Ego and the Id*, [1927] 1950, 86.
13 *Will*, 1980, 354.
14 *The Rebel*, [1954] 1967, 47.
15 *Civilization and Its Discontents*, [1930] 1961, 68.
16 *Life Against Death*, 1959, x.
17 *Culture Against Man*, 1965, 475.
18 *Self, God, and Immortality*, 1986, 222.
19 *African Genesis*, [1961] 1967, 246–47.
20 *The Fate of the Earth*, 1982, 113.
21 court statement, Aug., 1970.
22 *Holy Bible*, Romans 6:23.
23 *The Courage to Be*, 1952, 170.
24 *The Sacred and the Profane*, 1959, 113.
25 Birmingham [Alabama] funeral sermon, Sept. 15, 1963.
26 *Self-Deception and Morality*, 1986, 75.
27 *Love and Will*, 1969, 103.
28 letter quoted in *Love and Will*, 1969, 99.
29 in *Les Chênes qu'on abat*, A. Malraux, 1971, 68.
30 *Way to Wisdom*, 1951, 126.
31 *The Fable of the Bees*, [1724] 1970, 223.
32 *The Image*, 1956, 72.
33 *Works*, vol. 14, [1915] 1953, 289.
34 *God, Guilt, and Death*, 1984, 98.
35 *The Broken Connection*, 1979, 91–92.
36 *How Does Analysis Cure?*, 1984, 19.
37 *Eros and Civilization*, [1955] 1966, 236.
38 *Philosophical Aspects of Thanatology*, 1978, vol. 1, 84–6.
39 *Modern Man in Search of a Soul*, 1933, 129.
40 *Man for Himself*, 1947, 91.
41 *Death and Western Thought*, 1963, 27.
42 *The Rebel*, [1954] 1967, 101.
43 *Being and Nothingness*, [1943] 1957, 539.
44 Ibid., 1957, 544.
45 *Note-Books*, 1912, XXIII.

Pages 189–95

6 *The Dragons of Eden*, 1977, chap. 4.
7 *African Genesis*, [1961] 1967, 355.
8 *The Second Sex*, [1949] 1964, 64.
9 *Beyond Power*, 1985, 90.
10 *Escape from Evil*, 1975, 102, 105.
11 *Men in Groups*, 1970, 229, 237.
12 *Sexual Suicide*, 1973, 259.
13 in *Take Back the Night*, 1980, L. Lederer ed., 289.
14 *Philosophical Dictionary*, 1764, "War."
15 *The Pursuit of Loneliness*, [1970] 1976, 144.
16 *Pensées d'un biologiste*, 1939, 116.
17 *The Heart of Man*, 1964, 40.
18 *The Biology of Peace and War*, 1979, 190.
19 *The Nature of Human Aggression*, 1976, 264.
20 *On Civil Disobedience and Non-Violence*, [c. 1900] 1967, 156.
21 quoted in *The Psychology of Dictatorship*, G. Gilbert, 1950, 256.
22 *Eichmann in Jerusalem*, [1963] 1977, 150.
23 quoted in *The Rise and Fall of the Third Reich*, W. Shirer, 1960, 982.
24 *Will*, 1980, 26.
25 *History and Human Survival*, 1970, 218.
26 *The Anatomy of Human Destructiveness*, 1973, 251.
27 *The Rebel*, [1954] 1967, 184.
28 *The Crime of Punishment*, 1968.
29 *Suicide*, [1897] 1951, 351.
30 in *Encounter*, May, 1966, 27.
31 *Will Therapy and Truth and Reality*, [1936] 1945, 130.
32 *The Pursuit of Loneliness*, [1970] 1976, 100.
33 *The War Myth*, 1967, 10–12.
34 *On Aggression*, 1966, 242.
35 *Generation of Vipers*, 1942, 284–85.
36 "Caesar" in *Caesar and Cleopatra*, 1898, act 4.
37 *The Rebel*, [1954] 1967, 4.
38 *Holy Bible*, Exodus 20:1.
39 *The Betrayal of the West*, 1978, 65.

Knowledge

1 *Metaphysics*, 11.
2 *A Brief History of Time*, 1988, 13.
3 *The Quest for Certainty*, [1929] 1960, 41.
4 *The Phenomenon of Man*, [1940] 1959, 248.
5 *The Human Soul*, [1959] 1973, 106.
6 *Megabrain*, 1986, 159.
7 *Folkways*, [1906] 1940, 44.
8 *The Phaedo* by Plato.
9 *Meditationes Sacrae*, 1597, "Of Heresies."
10 *Power Shift*, 1990, 20, 277.
11 *A Grammar of Politics*, [1925] 1938, 240.
12 *The Meaning of the 20th Century*, 1964, 107.
13 *The Image*, 1956, 130.
14 *Homo Ludens*, 1955, 105.
15 quoted in *Information Anxiety*, R. Wurman, 1989, 29.
16 *Megatrends*, 1984, 17.
17 *Against Method*, 1975, 261.
18 *The Meaning of the 20th Century*, 1964, 71.
19 in *This World*, May 24, 1987.
20 *Power Shift*, 1990, 20, 277.
21 *The Will to Power*, [1901] 1967, 266, s. 480.
22 *The Power Elite*, 1956, 351.
23 *Marriage and Morals*, [1929] 1959, 201.
24 *The Realm of Spirit*, 1940, 171.
25 *The Open Society and Its Enemies*, 1950, 195.
26 *Holy Bible*, Genesis 2:17.
27 *The Fate of the Earth*, 1982, 115.
28 *Parables and Paradoxes*, 1935, "Paradise."
29 *Guilt*, 1985, 227.
30 *Sociobiology*, 1980, 300.
31 *Technology and Justice*, 1986, 22.
32 *Mindstorms*, 1980, 171.
33 *Personal Knowledge*, 1962, 214.
34 *The Future of an Illusion*, 1927, 69.
35 *A Vindication of the Rights of Woman*, 1791, chap. 4.
36 *Rasselas*, 1759, chap. 41.
37 *Mind and Nature*, 1980, 98, 149.
38 *The Problems of Philosophy*, 1912, 158.
39 *Tragic Sense of Life*, [1912] 1954, 235.
40 *Being and Nothingness*, [1943] 1957, 577.
41 *Personal Knowledge*, 1962, 312.
42 *The Study of Man*, 1959, 11.
43 *The Art of Loving*, 1956, 29.
44 *Biology and Knowledge*, 1971, 6.
45 *The Quest for Certainty*, [1929] 1960, 221.
46 *The Psychology of Science*, 1966, 128.
47 *Miscellaneous Writings of Lord Macaulay*, 1860, vol. 1, "History."
48 *Discourse on the Method*, 1637, Part II.
49 [1963] in *Quotations from Chairman Mao*, 1967, chap. 22.
50 *Homo Ludens*, 1955, 155.
51 *Being and Nothingness*, [1943] 1957, 172.
52 *The Quest for Certainty*, [1929] 1960, 197.
53 *The Basic Writings of C. G. Jung*, 1959, 41.
54 *A Primer of Freudian Psychology*, 1954, 42.
55 [1937] in *Quotations from Chairman Mao*, 1967, chap. 22.
56 *The Order of Things*, 1973, 40.
57 *An Essay on Man*, [1944] 1970, 62.
58 *Democracy and Education*, [1916] 1961, 339–40.
59 *The Gay Science*, [1882] 1974, s. 355, 300.
60 *The Cult of Information*, 1986, 132.
61 *The Decline of the West*, [1932] 1965, 321.
62 *Science and Human Values*, [1956] 1965, 57.
63 in *Popular Scientific Lectures*, 1895, 197–98.
64 *The Order of Things*, 1970, 373.
65 Ibid., 87–88.
66 *The Image*, 1956, 78.
67 Ibid., 81.
68 *Tragic Sense of Life*, [1912] 1954, 15.
69 *The Crowd*, [1895] 1960, 93.
70 *Man in the Modern Age*, [1931] 1951, 181.
71 *In Praise of Idleness*, 1935, 48.
72 "Science and Culture," 1880.

21 in *C. G. Jung*, A. Jaffe ed., 1979, 78, 92.
22 *The Ego and the Self*, 1951, 68.
23 *The Problem of Being Human*, 1974, 140–41.
24 *Meditations*, [c. 161–80 A.D.] 1898, Book 8, par. 61.
25 *The Passions*, 1976, 103.
26 *Beyond Theology*, 1964, 202.
27 *Mind, Self and Society*, 1934, 91, 140, 324.
28 *The Courage to Be*, 1952, 150.
29 *The Aquarian Conspiracy*, 1980, 100.
30 *Coming to Our Senses*, 1989, 25.
31 in *Canadian Journal of Philosophy*, vol. 9, Mar., 1979, 407–08.
32 in *The Psychology of Women*, M. Walsh ed., 1987, 257.
33 *The True Believer*, 1951, 14.
34 *The Passions*, 1976, 87.
35 in *The Self*, T. Mischel ed., 1977, 279.
36 *Memories, Dreams, Reflections*, 1961, 338.
37 *The Problem of Being Human*, 1974, 89.
38 *Freud: The Mind of the Moralist*, 1961, 391–92.
39 *Basic Writings*, 1959, 439.
40 *Man for Himself*, 1947, 19.
41 *The Gutenberg Galaxy*, 1962, 249.
42 *Culture Against Man*, 1965, 379.
43 *Revolution from Within*, 1992, 277.
44 *The Greening of America*, 1970, 225, 295.
45 *Man for Himself*, 1947, 139.
46 *Summerhill*, 1960, 246.
47 *Hamlet*, 1601, act 1, scene 1.
48 *The Cultural Contradictions of Capitalism*, 1976, 13.
49 *Process and Reality*, [1929] 1978, 222.
50 [d. 1930] *Selected Essays*.
51 *Being and Nothingness*, [1943] 1957, 93.
52 in *The American Journal of Psychoanalysis*, 1961, vol. 1, 254–60.
53 *Ideas and Opinions*, 1954, 12.
54 *Life Against Death*, 1966, 47.
55 *Way to Wisdom*, 1951, 45, 84.
56 *The Sickness Unto Death*, [1849] 1944, 31, 44.

Self-consciousness / Self-knowledge

1 *The Rebel*, [1954] 1967, 138.
2 *The Social Bond*, 1977, 51.
3 *Ends and Means*, 1938, 325.
4 *The Sickness Unto Death*, [1849] 1944, 43.
5 *The Basic Writings of C. G. Jung*, 1959, 148.
6 in *Psychiatry*, 1957, 128.
7 *The Disowned Self*, 1971, 104–06.
8 *An Introduction to Social Psychology*, [1908] 1931, 194.
9 *The Power of Positive Thinking*, 1952, 182.
10 *The Warriors*, [1959] 1970, 176.
11 in *New Directions in Psycho-Analysis*, M. Klein ed., 1955, 435.
12 *The City in History*, 1961, 50.
13 *The Lonely Crowd*, [1950] 1965, 305.
14 *Mind, Self and Society*, 1934, 134.
15 *The Phenomenon of Man*, [1940] 1959, 165.
16 *Neurosis and Human Growth*, [1950] 1991, 15.
17 *A Grammar of Politics*, [1925] 1938, 263.
18 *Man's Search for Himself*, 1953, 160–61.
19 *The Psychology of Science*, 1966, 43.
20 *The Concept of Mind*, 1949, 194.
21 *Moral Man and Immoral Society*, 1932, 41.
22 *The Drama of the Gifted Child*, 1981, 112.
23 *The Philosophy of Mind*, 1817, sec. 435.
24 *The Phenomenology of Spirit*, 1807, Part 4a, sec. 187.
25 *Introduction to the Reading of Hegel*, [1947] 1969, 14.
26 *Life Against Death*, 1966, 174–75.
27 preface to *Tropic of Cancer*, Henry Miller, 1934.
28 *Understanding Media*, 1966, 93.
29 *A Choice of Heroes*, 1982, 116.
30 *Memories, Dreams, Reflections*, 1961, 325.
31 *A Theory of Objective Self-Awareness*, 1972, 2–5.
32 *The Life of Reason*, 1954, 151.
33 *Journal of General Psychology*, 1963, 68, 118–19.
34 *Psychology and the Soul*, 1931, 10.
35 *The Psychology of Science*, 1966, 16.
36 *Love and Will*, 1969, 165.
37 *The Divided Self*, 1960, 214.
38 in *The Self*, T. Mischel ed., 1977, 317.
39 in *First Alcibiades*, by Plato.
40 in *Apology*, 38a, by Plato.
41 *The Sickness Unto Death*, [1849] 1944, 40.
42 [d. 1930] "Pornography and Obscenity."
43 *Existence*, 1958, 74.
44 *Ends and Means*, 1938, 323.

Self-esteem

1 *The Birth and Death of Meaning*, 1962, 79–80.
2 *Revolution from Within*, 1992, 322.
3 in *Current Anthropology*, 1975, no. 16, 553–72.
4 *Ends and Means*, 1938, 97.
5 *Discourses on Davila*, 1805, 29–30.
6 *How to Win Friends and Influence People*, 1936, 30, 36.
7 *Motivation and Personality*, 1954, 90–91.
8 *Psychology*, 1892, chap. 12.
9 *The Passions*, 1976, 96.
10 *Man for Himself*, 1947, 72.
11 in *The Self*, 1977, T. Mischel ed., 218–19.
12 *The Birth and Death of Meaning*, 1962, 79–81.
13 *The Disowned Self*, 1971, 89.
14 *The Ego and the Self*, 1951, 43.
15 in *The Self*, T. Mischel ed., 1977, 139.
16 *The Ego and the Self*, 1951, 106.
17 *Self-Esteem and Meaning*, 1984, 62, 79, 89, 123.
18 *The Nature of Human Values*, 1973, 13.
19 "John Galt" in *Atlas Shrugged*, 1957, 1021.
20 *Ethics*, 1675, Part 3, prop. 30.
21 *For The New Intellectual*, 1961, 25, 37, 47.
22 in *Readings About the Social Animal*, 1984, 188.

The true value of a human being is determined by the measure and the sense in which he has attained liberation from the self. 53
Albert Einstein

[H]uman perfection consists in an expansion of the self until it enjoys the world as it enjoys itself. 54 *Norman O. Brown*

If I do not experience the miracle of selfhood, I need no relation to God, I am content with the empirical existence of nature.... Only in devotion to God and not to the world is this selfhood granted and received as the freedom to assert it in the world. 55 *Karl Jaspers*

The self is the conscious synthesis of infinitude and finitude ... which can be performed only by means of a relationship to God.... [T]o be a self is the greatest concession made to man, but at the same time it is eternity's demand upon him. 56 *Søren Kierkegaard*

Self-consciousness Self-knowledge

The only thing in the world that is distinct from nature is, precisely, self-consciousness. 1
Albert Camus

Nothing is more distinctively human than consciousness of self. 2
Robert Nisbet & Robert Perrin

[W]e cannot become persons unless we make ourselves self-conscious. 3 *Aldous Huxley*

Generally speaking, consciousness, i.e. consciousness of self, is the decisive criterion of the self. The more consciousness, the more self.... 4
Søren Kierkegaard

[T]he more we become conscious of ourselves through self-knowledge ... the more ... the personal unconscious ... will be diminished. In this way there arises a consciousness which is no longer imprisoned in the petty, oversensitive, personal world of the ego.... This widened consciousness is no longer that touchy, egotistical bundle of personal wishes, fears, hopes, and ambitions ... [but instead brings] the individual into absolute, binding, and indissoluble communion with the world at large. 5 *Carl Jung*

Only when the human person himself overcomes his inner resistance can he attain to self-illumination. The "opening door" of self-illumination leads us into ... the interior of the law. It is the law of man in which we then stand: the law of the identity of the human person as such with himself, the one who recognizes guilt with the one who bears guilt, the one in light with the one in darkness.... 6 *Martin Buber*

The more a person grows in self-awareness, the more he is prepared to acknowledge responsibility for his actions.... The essence of morality ... is a dedication to awareness.... 7
Nathaniel Branden

Even the purely altruistic sentiments, the love of beneficence or of mankind in general, will not necessarily suffice to enable a man to reach the highest plane of conduct.... The habit of self-criticism is required, and this implies, and arises from, a strong self-regarding sentiment. The special moral sentiments must be brought into connection with, and organized within, the system of a more comprehensive sentiment—which may be called the master sentiment among all moral sentiments, namely the sentiment for a perfected or completely moral life.... In this sentiment, then, the altruistic and egoistic emotions and sentiments may find some sort of reconciliation; that is to say, they may become synthesized in the larger sentiment of love for an ideal of conduct. 8 *William McDougall*

Self-knowledge is the beginning of self-correction. 9 *Norman Vincent Peale*

[A]n important function of guiltiness is to make us aware of our selves.... Conscience is thus in the first instance a form of self-consciousness.... Therewith the life of reflection begins, and the inner history of the individual no longer corresponds to his outer fate. 10 *J. Glenn Gray*

[A] movement away from the authoritarian and towards the humanist type of conscience is the moral effect of any increase in that kind

Self-consciousness / Self-knowledge

of wisdom which consists in insight or self-knowledge. 11 *R. E. Money-Kyrle*

The growth of self-consciousness in the city, through the clash of village customs and regional differences, produced the beginnings of reflective morality.... 12 *Lewis Mumford*

[A]s the inner-directed man is more self-conscious than his tradition-directed predecessor and as the other-directed man is more self-conscious still, the autonomous man ... can disentangle himself from the adjusted others only by a further move toward even greater self-consciousness. His autonomy depends ... upon the success of his effort to recognize and respect his own feelings, his own potentialities, his own limitations. 13 *David Riesman*

It is by means of reflexiveness—the turning-back of the experience of the individual upon himself—that the whole social process is ... brought into the experience of the individuals involved in it; it is by such means, which enable the individual to take the attitude of the other toward himself, that ... the individual becomes self-conscious and has a mind.... Reflexiveness, then, is the essential condition, within the social process, for the development of mind. 14 *George H. Mead*

If we wish to settle this question of the "superiority" of man over the animals ... [go] straight for the central phenomenon, *reflection*.... [R]eflection is, as the word indicates, the power acquired by a consciousness to turn in upon itself, to take possession of itself *as of an object* ... and fuse into a unity that is conscious of its own organisation....The being who is the object of his own reflection, in consequence of that very doubling back upon himself, becomes in a flash able to raise himself into a new sphere. In reality, another world is born. Abstraction, logic, reasoned choice and inventions, mathematics, art, calculation of space and time, anxieties and dreams of love—all these activities of *inner life* are nothing else than the effervescence of the newly-formed centre as it explodes onto itself. 15
Pierre Teilhard de Chardin

Self-knowledge, then, is not an aim in itself, but a means of liberating the forces of spontaneous growth. 16 *Karen Horney*

[I]t is when I am guided by self-knowledge to the sense of what I may become that I begin most genuinely to enter my inheritance. 17
Harold Laski

Consciousness of self gives us the power to stand outside the rigid chain of stimulus and response.... Freedom is man's capacity to take a hand in his own development.... [C]onsciousness of self and freedom go together. 18
Rollo May

[S]elf-knowledge decreases control from outside the person and increases control from within the person.... Freedom has now become ... the freedom to embrace and to love one's own destiny.... 19 *Abraham Maslow*

Self-consciousness, if the word is to be used at all, must not be described on the hallowed para-optical model, as a torch that illuminates itself by beams of its own light reflected from a mirror in its own insides. On the contrary, it is simply a special case of an ordinary more or less efficient handling of a less or more honest and intelligent witness. 20 *Gilbert Ryle*

Human self-consciousness is the fruit of reason. Men become conscious of themselves as they see themselves in relation to other life and to their environment. This self-consciousness increases the urge to preserve and to extend life. 21 *Reinhold Niebuhr*

[A] person who has consciously worked through the whole tragedy of his own fate will recognize another's suffering more clearly.... He surely will not help to keep the vicious circle of contempt turning. 22 *Alice Miller*

The servant ... works off the singularity and egoism of his will in the service of the master ... and through his privation and fear of the Lord makes—and it is the beginning of wisdom—the transition to universal self-consciousness. 23 *G. W. F. Hegel*

It is solely by risking one's life that freedom is attained ... and the essential nature of self-

consciousness revealed.... The individual who has not staked his life may be recognized as a person, but has not attained the truth of this recognition as an independent self-consciousness. 24
G. W. F. Hegel

All human, anthropocentric desire—the desire that generates self-consciousness, the human reality—is, finally, a function of the desire for "recognition." And the risk of life by which the human reality "comes to light" is a risk for the sake of such a desire. Therefore, to speak of the "origin" of self-consciousness is necessarily to speak of a fight to the death for "recognition." 25
Alexandre Kojève

Apollonian form is form negating matter ... form as the negation of instinct ... that is to say, by the irony that overtakes all flight from death, deathly form.... Dionysus reunifies male and female, Self and Other, life and death. Dionysus is the image of the instinctual reality.... [One is] right in saying that the Apollonian preserves, the Dionysian destroys self-consciousness. 26 *Norman O. Brown*

[E]xperience [is the] prime source of wisdom and creation.... In the anaesthesia produced by self-knowledge, life is passing, art is passing, slipping from us: we are drifting with time and our fight is with shadows.... In a world grown paralyzed with introspection ... the tragedy of our world is precisely that nothing any longer is capable of rousing it from its lethargy. 27
Anaïs Nin

Self-consciousness of the causes and limits of one's own culture seems to threaten the ego structure and is, therefore, avoided. Nietzsche said understanding stops action, and men of action seem to have an intuition of the fact in their shunning the dangers of comprehension. 28
Marshall McLuhan

Our survival depends on the emergence of a new kind of leader, who has worked not only for power, but for self-awareness. 29 *Mark Gerzon*

Attainment of consciousness is culture in the broadest sense, and self-knowledge is therefore the heart and essence of this process. 30
Carl Jung

In contrast to egocentrism is the self-conscious state.... [It is] a consciousness that one's point of view is unique, and therefore subject to error.... [T]he state of objective self-awareness will lead to a negative self-evaluation and negative affect whenever the person is aware of a self-contradiction.... [At] such point he will prefer to revert to the subjective state ... [and] a feeling of control and mastery, for it is only in objective awareness that he will think about himself as falling short of the [ego] ideal of exerting control over the environment. 31
S. Duval & R. A. Wicklund

The more reflective and self-conscious a man is the more completely will his experience be subsumed and absorbed in his perennial "I." ... But the more successful he is in stuffing everything into his self-consciousness, the more desolate will the void become which surrounds him. 32 *George Santayana*

Freud's greatest discovery, the one which lies at the root of psychodynamics, is that *the* great cause of much psychological illness is the fear of knowledge of oneself ... [which] is very often isomorphic with, and parallel with, fear of the outside world. 33
Abraham Maslow

On the whole, psychoanalysis failed therapeutically because it ... sent the self-conscious neurotic back to the very self-knowledge from which he wanted to escape. 34 *Otto Rank*

More than any other kind of knowledge we fear knowledge of ourselves, knowledge that might transform our self-esteem and our self-image. 35
Abraham Maslow

How much *self-knowledge* can a human being bear? 36 *Rollo May*

Personal unity is a prerequisite of reflective awareness, that is, the ability to be aware of one's own self.... 37 *R. D. Laing*

[T]he cohesiveness and autonomy of the individual's so-called "self" is ... a practical measure of the extent to which he succeeds, on every level ... to "know himself." 38
Stephen Toulmin

Self-consciousness / Self-knowledge

He is not to be lightly esteemed who inscribed the text on the temple of Delphi, "Know Thyself." ... Self-knowledge, however, is not an easy thing.... Whether easy or difficult, there is still no other way. 39 *Socrates*

The unexamined life is not worth living. 40 *Socrates*

[O]nly that man's life is wasted who ... never became eternally and decisively conscious of himself as spirit, as self, or ... that there is a God, and that he, he himself, his self, exists before this God, this gain of infinity.... 41 *Søren Kierkegaard*

[I]n his adventure of self-consciousness a man must come to the limits of himself and become aware of something beyond him.... And that is freedom and the fight for freedom. 42 *D. H. Lawrence*

Self-consciousness implies self-transcendence. 43 *Rollo May*

Self-transcendence is through self-consciousness. 44 *Aldous Huxley*

Self-esteem

If we had to give one definition of "human nature," it would derive from this crucial need: Man is the only animal who needs a symbolic constitution of his worth.... [T]he seemingly trite words "self-esteem" are at the *very core* of human adaptation. 1 *Ernest Becker*

[S]elf-esteem starts out as a blessing, but it becomes nothing less than an evolutionary force. 2 *Gloria Steinem*

With the development of a sense of self, our ancestors' primate tendency to seek high social rank would have been transformed ... [and] taken the form of an imperative to evaluate the self as higher in rank than others: to evaluate the self as higher than others is to maintain self-esteem. 3 *Jerome Barkov*

Self-esteem has as its complement disparagement of others. 4 *Aldous Huxley*

The rewards ... in this life are *esteem* and *admiration* of others—the punishments are *neglect* and *contempt*.... Every personal quality, and every blessing of fortune, is cherished in proportion to its capacity of gratifying this universal affection for the esteem, the sympthy, admiration and congratulations of the public.... 5 *John Adams*

We nourish the bodies of our children and friends and employees; but how seldom do we nourish their self-esteem.... Here is a gnawing and unfaltering human hunger; and the rare individual who honestly satisfies this heart-hunger will hold people in the palm of his hand.... 6 *Dale Carnegie*

All people in our society (with a few pathological exceptions) have a need or desire for a stable, firmly based ... self-respect, or self-esteem.... The most stable and therefore most healthy self-esteem is based on *deserved* respect from others rather than on external fame or celebrity and unwarranted adulation. 7 *Abraham Maslow*

Self-esteem equals Success divided by Pretensions. 8 *William James*

Self-esteem, it would seem, turns on ... indispensability. So to salvage our sense of worth, we try desperate schemes.... We strive to make ourselves indispensable through power, money, violence, *success*. But ... men and women who do succeed in becoming the most prosperous and powerful and therefore, we would think, worthy of the highest self-esteem in fact despise themselves the most and are the most likely to take their own lives. 9 *Robert C. Solomon*

Since modern man experiences himself both as the seller and as the commodity to be sold on the market, his self-esteem depends on conditions beyond his control. If he is "successful," he is valuable; if he is not, he is worthless. The degree of insecurity which results from this orientation can hardly be overestimated. 10 *Erich Fromm*

A fragmentation of the self ... is experienced as feelings of depression or even deadness.... Even transient and relatively minor losses of cohesion are manifested by ... disturbances of self-esteem.... Achieving an irreversible cohesive self is concomitant with achieving freedom from the imperative intrusions of narcissistic tensions. 11 *Ernest S. Wolf*

Self-esteem ... takes shape as the continued disposal of power to act without anxiety.... Self-esteem, then, is an aspect of self-consciousness that permits the self to handle not only present anxieties *but past and future ones as well.* 12 *Ernest Becker*

When a person represses certain of his emotions, because they threaten his sense of control ... he disowns a part of himself.... Self-esteem cannot be built on a foundation of self-alienation. The consequences of such attempts is ... self-betrayal, the anxious need always to be on guard against dark, frightening forces which might erupt from the limbo of one's denied self to threaten the structure of one's existence—and the subversion of one's self-esteem. 13
Nathaniel Branden

Integration depends upon self-regarding feelings. As self-esteem becomes greater the individual is able to reconcile different elements of his personality, whereas an individual with feelings of inferiority ... must destroy his own capacity for self-integration. 14 *Percival M. Symonds*

The search then, seems to be for a stable and unifying core of existence, a firm touchstone which can provide us with a sense of authenticity and coherence.... 15 *Kenneth Gergen*

Many of the defense mechanisms have as their main purpose maintaining the integrity of the self. 16 *Percival M. Symonds*

[There is a] difference between genuine and defensive self-esteem.... [D]efensive self-esteem is signified by disruptions in meaning.... [It] involves an attempt to live out a contradiction ... [which] is aimed at keeping the reorganization which solves the central conflict from spreading to include a painful reevaluation of self and world.... An experience of self-esteem can be regarded as non-defensive insofar as it involves a resolution of a central conflict that includes a change in the way one thinks about one's own identity and the world. 17 *Michael R. Jackson*

It is ... self-justification on the one hand and self-deception on the other that enables us to maintain and enhance our self-esteem.... Values provide a basis for rational self-justification insofar as possible but also as a basis for rationalized self-justification insofar as necessary. Either way, values serve to maintain and enhance self-esteem. 18 *Milton Rokeach*

"[T]he first precondition of self-esteem is that radiant selfishness of soul which desires the best in all things, in values of matter and spirit, a soul that seeks above all else to achieve its own moral perfection, valuing nothing higher than itself." ... 19 *Ayn Rand*

I shall call Joy accompanied by the idea of an internal cause, Self-esteem.... 20
Baruch Spinoza

Reason requires freedom, self-confidence and self-esteem.... [T]he man who doubts the validity of his mind, will not achieve the self-esteem necessary to uphold the value of his person and to discover the moral premises that make man's value possible.... [N]o man of self-esteem can accept ... altruistic morality.... 21
Ayn Rand

[T]he development of high self-esteem in the individual may be crucial in his choosing a moral rather than an immoral mode of behaving. 22 *E. Aronson & D. R. Mettee*

The more a person esteems himself, the more he tends to esteem others. 23
Percival M. Symonds

A theology of self-esteem ... will return our focus to the sacred right of every person to self-esteem. The fact is, the church will never succeed until it satisfies the human being's hunger for self-value. 24 *Rev. Robert Schuller*

Schuller's critics are probably right in seeing the "theology of self-esteem" as a strategy according to which ... secular values inform, and eventually replace, religious ones.... His reinvented God is the mirror image of humanistic modern man.... He makes the new narcissism respectable to Christian conservatives.... 25
Malise Ruthven

Self-esteem

The problem with the present-day self-esteem movement is that its members ... are seldom willing to make choices concerning what should be esteemed.... To truly esteem oneself means that one must be capable of feeling shame or self-disgust when one does not live up to a certain standard. 26 *Francis Fukuyama*

"[M]an, who has ... no automatic sense of self-esteem ... must earn it by shaping his soul in the image of his moral ideal." ... 27 *Ayn Rand*

Healthy self-esteem means that an individual lives in accordance with the ideals, values, and moral and ethical standards that he himself has formulated as part of the process of psychological maturation. 28 *Althea Horner*

Self-esteem is really the highest thing we can hope for. 29 *Baruch Spinoza*

[S]elf-esteem isn't everything; it's just that there's nothing without it. 30 *Gloria Steinem*

~ Sex ~

I regard sex as the central problem of life.... Sex lies at the root of life, and we can never learn to reverence life until we know how to understand sex. 1 *Havelock Ellis*

The core of happiness in life is *sexual* happiness. 2 *Wilhelm Reich*

Normal sex life ... strengthens the feeling of unity and identity. This state is described as one of complete harmony, and is extolled as a great happiness ("one heart and one soul")—not without good reason, since the return to that original condition of unconscious oneness is like a return to childhood. Hence the childish gestures of all lovers. Even more it is a return to the mother's womb, into the teeming depths of an as yet unconscious creativity. It is, in truth, a genuine and incontestable experience of the Divine, whose transcendent face obliterates and consumes everything individual; a real communion with life and the impersonal power of fate. 3 *Carl Jung*

Sexual union that occurs in the context of a powerful emotional bond can ... be experienced as a spiritual union of the feminine and masculine principles and appear to have divine dimensions. 4 *Christina & Stanislov Grof*

Sex is sacred. 5 *Timothy Leary*

Sex means the being divided into male and female, and the magnetic drive or impulse which puts male apart from female ... but which also draws male and female together in a long and infinitely varied approach toward the critical act of coition. 6 *D. H. Lawrence*

Lovers are seeking their other half. 7 *Diotima*

To make love is to return to paradise, it is to plunge again into the world before birth, before the great separation. It is to find again the primordial slowness, the blind and all-powerful rhythm of ... the great ocean. 8 *Frederick Leboyer*

[T]he modern Western preoccupation with sex is really a symptom of continuum rupture. The search for a universe that is loving ... is the real issue here. 9 *Morris Berman*

The loss of [the] infant illusion of omnipotence—the discovery that ... the infant does not own or control the mother's body ... is an original and basic human grief.... In lovemaking, both man and woman make [a] direct attempt to repair the old loss. 10 *Dorothy Dinnerstein*

In heterosexual love ... a dual transference may be in progress in which each partner is also reunited with the longed-for mother.... For both, sex serves as a highly charged symbolic expression of generally inarticulated dependency needs. 11 *Luise Eichenbaum & Susie Orbach*

Sex ... is a proven antidote to the fears of abandonment and non-being. 12 *Reuven Bar-Levav*

[M]any behavior patterns that are regarded as typically sexual, such as kissing and caressing, are actually in origin actions of parental care.... A mother looks after her children with the actions of parental care; these she also uses to woo her husband. 13 *Irenäus Eibl-Eibesfeldt*

[E]rotic and maternal love flow through the same breasts and vagina. 14 *Beryl Benderly*

Woman's love ... is always compassionate in its essence—maternal. Woman yields herself to the lover because she feels that his desire makes him suffer. 15 *Miguel de Unamuno*

Although cultural and social causes have led to the association in the male of the two forms of sexual attraction, that which views the woman as a sexual prey and that which regards her as a surrogate for the mother, they are distinct in origin and function, and remain essentially opposed. 16 *Robert Briffault*

The paradox of female sexuality being the vehicle for a woman to find a home, so to speak, and yet once she has found that home needing to hide her sexuality or channel it into producing babies, means that all women live with the split of simultaneously having to be sexual and yet having to curb their sexuality. 17
Luise Eichenbaum & Susie Orbach

[W]e must keep in mind a fundamental difference between the two sexes—namely, that the two components, sexual satisfaction and service to the species are not present in the same quantitative relation in man and in woman. In man, the reproductive function is appended to the sexual satisfaction; in woman, the sexual act is a pleasure prize that is appended to her service to the species. 18 *Helene Deutsch*

The vast bulk of copulation in our species is obviously concerned, not with producing offspring, but with cementing the pair-bond by providing mutual rewards for the sexual partners.... The simplest and most direct method of doing this was ... to make sex sexier.... Clearly, the naked ape is the sexiest primate alive. 19 *Desmond Morris*

[T]here is no higher form of love than this total involvement of a man and a woman in each other. No other kind can grant us deeper glimpses into the nature of man. 20 *J. Glenn Gray*

Sex and the imagery of sex seem to me to be the very heart of, the very best of who we are. 21
Hugh Hefner

Lovers in their play are moving amongst the highest human activities, alike of the body and of the soul. They are passing to each other the sacramental chalice of that wine which imparts the deepest joy men and women can know. 22
Havelock Ellis

Sexual attraction between the sexes is only partly motivated by the need for removal of tension; it is mainly the need for union with the other sexual pole. 23 *Erich Fromm*

The ideal of the sex act ... is a double merging—of the physical and psychological into a unique blend of feeling, and of two individuals into something like a single, transcendent entity.... When the ideal is approached, the self is both nonexistent and most alive. 24
Robert Jay Lifton

Physical and spiritual castration is the danger every man runs in intercourse with a woman. Love is the spell by which he puts his sexual fear to sleep. 25 *Camille Paglia*

Men dislike the idea of woman's enjoying sex because it suggests to them the treasonous thought that perhaps man was made for woman's pleasure and not woman for man's convenience. 26 *Elizabeth Gould Davis*

The desire of a man for a woman is not directed at her because she is a human being, but because she is a woman. That she is a human being is of no concern to him. 27 *Immanuel Kant*

Man, taking her body, the mind is left to rust; so that while physical love enervates man, as being his favorite recreation, he will endeavour to enslave woman.... 28
Mary Wollstonecraft

Woman's degradation is in man's idea of his sexual rights. 29 *Elizabeth Cady Stanton*

[W]hat is called sexuality is the dynamic of control by which male dominance ... eroticizes and thus defines man and woman.... [M]ale force is romanticized, even sacralized ... by being submerged into sex itself. 30
Catherine MacKinnon

Sex

The sex of domination leads to death: it is ... annihilation; sex, violence, death—that is pure sex; and it is the slow annihilation of the woman's will.... Annihilation is sexy, and sex tends toward it; women are the preferred victims of record. 31 *Andrea Dworkin*

What pornography is really about, ultimately, isn't sex but death. 32 *Susan Sontag*

[D]eath is the ultimate sexual act, the ultimate making of a person into a thing. 33
Catherine MacKinnon

[F]rom the moment when sexual crime destroys the object of desire, it also destroys desire, which exists only at the precise moment of destruction. Then another object must be brought under subjection and killed again.... 34 *Albert Camus*

Sex crimes are always male, never female, because such crimes are conceptualizing assaults on the unreachable omnipotence of women and nature. 35 *Camille Paglia*

My theory: when political and religious authority weakens, hierarchy reasserts itself in sex, as the archaizing phenomenon of sadomasochism. Freedom makes new prisons. We cannot escape our life in these fascist bodies. 36
Camille Paglia

However muted its present appearance may be, sexual dominion obtains nevertheless as perhaps the most pervasive ideology of our culture and provides its most fundamental concept of power. 37 *Kate Millet*

Sex *is* power. 38 *Camille Paglia*

It is through intercourse in particular that men express and maintain their power and dominance over women.... The woman who says no to her husband, whatever her reasons, also says no to the state. 39 *Andrea Dworkin*

[The] patriarchal sexual order ... became the basis of authoritarian ideology by depriving women, children and adolescents of sexual freedom, by making a commodity out of sexuality, and by putting sexuality in the service of economic suppression.... [F]ilthy sexuality is not natural sexuality but the specific sexuality of patriarchy. 40 *Wilhelm Reich*

The question is: *what* sexuality are women to be liberated to enjoy? Merely to remove the onus placed upon the sexual expressiveness of women is a hollow victory if the sexuality they become freer to enjoy remains the old one that converts women into objects.... This already "freer" sexuality mostly reflects a spurious idea of freedom: the right of each person, briefly, to exploit and dehumanize someone else. Without a change in the very norms of sexuality, the liberation of women is a meaningless goal. Sex as such is not liberating for women. Neither is more sex. 41 *Susan Sontag*

Empirically speaking, sexual liberation ... did not free women. Its purpose—it turned out—was to free men to use women without bourgeois constraints, and in that it was successful. 42
Andrea Dworkin

The decline of childrearing as a major preoccupation has freed sex from its bondage to procreation and made it possible for people to value erotic life for its own sake. 43
Christopher Lasch

And now sexuality has become a major commodity. The sex merchants have a huge market among sexually repressed and starved people.... [N]ow that the sexual revolution has released us from the compulsions of secrecy, sexual commodities are flooding the market and are becoming the most profitable area of capitalism next to the market of aggression—the armaments industry. 44 *George Frankl*

Sex is the lubricant of the consumer economy, but in order to fulfill that function the very character of human sexuality itself must undergo special conditioning.... Sex, which is a feature of the whole personality, must be localized and controlled. Fantasy ... must be expanded, elaborated and exploited. 45
Germaine Greer

The sellers ... have sexed the sex out of sex. 46
Betty Friedan

Sex

It is a favorite neurotic misunderstanding that the right attitude to the world is found by indulgence in sex. 47 *Carl Jung*

[T]he U.S.A. is technically insane in the matter of sex. 48 *Philip Wylie*

Copulo, ergo sum. 49 *Malcolm Muggeridge*

The orgasm has replaced the Cross as the focus of longing and the image of fulfillment. 50 *Malcolm Muggeridge*

Sex is the ersatz or substitute religion of the 20th century. 51 *Malcolm Muggeridge*

Nowadays we have no real sexual morality.... We are not yet far enough advanced to distinguish between moral and immoral behavior in the realm of free sexual activity. 52 *Carl Jung*

Sex is daemonic. 53 *Camille Paglia*

The continuum of sex leads to sadomasochism. Failure to realize that was the error of the Dionysian Sixties. Dionysus expands identity but crushes individuals. There is no liberal dignity of the person in the Dionysian. 54 *Camille Paglia*

Sex—like death—is an activity that is both animal and human.... When sex is a public spectacle, a human relationship has been debased into a mere animal connection. 55 *Irving Kristol*

[H]uman sex is always more than mere sex. And it is more than mere sex precisely to the extent that it serves as *the physical expression of something metasexual....* And only to the extent that sex carries out this function ... will it climax in a truly rewarding experience. 56 *Viktor Frankl*

Sex is metaphysical for men, as it is not for women. Women have no problem to solve by sex. 57 *Camille Paglia*

Sex expression is an art. To become artists in love, men and women must learn to master and control the instruments by which this art is expressed. These instruments are not merely the so-called sex organs, isolated and unrelated to the body or personality. If marriage is to be fully consummated, the entire body and spirit as units must participate in the union. 58 *Margaret Sanger*

Sex is human if it is experienced as a vehicle of love.... 59 *Viktor Frankl*

[W]ithout virtue a sexual attachment must expire, like a tallow candle in the socket, creating intolerable disgust. To prove this, I need only observe that men who have wasted a great part of their lives with women, and with whom they have sought for pleasure with eager thirst, entertain the meanest opinion of the sex. 60 *Mary Wollstonecraft*

Sex without self, enshrined by the feminine mystique, casts an ever-darkening shadow over man's image of woman and woman's image of herself.... Instead of fulfilling the promise of infinite orgastic bliss, sex in the America of the feminine mystique is becoming a strangely joyless national compulsion, if not a contemptuous mockery. 61 *Betty Friedan*

By the time an American boy or girl reaches maturity he or she has so much symbolic language attached to the sexual impulse that the mere mutual stimulation of two human bodies seems almost meaningless. 62 *Philip Slater*

[M]uch of the frankness about sex in this generation is a sign of our chaos, of a world in which our human connections are in a state of serious disorganization, a world in which little that is really human is left. 63 *Lloyd J. Averill*

Beyond all question, there is a marked disturbance today in the realms of sexual life.... It is an over-emphasized sexuality piled behind a dam; and it shrinks at once to normal proportions as soon as the way to development is opened. 64 *Carl Jung*

What pornographic literature does is precisely to drive a wedge between one's existence as a full human being and one's existence as a sexual being—while in ordinary life a healthy person is one who prevents such a gap from opening up. 65 *Susan Sontag*

Sex

In some of its more extreme aspects the sexual revolution seems to have passed the point of campaigning for the liberation of a natural appetite, and reached the vomitorial stage of trying to reactivate an exhausted one. 66
Elaine Morgan

[M]en and women enjoy more sexual liberty than ever before. But the truth is that this freedom and satisfaction are transforming the earth into hell. 67 *Herbert Marcuse*

An excess of sexual enjoyment is far more harmful than the want of same. 68
August Bebel

Certainly men and women require a certain amount of sexual intercourse ... but there are few signs that either men or women want to indulge in sexual intercourse to an extent that is damaging either to themselves or society. 69
Rebecca West

One of the weaknesses of the argument that sexual freedom dooms America to destruction and oblivion is that it mistakes the sources of the American absorption with sex. It derives less from sexual freedom itself than from the centuries of the Puritan heritage of repression. 70
Max Lerner

The sex passion affects the weal or woe of human beings far more than hunger.... It has two opposite extremes—renunciation and licence. In neither one of these can peace and satisfaction be found.... The truth is that licence stimulates desire without limit, and ends in impotent agony. Renunciation produces agony of another kind. 71 *William Graham Sumner*

The negative renunciation of polygamous eroticism is the outcome of a positive which, as contemporary love, is only sincere when it includes the whole of life; and the negative determination not to squander oneself is the outcome of an uncompromising readiness for this loyalty on the part of a possible selfhood. Without strictness in erotic matters, there is no selfhood.... 72 *Karl Jaspers*

[W]hen there is absolute physical suppression on the sexual side, it seems probable that thereby a greater intensity of spiritual fervor is caused. Many eminent thinkers seem to have been without sexual desire. 73 *Havelock Ellis*

The idea of placing restrictions on sexuality was a stunning cultural invention, as important as the acquisition of fire. In it men found a source of energy that was limitless and unflagging—one that enabled them to build empires on earth. 74 *Philip Slater*

In brief, the goal of sexual suppression is that of producing an individual who is adjusted to the authoritarian order and who will submit to it in spite of all misery and degradation.... The suppression of natural sexual gratification leads to various kinds of substitute gratifications. Natural aggression, for example, becomes brutal sadism which then is an essential mass-psychological factor in imperialistic wars. 75
Wilhelm Reich

Chastity ... is the necessary pre-condition to any kind of moral life superior to that of the animal. At the same time, the energy created by chastity has a natural tendency to be, on the whole, more evil than good. 76 *Aldous Huxley*

The sex taboo is the root evil in the suppression of children. 77 *A. S. Neill*

The doctrine that there is something sinful about sex is one which has done untold harm to individual character.... By keeping sex love in a prison, conventional morality has done much to imprison all other forms of friendly feeling, and to make men less generous, less kindly, more self-assertive and more cruel. 78 *Bertrand Russell*

[T]he more isolated and polarized the roles of men and women ... the more sex becomes an obsession.... And in such societies, where basic human sexual needs for intimacy are alienated, violence breeds. 79 *Betty Friedan*

Only a fully sexual person can be loving. 80
Arthur Janov

[T]o pour contempt on the sexual life, to throw the veil of "impurity" over it, is ... the unpardonable sin against the Holy Ghost of Life. 81
Havelock Ellis

Sex

Hate sex and you hate life. 82 *A. S. Neill*

Joy of life … depends upon a certain spontaneity in regard to sex. 83 *Bertrand Russell*

Being a sexual object to the opposite sex is part of what makes the world go around. Without it, we'd live on a sterile and pathetic planet. 84 *Hugh Hefner*

Sexual activity is the most ready way to silence the inner dread of death.… Repression of death equals obsession with sex. Sex is the easiest way to prove our vitality, to prove we are still "young," attractive, and virile, to prove we are not dead yet. 85 *Rollo May*

Masturbation: the primary sexual activity of mankind. In the nineteenth century, it was a disease; in the twentieth, it's a cure. 86 *Thomas Szasz*

You wicked fools, you cretins who promote sexology and sex education and universal sexualization.… What you are preparing the way for with your sexology is a human being who is disgusted with sex, who will no longer have the slightest idea of what love is.… Your sex education in the schools is training a generation of torturers who will end in suicide. You are taking from them the passion of love … but then they will develop a passion for death. Those are the only two passions possible. 87 *Jacques Ellul*

[W]hat underlies our emasculation of sex is the separation of sex from eros.… We are in a flight from eros—and we use sex as the vehicle for the flight.… We fly to the sensation of sex in order to avoid the passion of eros. 88 *Rollo May*

The separation of sex from emotion is at the very foundations of Western culture and civilization. 89 *Shulamith Firestone*

The Victorian person sought to have love without falling into sex; the modern person seeks to have sex without falling into love. 90 *Rollo May*

Our present-day culture … encourages the "acting out" of sexual impulses in the name of liberation, but minimizes the importance of feeling. The result is narcissism. 91 *Alexander Lowen*

In the realm of sexuality, narcissism withdraws physical love from any kind of commitment, personal or social. The sheer fact of commitment on a person's part seems to him or her to limit the opportunities for "enough" experience to know who he or she is.… Every sexual relationship under the sway of narcissism becomes less fulfilling the longer the partners are together. 92 *Richard Sennett*

Narcissists use sex as a substitute for love and intimacy. 93 *Alexander Lowen*

Sex is a built-in mechanism driving us to relatedness. 94 *Bernard Loomer*

Sexual desires do not unite men but divide them. 95 *Sigmund Freud*

Sex is an antisocial force in evolution. Bonds are formed between individuals in spite of sex and not because of it. 96 *E. O. Wilson*

In vain have I looked for one whose desire to build up his moral power was as strong as sexual desire. 97 *Confucius*

The supreme delight of begetting is perhaps nothing but a foretaste of death, the eradication of our own vital essence. We unite with another, but it is to divide ourselves; this most intimate embrace is only a most intimate sundering. In its essence, the delight of sexual love, the genetic spasm, is a sensation of resurrection, or renewing our life in another, for only in others can we renew our life and so perpetuate ourselves. 98 *Miguel de Unamuno*

The ecstacy of love can absorb one's self in its union with the other self, and separation seems to be overcome. But after these moments, the isolation of self from self is felt even more deeply than before, sometimes even to the point of mutual repulsion. We have given too much of ourselves, and now we long to take back what was given. 99 *Paul Tillich*

Freud's conception of sexuality as an exchange

Sex

suggests a bargain of fools each of whom is bound to find out that he has invested far more libido than the "object" was really worth. Objects disappoint, instincts are stupid, love cheats when it does not delude. 100 *Philip Rieff*

Every lover, after the ultimate consummation of the great work, finds himself cheated; for the illusion has vanished by means of which the individual was here the dupe of the species. 101
Arthur Schopenhauer

It is my belief that, however strange it may sound, we must reckon with the possibility that something in the nature of the sexual instinct itself is unfavourable to the realization of complete satisfaction. 102 *Sigmund Freud*

To have a pleasurable and satisfying sexual experience one must be able to let go, and to merge with another one must have a defined sense of self to return to. 103
Luise Eichenbaum & Susie Orbach

Lovers never attain to a love of self abandonment, of true fusion of soul and not merely of body, until the heavy pestle of sorrow has bruised their hearts and crushed them in the same mortar of suffering. Sensual love joined their bodies but disjoined their souls; it kept their souls strangers to one another.... For to love is to pity; and if bodies are united by pleasure, souls are united by pain. 104
Miguel de Unamuno

Human beings are so constructed that each sex has much to learn from the other, but mere sex relations, even when they are passionate, do not suffice for these lessons. 105
Bertrand Russell

One has to say that mutual sexuality is healthy and a great help, but it would be wrong to assume that the only solution to life's problems is in mutual sex. 106 *D. W. Winnicott*

So intense are the pleasures of sexuality ... that sexual desire can drive love out from its presence. It can become the rock of "reality" on which the search for the beauty of the world founders. 107 *George Grant*

Without—in its true sense—the lustiness of sex, religion is joyless and abstract; without the self-abandonment of religion, sex is a mechanical masturbation. 108 *Alan Watts*

To strangers from another planet, what would be the most striking thing is that sexual passion no longer includes the illusion of eternity. 109
Allan Bloom

It can easily be shown that the psychical value of erotic needs is reduced as soon as their satisfaction becomes easy.... In times in which there were no difficulties standing in the way of sexual satisfaction ... love became worthless and life empty. 110 *Sigmund Freud*

[S]exual libido most often becomes rampant in an existential vacuum.... 111 *Viktor Frankl*

In sex, man is driven into the very abyss which he flees. He makes a voyage to nothing and back. 112 *Camille Paglia*

A good part of our life is passed in plugging up holes, in filling empty places, in realizing and symbolically establishing a plenitude.... Here at its origin we grasp one of the most fundamental tendencies of human reality.... It is only from this standpoint that we can pass on to sexuality ... because sex is a hole.... It is an appeal to being as all holes are. 113
Jean-Paul Sartre

~ Society ~

Man was formed for society. 1
Sir William Blackstone

Man managed to live a human life only in the measure he *organized* himself into a *society*. 2
Jacques Ellul

[T]he totality—the fullness of man—is not in the separate member, but in the body of the society as a whole; the individual can only be an organ.... If he presumes to cut himself off, either in deed or in thought and feeling, he only breaks connection with the sources of his existence. 3 *Joseph Campbell*

SOCIETY

Where the end of anything consists, therein also does its good consist. Society is therefore the proper good of a rational creature. 4
Marcus Aurelius

[S]ocial man is the essence of civilized man; he is the masterpiece of existence. 5
Émile Durkheim

He who first established civil society was the cause of the greatest benefit; for as man, thus perfected, is the most excellent of all living beings, so without law and justice he would be the worst. 6 *Aristotle*

All failures—neurotics, psychotics, criminals, drunkards, problem children, suicides, perverts and prostitutes—are failures because they are lacking in social interest. 7 *Alfred Adler*

He who is unable to live in society, or who has no need of it because he is sufficient unto himself, must be either a beast or a god. 8 *Aristotle*

The problem is not how to produce great men, but how to produce great societies. The great society will put up the men for the occasions. 9
Alfred N. Whitehead

The main cause of the superiority of the social to the individual organization is ... the more marked specialty of the various functions fulfilled by organs more and more distant but interconnected, so that unity of aim is more and more combined with diversity of means. 10 *Auguste Comte*

Human society, as a society, possesses senses which the individual, but for his existence in society, would lack, just as the individual man, who is in his turn a kind of society, possesses senses lacking in the cells of which he is composed. 11 *Miguel de Unamuno*

[T]he social membrane has a function in adult life parallel to the function of the social womb for the infant: both foster a biological and emotional life that is ... human.... [O]ther people are necessary to remind us that we feel ... how we feel and what we feel. 12
James Lynch

Society is the total network of relations between human beings. 13 *Arnold Toynbee*

A society consists of individuals and groups which communicate with one another. 14
Claude Lévi-Strauss

Reciprocation among distantly related or unrelated individuals is the key to human society. The perfection of the social contract has broken the ancient vertebrate constraints imposed by rigid kin selection. 15 *E. O. Wilson*

Society is indeed a contract.... [I]t becomes a partnership not only between those who are living, but between those who are living, those who are dead, and those who are to be born. 16
Edmund Burke

A true social system ... begins when animals respond differentially to other members of the species as individuals. They begin to *select* other members for specific kinds of relatively permanent interaction ... [that] can be called bonds. 17
Lionel Tiger & Robin Fox

The advantages of social organization reach not only outward ... but inward as well.... By clearly defining the status of each member, it reduces friction to a minimum.... [I]nternal harmony is ensured when all members accept the status assigned to them. 18 *Stanley Milgram*

Consensus is the basis of every society.... 19
Philip Rieff

Society, not the state, is the source of law. The state is only a clerk to the society, whose duty it is to measure and dispense the law. 20
August Bebel

The chief Thing ... which Law-givers and other Wise Men, that have laboured for the Establishment of Society, have endeavour'd, has been to make the People they were to govern, believe, that it was more beneficial for every body to conquer than to indulge his Appetites, and much better to mind the Publick than what seem'd his private Interest. 21 *Bernard Mandeville*

Society is produced by our wants, and government by our wickedness; the former promotes

Society

our happiness *positively* by uniting our affections, the latter *negatively* by restraining our vices. Society in every state is a blessing, but government even at its very best is but a necessary evil. 22 *Thomas Paine*

A society holds together by the respect which man gives to man; it fails in fact, it falls apart into groups of fear and power, when its concept of man is false. We find the drive which makes a society stable at last in the search for what makes us men. 23 *Jacob Bronowski*

A true society is sustained by the sense of human dignity. 24 *Jacob Bronowski*

[T]he good society [is] one that gives to its members the greatest possibility of becoming sound and self-actualizing human beings. 25 *Abraham Maslow*

If there is going to be a victory over human incompleteness and limitation, it has to be a social project and not an individual one. 26 *Ernest Becker*

The ideal of human society is one which does bring people so closely together in their interrelationships ... that the individuals who exercise their own peculiar functions can take the attitude of those whom they affect.... The ideal of human society cannot exist as long as it is impossible for individuals to enter into the attitudes of those whom they are affecting.... 27 *George H. Mead*

The human mind exists only within an articulate framework provided for it by society; society both fosters thought and is in its turn largely controlled by thought. Hence the responsibility for every major mental decision is in part a social responsibility.... 28 *Michael Polanyi*

Men are what society has made them. 29 *August Bebel*

It is man's social being that determines his thinking. Once the correct ideas characteristic of the advanced class are grasped by the masses, these ideas turn into a material force which changes society and changes the world. 30 *Mao Tse-tung*

[I]f society is to be healthy, men must regard themselves not as the owners of rights, but as trustees for the discharge of functions and the instruments of a social purpose. 31 *R. H. Tawney*

[S]ociety cannot afford the absence among its members of *virtue* with its readiness for sacrifice beyond defined duty. Since its presence—that is say, that of personal idealism—is a matter of grace and not decree, we have the paradox that society depends for its existence on intangibles of nothing less than a religious order, for which it can hope, but which it cannot enforce. 32 *Hans Jonas*

If society is treated as a simple contraption to be managed on mathematical lines ... then man will be degraded into something much less than a partner in the immortal contract that unites the dead, the living, and those yet unborn, the bond between God and man. Order in this world is contingent upon order above. 33 *Russell Kirk*

The mind of the universe is social. 34 *Marcus Aurelius*

Society is the nexus and cradle of aspirations and visions which are certainly transindividual. Society is ultimately one of the modes of man's spiritual being. 35 *Henryk Skolimowski*

The first duty of society is to give each of its members the possibility of fulfilling his destiny. When it becomes incapable of performing this duty it must be transformed. 36 *Alexis Carrel*

A society is mad when its actions are no longer guided by what will make men healthier and happier, when its power is no longer in the service of life. 37 *Charles A. Reich*

All societies on the verge of death are masculine.... The masculinization of societies in decline is often caused by the loss of women.... A society can survive with only one man; no society will survive a shortage of women. 38 *Germaine Greer*

[There exists] a problem of social entropy in man's own nature and ... in the social organiza-

tions which he creates. Man is a highly improbable being and he constantly tends to slip down into more probable and less highly organized states.... His own constitution, therefore, and the societies which he creates are precarious, in the sense that their equilibrium, maintenance, and development require constant vigilance, attention and work. 39
Kenneth Boulding

[T]he machinery of society is at least as delicate as that of a spinning-jenny, and as little likely to be improved by the meddling of those who have not taken the trouble to master the principles of its action. 40 *T. H. Huxley*

[I]n modern society, people have become actors without an art. Society and social relations may continue to be abstractly imagined in dramatic terms, but men have ceased themselves to perform. 41 *Richard Sennett*

There is no such thing as Society. There are individual men and women, and there are families. 42 *Margaret Thatcher*

One of the great lessons ... which society has to teach its members is that society exists.... The mind is naturally its own world and its solipsism needs to be broken down by social influence. 43 *George Santayana*

What will not be built any more henceforth, and *cannot* be built any more is—a society in the old sense of that word; to build that, everything is lacking, above all the material. All of us are no longer material for a society. 44
Friedrich Nietzsche

Men must strive to realise their individual ideals in their common life but they will learn in the end that society remains man's great fulfillment and his great frustration. 45
Reinhold Niebuhr

Among the laws controlling human societies there is one more precise and clearer, it seems to me, than all the others. If men are to remain civilized or to become civilized, the art of association must develop and improve among them.... 46 *Alexis de Tocqueville*

Soul

To HAVE A SOUL is the whole venture of life, for soul is a life-giving daemon.... 1 *Carl Jung*

The definition of man is the definition of his soul. 2 *Aristotle*

The differentiation between "mind" and "soul" is a preliminary step towards a first understanding of the human being.... [T]he mind develops out of the soul's existence.... The soul enshrines the whole becoming of man. 3
Karl König

If a human being were to lose his soul, he would cease to be human; for the essence of being human is an awareness of a spiritual presence behind the phenomena.... 4 *Arnold Toynbee*

Neither man nor nation can exist without a sublime idea. And on earth there is *but one* supreme idea—namely, the idea of the immortality of man's soul—since all other "sublime" ideas of life, which gives life to man, *are merely derived from this one idea....* [W]ithout the belief in the existence of soul and its immortality human existence is "unnatural and unbearable." 5 *Feodor Dostoevsky*

[W]hat we hold most precious [is] the eternal essence of our soul.... There is a passionate desire in our souls, to stay related or to reestablish relations with humanity as such. 6
Karl Jaspers

The development of the child's soul is connected indissolubly with his craving for the You.... In the beginning is the relation—as category of being ... as a form that reaches out to be filled ... *the innate You.* 7 *Martin Buber*

The designation "soul" is merely a term used to denote the individual consciousness in its integrity and continuity; and that this soul undergoes change, that in like manner as it is integrated so it is disintegrated, is a thing very evident. 8 *Miguel de Unamuno*

Metaphysics or theology may prove the Soul to exist; but for psychology the hypothesis of

Soul

such a substantial principle of unity is superfluous. 9 *William James*

If our civilization is not the first to deny the immortality of the soul, it is certainly the first for which the soul has no importance. 10
André Malraux

To grant the substantiality of the soul … is repugnant to the spirit of the age, for to do so would be heresy. 11 *Carl Jung*

I have failed in my foremost task—to open people's eyes to the fact that man has a soul, that there is a buried treasure in the field.… 12
Carl Jung

The word soul or psyche is a literary symbol standing for the unconscious organic destiny present in living seeds and in living bodies. 13
George Santayana

[T]he soul of the living organism is its genetic code.… 14 *Timothy Leary*

Our reasonings have not established the nonexistence of the Soul; they have only proved its superfluity for scientific purposes. 15
William James

I maintain … that scientific psychology, in its inability to discover or even approach the essence of the soul … has put a *mechanism* in place of an *organism*. 16 *Oswald Spengler*

The same thing that looked at from the outside or biologically is called the psyche, looked at morally from within is called the soul. 17
George Santayana

The soul—or psyche—is that which constitutes our powers of sensing, feeling, and thought, the entirety of our experiences and all our memories.… Or, to put it another way: Our soul is the outward expression of that which moves us, raising it to the surface for the maintenance and defence of life. 18 *Conrad Stettbacher*

Soul is love; soul is the future.… The great saints and preachers followed it, the heroes and sufferers, the great generals and conquerors; the great magicians and artists followed it, and all those whose way began in the commonplace and ended in the holy heights. The way of millionaires is a different way and ends in the sanitarium.… [A]nd when it is cheated, when you win success at its expense, no happiness blossoms for you. For "happiness" can be felt only by the soul, not by the intellect, the belly, the head, or the purse. 19 *Hermann Hesse*

[T]o think of the soul as something simple is quite permissible in order, by the help of this *Idea*, to make the complete and necessary unity of all spiritual forces … the principle of our judgment. 20 *Immanuel Kant*

[It is] a fact of experience that supreme values reside in the soul.… 21 *Carl Jung*

One cannot do evil with his whole soul, one can do good only with his whole soul. 22
Martin Buber

Every human soul is still the battlefield of the powers of light and darkness. 23 *Karl König*

Everywhere the human soul stands between a hemisphere of light and another of darkness; on the confines of the two everlasting empires, necessity and free will. 24 *Thomas Carlyle*

If death had only been the end of all, dying would have been a godsend to the wicked, for they would have been happily rid not only of their body, but of their own evil together with their souls. But now, inasmuch as the soul is manifestly immortal, there is for her no release or salvation from evil except the attainment of the highest virtue and wisdom. 25 *Socrates*

The Good of man is the active exercise of his soul's faculties in conformity with excellence or virtue. 26 *Aristotle*

[T]he soul's hope has not been for more of the same, but for something altogether higher and better. 27 *John Baillie*

And it happens that the less a man believes in the soul … the more he will exaggerate the worth of this poor transitory life. 28
Miguel de Unamuno

Verily the lust for comfort murders the passion of the soul, and then walks grinning in the funeral. 29 *Kahlil Gibran*

From that awful encounter of the soul with the outer world, renunciation, wisdom, and charity are born; and with their birth a new life begins. To take into the inmost shrine of the soul the irresistible forces whose puppets we seem to be—Death and change … is to conquer them. 30 *Bertrand Russell*

In many primitive societies the soul is imagined to leave the body at death or just prior to it; here, on the other hand, society drives out the remnants of the soul of the institutionalized old person while it struggles to keep his body alive. 31 *Jules Henry*

And be not afraid of them who kill the body, but are not able to kill the soul; but rather fear him who is able to destroy both soul and body. 32 *Holy Bible*

Our souls are diseased, pursuing things that ultimately repel them. And the approach to health cannot come by rescinding our nature but by disentangling and harmonizing it as much as possible, as indeed it naturally endeavours to harmonize itself. 33 *George Santayana*

We have cancer—cancer of the soul. 34
Philip Wylie

"[U]ncertainty in the strivings of the soul" is perhaps one of the aptest descriptions of man's condition in our modern crisis.… 35
Marshall McLuhan

People will do anything, no matter how absurd, in order to avoid facing their own souls. 36
Carl Jung

As a result of the … triumphs of science, we are shaken by secret shadows and dark forebodings; but we know no way out, and very few persons indeed draw the conclusion that this time the issue is the long-since-forgotten *soul of man*. 37 *Carl Jung*

I think that the highly industrialized Western world has neglected to the utmost degree to leave room for man. The infernal production—consumption cycle has completely dehumanized life. The individual has become a tool. He hardly has any contact with nature anymore. That is, with himself. He has lost his soul and is not even trying to find it again. 38 *Indira Gandhi*

The scientific age has dawned, and we recognize that man himself is the master of his fate, the captain of his soul. He … is free to navigate it into fair waters or foul, or even to run it on to the rocks. 39 *Sir James Jeans*

[T]here is justifiable hope that regardless of the ever-increasing application of technology to the field of psychological knowledge … the human soul is virtually indestructible, and its ability to rise from the ashes remains so long as the body draws breath. 40 *Alice Miller*

[R]eturn to the depths of your soul: that is where you will rediscover the source of the sacred fire which inflames us with a love of the sublime; and that is where you will find the eternal image of true beauty, the contemplation of which inspires us with a holy joy. 41
Jean-Jacques Rousseau

SPIRIT

MAN IS SPIRIT. 1 *Søren Kierkegaard*

[T]he "spiritual" is what is human in man. 2
Viktor Frankl

When the organization called soul is free, moving and operative … it is spirit.… Spirit quickens; it is not only alive, but spirit gives life.… It is the moving function of that of which soul is the substance. 3 *John Dewey*

[T]he spirit giveth life. 4 *Saint Paul*

To … break a man's spirit is devil's work. 5
George Bernard Shaw

Spirit … sets up a moral centre for the universe. 6 *George Santayana*

[L]ove is the deepest ground of the life of the spirit. 7 *Søren Kierkegaard*

Spirit

[L]ove needs the spirit, and the spirit love, for their fulfillment. 8 *Carl Jung*

Man lives in the spirit when he is able to respond to his You.... [W]ithout It a human being cannot live. But whoever lives only with that [It] is not human. 9 *Martin Buber*

Spirit is not in the I but between I and You.... Spirit in its human manifestation is man's response to his You.... It is solely by virtue of his power to relate that man is able to live in the spirit. 10 *Martin Buber*

Spirit is the self.... The self is a relation. 11 *Søren Kierkegaard*

[S]pirit, by definition, is domination by the not-self.... So that to talk of selfishness in the spirit, in this ideal sense, would be a contradiction in terms. To be concerned with the self at all, for spirit, is a horrible distraction, the great disease, the eternal torment. 12 *George Santayana*

Spiritual powers are a form of wealth. They must go into circulation so that others can enjoy them; they must be expressed, utilized, to complete the cycle of human relations. 13 *Maria Montessori*

Spirit is like a child with eyes wide open, heart simple, faith ready, intellect pure.... Spirit is infinitely open. 14 *George Santayana*

A man is spiritual when he lives in the presence of the ideal, and whether he eat or drink does so for the sake of a true and ultimate good.... Spirituality is nobler than piety, because what would fulfil our being and make it worth having is what alone lends value to that being's source. 15 *George Santayana*

It is only from the presence of the spirit that significance and joy can flow into all work, and reverence and the strength to sacrifice into all possessions.... 16 *Martin Buber*

[T]he fruit of the Spirit is love, joy, peace.... 17 *Saint Paul*

Let the spirit come to the aid of the flesh and so recover the support of the flesh, and let the flesh submit to the spirit and thus recover peace. There lies the way. 18 *Denis de Rougemont*

The spirit lives in the word of language and in the mythical image.... [I]t uses them both as *organs* of its own, and thereby recognizes them for what they really are: forms of its own self-revelation. 19 *Ernst Cassirer*

The science of Pure Mathematics ... may claim to be the most original creation of the human spirit. Another claimant for this position is music. 20 *Alfred N. Whitehead*

Spirit speaks not for the truth or for the intellect ... but speaks for all life, in so far as life has been perfected and harmonized. 21 *George Santayana*

As a being in an active relation to the world [man] comes into a spiritual relation with it by not living for himself alone, but feeling himself one with all life that comes within his reach.... The stronger the reverence for natural life, the stronger grows also that for spiritual life. 22 *Albert Schweitzer*

[T]he spiritual life is part of our biological life. It is the "highest" part of it, but part of it. 23 *Abraham Maslow*

It would be strange, indeed, if the order of material things were to reflect more of divine wisdom than that of spiritual things. The contrary is true. 24 *Simone Weil*

[E]verything that is physical around us is actually an outcome of the spiritual. Spirit is always there first. And it is the spirit that sets everything going. 25 *Rudolf Steiner*

Spiritual development is an innate evolutionary capacity of all human beings. It is a movement toward wholeness, the discovery of one's true potential. 26 *Christina & Stanislov Grof*

Spiritual growth is a journey out of the microcosm into an ever greater macrocosm. 27 *M. Scott Peck*

By spiritual being we mean that state of being where the self excels into the universe, and

knows all things by passing into all things. 28
D. H. Lawrence

Spirituality is something that characterizes the relationship of an individual to the universe.... 29 *Christina & Stanislov Grof*

The spiritual quest begins, for most people, as a search for meaning. 30 *Marilyn Ferguson*

Spiritual self-affirmation occurs in every moment in which man lives creatively in the various spheres of meaning. 31 *Paul Tillich*

[O]nly the spirit can give life its highest meaning. 32 *Carl Jung*

[J]ust as our primary wide-awake consciousness throws open our senses to the touch of things material, so it is logically conceivable that *if there be* higher spiritual agencies that can directly touch us, the psychological condition of their doing so *might be* our possession of a subconscious region which alone should yield access to them. The hubbub of the waking life might close a door which in the dreamy Subliminal might remain ajar or open. 33 *William James*

[I]n the last analysis the "spirit" of persons or things comes down to their capacity to be remembered and imagined after perception of them has ceased. 34 *Sigmund Freud*

We live in memory and by memory, and our spiritual life is at bottom simply the effort of our memory to persist, to transform itself into hope, the effort of our past to transform itself into our future. 35 *Miguel de Unamuno*

Every great culture that embraces more than one people rests upon some original encounter, an event at the source when a response was made to a You, an essential act of the spirit. 36
Martin Buber

[T]o obstruct useful, if merely technological and instrumental, progress in the name of spiritual values is to ascribe to the superficial trappings of our lives an importance far beyond their deserts. It is also to risk ultimate economic failures that imperil the future of free societies. 37 *George Gilder*

Nihilism and scientism ... enshrined Facts as deities, and condemned all products of the human spirit as "meaningless." ... 38
Henryk Skolimowski

In our time ... the transformational journey of spiritual development becomes ... almost viewed through the lens of disease. 39
Christina & Stanislov Grof

[I]n our age it is a crime to have spirit.... 40
Søren Kierkegaard

We moderns are faced with the necessity of rediscovering the life of the spirit.... 41 *Carl Jung*

For the time being at least, in the moment of profound change at the end of the cold war, the advantage lies not with the policies of fear and restraint but with the reaching of the human spirit.... 42 *Lewis Lapham*

The spiritual life is really built upon the fundamental basis of a unified personality, well attuned to the outer world. 43
Maria Montessori

Spirit ... speaks for a soul reduced to harmony and for the sane mind. This sanity implies not only integrity within, but also adjustment to the outer universe. So that whilst spirit is physically the voice of the soul crying in the wilderness, it becomes vicariously and morally the voice of the wilderness admonishing the soul. 44
George Santayana

The spirit is the true self. 45 *Cicero*

Spirituality is ... an instrument, enabling man to refine himself further and further. Thus ... spirituality is an instrument of the perfectibility of man. In a sense, spirituality is synonymous with the quality of humanity. 46
Henryk Skolimowski

[M]an, oblivious to the existence of spiritual powers ... ceases to be human. 47 *Russell Kirk*

[W]e must look to the spiritual world to find the impulse to carry forward what we know to be the evolutionary course of humanity.... Spiritual science will become the great impulse

State

The preservation of the national character and, more particularly, the development of its creative faculties is the supreme task of the nation. In order to fulfill this task, the nation needs power that will protect it against other nations and will stimulate its own development. In other words, the nation needs a state. "One nation—one state" is thus the political postulate of nationalism; the nation state is its ideal. 17
Hans Morgenthau

The state has thus become a modern idol whose suggestive power few men are able to escape. 18 *Albert Einstein*

[D]uring the time that men live without a common power to keep them all in awe, they are in that condition which is … a war … of every man against every man.… In such condition … the life of man [is] solitary, poor, nasty, brutish, and short.… [I]n the introduction of that restraint upon themselves in which we see them live in commonwealths … [men get] themselves out from that miserable condition … when there is no visible power to keep them in awe and tie them by fear of punishment to the performance of their covenants.… 19
Thomas Hobbes

The State is the keystone of the social arch. 20
Harold Laski

The political state is founded not for the purpose of men's merely living together, but for their living together as men ought.… 21 *Aristotle*

It is through the appearance of struggle for recognition and submission to a master, that states have been initiated out of the social life of men. 22 *G. W. F. Hegel*

[I]s masculinity inherent in the state form as such?… Formally, the state is male in that objectivity is its norm.… Objectivist epistemology is the law of law. It ensures that the law will most reinforce existing distributions of power when it most closely adheres to its own highest ideal of fairness.… Such law not only reflects a society in which men rule women; it rules in a male way.… It is because the state, in part through law, institutionalizes male power. 23
Catherine MacKinnon

Society is founded on love, but the state is not because the state is a collection of minorities with different, even irreconcilable common goods.… [T]he state must bring harmony among the warring groups, not through love, but external discipline. 24
Germaine Greer

The State is a cold concern which cannot inspire love, but itself kills, suppresses everything that might be loved; so one is forced to love it, because there is nothing else. That is the moral torment to which all of us today are exposed. 25 *Simone Weil*

The state came into existence as a necessary product of the new social order based on conflicting interests. Its direction naturally was assumed by those who had the greatest interest in its founding and who, thanks to their social power, were most influential: *the propertied classes.* 26 *August Bebel*

[T]he bourgeoisie has at last, since the establishment of modern industry and of the world market, conquered for itself, in the modern representative State, exclusive political sway. The executive of the modern State is but a committee for managing the affairs of the whole bourgeoisie. 27 *Karl Marx*

[T]he basic function of the State remains the regulation of domestic and international affairs in the interest of the masters of the private economy.… 28 *Noam Chomsky*

Society, that it may live better, creates the State as an instrument. Then the State gets the upper hand and society has to begin to live for the State. 29 *José Ortega y Gasset*

The national state was designed to be the guardian of civil society. The Megastate became its master. 30 *Peter F. Drucker*

[T]he State, which claimed to be the embodiment of … unity and yet desired to be independent of, and superior to, the nation … [is] but a parasitic excrescence on the body of the nation.… 31 *Karl Marx*

The state no longer exists to serve man; men exist

STATE

in order to worship a state.... It is now an end and no longer a means. 32 *Adolf Hitler*

[T]he altogether un-Socratic and un-Christian teaching that the end justifies the means is the basis on which governments, in all times, have licensed themselves to commit crimes of every sort; the *raison d'état* of governments ... holds that states may do virtually anything whatever in the name of survival. 33 *Jonathan Schell*

The State is the enemy not merely because of oppression, injustice, and war, but because it has made itself the enemy of life itself. 34 *Charles A. Reich*

[A] minimal state, limited to the narrow functions of protection against force, theft, fraud, enforcement of contracts, and so on, is justified.... [A]ny more extensive state will violate persons' rights not to be forced to do certain things, and is unjustified.... 35 *Robert Nozick*

A society striving for true democracy should never lose sight of the principle that it is the task of the state to make itself progressively unnecessary.... The state must not only further the strongest longings for freedom ... [but] it also has the task of adding to it the *capacity for freedom*. If it fails to do so ... it proves its fascist character. 36 *Wilhelm Reich*

[S]o long as the state exists there is no freedom. When there is freedom, there will be no state. 37 *V. I. Lenin*

The state withers away in so far as there are no longer any capitalists, any classes, and, consequently, no *class* can be *suppressed*.... For the state to wither away completely complete Communism is necessary. 38 *V. I. Lenin*

[O]nly under Communism will the State become quite unnecessary, for there will be *no one* to suppress.... 39 *V. I. Lenin*

All modern revolutions have ended in a reinforcement of the State. 40 *Albert Camus*

Most theories of the state are merely intellectual devices invented by philosophers for the purpose of proving that the people who actually wield power are precisely the people who ought to wield it. 41 *Aldous Huxley*

To the extent that the twentieth century has rescued itself from barbarianism, it is because the hopes of ordinary people have prevailed over the interests of the state. 42 *Lewis Lapham*

The degree of statism in a country's political system, is the degree to which it breaks up the country into rival gangs and sets men against one another.... In order to survive under such a system, men have no choice but to fear, hate, and destroy one another; it is a system of underground plotting, of secret conspiracies, of deals, favors, betrayals, and sudden, bloody coups.... Statism *needs* war.... If nuclear weapons are a dreadful threat and mankind cannot afford war any longer, then *mankind cannot afford statism any longer*. 43 *Ayn Rand*

The only ultimate cure for war is the creation of a world-state or superstate, strong enough to decide by law all disputes between nations. 44 *Bertrand Russell*

[T]he proponents of a "world superstate" are asking us voluntarily to surrender [our] independence for the sake of a "world government," which is nothing but a flamboyant signboard for the world supremacy of the capitalist monopolies. 45 *Soviet editorial*

Do I fear the tyranny of a world government? Of course I do. But I fear still more the coming of another war or wars. 46 *Albert Einstein*

There is only *one* path to peace and security: the path of the supranational organization. 47 *Albert Einstein*

The problem before us has become, because of the unified interests of mankind, that of bending the modern State to the interests of humanity. 48 *Harold Laski*

SUFFERING & CHALLENGE

THERE IS NOT MUCH SENSE in suffering, since drugs can be given for pain.... The belief has long died that suffering here on earth will be rewarded in heaven. Suffering has lost its meaning. 1 *Elizabeth Kübler-Ross*

Whatever its nature and whatever its apparent cause, [archaic man's] suffering had a meaning.... [H]e tolerates it morally because *it is not absurd*.... If it was possible to tolerate such sufferings, it was precisely because they seemed neither gratuitous nor arbitrary.... [N]owhere—within the frame of the archaic civilizations—are suffering and pain regarded as "blind" and without meaning. 2 *Mircea Eliade*

[O]ne assumes that elimination of suffering is an essential or even *the* essential drive of man. But ... [the] idea of the pleasure principle, particularly when applied to normal life, overlooks the enormous significance of tension for self-realization in its highest forms.... [We] are in a dilemma that demands a *choice* between [not] accepting and enduring suffering and getting fuller self-realization. 3 *Kurt Goldstein*

Some sick people are capable of making the almost superhuman effort that will transform the disaster of bodily defect into spiritual triumph. 4 *Aldous Huxley*

My existence is a terrible burden; I would have thrown it away long ago, if I had not made the most enlightening tests and experiments in the spiritual and moral domain precisely in this state of suffering. 5 *Friedrich Nietzsche*

[F]ar from confirming the current idea that suicide is due to life's burdens ... on the contrary, it diminishes as these burdens increase. 6 *Émile Durkheim*

It is ... only in the state of complete abandonment and loneliness that we experience the helpful powers of our own natures. 7 *Carl Jung*

The sorrows and distresses of life ... seem to be necessary ... to soften and humanize the heart.... The heart that has never known sorrow will seldom be feelingly alive to the pains and pleasures, the wants and wishes, of its fellow beings. 8 *Thomas Malthus*

Suffering and understanding are deeply connected.... Kindness is a stranger to those who have not suffered. 9 *Denis de Rougemont*

Your pain is the breaking of the shell that encloses your understanding. 10 *Kahlil Gibran*

[M]en must learn wisdom by suffering. Drop by drop in sleep upon the heart ... against one's will comes wisdom. 11 *Aeschylus*

[E]ven on the lowest plane we may say that to suffer is to learn. 12 *George Santayana*

[B]y death, by illness, by poverty ... we must learn, each one of us, that ... however beautiful may be the things we crave, Fate may nevertheless forbid them. It is the part of courage, when misfortune comes, to bear without repining the ruin of our hopes.... This degree of submission to Power is only just and right: it is the very gate of wisdom. 13 *Bertrand Russell*

Man is never helped in his suffering by what he thinks for himself, but only by revelations of a wisdom greater than his own. 14 *Carl Jung*

At first we cannot see beyond the path that leads downward to dark and hateful things—but no light or beauty will ever come from the man who cannot bear this sight. 15 *Carl Jung*

Deep, unspeakable suffering may well be called a baptism, a regeneration, the initiation into a new state. 16 *George Eliot*

Only through experience of the impossibility of achieving fulfilment does man become enabled to perform his allotted task. 17 *Karl Jaspers*

There is no such thing as fulfillment where there is no risk of failure.... 18 *John Dewey*

A successful life is not one without ordeals, failures, and tragedies, but one during which the person has made an adequate number of effective responses to the constant challenges of his physical and social environment. 19 *René Dubos*

Suffering & Challenge

He who has never failed somewhere, that man can not be great. 20 *Herman Melville*

I believe … that many of the greatest heroes, perhaps the greatest of all, have been men of despair and that by despair they have accomplished their mighty works. 21
Miguel de Unamuno

Experience suggests that if men cannot struggle on behalf of a just cause … then they will struggle *against* the just cause. They will struggle for the sake of struggle … for they cannot imagine living in a world without struggle. 22
Francis Fukuyama

All life is the struggle, the effort to be itself. The difficulties which I meet with in order to realize my existence are precisely what awaken and mobilize my activities, my capacities. 23
José Ortega y Gasset

The spiritual value of our disappointments does not lie merely in producing resignation, or reconciling our chastened wills.… But the chief good in having been disappointed is that, if we are firm, we remain inconsolable, having aspired and still aspiring to something better than the event. Then against its Will, fortune will have wedded us to beauties it had no power to create, but only to promise. That promise, externally so foolish, has made us inwardly wise, enabling us to break in spirit through the veil of time, and to recognize a sublime nocturnal firmament above the sky. 24
George Santayana

Indeed life is a battle … but in fighting the difficulties the inmost strength of the heart is developed. 25 *Vincent van Gogh*

The advent of spirit cannot abolish … vital impulses and mortal dangers; but in raising them into conscious suffering and love, spirit turns the ignominy of blind existence into nobleness, setting before us some object to suffer for and to pursue. In the very act of becoming painful, life has become worth living in its own eyes. 26 *George Santayana*

It is not true that suffering ennobles the character; happiness does that sometimes, but suffering, for the most part, makes men petty and vindictive. 27 *W. Somerset Maugham*

In the last resort it is highly improbable that there could ever be a therapy which got rid of all difficulties. Man needs difficulties; they are necessary for health. What concerns us here is only an excessive amount of them. 28 *Carl Jung*

The great enigma of human life is not suffering but affliction.… There is not really affliction where there is not social degradation or the fear of it in some form or another. 29 *Simone Weil*

It is not the fate that overtakes us that makes our dignity but the detachment with which we suffer it. 30 *George Santayana*

We begin to live when we have conceived life as tragedy. 31 *W. B. Yeats*

[L]ife is always difficult and is full of pain as well as joy. Yet it is in this whole process of meeting and solving problems that life has its meaning.… It is only because of problems that we grow mentally and spiritually. 32 *M. Scott Peck*

[H]appiness is not a characteristic of spirit. 33
Søren Kierkegaard

He who suffers lives, and he who lives suffering … loves and hopes. It is better to live in pain than to cease to be in peace. 34
Miguel de Unamuno

Everything that the human race has done and thought is concerned with the satisfaction of deeply felt needs and the assuagement of pain. One has to keep this constantly in mind if one wishes to understand spiritual movements and their development. 35 *Albert Einstein*

Suffering is never provisional for the man who does not believe in the future. 36 *Albert Camus*

Myths tell us how to confront and bear and interpret suffering, but they do not say that in life there can or should be no suffering. 37
Joseph Campbell

There are times when sorrow seems to me to be the only truth. Other things may be illusions …

but out of sorrow have the worlds been built.... For the secret of life is suffering. It is what is hidden behind everything. 38 *Oscar Wilde*

[R]eal change is difficult and painful, which perhaps explains why Americans have abandoned all responsibility for initiating it.... 39 *Philip Slater*

We wish to make our lives simple, certain and smooth—and for that reason problems are *tabu*.... The artful denial of a problem will not produce conviction; on the contrary, a wider and higher consciousness is called for.... 40 *Carl Jung*

[T]he evolution of organic beings is simply a struggle to realize fullness of consciousness through suffering.... 41 *Miguel de Unamuno*

We perceive that *Homo sapiens* has the capacity to extort new adaptations from his suffering, and that if he does not destroy himself too soon, he may eventually come upon a destiny of great beauty. 42 *Jules Henry*

Without matter there is no spirit, but matter makes spirit suffer by limiting it. And suffering is simply the obstacle which matter opposes to spirit.... Suffering is, in effect, the barrier which unconsciousness, matter, sets up against consciousness, spirit; it is the resistance to will, the limit which the visible universe imposes upon God.... 43 *Miguel de Unamuno*

[W]hat all the strongest of human souls have observed and reported as a fact of experience [is] that through the endurance and the conquest over its own internal ills the spirit wins its best conscious fulfilment. What if this moment of despair be but the beginning ... of your whole life.... That the fulfilment of the whole of a purpose may involve the defeat of a part of this very purpose, every experience of the beauty of tragedy, of the glory of courage, of the nobility of endurance, of the triumph over our own selves, empirically illustrates.... Whoever has not faced problems as problems ... [or] defeats as defeats, knows not what the completer possession of his own life means.... For in the victorious warfare with finitude consists the perfection of the spirit. 44 *Josiah Royce*

God is revealed to us because He suffers and because we suffer.... He sent His Son in order that he might redeem us by suffering and dying. It was the revelation of the divine in suffering, for only that which suffers is divine. 45 *Miguel de Unamuno*

Where there is sorrow there is holy ground. 46 *Oscar Wilde*

Suffering is the substance of life and the root of personality, for it is only suffering that makes us persons. And suffering is that which unites all us living beings together; it is the universal or divine blood that flows through us all. 47 *Miguel de Unamuno*

Pleasure for the beautiful body, but pain for the beautiful soul. 48 *Oscar Wilde*

Symbols

The essential act of thought is symbolization. 1 *A. D. Ritchie*

I believe there is a primary need in man, which other creatures probably do not have, and which actuates all his apparently unzoölogical aims, his wistful fantasies, his consciousness of value, his utterly impractical enthusiasms, and his awareness of a "Beyond" filled with holiness.... This basic need, which certainly is obvious only in man, is the *need of symbolization.* 2 *Susanne Langer*

It is this ability to proliferate and elaborate the image into a symbolic universe that is the peculiarity and the glory of man. 3 *Kenneth Boulding*

No longer in a merely physical universe, man lives in a symbolic universe.... [T]his appears to be the distinctive mark of human life.... No longer can man confront reality immediately ... [but rather] he lives, so to speak, in a new *dimension* of reality.... Instead of dealing with the things themselves man is in a sense constantly conversing with himself. 4 *Ernst Cassirer*

The symbol has become an automatic register of the dimensions of the self.... 5 *Herbert Read*

Symbols

[T]he deepening humanization of man in society depends upon his capacity to turn experiences into symbols and symbols into life-experiences.... Only by means of symbols can man widen the powers of discrimination and the acts of choice.... Thus symbols are not vicarious substitutes for experience but a means of enhancing it and enlarging its domain. 6
Lewis Mumford

Symbols pave the royal route from raw intelligences to finished cultures. 7
Howard Gardner

[W]here masses of people must cooperate in an uncertain and eruptive environment, it is usually necessary to secure unity and flexibility without real consent. The symbol does that.... It renders the mass mobile though it immobilizes personality. 8 *Walter Lippmann*

Because of its power to siphon emotion out of distinct ideas, the symbol is both a mechanism of solidarity, and a mechanism of exploitation. 9 *Walter Lippmann*

The power to dominate a culture's symbol-producing apparatus is the power to create the ambiance that forms human consciousness. 10
Rose Goldsen

Any miscarriage of the symbolic process is an abrogation of our human freedom.... All such obstacles may block the free functioning of mind. 11 *Susanne Langer*

The essence of the use of symbols ... is the capacity to transcend the immediate, concrete situation.... [T]his capacity for transcending the immediate situation is the basis of human freedom. 12 *Rollo May*

Symbols ... afford the only way of escape from submergence in existence. 13 *John Dewey*

Symbols awaken individual experience and transmute it into a spiritual act, into metaphysical comprehension of the world. 14
Mircea Eliade

It is a peculiar fact that every major advance in thinking, every epoch-making new insight, springs from a new type of symbolic transformation. 15 *Susanne Langer*

[T]he special symbolic forms are not imitations but *organs* of reality, since it is solely by their agency that anything real becomes an object for intellectual apprehension.... 16 *Ernst Cassirer*

The world which the human mind knows and explores does not survive if it is emptied of thought. And thought does not survive without symbolic concepts. The symbol and the metaphor are as necessary to science as to poetry. 17
Jacob Bronowski

[O]nce the idea of possible operations, indicated by symbols and performed *only* by means of symbols, is discovered, the road is opened to operations of ever increasing definiteness and comprehensiveness. 18 *John Dewey*

Symbols are sensible signs, final, indivisible and, above all, unsought impressions of definite meaning. A symbol is a trait of actuality that for the sensuously alert man has an immediate and inwardly sure significance, and that is incommunicable by process of reason. 19
Oswald Spengler

Symbols are only the *vehicles* of communication; they must not be mistaken for the final term, the *tenor* of their reference.... [T]hey remain but convenient means, accommodated to the understanding.... The problem of the theologian is to keep his symbol translucent, so that it may not block out the very light it is supposed to convey. 20 *Joseph Campbell*

Knowledge is assimilation.... The symbol represents the dream of a non-destructive assimilation. 21 *Jean-Paul Sartre*

The requisites for symbolism are that there be two species of percepta; and that a perceptum of one species has some "ground" in common with a perceptum of another species, so that a correlation between the pair of percepta is established. 22 *Alfred N. Whitehead*

A symbol is nothing but the stimulus whose response is given in advance. 23
George H. Mead

The modern age ... has turned from symbolism to extreme realism.... It is inevitable, however, in this effort after exact realism of detail that the sense of the larger unity of things should be obscured.... For symbolism is, in its highest aspect, a reverential search after the highest truth, an acknowledgment of the broad unity of things. 24 *Ruth Benedict*

[T]he distinction between what exists in time, what is irreversible, and, on the other hand, what is outside of time, what is eternal, is at the origin of human symbolic activity. 25
Ilya Prigogine

[B]eyond [the intellect] there is a thinking in primordial images—in symbols which ... still make up the groundwork of the human psyche. It is only possible to live the fullest life when we are in harmony with these symbols; wisdom is a return to them. 26 *Carl Jung*

Mythological symbols ... have to be followed through all their implications before they open out the full system of correspondences through which they represent, by analogy, the millennial adventure of the soul. 27 *Joseph Campbell*

Man is still in his childhood.... His moral life, to take shape at all, must appear to him in fantastic symbols. The history of these symbols is therefore the history of his soul. 28
George Santayana

[W]e are dealing with a breakdown in man's sense of symbolic unity and impairment of his sense of immortality.... [G]eneral or historical desymbolization ... is characterized by an inability to believe in larger connections, by pervasive expressions of psychic numbing. These states can be directly manifested in various kinds of apathy, unrelatedness, and a general absence of trust or faith.... 29 *Robert Jay Lifton*

All old symbols are gone.... 30
Susanne Langer

Western culture is changing already into a symbol system unprecedented in its plasticity and absorptive capacity. Nothing much can oppose it really, and it welcomes all criticism, for, in a sense, it stands for nothing. 31 *Philip Rieff*

TECHNOLOGY

EVERY TECHNOLOGY ever conceived by the genius of humankind is nothing more than a transformer of energy from nature's storehouse. In the process of that transformation ... the energy eventually ends up as dissipated waste.... The faster we streamline our technology, the faster we speed up the transforming process, the faster available energy is dissipated, the more pollution and waste mounts. 1 *Jeremy Rifkin*

When critics charge that technocratic planning is anti-human, in the sense that it neglects social, cultural, and psychological values in its headlong rush to maximize economic gain, they are usually right.... [T]echnological questions can no longer be answered in technological terms alone.... And we cannot casually delegate responsibility for such decisions to businessmen, scientists, engineers or administrators who are unaware of the profound consequences of their own actions. 2 *Alvin Toffler*

Technological reason ... abolishes contradiction ... and permits vague anxieties to be replaced by definite fears which supposedly can be mastered. But the ethical, social and existential issues of ultimate concern require a totally different kind of reasoning.... 3
Charles Hampden-Turner

Science, the parent, is consumed by its technological offspring. What results is an impulse—never stronger and never more dangerous than now—to substitute a brilliant technological vision for the more recalcitrant problems of human continuity, of ... symbolic immortality.... Within this scientific aberration, "knowing" ... becomes only solving puzzles or manipulating the environment. 4
Robert Jay Lifton

It is my judgment in these things that when you see something that is technically sweet, you go ahead and do it.... That is the way it was with the atomic bomb. 5 *Robert Oppenheimer*

In our technological society, *technique* is the totality of methods rationally arrived at and having absolute efficiency ... in every field of

Technology

human activity.... [T]echnique transforms everything it touches into a machine.... Technique integrates the machine into society. It constructs the kind of world the machine needs.... Technique has become autonomous; it ... obeys its own laws.... Technique requires predictability.... It is necessary, then, that technique prevail over the human being.... Technique must reduce man to a technical animal.... [T]here can be no human autonomy in the face of technical autonomy. 6 *Jacques Ellul*

[Out] of modern technological development ... emerges a new type of man—the uncritical recipient of orders.... The more mechanized the world becomes, the more essential is a counterbalancing influence of individual freedom and responsibility. 7 *Albert Speer*

In our minds, at least, technology is always on the verge of liberating us from personal discipline and responsibility. Only it never does and it never will. 8 *John Naisbitt*

Today's real world of technology is characterized by the dominance of prescriptive technologies.... [P]rescriptive technologies eliminate the occasions for decision-making and judgement in general and especially for the making of *principled* decisions.... At the same time they have created a culture of compliance ... [and] diminished resistance to the programming of people. 9 *Ursula Franklin*

Technical progress is putting man's freedom of mind in jeopardy. 10 *Susanne Langer*

In the technetronic society the trend would seem to be towards ... attractive personalities effectively exploiting the latest communication techniques to manipulate emotions and control reason. 11 *Zbigniew Brzezinski*

Machines are an extension of man's mind.... The demand to "restrict" technology is the demand to restrict man's mind.... [L]ife in nature, without technology, is wholesale death. 12 *Ayn Rand*

Technology is the very strategy of life: the essential form of action in the battle that is life itself. 13 *Oswald Spengler*

We must realize that technology was not put into the universe by man. The universe is the most comprehensive system of technology. Humanity is discovering and beginning to employ it.... 14 *R. Buckminster Fuller*

The world populace identifies technology with (1) weapons and (2) machines that compete with them for their jobs. Most people therefore think they are against technology, not knowing that the technology they don't understand is their only means of exercising their option to "make it" on this planet and in this life. 15 *R. Buckminster Fuller*

Electromagnetic technology requires utter human docility and quiescence of meditation such as befits an organism that now wears its brain outside its skull and its nerves outside its hide.... By continuously embracing technologies, we relate ourselves to them as servomechanisms. That is why we must, to use them at all, serve these objects, these extensions of ourselves, as gods or minor religions.... [L]ike the bees in the plant world, men have always been the sex organs of the technological world. 16 *Marshall McLuhan*

Just as scientific knowledge is becoming alienated from human experience, so are its technological applications becoming increasingly alienated from human needs. 17 *René Dubos*

New needs are being produced every minute; there is no end to them; and humankind, like an eternal suckling babe, waits with open mouth, expecting to be fed more and more and more. This is a paradise of total gratification.... Technology is the new God ... assuming the role of a Great Mother who will feed all her children and satisfy all their demands.... 18 *Erich Fromm*

The more technical our society becomes, the less natural we become as mothers, the greater the potential harm there is for our children.... 19 *Natalie Shainess*

[I]n technological societies ... we find the greatest terror of the organic, in fact ... hatred and fear of life. 20 *Morris Berman*

Technology

[T]he *specialist* [is] the man who knows more and more about less and less.... As he grows more expert in his special bit of information the specialist tends to decline in his competence as a human being. In a world in which the technologist is as highly valued as our own, the danger to us all of becoming technologized out of existence is great. Humanity must protect itself from the technologists, and do everything in its power to protect the technologists from themselves. 21 *Ashley Montagu*

Man has now decisively overcome Nature by his technology, but the victor has been technology, not Man himself. Man has merely exchanged one master for another, and his new master is more overbearing than his former. 22
Arnold Toynbee

We pride ourselves on being a democracy but we are in fact slaves. We submit to an absolute ruler whose edicts and whims we never question.... [F]or technology is a harsh and capricious king, demanding prompt and absolute obedience.... Technology makes core policy in every industrialized nation, and the humans adjust as best they can. 23 *Philip Slater*

In the construction of the technological reality, there is no such thing as a purely rational scientific order; the process of technological rationality is a political process. 24
Herbert Marcuse

No doubt every technological revolution is also a social one in the sense that technological changes are both consequences and causes of social changes. 25 *Arnold Toynbee*

What makes the drive to technology so strong is that it is carried on by men who still identify what they are doing with the liberation of mankind. Our ruling managers are able to do what they do just because among sufficient of them technology and liberalism support each other as identified. It is this identification which makes our drive to technology still more dynamic than the nihilistic will to will which is emptied of all conceptions of purpose. 26 *George Grant*

One of the major goals of technology in America is to "free" us from the necessity of relating to, submitting to, depending upon, or controlling other people. Unfortunately, the more we have succeeded in doing this the more we have felt disconnected, bored, lonely, unprotected, unnecessary, and unsafe. 27 *Philip Slater*

The greatest danger of our machine made wealth grows out of this: ... material comfort is possible for almost everyone. But if this, because it is so much more available, is sought not in addition to emotional contentment but in lieu of it, then there is the danger of our becoming addicted to it. We will need more and more technological progress to cover up our emotional want and discomfort. 28
Bruno Bettelheim

In this age, in which technics is invading and conquering the last enemy—man's inner life, the psyche itself—a suitable new character type has arrived on the scene: the psychological man ... a child not of nature but of technology ... : he is anti-heroic, shrewd, carefully counting his satisfactions and dissatisfactions, studying unprofitable commitments as the sins most to be avoided.... Psychological man has withdrawn into a world always at war, where the ego is an armed force capable of achieving armistices but not peace.... 29 *Philip Rieff*

At this point, technology diminishes consciousness and demolishes eros. Tools are no longer an enlargement of consciousness but a substitute for it.... 30 *Rollo May*

The effects of technology do not occur at the level of opinions or concepts, but alter sense ratios or patterns of perception steadily and without any resistance.... It goes without saying that the universal ignoring of the psychic action of technology bespeaks some inherent function, some essential numbing of consciousness.... 31 *Marshall McLuhan*

Only man, through his technology, could render the meaningful totally meaningless. 32
Robert Jay Lifton

Technology demands of man a new mind—a higher, transcendent reason—if it is to be controlled and guided rather than to become an unthinking monster. It demands a new

TECHNOLOGY

individual responsibility for values, or it will dictate all values. 33 *Charles A. Reich*

[T]he progress of the technological world depends upon the obliteration of moral questions—the advancement of value-free judgments. 34 *Abraham Maslow*

The coming to be of technology has required changes in what we think is good ... how we conceive sanity and madness, justice and injustice, rationality and irrationality, beauty and ugliness.... [We] apprehend our destiny by forms of thought which are themselves the very core of that destiny. 35 *George Grant*

[T]echnology as a mode of revealing truth determines the character of that truth, and leaves out other truths. The danger lies not in the technology itself, but in a misunderstanding of technology's impact on man and knowledge, and in the loss of control. 36
R. G. Lazar & M. D. Lazar

The power which man has achieved through technology has been transformed into spiritual and moral impotence. 37 *Ruth N. Anshen*

We must learn to balance the material wonders of technology with the spiritual demands of our human nature. 38 *John Naisbitt*

Is technological man still a part of Gaia or are we in some or in many ways alienated from her?... [I]n a Gaian world our species with its technology is simply an inevitable part of the natural scene. Yet our relationship with our technology releases ever-increasing amounts of energy and provides us with a similarly increasing capacity to channel and process information. Cybernetics tells us that we might safely pass through these turbulent times if our skills in handling information develop faster than our capacity to produce more energy. In other words, if we can always control the genie we have let out of the bottle. 39 *J. E. Lovelock*

The horrifying truth is that, so far as much technology is concerned, no one is in charge. 40
Alvin Toffler

[T]here can only be disaster arising from unawareness of the causalities and effects inherent in our own technologies. 41
Marshall McLuhan

Technology has muddled or even destroyed the traditional social compass.... [To] shape and direct technology will [require] a renewed emphasis on the concept of justice. The viability of technology, like democracy, depends in the end on the practice of justice and on the enforcement of limits to power. 42 *Ursula Franklin*

The Big Technology has been for Americans what the Cross was for the Emperor Constantine: *In hoc signo vincas*. It set the pace for an impressively swift and thorough conquest of a new environment and of world leadership. 43 *Max Lerner*

[T]he quest for control is inherent in all technology. 44 *Joseph Weizenbaum*

The human dilemma is as it has always been, and we solve nothing fundamental by cloaking ourselves in technological glory. 45
Neil Postman

Technology is materialized fantasy. We are ruled today by the materialized fantasies of previous generations. 46 *Philip Slater*

Technological progress is accompanied by a progressive rationalization and even realization of the imaginary. The archetypes of horror as well as of joy, of war as well as of peace lose their catastrophic character.... When technical progress cancels this separation, it invests the images with its own logic and its own truth; it reduces the free faculty of the mind. But it also reduces the gap between imagination and Reason. 47 *Herbert Marcuse*

The Technopoly story is without a moral center. It puts in its place efficiency, interest, and economic advance. It promises heaven on earth through the conveniences of technological progress. It casts aside all traditional narratives and symbols that suggest stability and orderliness, and tells instead, of a life of skills, technical expertise, and the ecstasy of consumption. Its purpose is to produce functionaries for an ongoing Technopoly. 48 *Neil Postman*

Technological advance has its own self-destruct mechanism built into it. For as change becomes more rapid, reaching the point of almost instant obsolescence, it becomes more and more impossible to plan for the future.... So as technology pushes into the future, it also *undermines* the future.... 49 *Philip Slater*

Unfortunately, what technology gives with one hand, it often takes away with the other. 50 *Michael Heim*

Technological advance is rapid. But without progress in charity, technological advance is useless. Indeed, it is worse than useless. Technological progress has merely provided us with more efficient means for going backwards. 51 *Aldous Huxley*

On the terms imposed by technocratic society, there is no hope for mankind except by "going with" its plans for accelerated technological progress, even though man's vital organs will all be cannibalized in order to prolong the megamachine's meaningless existence. But for those of us who have thrown off the myth of the machine ... the gates of the technocratic prison will open automatically ... as soon as we choose to walk out. 52 *Lewis Mumford*

The turn in our destinies will come from the realization that technology, know-how, achievements, are not enough. The science and technologies of man must become parts of an encompassing whole.... Our age must learn that some things are beyond "doing." 53 *Karl Jaspers*

To accept the limitation of our abilities, seems to be the most difficult idea that Promethean man must learn. But learn it he must and learn it he will. The only question is whether the teacher will be history or ourselves. 54 *Robert Heilbroner*

TRUTH

THE NEED OF TRUTH is more sacred than any other need. 1 *Simone Weil*

We cannot shirk the historic question, What is truth? On the contrary: the civilization we take pride in took a new strength on the day the question was asked. 2 *Jacob Bronowski*

A scientific civilization like ours cannot exist unless it accepts truth ... as its cardinal value. 3 *Jacob Bronowski*

It is the knowledge of the necessary and eternal truths which distinguishes us from mere animals, and gives us *Reason* and the sciences, raising us to knowledge of ourselves and of God. 4 *Gottfried Wilhelm von Leibniz*

[T]he average person today knows far more facts about the world than Isaac Newton ever did, though considerably less truth. 5 *Studs Terkel*

It does not appear that the experience of life teaches truthfulness.... The truthful peoples are generally the isolated, unwarlike, and simple. Warfare and strength produce cunning and craft.... That honesty is the best policy is current doctrine, but not established practice now. 6 *William Graham Sumner*

[T]here is a principle which binds society together, because without it the individual would be helpless.... This principle is truthfulness. 7 *Jacob Bronowski*

I believe that truth is the glue that holds government together, not only our government, but civilization itself. 8 *Gerald Ford*

We are not afraid to entrust the American people with unpleasant facts, foreign ideas, alien philosophies and competitive values. For a nation that is afraid to let its people judge the truth and falsehood in an open market is a nation that is afraid of its people. 9 *John F. Kennedy*

Truth is what is beneficial to the Fatherland and to the people.... To strive to serve the Fatherland and the people is to obey the truth. 10 *Ho Chi Minh*

The truth is often a terrible weapon of aggression. It is possible to lie, and even to murder, for the truth. 11 *Alfred Adler*

Truths have ... [a] desperate instinct of self-

Truth

preservation and of desire to extinguish whatever contradicts them. 12 *William James*

Nothing causes as much destruction, misery, and death as obsession with a truth believed absolute. Every crime in history is the product of some fanaticism. Every massacre is performed in the name of virtue; in the name of legitimate nationalism, a true religion, a just ideology, the fight against Satan. 13 *François Jacob*

The blind willingness to sacrifice people to truth … has always been the danger of an ethics abstracted from life.… [M]oral truth is complicated by psychological truth.… [T]he awareness of multiple truths leads to … an ethic of generosity and care. 14 *Carol Gilligan*

Convictions are more dangerous enemies of truth than lies. 15 *Friedrich Nietzsche*

The surest way to lose truth is to pretend that one already wholly possesses it. 16
Gordon W. Allport

Irrationally held truths may be more harmful than reasoned errors. 17 *T. H. Huxley*

It goes without saying that it is not a matter of possessing truth but of striving for it. 18
Alfred Adler

To be in possession of an absolute truth is to have a net of familiarity spread over the whole of eternity. 19 *Eric Hoffer*

The basic spiritual principle … [offers] the opportunity to be reborn into a timeless realm of ultimate, death-transcending truths. In that realm one can share the immortality of the deity, obtain membership in a sacred community or a "covenant with God." … [I]ts final meaning is life-power and power over death. 20
Robert Jay Lifton

[T]he passion of the infinite is the truth. But the passion of the infinite is precisely subjectivity, and thus subjectivity becomes the truth. 21
Søren Kierkegaard

"Truth" is … not something … that might be found or discovered—but something that must be created.… Man projects his drive to truth, his "goal" in a certain sense, outside himself as a world that has being, as a metaphysical world.… His needs as creator invent the world upon which he works, and anticipate being; this anticipation (this "belief" in truth) is his support. 22 *Friedrich Nietzsche*

When I say that a thing is true, I mean that I cannot help believing it. 23
Oliver Wendell Holmes Jr.

[T]he stress on the abstract visual evoked as standards of truth the mere matching of object with object. So unconscious were people of this … that when a Pope or a Blake pointed out that truth is a ratio between the mind and things, a ratio made by the shaping imagination, there was nobody to note or comprehend. 24
Marshall McLuhan

Mathematics is … the chief source of the belief in eternal and exact truth.… This suggests the view that all exact reasoning applies to the ideal as opposed to sensible objects … [and] the objects of thought [are] more real than those of sense perception. 25 *Bertrand Russell*

But as for certain truth, no man has known it. Nor will he know it.… And even by chance he were to utter the perfect truth, he would himself not know it, for all is but a woven web of guesses. 26 *Xenophanes*

The present age … has witnessed a definite regression … in men's regard for truth. At no period of the world's history has organized lying been practised so shamelessly or, thanks to modern technology, so efficiently or on so vast a scale.… 27 *Aldous Huxley*

[W]e may argue that what we mean by truth, or at least the progress toward truth, is an orderly development of the image, especially of the public and transcribed image through its confirmation by feedback messages. 28
Kenneth Boulding

[W]e live in a world of pseudo-events and quasi-information, in which the air is saturated with statements that are neither true nor false but merely credible. 29 *Christopher Lasch*

Truth

Advertising, from its modern American beginnings, was a classic example of the pseudo-event.... We think it has meant an increase of untruthfulness. In fact it has meant a reshaping of our very concept of truth. 30 *Daniel J. Boorstin*

Feminism distinctively as such comprehends that what counts as truth is produced in the interest of those with power to shape reality. 31
Catherine MacKinnon

If you would be a real seeker after truth, it is necessary that at least once in your life you doubt, as far as possible, all things. 32 *René Descartes*

[I]f we are empiricists, if we believe that no bell in us tolls to let us know for certain when truth is in our grasp, then it seems a piece of idle fantasticality to preach so solemnly our duty of waiting for the bell. Indeed, we *may* wait ... but if we do so, we do so at our peril as much as if we believed. In either case we *act*, taking our life in our hands. 33 *William James*

[T]ruth is something that can be thought of only by believing it. 34 *Michael Polanyi*

All truth is a species of revelation. 35
Samuel Taylor Coleridge

Dasein is "in the truth." ... Before there was any Dasein, there was no truth; nor will there be any after Dasein is no more. For in such a case truth as disclosedness, uncovering, and uncoveredness, *cannot* be. 36 *Martin Heidegger*

"Being-true" ("truth") means being-uncovering. 37
Martin Heidegger

[E]very step towards Truth is a step away from vague possibilities, and towards determinateness of idea and of experience. 38 *Josiah Royce*

Truth is coherence. But as regards the whole system, the aggregate, as there is nothing outside of it which we have knowledge, we cannot say whether it is true or not. 39
Miguel de Unamuno

[S]ince we are inside truth and cannot get outside it, all that I can do is define a truth within the situation. 40 *Maurice Merleau-Ponty*

[W]e must remember that "true" means true for mankind, true for the purposes and aims of human beings. There is no other truth than this; and if another truth existed, it could never concern us; we could never know it; it would be meaningless. 41 *Alfred Adler*

Truth is *made* ... in the course of experience. 42
William James

Although pragmatism may not contain ultimate philosophical truth ... it realizes that the truth that *we* can attain to is merely human truth, fallible and changeable like everything human. What lies outside the cycle of human occurrences is not truth, but fact (of certain kinds). Truth is a property of beliefs, and beliefs are psychical events. 43 *Bertrand Russell*

Whatever satisfies the soul is truth. 44
Walt Whitman

Everything to be true must become a religion. 45
Oscar Wilde

It is the customary fate of new truths to begin as heresies and to end as superstitions. 46
T. H. Huxley

All great truths begin as blasphemies. 47
George Bernard Shaw

There are trivial truths and the great truths. The opposite of a trivial truth is plainly false. The opposite of a great truth is also true. 48
Niels Bohr

[N]o passion is warmer than the zeal to see, to discover, to master the truth, to rescue the spirit from confusion and slavery, even at the price of perceiving the vanity of life. 49
George Santayana

While men believe themselves to be seeking truth for its own sake, they are in fact seeking life in truth. 50 *Miguel de Unamuno*

To desire truth is to desire direct contact with a piece of reality. To desire contact with a piece of reality is to love. We desire truth only in order to love in truth. 51 *Simone Weil*

Truth

Truth means the fulfillment of our self.... 52
Tze-sze

Deep doubts about the self are displaced on to doubts about the world outside, and these doubts are sought to be allayed by ostentatious preoccupation with truth. 53 *Harold D. Lasswell*

[T]he human mind seems to operate *as if* the elimination of ambiguity is an innate goal of the system.... Truth is valued ... as a means of avoiding the discomfort of ambiguity. 54 *George E. Pugh*

Man's choice is not whether he needs a comprehensive view of life, but only whether his view is true or false. 55 *Ayn Rand*

What an asserted sentence expresses is a *belief*; what makes it true or false is a *fact*.... 56
Bertrand Russell

The very notion of truth is a culturally given direction, a part of the pervasive nostalgia for an earlier certainty.... What was then an augury for direction of action among the ruins of an archaic mentality is now the search for an innocence of certainty among the mythologies of facts. 57 *Julian Jaynes*

There are two kinds of truths: *those of reasoning* and *those of fact*. The truths of reasoning are necessary and their opposite is impossible; the truths of fact are contingent and their opposites are possible. 58
Gottfried Wilhelm von Leibniz

"Truth is the recognition of reality; reason, man's only means of knowledge, is the only standard of truth.... [D]evotion to truth is the hallmark of morality." 59 *Ayn Rand*

[O]ne of the most common ways of avoiding seeing truth ... is to make an abstract or logical principle out of the problem.... Seeing truth is not a function of the separate intellect, but of the whole man.... 60 *Rollo May*

We come to know truth not only by reason, but even more by our heart; it is through this second way that we know first principles, and reason, which has no part in it, tries in vain to undermine them. 61 *Blaise Pascal*

[W]hen Jesus was taken before Pilate, then *the world of facts and the world of truths were face to face in immediate and implacable hostility*. It is a scene ... such as the world's history had never before and has never since looked at. 62
Oswald Spengler

The truth must essentially be regarded as in conflict with this world; the world has never been so good, and will never become so good that the majority will desire the truth. 63
Søren Kierkegaard

There are very few lovers of truth.... 64
John Locke

Truth far outruns actual knowledge.... 65
George Santayana

The knowledge of truth as such is wonderful, but it is so little capable of acting as a guide that it cannot prove even the justification and the value of the aspiration toward that very knowledge of truth. 66 *Albert Einstein*

The highest violation of the duty owed by man to himself ... is a departure from truth, or lying.... A lie may be either external or internal: by means of the former he falls under the contempt of others; but by means of the latter, falls, which is much worse, under his own, and violates the dignity of humanity in his own person.... A lie is the abandonment, and, as it were, the annihilation, of the dignity of a man. 67
Immanuel Kant

The lie is the specific evil which man has introduced into nature.... In a lie the spirit practices treason against itself. 68 *Martin Buber*

The lie in the soul is a true lie. 69
Benjamin Jowett

Speaking a lie is a minor frailty; living a lie is a major calamity. 70 *A. S. Neill*

[T]he foundation of morality is to have done, once and for all, with lying. 71 *T. H. Huxley*

Our age is so poisoned by lies that it converts everything it touches into a lie. 72
Simone Weil

Every violation of truth is not only a sort of suicide in the liar, but is a stab at the health of human society. 73 *Ralph Waldo Emerson*

There is a taint of death, a flavor of mortality in lies.... 74 *Joseph Conrad*

"Beauty is truth, truth beauty," —that is all ye know on earth, and all ye need to know. 75 *John Keats*

The truth is God's alone, but there is a human truth, namely, to be devoted to the truth. 76 *Martin Buber*

The nearest each of us can come to God is by loving the truth. 77 *R. Buckminster Fuller*

[T]ruth ought not to be seen as the property of a proposition, but of the person. 78 *Theodore Roszak*

The truth will set you free. 79 *Holy Bible*

UNCONSCIOUS / SUBCONSCIOUS

THE UNCONSCIOUS is the unwritten history of mankind from time unrecorded. 1 *Carl Jung*

We mean by collective unconscious, a certain psychic disposition shaped by the forces of heredity; from it consciousness has developed. 2 *Carl Jung*

Consciousness, no matter how extensive it may be, must always remain the smaller circle within the greater circle of the unconscious, an island surrounded by the sea. 3 *Carl Jung*

It is essential to abandon the overvaluation of the property of being conscious.... You behave like an absolute ruler who is content with the information supplied him by his highest officials and never goes among the people to hear their voice. Turn your eyes inward, look into your own depths, learn first to know yourself.... The unconscious is the true psychical reality. 4 *Sigmund Freud*

The division of the psychical into what is conscious and what is unconscious is the fundamental premise of psychoanalysis; and it alone makes it possible for psychoanalysis to understand the pathological processes in mental life. 5 *Sigmund Freud*

Freud's postulation of an unconscious realm challenged Western notions of control, for the unconscious cannot be controlled.... Indeed, much of ... psychology since Freud can be interpreted as a frantic revision asserting the possibility of finding methods of control of this unruly dimension of self. 6 *Marilyn French*

This book [*The Hidden Persuaders*] ... is about the large-scale efforts made to ... channel our unthinking habits, our purchasing decisions, and our thought processes by the use of insights gleaned from psychiatry and the social sciences. Typically these efforts take place beneath our level of awareness.... The result is that many of us are being influenced and manipulated, far more than we realize.... 7 *Vance Packard*

The unconscious is a direct creation of print technology, the ever-mounting slag-heap of rejected awareness.... The denuding of conscious life and its reduction to a single level created the new world of the unconscious in the 17th century. 8 *Marshall McLuhan*

If it is adaptive to act so as to conceal one's intentions, one could expect the evolution of unconscious mechanisms of emotion. 9 *James Weinrich*

Most of the unconscious consists of what were once highly emotional conscious thoughts, which have now become buried. It is possible to do this process of burying deliberately, and in this way the unconscious can be led to do a lot of useful work.... After some months I return consciously to the topic and find that the work has been done. 10 *Bertrand Russell*

The mores are social ritual in which we all participate unconsciously.... The great mass of the folkways give us discipline and all the support of routine and habit. If we had to form judgments as to all these cases before we could act in them, and were forced always to act

Unconscious / Subconscious

rationally, the burden would be unendurable. 11
William Graham Sumner

[T]he unconscious mind is capable at times of assuming an intelligence and purposiveness which are superior to actual conscious insight. 12
Carl Jung

[T]he unconscious is wiser than we are about other people as well as ourselves. The fact of the matter is that our unconscious is wiser than we are about everything. 13 *M. Scott Peck*

The great decisions of human life have as a rule far more to do with the instincts and other mysterious unconscious factors than with conscious will.... 14 *Carl Jung*

Man cannot long endure the state of awareness or consciousness. He must ever again escape into the unconscious, for there live his roots. 15
Goethe

He who is rooted in the soil endures. Alienation from the unconscious and from its historical conditions spells rootlessness. That is the danger that lies in wait for ... every individual who ... loses touch with the dark, maternal, earthy ground of his being. 16 *Carl Jung*

The difference between Socrates and Jesus Christ? The Great Conscious; the immeasurably great Unconscious. 17 *Thomas Carlyle*

History organizes its data in relation to conscious expressions of social life, while anthropology proceeds by examining its unconscious foundations.... [If] the unconscious activity of the mind consists in imposing forms upon content, and if these forms are fundamentally the same for all minds ... it is necessary and sufficient to grasp the unconscious structure underlying each institution and each custom, in order to obtain a principle of interpretation valid for other institutions and other customs.... 18
Claude Lévi-Strauss

On the horizon of any human science, there is the project of bringing man's consciousness back to its real conditions, of restoring it to the contents and forms that brought it into being.... [T]his is why the problem of the unconscious ... is not simply a problem within the human sciences which they can be thought of as encountering by chance in their steps; it is a problem that is ultimately coextensive with their very existence. A transcendental raising of level that is, on the other side, an unveiling of the non-conscious is constitutive of all the sciences of man. 19 *Michel Foucault*

The world comes into being when man discovers it. But he only discovers it when he sacrifices his containment in the primal mother, the virginal state of unconsciousness. 20 *Carl Jung*

We have become conscious of ourselves but in having achieved this, we subconsciously feel that we have lost a vast kingdom in order to gain the tiny cell of consciousness. This is the destiny of man on earth; he had to become a prodigal son who left his father's house to descend into poverty and need. 21 *Karl König*

[T]he courage required to explore a dangerous coast is like the courage one must muster in order to probe one's unconscious, to take into one's heart and mind what it washes up on the shore of consciousness, and to examine it in spite of one's fears. For the unconscious washes up not only the material of creativity ... but also the darkest truths about one's self. These too must be examined, understood, and somehow incorporated into one's life. If the teacher, if anyone, is to be an example of a whole person to others, he must first strive to be a whole person. Without the courage to confront one's inner as well as one's outer worlds, such wholeness is impossible to achieve.... Man, in order to become whole, must be forever an explorer of both his inner and outer realities. 22 *Joseph Weizenbaum*

It is because our conscious self resists our unconscious wisdom that we become ill. 23
M. Scott Peck

The unconscious is not a demoniacal monster.... It only becomes dangerous when our conscious attitude to it is hopelessly wrong. To the degree that we repress it, its danger increases. 24 *Carl Jung*

Freud was right: our real desires are unconscious. It also begins to be apparent that mankind, unconscious of its real desires and therefore unable to obtain satisfaction, is hostile to life and ready to destroy itself. 25

Norman O. Brown

My experience in the [concentration] camps taught me ... that my actions were much more my "true" self than my unconscious or preconscious motives.... What goes on in his unconscious is certainly true of man, it is a part of him and his life, but it is not the "true" man. 26

Bruno Bettelheim

At this stage in our culture the price of awareness seems to be far smaller than the incredibly high price ... for the dubious bliss of unconsciousness. 27 *Herb Goldberg*

UNDERSTANDING

NO LIFE IS RATIONAL without understanding, and things are good only insofar as they aid man to enjoy the life of the Mind, which is defined by understanding. 1 *Baruch Spinoza*

The struggle for understanding is one of the characteristic features of our species.... The satisfaction of this urge is our destiny. 2 *Hans Selye*

The more the universe seems comprehensible, the more it seems pointless. But if there is no solace in the fruits of our research, there is at least some consolation in the research itself.... The effort to understand the universe is one of the very few things that lifts human life above the level of farce, and gives it some of the grace of tragedy. 3 *Steven Weinberg*

Science cannot and should not attempt to embrace the purpose of the original Creator; but it can and constantly must examine teleologic motives in the objects of creation. Only by doing this can science progress from the mere accumulation of unintelligible facts to what we call *understanding*. 4 *Hans Selye*

[S]cience has become the sole legitimate form of understanding. 5 *Joseph Weizenbaum*

We neither need nor will get "polymaths" who are at home in many knowledges.... But what we do need—and what will define the educated person in the knowledge society—is the ability to *understand* the various knowledges.... Without such understanding, the knowledges themselves will become sterile, will indeed cease to be "knowledges." 6 *Peter F. Drucker*

Intellectual knowledge is no guarantee of understanding.... 7 *Alice Miller*

Understanding ... is in general not identical with scientific knowledge or with opinion.... For understanding is concerned neither with eternal and unchangeable truth nor with anything and everything that comes into being.... Understanding, on the other hand, only passes judgment. 8 *Aristotle*

Information without human understanding is like an answer without its question—meaningless. 9 *Archibald MacLeish*

[T]he difference between understanding and explanation is that between meaningful connections and causal connections. 10

Merold Westphal

To reach understanding, we must always discover the simple by examining the complex, and then reconstruct the complex by starting from the simple. 11 *Gaston Viaud*

Understanding is nothing but seeing under and seeing far. 12 *George Santayana*

Understanding a thing is to arrive at a metaphor for that thing by substituting something more familiar to us. And the feeling of familiarity is the feeling of understanding. 13

Julian Jaynes

The subjective thinker has the task of understanding himself in his existence.... To remain in existence so as to understand one thing in one moment and another thing in another moment, is not to understand oneself. But [rather it is] to understand the greatest oppositions together, and to understand oneself existing in them.... 14 *Søren Kierkegaard*

Understanding is the existential Being of Dasein's own potentiality-for-Being; and ...

Understanding

this Being discloses in itself what its Being is capable of.... The kind of Being which Dasein has, as potentiality-for-Being, lies existentially in understanding.... As understanding, Dasein projects its Being upon possibilities. 15
Martin Heidegger

[A]cknowledgment of understanding as a valid form of knowing foreshadows the promised transition from the study of nature to a confrontation with man acting responsibly, under an over-arching firmament of universal ideals. 16
Michael Polanyi

The healthy Understanding ... is not the Logical, argumentative, but the Intuitive; for the end of Understanding is not to prove and find reasons, but to know and believe. 17
Thomas Carlyle

We can be absolutely certain only about things we do not understand. A doctrine that is understood is shorn of its strength. 18 *Eric Hoffer*

[U]nderstanding is what you need to master life, but understanding may also make you lose your mastery. 19 *Paul Kecskemeti*

[U]nderstanding is only one of our faculties. It can increase beyond a certain point only to the detriment of the practical faculties, disrupting sentiments, beliefs, customs, with which we live, and such a rupture of equilibrium cannot take place without troublesome consequences. 20 *Émile Durkheim*

Understanding itself is a social factor.... 21
Alfred Adler

To be totally understanding makes one very indulgent. 22 *Madame de Staël*

[T]he therapist must have the plasticity to transpose himself into another strange and even alien view.... Only thus can he arrive at an understanding of the patient's existential position.... [B]y "understanding" I do not mean a purely intellectual process. For understanding I might say love. 23 *R. D. Laing*

[O]ne can really understand people only to the extent that one loves them, and one will love them better if one understands them better. 24
Josef Rattner

Knowledge has been the liberator.... Science [however], it may be said, has now entered upon a new realm of destruction which threatens mankind.... If salvation is to be found ... it must be by an understanding of man. 25
Bertrand Russell

Of course, *understanding* of our fellow-beings is important. But this understanding becomes fruitful only when it is sustained by sympathetic feeling in joy and sorrow. 26
Albert Einstein

Freedom is knowing and understanding and respecting things quite other than ourselves. 27
Iris Murdoch

If civilization is to survive, the expansion of understanding is a prime necessity.... 28
Alfred N. Whitehead

To change the world in a conscious way one must first have a conscious understanding of what the world is like. Lack of such an understanding is a dismal portent. 29 *Marvin Harris*

Any attempt to reduce the world to the dimensions of our own understanding will exclude novelty and progress. 30 *George Gilder*

[T]oo many hypotheses and systems of thought in philosophy ... are based on the bizarre view that we, at this point in history, are in possession of the basic forms of understanding needed to comprehend absolutely everything. I believe that the methods needed to understand ourselves do not yet exist. 31
Thomas Nagel

It is inevitable also in this restless inquiry into all things for the sake of complete understanding that the sense of reverence and awe should also be lost. 32 *Ruth Benedict*

Understanding is the well-known feeling of pleasure due to the empirical transformation of sensations into categories. It is quite meaningless to try to extend this feeling of pleasure beyond its possible limits.... The wish to understand the world is not only unrealizable, but it is also a very stupid wish. 33 *Hans Vaihinger*

[I]n renouncing the factitious unity which the understanding imposes on nature from outside, we shall perhaps find its true, inward and living unity. For the effort we make to transcend the pure understanding introduces us into that more vast something out of which our understanding is cut, and from which it has detached itself. 34 *Henri Bergson*

The absolute virtue of the Mind ... is understanding. But the greatest thing the Mind can understand is God. 35 *Baruch Spinoza*

Unity / Wholeness

GOOD IS THAT WHICH makes for unity; Evil is that which makes for separateness. 1
Aldous Huxley

Good and evil ... and all the opposites have their place and value in the scheme of things, and the whole man must experience and master them all. He does this not by trying to banish his "demons" ... but by reconciling his good and evil selves in the unity of his true, higher self. 2 *Richard Cavendish*

Human insurrection ... is always directed at everything in creation which is dissonant.... Essentially, then, we are dealing with a perpetual demand for unity.... The insurrection against evil is, above all, a demand for unity. 3
Albert Camus

God is love, and he that remains in love remains in union with God and God remains in union with him. 4 *Holy Bible*

There is neither Jew nor Greek, there is neither slave nor freeman, there is neither male nor female; for you are all one in union with Christ Jesus. 5 *Holy Bible*

The soul that has caught the vision of unity, and has seen the unifying spirit as love, is spiritually prepared to perceive, and to respond to, the challenge of an "other world" ... a world of a different order of reality. 6 *Arnold Toynbee*

At Stage 6 ... universal ethical principles cannot be ... justified by the realities of the human social order. Such a morality uniquely "requires" an ultimate stage of religious orientation.... One part of the notion of a "Stage 7" comes from [Erik] Erikson's discussion of an ultimate stage in the life cycle in which integrity is found and despair ultimately confronted.... In religious writing, the movement to "Stage 7" starts with despair. Such despair involves the beginning of a cosmic perspective.... In despair we are the self seen from the distance of the cosmic or infinite. In ... Stage 7 we identify ourselves with the cosmic.... We sense the unity of the whole and ourselves as part of that unity. 7 *Lawrence Kohlberg*

Fuller being in closer union.... But let us emphasize the point: union increases only through an increase in consciousness; that is to say, in vision. And that, doubtless, is why the history of the living world can be summarized as the elaboration of ever more perfect eyes.... 8
Pierre Teilhard de Chardin

Unconscious wholeness ... seems to me the true *spiritus rector* of all biological and psychic events. Here is a principle which strives for total realization—which in man's case signifies the attainment of total consciousness. 9
Carl Jung

In an improving state of the human mind, the influences are constantly on the increase, which tend to generate in each individual a feeling of unity with all the rest; which, if perfect, would make him never think of, or desire, any beneficial condition for himself, in the benefits of which they are not included. 10
John Stuart Mill

Only man*kind* is the true man, and the individual can be joyous and happy only when he has the courage to feel himself in the whole. 11
Goethe

[A]ll true "meanings of life" ... are common meanings.... Life means—to contribute to the whole. 12 *Alfred Adler*

Perfection in oneself means ... the perfect participation in the whole. 13 *Søren Kierkegaard*

which could be ... set against the Chinese concept of Tao. 28 *Carl Jung*

[T]he only spiritual union that can be certain, obvious, and intrinsically blissful, must be not a union between two spirits but the unity of a spirit within itself. 29 *George Santayana*

The necessity to find ever-new solutions for the contradictions in his existence, to find ever-higher forms of unity with nature, his fellow men and himself, is the source of all psychic forces which motivate man.... 30
Erich Fromm

Wholeness can only exist by maintaining contradiction, but this is not easy. 31
Jessica Benjamin

[M]an's adaptation to the world is the result, paradoxically, of *not* being perfectly adjusted to the environment, of *not* being in a state of psychological equilibrium. The ecstatic sense of wholeness is bound to be transient because it has no part in the total pattern of "adaptation through maladaptation" which is characteristic of our species. 32 *Anthony Storr*

[H]as any man ever been completely at one with himself?... That a man shall attain this inner unity is the impossible and inconsistent pretension put forward by almost all philosophers. For as a man it is rational to him to be at war with himself as long as he lives. While he can be only one thing thoroughly, he has the disposition to be everything else.... [A]s a man, he is the possibility of many contradictions. 33
Arthur Schopenhauer

Selfhood is the painful awareness of the tension between our unlimited aspirations and our limited understanding, between our original intimations of immortality and our fallen state, between oneness and separation.... A new culture—a postindustrial culture ... has to be based on a recognition of these contradictions in human experience, not on a technology that tries to restore the illusion of self-sufficiency or, on the other hand, on a radical denial of selfhood that tries to restore the illusion of absolute unity with nature. Neither Prometheus nor Narcissus will lead us out of our present predicament. 34
Christopher Lasch

The West has been determined to reduce everything to unity, to pull everything together into a coherent whole.... The passion for unity simply annihilated whatever continued to resist assimilation.... [T]his search for unity at any price was to make a single whole out of the insane and the reasonable.... Now madness is enthroned at the very heart of western efficiency, in the ... marvellous combination that provides utopia as its splendid proof. 35
Jacques Ellul

Union cannot be attained by sacrificing integrity. 36 *George Santayana*

In any domain—whether it be the cells of a body, the members of a society or the elements of a spiritual synthesis—*union differentiates*. In every organised whole, the parts perfect themselves and fulfil themselves. Through neglect of this universal rule many a system of pantheism has led us astray to the cult of a great All in which individuals were supposed to be merged like a drop in the ocean.... 37
Pierre Teilhard de Chardin

When the pantheists try to conceive all the parts of nature as forming a single being, which shall contain them all and yet have absolute unity, they find themselves soon defying the existence of the world they are trying to deify; for nature, reduced to the unity it would assume in an omniscient mind, is no longer nature, but something simple and impossible, the exact opposite to the real world. 38
George Santayana

We live in a life in which our percepts are perhaps always the perception of *parts*, and our guesses about wholes are continually being verified or contradicted by the later presentation of other parts. It is perhaps so, that *wholes* can never be presented; for *that* would involve direct communication. 39 *Gregory Bateson*

Being a part, man cannot grasp the whole. He is at its mercy. He may assent to it, or rebel against it; but he is always caught up by it and is sustained by it. 40 *Carl Jung*

Unity / Wholeness

Whether the universe is atoms or a system, let it first be established: I am part of the whole which is governed by nature.... [I]nasmuch as I am a part, I shall be discontented with none of the things which are assigned to me out of the whole; for nothing is injurious to the part, if it is for the advantage of the whole. For the whole contains nothing which is not for its advantage.... By remembering, then, that I am part of such a whole, I shall be content with everything that happens. 41

Marcus Aurelius

[In] the world view emerging from modern physics ... the universe is no longer seen as a machine, made up of a multitude of objects, but has to be pictured as one indivisible, dynamic whole whose parts are essentially interrelated and can be understood only as patterns of a cosmic process.... This is how modern physics reveals the basic oneness of the universe. 42 *Fritjof Capra*

The farther and more deeply we penetrate into matter, by means of increasingly powerful methods, the more we are confounded by the interdependence of its parts. Each element of the cosmos is positively woven from all the others.... [T]he more we split and pulverise matter artificially, the more insistently it proclaims its *fundamental unity.* 43

Pierre Teilhard de Chardin

The universe as a whole could have a cause and a purpose only if it were itself created by a conscious agent which transcended it.... If this transcendent conscious being were the source of the universe and of everything within it, all created things would in some sense participate in its nature. The more or less limited "wholeness" of organisms at all levels of complexity could then be seen as a reflection of the transcendent unity on which they depended, and from which they were ultimately derived. 44

Rupert Sheldrake

There is no reason ... [why] a form of existence like our own, should not be attributed to the systems that science isolates, provided such systems are reintegrated into the Whole. But they must be so reintegrated. 45

Henri Bergson

Being-in-the-world is a structure which is primordially and constantly *whole.* 46

Martin Heidegger

[O]ur world, however many and various its objects, possesses what we may call Ontological Unity, in so far as all its types of Being, concrete and abstract, appear as various aspects of one type of Being.... All varieties of individuals and of individual ideas must be subordinate to the unity of this system. 47

Josiah Royce

[O]nly by looking at the whole can we really find the best alternative, with the least prospect of conflict and misery in the longer term. 48

John Gribbin

It is the whole human being, closed in its wholeness, at rest in its wholeness, that is ... able to venture forth toward the supreme encounter. 49 *Martin Buber*

To confront the undivided mystery undivided, that is the primal condition of salvation. 50

Martin Buber

I still think that in a species of man, wherein I count myself, nothing so much matters as Unity of Being, but ... [little] did I understand as yet how little that Unity, however wisely sought, is possible without a Unity of Culture in class or people that is no longer possible at all. 51

W. B. Yeats

The unity and structure of the complete self reflects the unity and structure of the social process as a whole.... 52 *George H. Mead*

Man's existence is made up of ... a multitude of conflicting voices ... which drowns conscience itself.... Pervasive throughout our world is a nostalgia for an imagined ethical wholeness, an existence in which man can declare himself to be sound and secure. 53

Joseph A. Amato

The time has come to realise that an interpretation of the universe ... remains unsatisfying unless it covers the interior as well as the exterior of things; mind as well as matter. The true physics is that which will, one day, achieve the inclusion of man in his wholeness in a coherent picture of the world. 54

Pierre Teilhard de Chardin

Most of us have lost that sense of unity of biosphere and humanity which would bind and reassure us all with an affirmation of beauty. Most of us do not today believe that ... the larger whole is primarily beautiful. 55 *Gregory Bateson*

[Man's] sense of wholeness and purpose has been severely fragmented as our egos have reveled in the individual power created by ownership of physical scientific knowledge.... [We need] a new "self image" for humankind, one that emphasizes the human wholeness and connectivity with everything around it. 56

William A. Tiller

We still await the larger symbolic image which will unite us all. 57 *Kenneth Boulding*

All things are linked and knitted together, and the knot is sacred.... For all things throughout, there is but one and the same order; and through all things, one and the same God, the same substance and the same law. 58

Marcus Aurelius

VALUES

VALUE IS A CHARACTERISTIC of the true being of man, of his essence.... 1 *Kurt Goldstein*

Value is man's essential being.... From this follows [that] ... knowledge of values is identical with the knowledge of one's essential being. 2 *Paul Tillich*

Only man placed values in things to preserve himself—he alone created a meaning for things, a human meaning. Therefore he calls himself "man." ... No people could live without first valuing.... Valuing is creating; hear it, ye creating ones!... Through valuation only is there value; and without value the nut of existence would be hollow. 3 *Friedrich Nietzsche*

When we survey the charnel-house of dead values, we realize that values live and die in conjunction with the vicissitudes of man. Like the individuals who express the highest values, they are man's form of defense; each hero, saint or sage stands for a victory over the human situation. 4 *André Malraux*

Value is beyond being.... It is the beyond which surpasses and which provides the foundation for all my surpassings.... Thus value taken in its origin, or the supreme value, is the beyond and the *for* of transcendence. 5

Jean-Paul Sartre

"Value" is the word I use for the intrinsic reality of an event.... Realization therefore is in itself the attainment of value. 6

Alfred N. Whitehead

Values express the objective will. 7

Thomas Nagel

Values are really a complex and compact repository of survival wisdom—an expression of those feelings, attitudes, actions, relationships that we have found to be most essential to our well-being. 8 *Tom Bender*

[E]volution ... [is] capable of creating new values. That the origin of a higher form of life from a simpler ancestor means an increase in values is a reality as undeniable as that of our own existence. 9 *Konrad Lorenz*

[I]nnate censors and motivators exist in the brain that deeply and unconsciously affect our ethical premises; from these roots, morality evolved as an instinct.... [S]cience may soon be in a position to investigate the very origin and meaning of human values, from which all ethical pronouncements and much of political practice flow. 10 *E. O. Wilson*

[I]t is precisely because value norms are anchored in the drives of human beings, or in their repression, that social organizations are so difficult to change. 11

Margarete Mitscherlich

Once a value is internalized it becomes, consciously or unconsciously, a standard or criterion for guiding action, for developing and maintaining attitudes ... for morally judging self

Values

and others, and for comparing self with others. 12
Milton Rokeach

Needs are cognitively transformed into values so that a person can end up smelling ... like a rose. 13 *Milton Rokeach*

The paradox of man's apparent ability to think rationally and his inability to behave rationally seems to originate in the conflict between rational thought and the irrational and variable innate value system.... [B]asic personal values cannot be derived by rational thought. 14
George E. Pugh

Questions of ends are questions of values, and on values reason is silent. 15
Alasdair MacIntyre

Like all other values, our morals are not a product but a presupposition of reason, part of the ends which the instrument of our intellect has been developed to serve. At any one stage of our evolution, the system of values into which we are born supplies the ends which our reason must serve. 16 *Friedrich von Hayek*

"[V]alues" are a matter of a person's affective responses.... [T]he person's affective system is the ultimate arbiter of value. 17 *Eric Klinger*

Our major values—love, protection, courage, honor, loyalty among them—were all nourished originally in the small contexts of human association: family, neighborhood, small community. 18 *Robert Nisbet*

The problem of values arises only when men try to fit together their need to be social animals with their need to be free men. There is no problem, and there are no values, until men want to do both. 19 *Jacob Bronowski*

The Objectivist ethics holds man's life as the *standard* of value—and *his own life* as the ethical purpose of every individual man.... The three cardinal values of the Objectivist ethics ... which together are the means to and realization of one's ultimate value, one's own life—are: Reason, Purpose, Self-Esteem.... 20
Ayn Rand

[T]he functions served by a person's values are to provide him with a comprehensive set of standards to guide actions, justifications, judgments, and comparisons of self and others.... In other words, the ultimate purpose of one's total belief system, which includes one's values, is to maintain and enhance ... the master of all sentiments, the sentiment of self-regard. 21
Milton Rokeach

[I]t looks as if there were a single ultimate value for mankind.... This is called variously by different authors self-actualization, self-realization, integration, psychological health, individuation, autonomy, creativity, productivity, but they all agree that this amounts to realizing the potentialities of the person.... 22
Abraham Maslow

You select values according to whatever is the aim of your life as you see it in broad outline.... The more values you adopt which yield only immediate composures and balances, or pleasures and entertainments, the more likely you are, of course, to overlook the values which give integration to the long trajectory of your years. 23 *Philip Wylie*

Might one's "real" self turn out to be simply the totality of one's values. Would self-knowledge then presuppose knowing what one really values? 24 *David Kipp*

The "As if" world ... the world of the "unreal" is just as important as the world of the so-called real or actual (in the ordinary sense of the word); indeed it is far more important for ethics and aesthetics. This aesthetic and ethical world of "As if," the world of the unreal, becomes finally for us a world of values.... 25
Hans Vaihinger

A "natural" value hierarchy, valid for all men, does not exist. 26 *Heinz Hartmann*

In sum, human values are conceptualized as consisting of a relatively small number of core ideas or cognitions present in every society about desirable end-states of existence and desirable modes of behavior instrumental to their attainment.... 27 *Milton Rokeach*

VALUES

Relativism—the doctrine that maintains that all values are merely relative and which attacks all "privileged perspectives"—must ultimately end up undermining democratic and tolerant values as well. 28 *Francis Fukuyama*

Stabilizing the present polytheism of values, there is the historic deconversion experience of the therapeutic, proposing an infinity of means transformed into their own ends. 29 *Philip Rieff*

[V]alues are ... being politicized.... In fact, values no longer serve us as criteria of judgment to determine good or evil: political considerations are now the pre-eminent value, and all others must adjust to them. 30 *Jacques Ellul*

[T]hrough the modern paradigm of knowledge the conception of good has been emptied ... [and] replaced in our ethical discourse by the word "value." 31 *George Grant*

No society can be stable unless there is a basic core of value judgments that are unthinkingly accepted by the great bulk of its members. 32 *Milton Friedman*

In the absence of any accepted set of intrinsic values, instrumental values tend to become more and more universal, and equated with the ultimate criterion of values.... The instrumental imperative eventually gives rise to the technological imperative, which demands that man should behave according to the modes dictated by technology's drive towards increased efficiency. 33 *Henryk Skolimowski*

Today the values of technology have so permeated the public mind that all too frequently what is seen as efficient is seen as the right thing to do. 34 *Ursula Franklin*

Making values explicit is essential to preserving a society in which diversity of values can flourish: an end that a soft energy path seems better suited to serve.... The dichotomies of social structures and values between soft and hard energy paths ... offer us a vivid metaphor for the wider tensions in our lives. 35 *Amory Lovins*

Not being able to make our values beautiful, we make them huge. 36 *Pliny*

There remains ... a vast field ... where scientific methods are inadequate. This field includes ultimate questions of value.... 37 *Bertrand Russell*

The pursuit of objectivity with respect to value runs the risk of leaving value behind altogether. We may reach a standpoint so removed from the perspective of human life that ... nothing seems to have value of the kind it appears to have from inside.... The problem is to know where and when to stop. 38 *Thomas Nagel*

[M]an, not technique, must become the ultimate source of value. 39 *Erich Fromm*

To suppress our concern for human values is to suppress the essence of life. 40 *George E. Pugh*

Only a new humanism can bring about ... the renaissance of the human spirit.... [It] must encourage the rise of new value systems to redress our inner balance, and ... to fill the emptiness of our life; it must be capable of restoring within us ... love, friendship, understanding, solidarity, a spirit of sacrifice, conviviality.... 41 *Aurelio Peccei*

Our remedy demands a complete change of the contemporary mentality, a fundamental transformation of our system of values, and the profoundest modification of our conduct toward other men, cultural values, and the world at large. 42 *Pitirim Sorokin*

For years I have labored with the idea of reforming the existing institutions of society, a little change here, a little there. Now I feel quite differently. I think you have got to have a reconstruction of the entire society, a revolution of values. 43 *Martin Luther King Jr.*

Values are the key to the evolution of a sustainable society.... [The] value changes that lead to a more harmonious relationship with nature may also lead to a more harmonious relationship with each other. 44 *Lester Brown*

Values

Sustainable development requires changes in values and attitudes ... new values that would stress individual and joint responsibility towards the environment and towards nurturing harmony between humanity and environment. 45
World Commission on Environment & Development

Human values shape human decisions that in turn govern human destiny. Any handle on human values becomes a potential handle on the future. 46 *Roger Sperry*

What I relate is the history of the next two centuries ... : *the advent of nihilism*.... For why has the advent of nihilism become *necessary*? Because the values we have had hitherto thus draw their final consequences; because ... we must experience nihilism before we can find out what value these "values" really had.—We require, sometime, *new values*. 47 *Friedrich Nietzsche*

[T]he chief thing lacking in our Western world is precisely an ethical code and a system of accepted values. So soon as there is even a tiny blossoming of values, the intellectuals rise up and reject it and jeer at it. In doing so, they ... have surrendered to the madness in which negation becomes an end in itself.... There is no longer anything to live for: that is what these intellectuals are saying without realizing it; the blinding light they shed is that of a sun on the point of sinking into the sea. 48
Jacques Ellul

[T]he ultimate disease of our time is valuelessness.... 49 *Abraham Maslow*

The nihilistic revolution has succeeded.... [T]here is no goal, nothing transcendent, no value to light the way.... 50 *Jacques Ellul*

[A] new symbolic universe of values must be found or an old reinstated if mankind is to be saved from the pit of meaninglessness, suicide, and atomic fire. 51 *Ludwig von Bertalanffy*

In essence, what a person or a society values determines what it does.... Simple logic says that future alterations in this single factor alone could spell the difference between utopia and social disaster. 52 *Roger Sperry*

War

[T]he condition of mere nature ... is a condition of war of every man against every man.... 1 *Thomas Hobbes*

The battlefield is symbolic of the field of life, where every creature lives on the death of another. 2 *Joseph Campbell*

War is a biological necessity.... 3
Friedrich von Bernhardi

With men, the state of nature is not a state of peace, but war.... Thus the state of peace must be *established*. 4 *Immanuel Kant*

War is not a law of nature, nor even a law of human nature. It exists because men wish it to exist; and we know ... that the intensity of that wish has varied from absolute zero to a frenzied maximum. 5 *Aldous Huxley*

When the world is declared under martial law, every Esau retakes his birthright, and what there is in him does not fail to appear.... [The] vice of men gets well represented and protected, but their virtue has none to plead its cause. 6
Henry David Thoreau

In all the rich catalogue of human hypocrisy it is difficult to find anything to compare with that dainty of dainties, that sugared delicacy, the belief that people do not like war. 7
Robert Ardrey

So many people are in love with death. They want war. 8 *Erich Fromm*

[T]he greater the tensions and the harder the daily repressions of civilization, the more useful war becomes as a safety valve.... [T]he invention of the military machine made war "necessary" and even desirable. 9 *Lewis Mumford*

[T]here is no likelihood of our being able to suppress humanity's aggressive tendencies.... [W]hat we may try is to divert it into a channel other than that of warfare. 10
Sigmund Freud

War

If wars were due to the arousal of instinctive drives, nations would not have to resort to conscription and the draft in order to raise armies. 11 *Ashley Montagu*

The first of the political causes of war is war itself.... War and violence are the prime causes of war and violence. 12 *Aldous Huxley*

[W]ar is not a human action but a male action; war is not a human problem but a male problem. 13 *Robin Fox & Lionel Tiger*

No one has found a primitive tribe where women are the warriors. War is a function of male bonding. 14 *Elaine Morgan*

Older men create wars.... Boys fight wars. Boys die in wars. Older men hate boys because boys still have the smell of women on them. War purifies, washes off the female stink.... The ones who survive the bloodbath will never again risk the empathy with women they experienced as children.... The child is dead. The boy has become a man. 15 *Andrea Dworkin*

In war, the seclusion of men from intimate daily relations with women as a virtual condition of the necessary violence has been taken for granted throughout history.... 16 *Betty Friedan*

Loyalty on the hunt has become loyalty in fighting, and war is born. Ironically, it is the evolution of a deep-seated urge to help our fellows that has been the main cause of all the major horrors of war. 17 *Desmond Morris*

[W]hat all wars have in common ... is the unmistakable moral lesson that homicide is an acceptable, or even praiseworthy, means to certain ends. 18 *D. Archer & R. Gartner*

[I]n the United States of America war is such a popular subject ... [because] there is an element of sanctity, even transcendence, attaching to it. To be concerned with war, as members of groups, is to be concerned with survival viewed as a cosmic fact.... 19 *Joseph Lopreato*

[All] wars are conducted as "holy" wars. 20 *Hugh D. Duncan*

One wages war in order to obtain a decision of holy validity.... [W]ar itself might conceivably be regarded as a form of divination. 21 *Johan Huizinga*

[T]here is nothing like the smell of gunpowder for making a nation perceive the fragrance of divinity in truth. 22 *Boston minister of mid-19th century*

If anything were needed to make the magical origins of war plausible, it is the fact that war, even when it is disguised by seemingly hard-headed economic demands, uniformly turns into a religious performance; nothing less than a wholesale ritual sacrifice. 23 *Lewis Mumford*

War is, in its strictest sense, the sanctification of homicide.... 24 *Miguel de Unamuno*

[T]he whole world is wet with mutual blood; and murder, which in the case of an individual is admitted to be a crime, is called a virtue when it is committed wholesale. 25 *Saint Cyprian*

To my mind, to kill in war is not a whit better than to commit ordinary murder. 26 *Albert Einstein*

You are surprised that soldiers are taught that it is right to kill people in certain cases and in war, while in the books admitted to be holy by those who so teach, there is nothing like such a permission, but, on the contrary, not only is all murder forbidden, but all insulting of others is forbidden also, and we are told not to do to others what we would not wish done to us. And you ask, is this not fraud? 27 *Leo Tolstoy*

I do not think it extreme to link the breakdown in moral standards in all spheres—economic, educational, and political, as well as in family life—to the effects of two major wars—celebrated wars!—in this century.... War also creates opportunity for what can only be called "licensed immorality." 28 *Robert Nisbet*

Laws are silent in time of war. 29 *Cicero*

[O]ne of the more distressing results of the degeneration of warfare in World War II has

War

been the loss of appreciation, on the part of many otherwise honorable people, of the distinction between right and wrong in matters of warfare. 30 *Guenter Lewy*

As war continues, both sides come more and more to resemble each other. 31 *R. D. Laing*

[I]n warfare anywhere, the law of violence is such that each side becomes equally vicious. To try to distinguish which is more vicious is to fail to recognize the logic of war. 32 *Bayard Rustin*

Once war begins, there are no moral limits, only practical ones, only … the "law of violence." 33 *Michael Walzer*

When you resorted to force as the arbiter of human difficulty, you didn't know where you were going.… If you got deeper and deeper, there was just no limit except what was imposed by the limitations of force itself. 34 *Dwight D. Eisenhower*

[I]f men are acting in the name of "their nation" they do not know moral limits but only expedient calculations. 35 *C. Wright Mills*

Man must not only be ready to sacrifice his life, but also the natural deeply rooted feelings of the human soul; he must devote his whole ego for the furtherance of a great patriotic idea: that is the moral sublimity of war. 36 *Heinrich von Treitschke*

[P]olicy which uses uninformed impulse for its purposes is always hostile to the well-being of society. That is why those who, for example, obey their government because it has declared war, cease to be moral beings. 37 *Harold Laski*

In war, man is much more a sheep than a wolf. He follows, he obeys. 38 *Jean Rostand*

To call war the soil of courage and virtue is like calling debauchery the soil of love. 39 *George Santayana*

For every war a motive of safety or revenge, of honor or zeal, of right or convenience, may be readily found in the jurisprudence of conquerors. 40 *Edward Gibbon*

War is the highest form of struggle for resolving contradictions, when they have developed to a certain stage, between classes, nations, states, or political groups, and it has existed ever since the emergence of private property and of classes. 41 *Mao Tse-tung*

It is the nature of wars for both sides to maintain that they are supporting a just cause. 42 *Alberico Gentili*

In a larger sense every just war is a *defensive* war.… 43 *William Paley*

[W]ith states the right of natural defense carries along with it sometimes the necessity of attacking.… The right therefore of war is derived from necessity and strict justice. 44 *Charles de Montesquieu*

The relatively simple American doctrine of the just war states that any defensive war is just, and any aggressive war is unjust. The only problem … is to determine who started the war.… Since history presents every nation, by its own lights, as the innocent victim, we are now in the position of having no negotiable criteria by which any war can be judged. 45 *Donald A. Wells*

If the cause and end of war be justifiable, all the means that appear necessary to the end, are justifiable also. 46 *William Paley*

In starting and waging a war, it is not Right that matters but Victory. 47 *Adolf Hitler*

Human warfare comes about when the defensive instinct of a determined territorial proprietor is challenged by the predatory compulsions of an equally determined territorial neighbor. 48 *Robert Ardrey*

To survive you often have to fight, and to fight you have to dirty yourself. War is evil, and it is often the lesser evil. 49 *George Orwell*

[W]ar is a necessary part of God's arrangement of the world.… Without war the world would

deteriorate into materialism. 50
Helmuth von Moltke

[O]nly war creates order. 51 *Bertolt Brecht*

War or the danger of war has ... contributed toward building the modern nation-states, toward spreading and developing modern civilization, toward preserving peace and stability within the states, and toward maintaining the international system of independent states. 52
Quincy Wright

War is the father of all things that actually arise, since they arise by the confluence of forces.... 53
George Santayana

War is never anything less than accelerated technological change.... War, in fact, can be seen as a process of achieving equilibrium among unequal technologies.... 54
Marshall McLuhan

War is an integral part of social development in history.... The fact that the way to win wars is changing is only a phase of the larger fact that society as a whole is changing. 55
James Burnham

War has always been the most effective factor of progress, even more than commerce. 56
Miguel de Unamuno

War is of course the health of the corporate economy.... 57 *C. Wright Mills*

In an era when war is technology the organization of the war economy is crucial. 58
Max Lerner

[T]he more completely capitalist the structure and attitude of a nation, the more pacifist—and the more prone to count the costs of war.... 59
Joseph Schumpeter

Modern war is so expensive that we feel trade to be a better avenue to plunder; but modern man inherits all the innate pugnacity and all the love of glory of his ancestors. Showing war's irrationality and horror is of no effect upon him. The horrors make the fascination. War is the *strong* life; it is life *in extremis*; war-taxes are the only ones men never hesitate to pay, as the budgets of all nations show us. 60
William James

The enthusiasm for war, and the predatory temper of which it is the index, prevail in the largest measure among the upper classes, especially among the hereditary leisure class. 61
Thorstein Veblen

The common man ... is the great protection against war. 62 *Ernest Bevin*

When the rich wage war it's the poor who die. 63 *Jean-Paul Sartre*

War should be the only study of a prince. He should consider peace only as a breathing-space.... 64 *Niccolò Machiavelli*

War is the trade of kings. 65 *John Dryden*

War is the continuation of diplomacy by other means. 66 *Carl von Clausewitz*

[States] seek acknowledgement of their value or dignity on dynastic, religious, nationalistic, or ideological grounds, and in the process force other states either to fight or to submit. The ultimate ground of war among states is therefore *thymos* rather than self-preservation. 67
Francis Fukuyama

If men want to oppose war, it is *statism* that they must oppose. So long as they hold the tribal notion that the individual is sacrificial fodder for the collective, that some men have the right to rule others by force, and that some (any) alleged "good" can justify it—there can be no peace *within* a nation and no peace among nations. 68 *Ayn Rand*

War is unthinkable in a society of autonomous people who have discovered the connectedness of all humanity, who are unafraid of alien ideas and alien cultures, who know that all revolutions begin within and that you cannot impose your brand of enlightenment on anyone else. 69
Marilyn Ferguson

[W]ar can no longer be an act of rape between nations; it must be a sadistic crime, the

War

possession of a dead victim.... [It is now an] irreversible perversion of passion, the "castration complex." 70 *Denis de Rougemont*

War is in truth a disease, in which the humors that ought to serve and sustain health go only to nourish something that is foreign to nature. 71 *Goethe*

The causes and consequences of war may have more to do with pathology than with politics, more to do with irrational pressures of pride and pain than with rational considerations of advantage and profit. 72 *J. William Fulbright*

Let me say ... that in the community it is the ill members who are compelled by unconscious motives to go to war and to attack as a defence against delusions of persecution, or else to destroy the world, a world that annihilated them, each one of them separately, in their infancy. 73 *D. W. Winnicott*

The act of going to war is an admission that reason has failed; hence war is a demonstration of infantilism in man. 74 *Philip Wylie*

We make war that we may live in peace. 75 *Aristotle*

To be prepared for war is one of the most effective means of preserving peace. 76 *George Washington*

The myth of war to end war, and of weapons to keep the peace, constitutes one of the chief obstacles to the future survival of mankind, and yet every nation engaged in armed conflict finds this fact the most difficult to comprehend. 77 *Donald A. Wells*

Every road towards a better state of society is blocked, sooner or later, by war, by threats of war, by preparations for war. 78 *Aldous Huxley*

[H]istory abounds with examples of the failure of deterrence as long-term policy to prevent war; at best, deterrence *defers* war. 79 *John Barber et al.*

[The] immediate cause of World War III is the preparation of it.... 80 *C. Wright Mills*

[W]e may say, without fear of exaggeration: *The next war will be the last war.* 81 *August Bebel*

The next World War will be fought with stones. 82 *Albert Einstein*

War in our time has become an anachronism. 83 *Dwight D. Eisenhower*

[B]efore 1914, it [was] firmly believed that war was virtually obsolete. 84 *Pitirim Sorokin*

[T]he tendency to destroy the adversary which lies at the bottom of the conception of War is in no way changed or modified through the progress of civilization. 85 *Carl von Clausewitz*

War is a more serious matter than it used to be. War can still settle problems, but it can only settle them the wrong way. 86 *Bertrand Russell*

In war ... there are no winners, but all are losers. 87 *Neville Chamberlain*

We hear war called murder. It is not: it is suicide. 88 *Ramsay MacDonald*

In the age of civilization war was a stable social institution, and for mankind as a whole, a tolerable one.... [But] man is now faced with the problem of getting rid of war, and this is a unique and unprecedented problem peculiar to the twentieth century. 89 *Kenneth Boulding*

Either war is obsolete or men are. 90 *R. Buckminster Fuller*

Mankind must put an end to war or war will put an end to mankind. 91 *John F. Kennedy*

If you have a nation of men who have risen to that height of moral cultivation that they will not declare war or carry arms ... you have a nation of lovers, of benefactors, of true, great and able men.... 92 *Ralph Waldo Emerson*

[E]very thoughtful citizen who despairs of war and wishes to bring peace, should begin by looking inward—by examining his own attitude toward the possibilities of peace.... 93 *John F. Kennedy*

The only cure for war is to change the hearts of men. 94 *Hal Lindsey*

Anything that encourages the growth of emotional ties between men must operate against war. 95 *Sigmund Freud*

War in the modern period does not grow out of a situation but out of a highly artificial interpretation of a situation.... War ... rests, in modern civilization, upon an elaborate ideological construction maintained through education in a system of language, law, symbols, and values. 96 *Quincy Wright*

War is an invention of the human mind. The human mind can invent peace. 97
Norman Cousins

To stop war will take exactly as much money, effort, unity, determination, planning, and sacrifice as war takes.... 98 *Philip Wylie*

We stand, therefore, at the parting of the ways. Whether we find the way of peace or continue along the old road of brute force, so unworthy of our civilization, depends on ourselves.... Our fate will be according to our deserts. 99
Albert Einstein

WILL

[THERE IS] ONE fundamental form of will—namely, the Will to Power.... The world seen from the inside ... would simply be "Will to Power" and nothing else. 1 *Friedrich Nietzsche*

Our human world is composed of an endless series of vicious circles, from which it is possible to escape only by an act, or rather a succession of acts, of intelligently directed will. 2
Aldous Huxley

One can do everything if one has the necessary will. 3 *Adolf Hitler*

The origins of the male monopoly over the formulation of mythic structures can be seen in the shift in creation myths from the paradigm of birth to that of creation by an act of will. 4
J. C. Smith

Through property man imbues his world with will. 5 *Roger Scruton*

Will begins in opposition.... [It makes] possible autonomy, freedom in the mature sense, and consequent responsibility.... It points toward maturity, integration, wholeness. None of these is ever achieved without relation to its opposite. 6 *Rollo May*

Woman is the will's first, overwhelming adversary. 7 *Dorothy Dinnerstein*

[S]exual satisfaction [is] the affirmation of the will-to-live.... By reason of all this, the genitals are the real focus of the will. 8
Arthur Schopenhauer

Life and the will to live are at bottom identical. 9
George Santayana

Will moves through desire. 10 *Aristotle*

The basis of all willing is need, deficiency and thus pain. 11 *Arthur Schopenhauer*

[T]he will is in the last resort motivated by instincts.... But at the ... upper limit of the psyche where the function breaks free from its original goal, the instincts lose their influence as movers of the will. 12 *Carl Jung*

Actions prompted by our inclination clearly do not involve an effort of will.... Efforts of the will are only in their right place for carrying out definite obligations. 13 *Simone Weil*

Each part and act of the Will remains nevertheless an original phase of the Will of nature. 14
George Santayana

The will has not preceded from knowledge.... On the contrary, the will is that which is first, the essence-in-itself.... [T]he organism is simply the will become visible.... 15
Arthur Schopenhauer

The will ... is a generalized impulse toward integrated affective expression which is prior to growth and development and which determines what the integrated personality will be. 16
Magda B. Arnold & John A. Gasson

Will

The will, to my mind, is nothing but a thirst for a complete and conscious self-possession.... And in terms of this its central motive, the will defines the truth that it endlessly seeks as a truth that possesses completeness, totality, self-possession, and therefore absoluteness. 17

Josiah Royce

Everything in nature works according to laws. Rational beings alone have the faculty of acting according to *the conception* of laws—that is, according to principles. This capacity is *will.* Since the deduction of actions from principles requires *reason*, the will is nothing but practical reason. 18 *Immanuel Kant*

The only resistance which our will can possibly experience is the resistance which ... an idea offers to being attended to at all. To attend to it is the volitional act.... Volition is primarily a relation, not between our Self and extra-mental matter ... but between our Self and our own states of mind. 19 *William James*

The essential achievement of will, in short, when it is most "voluntary," is to attend to a difficult object and hold it fast before the mind.... Effort of attention is thus the essential phenomenon of will. 20 *William James*

This power which the mind has thus to order the consideration of any idea, or the forbearing to consider it ... is that which we call the will. 21 *John Locke*

Willing is that psychic activity of man, whereby he tends toward or away from certain objectives reflectively adopted.... 22 *V. J. Bourke*

By the will, I understand a faculty ... by which the mind affirms and denies that which is true or false, and not a desire by which the mind seeks a thing or turns away from it. 23

Baruch Spinoza

[W]hat the idea always aims to find in its object is nothing whatever but the idea's own conscious purpose or will.... When I have an idea of the world, my idea is a will, and the world of my idea is simply my own will itself determinately embodied. 24 *Josiah Royce*

When we put our being into our will, and our will itself into the impulsion it prolongs, we understand, we feel, that reality is a perpetual growth, a creation pursued without end. Our will ... performs this miracle. 25

Henri Bergson

The will is not an abstract power of man which he possesses apart from his character. On the contrary, the will is nothing but the expression of his character. 26 *Erich Fromm*

[I]t has long been recognized that the will, regarded as a motive force that impels men to action, also has to be considered as part of morality. 27 *Ervin Staub*

[In the] ethics of Agape ... the opposition between good and evil is conceived exclusively in terms of the will. Sin has nothing to do with the bodily or sensual nature.... Sin is the perversion of the will.... [I]t is man's self-centred rebellion against God. Hence "conversion" ... signifies a complete change of heart, whereby the selfish will is transformed into a theocentric will, a will determined by God. 28

Anders Nygren

Every will which enters into selfhood ... denies union with the Will of God and ... goes out from unity into a desire for self ... then greed, envy, strife ... arise. 29 *Jacob Boehme*

Nothing in the whole world, or even outside of the world, can possibly be regarded as good without limitation, except a *good will.* 30

Immanuel Kant

If we could gain control of the willed processes (including meditation and attitude change), the possibility of changing society from within rather than purely by external social engineering would become a real one. 31

John H. Crook

There is no such thing as "will." ... All actions must first be made possible mechanically before they are willed. Or: the "purpose" *usually* comes into the mind only after everything has been prepared for its execution. The end is an "inner stimulus"—no more. 32

Friedrich Nietzsche

Electrical stimulation creates impulses similar to physiological functions in that the evoked effects not only resembled spontaneous activities, but also combined or competed with them. Electronic command overwhelmed the "will" of the experimental subject and always prevailed if sufficient intensity was applied.... These facts would seem to support the distasteful conclusion that motion, emotion, and behavior can be directed by electric forces and that animals and humans can be controlled like robots by pushbuttons. 33 *José Delgado*

The world is independent of my will.... Even if all that we wish for were to happen, still this would only be a favour granted by fate, so to speak: for there is no *logical* connexion between the will and the world, which would guarantee it, and the supposed physical connexion itself is surely not something that we could will. 34
Ludwig Wittgenstein

The strongest wills cannot elicit non-existent forces from nothingness and the shocks of experience constantly dissipate these facile illusions. 35 *Émile Durkheim*

In [some] sense, will is an observable phenomenon. But as a faculty, as a separate occurrence, it is, I think, a delusion. 36 *Bertrand Russell*

Our will merely accompanies our adjustment to the environment, and constitutes our own consciousness of the meaning of a certain portion of this adjustment. Our will is not itself one of the forces or powers of nature. 37
Josiah Royce

Since the differentiated consciousness of civilized man has been granted an effective instrument for the practical realization of its contents through the dynamics of his will, there is all the more danger, the more he trains his will, of his getting lost in one-sidedness and deviating further and further from the laws and roots of his being. 38 *Carl Jung*

The education of the will is the object of our existence. 39 *Ralph Waldo Emerson*

[W]hen the intelligence has become duly darkened, the intelligence and the will can understand one another better; at last they agree entirely, for now the intelligence has gone over to the side of the will and acknowledges that the thing is quite right as it would have it. 40
Søren Kierkegaard

If the will is to be freedom, then it is of necessity negativity and the power of nihilation.... If the will is nihilation, then the ensemble of the psychic must likewise be nihilation. 41
Jean-Paul Sartre

The will cannot produce any good in the soul. 42
Simone Weil

For the Will in spirit is precisely *not to will*, but to understand the lure and the sorrow in all willing. 43 *George Santayana*

In His will is perfected our peace. 44 *Dante*

The complete union between the soul and the object ... creates the temporary extinction of the ... will. 45 *Karl König*

Without intentionality we are indeed nothing. 46
Rollo May

~ WISDOM ~

AS WE HURTLE into tomorrow ... past experience will offer little clue to wisdom. 1
Alvin Toffler

With society wielding more power than ever, and himself more anxious than before, the individual must rely for his very survival on the wisdom of the managers of society. 2
Bruno Bettelheim

And where are the great and wise men who do not merely talk about the meaning of life and of the world, but really possess it? 3 *Carl Jung*

The leading intellects lack balance.... Wisdom is the fruit of a balanced development.... [W]e are left with no expansion of wisdom and with greater need of it. 4 *Alfred N. Whitehead*

[T]he professors ... have let the teaching of wisdom disappear altogether from the curriculum,

Wisdom

because, doubtless, they no longer have any to teach. 5 *Philip Wylie*

Neither science nor philosophy now aspires to give us wisdom. 6 *Ernest Becker*

The neglect, indeed the rejection, of wisdom has gone so far that some of our intellectuals have not even the faintest idea what the term could mean. 7 *E. F. Schumacher*

[T]he love of wisdom, I suppose, is like any other sort of love—the professionals are the ones who know least about it. 8 *Abraham Kaplan*

Skill without wisdom is the cause of our troubles. 9 *Bertrand Russell*

Nothing more doth hurt in a state than that cunning men pass for wise. 10 *Francis Bacon*

What the world admires as shrewdness is really an understanding of evil—wisdom is an understanding of the good. 11 *Søren Kierkegaard*

Wisdom is the union of intuitive reason and science.... It may be defined as the capital science of honorable matters. 12 *Aristotle*

Growth in philosophical understanding, or just plain wisdom, is ... a matter of being able to distinguish between levels of truth and frames of reference. 13 *Alan Watts*

The more comprehensive the meaning, the less comprehensible it is.... Here is the point at which science gives up and wisdom takes over.... Wisdom is knowledge plus: knowledge—and the knowledge of its own limits. 14 *Viktor Frankl*

I want, once and for all, *not* to know many things. Wisdom sets limits to knowledge too. 15 *Friedrich Nietzsche*

The art of being wise is the art of knowing what to overlook. 16 *William James*

We have become rich in knowledge, but poor in wisdom. 17 *Carl Jung*

More education can help us only if it produces more wisdom. 18 *E. F. Schumacher*

Wisdom must be the most precise and perfect form of knowledge. Consequently, a wise man must not only know what follows from fundamental principles, but he must also have true knowledge of the fundamental principles themselves. 19 *Aristotle*

The leading notion that runs through Greek philosophy is the *logos*.... Wisdom, then, consists in grasping the underlying formula which is common to all things. 20 *Bertrand Russell*

The name of being wise is reserved to him alone whose consideration is about the end of the universe, which end is also the beginning of the universe. 21 *Saint Thomas Aquinas*

I mean by wisdom a right conception of the ends of life. 22 *Bertrand Russell*

Wisdom denotes the pursuing of the best ends by the best means. 23 *Francis Hutcheson*

What is called wisdom is the attainment of this optimal strategy, the "harmony of the soul." 24 *Robert C. Solomon*

In man everything else depends on the soul; but the things of the soul itself depend on wisdom, if it is to be good.... 25 *Socrates*

For not only is the ignorant man troubled in many ways by external causes, and unable ever to possess true peace of mind, but he also lives as if he knew neither himself, nor God, nor things; and as soon as he ceases to be acted on, he ceases to be. On the other hand, the wise man ... is hardly troubled in spirit, but being, by a certain eternal necessity, conscious of himself, and of God, and of things, he never ceases to be, but always possess true peace of mind. 26 *Baruch Spinoza*

[W]isdom ... enables [one] to maintain his self-esteem despite the recognition of his limitations.... 27 *Heinz Kohut*

Wisdom may thus be defined as a stable attitude of the personality toward life and the world … the victorious outcome of the lifework of the total personality in acquiring broadly based knowledge and in transforming archaic forms of narcissism into ideals, humor, and a sense of supraindividual participation in the world. 28 *Heinz Kohut*

[T]he eternal laws of nature and order do exist. For the wise man, they take the place of positive law. They are written in the depth of his heart by conscience and reason. It is to these that he ought to enslave himself in order to be free. 29 *Jean-Jacques Rousseau*

Make men wise, and by that very operation you make them free. 30 *William Godwin*

The point is to have expressed and discharged all that was latent in us.… Wisdom and genius lie in discerning this prescribed task and in doing it readily, cleanly, and without distraction. 31 *George Santayana*

The achievement of wisdom is a feat that we must not expect … of ourselves. Since its full attainment includes the emotional acceptance of the transience of individual existence, we must admit that it can probably be reached by only a few and that its stable integration may well be beyond the compass of man's psychological capacity. 32 *Heinz Kohut*

[A] genuine love of wisdom is a relatively rare thing in human life. 33 *Blaise Pascal*

Knowledge is the first concern of the scientist … but wisdom is the ultimate intellectual goal of everybody.… 34 *Hans Selye*

Wisdom is better than mightiness; yet the wisdom of the needy one is despised, and his words are not listened to. 35 *Holy Bible*

The more unique each person is, the more he contributes to the wisdom of others. Such a community makes possible and fosters that ultimate quest for wisdom—the search for self.… In a community devoted to the search for wisdom, the true relationship between people is that all are students and all are teachers. 36 *Charles A. Reich*

In seeking wisdom, men's interests are not antagonistic.… Wisdom is the one commodity that is unlimited in supply. 37 *Charles A. Reich*

By wisdom we mean not systematic and proved knowledge of fact and truth, but a conviction about moral values, a sense for the better kind of life to be led. Wisdom is a moral term, and like every moral term refers … not to accomplished reality but to a desired future which our desires, when translated into articulate conviction, may help bring into existence. 38 *John Dewey*

The real value of the accumulated wisdom of a lifetime is that it can be handed on to future generations. Our society, however, has lost this conception of wisdom and knowledge. It holds an instrumental view of knowledge.… 39 *Christopher Lasch*

Wisdom is the possession of *right* knowledge. Right knowledge must be based on a proper understanding of the structural hierarchies within which life cycles and human cycles are nested and nurtured.… Ultimately wisdom must be related to our understanding of the awesome and fragile fabric of life. 40 *Henryk Skolimowski*

Death never takes the wise man by surprise; he is always ready to go. 41 *Jean de la Fontaine*

A wise man never complains of the destiny of Providence, nor thinks the universe in confusion when he is out of order.… [He] considers himself as an atom, a particle, of an immense and infinite system, which must and ought to be disposed of according to the conveniency of the whole. 42 *Adam Smith*

Human history is replete with evidence that devolutionary processes also operate, with deterioration of the human condition, unless foresight … and wisdom are brought to bear, to increase self-awareness and self-discipline in the choice of ends as well as means.… By suggesting the idea of the survival of the wisest I mean … that the survival of Man, with a life of high quality, depends upon the prevalence of respect for wisdom and for those possessing a sense of the BEING of Man and of the laws of Nature. 43 *Jonas Salk*

Wisdom

[W]e should reject the small souls who know only how to be correct, and cleave to the great who know how to be wise. 44 *Theodore Roszak*

We do not know of any part of our souls which is more divine than that which has to do with wisdom.... 45 *Socrates*

Wisdom is the principal thing; therefore get wisdom. 46 *Holy Bible*

Woman

In the most intelligent races ... there are a large number of women whose brains are closer in size to those of gorillas than to the most developed male brains. This inferiority is so obvious that no one can contest it for a moment; only its degree is worth discussion. All psychologists who have studied the intelligence of women ... recognize today that they represent the most inferior forms of human evolution and that they are closer to children and savages than to an adult, civilized man. They excel in fickleness, inconstancy, absence of thought and logic, and incapacity to reason. Without doubt there exist some distinguished women ... but they are as exceptional as the birth of any monstrosity, as, for example, of a gorilla with two heads; consequently, we may neglect them entirely. 1 *Gustave Le Bon*

[W]omen have progressed farther from the apes than men.... 2 *Kent G. Bailey*

Women were the originators and repositors of all culture ... and the source of the first civilization. 3 *J. J. Bachofen*

The man *makes* History, the woman *is* History. 4 *Oswald Spengler*

Woman is the primeval fabricator, the real First Mover. She turns a gob of refuse into a spreading web of sentient being, floating on the snaky umbilical by which she leashes every man. 5 *Camille Paglia*

[W]omen have plenty of influence but not much authority. 6 *Carol Tavris & Carole Wade*

A Positive Woman cannot defeat a man in a wrestling or boxing match, but she can motivate him, inspire him, encourage him, teach him, restrain him, reward him, and have power over him that he can never achieve over her with all his muscles. 7 *Phyllis Schlafly*

Your man needs to feel important, loved, and accepted.... A Total Woman caters to her man's special quirks, whether it be in salads, sex, or sports. She makes his home his haven, a place to which he can run. She allows him that priceless luxury of unqualified acceptance. 8 *Marabel Morgan*

The Total Woman recipe for eternal marital bliss can be boiled down to this: Be your husband's ideal mother. Cater to him. Indulge him. Treat him like a child. 9 *Mark Gerzon*

Throughout the ages, the problem of woman has puzzled people of every kind. 10 *Sigmund Freud*

The great question that has never been answered ... despite my thirty years of research into the feminine soul, is: What does a woman want? 11 *Sigmund Freud*

What do these feminists want? You may be equal in the eyes of the law but not in ability. You have never even produced a good cook.... [Y]ou have produced nothing great, nothing. 12 *Shah of Iran*

The devaluation of woman represents a necessary stage in the history of humanity, for it is not upon her positive value but upon man's weakness that her prestige is founded. In woman are incarnated the disturbing mysteries of nature, and man escapes her hold when he frees himself from nature.... [W]oman is necessary in so far as she remains an Idea into which man projects his own transcendence. 13 *Simone de Beauvoir*

Women have served all these centuries as looking-glasses possessing the magic and delirious power of reflecting the figure of man at twice its natural size. Without that power probably the earth would still be swamp and jungle.... Whatever may be their use in civilized societies, mirrors are essential to all violent and heroic action. 14 *Virginia Woolf*

A woman is a being who identifies and is identified as one whose sexuality exists for someone else.... If women are socially defined such that female sexuality cannot be lived or spoken or felt or even somatically sensed apart from its enforced definition ... then there is no such thing as a woman as such, there are only walking embodiments of men's projected needs. 15 *Catherine MacKinnon*

Woman is made specially to please man. 16
Jean-Jacques Rousseau

Our religion, laws, customs, are all founded on the belief that woman was made for man. 17
Elizabeth Cady Stanton

The extension of women's rights is the basic principle of all social progress. 18
Charles Fourier

No woman can call herself free who does not own or control her body. 19 *Margaret Sanger*

By law, public sentiment, and religion—from the time of Moses down to the present day—woman has never been thought of as other than a piece of property, to be disposed of at the will and pleasure of man.... 20 *Susan B. Anthony*

[T]he human breakthrough involves the evolution of the notion of women as property—perhaps the most primitive form of property. 21
Lionel Tiger & Robin Fox

Under capitalism, women appear as commodities.... Under true communism, women would be collective sex objects.... If women have always been things, it is also true that things have not always had the same meaning. 22
Catherine MacKinnon

And since women exist in the main solely for the propagation of the species ... they live, as a rule, more for the species than for the individual, and in their hearts take the affairs of the species more seriously than those of the individual. 23 *Arthur Schopenhauer*

If superiority consists in adaptation to the present environment, then man is superior; if it consists in the possession of those underlying qualities which are essential to the race—past, present, and future—then woman is superior.... Every woman is, as it were, a composite picture of the race, never much worse nor much better than all. Man is, as it were, Nature's experiment.... 24 *G. T. W. Patrick*

Except for their long-range contribution to the population problem, women are in fact a better cost/benefit bargain than men. 25
Marvin Harris

[I]n almost all societies women work harder than men. 26 *Marilyn French*

Until this day no great and important movement has taken place in all the world in which women did not figure as heroines and martyrs. 27
August Bebel

From Robespierre to Lenin all the great revolutionary theorists and organizers have been men. When the time has come for a revolution to be actually launched and for the masses to ... break the bond, then a *woman* has always stood in the front ranks.... 28 *Hanns Sachs*

There was not a type of war in which women did not participate. 29 *Mary R. Beard*

A man without pity is a monster; so is a woman without courage. 30 *Mary Midgley*

[F]or women the level of what is ethically normal is different from what it is in men. Their super-ego is never so inexorable, so independent of its emotional origins as we require it to be in men. [Thus] critics of every epoch have brought up against women [the charge] that they show less sense of justice than men. 31
Sigmund Freud

Sensitivity to the needs of others and the assumption of responsibility for taking care lead women to attend to voices other than their own and to include in their judgment other points of view. Women's moral weakness, manifest in an apparent diffusion and confusion of judgment, is thus inseparable from women's moral

Woman

strength, an overriding concern with relationships and responsibilities.... [H]erein lies a paradox ... [:]the very traits that have traditionally defined the "goodness" of women, their care for and sensitivity to the needs of others, are those that mark them as deficient in moral development. 32 *Carol Gilligan*

Are having and rearing children and a sense of emotional connection with, and responsibility for others, capacities that women must be liberated from in order to become human—that is, to become equal to men? 33 *Ann Oakley*

Woman manifests justice unconsciously but with full certainty; she is naturally in herself just, wise. 34 *J. J. Bachofen*

Every poll in the U. S. confirms the view that significantly more women than men support the twin causes of peace and justice. 35
F. H. Knelman

[W]omen are more democratic than men. 36
Vicky Randall

[W]hile there are more brilliant men than brilliant women, there are more good women than good men. 37 *Steven Goldberg*

The existence of "good" women—according to male standards of being unmolested private property—has required the existence of "bad" women, who have been scapegoats for male sexual guilt. 38 *Mary Daly*

Zeus designed women as the greatest of all evils—and bound us to her in unbreakable fetters of need and desire. 39
Semonides of Amorgos

Woman as a source of danger, as a repository of externalized evil, is an image that runs through patriarchal history. 40 *Eva Figes*

The psychic life of woman ... [includes] a strong feeling of inferiority because of their situation in the scheme of things. 41
Alfred Adler

Woman's basic fear is that she will lose love. 42
Sigmund Freud

Man's love is of man's life a thing apart,
'Tis woman's whole existence. 43
Lord Byron

Woman has neither the selfishly developed conception of the self nor the intellectuality of man; for all that she is his superior in tenderness and fineness of feeling. On the other hand, woman's nature is devotion, submission, and it is unwomanly if it is not so.... But the fact that devotion is woman's nature comes again to evidence in despair. By devotion she has lost herself, and only thus is she happy, only thus is she herself.... 44 *Søren Kierkegaard*

The conduct and manners of women, in fact, evidently prove that their minds are not in a healthy state; for, like the flowers which are planted in too rich a soil, strength and usefulness are sacrificed to beauty; and the flaunting leaves, after having pleased a fastidious eye, fade, disregarded on the stalk, long before the season when they ought to have arrived at maturity. 45 *Mary Wollstonecraft*

It is time to effect a revolution in female manners—time to restore to them their lost dignity—and make them, as a part of the human species, labour by reforming themselves to reform the world. 46 *Mary Wollstonecraft*

[W]omen's character formation is more directly tied to the memory of interdependence and harmony in relation to a mother. Women, therefore, have character resources to counter the isolation and detachment of psychological man.... 47 *Mary Ellen Ross*

Ultimately, the greatest service a woman can do her community is to be happy.... 48
Germaine Greer

We learn it at last—that the one gift in our treasure house is love—love—love. If we may not give it ... we may indeed collect ourselves and offer our second-best to the world, and the world may applaud. But the vital principle is gone from our lives. 49 *Ruth Benedict*

The beauty of the woman, and the happiness she promises are fatal in the work-world of civilization. 50 *Herbert Marcuse*

The woman who stands outside the family, the single woman, the woman who is not attached within a sexual relationship, represents women's unharnessed sexuality. She carries an aura that both men and women respond to with awe and fear; she represents a threat to the given order. 51 *Luise Eichenbaum & Susie Orbach*

[A] man gives evidence of his love for a woman by treating her as a completely human person, not as if she were the spirit of the legend—half goddess, half bacchante, a compound of dreams and sex. 52 *Denis de Rougemont*

Rarely in historic civilization have women been as free, expressive, and powerful as in America: yet rarely also has the burden of being a woman, and trying to be a fulfilled one, been as heavy to carry. 53 *Max Lerner*

The woman, as the cement of society, the head of the family, and the centre of cohesion, has, for all intents and purposes, ceased to exist. She has become a wandering isolated unit, rather a dispersive than a collective force. 54
Henry Brooks Adams

Educated women have shown a tendency to raise questions rather than children. 55
Elizabeth Hawes

[T]here is something mysterious and oracular about a woman's mind which inspires a certain deference and puts it out of the question to judge what she says by masculine standards. 56
George Santayana

[We] need [women] in our vision of affairs, as we have never needed them before.... We shall need their moral sense to preserve what is right and fine and worthy in our system of life.... Without their counsellings we shall be only half wise.... 57 *Woodrow Wilson*

Women are wiser than men because they know less and understand more. 58 *James Stevens*

The significant innovations today are being made by women—most men are merely running minor variations on familiar ego-themes. 59
Philip Slater

Because women have had to be unselfish, forbearing, self-sacrificing, and maternal, they possess a deeper understanding than men of what it means to be human. Women live the whole spectrum of life.... It is the function of women to teach men how to be human. 60
Ashley Montagu

When woman, after she had tamed man, extended her love for her children to include their father, then perhaps man began to learn for the first time what love was.... Eventually he came to depend on woman's love as one of the basic necessities of life. Yet she is still trying to teach him what love really is. 61 *Elizabeth Gould Davis*

Women all over the world are taking the lead in defending the forces of life.... We must show that we have the power to change the world. 62
Petra Kelly

The overriding psychological need of a woman is to love something alive. 63 *Phyllis Schlafly*

Although [anima] may be the chaotic urge to life, something strangely meaningful clings to her, a secret knowledge or hidden wisdom ... like a hidden purpose which seems to reflect a superior knowledge of life's laws. 64 *Carl Jung*

Women ... tend to feel rather more in tune with the universe than men. 65 *Ashley Montagu*

The central role will forever belong to women.... Nature has bestowed on women the biological abilities and bio-psychological propensities that enable the species to sustain itself. Men must forever stand at the periphery, questing after the surrogate powers, creativity, and meaning that nature has not seen fit to make innate functions of their biology. 66
Steven Goldberg

No man has yet been born, even Jesus himself, who was not spun on the secret loom within a woman's body. That body is the cradle and soft pillow of woman's love, but it is also the torture rack of nature. 67 *Camille Paglia*

To call women the weaker sex is a libel.... If by strength is meant brute strength, then, indeed, is woman less brute than man. If by strength is

strong Uncertainty Avoidance countries like Austria, working hard is caused by an inner urge; it is a way of stress release. 16

Geert Hofstede

What most workers want ... is to become masters of their immediate environments and to feel that their work and they themselves are important—the twin ingredients of self-esteem. 17

U. S. Dept. of Health, Education, and Welfare

The great majority of criminals are *untrained and unskilled workers*.... They find work terrible.... A useful occupation implies an interest in other people and a contribution to their welfare; but this is exactly what we miss in the criminal personality. 18 *Alfred Adler*

[O]ccupational therapy [is] now used to restore neurotic patients ... [through] weaving, modelling, carpentry, pottery-making. The repetitive nature of these formative tasks helps control the erratic unchannelled impulses of the personality and provides in the end a gratifying reward.... That lesson we forget at our peril. 19

Lewis Mumford

Whoever controls work and wages, controls morals. 20 *Susan B. Anthony*

[A] man's work must be permeated by his personality. Just as his choice of work must not be due to mere convenience, chance or expediency, but should directly reflect how he reaches for self realization in this world of ours, so the results of his work, besides being objectively purposeful, should also reflect his own purposes in life. 21 *Bruno Bettelheim*

Consistent purpose is not enough to make life happy, but it is an almost indispensable condition of a happy life. And consistent purpose embodies itself mainly in work. 22

Bertrand Russell

The reward of labour is life. 23 *William Morris*

Work is psychologically simply an activity which consciously includes regard for consequences as a part of itself; it becomes constrained labor when the consequences are outside of the activity as an end to which activity is merely a means. Work which remains permeated with the play attitude is art.... 24

John Dewey

The principle of playing means that what is done, is done for its own sake; gratification lies in the activity itself. The principle of working means that an action is not undertaken for its own sake, but for some other purpose, serving the ends of self-preservation. 25

Barbara Lantos

Independence truly occurs only when we are able to recognize ourselves in the creations of our labor, and this happens only in unalienated labor. 26 *Mitchell Aboulafia*

[T]he alienated character of work for the worker appears in the fact that it is not his work but work for someone else, that in work he does not belong to himself but to another person.... It is another's activity, and a loss of his own spontaneity.... [C]onsequently he does not fulfil himself in his work but denies himself.... 27

Karl Marx

The elimination of human potentialities from the world of (alienated) labor creates the preconditions for the elimination of labor from the world of human potentialities. 28

Herbert Marcuse

The majority of workmen have ... experienced the sensation of no longer existing, accompanied by a sort of inner vertigo, such as intellectuals or *bourgeois*, even in their greatest sufferings, have rarely had the opportunity of knowing. This first shock, received at ... early an age, often leaves an indelible mark. It can rule out all love of work once and for all. 29

Simone Weil

The natural price of labor is that price which is necessary to enable the laborers ... to subsist and to perpetuate their race, without either increase or diminution. 30 *David Ricardo*

No business which depends for existence by paying less than living wages to its workers has any right to continue in this country. 31

Franklin D. Roosevelt

Work / Labour

A society that gives to one class all the opportunities of leisure, and to another all the burdens of work, dooms both classes to a partial spiritual sterility.... 32 *Lewis Mumford*

[T]he characteristic feature of leisure-class life is a conspicuous exemption from all useful employment.... Abstention from labour is the conventional evidence of wealth and ... social standing; and ... it presently comes to be a requisite of decency. 33 *Thorstein Veblen*

Labor is prior to, and independent of, capital. Capital is only the fruit of labor, and could never have existed if labor had not first existed. Labor is the superior of capital, and deserves much the higher consideration. 34 *Abraham Lincoln*

Trade in general being nothing else but the exchange of labor for labor, the value of all things is ... most justly measured by labor. 35 *Benjamin Franklin*

In a higher phase of communist society, after the enslaving subordination of the individual to the division of labor ... has vanished; after labor has become not only a means of life but life's prime want; after ... all the springs of co-operative wealth flow more abundantly—only then can ... society inscribe on its banners: From each according to his ability, to each according to his needs! 36 *Karl Marx*

[C]entral planning undermines an all-important aspect of human capital, the work ethic. 37 *Francis Fukuyama*

The silly assertion that the Socialists wish to abolish work is an absurdity. Lazy persons, shirkers of work, are met in bourgeois society *only*. Socialism is agreed with the Bible in asserting that "he who will not work neither shall he eat." But work shall be useful, productive activity. 38 *August Bebel*

The Russian Soviet Republic considers work the duty of every citizen of the Republic, and proclaims as its motto: He shall not eat who does not work. 39 *Russian Soviet Constitution*

In proportion as the principle of the division of labor is more extensively applied, the workman becomes more weak, more narrow-minded, and more dependent.... He every day becomes more adroit and less industrious; so it may be said of him that in proportion as the workman improves, the man is degraded. 40 *Alexis de Tocqueville*

Labor is the curse of the world, and nobody can meddle with it without becoming proportionately brutified. 41 *Nathaniel Hawthorne*

To crush, to annihilate a man utterly ... one need only give him work of an absolutely, completely useless and irrational character. 42 *Feodor Dostoevsky*

In hunting and agriculture work had been a sacred function.... But for those who were drafted into the megamachine, work ceased to be a sacred function, willingly performed ... : it became a curse. 43 *Lewis Mumford*

The curse of work was a real affliction for those who came under the rule of authoritarian technics. But the idea of abolishing all work, of transferring the skill of the hand without the imagination of the mind to a machine—that idea was only a slave's dream ... for it ignored the fact that work which is not confined to the muscles, but incorporates all the functions of the mind, is not a curse but a blessing. No one who has ever found his life-work and tasted its reward would entertain such a fantasy, for it would mean suicide. 44 *Lewis Mumford*

The ongoing military-industrial drive toward rationalizing, disciplining, and ultimately dehumanizing the workplace is among the foundation stones of information technology. 45 *Theodore Roszak*

When the worker feels that he is in a hostile environment and in an economic system opposed to his interests, he will not work (and this is involuntary) with the same ardor and skill. 46 *Jacques Ellul*

The modern worker is outraged by the inhumanity and the hypocrisy of the existing order.... The roots of loyalty are gone. 47 *Harold Laski*

The second stage must establish the real value of "woman's work" to life and to society, whether it is done by women or men, inside the home or out. 48 *Betty Friedan*

Can we accept that democratic government, which requires of the individual independent judgment and active participation in deciding important social issues, will flourish when in one of the most important spheres of life—that of work and economic production—the great majority of individuals are denied the opportunity to take an effective part in the decisions which vitally affect their lives? 49
T. B. Bottomore

The struggle of the working class is like the growth of a plant. The plant is blind and stupid, but it knows enough to keep pushing upwards towards the light, and it will do this in the face of endless discouragements. What are the workers struggling for? Simply for the decent life which they are more and more aware is now technically possible. Their consciousness of this aim ebbs and flows. 50
George Orwell

In the developed capitalist countries a true proletariat still exists, but it has become a minority, and furthermore, unfortunately, an impotent minority.... The working class indeed has become a fiction.... The industrial worker indeed, who was seen by Marx as the man of the future, rapidly becomes the man of the past. 51
Kenneth Boulding

The fundamental crisis of the American labor movement is a crisis of human obsolescence.... [T]he byproduct of efficiency and increased productivity is the superfluous man whose only social function is to consume. 52
R. J. Barnet & R. E. Muller

One of the most striking things about America is its total failure to afford any means of recognition to work at any but the "highest" level.... "Lower" people simply do not exist; and their work does not exist. 53 *Charles A. Reich*

Seeing in the economic world only the drive for profits and dividends, for power and efficiency, the worker finds his own drive becoming one for wages and job protection rather than an interest and joy in the work itself. 54 *Max Lerner*

Nothing in the world can make up for the loss of joy in one's work. 55 *Simone Weil*

Labour without joy is base. 56 *John Ruskin*

While work in its generic sense continues to be valued, it seems clear that many Americans, youth and adults alike, no longer embrace the axiom that work for its own sake is rewarding and ennobling. 57 *Henry Borow*

When work ... loses all its romance we are doomed. 58 *Alistair Mant*

The relationship of an individual to his work, if he enjoys it, is *libidinous*.... Work and sexuality derive from the same biological energy.... The safeguarding of a fully gratifying sexual life of the working masses is the most important prerequisite for joyful work. 59 *Wilhelm Reich*

The basic problem of a true democracy, of a *work* democracy ... is the problem of whether work is really so changed that from a *burdensome duty* it can become the pleasurable *gratification of a need.* 60 *Wilhelm Reich*

The essential point is that in work, as contrasted with purposeless destruction, the aggressive impulses are molded and guided in a constructive direction by the influence of the creative (erotic) instinct. 61 *Karl Menninger*

The long record of man on earth has been a history of the blind conquest of nature through work.... Like many other human characteristics, the ability to work has dual aspects. We can use it to destroy ourselves as a life species, or we can use it to improve our lot on earth. 62
Walter S. Neff

If on the one hand the whole spiritual life of the soul, and on the other hand all the scientific knowledge acquired concerning the material universe, are made to converge upon the act of work, work occupies its rightful place in man's thoughts. Instead of being a kind of prison, it becomes a point of contact between this world and the world beyond. 63 *Simone Weil*

Work / Labour

Where the whole man is involved there is no work. 64 *Marshall McLuhan*

The fullness of life must be found in the nature of work itself. 65 *Daniel Bell*

Work is the keystone of a perfect life. Work and trust in God. 66 *Woodrow Wilson*

[A]ll knowledge is vain save when there is work, and all work is empty save when there is love; and when you work with love you bind yourself to yourself, and to one another, and to God. 67 *Kahlil Gibran*

It is not difficult to define the place that physical labour should occupy in a well-ordered social life. It should be its spiritual core.... The contemporary form of true greatness lies in a civilization founded upon the spirituality of work. 68 *Simone Weil*

Without work all life goes rotten. But when work is soulless, life stifles and dies. 69 *Albert Camus*

Youth / Children

In the eye of nature, it would seem, a child is a more important object than an old man.... Every thing may be expected, or at least hoped, from the child. 1 *Adam Smith*

To understand our attachment to the world, it is necessary to add a childhood, our childhood, to each archetype. We cannot love water, fire, the tree without putting a love into them, a friendship which goes back to our childhood. We love them with childhood. 2 *Gaston Bachelard*

Childhood remains within us as a principle of deep life, of life always in harmony with the possibility of new beginnings.... The archetype is a reserve of enthusiasm which helps us to believe in the world, love the world, create our world. 3 *Carl Kerényi*

Youth's the season made for joys.... 4 *John Gay*

One of the exciting things about adolescent boys and girls can be said to be their idealism. They have not yet settled down into disillusionment, and the corollary of this is that they are free to formulate ideal plans.... It is not for the adolescent to take a long-term view.... 5 *D. W. Winnicott*

No young man ever thinks he shall die. 6 *William Hazlitt*

In no other stage of the life cycle ... are the promise of finding oneself and the threat of losing oneself so closely allied. 7 *Erik Erikson*

The child is the spiritual builder of mankind, and obstacles to his free development are the stones in the wall by which the soul of man has become imprisoned. 8 *Maria Montessori*

Following the models of the ancients, the most modern of dictators, such as Hitler, Mussolini, Lenin and Stalin, have taxed their ingenuity to find ways to seize the child in the cradle and mold him according to their will. 9 *Pitirim Sorokin*

Over the years children forget everything that happened to them in early childhood. If their wills can be broken at this time, they will never remember afterwards that they had a will. 10 *Johann Sulzer*

Children are repressed at every waking minute. *Childhood is hell.* 11 *Shulamith Firestone*

We find ideal the kind of "good" children who are just enough afraid of us to do everything we want, without making us feel that fear of us is what is making them do it. 12 *John Holt*

If there is anything that we wish to change in the child, we should first examine it and see whether it is not something that could better be changed in ourselves. 13 *Carl Jung*

Our children are not individuals whose rights and tastes are casually respected from infancy ... but special responsibilities, like our possessions, to which we succumb or in which we glory.... They are fundamentally extensions of our egos and give a special opportunity for the display of authority. The pattern is not inherent in the parent-children situations ... [but] is impressed upon the situation by the major drives of our culture.... 14 *Ruth Benedict*

I find children, up to the time they are spoiled ... by culture, nicer, better, more attractive human beings than their elders.... The "taming and transforming" that they undergo seems to hurt rather than help. 15 *Abraham Maslow*

We are a nation ... that sentimentalizes children or dismisses them, but we do not take them seriously. Nor do we have much regard for people who do. 16 *Katherine Paterson*

The folkish state must make up for what everyone else today has neglected.... It must declare the child to be only the most precious treasure of the people. 17 *Adolf Hitler*

Treat even the youngest baby with respect, as a person who will have to take his place in the world. Do not sacrifice his future to your convenience, or to your pleasure in making much of him: the one is as harmful as the other. 18
Bertrand Russell

Your children are not your children. They are the sons and daughters of Life's longing for itself. They came through you but not from you. 19 *Kahlil Gibran*

I can imagine that someday we will regard our children not as creatures to manipulate or to change but rather as messengers from a world we once deeply knew, but which we have long since forgotten, who can reveal to us more about the true secrets of life, and also our own lives, than our parents were ever able to. 20
Alice Miller

Learning from their children is the best opportunity most people have to assure themselves of a meaningful old age. Sadly, most do not take this opportunity. 21 *M. Scott Peck*

No one can understand the grown-up who does not learn to understand the child. 22
Alfred Adler

The Child is the Father of the Man.... 23
William Wordsworth

[T]he child explains the man as well as and often better than the man explains the child. 24
Jean Piaget & Bärbel Inhelder

The most important condition for the development of the love of life in the child is for him to be with people who love life.... 25
Erich Fromm

[A]ll children need the love of someone for whom they are a miracle.... 26
Christine Downing

Children who have grown up without love become adults filled with hate.... 27 *R. A. Spitz*

Children are wise. They will react to love with love, and will react to hate with hate. 28
A. S. Neill

We are now working toward ... a world in which the harvest of democracy may be reaped. But if we want to make the world safe for democracy, we must first make democracy safe for the healthy child.... [W]e must now learn not to break his growing spirit by making him the victim of our anxieties. 29 *Erik Erikson*

The basic postulate of the Id is Impulse release is right (Pleasure is truth).... Adolescents have a philosophical system ... based on the efforts of the Id to free itself from the restrictions of conscience and of the adult world. 30
Jules Henry

[F]or children to develop the capacity to delay gratification, it is necessary for them to have self-disciplined role models, a sense of self-worth, and a degree of trust in the safety of their existence. 31 *M. Scott Peck*

The growing child must, at every step, derive a vitalizing sense of actuality from the awareness that his individual way of mastering experience (his ego synthesis) is a successful variant of a group identity.... They may have to accept artificial bolstering of their self-esteem in lieu of something better, but their ego identity gains real strength only from wholehearted and consistent recognition of real accomplishment—i.e., of achievement that has meaning in the culture. 32 *Erik Erikson*

Youth / Children

Young people seem to be unable to accept the values held in honor by the older generation, unless they are in close contact with at least one of its representatives who commands their unrestricted respect and love. 33 *Konrad Lorenz*

Old age is happiest when it can take youth up to the threshold of the good and ... point out the Promised Land to its children.... Youth, on the other hand, is happiest when it feels it is fighting to reach goals that were conceived of but not realized by the generation before them. 34
Bruno Bettelheim

American adults ... can be seen as having abdicated their ideal roles of structuring the world for the child, of providing him with a clear set of values.... This, we conceive, breeds in him, not only insecurity and anxiety, but also a deeply "justified" hostility, contempt and resentment against the parents.... 35 *Abraham Maslow*

[W]e cannot expect to have secure adolescents in a culture which offers no definitive path from adolescence to adulthood. 36 *Seymour Lipset*

The young not only live in a world of their own.... They now live—an increasing number now live—in an *anti*-world, one whose existence challenges the legitimacy of the adult world. 37 *Irving Kristol*

[E]ven as [the young] attack the adult world they become trapped in destroying themselves; if they make their parents irrelevant, they will surely make themselves irrelevant. 38
Seymour L. Halleck

[N]o longer is it merely for the old to teach the young the meaning of life. It is the young who, by their responses and actions, tell the old whether life as represented to them has some vital promise.... 39 *Erik Erikson*

Perhaps the most significant fact about current youth culture is its concern with meaningfulness. 40 *Talcott Parsons*

The buoyancy of youth is fed by the conviction of a full life to come, one in which all great things are theoretically attainable.... If there is no certainty of fulfillment, then it is better not to give up the promise of youth.... Youth at least offers the chance to escape the premature death of rigidity or the anxious confusion of a life that is disgraceful when it is without direction.... Better to be committed to such uncommittedness than to commit oneself to spending the rest of one's life as a hollow man. 41
Bruno Bettelheim

We are living in a world in which nothing is made to man's measure; there exists a monstrous discrepancy between man's body, man's mind and the things which at the present time constitute the elements of human existence; everything is disequilibrium ... and the younger generation, who have grown up in it and are growing up in it, inwardly reflect the chaos surrounding them more than do their elders. 42
Simone Weil

It is the young, arriving with eyes that can see the obvious, who must remake the lethal culture of their elders, and who must remake it in desperate haste. 43 *Theodore Roszak*

"By nature," the young are in the forefront of those who live and fight for Eros against Death, and against a civilization which strives to shorten the "detour to death" while controlling the means for lengthening the detour. 44
Herbert Marcuse

Long before a thermonuclear war can come about, we have had to lay waste to our own sanity. We begin with the children. It is imperative to catch them in time. Without the most thorough and rapid brain-washing their dirty minds would see through our dirty tricks. 45
R. D. Laing

It is quite certain that unless we can regulate our behaviour much more satisfactorily than at present, then we are going to exterminate ourselves.... [Yet] each time a new baby is born there is a possibility of reprieve. Each child is a new being, a potential prophet, a new spiritual prince, a new spark of light, precipitated into the outer darkness. Who are we to decide that it is hopeless? 46 *R. D. Laing*

[T]he stage of life [one] calls "youth" is better described as the stage of education. "Youth" in this sense must now of necessity continue all through life. 47 *Charles A. Reich*

Flexibility is the hallmark of human evolution. If humans evolved, as I believe, by neotony, then we are, in a more than metaphorical sense, permanent children.... We retain not only the anatomical stamp of childhood, but its mental flexibility as well. 48 *Stephen Jay Gould*

It is human to have a long childhood; it is civilized to have an ever longer childhood. Long childhood makes a technical and mental virtuoso out of man, but it also leaves a lifelong residue of emotional immaturity in him. 49
Erik Erikson

Modern social life is being dominated to an ever-increasing extent by a quality ... I have ventured to call by the name of Puerilism, as being the most appropriate appellation for that blend of adolescence and barbarity which has been rampant all over the world for the last two or three decades. It would seem as if the mentality and conduct of the adolescent now reigned supreme over large areas of civilized life which had formerly been the province of responsible adults. 50 *Johan Huizinga*

The cult of the abused Inner Child has a very important use in modern America: it tells you that the ... upward production curve of maudlin narcissism need not intersect with the descending spiral of cultural triviality. Thus the pursuit of the Inner Child has taken over just at the moment when Americans ought to be figuring out where their Inner Adult is.... 51
Robert Hughes

The very frequent disturbances of adult years all have one thing in common: they want to carry the psychology of the youthful phase over the threshold.... Whoever carries over into the afternoon the law of the morning ... must pay for it with damage to his soul. 52 *Carl Jung*

When I was a child, I spoke as a child, I understood as a child, I thought as a child: but when I became an adult, I put away childish things. 53 *Saint Paul*

Let the young alter society and teach grown-ups how to see the world afresh; but, where there is the challenge of the growing boy or girl, there let an adult meet the challenge. 54
D. W. Winnicott

[T]he child ... makes everything possible. On his work stands civilization. This is why we must offer the child the help he needs, and be at his service so that he does not have to walk alone. 55 *Maria Montessori*

The increasing dislike of human beings by human beings concentrates itself in the current neglect of children. Perhaps this is the first time in human history that children, en masse, have picked up the idea that they are not wanted, not needed. 56 *Robert Bly*

Whenever the older generation has lost its bearings, the younger generation is lost with it. 57
Bruno Bettelheim

References

Pages 1–7

Aggression / Violence

1 *The Broken Connection*, 1979, 333.
2 report to The [U.S.] National Commission on the Causes and Prevention of Violence, June, 1969.
3 *Aggression American Style*, 1978, 238.
4 Washington speech, July 27, 1967.
5 *Psychology for Our Times*, 1973, 363.
6 in 1972 report to U.S. Senate committee.
7 *The Pursuit of Loneliness*, [1970] 1976, 40.
8 Ibid., 42.
9 *Suicide*, [1897] 1951, 356.
10 *The Broken Connection*, 1979, 330.
11 *The Gulag Archipelago*, 1974, 14.
12 *Civilization and Its Discontents*, [1930] 1961, 58–69.
13 [1955] in *On Aggression*, 1966, 243.
14 *The Anatomy of Human Destructiveness*, 1973, 198.
15 *Frustration and Aggression*, 1939, 1.
16 *The Cultured Man*, 1958, 34–35.
17 *Physical Control of the Mind*, 1969, 122.
18 *The Nature of Human Aggression*, 1976, 236, 318.
19 in *The Psychology of Women*, M. Walsh ed., 1987, 76.
20 *American Behavioral Scientist*, 1978, vol. 21, 695–96.
21 *Sociobiology*, 1980, 126.
22 *Violent Men*, 1969, 234.
23 *Violent Men*, [1969] 1992, 221–28.
24 *Power and Innocence*, 1972, 23.
25 *The Male Machine*, 1975, 157.
26 *Love and Will*, 1969, 30.
27 *The Heart of Man*, 1964, 30.
28 *Pornography*, 1989, 51–55.
29 *Introduction to Psychology*, 1986, 338.
30 *Men in Groups*, 1970, 204, 224.
31 *The Imperial Animal*, 1974, 263.
32 *The Broken Connection*, 1979, 333.
33 in *Men in Transition*, K. Solomon ed., 1982, 479.
34 *Human Aggression*, 1968, 60–62.
35 *Ethology*, 1975, 509.
36 in *Christian Century*, 77, Apr. 13, 1960, 439–41.
37 in *New York Times Magazine*, Sept. 10, 1961, 25ff.
38 *Fighting for Hope*, 1984, 27.
39 final speech, Memphis, Tenn., Apr. 3, 1968.
40 *Science, Liberty and Peace*, 1946, 8.
41 *Ends and Means*, 1938, 27.
42 *The Rebel*, [1954] 1967, 291.
43 *The Varieties of Religious Experience*, [1902] 1958, 289.
44 *I and Thou*, [1922] 1970, 75.
45 *The Search for the Self*, 1978, 635.
46 *Mein Kampf*, [1924] 1943, 171.
47 Address to the Nation, Jan. 4, 1980.
48 in *New York Review of Books*, Oct. 20, 1966, 3.
49 *On Civil Disobedience and Non-Violence*, [c. 1900] 1967, 259.
50 Ibid., 1967, 285.

Alienation

1 *The Problem of Being Human*, 1974, 89.
2 *The Politics of Experience*, 1967, 12–29.
3 *The Making of a Counter Culture*, 1969, 58.
4 [1844] in *Karl Marx*, 1964, 169–71.
5 *For the Love of Life*, 1986, 137.
6 *A Study of History*, vol. 2, 1957, 318.
7 quoted in *Man Alone*, E. Josephson ed., 1962, 21.
8 *Political Pilgrims*, 1981, 24.
9 *The Sane Society*, 1955, 120, 360.
10 *Guilt and Gratitude*, 1982, 201.
11 *The Warriors*, [1959] 1970, 211.
12 in *The Basic Writings of C. G. Jung*, V. de Laslo ed., 1959, 137.
13 *The Minimal Self*, 1984, 162–63.
14 *Being and Nothingness*, [1943] 1957, 263.
15 in *Capitalism*, A. Rand, 1966, 281.
16 *The Betrayal of the West*, 1978, 134.
17 in *Daedalus*, vol. 94, 1965, 223–44.
18 *Human Paleopsychology*, 1987, 196.
19 *The Nature of Woman*, 1980, 110.
20 *The Peaceable Sex*, 1987, 153.
21 *The View from Nowhere*, 1986, 198.
22 *The Betrayal of the West*, 1978, 138.

Altruism

1 *Sociobiology*, 1980, 55.
2 *The Evolution of Cooperation*, 1984, 135.
3 in *New Knowledge in Human Values*, A. Maslow ed., 1959, 5.
4 *The Division of Labor in Society*, [1893] 1964, 228.
5 *Tragic Sense of Life*, [1912] 1954, 133.
6 *The Future of Mankind*, 1961, 42.
7 *The Warriors*, [1959] 1970, 50.
8 *Holy Bible*, John 15:13.
9 *Mein Kampf*, [1924] 1943, 298.
10 *Capitalism*, 1966, 130.
11 *The Church and the Changing Order*, 1907, 166.
12 "Roark" in *The Fountainhead*, A. Rand, 1943, 715.
13 *The Virtue of Selfishness*, 1964, 33–34, 127.
14 *The Gay Science*, [1882] 1974, s. 345, 283.
15 *The Psychology of Moral Behavior*, 1971, 145.
16 *An Introduction to Social Psychology*, [1908] 1931, 175.
17 *Summerhill*, 1960, 250.
18 in *Explorations in Altruistic Love and Behavior*, P. Sorokin ed., 1950, 63–68.
19 *The Biological Origin of Human Values*, 1977, 420.
20 *On Human Nature*, 1978, 157.
21 *Eco-Philosophy*, 1981, 80.
22 *The Selfish Gene*, 1976, 103.
23 [1976] quoted in *The Battle for Human Nature*, 1986, 85.
24 *The Biology of Moral Systems*, 1987, 93, 114.
25 *Sociobiology*, 1980, 120.

Pages 7–12

26 *Attachment and Loss*, vol. 1, 1969, 132.
27 *The Selfish Gene*, 1976, 215.
28 *The Limits of Altruism*, 1977, 132.
29 quoted in *The Politics of Greed*, M. Loney, 1981, 136.
30 *The Theory of Moral Sentiments*, 1759, Part II, sec. 2, chap. 3, par. 1.
31 *The Gift Relationship*, 1970, 245.
32 *Ideas and Opinions*, [1936] 1954, 62.
33 "Dejection: An Ode," 1802, stanza 4.
34 *The Art of Loving*, 1956, 18.
35 *Holy Bible*, Acts 20:35.
36 *The Prophet*, 1923, 64.
37 *Nature, Man, and Woman*, 1958, 92.
38 *Love in the Western World*, [1940] 1956, 310.
39 *Agape and Eros*, 1953, xxi–xxii.
40 *Airman's Odyssey*, 1942, 428.
41 *Psychology and Religion*, 1938, 94.
42 *Animal Liberation*, [1975] 1990, 247.

Anxiety / Fear / Neurosis

1 *The Birth and Death of Meaning*, 1962, 39.
2 *Time*, Mar. 31, 1961, 46.
3 *Civilization and Its Discontents*, [1930] 1961, 91.
4 *Our Inner Conflicts*, [1945] 1966, 161.
5 *Reason and Emotion in Psychotherapy*, 1962, 94.
6 *The Pursuit of Loneliness*, [1970] 1976, 88.
7 *America As a Civilization*, 1957, 694.
8 *The Politics of Ecstasy*, 1968, 296.
9 *Culture Against Man*, 1965, 312.
10 *America As a Civilization*, 1957, 698.
11 *Civilization and its Discontents*, [1930] 1961, 92.
12 *Philosophy in a New Key*, [1942] 1957, 158.
13 *The Denial of Death*, 1973, 17–18.
14 *A Grammar of Politics*, [1925] 1938, 20.
15 *Why I Am Not a Christian*, 1927, 29.
16 *Summerhill*, 1960, 124.
17 *The Birth and Death of Meaning*, 1962, 39.
18 quoted in *New York Times Magazine*, May 6, 1956.
19 *Summerhill*, 1960, 125.
20 in *New Knowledge in Human Values*, A. Maslow ed., 1959, 141.
21 *Psychological Reflections*, [1912] [1953] 1970, 150.
22 *Thinking in the Shadow of Feelings*, 1988, 17, 73.
23 *Man for Himself*, 1947, 157.
24 *Attachment and Loss*, vol. 2, 1969, 23, 86, 181.
25 *Escape from Freedom*, 1941, 45.
26 in *New Knowledge in Human Values*, A. Maslow ed., 1959, 133.
27 *Inhibitions, Symptoms and Anxiety*, 1926, in *Works*, vol. 20, 1959, 136–37.
28 *The Primal Scream*, [1970] 1980, 103.
29 *A Primer of Freudian Psychology*, 1954, 64.
30 *The Neurotic Personality of Our Time*, 1937, 89.
31 *The Minimal Self*, 1984, 193.
32 *The Origin and Function of Culture*, 1943, 93.
33 *The Lonely Crowd*, [1950] 1965, 26.
34 *Maps of the Mind*, 1981, 59.
35 *The Psychology of Science*, 1966, 30.
36 *Information Anxiety*, 1989, 34.
37 in *Future Shock*, A. Toffler, 1970, 298.
38 *The Primal Scream*, [1970] 1980, 64.
39 *Psychology and Religion*, 1938, 92.
40 *Reason and Emotion in Psychotherapy*, 1962, 55.
41 *About Men*, 1978, xviii.
42 *Love and Hate*, 1972, 167.
43 *Thoughts on Government*, 1776, par. 6.
44 *The True Believer*, 1951, 122, 125.
45 in *The Psychoanalytic Theory of Neurosis*, O. Fenichel, 1945.
46 *Nicomachean Ethics*, Book 3, part 9.
47 *The Human Soul*, [1959] 1973, 63.
48 *Client-Centered Therapy*, 1951, 507.
49 *The Primal Scream*, [1970] 1980, 347.
50 *Man's Search for Himself*, 1953, 40.
51 *Existence*, 1958, 50.
52 *The Courage to Be*, 1952, 35.
53 Ibid., 66.
54 *Being and Time*, [1931] 1962, 180.
55 Ibid., 232.
56 *Modern Man in Search of a Soul*, 1933, 273.
57 *Man for Himself*, 1960, viii.
58 *The Need for Roots*, 1952, 32.
59 *The Human Soul*, [1959] 1973, 49.
60 *On the Sublime and Beautiful*, 1757, Part 2, sec. 2.
61 *The Cinderella Complex*, 1981, 64–65.
62 *Man for Himself*, 1947, 220.
63 London lecture, May, 1840.
64 Inaugural address, Washington, Mar. 4, 1933.
65 *On Heroes*, lecture 1, [1840] 1902, 36.
66 *On the Evils Due to Fear*, 1929, 228.
67 *The Denial of Death*, 1973, 92.
68 *Remembrance of Things Past*, 1913–26, vol. 3, "The Guermantes Way."
69 *Motivation and Personality*, 1954, 145.
70 *The Denial of Death*, 1973, 197–98.
71 in *New Knowledge in Human Values*, A. Maslow ed., 1959, 73.
72 *Physical Control of the Mind*, 1969, 136.

Art

1 *The Life of Reason*, 1954, 303.
2 *Science and the Modern World*, 1925, 290–91.
3 *Icon and Image*, [1954] 1965, 17.
4 *Nicomachean Ethics*, Book 6, chap. 4.
5 *The Power of Myth*, 1988, 228.
6 *The Will to Power*, 1900, Aph. 821.
7 *Waiting for God*, 1951, 106.
8 *Doctor Zhivago*, 1958, Part 2, chap. 14, sec. 14.
9 *Eco-Philosophy*, 1981, 34.
10 *Principles of Social Reconstruction*, 1916, 226.
11 *The Varieties of Religious Experience*, [1902] 1958, 295.
12 *Process and Reality*, [1929] 1978, 317.

Pages 12–18

13 *Experience and Nature*, [1922] 1958, 388.
14 *The Death and Life of Great American Cities*, [1961] 1969, 372.
15 *The Life of Reason*, 1905, "Reason in Art."
16 *An Essay on Man*, 1970, 175.
17 *Totem and Taboo*, [1913] 1950, 90.
18 *Eros and Civilization*, [1955] 1966, 185.
19 Ibid., 105.
20 *An Essay on Man*, 1970, 158.
21 [d. 1832] in *Goethe's World View*, 1963, 175.
22 *The Spying Heart*, 1989, 102.
23 *Eros and Civilization*, [1955] 1966, 145.
24 *Experience and Nature*, [1925] 1958, 363.
25 *One-Dimensional Man*, 1964, 62.
26 *Life Against Death*, 1966, 67.
27 Ibid., 63.
28 *Marriage and Morals*, [1929] 1959, 199–200.
29 *The Cultural Contradictions of Capitalism*, 1976, 20, 51.
30 Ibid., 51–53.
31 *Personal Knowledge*, 1962, 200.
32 *Adventures of Ideas*, 1933, Part 4, chap. 17.
33 *Between Myth and Morning*, 1974, 6.
34 *The Ominous Parallels*, 1982, 173.
35 *The Courage to Be*, 1952, 147.
36 *Neurosis and Human Growth*, [1950] 1991, 332.
37 *Sexual Personae*, 1990, 289.
38 *Solitude*, 1988, 199.
39 *The Triumph of the Therapeutic*, 1966, 225.
40 Ibid., 10.
41 quoted in *The Arts*, 1923.
42 *The Will to Power*, 1900, Aph. 822.
43 Ibid., Aph. 809.
44 *Order Out of Chaos*, 1984, 312.
45 *The Life of Reason*, 1954, 301.
46 *The Meaning of Art*, 1955, chap. 1.
47 *Dialogues*, [June 10, 1943] 1954.
48 *Critical Path*, 1981, 236.
49 *The Savage Mind* , 1966, 22.
50 *The Mind of Primitive Man*, [1911] 1938, 242–43.
51 *The Savage Mind* , 1966, 29.
52 *The Hunters*, 1966, 77.
53 *Sexual Personae*, 1990, 29.
54 *Ego Psychology and Adaptation*, [1937] 1958, 77.
55 *Sexual Personae*, 1990, 39.
56 in *Writers At Work*, G. Plimpton ed., 1967, 3rd Series, 190.
57 *The Voices of Silence*, 1953, 630.
58 "Hyperion," 1839.
59 *Dear Theo: An Autobiography*, 1937, 63.
60 *The Realm of Spirit*, 1940, 150.
61 *The Spying Heart*, 1989, 114.
62 *Technics and Human Development*, 1967, 252.
63 *Note-Books*, 1912, chap. 11.
64 *The Meaning of the 20th Century*, 1964, 196.
65 *Under Western Eyes*, 1911, preface.
66 *I Believe*, C. Fadiman ed., 1940, 299.
67 in *Modern Man and Mortality*, J. Choron, 1964, 185.
68 *The Voices of Silence*, 1953, 630, 639.
69 in *I Believe*, Clifton Fadiman ed., 1940, 220.
70 *Mind*, 1967, 87.
71 *What Is Art?*, 1898, chap. 8.
72 in *Saturday Review*, Dec. 24, 1960, 9.
73 *Inward Vision*, 1958, "Creative Credo" [1920].
74 *The Sense of Beauty*, 1955, 151.
75 *Meditations*, c. 161–80 A.D., Book 11, IX.
76 *The Life of Reason*, 1954, 366.
77 Ibid., 378–79.
78 [d. 1930] "Art and the Individual."
79 *De Profundis*, 1897.
80 *Adventures of Ideas*, 1933, Part 4, chap. 18.
81 lecture, New York, Jan. 9, 1882.
82 *The Life of Reason*, 1954, 302.
83 *Man in the Modern Age*, [1931] 1951, 131.
84 letter to Charles Bray, July 5, 1859.
85 *The Romantic Manifesto*, 1969, 25.
86 *Sexual Personae*, 1990, 137.
87 *Intentions*, 1891, "The Critic as Artist," Part 2.
88 *Sexual Personae*, 1990, 29.
89 *Tropic of Cancer*, [1934] 1961, 253.
90 *The Gutenberg Galaxy*, 1962, 275.
91 speech, Amherst College, Oct. 26, 1963.
92 in *The Sketch*, Jan. 9, 1895.
93 *Homo Ludens*, 1955, 201.
94 *The Voices of Silence*, 1953, 616.
95 [1942] in *Quotations from Chairman Mao*, 1967, chap. 32.
96 *Solitude*, 1988, 75–80.
97 *Strong Opinions*, 1973, 33.
98 *Icon and Image*, [1954] 1965, 65.
99 *The End of History and the Last Man*, 1992, 320.
100 *The Aquarian Conspiracy*, 1980, 177.
101 *The Life of Reason*, 1954, 373.
102 *Art*, 1914, Part 2, chap. 1.
103 *The Voices of Silence*, 1953, 639.
104 *The Life of Reason*, 1954, 378.
105 *The Spying Heart*, 1989, 114.
106 *Modern Man in Search of a Soul*, 1933, 194.
107 *The Life of Reason*, 1954, 370.
108 *Dear Theo: An Autobiography*, 1937, 44.
109 *Sand and Foam*, 1926, 83.

Authority

1 *Modern Education*, 1932, 13.
2 *An Inquiry into the Human Prospect*, 1975, 162–64.
3 *Authority*, 1980, 3, 120.
4 *The Minimal Self*, 1984, 204.
5 *The Authoritarian Personality*, 1950, 971.
6 *Mein Kampf*, [1924] 1943, 669–71.
7 *The Philosophy of Fascism*, 1936, 140–41.
8 in *Explorations in Altruistic Love and Behavior*, P. Sorokin ed., 1950, 160–61.
9 in *Dimensions of Personality*, 1981, 23.
10 *Man for Himself*, 1947, 9.

11 *The Decay of Capitalist Civilisation*, 1923, 144.
12 *Economy and Society*, [1918] 1968, 220–23.
13 *The Image*, 1956, 101.
14 *Selected Correspondence*, [1877] 1961, 310.
15 in *A Study of Bolshevism*, N. Leites, 1953, 288.
16 letter to Mandell Creighton, 1887.
17 *The Mass Psychology of Fascism*, 1946, 213, 231.
18 *Summerhill*, 1960, 210.
19 *Guilt*, 1985, 165, 201, 213.
20 *The Mermaid and the Minotaur*, 1976, 176.
21 *Public Opinion*, [1922] 1957, 222.
22 *On the Democratic Idea in America*, 1972, 68.
23 *The Meaning of Conservatism*, 1984, 19.
24 *The Open Society and Its Enemies*, vol. 1, 1962, 72.
25 *The Crisis of Democracy*, 1975, 163–69.
26 *America As a Civilization*, 1957, 373–74.
27 in *Handbook of Political Psychology*, J. Knutson ed., 1973, 111.
28 in *International Journal of Law and Psychiatry*, 1983, vol. 6, 235.
29 *Law, Legislation and Liberty*, vol. 1, 1973, 95.
30 *Economy and Society*, [1918] 1968, 263.
31 *The Power Elite*, 1956, 89.
32 *The Crowd*, [1895] 1960, 130.
33 *Le Fil de l'épée*, 1932, "Du caractère," sec. 2.
34 in *Objections to Conservatism*, Heritage Foundation, 1981, 72.
35 *Police State*, 1970, 95.
36 *Obedience to Authority*, 1973, 178.
37 *The Manufacture of Madness*, 1970, 41.
38 *The Dangers of Obedience*, 1968, 13.
39 *Unpopular Essays*, 1951, 81.
40 "Lay Sermons," 1870–75.
41 *Summerhill*, 1960, 297.
42 *The Culture of Narcissism*, 1979, 316.
43 *A Grammar of Politics*, [1925] 1938, 252.
44 *The Biological Origin of Human Values*, 1977, 364.
45 *A Grammar of Politics*, [1925] 1938, 263.

Beauty

1 *Waiting On God*, 1951, 110.
2 in Plato's *Symposium*, 201a.
3 *Waiting On God*, 1951, 101.
4 *Nature*, 1836, chap. 3.
5 *Waiting On God*, 1951, 104.
6 Ibid., 102.
7 *The Concept of Dread*, [1844] 1946, 62.
8 *A Sand County Almanac*, 1949, 96.
9 in *Life Against Death*, Norman O. Brown, 1966, 73.
10 *Notebooks*, I, 1935–42.
11 *Waiting On God*, 1951, 102.
12 *The Prophet*, 1923, 76.
13 *Tragic Sense of Life*, [1912] 1954, 201.
14 Ibid., 202.
15 *The Sense of Beauty*, [1896] 1955, 263.
16 *The Need for Roots*, 1952, 10.
17 in *Living Philosophies*, Clifton Fadiman ed., 1931, 302.
18 *Letters*, to Maupassant, Oct. 26, 1871.
19 in *New Knowledge in Human Values*, A. Maslow ed., 1959, 230.
20 *Endymion*, 188, Book 1, line 1.
21 [d. 1930] "Return to Bestwood."
22 *The View from Nowhere*, 1986, 223.
23 quoted in *Saturday Review*, Oct. 2, 1976 36.
24 in *Symposium*, by Plato.
25 *Symbols of Transformation*, 1952, in *Collected Works*, vol. 5, par. 253.
26 *Confessions*, 397 A.D., Book 10, chap. 27.
27 *Technology and Justice*, 1986, 50.
28 *Stones of Venice*, 1852, vol. 1, chap. 2, sec. 17.
29 *Civilization and Its Discontents*, [1930] 1961, 29.
30 *The Rebel*, [1954] 1967, 277.

Belief

1 speech in *The Times* of London, Nov. 26, 1864.
2 *Wish and Wisdom*, 1935, 2–3.
3 in *The Case for and Against Psychical Belief*, 1927, 284.
4 *Chance, Love and Logic*, 1923, 41.
5 Ibid., 38.
6 *The Varieties of Religious Experience*, [1902] 1958, 339.
7 *Wealth and Poverty*, 1981, 261.
8 *The Social Brain*, 1985, 3.
9 Ibid., 99.
10 *The Open and Closed Mind*, 1960, 67–68.
11 *An American Dilemma*, [1944] 1962, 1030.
12 *An American Dilemma*, 1944, xlix.
13 *Self-Deception and Morality*, 1986, 119.
14 in *Beliefs, Attitudes, and Values*, M. Rokeach, 1968, 254.
15 *Novum Organum*, 1620, Book 1, Aph. 49.
16 in *Penthouse*, March, 1981.
17 *The Broken Connection*, 1979, 112.
18 *The Basic Writings of C. G. Jung*, 1959, 89.
19 *Aids to Reflection*, 1825, "On Spiritual Religion," Aph. V.
20 *Prosologion*, c. 1100, chap. 1.
21 *The Sickness Unto Death*, [1849] 1944, 58.
22 in *U.S. News & World Report*, Oct. 26, 1981, 70.
23 *The True Believer*, 1951, 78.
24 Ibid., 125.
25 *The Anti-Christ*, 1888, Aph. 54.
26 *The Theory of Moral Sentiments*, 1759, Part VII, sec. 4.
27 *The Open and Closed Mind*, 1960, 58.
28 *Lectures and Essays*, vol. 2, 1879, 163–76.
29 *The Image*, 1962, 227.
30 *Reason and Emotion in Psychotherapy*, 1962, 105.
31 *Law, Legislation and Liberty*, vol. 1, 1973, 12.
32 *Personal Knowledge*, 1962, 268.
33 Ibid., 266.

34 *Ends and Means*, 1938, 329.
35 *The Crowd*, [1895] 1960, 142.
36 Ibid., 143–49.
37 Ibid., 143.
38 in *Living Philosophies*, Clifton Fadiman ed., 1931, 186.
39 *Home Is Where We Start From*, 1986, 143.
40 *The Closing of the American Mind*, 1987, 143.
41 *Tragic Sense of Life*, [1912] 1954, 117.
42 *The Fall of Public Man*, 1977, 151.
43 *Revolution from Within*, 1992, 318.
44 Inaugural Address, Washington, Jan. 20, 1965.

Bonding

1 *Man in the Modern Age*, [1931] 1951, 182.
2 *Suicide*, [1897] 1951, 252.
3 *God, Guilt, and Death*, 1984, 87.
4 *Being and Nothingness*, [1943] 1957, 175.
5 *The Territorial Imperative*, 1973, 5–6.
6 *On Aggression*, 1966, 190.
7 *Men in Groups*, 1970, 168.
8 *The Imperial Animal*, 1974, 82.
9 *Works*, 1915, vol. 8, 138.
10 *Leadership*, 1978, 292.
11 *Ethology*, 1975, 503.
12 *Men in Groups*, 1970, 218, 224.
13 *Against Our Will*, 1976, 211.
14 Ibid., 5.
15 *Sexual Personae*, 1990, 12.
16 *The Myth of Masculinity*, 1981, 150.
17 *The Imperial Animal*, 1974, 132–38.
18 *Origins*, 1982, 58.
19 *The Evolution of Love*, 1981, 267.
20 *Attachment and Loss*, vol. 3, 1980, 40.
21 *The Imperial Animal*, 1974, 84.
22 *The Pursuit of Loneliness*, [1970] 1976, 95.
23 in *Dimensions of Personality*, R. Lynn ed., 1981, 7.
24 *The Dialectic of Sex*, 1970, 80.
25 *The Mermaid and the Minotaur*, 1976, 77.
26 *Escape from Freedom*, 1941, 52.
27 *Revolution from Within*, 1992, 302.
28 *The Image*, 1956, 64.
29 *An Inquiry into the Human Prospect*, 1975, 114–15.

Bureaucracy

1 *Economy and Society*, [1918] 1968, 973.
2 Ibid., 1968, 225.
3 *America As a Civilization*, 1957, 409.
4 *Economy and Society*, [1918] 1968, 975.
5 *Leadership*, 1978, 301.
6 *Eichmann in Jerusalem*, 1964, 289.
7 *The Real World of Technology*, 1990, 116.
8 *The Age of Charisma*, 1984, 285.
9 *Eichmann in Jerusalem*, 1964, 290.
10 *Working Through Narcissism*, 1981, 311.
11 *Technics and Human Development*, 1967, 200.
12 *For The Love of Life*, 1986, 57.
13 *Freud: The Mind of the Moralist*, 1961, 258.
14 *The Culture of Narcissism*, 1979, 91–99.
15 *The Origins of Totalitarianism*, 1958, 207.
16 *The Pursuit of Loneliness*, [1970] 1976, 12.
17 quoted in *A Study of Bolshevism*, N. Leites, 1953, 574.
18 *The New Class*, 1957, 97.
19 *The State and Revolution*, 1917, chap. 6, part 2.
20 Ibid., chap. 3, part 3.
21 *The Political Illusion*, 1967, 160.
22 *Economy and Society*, [1918] 1968, 991.
23 *The State and Revolution*, 1917, chap. 6, part 3.
24 *The Political Illusion*, 1967, 155.
25 *America As a Civilization*, 1957, 410.
26 *The Origins of Totalitarianism*, 1958, 243.
27 in *The New Yorker*, Oct. 18, 1958, 186.
28 *Capitalism, Socialism, and Democracy*, [1942] 1950, 293.
29 *Economy and Society*, [1918] 1968, 1393.
30 Ibid., 987.
31 *Political Man*, 1063, 393.
32 *The End of History and the Last Man*, 1992, 78.
33 in *Political Psychology*, M. Hermann ed., 1986, 17.
34 *Sex and Destiny*, 1984, 279.
35 *The Imperial Animal*, 1974, 70.
36 *The Anti-Man Culture*, 1972, 218.
37 *Ideas and Opinions*, [1934] 1954, 93.

Capitalism

1 *The Protestant Ethic and the Spirit of Capitalism*, [1904] 1958, 17.
2 *Folkways*, 1906, 23.
3 *An Introduction to Social Psychology*, 1926, 330.
4 *Wealth and Poverty*, 1981, 265.
5 Ibid., 255.
6 *Capitalism, Socialism, and Democracy*, [1942]1950, 127.
7 in *Sexual Politics of Gender*, 1981, 64.
8 *Toward a Feminist Theory of the State*, 1989, 4.
9 *The Culture of Narcissism*, 1979, 132.
10 *Capital*, 1867, vol. 1, chap. 25, 4.
11 *Technics and Human Development*, 1967, 277.
12 in *Nehru: The Years of Power*, V. Shean, 1960.
13 *Capital*, 1867, vol. 1, chap. 6, 7.
14 *The Decay of Capitalist Civilisation*, 1923, 6.
15 Ibid., 163.
16 *Woman and Socialism*, 1910, 341.
17 in *Monthly Review*, May, 1949, "Why Socialism," par. 18.
18 *The Art of Loving*, 1956, 85.
19 *The Passions*, 1976, 8.
20 *Patterns of Culture*, [1934] 1960, 217.
21 *Corporate Liberalism*, 1982, 15.
22 *Libertarianism*, 1971, 90.

23 *The Culture of Narcissism*, 1979, 391.
24 *The Permissive Society*, 1971, 168–69.
25 *The Meaning of the 20th Century*, 1964, 178–79.
26 *Capitalism, Socialism, and Democracy*, [1942] 1950, 144.
27 *Capitalist Society*, 1979, 421.
28 in *From Max Weber*, H. Gerth ed., 1946, 322.
29 *The End of History and the Last Man*, 1992, 335.
30 *The Protestant Ethic and the Spirit of Capitalism*, [1904] 1958, 172–74.
31 *Religion and the Rise of Capitalism*, [1926] 1961, 280.
32 *Listen, America!*, 1980, 13.
33 address, Sept. 1956.
34 *Life Against Death*, 1966, 221.
35 *Maps of the Mind*, 1981, 184.
36 *The Cultural Contradictions of Capitalism*, 1976, 78.
37 in *Collected Essays*, 1959, 266.
38 *The Making of a Counter Culture*, 1969, 18.
39 *America As a Civilization*, 1957, 292–93.
40 *The Culture of Contentment*, 1992, 53, 59.
41 *Capitalism, Socialism, and Democracy*, [1942] 1950, 31, 83.
42 *On the Democratic Idea in America*, 1972, 92.
43 *The March of Folly*, 1984, 4.
44 *The City in History*, 1961, 438.
45 in *Time*, Feb. 20, 1995, 44.
46 *Global Reach*, 1974, 386.
47 *The Virtue of Selfishness*, 1964, 32.
48 *A Study of War*, [1942] 1964, 302.
49 *The Decay of Capitalist Civilisation*, 1923, 84.
50 in *Capitalism*, A. Rand, 1966, 116.
51 *The Neoconservatives*, 1979, 138.
52 *Wealth and Poverty*, 1981, 24.
53 *America As a Civilization*, 1957, 269.
54 *An Inquiry into the Human Prospect*, 1975, 70.
55 *The Human Prospect*, 1955, 316.
56 *Wealth and Poverty*, 1981, 3.
57 *Power and Personality*, 1948, 210.
58 *Capitalism, Socialism, and Democracy*, [1942] 1950, 424.

Chaos / Order

1 in *New Dimensions in Psychoanalysis*, 1955, 312.
2 *Good and Evil*, 1953, 139.
3 *The Need for Roots*, 1952, 9.
4 *The Realm of Spirit*, 1940, 41.
5 *Solitude*, 1988, 167.
6 *Civilization and Its Discontents*, 1930, chap. 3.
7 *I Believe*, C. Fadiman ed., 1940, 35.
8 *Meditations*, c. 161–80 A.D., Book VII, par. 75.
9 *The End of Nature*, 1989, 73.
10 *Émile*, [1762] 1979, 282
11 *Reflections on the Revolution in France*, 1790, 351.
12 *Works*, 1915, vol. 8, 80.
13 *The Authoritarian Personality*, 1950, 675.
14 in *Moral Values and the Superego Concept in Psychoanalysis*, S. Post ed., 1968, 129.
15 *The Real War*, 1981, 46.
16 "My Political Testament," in *Aus Metternich's Nachgelassenen Papieren*, 1880, vol. 7, 636.
17 Whitney *v* California, [1927] 274 U.S. 357.
18 Letter from Birmingham [Alabama] Jail, in *Atlantic Monthly*, Aug., 1963, 81.
19 *Aggression American Style*, 1978, 291.
20 *Information Anxiety*, 1989, 49.
21 *The Sexual Revolution*, [1929] 1974, 202.
22 *The Philosopher's Stone*, 1991, 161.
23 *Tropic of Cancer*, [1934] 1961, 2.
24 *Order Out of Chaos*, 1984, 292.
25 *The Philosopher's Stone*, 1991, 196.
26 *Against Method*, 1975, 179.
27 *Process and Reality*, [1929] 1978, 111–12.
28 *Thus Spake Zarathustra*, 1881, Prologue, No. 5.
29 *For the Love of Life*, 1986, 56.
30 *I and Thou*, [1922] 1970, 82.
31 *The Technological Society*, 1964, 5, 79.
32 in *International Journal of Law and Psychiatry*, 1979, vol. 2, 220.
33 *The Triumph of the Therapeutic*, 1966, 40.
34 *The New Left*, 1975, 194.
35 in *Nietzsche*, by W. Kaufman, 1950, 140.
36 *Creative Evolution*, [1907] 1944, 254.
37 *Post-Capitalist Society*, 1993, 113.
38 *The Being of Man and His Future Evolution*, [1908] 1981, 74.
39 *The Life of Reason*, 1954, 3.
40 *Émile*, [1762] 1979, 473.
41 *The Varieties of Religious Experience*, [1902] 1958, 58.
42 "Science and Culture," 1880.

Christianity

1 *The Rebel*, [1954] 1967, 189.
2 *Philosophical Dictionary*, 1764, "Christianity."
3 *The Life of Reason*, 1954, 219–22.
4 *Woman and Socialism*, 1910, 58.
5 in *Self Deception and Self-Understanding*, M. Martin, 1985, 267.
6 *The Will to Power*, [1901] 1967, 142.
7 *The Basic Writings of C. G. Jung*, 1959, 442.
8 *The Age of Faith*, 1950, 829.
9 First Crusade, Nov. 26, 1095.
10 [d. 1153] quoted in *A Survey of European History*, W. Ferguson ed., 1969, 203.
11 *Ends and Means*, 1938, 93.
12 *Altruistic Love*, 1950, 47.
13 *Secular Authority*, 1523, Book 3.
14 *Writings on Civil Disobedience and Nonviolence*, [c. 1900] 1987, 172.
15 *On Civil Disobedience and Non-Violence*, [c. 1900] 1967, 206, 240.
16 Ibid., 11.

Pages 37–43

17 *The Betrayal of the West*, 1978, 69.
18 *Beyond Theology*, 1964, 143.
19 *Prophesy and Politics*, 1986, 197.
20 *Process and Reality*, [1929] 1978, 342.
21 *The Triumph of the Therapeutic*, 1966, 19.
22 Ibid., 250.
23 *Why I Am Not a Christian*, [1927] in *Basic Writings*, 1961, 595.
24 *The Psychology of Moral Behaviour*, 1971, 147.
25 quoted in *Boston Globe*, Nov. 15, 1980.
26 *Nature, Man, and Woman*, 1958, 51–52.
27 *The Rebel*, [1954] 1967, 32.
28 *Beyond Theology*, 1964, 143.
29 *Thoughts*, [1670] 1962, Fragments 382–83.
30 *The Myth of the Eternal Return*, [1949] 1971, 96.
31 [1623–62], in a biography by his sister.
32 *Christianity*, 1958, 26.
33 *Agape and Eros*, [1953] 1982, 734–35.
34 *De Profundis*, 1897.
35 *Works of Love*, [1848] 1962, 112.
36 Ibid., 1962, 351–52.
37 *On Civil Disobedience and Non-Violence*, [c. 1900] 1967, 14.
38 *Agape and Eros*, [1932] 1982, 46.
39 *Les Faux Monnayeurs*, 1925, Part 1, chap. 13.
40 *The Realm of Spirit*, 1940, 212.
41 *The Being of Man and His Future Evolution*, [1909] 1981, 144.
42 *The Power of Myth*, 1988, 220.
43 *The Phenomenon of Man*, [1940] 1959, 294.
44 *Memories, Dreams, Reflections*, 1961, 328.
45 *The Denial of Death*, 1973, 160.
46 *The Realm of Spirit*, 1940, 205.
47 *Generation of Vipers*, 1942, 276.
48 *Mind, Self, and Society*, 1934, 293.
49 speech to Free World Association, Mar. 8, 1942.
50 *De Profundis*, 1897.
51 *The Myth of the Eternal Return*, [1949] 1971, 161.
52 *Orthodoxy*, [1908] 1959, 245–46.
53 *Waiting for God*, 1951, 28.
54 *Woman and Socialism*, 1910, 58.
55 *The First Sex*, 1971, 246.
56 *Note-Books*, 1912, XXI.
57 *The Anti-Christ*, 1888, Aph. 5.
58 *The End of History and the Last Man*, 1992, 197.
59 *The Need for Roots*, 1952, 208.
60 *Armed Neutrality and an Open Letter*, [1851] 1968, 49–51.
61 *The Unfinished Temple*, 1910, i., 5.
62 *Generation of Vipers*, 1942, 276.

Civilization

1 *The Meaning of the 20th Century*, 1964, 84.
2 *The Third Wave*, 1980, 383.
3 *Politics Among Nations*, [1948] 1967, 370.
4 *The Politics of Experience*, 1967, 61–64.
5 *America As a Civilization*, 1957, 42.
6 *Alexandria Quartet*, 1979, 764.
7 *Civilization*, 1969, 347.
8 *Life Against Death*, 1966, 286, 297.
9 *Eros and Civilization*, [1955] 1966, 51.
10 *Civilization and Its Discontents*, 1930, 63.
11 *Civilization and Its Discontents*, [1930] 1961, 83.
12 *The Conservative Mind*, [1953] 1986, 421.
13 *Mon Coeur Mis à Nu*, 1887, XXXII.
14 *The Origin and Function of Culture*, 1943, 100.
15 Ibid., 98–99.
16 *Love and Will*, 1969, 98.
17 *The Decline of the West*, 1932, 250.
18 *Introduction to Mathematics*, 1911, 61.
19 *The Constitution of Liberty*, 1960, 22, 26.
20 *In Praise of Idleness*, 1935, 183.
21 *Capitalism*, [1946] 1966, 296.
22 *The Revolt of the Masses*, 1932, 75.
23 Nobel Prize acceptance speech, Dec. 10, 1964.
24 *The Rebel*, [1954] 1967, 273.
25 *The City in History*, 1961, 52.
26 *Physics and Politics*, 1873, chap. 2.
27 quoted in *The Biology of Moral Systems*, R. Alexander, 1987, 227.
28 *The Anatomy of Human Destructiveness*, 1973, 166.
29 *The Psychology of Dictatorship*, 1950, 298.
30 *Sex and Temperament in Three Primitive Societies*, [1935] 1963, 168.
31 *Wealth and Poverty*, 1981, 70.
32 *The Power of the Positive Woman*, 1977, 177.
33 *Woman As Force in History*, [1946] 1973, 285.
34 *Sexual Personae*, 1990, 38.
35 *Civilization and Its Discontents*, [1930] 1961, 50.
36 *Where Is Industrialism Going?*, 1923, 143.
37 *The Crowd*, [1895] 1960, 67–68.
38 *The Decline of the West*, [1932] 1965, 185.
39 Ibid., 406–07.
40 *The Origin of Family, Private Property and State*, [1884] chap. 9.
41 *Capitalism, Socialism, and Democracy*, [1942] 1950, 125.
42 *The Communist Manifesto*, 1848.
43 *Experience and Education*, [1938] 1963, 39.
44 *Folkways*, [1906] 1940, 109.
45 *The Meaning of the 20th Century*, 1964, 184.
46 *A Discourse on the Origin and Foundations of Inequality Among Men*, [1754] 1984, 136.
47 *An Outline of Psychoanalysis*, 1940, chap. 7.
48 *The Mind of Primitive Man*, [1911] 1938, 137.
49 *The Public Philosophy*, [1955] 1989, 86.
50 *The Origin of Consciousness in the Breakdown of the Bicameral Mind*, 1976, 126.
51 *Understanding Media*, 1966, 86.
52 *The Mind of Primitive Man*, [1911] 1938, 252.
53 *The Gutenberg Galaxy*, 1962, 27.
54 *Mind, Self and Society*, 1934, 221.
55 "Roark" in *The Fountainhead*, A. Rand, 1943, 715.
56 *Capitalism and Freedom*, 1962, 3–4.

Pages 43–50

57 *Icon and Image,* [1954] 1965, 20.
58 *The Human Revolution,* 1972, 159.
59 *The Public Philosophy,* [1955] 1989, 137.
60 *A Grammar of Politics,* [1925] 1938, 20.
61 Ibid., 100.
62 *So Human an Animal,* 1968, 211.
63 *Profiles of the Future,* 1982, 177.
64 *The Conquest of Happiness,* 1930, chap. 14.
65 *Homo Ludens,* 1955, 211.
66 *Airman's Odyssey,* 1942, 433.
67 *Group Psychology and the Analysis of the Ego,* [1921] 1959, 35.
68 *A Study of History,* [1934] 1972, 44.
69 *The City in History,* 1961, 558.
70 *The Revolt of the Masses,* 1932, 67, 81.
71 *Eco-Philosophy,* 1981, 22.
72 *Caesar and Christ,* 1944, 665.
73 *America As a Civilization,* 1957, 950.

Community

1 *Post-Capitalist Society,* 1993, 154.
2 *The Fall of Public Man,* 1977, 222.
3 *Twilight of Authority,* 1975, 87.
4 *The Closing of the American Mind,* 1987, 154.
5 *The End of History and the Last Man,* 1992, 328.
6 *The Conservative Mind,* [1953] 1986, 242, 487.
7 *An Inquiry into the Human Prospect,* 1975, 160.
8 *The Triumph of the Therapeutic,* 1966, 52.
9 *The Human Problems of an Industrial Civilization,* [1933] 1960, 137.
10 *Generation of Vipers,* 1942, 101.
11 *Global Reach,* 1974, 365.
12 *The Triumph of the Therapeutic,* 1966, 245.
13 *Ends and Means,* 1938, 78.
14 in *Cyberspace,* 1991, Michael Benedikt ed., 74.
15 *Post-Capitalist Society,* 1993, 61.
16 *The Greening of America,* 1970, 8.
17 *The Courage to Be,* 1952, 91.
18 *Mind, Self and Society,* 1934, 316.
19 in *The Development of a Research Agenda on White-Collar Crime,* H. Edelhertz ed., 1980, 28.
20 *Suicide,* [1897] 1951, 209–12.
21 *The Pursuit of Loneliness,* [1970] 1976, 191.
22 *What I Believe,* 1925, 60–61.
23 [1845] in *Karl Marx,* T. B. Bottomore ed., 1963, 253.
24 *The Will to Believe,* 1897, 174.
25 *The Managers,* 1979, 226.
26 *I and Thou,* [1922] 1970, 94.
27 *Ends and Means,* 1938, 131.
28 *A Grammar of Politics,* [1925] 1938, 24.
29 *Mein Kampf,* [1924] 1943, 298.
30 in *Political Psychology,* M. Hermann ed., 1986, 483.
31 *The Fall of Public Man,* 1977, 310.
32 Ibid., 309.
33 *The Pursuit of Loneliness,* [1970] 1976, 166.
34 *An Introduction to the Principles of Morals and Legislation,* 1823, chap. 1, sec. 4.
35 *The Problem of Christianity,* 1914, vol. 2, 60.
36 *The Managers,* 1979, 205.
37 *The Need for Roots,* 1952, 41.
38 *Post-Capitalist Society,* 1993, 173–74.
39 *The Pursuit of Loneliness,* [1970] 1976, 169.
40 *The End of History and the Last Man,* 1992, 323–26.

Computers

1 *The Second Self,* 1984, 307.
2 in *Psychology Today,* Dec. 1983, 34–35.
3 *The Enchanted Loom,* 1981, 159.
4 *The Revolution of Hope,* 1968, 43.
5 *Learning With Logo,* 1983, chap. 13.
6 in *Creative Intelligences,* R. Gregory ed., 1987, 119–20.
7 *Computer Power and Human Reason,* 1976, 115, 126.
8 *The Cult of Information,* 1986, 179, 217.
9 *The Electronic Sweatshop,* 1988, 171.
10 quoted in *The Electronic Sweatshop,* B. Garson, 1988, 202.
11 *The Myth of the Machine,* 1970, 192.
12 *Technology and Justice,* 1986, 22, 26.
13 *Making Babies,* 1985, 31.
14 *Beliefs, Attitudes, and Values,* 1968, 224.
15 *Mindstorms,* 1980, 5.
16 quoted in *Information Anxiety,* R. Wurman, 1989, 86.
17 *Megatrends,* 1984, 282.
18 *Critical Path,* 1981, xxx.
19 Ibid., xxvi.
20 Ibid., xxxv.
21 *Understanding Media,* 1966, 84.
22 in *Discover,* Oct., 1989, 58.
23 *Mind Children,* 1988, 110–12.
24 *The Enchanted Loom,* 1981, 166–67.
25 *The Cerebral Symphony,* 1990, 330.
26 *The Enchanted Loom,* 1981, 162.
27 [1971] quoted in *The Cerebral Symphony,* W. Calvin, 1990, 330.
28 in *Through the 80's,* F. Feather ed., 1980, 19.
29 *Saturday Review,* July 23, 1966, 42.
30 speech to German Information Society, Stuttgart, Oct. 11, 1990.
31 *Computer Power and Human Reason,* 1976, 227.
32 *Preparing for The Twenty-First Century,* 1993, 162.
33 *Mindstorms,* 1980, 28.
34 *Frames of Mind,* 1983, 391.
35 *Mindstorms,* 1980, 35.
36 *Technics and Human Development,* 1967, 93.
37 in *Creative Intelligences,* R. Gregory ed., 1987, 111, 19.
38 *Computer Power and Human Reason,* 1976, 250.
39 *For Your Own Good,* 1984, 277.
40 *Mindstorms,* 1980, 189.

~ Conflict ~

1 *Patterns of Culture*, [1934] 1960, 58–59.
2 *Ego Psychology and Adaptation*, [1937] 1958, 12.
3 *The Marriage of Heaven and Hell*, 1790, "The Argument."
4 in *The Early Philosophers of Greece*, 1935, 119.
5 quoted in *From Luther to Hitler*, W. McGovern, 1941, 539.
6 *1999: Victory Without War*, 1988, 21, 27.
7 *Mein Kampf*, [1924] 1943, 135, 289.
8 *Politics*, vol. 1, 1916, 19–21.
9 *Leadership*, 1978, 36.
10 Ibid., 453.
11 *Being and Nothingness*, [1943] 1957, 429.
12 *Political Ensembles*, 1985, 7, 196.
13 *The Origin of the Family*, 1884, chap. 2.
14 *The Inevitability of Patriarchy*, 1973, 35.
15 in *Men in Transition*, K. Solomon ed., 1982, 56.
16 *The Peaceable Sex*, 1987, 95.
17 *Our Inner Conflicts*, [1945] 1966, 46.
18 *Love's Coming of Age*, 1896, 28.
19 *The Philosopher's Stone*, 1991, 118.
20 *An American Dilemma*, [1944] 1962, LXXI.
21 in *The Basic Writings of C. G. Jung*, V. de Laslo ed.,1959, 355.
22 *Origins*, 1982, 9.
23 *Small Is Beautiful*, 1973, 39.
24 *The Informed Heart*, 1960, 45.
25 *Man's Search for Himself*, 1953, 138.
26 *Client-Centered Therapy*, 1951, 4, 192.
27 *The Closing of the American Mind*, 1987, 228–29.
28 *Moral Man and Immoral Society*, 1932, 48.
29 *Economic and Philosophical Manuscripts of 1844*, 1964, 135.
30 [1957] in *Quotations from Chairman Mao*, 1967, chap. 22.
31 *Creative Evolution*, [1907] 1944, 277.
32 in *I Believe*, C. Fadiman ed., 1940, 89.
33 in *Physical Control of the Mind*, J. Delgado, 1969, xiv.
34 *The Meaning of the 20th Century*, 1964, 92.
35 *On the Origin of Species*, 1859, chap. 3.
36 *Germany and the Next War*, 1914, 18.
37 *Modern Man in Search of a Soul*, 1933, 219.
38 *The Psychology of the Child*, 1969, 158.
39 *Essays*, vol. 2, [1772] 1930, 203.
40 *The Denial of Death*, 1973, 173.
41 *Collected Works*, [1939] 1953, H. Read ed., vol. 9, Part I, par. 179.

~ Conscience ~

1 *The Descent of Man*, 1871, chap. 4.
2 in *I Believe*, C. Fadiman ed., 1940, 218.
3 *The Genealogy of Morals*, 1887, Second Essay, s. 18.
4 *The Unconscious God*, 1975, 115.
5 *The Psychology of Moral Behaviour*, 1971, 29.
6 "Essay on Faith," 1838.
7 *Metaphysic of Ethics*, 1781 Book 4, chap. 3, sec. 13.
8 *Émile*, [1762] 1979 Book 4, 1979, 252.
9 *The Art of Loving*, 1956, 37.
10 "Disobedience as a Psychological and Moral Problem," 1963.
11 *Psychic War in Men and Women*, 1976, 212.
12 *Being and Time*, [1927] 1962, 322.
13 in *Whistle Blowing*, R. Nader ed., 1972, 3.
14 quoted in *The Russians*, H. Smith, 1976, 273.
15 *Inside the Third Reich*, 1971, 33.
16 *The Psychology of Moral Behaviour*, 1971, 36.
17 *African Genesis*, [1961] 1967, 355–59.
18 *The Biology of Peace and War*, 1979, 193.
19 *Obedience to Authority*, 1974, 128.
20 *The Biology of Moral Systems*, 1987, 107.
21 quoted in *The Unconscious God*, V. Frankl, 1975, 56.
22 *Escape from Freedom*, 1941, 189.
23 in *Men in Transition*, K. Solomon, 1982, 244.
24 in *New Directions in Psycho-Analysis*, M. Klein ed., 1955, 435.
25 *The Minimal Self*, 1984, 258.
26 *The Betrayal of the West*, 1978, 22.
27 *Psychology and Religion*, 1938, 61.
28 *The Genealogy of Morals*, 1887, Second Essay, s. 19.
29 *Man for Himself*, 1947, 233.
30 Ibid., 158–59.
31 *The Courage to Be*, 1952, 148.
32 *Being and Time*, [1931] 1962, 277, 314.
33 *No Man Is an Island*, 1955, 30–31.
34 *Émile*, 1762, Book 4.
35 *Dear Theo: An Autobiography*, 1937, 208.
36 *Man's Search for Himself*, 1953, 215.
37 *Neurosis and Human Growth*, [1950] 1991, 131.
38 *Becoming*, 1955, 68, 74.
39 *The Division of Labor in Society*, [1893] 1933, 96.
40 *On Civil Disobedience and Non-Violence*, [c. 1900] 1967, 153.
41 *The Warriors*, [1959] 1970, 207.
42 *Collection of Letters on the Miracles*, 1767.
43 in *The Works of Joseph Butler*, 1896, 17.
44 quoted in *The Unconscious God*, V. Frankl, 1975, 52.

~ Consciousness ~

1 "On the Nature of the Psyche," [1947] in *Collected Works*, 1953, vol. 8, par. 412.
2 *The Evolution of Human Consciousness*, 1980, 5, 29.
3 *An Essay Concerning Human Understanding*, 1694, Book 2, chap. 27.
4 *The Pessimist's Handbook*, [1893] 1964, 6.
5 *Making Babies*, 1985, 79.
6 *Experience and Nature*, [1925] 1958, 303.
7 *The Gay Science*, [1882] 1974, sec. 354, 298.
8 quoted in *Sigmund Freud*, E. Jones, 1957, 57–58.

Pages 55–62

9 *The World As Will and Idea*, vol. 2, 1883, 328.
10 *The Self and Its Brain*, 1977, 431.
11 *Preconscious Processing*, 1981, 235.
12 in *Handbook of Political Psychology*, J. Knutson ed., 1973, 94.
13 *The Basic Writings of C. G. Jung*, 1959, 306.
14 *Mind and Brain*, 1984, 477.
15 *The Evolution of Human Consciousness*, 1980, 31–32.
16 *Mind, Self and Society*, 1934, 332–33.
17 [1859] in *Karl Marx*, T. Bottomore ed., 1963, 67.
18 *The Greening of America*, 1970, 253–55.
19 *Nature, Man, and Woman*, 1958, 89.
20 *The Gutenberg Galaxy*, 1962, 249.
21 *The Psychology of Consciousness*, 1977, 193.
22 *Living Philosophies*, C. Fadiman ed., 1931, 206.
23 *The Varieties of Religious Experience*, [1902] 1985, 308.
24 *The Politics of Ecstasy* 1968, 94–95.
25 quoted in *The Passions*, R. Solomon, 1976, 8.
26 *The Politics of Ecstasy*, 1968, 342.
27 *The Greening of America*, 1970, 4–16.
28 in *The Nature of Human Consciousness*, R. Ornstein ed., 1973, xii.
29 in *The Harvey Lectures*, Series 62, 1968, 318.
30 in *American Psychologist*, vol. 23, 1968, 723–33.
31 *The Analysis of Mind*, 1921, 40.
32 *Tragic Sense of Life*, [1912] 1954, 18.
33 *Adventures of Ideas*, 1933, chap. 20.
34 *Modern Man in Search of a Soul*, 1933, 110.
35 *Sexual Personae*, 1990, 16.
36 *Modern Man in Search of a Soul*, 1933, 243.
37 "The Meaning of Psychology for Modern Man," [1933] in *Collected Works*, 1953, vol. 10, par. 289.
38 quoted in *British Journal of Psychology*, 1962, 53:3.
39 *Preconscious Processing*, 1981, 185.
40 "John Galt" in *Atlas Shrugged*, A. Rand, 1957, 1015.
41 quoted in *The Cerebral Symphony*, W. Calvin, 1990, 2.
42 *Understanding Media*, 1966, 19, 202.
43 *The Philosopher's Stone*, 1991, 83.
44 *Stalking the Wild Pendulum*, 1977, 108, 112.
45 *The Phenomenon of Man*, [1940] 1959, 151, 178.
46 *Creative Evolution*, [1907] 1944, 284.
47 Ibid., 197.
48 *Being and Nothingness*, [1943] 1957, 620.
49 Ibid., li.
50 Ibid., 74.
51 *I and Thou*, [1922] 1970, 75.
52 "The Undiscovered Self," [1957] in *Collected Works*, 1953, vol. 10, par. 528.
53 *The View from Nowhere*, 1986, 6.
54 *Memories, Dreams, Reflections*, 1961, 256.
55 *Technics and Human Development*, 1967, 31.
56 *The Emperor's New Mind*, 1989, chap. 10, conclusion.
57 *The Symbiotic Universe*, 1988, 238.
58 in *The Conscious Mind*, K. Walker, 1962, 166.
59 *Man in the Modern Age*, [1931] 1951, 143.
60 *Tragic Sense of Life*, [1912] 1954, 13.

Conservatism

1 in *Objections to Conservatism*, Heritage Foundation, 1981, 10.
2 *Rationalism in Politics and Other Essays*, 1962, 172.
3 in *The International Journal of Ethics*, Apr., 1916.
4 *The Constitution of Liberty*, 1960, 400–01.
5 *The New Right*, 1987, 136.
6 quoted in *Maps of the Mind*, C. Hamden-Turner, 1981, 71.
7 *The Open and Closed Mind*, 1960, 122.
8 *Years of Upheaval*, 1982, 239.
9 *God in The White House*, 1988, 182.
10 in *Journal of International Affairs*, 1985, vol. 38, no. 2, 159.
11 in *Essays on Sociology*, P. Kecskemeti ed., 1953, 106.
12 *The Constitution of Liberty*, 1960, 402–04.
13 *On the Democratic Idea in America*, 1973, 97–98.
14 *The Power Elite*, 1956, 326.
15 *Political Man*, 1963, 124.
16 *The Meaning of Conservatism*, 1980, 16.
17 *The Neoconservatives*, 1979, 66, 212.
18 in *Conservative Essays*, M. Cowling ed., 1978, xx.
19 *The Psychology of Conservatism*, 1973, 288.
20 *On the Democratic Idea in America*, 1973, 105.
21 *The Triumph of the Therapeutic*, 1966, 41.
22 *Capitalism*, 1966, 196–99.
23 *The Conservative Mind*, [1953] 1986, 460.
24 *Twilight of Authority*, 1975, 51.
25 *The Power Elite*, 1956, 326.
26 *The (Guilty) Conscience of a Conservative*, 1978, 149.
27 *1999: Victory Without War*, 1988, 304.
28 in *Modern Age*, Winter, 1974, 11.
29 *The Conservative Mind*, [1953]1960, 539.
30 *The Conservative Mind*, [1953] 1986, 492.

Consumerism

1 *The Gutenberg Galaxy*, 1962, 125, 250.
2 *The Cultural Contradictions of Capitalism*, 1976, 65.
3 *Libertarianism*, 1971, 105.
4 *Wealth of Nations*, 1776, Book 5, chap. 1, part 3.
5 *The General Theory of Employment, Interest and Money*, 1936, 104.
6 *The End of History and the Last Man*, 1992, 126.
7 *The Culture of Narcissism*, 1979, 60, 138.
8 *The Minimal Self*, 1984, 28, 34.
9 *The Sane Society*, 1955, 164–66.
10 *The Revolution of Hope*, 1968, 119.
11 *Global Reach*, 1974, 71, 89.
12 *Culture Against Man*, 1965, 20.
13 *Tools for Conviviality*, 1973, chap. 3.
14 *For The Love of Life*, 1986, 20.
15 *The Theory of the Leisure Class*, [1899] 1934, 33.
16 Ibid., 157.

Pages 62–69

17 *America As a Civilization*, 1957, 257.
18 *The Status Seekers*, 1959, 317.
19 *The Waste Makers*, 1963, 203.
20 *Maps of the Mind*, 1981, 50.
21 *The Lonely Crowd*, [1950] 1965, 78, 82, 122.
22 *Sex and Destiny*, 1984, 247.
23 Ibid., 246, 301.
24 *Media Sexploitation*, 1976, 2.
25 *A Grammar of Politics*, [1925] 1938, 69, 77.
26 *The Greening of America*, 1970, 189–92.
27 *Small Is Beautiful*, 1973, 56.
28 *The End of History and the Last Man*, 1992, 169.
29 *Technology—The God That Failed*, 1971, 160.
30 in *Capitalism*, A. Rand, 1966, 112–13.
31 *Economics*, 1970, 55.
32 in *Arizona Law Review*, vol. 23, 1981, 1283–98.
33 *The Structure of Evil*, 1968, 51.
34 *The Culture of Narcissism*, 1979, 33.
35 *Creed or Chaos?*, 1947, chap. 6.
36 *So Human an Animal*, 1968, 191.

Control

1 in *Science*, vol. 124, Nov. 30, 1956, 1060.
2 *The Ways of Behaviorism*, 1926, 11.
3 in *Science*, vol. 124, Nov. 30, 1956, 1062.
4 *Social Psychology*, 1981, 202.
5 *Maps of the Mind*, 1981, 36–38.
6 *Forces of Production*, 1984, 328.
7 *Technics and Human Development*, 1967, 199.
8 *The Dehumanization of Man*, 1983, 112.
9 *The Minimal Self*, 1984, 48.
10 *The Greening of America*, 1970, 69–70.
11 *The Myth of The Machine*, 1970, 306.
12 *The Philosopher's Stone*, 1991, 34.
13 *Legacy of Hiroshima*, 1962, 56.
14 *The Heart of Man*, 1964, 41.
15 *The Bonds of Love*, 1988, 193.
16 *Beyond Power*, 1985, 76.
17 Ibid., 78.
18 *The Bonds of Love*, 1988, 53.
19 *The Passions*, 1976, 356.
20 in *The Search for the Self*, P. Ornstein ed., 1978, 645.
21 in *Men in Transition*, K. Solomon ed., 1982, 29.
22 *The Crisis of Our Age*, 1957, 240.
23 *Marriage and Morals*, [1929] 1959, 161.
24 in *The Quest for Self-Control*, S. Klausner ed., 1965, 5.
25 *The Descent of Man*, 1871, chap. 4.
26 *The Sexual Revolution*, [1929] 1974, 6, 21, 191.
27 *The Informed Heart*, 1960, 96.
28 *The Triumph of the Therapeutic*, 1966, 233.
29 *Control Theory*, 1984, 43.
30 *The Quest for Certainty*, [1929] 1960, 101.
31 *I Believe*, C. Fadiman ed., 1940, 18.
32 *Stalking The Wild Pendulum*, 1977, 135.
33 in *Stalking The Wild Pendulum*, I. Bentov, 1977, 16.
34 *The Sickness Unto Death*, [1849] 1944, 64.
35 *I Believe*, 1940, 21.
36 *The Courage to Be*, 1952, 138.
37 *Elites and Society*, 1964, 124.
38 *About Behaviorism*, 1974, 234, 251.
39 *Megabrain*, 1986, 312.
40 *Principles of Political Economy*, 1848.

Corporations

1 in *Saturday Review*, Jan. 21, 1978, 30.
2 *The Age of Uncertainty*, 1977, 258.
3 *The New Industrial State*, 1967, 196.
4 *Global Reach*, 1974, 14.
5 in *New York Times*, May 6, 1967.
6 *Building A Sustainable Society*, 1981, 322.
7 *Global Reach*, 1974, 364.
8 *White Collar Crime*, [1949] 1961, 88.
9 *White Collar Crime*, [1949] 1983, 191.
10 *Corporate Liberalism*, 1982, 256.
11 *White Collar Crime*, [1949] 1961, 224.
12 in *Corporate Violence*, S. Mills ed., 1987, 203.
13 *The Power Elite*, 1956, 342–43.
14 *Capitalism and Freedom*, 1962, 133.
15 *Post-Capitalist Society*, 1993, 101.
16 *The End of Ideology*, 1962, 41.
17 *The Pyramid Climbers*, 1962, 20.
18 *Corporate Violence*, 1987, 8.
19 *The Turning Point*, 1982, 221.
20 *America As a Civilization*, 1957, 284.
21 *The Managers*, 1979, 89, 106, 138.
22 *Brave New Workplace*, 1985, 121.
23 *Suicide*, [1897] 1951, 378–79.
24 *The Status Seekers*, 1959, 114.
25 *America As a Civilization*, 1957, 287.
26 *The Managers*, 1979, 267.
27 *Beyond Power*, 1985, 407.
28 *The Cult of Information*, 1986, 217.
29 in *Nation*, Feb. 6, 1982, 143.
30 *The Neoconservatives*, 1979, 294.
31 *America As a Civilization*, 1957, 287.
32 *Capitalism, Socialism, and Democracy*, [1942] 1950, 156.
33 *The Culture of Contentment*, 1992, 68–69.
34 *The Pursuit of Loneliness*, [1970] 1976, 174.
35 *The Managers*, 1979, 269.
36 *The Division of Labor in Society*, [1893] 1964, 31.

Culture

1 *The Decline of the West*, [1932] 1965, 73–74.
2 *The Human Revolution*, 1972, 160.
3 *Technics and Human Development*, 1967, 46.
4 in *Bulletin of Atomic Scientists*, 1966, 22, 2.
5 *Living Philosophies*, C. Fadiman ed., 1931, 213.

Pages 75–82

46 *The World and the Individual*, 1900, 380.
47 *Being and Time*, [1931] 1962, 294, 306.
48 Ibid., 357.
49 *America As a Civilization*, 1957, 618–20.
50 in *New York Times*, May 19, 1968, sec. 2, 1.
51 *The Realm of Spirit*, 1940, 127.
52 *Childhood and Society*, [1950] 1963, 269.
53 in *The Search for the Self*, P. Ornstein ed., 1978, 757.
54 *Markings*, 1961.
55 speech, June 23, 1963.

Deception / Self-deception

1 *Self-Deception*, 1969, 1.
2 quoted in *The Philosophy of "As If,"* H. Vaihinger, 1935, 355.
3 *Third Olynthiac*, 349 B.C., sec. 19.
4 *Culture and Value*, 1980.
5 *Thoughts*, [1670] 1962, Fragment 99.
6 *The Selfish Gene*, 1976, 70.
7 *Human Nature and Biocultural Evolution*, 1984, 58–59.
8 *The Politics of Experience*, 1967, 61.
9 *The Origin of Consciousness in the Breakdown of the Bicameral Mind*, 1976, 219.
10 *Self-Deception and Self-Understanding*, 1985, 7.
11 in *Inquiry*, 1975, 18, 22.
12 in *Self-Deception and Self-Understanding*, M. Martin ed., 1985, 161–62.
13 in *Perspectives on Self-Deception*, A. Rorty ed., 1988, 13.
14 *Critical Path*, 1981, xxxviii.
15 *Self-Deception and Self-Understanding*, 1985, 13.
16 *Self-Deception and Morality*, 1986, 98.
17 [d. 1274] *Summa Theologica*, Q. 76, art. 3.
18 *The Psychology of Dictatorship*, 1950, 119, 202.
19 *Moral Man and Immoral Society*, 1932, 42.
20 *Truth and Power*, 1970, 14.
21 *Aggression American Style*, 1978, 4, 5.
22 *Presidential Secrecy and Deception*, 1980, 4
23 *The Political Writings of H. D. Lasswell*, 1951, 50.
24 *Christmas Holiday*, 1939, "Stranger in Paris."
25 *For Your Own Good*, 1984, 36.
26 *Gyn/Ecology*, 1978, 30.
27 *Self and Others*, 1969, 124.
28 *Papers on the War*, 1972, 18.
29 *The Politics of Lying*, 1973, 344.
30 *The CIA and the Cult of Intelligence*, 1974, 4–6.
31 *Twilight of Authority*, 1975, 16–18.
32 *Critical Path*, 1981, 188.
33 quoted in *The CIA and the Cult of Intelligence*, V. Marchetti, 1974, 366.
34 *Crimes of War*, 1971, 428.
35 *The Cult of Information*, 1986, 165.
36 in *NewYork Times Co. v U.S.*, [1971] 403 U.S. 713.
37 *The Gutenberg Galaxy*, 1962, 262.
38 *The Wealth of Nations*, [1776] 1937, Book 1, chap XI, conclusion.
39 *The Public Philosophy*, 1955, 99.
40 *Folkways*, [1906] 1940, 529.
41 *The Image*, 1962, 209.
42 *The Prince*, 1513, chap. 18.
43 *A Tale of a Tub*, 1704, sec. 9.
44 *The Wild Duck*, 1884, act V.
45 in *Perspectives on Self-Deception*, A. Rorty ed., 1988, 399.
46 *The Image*, 1962, 260.
47 *Being and Nothingness*, [1943] 1957, 49.
48 *The Brothers Karamazov*, [1880] 1957, 49.
49 *The Realm of Spirit*, 1940, 264.
50 *Aggression American Style*, 1978, 297.
51 in *Cratylus* by Plato.
52 in *Perspectives on Self-Deception*, A. Rorty ed., 1988, 416.
53 *Critical Path*, 1981, xxxviii.

Dehumanization

1 in *Oui*, 1975, "Conversations with Indira Gandhi."
2 in *The Technological Society*, J. Ellul, 1964, v–viii.
3 *The Myth of the Machine*, 1970, 24.
4 *Das Capital*, 1867, vol. 1, Appendix (part II).
5 *The Cult of Information*, 1986, 179.
6 *Computer Power and Human Reason*, 1976, 266.
7 *Nobody Wanted War*, 1968, 208.
8 *The Origins of Totalitarianism*, 1958, 438.
9 *Ideas and Opinions*, [1945] 1954, 126.
10 on his fellow soldiers at My Lai, quoted in *Sanctions for Evil*, N. Sanford ed., 1971, 66.
11 *Torture*, 1978, 285.
12 *Ethology*, 2nd ed., 1975, 511.
13 in *Collected Essays*, 1959, 254.
14 *Love and Hate*, 1972, 101.
15 *The Evolution of Human Consciousness*, 1980, 176.
16 *The Imperial Animal*, 1974, 255.
17 *The Arrogance of Power*, 1966, 137.
18 *The Spying Heart*, 1989, 105.
19 in *American Political Science Review*, vol. 55, 1961, 2–23.
20 quoted in *Man and God*, Victor Gollancz ed.
21 *A Study of History*, [1934] 1972, 430.
22 *The Dehumanization of Man*, 1983, xxx.
23 in *Sanctions for Evil*, N. Sanford ed., 1971, 265.
24 *Against Our Will*, 1975, 377, 394.
25 *The First Sex*, 1971, 115.
26 *The Corrupt Society*, 1975, 6, 14, 42.
27 in *Sanctions for Evil*, N. Sanford ed., 1971, 102.
28 *Aggression American Style*, 1978, 7–9.
29 *Obedience to Authority*, 1973, 188.
30 *The Revolution of Hope*, 1968, 89.
31 *The Courage to Be*, 1952, 139.
32 *The Politics of Experience*, 1967, 37.
33 *The Phenomenon of Man*, [1940] 1959, 258, 290.
34 *The Dehumanization of Man*, 1983, 219.
35 *The City in History*, 1961, 4.

Pages 82–87

Democracy

1 [1937] quoted in *Sources of Democracy*, S. Padover ed., 1973, 37.
2 *Power and Personality*, 1948, 108, 150.
3 *The Political Writings of Harold D. Lasswell*, 1951, 495.
4 quoted in *Why Men Hate*, S. Tenenbaum, 1947, 161.
5 *Home Is Where We Start From*, 1986, 246.
6 *Revolution from Within*, 1992, 10.
7 *Profiles in Courage*, 1957, 208.
8 *A New History of the United States*, 1958.
9 *America As a Civilization*, 1957, 362–63.
10 *Politics*, Book 7.
11 *Politics*, Book 6, chap. 2.
12 *The State and Revolution*, 1917, chap. 4, part 6.
13 Ibid., chap. 5, part 2.
14 *Compendium of General Sociology*, [1920] 1980, 337.
15 *The State and Revolution*, 1917, chap. 5, part 4.
16 in *The Voice of Destruction*, H. Rauschning, 1940, 107–9.
17 *The Real War*, 1981, 340.
18 *The Crisis of Democracy*, 1975, 113, 162.
19 *Proper Studies*, 1927, 24–28.
20 *Reflections on the Revolution in France*, 1790, 139.
21 [1857] in *The Conservative Mind*, R. Kirk, [1953] 1986, 188.
22 *The Federalist Papers*, 1788, Paper no. 10.
23 *Megatrends*, 1984, 176.
24 *The Politics of Ecstasy*, 1968, 276.
25 *The Political Writings of Harold D. Lasswell* 1951, 194.
26 *Capitalism, Socialism, and Democracy*, [1942] 1950, 184, 297.
27 *The Crisis of Democracy*, 1975, 175.
28 *The Decline of the West*, [1932] 1965, 393.
29 speech to Council of the Americas, Dec. 5, 1972.
30 *The Cultured Man*, 1958, 31.
31 *Global Reach*, 1974, 361.
32 quoted in *The Hidden Persuaders*, V. Packard, 1980, 169.
33 *One-Dimensional Man*, 1964, 52.
34 *The Hero in History*, [1943] 1955, 245.
35 *Last Chance*, 1948, 78.
36 in *I Believe*, 1940, C. Fadiman ed., 101–02.
37 *Maps of the Mind*, 1981, 200.
38 *Corporate Liberalism*, 1982, 264.
39 *The Open Society and Its Enemies*, 1962, vol. 2, 126–27.
40 *Political Man*, 1963, 402.
41 quoted in *Anything But The Truth*, W. McGaffin, 1968, 78.
42 *The New Priesthood*, 1965, 3.
43 *Rational Evolution*, 1930.
44 *Children of Light and Children of Darkness*, 1944, foreword.
45 *The Constitution of Liberty*, 1960, 116.
46 in *Journal of International Affairs*, 1985, vol. 38, no. 2, 152.
47 *The Myth of the Machine*, 1967, 236.
48 *Political Man*, 1963, xxxii.
49 *Religion and the Rise of Capitalism*, [1926] 1961, 269.
50 *Beyond Freedom and Dignity*, 1972, 172.
51 *Human Aggression*, 1968, 121.
52 *Capitalism, Socialism, and Democracy*, [1942] 1950, 269.
53 *Wealth and Poverty*, 1981, 38.
54 *Psychology of the Normal and Subnormal*, 1919, 237.
55 *The Future of Mankind*, 1961, 297.
56 *Twilight of Authority*, 1975, 139.
57 *An American Dilemma*, [1944] 1962, 1029.
58 *The Pursuit of Loneliness*, [1970] 1976, 163.
59 *The End of History and the Last Man*, 1992, 305.
60 *The American Style*, 1958, 321.
61 *The Power Game*, 1988, 726.
62 in *Anticipatory Democracy*, C. Bezold ed., 1978, xviii.
63 *Future Shock*, 1970, 420.
64 *Home Is Where We Start From*, 1986, 241.
65 *Democracy*, 1971, 209.
66 *Power*, 1938, 274
67 quoted in *On the Democratic Idea in America*, I. Kristol, 1972, 54.
68 in *From Max Weber*, H. Gerth, 1946, 149.
69 *A Grammar of Politics*, [1925] 1938, 101.
70 *The Wish for Kings*, 1993, 41.
71 *The Pursuit of Loneliness*, [1970] 1976, 161.
72 *Corporate Liberalism*, 1982, 262.
73 *Footholds*, 1977, 48.
74 in *Beyond Domination*, C. Gould ed., 1983, 7–8.
75 in *Collected Essays*, 1959, 260.
76 *Atlantic Monthly*, March, 1901.
77 quoted in *Men and Atoms*, W. Laurence, 1959, 319.
78 Third Inaugural Address, Washington, Jan. 20, 1941.
79 *The End of History and the Last Man*, 1992, 42.
80 Commons speech, London, Nov. 11, 1947.

Dependency / Autonomy

1 *Childhood and Society*, [1950] 1963, 405.
2 *Self-Deception and Morality*, 1986, 42.
3 *Being and Loving*, 1978, 13.
4 Seneca Falls, New York, 1848.
5 *The First Sex*, 1971, 329.
6 *Against Our Will*, 1976, 6.
7 *The Cinderella Complex*, 1981, 15.
8 Ibid., 105.
9 Ibid., 159.
10 *Man for Himself*, 1947, 155.
11 *Solitude*, 1988, 127.
12 *Understanding Women*, 1985, 87.
13 Ibid.

Pages 87–94

14 *The Hazards of Being Male*, 1976, 12.
15 *Home Is Where We Start From*, 1986, 125.
16 *International Journal of Law and Psychiatry*, 1964, vol. 7, 230.
17 *The Anatomy of Human Destructiveness*, 1973, 323.
18 *Life Against Death*, 1966, 280.
19 [1942] in *Psychology of Women*, J. Williams ed., 2nd ed., 1985, 71.
20 *Woman and Socialism*, 1910, 10.
21 quoted in *Family Farm*, [Wisconsin] 1957, 78.
22 *The Second Stage*, 1981, 311.
23 *Authority*, 1980, 44–47.
24 *Wealth and Poverty*, 1981, 12.
25 *The Art of Japanese Management*, 1981, 197, 235.
26 *Megatrends*, 1984, 79.
27 *The Quest for Certainty*, [1929] 1960, 308.
28 *The Bonds of Love*, 1988, 52.
29 *The Meaning of Despair*, 1968, 391.

Devil

1 *Works*, J. Strachey ed., vol. 9, [1908] 1959, 174.
2 *Nature, Man, and Woman*, 1959, 25.
3 *A Commentary on the Galatians*, [1531] 1953, 21–28.
4 *Life Against Death*, 1966, 219.
5 *Tribes on the Hill*, 1981, 69.
6 *Truth and Power*, 1970, 6.
7 *The Paranoid Style in American Politics*, 1965, 14, 32.
8 *The Brothers Karamazov*, 1880, Book 5, chap. 4.
9 *Escape from Evil*, 1975, 123.
10 *The True Believer*, 1951, 89.
11 *Fountain of Life*, 1930, 22.
12 *The Late Great Planet Earth*, 1970, 120.
13 *Love and Will*, 1969, 139.
14 *The Duality of Human Existence*, 1966, 39–48.
15 *Neurosis and Human Growth*, [1950] 1991, 39, 154.
16 *Love and Will*, 1969, 123.
17 *The Realm of Spirit*, 1940, 166.
18 in *The Basic Writings of C. G. Jung*, V. de Laslo ed., 1959, 353.
19 *The Hero with a Thousand Faces*, 1956, 338.
20 in *Saturday Review*, Mar. 26, 1966, 42.
21 *The Realm of Spirit*, 1940, 165.
22 Ibid., 194.
23 *The Cultural Contradictions of Capitalism*, 1976, 157.
24 *Narcissism*, 1983, 121.
25 *Religion and the Rise of Capitalism*, [1926] 1961, 229.
26 *Challenge to Reason*, 1968, 108.
27 *Man in the Modern Age*, [1931] 1951, 173.
28 *Psychological Reflections*, [1953] 1970, 152.

Dominance / Hierarchy

1 *Nebraska Symposium on Motivation*, Univ. of Nebraska, 1972, 30.
2 *Economy and Society*, [1918] 1968, 941.
3 *The Imperial Animal*, 1974, 51–52.
4 *The Need for Roots*, 1952, 18.
5 *Essay on Man*, 1733, Epistle IV, lines 49–50.
6 *The Mismeasure of Man*, 1981, 30.
7 *Revolution from Within*, 1992, 33.
8 *Politics*, Book 1, chap. 5.
9 *Against Our Will*, 1976, 437.
10 *Beyond Power*, 1985, 299–304.
11 *Cannibals and Kings*, 1977, 81.
12 *Human Paleopsychology*, 1987, 153.
13 *The Origin of the Family*, [1884] 1902, 79–80.
14 *The Second Sex*, 1964, 58.
15 *Origins*, 1982, 152.
16 *Eros and Civilization*, [1955] 1966, 90.
17 *Beyond Power*, 1985, 79, 128.
18 *International Journal of Law and Psychiatry*, 1983, vol. 6, 255.
19 in *Sexual Politics of Gender*, 1981, 55.
20 *International Journal of Law and Psychiatry*, 1984, vol. 7, 215–34.
21 *The Inevitability of Patriarchy*, 1973, 42.
22 *The Mermaid and the Minotaur*, 1976, 191.
23 *The Bonds of Love*, 1988, 52.
24 *The Child, the Family, and the Outside World*, 1964, 10.
25 *Aggression American Style*, 1978, 275.
26 *What Life Should Mean to You*, 1931, 53.
27 *The Origins of Totalitarianism*, 1958, 456–64.
28 *The Origins of Totalitarianism*, [1958] 1966, 478.
29 *Maps of the Mind*, 1981, 177.
30 *What Life Should Mean to You*, 1931, 50.
31 Ibid., 55.
32 *Man for Himself*, 1947, 88.
33 *City of God*, 426 A.D., Book 5, part 19.
34 in *Emotion*, R. Plutchik ed., 1980, 27.
35 *The Greening of America*, 1970, 195–96.
36 *Eros and Civilization*, [1955] 1966, 93, 100.
37 *One-Dimensional Man*, 1964, 158.
38 *Human Aggression*, 1968, 19.
39 *African Genesis*, [1961] 1967, 114.
40 Ibid., 111.
41 *The End of History and the Last Man*, 1992, 315.
42 *What Life Should Mean to You*, 1931, 69.
43 *Economy and Society*, [1918] 1968, 954.
44 *The Neoconservatives*, 1979, 246.
45 *Obedience to Authority*, 1974, 111–12.
46 *The State and Revolution*, 1917, chap. 3, part 3.
47 Ibid., chap. 4, part 6.
48 *Economy and Society*, [1918] 1968, 1002.
49 *The Peter Principle*, 1970, 28.
50 Ibid., 7.
51 *The Status Seekers*, 1959, 123.
52 Ibid., 127.
53 *Megatrends*, 1984, 221.
54 *The Underside of History*, 1976, 783.
55 *The Pyramid Climbers*, 1962, 265–56.
56 *The Underside of History*, 1976, 784.

Pages 94–100

57 *The Descent of Woman*, 1979, 268.
58 *The Realm of Spirit*, 1940, 89.
59 in *Guilt*, J. Carroll, 1971, 167–70.

Duty

1 *The Foundations of the Metaphysics of Morals*, 1785, First Section.
2 *Self-Deception and Morality*, 1986, 55.
3 *An Inquiry Concerning Political Justice*, 1793, Book 6, chap. 3.
4 *The Division of Labor in Society*, [1893] 1964, 409.
5 *A Grammar of Politics*, [1925] 1938, 289.
6 *Holy Bible*, Ecclesiastes 12:13.
7 *The Moor's Revenge*, 1677, act 3, scene 3.
8 *The Revolution of Hope*, 1968, 81.
9 *The Social Contract*, [1762] 1913, 6.
10 *The Age of Charisma*, 1984, 34.
11 *Philosophy of Right*, 1821, sec. 325.
12 quoted in *From Luther to Hitler*, W. McGovern, 1941, 555.
13 *Mein Kampf*, [1924] 1943, 530.
14 *The Psychology of Moral Behavior*, 1971, 219.
15 *Escape from Freedom*, 1941, 185.
16 *Eichmann in Jerusalem*, [1963] 1977, 135.
17 *Personal Knowledge*, 1962, 245.
18 *Iron John*, 1990, 130.
19 *Peer Gynt*, 1867, act 4, scene 1.
20 *Émile*, [1762] 1979, 97, Book II.
21 Ibid.
22 *The Need for Roots*, 1952, 5.
23 *Scouting for Boys*, 1908, Part 1.
24 *A Vindication of the Rights of Woman*, 1791, chap. 9.
25 [d. 479 B.C.] *The Doctrine of Mean*, chap. 20, 8.
26 *A Vindication of the Rights of Woman*, 1791, chap. 9.
27 *The Power of the Positive Woman*, 1977, 94.
28 *America As a Civilization*, 1957, 623.
29 in *Life of Samuel Johnson*, J. Boswell, 1766, vol. 2, 10.
30 *The Hope of the Great Community*, 1916, 1.
31 *L'Enracinement*, 1949, "Les Besoins de l'âme."
32 *The End of History and the Last Man*, 1992, 323.
33 *Advancement of Learning*, 1623, Book 7, chap. 2
34 *Airman's Odyssey*, 1942, 398.
35 *The Need for Roots*, 1952, 151.

Economics

1 *The General Theory of Employment, Interest, and Money*, 1936, 383.
2 *Generation of Vipers*, 1942, 15.
3 *Thoughts and Details on Scarcity*, 1800, 31.
4 *The Decline of the West*, [1932] 1965, 399.
5 *Religion and the Rise of Capitalism*, [1922] 1961, 273.
6 *The Technological Society*, 1964, 226.
7 *Die Deutsche Ideologie*, 1859.
8 *The New Industrial State*, 1967, 398.
9 *The Dehumanization of Man*, 1983, 112.
10 *The Pursuit of Loneliness*, [1970] 1976, 171.
11 *Culture Against Man*, 1965, 45, 48.
12 *The New Industrial State*, 1967, 293, 325.
13 *The Battle for Human Nature*, 1986, 249, 292.
14 *The Ethics of Competition*, 1935, 282.
15 *Economy and Society*, [1918] 1968, 636–37.
16 Ibid., 585.
17 *Reason in Society*, 1962, chap. 1, n. 15.
18 *The Theory of the Leisure Class*, [1899] 1934, 223.
19 *The Acquisitive Society*, 1920, 33.
20 *The Transformation of Man*, 1956, 104.
21 *Home Is Where We Start From*, 1986, 170.
22 Ibid.
23 *Suicide*, [1897] 1951, 254–55.
24 *The Closing of the American Mind*, 1987, 84.
25 *Essays in Persuasion*, [1931] 1972, 327–31.
26 *Collected Works of John Stuart Mill*, 1965, 754.
27 *Folkways*, [1906] 1940, 500.
28 *The Electronic Sweatshop*, 1988, 262.
29 *The Revolution of Hope*, 1968, 2.
30 *The Pursuit of Loneliness*, [1970] 1976, 171.
31 *Small Is Beautiful*, 1973, 42.
32 *The Division of Labor in Society*, [1893] 1964, 51.
33 *Culture Against Man*, 1965, 41
34 quoted in *Money and Class in America*, L. Lapham, 1988, 37.
35 *Hard Heads, Soft Hearts*, 1987, 15.
36 *Working Through Narcissism*, 1981, 308.
37 *The Open Society and Its Enemies*, 1950, 314–15.
38 *Post-Capitalist Society*, 1993, 164.
39 *A Study of War*, [1942] 1964, 299.
40 *Capitalism*, 1966, 42.
41 *A Grammar of Politics*, [1925] 1938, 489.
42 *The Culture of Contentment*, 1992, 82.
43 *The Quest for Certainty*, [1929] 1960, 212.
44 *The Cultural Contradictions of Capitalism*, 1976, 26.
45 *Capitalism and Freedom*, 1962, 12–13.
46 *Capitalism*, [1946] 1966, 41.
47 *Capitalism and Freedom*, 1962, 15.
48 *Religion and the Rise of Capitalism*, [1926] 1961, 264.
49 *The Fate of the Earth*, 1982, 69.
50 *The Gutenberg Galaxy*, 1962, 272.
51 *The General Theory of Employment, Interest and Money*, 1936, 162.
52 *Capitalism and Freedom*, 1962, 9.
53 *Moral Man and Immoral Society*, 1932, 15.
54 *The Open Society and Its Enemies*, [1950] 1962, vol. 2, 126.
55 *The Pursuit of Loneliness*, [1970] 1976, 183.
56 *The Challenge of Facts and Other Essays*, 1914, 90.
57 quoted in *Time*, Aug. 16, 1976, 54.
58 *The Theory of the Leisure Class*, 1934, 33.
59 *The Culture of Contentment*, 1992, 75.
60 *Profiles of the Future*, 1982, 9–10.
61 *Generation of Vipers*, 1942, 221.
62 *Sceptical Essays*, 1928, 235–36.

Pages 100–106

63 *The Affluent Society*, 1958, 309.
64 *Escape from Evil*, 1975, 89.
65 *The Biological Origin of Human Values*, 1977, 441.
66 *The Battle for Human Nature*, 1986, 325.
67 *The Farther Reaches of Human Nature*, 1971, 321, 349.
68 "Centesimus Annus," May, 1991.
69 *Capitalism, Socialism, and Democracy*, [1942] 1950, 137.
70 *The End of Nature*, 1989, 173.
71 *The Hidden Persuaders*, 1958, 225.
72 *The Turning Point*, 1982, 192–93.
73 *The Aquarian Conspiracy*, 1980, 326.
74 *The Future: As If It Really Mattered*, 1988, 23.
75 *Unsafe At Any Speed*, 1972, xci.
76 *Ends and Means*, 1938, 39.
77 Ibid., 161.
78 *I Believe*, C. Fadiman ed., 1940, 377.
79 *A Grammar of Politics*, [1925] 1938, 539.
80 *Generation of Vipers*, 1942, 91, 221.
81 *Suicide*, [1897] 1951, 253–54.
82 "Science and Culture," 1880.
83 *The Order of Things*, 1970, 257.
84 *Religion and the Rise of Capitalism*, 1926, conclusion.
85 *An Inquiry into the Human Prospect*, 1975, 160.
86 *The Quest for Certainty*, [1929] 1960, 282.
87 *A Sand County Almanac*, 1949, ix.

Education

1 "A Liberal Education," 1868.
2 in *Living Philosophies*, C. Fadiman ed., 1931, 321.
3 in *Cambridge Essays on Education*, 1917, chap. 2.
4 *Laws*, Book 1, 641.
5 *Social Statics*, 1850, Part 2, chap. 17, sec. 4.
6 *The Philosophy of Moral Development*, 1981, 94–95.
7 *The Power Elite*, 1956, 318.
8 *The Dragons of Eden*, 1977, 192.
9 *The Cultured Man*, 1958, 43.
10 *The Biological Origin of Human Values*, 1977, 443.
11 *The Anti-Man Culture*, 1972, ix, 216–18.
12 *The Gutenberg Galaxy*, 1962, 247.
13 *Culture Against Man*, 1965, 297.
14 *The Basic Writings of Bertrand Russell*, [1957] 1961, 378.
15 [d. 1945] in letter to wife Gerda.
16 *I Believe*, C. Fadiman ed., 1940, 24.
17 *A Grammar of Politics*, [1925] 1938, 78.
18 *The Culture of Narcissism*, 1979, 140.
19 *Culture Against Man*, 1963, 293.
20 *The Politics of Ecstasy*, 1968, 245.
21 *A Sand County Almanac*, 1949, 158.
22 *Culture Against Man*, 1965, 286.
23 *Folkways*, [1906] 1940, 446.
24 *The Conservative Mind*, [1953] 1986, 289.
25 *Democracy and Education*, [1916] 1963, 95.
26 *The Human Problems of an Industrial Civilization*, [1933] 1960, 155.
27 *Ends and Means*, 1938, 323.
28 *Understanding Media*, 1966, 101, 119.
29 *Summerhill*, 1960, 28.
30 *Suicide*, [1897] 1951, 372.
31 *My Pedagogic Creed*, 1897, 16.
32 *Suicide*, [1897] 1951, 373.
33 *Man in the Modern Age*, [1931] 1951, 108.
34 *The Absorbent Mind*, [1949] 1984, 259.
35 *Icon and Image*, [1954] 1965, 138.
36 *Mysticism and Logic*, 1918, 39.
37 *Ends and Means*, 1938, 219.
38 *Psychology*, 1892, chap. 10.
39 in *New Scientist*, May 21, 1964, 484.
40 in *Progress in Psychobiology*, J. Sprague ed., 1976, 245.
41 *The Amazing Brain*, 1984, 163.
42 *What Life Should Mean to You*, 1931, 165.
43 *The Absorbent Mind*, [1949] 1984, 275.
44 *What Life Should Mean to You*, 1931, 181.
45 *The Education of Henry Adams*, 1907, chap. 20.
46 *Unpopular Essays*, 1951, 117.
47 *July 20, 2019*, 1986, 76, 85.
48 *Post-Capitalist Society*, 1993, 199.
49 quoted in *The New Priesthood*, R. Lapp, 1965, 9.
50 *The Human Problems of an Industrial Civilization*, [1933] 1960, 175.
51 *Post-Capitalist Society*, 1993, 198.
52 *Generation of Vipers*, 1942, 312.
53 *Critical Path*, 1981, 266.
54 *Experience and Education*, [1938] 1963, 64.
55 *The Education of the Individual*, 1958, 109.
56 *Saturday Review*, June 7, 1969, 19.
57 *Man in the Modern Age*, [1931] 1951, 142.
58 *The Late Great Planet Earth*, 1970, 121.
59 *Ideas and Opinions*, [1936] 1954, 60.
60 Message to U. S. Congress, Feb. 20, 1961.
61 [1816] in *Writings of Thomas Jefferson*, P. Ford ed., 1899, vol. 10, 4.
62 *Democracy in America*, [1835] 1966, 498.
63 *The Outline of History*, 1921, 1100.

Egoism / Selfishness

1 *Holy Bible*, Galatians 5:26.
2 in *The City of God*, 1950, xii.
3 *Civilization and its Discontents*, [1930] 1961, 14–15.
4 *The World As Will and Idea*, [1819] 1948, vol. 1, 428.
5 *The Stress of Life*, 1976, xviii, 450.
6 *Civilization and Its Discontents*, [1930] 1961, 87.
7 *Freud: The Mind of the Moralist*, 1961, 361.
8 *The Closing of the American Mind*, 1987, 178.
9 *The Varieties of Religious Experience*, [1902] 1958, 377.
10 *Tragic Sense of Life*, [1912] 1954, 45.
11 *The Will to Power*, 1901, Book 2, sec. 369.
12 *Psychology*, 1892, chap. 12.

Pages 107–13

13 *The Selfish Gene*, 1976, 38–39.
14 *The Virtue of Selfishness*, 1964, xv, 19, 23.
15 *Ayn Rand*, 1987, 149.
16 *Libertarianism*, 1971, 112.
17 *On Human Nature*, 1978, 157.
18 [d. 1906] *Letters of Henrik Ibsen.*
19 *The Wealth of Nations*, vol. 1, [1776] 1910, 13.
20 *The Ominous Parallels*, 1982, 308.
21 in *Capitalism*, A. Rand, 1966, 279.
22 *Looking Out for #1*, 1977, 10, 45, 52.
23 *The Disowned Self*, 1971, 173.
24 *The Sense of Beauty*, 1955, 235.
25 *Beyond Good and Evil*, 1886, no. 265.
26 *Patterns of Culture*, [1934] 1960, 238–39.
27 *The Realm of Spirit*, 1940, 176.
28 *Psychoanalysis and Moral Values*, 1960, 33, 77.
29 *The Pessimist's Handbook*, [1893] 1964, 623.
30 *The Power of Positive Thinking*, 1952, 192.
31 *The Realm of Spirit*, 1940, 161.
32 *Generation of Vipers*, 1942, 130.
33 *Beyond Culture*, 1976, Introduction.
34 *The Battle for Human Nature*, 1986, 300–01.
35 *Moral Man and Immoral Society*, 1932, 48, 91.
36 *Suicide*, [1897] 1951, 360.
37 *The Evolution of Human Consciousness*, 1980, 185.
38 *The Stress of Life*, 1976, 450.
39 *The Limits of Altruism*, 1977, 27.
40 *Democracy in America*, [1835] 1966, 498.
41 *The Sense of Beauty*, 1955, 42.
42 *The True Believer*, 1951, 47.
43 *The Culture of Narcissism*, 1979, 107, 131.
44 *Coming to Our Senses*, 1989, 41.
45 *Mind, Self and Society*, 1934, 388.
46 *I and Thou*, [1922] 1970, 112–14.
47 *Ultimate Concern*, 1965, 3, 48, 143.
48 *The Art of Loving*, 1956, 48, 51.
49 [d. 1805] *Philosophical Letters*, IV, "Sacrifice."
50 *Agape and Eros*, [1953] 1982, 740.
51 *Mein Kampf*, [1924] 1943, 300.
52 *Money and Class in America*, 1988, 225.
53 *The Late Great Planet Earth*, 1970, 137.
54 *Ideas and Opinions*, [1934] 1954, 114.
55 *In a Different Voice*, 1982, 79.
56 *Democracy in America*, [1835] 1966, 477.
57 *A Study of History*, [1934] 1972, 87–88.
58 in *The Book of Angelus Silesius*, 25–26.
59 *The Integrity of the Personality*, 1963, 171.
60 *The Politics of Ecstasy*, 1968, 37.
61 *Generation of Vipers*, 1942, 130.
62 *The Phenomenon of Man*, [1940] 1959, 244.
63 *The Conquest of Happiness*, 1930, 248.
64 *Critical Path*, 1981, 276.
65 *The Revolt of the Masses*, 1932, 142.
66 *The Limits of Altruism*, 1977, 39.

Emotion

1 *Being and Nothingness*, [1943] 1957, 615.
2 *The Passions*, 1976, 14.
3 in *Delusion and Dream and Other Essays*, 1956, 70.
4 *Concluding Unscientific Postscript*, [1846] 1944, 176.
5 in *The Psychobiology of Consciousness*, J. Davidson ed., 1980, 193.
6 *The Biological Origin of Human Values*, 1977, 279.
7 *The Face of Emotion*, 1971, 183.
8 *The Human Soul*, [1959] 1973, 56–57.
9 *The Politics of Ecstasy*, 1968, 38–39.
10 *Holy Bible*, I Peter 2:11.
11 *Icarus, or the Future of Science*, 1924, 63.
12 *Ends and Means*, 1938, 319.
13 *Émile*, [1762] 1979, 445, Book V.
14 *Nicomachean Ethics*, Book 3, part 3.
15 *The Open Society and its Enemies*, 1950, 419–22.
16 *The Life of Reason*, 1954, 373.
17 in *Living Philosophies*, C. Fadiman ed., 1931, 13.
18 *Our Inner Conflicts*, [1945] 1966, 138.
19 *The Informed Heart*, 1960, 66.
20 *The Prophet*, 1923, 50.
21 *The Sense of Beauty*, 1955, 23.
22 *De Profundis*, 1897.
23 *The Varieties of Religious Experience*, [1902] 1958, 379.
24 Ibid., 128.
25 *Being and Nothingness*, [1943] 1957, 391.
26 [1939] in *Collected Works*, vol. 9, Part I, par. 179.
27 "John Galt" in *Atlas Shrugged*, A. Rand, 1957, 1021.
28 in *Capitalism*, A. Rand, 1966, 281.
29 *The Varieties of Religious Experience*, 1902, Lec. 14.
30 *Science and Immortality*, 1904, chap. 2.
31 *The Politics of Experience*, 1967, 83.
32 *Totemism*, 1963, 70–1.
33 *Psychology*, 1892, chap. 24.
34 *The Cultural Contradictions of Capitalism*, 1976, 134.
35 *Culture of Complaint*, 1993, 10.
36 *Power*, 1938, 301–02.
37 *Summerhill*, 1960, 100.
38 *The Sketch Book*, 1820, "The Broken Heart."
39 *The Natural Superiority of Women*, [1952] 1968, 85–86.
40 *Modern Man in Search of a Soul*, 1933, 39.
41 *Culture Against Man*, 1965, 12.

Enemy

1 *The Broken Connection*, 1979, 304.
2 in *Encounter*, May, 1966, 27.
3 *Fighting for Hope*, 1984, 48.
4 *Papers On The War*, 1972, 251.
5 quoted in *The Psychology of Moral Development*, L. Kohlberg, 1984, 567.

6 *Communication and Social Order*, 1962, 132.
7 *Escape from Evil*, 1975, 114.
8 quoted in *The New Yorker*, May 18, 1981, 10.
9 *A Study of Bolshevism*, 1953, 28.
10 *Dictatorships and Double Standards*, 1982, 52.
11 quoted in *The Voice of Destruction*, H. Rauschning, 1940, 234.
12 *Mein Kampf*, [1924] 1939, 110.
13 quoted in *Maps of the Mind*, C. Hampden-Turner, 1981, 176.
14 *Men in Groups*, 1970, 210.
15 *The Rebel*, [1954] 1967, 183.
16 KKK literature, quoted in *The New Fascists*, P. Wilkinson, 1983, 142.
17 *The Paranoid Style in American Politics*, 1965, 32.
18 *The Will to Believe*, [1897] 1979, 71.
19 *Iron John*, 1990, 1.
20 *One-Dimensional Man*, 1964, 51.
21 *The Real World of Technology*, 1990, 78.
22 *Home Is Where We Start From*, 1986, 213.
23 *The Heart of Man*, 1964, 89.
24 *Holy Bible*, Matthew 5:43.

Equality

1 by Thomas Jefferson, July, 4, 1776, preamble.
2 Seneca Falls, New York, July 19, 1848.
3 *The Rich Nations and the Poor Nations*, 1962, 15.
4 *Democracy in America*, [1835] 1966, 678.
5 *Group Psychology and the Analysis of the Ego*, [1921] 1959, 52.
6 [1976] quoted in *The Soviet System in Theory and Practice*, H. Shaffer, 1984, 52.
7 *Science and Human Values*, 1956, 83.
8 *The End of History and the Last Man*, 1992, 289.
9 *Free to Choose*, 1980, 128, 148.
10 *Dictatorships and Double Standards*, 1982, 15.
11 *Democracy*, 1971, 273–74.
12 [d. 1876] *Complete Works*, II.
13 *The True Believer*, 1951, 32.
14 *Detroit Free Press*, Aug. 10, 1967.
15 *Leviathan*, 1651, chap. 13.
16 *The Constitution of Liberty*, 1960, 93.
17 *Democracy in America*, 1835, Part 4, chap. 1.
18 [1918] in *Characters and Events*, 1929, 852.
19 *Democracy in America*, 1835, vol. 1, part 2, chap. 3.
20 *The Crisis of Democracy*, 1975, 162.
21 *Man for Himself*, 1947, 74.
22 *Twilight of Authority*, 1975, 213.
23 *Reflections on the Revolution in France*, 1790, 72.
24 "Commandment" in *Animal Farm*, [1945] 1951, 114.
25 *The Cultural Contradictions of Capitalism*, 1976, 260.
26 *A Grammar of Politics*, [1925] 1938, 153.
27 *The Social Contract*, 1762, Book 2, chap. 2.
28 *Capitalism and Freedom*, 1962, 169.
29 *Ends and Means*, 1938, 169.
30 *Works of Love*, 1962, 72.
31 U.S. Senate speech, Jan. 22, 1917.
32 *The Second Sex*, 1964, 686.
33 Seneca Falls, New York, July 19, 1848.
34 *Time*, Aug. 31, 1970, Essay.
35 [1842] in *Auguste Comte and Positivism*, 1975, 268.
36 *Sexual Personae*, 1990, 21.
37 *Toward a Feminist Theory of the State*, 1989, 145.
38 *Love in the Western World*, [1940] 1956, 312.
39 *Woman and Socialism*, [1885] 1910, 7.
40 "Women and Society," in *The Woman Question*, 1975, 52.
41 [1955] in *Quotations from Chairman Mao*, 1967, chap. 31.
42 *The Imperial Animal*, 1974, 129.
43 *The Conservative Mind*, [1953] 1986, 58.
44 *Elites and Society*, 1964, 123.
45 *Beyond Power*, 1985, 484.
46 *The Human Brain*, 1983, 70.
47 *The Hunters*, 1966, 32.
48 Douglas debates, 1858.
49 *The Open Society and Its Enemies*, 1950, 421.
50 *Waiting for God*, 1951, 86.
51 *The Subjection of Women*, 1869, chap. 2.
52 *The Origins of Totalitarianism*, 1958, 301.
53 *Animal Liberation*, [1975] 1990, 4.
54 in *New Knowledge in Human Values*, A. Maslow ed., 1959, 82.
55 *Animal Liberation*, [1975] 1990, 5.
56 in *Charles Darwin's Notebooks 1836–1844*, 1987, Notebook B [1837–1838].
57 *Animal Liberation*, [1975] 1990, 7, 15.

Eros

1 *The World As Will and Idea*, 1819, Book 3.
2 Plato's *Symposium*, 211.
3 *Agape and Eros*, [1937] 1953, 49, 218.
4 *Explorations in Altruistic Love and Behavior*, 1950, 5.
5 in *Agape and Eros*, A. Nygren, 1953, xxi.
6 *The Denial of Death*, 1973, 173.
7 *Agape and Eros*, [1932] 1953, chap. 3.
8 *Primary Love and Psycho-Analytic Technique*, 1965, 50.
9 *Love in the Western World*, [1940] 1956, 62.
10 in *Take Back the Night*, 1980, L. Lederer ed., 297.
11 *The Second Sex*, 1964, 446.
12 *Inhibitions, Symptoms and Anxiety*, [1926] 1959, 48.
13 *The Power of Myth*, 1988, 186.
14 *The Duality of Human Existence*, 1966, 133.
15 *Psychological Reflections*, [1953] 1970, 121.
16 *The Female Eunuch*, 1971, 89.
17 *Love's Body*, 1966, 80.
18 *Eros and Civilization*, [1955] 1966, 109.
19 *Love in the Western World*, [1940] 1956, 311–13.
20 *Negations*, 1968, 257.

Pages 119–24

21 "Why War?" [letter to Albert Einstein], 1932.
22 *Civilization and its Discontents*, 1961, 92.
23 *The Second Sex*, 1964, 187.
24 *The Closing of the American Mind*, 1987, 122.
25 *The Betrayal of the West*, 1978, 79.
26 *The Realm of Spirit*, 1940, 242.
27 *Love and Will*, 1969, 74, 305.
28 *Psychological Reflections*, [1953] 1970, 105.
29 in Plato's *Symposium*.

Evil

1 *Aids to Reflection*, 1825, "On Spiritual Religion," Aphorism XII.
2 in *Saturday Review*, Jan. 4, 1964, 23.
3 in *Sanctions for Evil*, N. Sanford ed., 1971, 243.
4 *Ends and Means*, 1938, 301.
5 *The Real War*, 1981, 341.
6 *Collected Works*, 1953, vol. 8, 170–01.
7 *The Greening of America*, 1970, 230.
8 *Escape from Evil*, 1975, xvii, 135–36.
9 *Sanctions for Evil*, 1971, 2.
10 in *Sanctions for Evil*, N. Sanford ed., 1971, 51.
11 *The Constitution of Liberty*, 1960, 146.
12 *Writings on Civil Disobedience and Nonviolence*, 1987, 272.
13 *Meditations*, [c. 160-81 A.D.] Book 7, XLI.
14 *Roads to Freedom*, 1917, 188.
15 *The Fable of the Bees*, [1724] 1970, 370.
16 *Democracy and the Student Left*, 1968, 10.
17 *The Powers of Evil*, 1975, 260.
18 *A Choice of Heroes*, 1982, 224.
19 *Characteristics*, 1831.
20 *The Concept of Dread*, [1844] 1946, 47.
21 *Way to Wisdom*, 1951, 61.
22 *The Philosophy of Mind*, 1817, Sec. 1, subsec. C, "Practical sense."
23 *Meditations*, 1898, Book IV, par. 39.
24 *Leviathan*, 1651, chap. 6.
25 *Confessions*, 399 A.D., Book VII, Sec. III.
26 *Ethics*, 1675, Part 4, prop. 8.
27 *Man for Himself*, 1947, 20.
28 Ibid., 218.
29 in *Living Philosophies*, C. Fadiman ed., 1931, 211.
30 *On Population*, 1798, chap. 19.
31 *Way to Wisdom*, 1951, 60.
32 *City of God*, 426 A.D., Book 12, parts 6–7.
33 *Good and Evil*, 1953, 58.
34 Ibid.
35 *Process and Reality*, [1929] 1978, 340.
36 *Tragic Sense of Life*, [1912] 1954, 264.
37 *Nicomachean Ethics*, Book II, vi.
38 *Tragic Sense of Life*, [1912] 1954, 291.
39 *The Unity of India*, 1937.
40 *The Gulag Archipelago*, 1974, 178.
41 *Capitalism*, 1966, 144.
42 *For the New Intellectual*, 1961, 173.
43 "Looking Back on the Spanish War," 1943.
44 *Holy Bible*, Matthew 5:38.
45 in *Crito*, by Plato, 49d.
46 *The Politics of Experience*, 1967, 63.
47 *Collected Works*, 1967, vol. 13, 47–48.
48 *The Varieties of Religious Experience*, [1902] 1958, 139.
49 *Summa Theologicae* [c. 1265], Part 1, qu. 22, art. 2.
50 *The Sense of Beauty*, 1955, 220.
51 *Why Does Evil Exist?*, 1974, 29.
52 in *Harijan*, Mar. 3, 1946.
53 *Process and Reality*, [1929] 1978, 340.
54 *Science and the Modern World*, 1925, 276.
55 *Stalking the Wild Pendulum*, 1977, 196.
56 *Holy Bible*, III John: 11.
57 *Diaries of Franz Kafka 1914–23*, Jan. 19, 1922.
58 *Meditations*, c. 161–80 A.D., Book II, 17.
59 *The Gulag Archipelago*, 1974, 168.
60 *Émile*, [1762] 1979, 282, Book V.
61 *Memories, Dreams, Reflections*, 1961, 330.
62 *The Heart of Man*, 1964, 148.
63 in *New Knowledge in Human Values*, 1959, 134.
64 in *Living Philosophies*, C. Fadiman ed., 1931, 212.
65 quoted in *Profiles in Courage*, J. F. Kennedy, 1957, 207.

Exploitation

1 *Sexual Personae*, 1990, 2.
2 *The Technological Society*, 1964, 324.
3 *Order Out of Chaos*, 1984, 91.
4 *The State and Revolution*, 1917, chap. 5, part 2.
5 *Woman and Socialism*, 1910, 479.
6 *The State and Revolution*, 1917, chap. 2, part 1.
7 *The Politics of Experience*, 1967, 49.
8 *The New Class*, 1965, 35.
9 *The Betrayal of the West*, 1078, 128–30.
10 *What Is Property?*, 1840 chap. 5.
11 "John Galt" in *Atlas Shrugged*, 1957, 1065.
12 *Christmas Holiday*, 1939, "Stranger in Paris."
13 speech, Feb., 1837.
14 *Civilized Man's Eight Deadly Sins*, 1974, 87–88.
15 *For The Love of Life*, 1986, 146.
16 *The Theory of the Leisure Class*, 1934, 44.
17 *Narcissism*, 1983, ix, 5.
18 *Violent Men*, [1969] 1992, 155.
19 *Psychic War in Men and Women*, 1976, xv.
20 *The War Myth*, 1967, 203.
21 in *The International Journal of Ethics*, Apr., 1916.
22 *The Imperial Animal*, 1974, 154–55.
23 *The Open Society*, 1950, 385.
24 *The Pursuit of Loneliness*, [1970] 1976, 148.

Faith

1 *Holy Bible*, Hebrews 11:1.
2 *Tragic Sense of Life*, [1912] 1954, 186–91.
3 *The True Believer*, 1951, 119.

Pages 124–30

4 *My Belief*, 1974, 189.
5 *Man in the Modern Age*, [1931] 1951, 193.
6 *The Sickness Unto Death*, [1849] 1944, 154, 171.
7 *Agape and Eros*, [1953] 1982, 740–41.
8 [1948] quoted in *Technology and Justice*, G. Grant, 1986, 38.
9 *Pensées*, 1670, No. 424.
10 *Critique of Pure Reason*, [1781] 1956, 29.
11 *The Decline of the West*, [1932] 1965, 189.
12 *The Denial of Death*, 1973, 201.
13 *Tragic Sense of Life*, 1913, chap. 6.
14 quoted in *From Luther to Hitler*, W. McGovern, 1941, 547.
15 *The Crowd*, [1895] 1960, 119.
16 *Tragic Sense of Life*, [1912] 1954, 192.
17 *Where Is Science Going?*, 1932, 218.
18 *Ends and Means*, 1938, 258.
19 *Tragic Sense of Life*, [1912] 1954, 75.
20 *Biblical Religion and the Search for Ultimate Reality*, 1955, 51.
21 *The Unconscious God*, 1975, 13.
22 *Identity*, 1968, 106.
23 *The Image*, 1956, 172.
24 *The Triumph of the Therapeutic*, 1966, 12.
25 in *The Basic Writings of C. G. Jung*, 1959, 402.
26 *The Anti-Christ*, 1888, Aph. 8.
27 *The True Believer*, 1951, 14.
28 *Escape from Freedom*, 1941, 78.
29 *The Problem of Being Human*, 1974, 88.
30 *Biblical Religion and the Search for Ultimate Reality*, 1955, 61.
31 *Ends and Means*, 1938, 285.
32 "Essay on Faith," 1838.
33 *The Courage to Be*, 1952, 172–73.
34 *City of God*, 426 A.D., Book 13, part 4.
35 *The Rebel*, [1954] 1967, 56.
36 *Life Against Death*, 1966, 84.
37 *Man for Himself*, 1947, 198.
38 *Way to Wisdom*, 1951, 93.
39 *The Myth of the Eternal Return*, [1949] 1971, 160.
40 *Man for Himself*, 1947, 210.
41 *Mein Kampf*, [1924] 1943, 379.
42 *Characteristics*, 1831.
43 *The Conservative Mind*, [1953] 1986, 135.
44 *The Courage to Be*, 1952, 188.
45 *Way to Wisdom*, 1951, 82.

Family

1 *The Life of Reason*, 1954, 104.
2 *Male and Female*, 1955, 150.
3 *Twilight of Authority*, 1975, 82.
4 *The Reproduction of Mothering*, 1978, 199.
5 *Sexual Politics*, 1969, 45.
6 *The Sexual Revolution*, [1929] 1974, 82.
7 *The Mass Psychology of Fascism*, [1946] 1970, 30.
8 *The Politics of Experience*, 1967, 55.
9 *The Dialectic of Sex*, 1970, 11, 12, 54.
10 *Summerhill*, 1960, 102.
11 *The Subjection of Women*, [1869] 1970, 37.
12 *The Power of the Positive Woman*, 1977, 121.
13 *Capitalism, Socialism, and Democracy*, [1942] 1950, 157.
14 *Capital*, 1867, vol. 1, 514.
15 *The Communist Manifesto*, 1848, sec. 3.
16 *The Greening of America*, 1970, 179–80.
17 *Suicide*, [1897] 1951, 377.
18 [d. 1918] quoted in *Pioneers in Criminology*, H. Mannheim ed., 1972, 227.
19 *Sex and Destiny*, 1984, 271.
20 *The Female Eunuch*, 1971, 230.
21 *She*, 1976, 48.
22 *The Fall of Public Man*, 1977, 180–81.
23 *Capitalism, Socialism, and Democracy*, [1942] 1950, 161.
24 *The Crisis of Our Age*, 1957, 188–90.
25 *The End of History and the Last Man*, 1992, 324.
26 *Twilight of Authority*, 1975, 260.
27 *The True Believer*, 1951, 36.
28 *The Psychology of Moral Development*, 1984, 75.
29 *The Inevitability of Patriarchy*, 1973, 154.
30 *Suicide*, [1897] 1951, 199–202.
31 *Future Shock*, 1970, 211.
32 *The Closing of the American Mind*, 1987, 119.
33 *The Second Stage*, 1981, 83, 99, 203.
34 *Post-Capitalist Society*, 1993, 173.
35 *Future Shock*, 1970, 221.
36 *Narcissism*, 1988, 182.
37 speech to British Conservative Party, Oct. 14, 1950.
38 *Love and Hate*, 1972, 242.
39 *The Biology of Peace and War*, 1979, 230.
40 *Moral Und Hypermoral*, 1969, 121.

Father

1 *Folkways*, [1906] 1940, 304–05.
2 *Male and Female*, 1955, 141.
3 *Marriage and Morals*, [1929] 1959, 16–17.
4 *An Introduction to Social Psychology*, [1908] 1931, 144.
5 *Escape from Evil*, 1975, 66–67.
6 in *International Journal of Law and Psychiatry*, vol. 6, 1983, 238.
7 *For Your Own Good*, 1984, 74–75.
8 *The Art of Loving*, 1956, 36.
9 in *Men in Transition*, K. Solomon ed., 1982, 488.
10 *The Pessimist's Handbook*, [1893] 1964, 213.
11 *The Bonds of Love*, 1988, 100.
12 Ibid., 171.
13 *Guilt*, 1985, 56.
14 *The Scientific Credibility of Freud's Theories and Therapy*, 1977, 209.
15 *The Bonds of Love*, 1988, 181.
16 *The Hazards of Being Male*, 1977, 153.

Pages 131–36

17 *Émile*, [1762] 1979, 49, Book I.
18 *What Life Should Mean to You*, 1931, 138.
19 *Baby and Child Care*, 1976, 47.
20 *Of Woman Born*, 1977, 282.
21 *Understanding Women*, 1985, 10.
22 *Of Woman Born*, 1977, 211.
23 in *Moral Values and the Superego Concept in Psychoanalysis*, S. Post ed., 1968, 355.
24 *Marriage and Morals*, [1929] 1959, 133–34.
25 *Les Mots*, 1964, "Lire."
26 *Iron John*, 1990, 121.
27 *The Brown Decades*, 1931, 3.

Female / Femininity

1 *Generation of Animals*, 4th century B.C.
2 *Life Against Death*, 1966, 130.
3 *Man and Woman/Boy and Girl*, 1972, 148.
4 *Human Paleopsychology*, 1987, 187.
5 *Sex and Society*, 1907, 51.
6 *International Journal of Law and Psychiatry*, 1984, vol. 7, 219–47.
7 *Human Paleopsychology*, 1987, 186.
8 *The Human Brain*, 1983, 72.
9 *Beyond Power*, 1985, 94.
10 *Identity*, 1968, 270–74.
11 *Childhood and Society*, [1950] 1963, 410.
12 quoted in *The Scientific Credibility of Freud's Theories and Therapy*, S. Fisher, 1977, 198.
13 *Beyond Power*, 1985, 93.
14 in *Men in Transition*, K. Solomon ed., 1982, 120.
15 *The Feminine Mystique*, 1963, 79.
16 *A Vindication of the Rights of Woman*, 1792, chap. 3.
17 *The First Sex*, 1971, 334.
18 in *Journal of Women in Culture and Society*, Spring, 1982, 530.
19 *The Female Eunuch*, 1970, 58, 68.
20 *Culture Against Man*, 1965, 82–85.
21 *The Female Eunuch*, [1970] 1991, foreword.
22 *The Selfish Gene*, 1976, 158.
23 *Émile*, [1762] 1979, 361, Book V.
24 *Civilization*, 1969, chap. 7, 177.
25 *Wealth and Poverty*, 1981, 70.
26 in *Psychology of Women*, J. Williams ed., 2nd ed., 1985, 386.
27 *Sexual Personae*, 1990, 10.
28 "The Female of the Species," 1911.
29 *The Decline of the West*, [1932] 1965, 354.

Freedom / Liberty

1 *The Need for Roots*, 1952, 12.
2 *The Philosophy of History*, [1832] 1944, 14–16.
3 [1945] in *Quotations from Chairman Mao*, 1967, chap. 22.
4 address at Columbia University, 1954.
5 jury address, Chicago, 1920.
6 *Philosophy of Mind*, [1817] 1971, 175.
7 Berlin speech, June 26, 1963.
8 *Charles Péguy*, 1947, 146.
9 *L'Ancien Régime*, 1856, foreword.
10 *Escape from Freedom*, 1941, 37.
11 *The Cultured Man*, 1958, 50.
12 *America As a Civilization*, 1957, 463.
13 *Beyond Domination*, 1983, 4.
14 *A Grammar of Politics*, [1925] 1938, 142.
15 *The Machinery of Freedom*, 1973, 65.
16 *On Liberty*, 1859, chap. 1.
17 *The Virtue of Selfishness*, 1964, 86.
18 *Libertarianism*, 1971, 249.
19 in *New Knowledge in Human Values*, A. Maslow ed., 1959, 60.
20 *Airman's Odyssey*, 1942, 429.
21 *The Constitution of Liberty*, 1960, 29, 32.
22 in *The Pornography of Power*, L. Rubinoff, 1968, 16.
23 *The Mass Psychology of Fascism*, 1946, 301.
24 speech to New York Press Club, Sept. 9, 1912.
25 *The (Guilty) Conscience of a Conservative*, 1978, 52.
26 *Two Concepts of Liberty*, 1958, 16.
27 Baltimore speech, Apr. 18, 1864.
28 *Taxation No Tyranny*, 1775, Yale ed.: vol. 10, 454.
29 *The State and Revolution*, 1917, chap. 4, part 6.
30 in *The British Magazine*, Jan., 1760.
31 *Money and Class in America*, 1988, 52.
32 [1877] quoted in *Sources of Democracy*, S. Padover ed., 1973, 52.
33 *The Betrayal of the West*, 1978, 148.
34 quoted in *The Soft War*, T. Barry, 1988, 3.
35 *The Perpetual Pessimist*, 1963, 58.
36 in *Histoire des Girondins*, A. de Lamartine, 1847, Book 51, chap. 8.
37 speech to Republican Convention, July 16, 1964.
38 *Persecution East and West*, 1983, 129.
39 "Women's Rights Convention" 1860, quoted in *Feminist Quotations*, 1979, 214.
40 *The Nature of Human Values*, 1973, 183.
41 [1937] quoted in *Sources of Democracy*, S. Padover ed., 1973, 37.
42 quoted in *Minneapolis Morning Tribune* [editorial], Mar. 17, 1950.
43 *Democracy in America*, [1835] 1969, 254.
44 *Corporate Liberalism*, 1982, 257.
45 *Beast and Man*, 1978, 288.
46 *Future Shock*, 1970, 167.
47 *The True Believer*, 1951, 32.
48 *Man and Superman*, 1903, Maxims: "Liberty and Equality."
49 *Home Is Where We Start From*, 1986, 215.
50 in *People, Penguins and Plastic Trees*, D. Van de Beer ed., 1986, 256.
51 *Love and Will*, 1969, 42.
52 *Maps of the Mind*, 1981, 54.
53 *The Journals of André Gide*, 1928, vol. 3, 26.
54 *Eros and Civilization*, [1955] 1966, 225.

Pages 136–42

55 *Being and Nothingness*, [1943] 1957, 439–40.
56 *The Philosophy of History*, [1832] 1944, 15.
57 *Psychological Reflections*, [1953] 1970, 161.
58 *Man for Himself*, 1947, 247.
59 *Explorations in Altruistic Love and Behavior*, 1950, 20.
60 *Summerhill*, 1960, 297.
61 *The Unconscious God*, 1975, 52.
62 *A Grammar of Politics*, [1925] 1938, 143.
63 *Philosophy in a New Key*, [1942] 1957, 290.
64 *Generation of Vipers*, 1942, 253.
65 *On Aggression*, 1966, 232.
66 *The Basic Writings of C. G. Jung*, 1959, 134.
67 quoted in *Twilight of Authority*, R. Nisbet, 1975, 72.
68 *The Crisis of Our Age*, 1957, 204.
69 *Love in the Western World*, [1940] 1956, 282.
70 *Capitalism and Freedom*, 1962, 33.
71 speech [1790] in *Speeches*, T. Davis ed., 1845, 94.
72 *The Good Want Power*, 1977, 142.
73 *Anarchism*, 1962, 476.
74 *The Conservative Mind*, [1953] 1986, 100.
75 *The Rebel*, [1954] 1967, 71.
76 *A Theory of Justice*, 1971, 215.
77 *The Courage to Be*, 1952, 152.
78 *The Spirit of Laws*, 1748, Book XI, 3.
79 *Beyond Freedom and Dignity*, 1972, 42.
80 *African Genesis*, [1961] 1967, 323.
81 *The Rebel*, [1954] 1967, 287.
82 *The Good Want Power*, 1977, 54.
83 *The Open Society and Its Enemies*, 1945, vol. 2, chap. 21, 177.
84 "Frazier," in *Walden Two*, B. F. Skinner, [1948] 1976, 246–48.
85 *Émile*, [1762] 1979, 120.
86 *Twilight of Authority*, 1975, 228.
87 *The Female Eunuch*, 1971, 328.
88 *Sexual Personae*, 1990, 39.
89 *Civilization and Its Discontents*, 1930, chap. 3.
90 *The True Believer*, 1951, 30.
91 [1809] in *Goethe's World View*, 1963, 139.
92 Ibid., 141.
93 *The Betrayal of the West*, 1978, 21, 66.
94 *Future Shock*, 1970, 282.
95 *The Prophet*, 1923, 47.
96 *The Basic Writings of Bertrand Russell*, [1903] 1961, 69.
97 *Man in the Modern Age*, [1931] 1951, 204.
98 *Small Is Beautiful*, 1973, 296.
99 quoted in *Love and Will*, R. May, 1969, 269.
100 *I and Thou*, [1922] 1970, 102.
101 quoted in *Man's Search for Himself*, R. May, 1953, 142.

Free Will

1 *The City of God*, 426 A.D., Book 5, part 9.
2 in *Living Philosophies*, C. Fadiman ed., 1931, 293.
3 *Insight and Responsibility*, 1964, 118.
4 *The Metaphysics of Morals*, 1785, Third Section.
5 *The Philosophy of "As If,"* 1935, 258.
6 *The Heart of Man*, 1964, 130.
7 *Smith v. United States*, 1929, 59 App. D.C.
8 *African Genesis*, [1961] 1967, 352–53.
9 quoted in *I Believe*, C. Fadiman ed., 1940, 69.
10 *The Quest for Certainty*, [1929] 1960, 250.
11 *Psychology*, 1892, chap. 26.
12 *On The Will in Nature*, [1836] 1992, 36.
13 *Our Knowledge of the External World*, 1914, 255–56.
14 *The Origins of Knowledge and Imagination*, 1978, 18.
15 *Supplements to "The World As Will and Idea,"* 1844, chap. 17.
16 *Theses for The Heidelburg Disputation*, 1518, no. 13.
17 [1889] in *The Portable Nietzsche*, W. Kaufman ed., 1954, 499.
18 *Human Society in Ethics and Politics*, 1954, 97.
19 *Beyond Good and Evil*, [1886] 1907, chap. 1, par. 19–21.
20 quoted in *The Voice of Destruction*, H. Rauschning, 1940, 225.
21 *The Dragons of Eden*, 1977, 209.
22 *Ethics*, 1675, Part II, prop. 48.
23 *Psychology*, 1892, chap. 13.
24 *Science and Human Behavior*, 1953, 447.
25 *Man in the Modern Age*, [1931] 1951, 203.
26 *De Profundis*, 1897.
27 *The Metaphysics of Morals*, 1785, Third Section.
28 *On Becoming a Person*, 1961, 193.
29 *Paradise Lost*, 1667, Book 7, line 172.
30 *The World and the Individual*, 1900, 468.
31 *The Dehumanization of Art*, 1956, 153.

Future

1 *The Revolt of the Masses*, 1932, 173.
2 *Pensées*, 1670, No. 47.
3 *The Unconscious God*, 1975, 139.
4 *The Image*, 1956, 125.
5 *Edifying Discourses*, 1847, "The Expectancy of Faith."
6 *Existence*, 1958, 69.
7 *Being and Nothingness*, [1943] 1957, 128–29.
8 Ibid., 124.
9 *Becoming*, 1955, 12.
10 in *I Believe*, C. Fadiman ed., 1940, 220.
11 *An Essay on Man*, [1944] 1970, 60.
12 *The Imperial Animal*, 1974, 56.
13 *The Decline of the West*, [1918] 1962, 187.
14 *The Rebel*, [1954] 1967, 166, 208.
15 in *Handbook of Political Psychology*, J. Knutson ed., 1973, 165.
16 *The Managers*, 1979, 166.
17 *Sex and Destiny*, 1984, 492.
18 *The Natural Superiority of Women*, [1952] 1968, 104.
19 *Love and Will*, 1969, 325.
20 *This Week Magazine*, Mar. 16, 1969, 7.

Pages 142–47

21 *The Biological Origin of Human Values*, 1977, 406.
22 *The Rebel*, [1954] 1967, 304.
23 *What Price Progress?*, 1926, 312.
24 *Man's Search for Himself*, 1953, 268.
25 *The Philosopher's Stone*, 1991, 154.
26 *Process and Reality*, [1929] 1978, 214.
27 *The Need for Roots*, 1952, 48.
28 *The Conservative Mind*, [1953] 1986, 303.
29 *Studies in the Psychology of Sex*, [1910] 1936, vol. 4, 1.
30 *Megatrends*, 1984, 37.
31 in *Collected Essays*, 1959, 296.
32 *A Tract on Monetary Reform*, 1923, chap. 3.
33 *The Fate of the Earth*, 1982, 168.
34 *Essay on the Principle of Population*, 1798.
35 *Autobiography*, 1873, chap. 7.
36 telegram quoted in *New York Times*, May 25, 1946.
37 *Order Out of Chaos*, 1984, 119.
38 *Science and the Modern World*, 1925, 298.
39 *The Pursuit of Loneliness*, [1970] 1976, 140.
40 *Future Shock*, 1970, 4, 290, 306.
41 *The Revolt of the Masses*, 1932, 181.
42 *The Open and Closed Mind*, 1960, 367.
43 *The Revolution of Hope*, 1968, 8.
44 *The Culture of Narcissism*, 1979, 23, 26, 357.
45 *Memories, Dreams, Reflections*, 1961, 326.
46 *Revolution from Within*, 1992, 103.
47 *Nineteen Eighty-Four*, 1949, chap. 3.
48 speech at Harvard, Sept. 6, 1943.
49 [1960] in *Perspectives on the Computer Revolution*, Z. Pylyshyn ed., 1970, 409–10.
50 *Mind Children*, 1988, 1, 115–16.
51 *Profiles of the Future*, 1982, 225.
52 *The Enchanted Loom*, 1981, 162.
53 [1969] in *The World of René Dubos*, 1990, 369.
54 [past President of World Future Society], quoted in *The Futurist*, vol. 14, Feb., 1980, 7.
55 in *The Futurists*, 1972, 129.
56 *So Human an Animal*, 1968, 238.
57 *No Limits to Learning*, 1979, xiii.
58 *The Fate of the Earth*, 1982, 178.
59 *100 Pages for the Future*, 1982, 12.
60 in *Science and Moral Priority*, R. Sperry, 1983, 147.

Gender

1 *Sex and Gender*, 1968, viii.
2 *Man and Woman/Boy and Girl*, 1972, 105, 107, 176.
3 in *International Journal of Law and Psychiatry*, 1984, 219.
4 in *Beyond Domination*, C. Gould ed., 1983, 49.
5 *Phoenix*, 1936, "Study of Thomas Hardy," chap. 7.
6 "Woman in Europe," 1927.
7 *Home Is Where We Start From*, 1986, 189.
8 *Understanding Women*, 1985, 22.
9 *The Life of Reason*, 1954, 155.
10 *The Reproduction of Mothering*, 1978, 169.
11 *In A Different Voice*, 1982, 8.
12 *Beyond Power*, 1985, 91–93.
13 [1951] in *Collected Works*, vol. 9, Part II, par. 30.
14 *The Art of Loving*, 1956, 36.
15 *Psychological Reflections*, [1953] 1970, 116.
16 "The Special Phenomenology of the Child Archetype," 1940.
17 *The Bonds of Love*, 1988, 82.
18 *Revolution from Within*, 1992, 258.
19 in *Signs*, 1983, no. 8, 598–616.
20 *The Evolution of Human Consciousness*, 1980, 223.
21 *The Cinderella Complex*, 1981, 204.
22 *Gender and Stress*, 1987, 356–60.
23 *Toward a Feminist Theory of the State*, 1989, 160.
24 *The Female Eunuch*, 1970, 16.
25 Ibid., 249–51.
26 in *International Journal of Law and Psychiatry*, vol. 6, 1983, 245.
27 *The Mermaid and the Minotaur*, 1976, 276.
28 *A Psychiatrist's World*, [1920] 1959, 611.
29 *The Second Sex*, 1964, 65.
30 *Three Contributions to the Theory of Sex*, 1910.
31 *The Origins and History of Consciousness*, 1954, xxii.
32 quoted in *Understanding Human Sexuality*, J. Hyde, 1986, 364.
33 in *Feminine Psychology*, K. Horney, 1967, 117.
34 quoted in *The Protestant Temperament*, P. Grevan, 1977, 243.
35 *Life Against Death*, 1966, 134.
36 *The Concept of Dread*, [1844] 1946, 71.
37 *Male and Female*, 1949, chap. 18.
38 *Man and Woman*, 1904, 451.

God

1 *Metaphysics*, 11, 1.
2 *Creative Evolution*, [1907] 1944, 271.
3 *Holy Bible*, John 4:24.
4 *Tragic Sense of Life*, [1912] 1954, 185.
5 *The Essence of Christianity*, 1841.
6 *The Power of Myth*, 1988, 24.
7 *The Nature and Destiny of Man*, vol. 1, 1941, 156.
8 *Personal Knowledge*, 1962, 324.
9 *Ethics*, 1675, Part 1, par. 6.
10 *Thoughts*, [1670] 1910, 233.
11 *I and Thou*, [1922] 1970, 127.
12 *Life Against Death*, 1966, 265.
13 *Denial of Death*, 1973, 174.
14 *The Sickness Unto Death*, [1849] 1944, 45, 58.
15 *The Meaning of Truth*, [1909] 1975, 6.
16 *Self, God, and Immortality*, 1986, 8, 198.
17 *Psychology and Religion*, 1938, 105.
18 *Agape and Eros*, [1953] 1982, 214–15.
19 *Ethics*, 1675, Part 5, prop. 18.
20 *Tragic Sense of Life*, [1912] 1954, 27.
21 *Opus Postumum*, 1884, vol. 21, 414.
22 *Way to Wisdom*, 1951, 90.

Pages 147–53

23 *Process and Reality*, [1929] 1978, 207.
24 *The Descent of Man*, 1871, chap. 5.
25 *The Biology of Moral Systems*, 1987, 207.
26 *The Realm of the Great Goddess*, 1962, 53.
27 *Beyond Power*, 1985, 74.
28 *Nature, Man, and Woman*, 1958, 45.
29 *Émile*, [1762] 1979, 285.
30 *A Brief History of Time*, 1988, 175.
31 *Process and Reality*, [1929] 1978, 341.
32 *Science and the Modern World*, 1925, 257.
33 *Note-Books*, 1912, xx.
34 *Folkways*, [1906] 1940, 526.
35 *Systematic Theology*, 1951, 237.
36 *The Decline of the West*, [1932] 1965, 206–07.
37 *Waiting on God*, 1951, 71.
38 in *The Psychobiology of Consciousness*, J. Davidson ed., 1980, 438.
39 *The Origin of Consciousness in the Breakdown of the Bicameral Mind*, 1976, 72–75.
40 *Psychology and Religion*, 1938, 98.
41 *The Phenomenon of Man*, [1940] 1959, 284.
42 *Épîtres*, 1771, no. 96.
43 *The Gay Science*, 1882, Aphorism 125.
44 *Psychology and Religion*, 1938, 103.
45 *The Basic Writings of C. G. Jung*, 1959, 40.
46 *The Order of Things*, 1970, 385.
47 address, San Francisco, Apr. 16, 1966.
48 *Harper's*, Oct. 1961, 178.
49 *The Betrayal of the West*, 1978, 81.
50 *Essays*, 1625, "Of Atheism."
51 *The Rebel*, [1954] 1967, 62.
52 *Existentialism and Humanism*, 1948, 33.
53 *The Courage to Be*, 1952, 190.
54 *The Myth of the Eternal Return*, [1949] 1971, 161–62.
55 *The Varieties of Religious Experience*, [1902] 1958, 390.
56 *The Tragic Sense of Life*, 1954, 319.
57 *The World and the Individual*, 1900, 427.
58 *Letter on a General Principle Useful in Explaining the Laws of Nature*, 1687.
59 *Process and Reality*, [1929] 1978, 343.
60 *The Road Less Traveled*, 1979, 269.
61 *Agape and Eros*, [1932] 1982, 740.
62 [d. 1109] *Proslogium*, chap. 1.
63 *Life After God*, 1994, 359.
64 *Tragic Sense of Life*, [1912] 1954, 155.
65 *I and Thou*, [1922] 1970, 130.
66 *The Varieties of Religious Experience*, [1902] 1958, 389.

Guilt

1 *Civilization and Its Discontents*, [1930] 1961, 81.
2 *The Imperial Animal*, 1974, 38.
3 *Life Against Death*, 1966, 269.
4 *The Denial of Death*, 1973, 135–40.
5 *Love and Hate*, 1972, 164.
6 *The Psychology of Moral Behaviour*, 1971, 124.
7 *Politics*, 1950, 227.
8 *On Death and Dying*, 1969, 161.
9 *Civilization and its Discontents*, [1930] 1961, 79.
10 *Life Against Death*, 1966, 268.
11 in *Psycho-Analysis and Contemporary Thought*, J. Sutherland ed., 1958, 17, 23.
12 *Reason and Emotion in Psychotherapy*, 1962, 142–45.
13 *The Genealogy of Morals*, 1887, Second Essay, s. 22.
14 in *Time*, Sept. 14, 1959, 69.
15 *The Neoconservatives*, 1978, 65–66.
16 *Freud: The Mind of the Moralist*, 1961, 274.
17 *For Your Own Good*, 1984, 195.
18 in *New Directions in Psycho-Analysis*, M. Klein ed., 1955, 432.
19 in *Carmichael's Manual of Child Development*, P. Mussen ed., 1970, 339.
20 in *The Analysis of Defense*, J. Sandler, 1985, 269.
21 *Positive Social Behavior and Morality*, vol. 1, 1978, 257.
22 *The Peaceable Sex*, 1987, 19.
23 *The Ego and the Id*, [1927] 1950, 75.
24 *Escape from Evil*, 1975, 157.
25 *Guilt and Gratitude*, 1982, 5.
26 Ibid., 23.
27 *Understanding Women*, 1985, 147.
28 *Being and Nothingness*, [1943] 1957, 410.
29 *Guilt*, 1971, 19.
30 in *Psychiatry*, 1957, vol. 20, 117.
31 *Love and Will*, 1969, 107.
32 *Guilt*, 1985, 1.
33 *Escape from Evil*, 1975, 158.
34 *Being and Time*, [1931] 1962, 329–53.
35 in *Crimes of War*, R. Lifton ed., 1947, 478.
36 *Theories of Personality*, 1978, 324.
37 *The Warriors*, [1959] 1970, 211.
38 *The Broken Connection*, 1979, 146.
39 *Ultimate Concern*, 1965, 184.
40 *Self and Others*, 1969, 133.
41 *God, Guilt, and Death*, 1984, 162.
42 *The Courage to Be*, 1952, 149.
43 Ibid., 122.
44 *Tragic Sense of Life*, [1912] 1954, 290.
45 *The Warriors*, [1959] 1970, 206, 212.

Happiness

1 *The Life of Reason*, 1954, 63.
2 *The Fall of Public Man*, 1977, 90.
3 *America As a Civilization*, 1957, 693.
4 in *The New Yorker*, Jan. 7, 1967.
5 *Candida*, 1898, act 1.
6 *The Virtue of Selfishness*, 1964, 19–24.
7 *Works*, [1822] 1962, vol. 10, 80.
8 *No Man Is an Island*, 1955, 3.
9 *Reason and Responsibility*, 6th ed., 1985, 484.
10 *Love in the Western World*, [1940] 1956, 280.
11 *Ethics*, 1675, Part 4, prop. 18.

Pages 154–59

12 *Utilitarianism*, 1867, chap. 2.
13 *Meaning in Life*, 1992, 102.
14 *Sartor Resartus*, 1834, 153.
15 *Civilization and Its Discontents*, [1930] 1961, 30.
16 *The Stress of Life*, 1976, 440.
17 *The Division of Labor in Society*, [1893] 1964, 243.
18 *An Introduction to Social Psychology*, [1908] 1931, 134–35.
19 *Lectures on Ethics*, [1779] 1930, 151–52.
20 *Human Society in Ethics and Politics*, 1954, 238.
21 *Works*, 1851, vol. 4, 193.
22 *Nicomachean Ethics*, Book 1, part 2.
23 *Meditations*, 161-80 A.D., Book 5, xxx.
24 [1982] in *The World of René Dubos*, 1990, 50.
25 *Constitutional Code*, 1827, Introduction, sec. II.
26 *Enquiry Concerning Political Justice*, 1798, Book 3, chap. 3.
27 in *Science*, vol. 124, Nov. 30, 1956, 1062.
28 *The Open Society and its Enemies*, 1950, 422.
29 "Mustapha Mond" in *Brave New World*, [1932] 1977, 192.
30 *I Believe*, C. Fadiman ed., 1940, 70.
31 *The House of Seven Gables*, chap. xx, 1851.
32 "John Galt" in *Atlas Shrugged*, 1957, 1022.
33 *The Life of Reason*, 1954, 463.
34 *The Varieties of Religious Experience*, [1902] 1958, 83.
35 *Beyond Power*, 1985, 271.
36 *An Inquiry into the Human Prospect*, 1975, 76–77.
37 *The Making of a Counter Culture*, 1969, 102.
38 *The Mass Psychology of Fascism*, 1946, 275.
39 *The Will to Power*, 1900, Aph. 1023.
40 *Sociobiology*, 1980, 127.
41 *The Varieties of Religious Experience*, [1902] 1958, 31.
42 *So Human an Animal*, 1968, 147.
43 *How to Win Friends and Influence People*, 1936, 70.
44 *One-Dimensional Man*, 1964, 82.
45 *Man for Himself*, 1947, 189.
46 [d. 1832] in *Goethe's World View*, 1963, 91.
47 *Becoming*, 1955, 68.
48 in *An Anthropologist at Work*, M. Mead, 1959, 144.
49 *What Is Happiness?*, 1939, 59.
50 *The Conquest of Happiness*, 1930, 157.
51 *Meditations*, 161-80 A.D., Book VII, 67.
52 *The Triumph of the Therapeutic*, 1966, 17.
53 *Solitude*, 1988, 202.
54 *The Division of Labor in Society*, [1893] 1964, 241.
55 *Civilization and Its Discontents*, 1930, 39.

HARMONY

1 *The Realm of Spirit*, 1940, 120.
2 Ibid., 258.
3 *The View from Nowhere*, 1986, 215.
4 *Solitude*, 1988, 188.
5 *Adventures of Ideas*, 1933, Part 4, chap. 17.
6 *Psychology and Religion*, 1938, 87.
7 *The Sense of Beauty*, 1955, 231.
8 *Education and the Social Order*, 1932, 237.
9 *Our Common Future*, 1987, 111.
10 *Building a Sustainable Society*, 1981, 371.
11 *Positive Social Behavior and Morality*, vol. 1, 1978, 180.
12 *The Second Sex*, 1964, 620.
13 *Iron John*, 1990, 177.
14 *Creative Evolution*, [1907] 1944, 115.
15 Ibid., 58.
16 in *Intelligence in the Modern World*, J. Rattner ed., 1939, 1016.
17 *System of Transcendental Idealism*, [1800] 1867, 159–65.
18 *An Essay on Man*, 1733, Epistle 1, line 289.
19 *The Pessimist's Handbook*, [1893] 1964, 624.
20 *Moral Man and Immoral Society*, 1932, 29.
21 *Science and the Modern World*, [1925] 1957, 40.
22 *Alfred Adler*, 1983, 55.
23 *The Philosophy of Moral Development*, 1981, 309.
24 *Critique of Teleological Judgement*, 1790 Part II, sec. 86.
25 *Origins*, 1982, 8.

HATE

1 *Ethics*, 1675, Part 3, Affect VII.
2 *Collected Papers*, vol. 4, [1915] 1953, 82.
3 *Anthony and Cleopatra*, 1606, act 1, scene 3.
4 *Human Society in Ethics and Politics*, 1952, 139.
5 *The Great Patriotic War of the Soviet Union*, 1945, 53.
6 in *The Vancouver Sun*, Oct. 8, 1988, sec. B7.
7 *Mein Kampf*, [1924] 1939, 391.
8 *Beyond Power*, 1985, 353.
9 *Man's Search for Himself*, 1953, 100.
10 *Why Men Hate*, 1947, 106.
11 *Demian*, 1925, chap. 6.
12 *Summerhill*, 1960, 375.
13 *Neurosis and Human Growth*, [1950] 1991, 114.
14 *The True Believer*, 1951, 93.
15 *Being and Nothingness*, [1943] 1957, 411.
16 *Holy Bible*, John 15:18.
17 *Being and Nothingness*, [1943] 1957, 411.
18 *The Quest for Certainty*, [1929] 1960, 226.
19 *Beyond Power*, 1985, 331.
20 *The New Middle East*, 1993.
21 *For Your Own Good*, 1984, 144.
22 *Summerhill*, 1960, 102–03.
23 quoted in *Why Men Hate*, S. Tenenbaum, 1947, 20.
24 *Pensées*, 1670, Fragment 210.
25 *Beyond Power*, 1985, 325.
26 in *Explorations in Altruistic Love and Behavior*, P. Sorokin ed., 1950, 147–48.
27 *Summerhill*, 1960, 301.
28 *Psychic War in Men and Women*, 1976, 169.
29 *The Ego and the Id*, [1923] 1950, 59.
30 *On Aggression*, 1966, 214.
31 in *Personal Character and Cultural Milieu*,

Pages 159–65

D. Haring, 1948, 395.
32 *Man's Search for Himself*, 1953, 149.
33 *Thinking in the Shadow of Feelings*, 1988, 168–69.
34 *I and Thou*, [1922] 1970, 68.
35 *Ethics*, 1675, Part 4, prop. 45.
36 *Way to Wisdom*, 1951, 60.
37 *The Warriors*, [1959] 1970, 229.
38 *Human Society in Ethics and Politics*, 1954, 212.
39 *A Grammar of Politics*, [1925] 1938, 238.
40 in *The Basic Writings of C. G. Jung*, 1959, 463.
41 David Frost interview, 1977.

Humanity

1 *The Sickness Unto Death*, [1849] 1944, 17.
2 *Pensées*, [1670] 1962, Fragment 390.
3 *Progress and Power*, 1936, chap. 3.
4 *The Voices of Silence*, 1953, 641.
5 *The Study of Man*, 1959, 86.
6 *A Vindication of the Rights of Woman*, 1791, chap. 7.
7 "Protagoras," in *Plato's Theaetetus*, 160d.
8 *The Fate of the Earth*, 1982, 129.
9 *Fundamental Principles of the Metaphysics of Mortals*, 1785, second section.
10 *Tragic Sense of Life*, [1912] 1954, 11.
11 *Existentialism and Humanism*, 1948, 28.
12 *Structural Anthropology*, 1963, 353.
13 [1882] in *Collected Works*, 1987, vol. 25, 460.
14 *Sartor Resartus*, 1834, Book 1, chap. 5.
15 *Science and the Modern World*, 1925, 298.
16 *The City of God*, c. 430 A.D., Book xxi, chap. 10.
17 *The Farther Reaches of Human Nature*, 1971, 325–27.
18 in *Psychiatry*, 1957, vol. 20, 97–129.
19 *Computer Power and Human Reason*, 1976, 223.
20 *The Birth and Death of Meaning*, 1962, 157.
21 *The Problem of Being Human*, 1974, 27.
22 *Human Paleopsychology*, 1987, 113.
23 *Persecution East and West*, 1983, 87.
24 *Auguste Comte and Positivism*, [1842] 1975, 279.
25 *Beast and Man*, 1978, 363.
26 in *The Futurists*, 1972, 235.
27 *The Greening of America*, 1970, 3–5.
28 *The Myth of the Machine*, 1970, 191, 413.
29 *The Sane Society*, 1955, 360.
30 *The Natural Superiority of Women*, 1968, 159.
31 *Heretics*, 1905.
32 *Beyond Freedom and Dignity*, 1972, 202.
33 *Computer Power and Human Reason*, 1976, 203.
34 *Being and Nothingness*, [1943] 1957, 566.
35 *Being and Nothingness*, [1943] 1957.
36 *On Aggression*, 1966, 229.
37 *Thus Spake Zarathustra*, 1881, Prologue, 4.
38 Ibid, sec. 3.
39 *The Scientific Outlook*, 1931, 122.
40 *The Faith of a Rationalist*, 1947, 4.
41 *Vocation of Man*, 1800, Book 3, II.
42 *The Genealogy of Morals*, 1887, First Essay, sec. 12.
43 *Post-Capitalist Society*, 1993, 12.
44 *The Order of Things*, 1970, xxiii.
45 Ibid., 342.
46 *Introduction to the Reading of Hegel*, [1947] 1969, 434 (note).
47 *The Politics of Experience*, 1967, 36.
48 *Being and Time*, [1931] 1962, 255.
49 *Being and Nothingness*, [1943] 1957, 24.
50 *Memories, Dreams, Reflections*, 1961, 326.
51 *The Voices of Silence*, 1953, 640.
52 *Being and Nothingness*, [1943] 1957, 24.
53 *Tragic Sense of Life*, [1912] 1954, 308.
54 *The Life of Reason*, 1954, 222.
55 in *The Encyclopédie of Diderot and D'Alembert*, [1751] 1954, 55–56.
56 *The Life of Reason*, 1954, 262.
57 *Die Stellung des Menschen im Kosmos*, 1928, 13.
58 *So Human an Animal*, 1968, 30.
59 in *New Knowledge in Human Values*, 1959, 231.
60 *Creative Evolution*, [1907] 1944, 200–03.
61 *The Phenomenon of Man*, [1940] 1959, 223.
62 *Technics and Human Development*, 1967, 93.
63 *The Phenomenon of Man*, 1959, 33.
64 *The Myth of the Machine*, 1970, 293.
65 *Client-Centered Therapy*, 1951, 323.
66 *Airman's Odyssey*, 1942, 421–22.
67 in *New Knowledge in Human Values*, 1959, 164.
68 *Saturday Review*, June 7, 1969, 18–19.
69 Ibid., 61.
70 *The Cultured Man*, 1958, 67.
71 *The Future of Mankind*, 1961, 307.

Hypocrisy

1 *Patriotism and Christianity*, 1896, 69.
2 *Paradise Lost*, 1667, Book 3, line 682.
3 *Holy Bible*, Matthew 6:1–6.
4 *The Metaphysic of Ethics*, 1796, Book 4, Part I, chap. 2, sec. 9.
5 *The Advancement of Learning*, 1623.
6 *Canadian Journal of Philosophy*, vol. 9, June, 1979, 197.
7 *On Revolution*, 1963, chap. 2, part 5.
8 *The Counterfeiters*, 1955, 394.
9 *Self-Deception and Morality*, 1986, 48.
10 *Moral Man and Immoral Society*, 1932, 95.
11 *Maxims*, 1665, maxim 218.
12 in *Time*, Apr. 27, 1992, 74.
13 in *Collected Essays*, 1959, 281.
14 *Wealth and Poverty*, 1981, 86.
15 *The Fable of the Bees*, [1724] 1970, 351.
16 *Works*, [1915]1953, vol. 14, 284.
17 *The Prince*, 1513, chap. xviii.
18 *Moral Man and Immoral Society*, 1932, 95.
19 in *Harper's*, July, 1988, 22.
20 [1842] quoted in *The Russians*, H. Smith, 1976, 344.
21 in *On Trial*, 1985, i.

Pages 165–72

22 *On the Democratic Idea in America*, 1972, 130.
23 *America As a Civilization*, 1957, 674.
24 *The Pornography of Power*, 1972, 31–32.
25 *So Human an Animal*, 1968, 198.
26 *The Betrayal of the West*, 1978, 55.
27 *Generation of Vipers*, 1942, 209.
28 *Moral Man and Immoral Society*, 1932, 117.
29 *Essays: First Series*, 1841, "Friendship."
30 *Works of Love*, [1847] 1962, 32.

Ideals

1 *Voices of Silence*, 1953, 642.
2 *Mein Kampf*, [1924] 1943, 299.
3 *Man for Himself*, 1947, 49.
4 *A Grammar of Politics*, [1925] 1938, 27.
5 *The Life of Reason*, 1954, 227.
6 *The Sense of Beauty*, 1955, 256.
7 *Meaning in Life*, 1992, 100.
8 *How Does Analysis Cure?*, 1984, 77.
9 *Becoming*, 1955, 68.
10 *The Stress of Life*, 1976, 450, 460.
11 *The Triumph of the Therapeutic*, 1966, 18.
12 *On the Democratic Idea in America*, 1972, 29.
13 in *Living Philosophies*, C. Fadiman ed., 1931, 33–34.
14 *Icon and Idea*, [1954] 1965, 34.
15 *The Image*, 1962, 181, 197.
16 *Narcissism*, 1983, 7.
17 *Woman and Socialism*, 1910, 449.
18 *Nature, Man, and Woman*, 1958, 64.
19 *The Will to Power*, 1901, Book 1, sec. 80.
20 in *Saturday Review*, Feb. 5, 1966, 73–74.
21 *Paris in the Terror*, 1964, 403.
22 *Memories, Dreams, Reflections*, 1961, 329.
23 *Shantung Compound*, 1966, 112.
24 *The Quest for Certainty*, [1929] 1960, 279.
25 *The Bonds of Love*, 1988, 213.
26 *The Life of Reason*, 1954, 57.
27 *Man for Himself*, 1947, 50.
28 *Experience and Nature*, [1925] 1958, 62.
29 *Mein Kampf*, [1924] 1943, 299.
30 *Ends and Means*, 1938, 288.
31 quoted in *Alfred Adler*, J. Rattner, 1983, 80.
32 *The Passions*, 1976, 90.
33 in *New Knowledge in Human Values*, 1959, 130.
34 *Meaning in Life*, 1992, 100.
35 *The Ego and the Id*, [1927] 1950, 49.
36 *Psychological Issues*, 1959, vol. 1, no. 1, 94.
37 *My Life and Thought*, 1949, 114.
38 *Personal Knowledge*, 1962, 334.
39 *Folkways*, [1906] 1940, 402.
40 *Psychology*, 1892, chap. 12.
41 *The Varieties of Religious Experience*, [1902] 1958, 389.
42 *Man for Himself*, 1947, 49.
43 *The Life of Reason*, 1954, 69.
44 *Meaning in Life*, 1992, 90.
45 *Human Immortality*, 2nd. ed., 1899, 2.
46 *Life of Reason*, 1913, vol. 3, 272.
47 *Guilt*, 1985, 235.
48 quoted in *The Philosophy of "As If,"* H. Vaihinger, 1935, 330.
49 *The Division of Labor in Society*, [1893] 1964, 408.

Identity

1 in *New Knowledge in Human Values*, A. Maslow ed., 1959, 157.
2 *I and Thou*, [1922] 1970, 115.
3 *Psychology*, 1892, chap. 12.
4 *The Cult of Information*, 1986, 96.
5 *Essays on the Intellectual Powers of Man*, 1785, Essay 3, chap. 4.
6 *The Persistent Problems of Philosophy*, 1907, 227.
7 quoted in *The Great Divide*, S. Terkel, 1988, xi.
8 *Childhood and Society*, [1950] 1963, 240.
9 in *Totalitarianism*, C. Friedrich ed., 1954, 169.
10 *Childhood and Society*, [1950] 1963, 238.
11 in *Capitalism*, A. Rand, 1966, 278.
12 *Identity*, 1968, 297–99.
13 *Emotion*, 1980, 29.
14 *Working Through Narcissism*, 1981, 7.
15 *Human Aggression*, 1968, 54.
16 *Self and Others*, 1969, 66–70.
17 *The Cultural Contradictions of Capitalism*, 1976, 89.
18 Ibid., 38.
19 *Narcissism*, 1938, 209.
20 *Man for Himself*, 1960, 73.
21 *The Birth and Death of Meaning*, 1962, 85.
22 *Systematic Sociology*, 1957.
23 *The Cultural Contradictions of Capitalism*, 1976, 36.
24 *Guilt and Gratitude*, 1982, 39.
25 *Twilight of Authority*, 1975, 72.
26 *Childhood and Society*, [1950] 1963, 412.
27 *Brave New Workplace*, 1985, 121.
28 *Sexual Personae*, 1990, 2, 5.
29 *The Inevitability of Patriarchy*, 1973, 229.
30 *Patriarchal Precedents*, 1983, 286.
31 *The Feminine Mystique*, 1963, 71–77.
32 *America As a Civilization*, 1957, 570.
33 in *Capitalism*, A. Rand, 1966, 280.
34 *Being and Nothingness*, [1943] 1957, 77–78.
35 *Gaia*, [1979] 1987, 125.
36 *The Savage Mind* , 1966, 249.

Ideology

1 *The Hunters*, 1966, 63.
2 *The Arrogance of Power*, 1966, 164.
3 *The Origins of Totalitarianism*, 1958, 470–71.
4 *The (Guilty) Conscience of a Conservative*, 1978, 65.
5 *The Gulag Archipelago*, 1974, 174.
6 *American Political Science Review*, vol. 55, 1961, 22–23.

Pages 172–78

7 *The Passions*, 1976, 323.
8 *For Your Own Good*, 1984, 86.
9 *Critical Path*, 1981, 234.
10 *Mortal Rivals*, 1987, 250.
11 *Capitalism*, 1966, 201, 257.
12 *Politics Among Nations*, [1948] 1967, 85.
13 *Hitler's Ideology*, 1975, 86.
14 *Escape from Evil*, 1975, 64, 116.
15 *Psychological Reflections*, [1953] 1970, 168.
16 *The Broken Connection*, 1979, 110.
17 *The Cultural Contradictions of Capitalism*, 1976, 60.
18 *The End of Ideology*, 1960, 370–71.
19 *Obedience to Authority*, 1973, 142–45.
20 [1945] in *Quotations from Chairman Mao*, 1967, chap. 12.
21 *The New Class*, 1957, 76–77.
22 *The Managerial Revolution*, [1941] 1960, 198–99.
23 *Beliefs, Attitudes, and Values*, 1968, 123.
24 in *Political Psychology*, M. Hermann ed., 1986, 391.
25 *The Meaning of the 20th Century*, 1964, 161.
26 in *Perspectives on Self-Deception*, A. Rorty ed., 1988, 306.
27 *International Journal of Law and Psychiatry*, vol. 2, 1979, 231.
28 *The Rebel*, [1954] 1967, 131.
29 *Self-Esteem and Meaning*, 1984, 45–48.
30 *Signs*, vol. 7, no. 3, Spring, 1982, 527.
31 in *Psychology for Our Times*, P. Zimbardo ed., 1973, 331–32.
32 *The Rebel*, [1954] 1967, 4.
33 *Political Man*, 1963, 456.
34 *The Meaning of the 20th Century*, 1964, 166.
35 Ibid., 161.

Immortality

1 *The Broken Connection*, 1979, 17–18.
2 *Human Immortality*, 2nd ed., 1899, 2.
3 *Self, God, and Immortality*, 1986, 168.
4 *The Religious Consciousness*, 1928, 252.
5 *The Myth of the Eternal Return*, [1949] 1971, 158.
6 *Diary of a Writer*, vol. 1, [1876] 1949, 541–42.
7 *The World as Will and Idea*, [1819] 1948, vol. 1, 356.
8 *The Life of Reason*, 1954, 294.
9 *The Faith of a Rationalist*, 1946, 5.
10 *Profiles of the Future*, 1982, 224.
11 *The Hero with a Thousand Faces*, [1949] 1968, 189.
12 *The Philosophy of Hegel*, 1955, 514.
13 *Tractatus Logico-Philosophicus*, [1921] 1961, 72, 6.4311.
14 [d. 1930] "The Crown," 1915.
15 *The Power of Myth*, 1988, 228.
16 in *Living Philosophies*, C. Fadiman ed., 1931, 82–83.
17 Ibid., 89.
18 *The Selfish Gene*, 1976, 37.
19 *Concluding Unscientific Postscript*, [1846] 1944, 154.
20 [1915] *Works*, vol. 14, 289.
21 *The Denial of Death*, 1973, 142.
22 *The Origins of Totalitarianism*, 1958, 145.
23 *Life Against Death*, 1966, 101, 106.
24 *The Broken Connection*, 1979, 283.
25 in *Alfred Adler*, J. Rattner, 1983, 18.
26 *Psychology and the Soul*, [1931] 1961, 87.
27 *Love in the Western World*, [1940] 1956, 63.
28 *Memories, Dreams, Reflections*, 1961, 325.
29 *Tragic Sense of Life*, [1912] 1954, 224.
30 *A Vindication of the Rights of Woman*, 1791, chap. 4.
31 *America As a Civilization*, 1957, 620.
32 *The Broken Connection*, 1979, 293.
33 "Looking Back on the Spanish War," 1943.
34 *Tragic Sense of Life*, [1912] 1954, 31.
35 in Plato's *Symposium*, 207a.
36 *The Brothers Karamazov*, 1879, Book 2, chap. 6.

Individuality

1 *Escape from Freedom*, 1941, 50.
2 *The Being of Man and His Future Evolution*, [1908] 1981, 46–47.
3 *The Rebel*, [1954] 1967, 55.
4 *The Open Society and Its Enemies*, 1950, 100.
5 *Democracy in America*, [1835] 1966, 477.
6 *The Courage to Be*, 1952, 117.
7 *The Mothers*, 1931, 65.
8 *Politics*, Book 1, chap. 2.
9 *The Gift*, [1925] 1967, 75.
10 *Economic and Philosophical Manuscripts of 1844*, 1964, 138.
11 in *Living Philosophies*, C. Fadiman ed., 1931, 208.
12 *An Essay on Man*, [1944] 1970, 246.
13 *The Problem of Being Human*, 1974, 71.
14 *The Division of Labor in Society*, [1893] 1964, 130.
15 in *I Believe*, C. Fadiman ed., 1940, 19.
16 *The Hope of the Great Community*, 1916, 46.
17 *Suicide*, [1897] 1951, 210.
18 *Will Therapy and Truth and Reality*, 1936, 92–93.
19 *Life Against Death*, 1966, 286.
20 in *Feelings and Emotions*, M. Reymart ed., 1950, 364.
21 *The Brothers Karamazov*, [1880] 1955, 363.
22 *Man for Himself*, 1947, 101.
23 *The Organization Man*, 1957, 14.
24 *Works*, Bohn edition, 1854–57, vol. 6, 145–47.
25 *Characteristics of the Present Age*, 1847, 33–36.
26 *The World As Will and Idea*, [1819] 1948, vol. 3, 286.
27 *The Limits of Altruism*, 1977, 104.
28 in *Natural History*, 78, 1969, 176.
29 *Creative Evolution*, [1907] 1944, 16.
30 *The Pursuit of Loneliness*, [1970] 1976, 15.
31 *Creative Evolution*, [1907] 1944, 18.
32 *The Triumph of the Therapeutic*, 1966, 50.
33 *Ideas and Opinions*, 1954, 43.
34 [1945] *Psychological Reflections*, [1953] 1970, 171.
35 *The World As Will and Idea*, [1819] 1948, vol. 1, 365.

Pages 178–84

36 *The World and the Individual*, 1900, 297–346.
37 *Psychological Reflections*, [1953] 1970, 156.
38 *Tragic Sense of Life*, [1912] 1954, 312.
39 *Man and His Symbols*, 1964, 45.
40 *Becoming*, 1955, 19–22.
41 *The Being of Man and His Future Evolution*, [1908] 1981, 43.
42 in *Living Philosophies*, C. Fadiman ed., 1931, 87.
43 Ibid., 89.
44 *The Origins of Totalitarianism*, 1958, 454.
45 *The Informed Heart*, 1960, 269.
46 in *Studies in Philosophy and Education*, no. 3, Summer, 1968, 267.
47 [1931] in *Class, Status and Power*, R. Bendix ed., 1953, 58.
48 in *Psychology of Women*, 2nd ed., J. Williams ed., 1985, 188.
49 *Megatrends*, 1984, 261.
50 *Ancient Law*, 1861, chap. 5.
51 *The Bonds of Love*, 1988, 200.
52 *Philosophical Sketches*, 1964, 113–14.
53 "A Propos of *Lady Chatterly's Lover*," in *Phoenix II*, 1968, 512–13.
54 *The Hero with a Thousand Faces*, [1949] 1968, 388.
55 *The Basic Writings of C. G. Jung*, 1959, 144.
56 *Motivation and Personality*, 1954, 256.

Institution

1 *Folkways*, [1906] 1940, 61.
2 Ibid., 57.
3 *Scientist and Citizen*, 1968, 10[5] 123–25.
4 *A Study of History*, [1934] 1972, 84.
5 *The Psychology of Moral Development*, 1984, 73.
6 *A Theory of Justice*, 1971, 54–55.
7 *The Philosophy of Moral Development*, 1981, 144.
8 *The American Inquisition*, 1982, 2, 243.
9 *The Study of Man*, 1959, 68.
10 *The Limits of Altruism*, 1977, 79–80.
11 *Beyond Power*, 1985, 111–13.
12 *International Journal of Law and Psychiatry*, vol. 6, 1983, 243.
13 *Corporate Liberalism*, 1982, 20.
14 *The Psychology of Moral Behaviour*, 1971, 236.
15 *The Open and Closed Mind*, 1960, 68.
16 *The Triumph of the Therapeutic*, 1966, 2.
17 *The Theory of the Leisure Class*, [1899] 1934, 190.
18 *An American Dilemma*, 1944, 80.
19 *Childhood and Society*, [1950] 1963, 251.
20 *The Power Elite*, 1956, 96.
21 *The Open Society and Its Enemies*, 1950, 332.
22 *Law, Legislation and Liberty*, vol. 1, 1973, 8–11.
23 *The Crowd*, [1895] 1960, 86.
24 *The Public Philosophy*, [1955] 1989, 102.
25 *The Real World of Technology*, 1990, 12.
26 in *Anticipatory Democracy*, C. Bezold ed., 1978, 240.
27 *Human Nature and the Social Order*, 1902, ch. 12.
28 *On the Democratic Idea in America*, 1972, 22–23.
29 *I and Thou*, [1922] 1970, 94.
30 *The Greening of America*, 1970, 356–57.
31 *The Problem of Being Human*, 1974, 71.
32 *The Pursuit of Loneliness*, [1970] 1976, 136.
33 *Canadian Journal of Philosophy*, vol. 18, no. 2, June, 1988, 230.
34 *A Grammar of Politics*, [1925] 1938, 20.
35 *Civilization*, 1969, 346.

Intelligence

1 *The Life of Reason*, 1954, 294.
2 *Gaia*, [1979] 1987, 146.
3 *The Quest for Certainty*, [1929] 1960, 215.
4 in *I Believe*, C. Fadiman ed., 1940, 19.
5 *Creative Intelligence*, [1907] 1944, 150–56.
6 *Origins*, 1982, 169.
7 *Mind, Self and Society*, 1934, 100.
8 *Process and Reality*, [1929] 1978, 168.
9 *How Children Fail*, 1964, 205.
10 *The Psychology of the Child*, 1969, 9.
11 *Nicomachean Ethics*, Book 6, part 6.
12 *Intelligence: Its Evolution and Forms*, 1960, 18.
13 *On the Improvement of the Understanding*, 1677, VI, 31.
14 *Creative Evolution*, [1907] 1944, 168.
15 *The Realm of Spirit*, 1940, 111.
16 *The Quest for Certainty*, [1929] 1960, 213.
17 *Philosophy in a New Key*, [1942] 1957, 86.
18 *Frames of Mind*, 1985, 56, 297.
19 *The Myth of Two Minds*, 1987, 117.
20 *The Crack-Up*, [1936] 1956, 69.
21 *Mindstorms*, 1980, 155.
22 *Ends and Means*, 1938, 321.
23 *Mind, Self and Society*, 1934, 99–100.
24 *Making Babies*, 1985, 143.
25 *Intelligence: Heredity and Environment*, 1979, 204, 213.
26 *The Mismeasure of Man*, 1981, 25.
27 *Frames of Mind*, 1985, 18.
28 *Understanding Media*, 1966, 31.
29 *The Pursuit of Loneliness*, [1970] 1976, 186.
30 *The Natural Superiority of Women*, [1952] 1968, 124–28.
31 *Creative Evolution*, [1907] 1944, 167.
32 *Human Society in Ethics and Politics*, 1954, 177.
33 *The Naked Ape*, 1969, 210–11.
34 *Ends and Means*, 1938, 211.
35 *Public Opinion*, [1922] 1957, 397.
36 in *New Knowledge in Human Values*, A. Maslow ed., 1959, 160.
37 *Ego Psychology and Adaptation*, [1937] 1958, 69.
38 in *Saturday Review*, Apr. 5, 1969, 24.
39 in *Living Philosophies*, C. Fadiman ed., 1931, 281.
40 quoted in *The New Priesthood*, R. Lapp, 1965, 9.
41 *Profiles of the Future*, 1982, 238.

42 *The Cerebral Symphony*, 1990, 271.
43 in *Daedelus*, Summer, 1986, 167.
44 *Sex and Destiny*, 1984, 450.
45 *Final Contributions*, 1955, 246.
46 interview in *Playboy*, June 18, 1971.
47 *Airman's Odyssey*, 1942, 411.
48 *The Human Revolution*, 1972, 156, 160, 162.
49 *Creative Evolution*, [1907] 1944, 181–82.
50 *Technics and Human Development*, 1967, 288.

Joy

1 *Orthodoxy*, [1908] 1959, 296.
2 *Man's Search for Himself*, 1953, 96.
3 *An Introduction to Social Psychology*, [1908] 1931, 134.
4 [d. 1951], *Pretexts.*
5 *The Courage to Be*, 1952, 14.
6 *Ethics*, 1675, Part 3, def. 2.
7 *Thus Spake Zarathustra*, 1927, chap. 79: 9–11.
8 *Being and Time*, [1931] 1962, 357–58.
9 *The Being of Man and His Future Evolution*, [1908] 1981, 103.
10 *The Prophet*, 1923, 29.
11 *Orthodoxy*, [1908] 1959, 296.
12 *Suicide*, [1897] 1951, 365.
13 "Auguries of Innocence," 1803, line 53.
14 *Meaning and Void*, 1977, 316.
15 *Emotion*, 1980, 29.
16 *The Passions*, 1976, 336.
17 *The Farther Reaches of Human Nature*, 1971, 188.
18 *Nature, Man, and Woman*, 1958, 172.
19 *Man for Himself*, 1947, 230
20 "An die Freude," 1785.
21 [d. 1832] in *Goethe's World View*, 1963, 145.
22 *Marriage and Morals*, 1929, 232.
23 *The Making of a Counter Culture*, 1969, 229.
24 *Escape from Evil*, 1975, 120.
25 *The Future of Mankind*, 1961, 112.
26 *She*, 1976, 70.
27 quoted in *The Vancouver Province*, June 7, 1995, sec. B2.

Justice

1 *Civilization and Its Discontents*, [1930] 1962, 42.
2 *Leviathan*, 1651, chap. 13.
3 Ibid., chap. 15.
4 *A Theory of Justice*, 1971, 3–4.
5 "Letter from Birmingham Jail," [Alabama], April 16, 1963.
6 *The Republic*, Book 1, 334.
7 *A Theory of Justice*, 1971, 11.
8 *The Philosophy of Moral Development*, 1981, 201.
9 San Diego address, Sept. 19, 1919.
10 *Technology and Justice*, 1986, 130.
11 *Nicomachean Ethics*, Book 5, part 13.
12 *Works*, [1925] 1961, vol. 10, 257.
13 *In A Different Voice*, 1982, 22, 73.
14 in *The New Republic*, Sept. 24, 1917.
15 *The Longest War*, 1984, 78.
16 *Moral Man and Immoral Society*, 1932, 29–57.
17 in *New Knowledge in Human Values*, A. Maslow ed., 1959, 195.
18 *Works of Love*, [1847] 1962, 248.
19 *What Is Justice?*, 1957, 2.
20 *Group Psychology and the Analysis of the Ego*, [1921] 1959, 52.
21 *The Psychology of the Child*, 1969, 127.
22 *An Introduction to Social Psychology*, 1931, 62.
23 *The Biological Origin of Human Values*, 1977, 398.
24 *The Origins of Totalitarianism*, 1958, 447.
25 [1933] in Nuremberg Documents [1946–49], "Nazi Conspiracy and Aggression," IV, 496.
26 *A Vindication of the Rights of Woman*, 1792, chap. 12.
27 *City of God*, 426 A.D., Book 4, sec. 4.
28 [1791] Wentworth Woodhouse Papers, book I, 623.
29 *Ethics*, vol. 75, 1965, 259–71.
30 *The End of History and the Last Man*, 1992, 311.
31 *The Philosophy of Moral Development*, 1981, xiv.
32 *Meditations*, 161-80 A.D., Book 11, IX.
33 *Émile*, 1762, Book IV.
34 "Letter from Birmingham Jail," [Alabama], April 16, 1963.
35 *A Grammar of Politics*, [1925] 1938, 275.
36 *The Prospects of Industrial Civilization*, 1923, 279.
37 *The Rebel*, [1954] 1967, 288–91.
38 Ibid., 105.
39 *The Gulag Archipelago*, 1974, 355.
40 *The Rebel*, 1956, 209.
41 *Neurosis and Human Growth*, [1950] 1991, 55.
42 *Summerhill*, 1960, 164.
43 *The Merchant of Venice*, 1596, act 4, scene 1.
44 *A Theory of Justice*, 1971, 476.
45 *Enquiry Concerning Political Justice*, 1798, Book 3, chap. 3.
46 *Institutes*, Book 1, chap. 1, par. 1.
47 *Essays: Second Series*, 1844, "Character."
48 British Commons speech, Feb. 11, 1851.
49 in *Rex v Sussex Justices* [England], Nov. 9, 1923.
50 *A Grammar of Politics*, [1925] 1938, 171.
51 Ibid., 541.
52 Montgomery [Alabama] address, Mar. 25, 1965.
53 *Philosophy of Moral Development*, 1981, 388.

Killing

1 [1968] quoted in *Anatomy of Human Destructiveness*, E. Fromm, 1973, xviii.
2 *Considérations sur la France*, 1796.
3 *Holy Bible*, Numbers 31:15–19.
4 *The First Sex*, 1971, 136.
5 *African Genesis*, [1961] 1967, 322.

Pages 195–201

73 *Democracy and Education*, [1916] 1961, 184.
74 *Ends and Means*, 1938, 287.
75 *Post-Capitalist Society*, 1993, 19.
76 *Metaphysics*, 11.
77 *Man in the Modern Age*, [1931] 1951, 159.
78 *Some Lessons in Metaphysics*, 1969, 23.
79 *The Anti-Man Culture*, 1972, 112.
80 *Eros and Civilization*, [1955] 1966, 104.
81 *On Becoming a Person*, 1961, 213.
82 in *Saturday Review*, June 7, 1969, 19.
83 *The Cultured Man*, 1958, 61.
84 *The Phenomenon of Man*, [1940] 1959, 250.
85 *Eco-Philosophy*, 1981, 112.
86 *Mind and Nature*, 1980, 98.
87 *Structural Anthropology*, 1963, 361.
88 *The Meaning of the 20th Century*, 1964, 23.
89 *On Human Nature*, 1978, 207.
90 *Ideas and Opinions*, 1954, 49.
91 in *Science*, Jan. 28, 1910.
92 *The Quest for Certainty*, [1929] 1960, 8.
93 *The Philosopher's Stone*, 1991, 160.
94 *The Quest for Certainty*, [1929] 1960, 313.
95 *A Letter to a Grandfather*, 1933, 10.
96 *Holy Bible*, Ecclesiastes 1:18.
97 *The Preservation of Life*, 3rd century B.C.
98 *A Treaty of Human Learning*, 1633, stanza 1.
99 *Sexual Personae*, 1990, 22.
100 *The Image*, 1956, 131.
101 *Way to Wisdom*, 1951, 77.
102 *Aims of Education and Other Essays*, 1929, chap. 3.

Language

1 *Philosophy in a New Key*, [1942] 1957, 103.
2 *The Human Revolution*, 1972, 76.
3 *Being and Time*, [1931] 1962, 204.
4 *The Image*, 1956, 45.
5 *Language and Myth*, 1946, 61.
6 *Structural Anthropology*, 1963, 56.
7 *One-Dimensional Man*, 1964, 193–94.
8 *The Absorbent Mind*, [1949] 1984, 113.
9 *Technics and Human Development*, 1967, 96.
10 *Mind, Self and Society*, 1934, 49, 69.
11 Ibid., 192.
12 *The Savage Mind*, 1966, 252.
13 *A Primer of Freudian Psychology*, 1954, 56.
14 *The Life of Reason*, 1954, 327.
15 *Mind, Self and Society*, 1934, 78.
16 *An Essay on Man*, [1944] 1970, 120–21.
17 *The Decline of the West*, [1932] 1965, 228–29.
18 *The Study of Man*, 1959, 14–17.
19 *De Sensu et Sensibili*, 1.
20 *The Evolution of Human Consciousness*, 1980, 130, 143.
21 *The Order of Things*, 1970, 82.
22 *Understanding Media*, 1966, 83.
23 *Folkways*, [1906] 1940, 160.
24 in *The New Yorker*, Aug. 24, 1968.
25 *Dictatorships and Double Standards*, 1982, 135–38.
26 "Syme," in *1984*, [1949] 1954, 45.
27 *Philosophy in a New Key*, [1942] 1957, 126.
28 *Philosophical Investigations*, 1953, Remark 115.
29 *The Gutenberg Galaxy*, 1962, 30.
30 *The Politics of Experience*, 1967, 34.
31 "Politics and the English Language," 1946.
32 *Computer Power and Human Reason*, 1976, 250.
33 *Works*, 1843, vol. 6, Book 3, chap. 1.
34 *Philosophische Untersuchungen*, 1953, Part 1, sec. 109.
35 *Tractatus Logico-Philosophicus*, [1921] 1961, 19, 4.002.
36 *Language and Myth*, 1946, 98.
37 *Technics and Human Development*, 1967, 74.
38 *The Drama of the Gifted Child*, 1981, 78.
39 *Reason and Emotion in Psychotherapy*, 1962, 21.
40 *The Special Phenomenology of the Child Archetype*, 1940.
41 *The Politics of Ecstasy*, 1968, 303.
42 *Leviathan*, 1651, chap. 4.
43 *Man in the Modern Age*, [1931] 1951, 119.
44 *The Cultural Contradictions of Capitalism*, 1976, 98.
45 *The Order of Things*, 1970, 87.
46 Ibid., 290.
47 Ibid.
48 *Philosophical Sketches*, 1962, 142.
49 *The Sense of Beauty*, 1955, 171.
50 *The Need for Roots*, 1952, 208.
51 *The Order of Things*, 1970, 382.
52 *Experience and Nature*, [1925] 1958, 186.
53 *Tragic Sense of Life*, [1912] 1954, 311.
54 *Tractatus Logico-Philosophicus*, [1921] 1961, 56, 5.6.
55 *The Courage to Be*, 1952, 91.
56 *Way to Wisdom*, 1951, 26.
57 *Language*, vol. 8, 1971, 3.

Leadership

1 *The Varieties of Religious Experience*, [1902] 1958, 287.
2 *Human Paleopsychology*, 1987, 413–15.
3 *The True Believer*, 1951, 112.
4 *Freud: The Mind of the Moralist*, 1961, 257–58.
5 *The Mass Psychology of Fascism*, 1946, 275.
6 *The Leadership Passion*, 1977, 3.
7 *Mein Kampf*, [1924] 1943, 580.
8 Nuremberg Trials, 1946.
9 *The Crowd*, [1895] 1960, 190–91.
10 *Totalitarianism*, 1968, vol. 3, 46.
11 *The Crowd*, [1895] 1960, 194.
12 in *Advances in Self Psychology*, A. Goldberg ed., 1978, 403.
13 *Nuclear Madness*, 1980, 78.
14 *Mein Kampf*, [1924] 1943, 80.
15 *Listen, America!*, 1980, 98.
16 *The Fall of Public Man*, 1977, 265.

Pages 201–7

17 *The True Believer*, 1951, 114.
18 *The Hidden Persuaders*, [1957] 1980, 1, 242–43.
19 *The Denial of Death*, 1973, 133.
20 *Arms and Insecurity*, 1960, 231.
21 *The True Believer*, 1951, 109.
22 *Leadership*, 1978, 50.
23 *The Second Stage*, 1981, 244–45.
24 *Leaders We Deserve*, 1983, 19.
25 *Men in Groups*, 1970, 97.
26 in *Time*, Mar. 16, 1992, 74.
27 letter from prison, Feb. 16, 1917.
28 *Political Ensembles*, 1985, 161.
29 *Leadership*, 1978, 43, 454.
30 *Client-Centered Therapy*, 1951, 334.
31 in *From Max Weber*, H. Gerth ed., 1946, 95.
32 *Megatrends*, 1984, 108, 209.
33 *The Lonely Crowd*, [1950] 1965, 265.
34 *An Inquiry into the Human Prospect*, 1975, 164.
35 *What Life Should Mean to You*, 1931, 177.
36 *America As a Civilization*, 1957, 947.
37 *The Cultural Contradictions of Capitalism*, 1976, 201.
38 *The Crisis of Democracy*, 1975, 161–75.
39 *A Study of History*, [1934] 1972, 166.
40 *Building a Sustainable Society*, 1981, 311.
41 *Generation of Vipers*, 1942, 100.
42 *Profiles in Courage*, 1957, 209.

Learning

1 *The Mismeasure of Man*, 1981, 331–33.
2 *Positive Social Behavior and Morality*, vol. 1, 1978, 27.
3 *Man, His First Two Million Years*, 1969, 117.
4 *The Nature of Human Aggression*, 1976, 72, 82.
5 *Sociobiology*, 1980, 79.
6 *Social Learning and Imitation*, 1941, 1–2.
7 *Mind, Self and Society*, 1934, 95.
8 *The Concept of Mind*, 1949, 147.
9 *The Quest for Self-Control*, 1965, 5.
10 *A New Science of Life*, 1981, 172.
11 *Becoming*, 1955, 27.
12 *Client-Centered Therapy*, 1951, 389.
13 "On a Regicide Peace," 1796.
14 *Origins*, 1982, 50.
15 *The Psychology of Moral Development*, 1984, 28.
16 *Experience and Education*, [1938] 1963, 67.
17 *On Becoming a Person*, 1961, 276.
18 *On Education Especially in Early Childhood*, 1926, 42.
19 *Post-Capitalist Society*, 1993, 201.
20 *Understanding Media*, 1966, 65.
21 *The Meaning of the 20th Century*, 1964, 123.
22 *Culture Against Man*, 1965, 281.
23 *An Essay on Criticism*, 1711, line 215.

Liberalism

1 *America As a Civilization*, 1957, 729.
2 quoted in *Profiles in Courage*, J. F. Kennedy, 1957, 190.
3 *The Good Want Power*, 1977, 59.
4 *The Constitution of Liberty*, 1960, 406.
5 *Unpopular Essays*, 1951, 15–16.
6 *Corporate Liberalism*, 1982, 89.
7 *The Problem of Being Human*, 1974, 35.
8 *The New Right*, 1987, 28.
9 *Studies in Philosophy*, 1967, 162.
10 *The Philosophy of Moral Development*, 1981, 233.
11 *Power*, 1938, 302.
12 *The Good Want Power*, 1977, 125.
13 *Twilight of Authority*, 1975, 49.
14 *The Cultural Contradictions of Capitalism*, 1976, 275.
15 in *Canadian Journal of Philosophy*, vol. 18, June, 1988, 187.
16 *The Meaning of Conservatism*, 1984, 120.
17 *The End of History and the Last Man*, 1992, 324.
18 *Esquire*, Sept. 1965, 28.
19 [1937] in *Quotations from Chairman Mao*, 1967, chap. 24.
20 *The Decay of Capitalist Civilisation*, 1923, 58.
21 *Capitalism and Freedom*, 1962, 5.
22 *The Authoritarian Personality*, 1950, 155.
23 *The End of History and the Last Man*, 1992, xx.
24 *God in the White House*, 1988, 87.
25 *The Revolt of the Masses*, 1932, 76.
26 *From Luther to Hitler*, 1941, 14.
27 in *Handbook of Political Psychology*, J. Knutson ed., 1973, 152.
28 *The End of History and the Last Man*, 1992, 48.

Life

1 *The Mysterious Universe*, 1930, chap. 1.
2 *What Mad Pursuit*, 1988, chap. 5.
3 *Creative Evolution*, [1907] 1944, 279.
4 Ibid., 274.
5 *Order Out of Chaos*, 1984, 175.
6 *The Philosopher's Stone*, 1991, 123.
7 *Creative Evolution*, [1907] 1944, 142.
8 *Mind*, 1967, vol. 1, 206.
9 *Process and Reality*, [1929] 1978, 105.
10 *Tractatus Logico-Philosophicus*, [1921] 1961, 72, 6.4312.
11 *The Phenomenon of Man*, [1940] 1959, 167.
12 *The Politics of Ecstasy*, 1968, 41.
13 *Order Out of Chaos*, 1984, 252.
14 *The Prophet*, 1923, 80.
15 *The Varieties of Religious Experience*, [1902] 1958, 138.
16 *Process and Reality*, [1929] 1978, 105.
17 *Man and His Symbols*, 1964, 75.
18 *De Rerum Natura*, Book 2, line 7.

Pages 207–13

19 *A Genealogy of Morals*, 1887, Second Essay, Aph. 11.
20 in *I Believe*, C. Fadiman ed., 1940, 35.
21 speech to the Pharmaceutical Manufacturers Association, Washington, 1966.
22 [chairman of the House Government Activities and Transportation Subcommittee], House speech, Dec. 16, 1982.
23 *Iacocca*, 1984, 161.
24 *Why Men Hate*, 1947, 160.
25 *Natalie, Natalia*, 1972.
26 *Meaning in Life*, 1992, 148.
27 *The Hero with a Thousand Faces*, [1949] 1968, 191.
28 *Coming to Our Senses*, 1989, 101.
29 *New Directions in Psycho-Analysis*, 1955, 310.
30 *The Woman in America*, 1967, 35, 49.
31 *The Natural Superiority of Women*, 1968, 98, 157.
32 *Gyn/Ecology*, 1978, 355.
33 *The Myth of the Machine*, 1970, 228.
34 *Computer Power and Human Reason*, 1976, 269.
35 *Some Lessons in Metaphysics*, 1969, 158.
36 *Holy Bible*, Ecclesiastes 9:4.
37 *The Revolution of Hope*, 1968, 12.
38 *My Life and Thought*, 1949, 188.
39 *The Closing Circle*, 1971, 298–99.
40 *The Fate of the Earth*, 1982, 230–31.
41 in *I Believe*, C. Fadiman ed., 1940, 37.
42 *The Heart of Man*, 1964, 38.
43 *Summerhill*, 1960, 103.
44 *Eco-Philosophy*, 1981, 106.
45 *Life Against Death*, 1966, 233.
46 *The Passions*, 1976, 116–19.

Logic

1 *Logic*, 1812, introduction.
2 *Tractatus Logico-Philosophicus*, [1921] 1961, 65, 6.13.
3 *Democracy and Education*, [1916] 1961, 219.
4 *Tractatus Logico-Philosophicus*, [1921] 1961, 67, 6.3.
5 *Tractatus Logico-Philosophicus*, [1921] 1961, 47, 5.4731.
6 "John Galt" in *Atlas Shrugged*, 1957, 1016.
7 *The Philosophy of "As If,"* 1935, 8, 162.
8 *The Being of Man and His Future Evolution*, [1908] 1981, 143.
9 *Life Against Death*, 1966, 320–21.
10 *Aggression American Style*, 1978, 143–44.
11 *Narcissism*, 1983, 137, 155.
12 *The Gay Science*, [1882] 1974, s. 370, 328.
13 *The Origins of Totalitarianism*, 1958, 477.
14 *Chance, Love and Logic*, 1923, 11.
15 *Passages*, 1977, 126.
16 *Surfacing*, 1973, 186.
17 U.S. military attaché, Nov. 1922; quoted in *The Rise and Fall of the Third Reich*, W. Shirer, 1960, 47.
18 *The Psychology of Moral Development*, 1984, 171.
19 *Beyond Power*, 1985, 183.
20 *Nature, Man, and Woman*, 1958, 67.
21 *Creative Evolution*, [1907] 1944, xix–xx.
22 *The Mind of Primitive Man*, [1911] 1938, 223.
23 *The Will to Power*, [1901] 1967, 283.
24 *The Philosophy of Alfred North Whitehead*, 1951, 699.
25 *Mind*, 1967, vol. 1, 148.
26 *Where Is Science Going?*, 1932, 66.
27 *The Will to Power*, 1901 Book 3, 1, 538.
28 *The Aquarian Conspiracy*, 1980, 38.
29 *The Political Writings of Harold D. Lasswell*, 1951, 31–32.
30 *Law, Legislation and Liberty*, 1973, 11.
31 *Chance, Love and Logic*, 1923, 31.

Love

1 *Tragic Sense of Life*, [1912] 1954, 202.
2 in *Saturday Review*, Apr. 5, 1969, 24.
3 *Hymn of the Universe*, 1965, 145.
4 *Ultimate Concern*, 1965, 3, 47, 48, 179.
5 *What I Believe*, 1929, 15.
6 *Beyond Good and Evil*, 1886, no. 153.
7 *Love and Will*, 1969, 100–02.
8 *The Broken Connection*, 1979, 123.
9 *The Protestant Era*, 1948, 160.
10 *Coming to Our Senses*, 1989, 21.
11 *The Neurotic Personality of Our Time*, 1937, 113.
12 *Man's Search for Himself*, 1953, 244.
13 *Being and Nothingness*, [1943] 1957, 375.
14 *The Need to Be Loved*, 1963, 20.
15 *The Nature of Human Aggression*, 1976, 325.
16 *The Art of Loving*, 1956, 38.
17 *No Man Is an Island*, 1955, xx, 5.
18 *Works of Love*, [1847] 1962, 39.
19 *Civilization and Its Discontents*, 1930, 139.
20 CBS interview, Nov. 14, 1967.
21 *The Open Society and Its Enemies*, 19, 420–23.
22 *The True Believer*, 1951, 34.
23 *I and Thou*, 1958, 14–15.
24 *For The Love of Life*, 1986, 147.
25 *The Phenomenon of Man*, [1940] 1959, 266.
26 *The Selfish Gene*, 1976, 2.
27 *The Natural Superiority of Women*, 1968, 159.
28 *Collected Works*, 1948, vol. 14, 553.
29 *The Dialectic of Sex*, 1970, 144.
30 *The Rebel*, [1954] 1967, 261.
31 *The Denial of Death*, 1973, 160.
32 [d. 1832] in *Goethe's World View*, 1963, 145.
33 *Civilization and its Discontents*, [1930] 1961, 56.
34 *The Virtue of Selfishness*, 1964, 29.
35 *The Passions*, 1976, 339.
36 [1914] in *Collected Papers*, vol. 4, 1951, 42.
37 in *New Knowledge in Human Values*, A. Maslow ed., 1959, 7.
38 *1948 International Congress on Mental Health*, vol. 4, 1948, 269.

Pages 213–19

39 *The Human Revolution*, 1972, 156.
40 *Man's Search for Himself*, 1953, 238.
41 *Identity*, 1968, 265.
42 *Beyond Tragedy*, 1937, 155.
43 *Tragic Sense of Life*, [1912] 1954, 137.
44 *The Revolution of Hope*, 1968, 40.
45 *The Problem of Being Human*, 1974, 166.
46 Ibid., 174.
47 *Man's Search for Himself*, 1953, 241.
48 *Self, God, and Immortality*, 1986, 159.
49 *The Cultured Man*, 1958, 37.
50 *The Second Sex*, 1964, 667.
51 *Narcissism*, 1983, 31.
52 *The Religion of Man*, 1961, 30.
53 *The Road Less Traveled*, 1979, 89.
54 *The Problem of Being Human*, 1974, 167.
55 *Prior Analytics*, 2: 22.
56 *Being and Nothingness*, [1943] 1957, 408.
57 *The Basic Writings of C. G. Jung*, 1959, 339.
58 *On Aggression*, 1966, 217.
59 *Love and Hate*, 1972, 124.
60 *The Evolution of Love*, 1981, 5.
61 *I Believe*, C. Fadiman ed., 1940, 296.
62 *Life Against Death*, 1959, 40.
63 *Tragic Sense of Life*, [1912] 1954, 132.
64 *Love in the Western World*, [1940] 1956, 16, 25.
65 *Civilization and Its Discontents*, [1930] 1961, 29.
66 *The Realm of Spirit*, 1940, 115.
67 *The Power of Myth*, 1988, 205.
68 *Marriage and Morals*, 1929, 224.
69 *Holy Bible*, 1 John 4:18.
70 *Tragic Sense of Life*, [1912] 1954, 205.
71 *Autobiography*, 1967, 146.
72 *Explorations in Altruistic Love and Behavior*, 1950, 6, 65.
73 *The Art of Loving*, 1956, 48.
74 in *Symposium on Love*, by Plato, 193a.
75 in *YMCA Magazine*, Dec. 1960, 4–6.
76 *The Meaning of the 20th Century*, 1964, 146.
77 *The Open Society and Its Enemies*, 1962, vol. 2, 235.
78 *A Study of History*, [1934] 1972, 47.
79 *Howard's End*, 1921, chap. 31.
80 *Marriage and Morals*, [1929] 1959, 193.
81 *Way to Wisdom*, 1951, 26.
82 *The Phenomenon of Man*, [1940] 1959, 264.
83 "On Love," 1815.
84 *The Primal Scream*, [1970] 1980, 279.
85 quoted in *A Psychologist's Look at Love*, T. Reik, 1944, 9.
86 *The Problem of Being Human*, 1974, 166.
87 *The Road Less Traveled*, 1979, 22.

Machines / Mechanics

1 *Entropy*, [1980] 1989, 31.
2 *The Myth of the Machine*, 1970, 95, 125.
3 *The Informed Heart*, 1960, 59.
4 *The Decline of the West*, [1932] 1965, 410–12.
5 [1890] quoted in *The Nature of Human Consciousness*, R. Ornstein ed., 1973, 12.
6 *The Condition of Man*, 1973, 194.
7 *Order Out of Chaos*, 1984, 50.
8 *The Making of a Counter Culture*, 1969, 230.
9 *Signs of the Times*, 1829, par. 13.
10 *The Third Wave*, 1980, 88.
11 *America As a Civilization*, 1957, 227.
12 *The Pursuit of Loneliness*, [1970] 1976, 61.
13 *Aggression American Style*, 1978, 7.
14 *Anti-Dühring*, 1878, part 2.
15 *Economic and Philosophical Manuscripts of 1844*, 1964, 149.
16 *Small Is Beautiful*, 1973, 37.
17 *America and the Future*, 1970, 7–12.
18 *Sceptical Essays*, 1928, 87.
19 *The Revolution of Hope*, 1968, 26.
20 *The Greening of America*, 1970, 157.
21 *Understanding Media*, 1966, 105.
22 *The Technological Society*, 1964, 325.
23 *The Mass Psychology of Fascism*, 1946, 287.
24 *The Anatomy of Human Destructiveness*, 1973, 10.
25 *Profiles of the Future*, 1982, 242–43.
26 *Escape from Evil*, 1975, 141.
27 "John Galt" in *Atlas Shrugged*, 1957, 1064.
28 *Ends and Means*, 1938, 158.
29 *The New Industrial State*, 1967, 7.
30 *The Acquisitive Society*, 1920, 45.
31 *The Mass Psychology of Fascism*, 1946, 287.
32 in *Living Philosophies*, C. Fadiman ed., 1931, 214.
33 *Politics Among Nations*, [1948] 1967, 370.
34 *A Study of History*, [1934] 1972, 166.
35 *Creative Evolution*, [1907] 1944, 104.
36 *Signs of the Times*, 1829.
37 *The Realm of Spirit*, 1940, 156.
38 *Science and the Modern World*, 1925, 292.
39 *Profiles of the Future*, 1982, 229.
40 *Adrienne Rich's Poetry*, 1975, 62.
41 *Characteristics*, 1831.
42 *Signs of the Times*, 1829.

Male / Masculinity

1 *Iron John*, 1990, 180.
2 *Cannibals and Christians*, 1966, 201.
3 *The Longest War*, 1984, 203.
4 *Sexual Politics of Gender*, 13–14.
5 *The Myth of Two Minds*, 1987, 225.
6 *The Reproduction of Mothering*, 1978, 181–82.
7 *Feminine Psychology*, 1967, 137.
8 *Sexual Personae*, 1990, 27.
9 *International Journal of Law and Psychiatry* 1983, vol. 6, 251–52.
10 *Alfred Adler*, 1983, 156.
11 *The Pursuit of Loneliness*, [1970] 1976, 3.
12 *Beyond Power*, 1985, 290.

Pages 219–26

13 *The Nature of Woman*, 1980, 279.
14 in *Signs*, Spring, 1982, 542.
15 *Understanding Human Nature*, 1927, 128.
16 *A Choice of Heroes*, 1982, 40.
17 *Psychic War in Men and Women*, 1976, 204.
18 *The Imperial Animal*, 1974, 258.
19 quoted in *Nazi Germany*, 1938, 116.
20 *Mothers in the Fatherland*, 1987, 387, 411.
21 quoted in *A Choice of Heroes*, M. Gerzon, 1982, 93.
22 *A Certain World*, 1970, 298.
23 *Identity*, 1968, 261.
24 *The Peaceable Sex*, 1987, ix.
25 *Pornography*, 1989, 68.
26 *A Choice of Heroes*, 1982, 12, 83.
27 *Psychic War in Men and Women*, 1976, xiii, 64.
28 *The Female Eunuch*, 1971, 108.
29 *In Defense of Women*, 1922, 6.
30 *The Inevitability of Patriarchy*, 1973, 98.
31 *Thinking About Women*, 1968, 23.
32 *The Amazing Brain*, 1984, 170.
33 *Male and Female*, 1949, 168.
34 *The Basic Writings of C. G. Jung*, 1959, 180.
35 *Studies in the Psychology of Sex*, [1910] 1936, vol. 4, 3.
36 *She*, 1976, 48.
37 *On Human Nature*, 1978, 124–25.
38 *The Selfish Gene*, 1976, 174.
39 *A Vindication of Women*, 1792, chap. 12.
40 *The Dialectic of Sex*, 1970, 127, 154.
41 in *Signs*, vol. 8, no. 4, 1983, 658.
42 *Toward a Feminist Theory of the State*, 1989, 114.
43 *Beyond Power*, 1985, 93, 101.
44 Ibid., 323.
45 in *Men in Transition*, K. Solomon ed., 1982, 480.
46 [1851] in *Auguste Comte and Positivism*, 1975, 374.
47 *Male and Female*, 1955, 282.
48 *Guilt*, 1985, 176–246.
49 *Woman and Socialism*, 1910, 179.
50 *Reason and Emotion in Psychotherapy*, 1962, 221.
51 *Generation of Vipers*, 1942, 205.
52 in *Men in Transition*, K. Solomon ed., 1982, 478.
53 *The Unquiet Grave*, 1944, part 2.
54 *She*, 1976, 25.
55 *About Men*, 1978, xiv–xvi.
56 *The Dialectic of Sex*, 1970, 143.
57 *Sexual Personae*, 1990, 19.
58 *The Closing of the American Mind*, 1987, 129.
59 *The Farther Reaches of Human Nature*, 1971, 162.
60 *Essays*, 1741–1742, "Of Polygamy and Divorces."
61 letter to John Adams, Mar. 31, 1776.

Marxism / Communism Socialism

1 [1844] *Karl Marx*, T. B. Bottomore ed., 1963, 249–52.
2 *A Study of History*, vol. 5, [1939] 1956, 178.
3 in *International Journal of Law and Psychiatry*, vol. 6, 1983, 256.
4 quoted in *Political Pilgrims*, Paul Hollander, 1981, 418.
5 *The Soviet Paradox*, 1986, 186.
6 *A Study of Bolshevism*, 1953, 350.
7 quoted in *Thinking Tuna Fish, Talking Death*, R. Scheer, [1962] 1988, 113.
8 quoted in *Time*, Dec. 18, 1950, 23.
9 quoted in *The Wolf of the Kremlin*, S. Kahan, 1987, 309.
10 quoted in *Moral Man and Immoral Society*, R. Niebuhr, 1932, 177.
11 quoted in *The Wolf of the Kremlin*, S. Kahan, 1987, 155.
12 *The New Class*, 1957, 87.
13 *A Grammar of Politics*, [1925] 1938, 15.
14 in *The New Republic*, Feb. 9, 1921.
15 *The Life and Death of Lenin*, 1964, 631.
16 [1904] in *The USSR*, D. P. Hammer, 1986, 66.
17 *All Stalin's Men*, 1983, viii.
18 *The Revolution Betrayed*, 1937, 278.
19 quoted in *Beyond 1984*, R. G. Lazar ed., 1985, 11.
20 *The Russian Revolution*, 1930.
21 [1972] quoted in *The Russians*, H. Smith, 1976, 102.
22 *Woman and Socialism*, 1910, 500.
23 quoted in *Russia in flux*, J. Maynard, 1948, 301.
24 *The Technological Society*, 1964, 389.
25 *The Soviet Viewpoint*, 1983, 157.
26 *The New Class*, 1957, 3.
27 *The Practice and Theory of Bolshevism*, 1920, 180.
28 [1929] quoted in *The Constitution of Liberty*, F. Hayek, 1960, 240.
29 *Man Versus the State*, [1884] 1940, 41.
30 Address to AFL–CIO, New York, July, 1978.
31 *Woman and Socialism*, 1910, 280.
32 *Communism*, 1927, 250.
33 "Humanist Socialism," 1960, in *On Disobedience*, E. Fromm, 1981, 76.
34 *The Open Society and its Enemies*, 1950, 385.
35 quoted in *Political Pilgrims*, P. Hollander, 1981, 121.
36 [1939] in *Quotations from Chairman Mao*, 1967, chap. 24.
37 "Quadragesimo Anno," 1931.
38 *African Genesis*, [1961] 1967, 157–59.
39 *On Human Nature*, 1978, 190–91.
40 Declaration, Sept. 11, 1846.
41 *Mein Kampf*, [1924] 1943, 64.
42 *Ends and Means*, 1938, 50.
43 *Why I am Not a Communist*, 1934, 134.
44 *The Rebel*, [1954] 1967, 226.
45 *The Betrayal of the West*, 1978, 126–28.
46 *The New Class*, 1957, 146.
47 *Socialism, Peace and Democracy*, 1987, 150.
48 [1883] in *Correspondence*, 1934, 472.
49 *The Myth of the Eternal Return*, [1949] 1971, 152.
50 Ibid., 149.
51 *The Culture of Narcissism*, 1979, 15.
52 *Wealth and Poverty*, 1981, 26.

53 quoted in *Time*, July 9, 1979, 33.
54 *The End of History and the Last Man*, 1992, xix.
55 Ibid., 168.
56 *Critical Path*, 1981, 196.
57 *The Great Ascent*, 1963, 138.
58 *Power Shift*, 1990, 420.
59 *The Open Society and Its Enemies*, 1950, 334.
60 *Culture of Complaint*, 1993, 74.
61 *Post-Capitalist Society*, 1993, 7.
62 *The Betrayal of the West*, 1978, 83.
63 *Progress and Poverty*, 1879, Book 6, chap. 1.
64 [1927] in *Weekly Articles*, 1981, vol. 3, 93.
65 *Representative Government*, 1861, chap. 3.
66 *Woman and Socialism*, 1910, 234.

Meaning

1 *Experience and Nature*, [1925] 1958, 362.
2 *Modern Man in Search of a Soul*, 1933, 75.
3 *Self-Esteem and Meaning*, 1984, 190.
4 *What Life Should Mean to You*, 1931, 3.
5 *The Politics of Experience*, 1967, 37.
6 *The Problem of Being Human*, 1974, 28.
7 *Death-Camp to Existentialism*, 1959, 99.
8 *Meaning and Void*, 1977, 9.
9 *Self, God, and Immortality*, 1986, 178.
10 *Memories, Dreams, Reflections*, 1961, 340.
11 *Ideas and Opinions*, 1954, 11.
12 *On Civil Disobedience and Non-Violence*, [c. 1900] 1967, 211.
13 *The Passions*, 1976, 24, 113.
14 *Self-Deception and Self-Understanding*, 1985, 30.
15 *The Unconscious God*, 1975, 79–84.
16 quoted in *The Wisdom of the Dream*, S. Segaller, 1989, 181.
17 in *Sanctions for Evil*, N. Sanford ed., 1971, 196.
18 *Escape from Evil*, 1975, 3.
19 in *New Republic*, Apr. 29, 1940, 568–73.
20 *Meaning and Void*, 1977, 314.
21 *The Biological Origins of Human Values*, 1977, 426.
22 *What Life Should Mean to You*, 1931, 9.
23 *Childhood and Society*, [1950] 1963, 249.
24 *Mind, Self and Society*, 1934, 73–77.
25 *Experience and Nature*, [1925] 1958, 299.
26 *What Life Should Mean to You*, 1931, 8.
27 *Mind, Self and Society*, 1934, 89.
28 *Preconscious Processing*, 1981, 246.
29 in *Emotion*, R. Plutchik ed., 1980, 228.
30 *Catastrophe or Cornucopia*, 1982, 26.
31 *The Battle for Human Nature*, 1986, 212.
32 quoted in *The Failure of the Sexual Revolution*, G. Frankl, 1974, 2.
33 *Meaning in Life*, 1992, 85.
34 *The Courage to Be*, 1952, 121.
35 Ibid., 47.
36 *Letters of Sigmund Freud*, [1926] 1960, 436.
37 *Behaviorism*, [1924] 1970, 249–50.
38 *Ends and Means*, 1938, 276.
39 *The Voice of Experience*, 1982, 66.
40 *The Cult of Information*, 1986, 100.
41 *The Passions*, 1976, xvi.
42 *The World and the Individual*, 1900, 367.
43 *Love and Will*, 1969, 226–34.
44 *Man for Himself*, 1947, 45.
45 *The World and the Individual*, 1900, 443.
46 *An Essay on Man*, 1970, 123.
47 *Being and Nothingness*, [1943] 1957, 510.
48 *Experience and Nature*, [1925] 1958, 188, 288.
49 *The Philosopher's Stone*, 1991, 109.
50 Ibid., 117.
51 *Understanding Media*, 1966, 39, 56.
52 *The Gutenberg Galaxy*, 1962, 50.
53 *The Philosopher's Stone*, 1991, 9.
54 *The Will to Power*, 1901, Book 1, sec. 13.
55 *Memories, Dreams, Reflections*, 1961, 359.

Military

1 *On War*, [1832] 1976, 22.
2 *Leaders We Deserve*, 1983, 145.
3 *The True Believer*, 1951, 66.
4 *I Believe*, C. Fadiman ed., 1940, 71.
5 attributed in *Clemenceau and the Third Republic*, H. Jackson, 1946, 228.
6 *Twilight of Authority*, 1975, 147.
7 *The Power Elite*, 1956, 195, 205.
8 *The Power Elite*, 1962, 198.
9 farewell address, Jan. 17, 1961.
10 former Presidential science advisor, quoted in *Reagan, God, and the Bomb*, F. Knelman, 1985, 192.
11 *America As a Civilization*, 1957, 907.
12 *Suicide*, [1897] 1951, 236.
13 to John K. Galbraith [1974] in *The Age of Uncertainty*, 1977, 227.
14 *The Culture of Contentment*, 1992, 182.
15 *The Warriors*, [1959] 1970, 181.
16 *The Varieties of Religious Experience*, [1902] 1958, 283.
17 *America As a Civilization*, 1957, 918.
18 [1944] in *Quotations from Chairman Mao*, 1967, chap. 22.
19 *Generation of Vipers*, 1942, 262.
20 World War II.
21 *Generation of Vipers*, 1942, 263.
22 *The War Myth*, 1967, 70.
23 *Economy and Society*, [1918] 1968, 1155.
24 *The Gutenberg Galaxy*, 1962, 208, 219.
25 to Gaspard Gourgaurd on St. Helena, 1815.
26 *Saint Joan*, 1923, preface.
27 *Obedience to Authority*, 1973, 181.
28 *The Rebel*, [1954] 1967, 183.
29 *Persons and Places*, 1944, vol. 1, chap. 2.
30 *Eichmann in Jerusalem*, [1964] 1977, 256.
31 in *American Political Science Review*, vol. 55, 1961, 3–23.

Pages 232–38

32 *Ideas and Opinions*, [1947] 1954, 133.
33 *Passages*, 1977, 165.
34 *New York Review of Books*, Oct. 21, 1971, 24.
35 *Iron John*, 1990, 147, 156.
36 in *Infantry Journal*, Mar., 1927.
37 *Rhetoric*, Book 1.
38 *Generation of Vipers*, 1942, 265.
39 *Politics Among Nations*, [1948] 1967, 28.
40 *On Civil Disobedience and Non-Violence*, [c. 1900] 1967, 115.
41 *The Real World of Technology*, 1990, 80.
42 *Fighting for Hope*, 1984, 12.
43 Washington speech, Apr. 16, 1953.
44 *Beyond Power*, 1985, 427.
45 *August 1914*, 1962, 33.
46 *The Acquisitive Society*, 1921, 47.
47 *Living Philosophies*, C. Fadiman ed., 1931, 91.

Modern

1 *The Cultural Contradictions of Capitalism*, 1976, 158.
2 *Sex and Destiny*, 1984, 234.
3 *The Cultural Contradictions of Capitalism*, 1976, 16.
4 *The Order of Things*, 1970, 319.
5 *The Biological Origin of Human Values*, 1977, 116.
6 *After Virtue*, 1981, 32.
7 *The Minimal Self*, 1984, 36–37.
8 *For The Love of Life*, 1986, 19–20.
9 *The Pursuit of Loneliness*, [1970] 1976, 177.
10 *Technology and Justice*, 1986, 70.
11 *The Conservative Mind*, [1953] 1986, 492.
12 *The Denial of Death*, 1973, 284.
13 *The Minimal Self*, 1984, 162.
14 *How Does Analysis Cure?*, 1984, 60.
15 *Man's Search for Himself*, 1953, 33.
16 *On Aggression*, 1966, 223.
17 *Modern Man in Search of a Soul*, 1933, 227–28.
18 *Psychology and Religion*, 1938, 41.
19 *The Myth of the Eternal Return*, [1949] 1971, 156.
20 *The Image*, 1956, 66.
21 *The Cultural Contradictions of Capitalism*, 1976, 13.
22 *The Order of Things*, 1970, 318.
23 *Folkways*, [1906] 1940, 519.
24 *Philosophy in a New Key*, [1942] 1957, 276.
25 *The Scientific Outlook*, 1931, 34.
26 quoted in *The Wisdom of the Dream*, S. Segaller, 1989, 166.
27 *The Cultural Contradictions of Capitalism*, 1976, 28.
28 *The Informed Heart*, 1960, 53.
29 *The Phenomenon of Man*, [1940] 1959, 228.
30 *The Rebel*, [1954] 1967, 30.
31 *The Phenomenon of Man*, [1940] 1959, 252.
32 *The Structure of Evil*, 1968, 39.
33 *On Civil Disobedience and Non-Violence*, [c. 1900] 1967, 253.
34 *So Human an Animal*, 1968, 14.
35 *Man for Himself*, 1947, 74.
36 *The Crowd*, [1895] 1960, 153.
37 *The Realm of Spirit*, 1940, 123.
38 *The Philosophy of Moral Development*, 1981, 395–97.
39 *The Cultural Contradictions of Capitalism*, 1976, 28.
40 *The Warriors*, [1959] 1970, xviii.
41 *The Order of Things*, 1970, 328.
42 quoted in *Man Alone*, E. Josephson ed., 1962, 43.
43 *Modern Man in Search of a Soul*, 1933, 230.
44 *The Wisdom of the Dream*, 1989, 177.
45 *The Technological Society*, 1964, 305, 321.

Money / Wealth

1 *Woman and Socialism*, 1910, 241.
2 *The Devil's Dictionary*, c. 1887.
3 *L'Île des Pingouins*, 1908, Part 6, chap. 2.
4 *Escape from Evil*, 1975, 81.
5 *Money and Class in America*, 1988, 78.
6 *The Broken Connection*, 1979, 320.
7 *Works*, vol. 9, [1908] 1959, 174.
8 *Life Against Death*, 1966, 266, 279.
9 *Folkways*, [1906] 1940, 144.
10 "Erewhonians" in *Erewhon*, 1872, chap. 20.
11 *Politics Among Nations*, [1948] 1967, 223.
12 *Economy and Society*, [1918] 1968, 636.
13 *The Selfish Gene*, 1976, 202.
14 *Essays: Moral and Political*, 1741, "Of Money."
15 *Megatrends*, 1984, 94.
16 *Understanding Media*, 1966, 127.
17 *The Order of Things*, 1970, 181.
18 *The General Theory of Employment, Interest and Money*, 1936, 294.
19 *The Life of Reason*, 1954, 116.
20 *The Pursuit of Loneliness*, [1970] 1976, 196.
21 *Wealth and Poverty*, 1981, 23.
22 *Being and Nothingness*, [1943] 1957, 586–90.
23 [1844] in *Karl Marx*, T. Bottomore ed., 1963, 179.
24 *Economic and Philosophical Manuscripts of 1844*, 1964, 168.
25 *Wealth and Poverty*, 1981, 50, 63.
26 quoted in *Newsweek*, Sept. 15, 1980, 35.
27 in *Los Angeles Times*, June 1, 1981.
28 speech to National Press Club, Washington, June 25, 1981.
29 quoted in *Money and Class in America*, L. Lapham, 1988, 32.
30 *The Rover*, 1681, Part 2, act 3.
31 "Francisco d'Anconia" in *Atlas Shrugged*, 1957, 414–15.
32 *Holy Bible*, 1 Timothy 6:10.
33 [d. 323 B.C.] in *Lives of Eminent Philosophers*, Diogenes Laërtius, "Diogenes."
34 *The Pursuit of Loneliness*, [1970] 1976, 171.
35 *The Power Elite*, 1956, 162.
36 *The Power Game*, 1988, 270.
37 *Politics and Money*, 1983, 4–5.

Pages 238–44

38 *Honest Graft*, 1988, 294–95.
39 *Capital Corruption*, 1984, 3, 55.
40 *The Decline of the West*, [1932] 1965, 396.
41 *The Corrupt Society*, 1975, 46–47.
42 *Technics and Human Development*, 1967, 281.
43 *Economic and Philosophical Manuscripts of 1844*, 1964, 167.
44 *Someone, No One*, 1979, 188.
45 *Escape from Freedom*, 1941, 79.
46 *The Evolution of Human Consciousness*, 1980, 222.
47 *The Need for Roots*, 1952, 42.
48 *Technics and Human Development*, 1967, 276.
49 *The Myth of the Machine*, 1970, 168.
50 *Essays in Persuasion*, [1931] 1972, 329.
51 *The Primal Scream*, [1970] 1980, 140.
52 *The Open Society and Its Enemies*, 1950, 318.
53 *Religion and the Rise of Capitalism*, [1926] 1961, 265.
54 *Works of Love*, [1847] 1962, 299.
55 *Economic and Philosophical Manuscripts of 1844*, 1964, 167.
56 *The Pessimist's Handbook*, [1893] 1964, 4, 11.
57 *The Life of Reason*, 1954, 118.
58 *Democracy and Liberty*, 1896, 501–02.
59 quoted in *God, Guilt, and Death*, M. Westphal, 1984, 154.
60 *House of the Dead*, 1862, Part 1, chap. 1.
61 *The Realm of Spirit*, 1940, 149.
62 *The Confessions of J. J. Rousseau*, 1781, Book 1.
63 [d. 1913] *Autobiography*.
64 in *North American Review*, June, 1889, "Wealth."
65 quoted in *Money and Class in America*, L. Lapham, 1988, 57.
66 *Laws*, Book 5, 742–43.
67 *On Population*, 1798, chap. 19.
68 *Human Paleopsychology*, 1987, 260.
69 quoted in *Money and Class in America*, L. Lapham, 1988, 9.
70 in *The Origins of Psychoanalysis*, M. Bonaparte ed., 1954, 244.
71 *Summerhill*, 1960, 199.
72 "The Yes People," 1936.
73 *Economic and Philosophical Manuscripts of 1844*, 1964, 147.
74 *Apology*, by Plato.
75 *Ideas and Opinions*, 1954, 12.
76 *Money and Class in America*, 1988, 239–43.
77 *The Philosophy of Money*, [1907] 1978, 255.
78 in *Fortune*, July 6, 1987, 31.
79 Inaugural Address, Washington, Mar. 4, 1933.
80 *Holy Bible*, Matthew 6:24.

Morality / Ethics

1 *Critique of Practical Reason*, 1788, 2.
2 *On Heroes*, lecture 1, [1840] 1902, 35.
3 *Man's Search for Himself*, 1953, 174.
4 *Fundamental Principles of the Metaphysics of Ethics*, 1785, Second Section.
5 in *New Knowledge in Human Values*, A. Maslow ed., 1959, 195.
6 *The Life of Reason*, 1954, 445.
7 *The Realm of Spirit*, 1940, 129.
8 *Woman and Socialism*, 1910, 439.
9 *The Structure of Evil*, 1968, 50.
10 in *Foreign Affairs*, Mar. 15, 1923.
11 quoted in *Women and Love*, 1987, xxvii.
12 *Love in the Western World*, [1940] 1956, 237.
13 "John Galt" in *Atlas Shrugged*, 1957, 1015.
14 *The Virtue of Selfishness*, 1964, xiii, 16.
15 *Twilight of the Idols*, [1888] 1968, 489–90.
16 *The Will to Power*, 1900, Aph. 897.
17 *The Sexual Revolution*, [1929] 1974, 25.
18 *The Rebel*, [1954] 1967, 124.
19 *Freud: The Mind of the Moralist*, 1961, 277, 306.
20 *The Ego and the Id*, [1927] 1950, 79.
21 *Self-Deception and Morality*, 1986, 55.
22 *Human Society in Ethics and Politics*, 1954, 15–37.
23 quoted in *The Psychology of Moral Development*, L. Kohlberg, 1984, 482.
24 *Canadian Journal of Philosophy*, vol. 9, 1979, 401–03.
25 *A Theory of Justice*, 1971, 475.
26 *In A Different Voice*, 1982, 22.
27 *Moral Man and Immoral Society*, 1932, 170–73.
28 *Holy Bible*, Matthew 22:36–40.
29 *Babylonian Talmud*, i, 42.
30 *Ms. Magazine*, Sept., 1987, 63.
31 *Guilt and Gratitude*, 1982, xviii.
32 *Mysticism and Logic*, 1918, 108.
33 *Fundamental Principles of the Metaphysics of Ethics*, 1785, First Section.
34 *The Life of Reason*, 1954, 456.
35 *Process and Reality*, [1929] 1978, 15.
36 *An Introduction to the Principles of Morals and Legislation*, 1780, chap. 19, sec. 2.
37 *Political Justice*, 1798, Book 2, chap. 1.
38 *Man for Himself*, 1947, 242.
39 *The Triumph of the Therapeutic*, 1966, 261.
40 *The Philosophy of Moral Development*, 1981, 54.
41 *The Biology of Moral Systems*, 1987, 142.
42 *On Human Nature*, 1978, 167.
43 *The Descent of Man*, 1871, chap. 5.
44 *The Gay Science*, 1882, Book 3, sec. 116.
45 *The Basic Writings of C. G. Jung*, 1959, 133.
46 in *Collected Essays*, 1959.
47 quoted in *The Psychology of Dictatorship*, G. Gilbert, 1950, 116.
48 *The Fable of the Bees*, [1724] 1970, 85.
49 *Folkways*, [1906] 1940, 48, 101.
50 *Psychology and Religion*, 1938, 93.
51 *The Conservative Mind*, [1953] 1986, 257.
52 *The Revolution of Hope*, 1968, 32.
53 *The Technological Society*, 1964, 97–99.
54 *The Division of Labor in Society*, [1893] 1964, 36.
55 *Folkways*, [1906] 1940, 539.

Pages 244–50

56 *Beyond Power*, 1985, 17.
57 in *New Knowledge in Human Values*, A. Maslow ed., 1959, 32.
58 *Tragic Sense of Life*, [1912] 1954, 263.
59 *Works*, vol. 1, [1895] 1966, 318.
60 *Obedience to Authority*, 1974, 13.
61 *The Sense of Beauty*, 1955, 28.
62 *The Principles of Morals and Legislation*, 1780, chap. XVII, sec. 1, par. 4 (note).
63 *A Sand County Almanac*, [1949] 1970, 239–62.
64 *Man for Himself*, 1947, 214.
65 *Ends and Means*, 1938, 299.
66 *Ultimate Concern*, 1965, 48.
67 *Man for Himself*, 1947, 224.
68 *The Realm of Spirit*, 1940, 73.
69 *Democracy and Education*, [1916] 1961, 358.
70 *Lectures on Ethics*, [1779] 1963, 152.
71 *City of God*, 426 A.D., Book 2, part 21.
72 *Sexual Personae*, 1990, 131.
73 *The Conservative Mind*, [1953] 1986, 400.
74 *The Origins of Totalitarianism*, 1958, 451.
75 in *Saturday Review*, Apr. 5, 1969, 23.
76 *The View from Nowhere*, 1986, 186.
77 *Politics Among Nations*, [1948] 1967, 235.
78 *Suicide*, [1897] 1951, 386.
79 *Man for Himself*, 1947, 248.
80 *The Triumph of the Therapeutic*, 1966, 239.
81 Ibid., 239.
82 *Science and the Modern World*, 1925, 281.
83 *America As a Civilization*, 1957, 674–75.
84 Ibid., 673.
85 *For the New Intellectual*, 1961, 54.
86 *Edinburgh Review*, 1828, No. XCVI.
87 *The Meaning of the 20th Century*, 1964, 147.
88 *On Aggression*, 1966, 254.
89 *Ideas and Opinions*, [1930] 1954, 94.
90 *Principles*, 1783, chap. XVII, No. 6.
91 *Ideas and Opinions*, [1930] 1954, 54.

Mother

1 in *New Knowledge in Human Values*, A. Maslow ed., 1959, 155.
2 *Home Is Where We Start From*, 1986, 123.
3 Ibid., 124.
4 *Woman and Socialism*, 1910, 303.
5 *Myth, Religion, and Mother Right*, [1926] 1967, 79.
6 in *Alfred Adler*, J. Rattner, 1983, 46.
7 *The Imperial Animal*, 1974, 87, 187.
8 *The First Sex*, 1971, 119.
9 by R. D. Laing, 1960, 186.
10 *Adam Bede*, 1859, chap. 43.
11 *The Art of Loving*, 1956, 34–41.
12 *Childhood and Society*, 1963, 79–80.
13 *Leaders We Deserve*, 1983, 46.
14 in *The Search for the Self*, P. Ornstein ed., 1978, 455.
15 in *Sanctions for Evil*, N. Sanford ed., 1971, 201.
16 *The Psychology of Moral Development*, 1984, 80.
17 *The Psychology of Moral Behaviour*, 1971, 64.
18 *Evolution and Ethics*, 1947, 110.
19 *The Mothers*, 1931, 51, 66.
20 *Attachment and Loss*, vol. 1, 1969, 357.
21 in *Understanding Women*, S. Orbach, 1983, 34.
22 *What Life Should Mean to You*, 1931, 17.
23 *Attachment and Loss*, vol. 3, 1980, 22.
24 in *New York Times*, May 8, 1960.
25 *Understanding Women*, 1985, 17.
26 *The Mermaid and the Minotaur*, 1976, 100.
27 *The Bonds of Love*, 1988, 206.
28 *The Reproduction of Mothering*, 1978, 75.
29 in *Psychology of Our Times*, P. Zimbardo ed., 1973, 341.
30 *What Life Should Mean to You*, 1931, 121.
31 *Of Woman Born*, 1977, 116, 286.
32 *The Reproduction of Mothering*, 1978, 209.
33 *The Child, the Family, and the Outside World*, 1964, 10.
34 *The Heart of Man*, 1964, 99.
35 *The Basic Writings of C. G. Jung*, 1959, 168.
36 *Reason and Emotion in Psychotherapy*, 1962, 221.
37 in London *Observer*, Sept. 12, 1982, "Sayings."
38 *The Second Stage*, 1981, 313–14.
39 *The Drama of the Gifted Child*, 1981, 28.
40 *The Pursuit of Loneliness*, [1970] 1976, 154.
41 *A Vindication of the Rights of Woman*, 1792, chap. 10.
42 Ibid., chap. 12.
43 *Happiness in Marriage*, [1926] 1969, 199.
44 quoted in *Parade*, Dec. 1, 1963.
45 *The Second Stage*, 1981, 90.
46 *The Dialectic of Sex*, 1970, 81, 226.
47 *The Descent of Woman*, 1972, 231.
48 *Right-Wing Women*, 1983, 181.
49 *The Bonds of Love*, 1988, 185.
50 Ibid., 205.
51 *An Introduction to Social Psychology*, 1931, 58.
52 *The Natural Superiority of Women*, [1952] 1968, 214–15.
53 *The Decline of the West*, [1932] 1965, 139.
54 *Sex and Dehumanization*, 1972, 66.

Myth

1 *Myth and Reality*, 1964, 5–6.
2 *The Sacred and the Profane*, 1959, 95.
3 *The Hero with a Thousand Faces*, [1949] 1968, 267.
4 *The Being of Man and His Future Evolution*, [1908] 1981, 94.
5 *Structural Anthropology*, 1963, 209.
6 [4th century], quoted in *The Dragons of Eden*, C. Sagan, 1977, 7.
7 *Philosophy in a New Key*, [1942] 1957, 201.
8 *The Savage Mind*, 1966, 18.
9 *Memories, Dreams, Reflections*, 1961, 311.

Pages 250–55

10 *Structural Anthropology*, 1963, 229.

11 *Introduction to the Science of Religion*, 1873, 353.

12 *Structural Anthropology*, 1963, 210.

13 *The Problem of Being Human*, 1974, 53.

14 *The Savage Mind*, 1966, 22.

15 *Televangelism*, 1988, 32.

16 *The Life of Reason*, 1954, 241.

17 *The Making of a Counter Culture*, 1969, 214.

18 *Works*, [1925] 1953, vol. 9, 152.

19 quoted in *Mussolini's Italy*, H. Finer, 1935, 218.

20 *The Second Sex*, 1964, 260.

21 *International Journal of Law and Psychiatry*, vol. 6, 1983, 237, 255.

22 *Working Through Narcissism*, 1981, 333.

23 *Breach of Faith*, 1975, 322.

24 *America As a Civilization*, 1957, 903.

25 *Patriarchal Precedents*, 1983, 227.

26 *Order and History*, vol. 4, 1974, 30.

27 Plato's *Symposium*, 1968, 1.

28 *An Essay on Man*, [1944] 1970, 92.

29 *Love in the Western World*, [1940] 1956, 19–21.

30 *The Life of Reason*, 1954, 203.

31 *The Decline of the West*, [1932] 1965, 201.

32 *The Power of Myth*, 1988, 5.

33 *The Hero with a Thousand Faces*, [1949] 1968, 11.

34 *Iron John*, 1990, 45.

35 *The Power of Myth*, 1988, 31.

36 *Philosophy in a New Key*, [1942] 1957, 176.

37 *The Myth of the Eternal Return*, [1949] 1971, xiv.

38 *Subtle Is The Lord*, 1982, 311.

39 *The Betrayal of the West*, 1078, 200.

40 *Memories, Dreams, Reflections*, 1961, 332.

41 *From Luther to Hitler*, 1941, 429.

Narcissism

1 *Narcissism*, 1983, IX, 25.

2 *The Culture of Narcissism*, 1979, 22, 52, 60.

3 *For the Love of Life*, 1986, 120.

4 *The Fall of Public Man*, 1977, 8–10.

5 *Narcissism*, 1988, 195.

6 *The Fall of Public Man*, 1977, 324.

7 in *Man Alone*, E. Josephson ed., 1962, 470.

8 *The Fall of Public Man*, 1977, 220.

9 in *New Left Review* 47, 1968, 79–97.

10 *The Fall of Public Man*, 1977, 325.

11 "The Bonds of Love: Rational Violence and Erotic Domination," 1981, note 12.

12 *Working Through Narcissism*, 1981, 7.

13 *The Culture of Narcissism*, 1979, 38.

14 *The Psychology of Self and Other*, 1985, 76.

15 *Political Ensembles*, 1985, 56.

16 in *Signs*, Spring, 1982, 530.

17 *The Peaceable Sex*, 1987, 180.

18 in *The Self*, T. Mischel ed., 1977, 219.

19 *Group Psychology and the Analysis of the Ego*, [1921] 1959, 55.

20 *Narcissism*, 1988, 3.

21 *Working Through Narcissism*, 1981, 288.

22 *The Heart of Man*, 1964, 87.

23 in *The Search for the Self*, P. Ornstein ed., 1978, 640–46.

24 in *Advances in Self Psychology*, A. Goldberg ed., 1978, 178.

25 in *The Search for the Self*, P. Ornstein ed., 1978, 639.

26 *The Heart of Man*, 1964, 70.

27 *Escape from Evil*, 1975, 157.

28 *Sexual Personae*, 1990, 523.

29 *The Heart of Man*, 1964, 66.

30 *The Fall of Public Man*, 1977, 335.

31 in *Theory and Society* 14, 1985, 271–319.

32 *The Fall of Public Man*, 1977, 315.

33 *The Culture of Narcissism*, 1979, 61.

34 *The Image*, 1962, 257.

35 *Narcissism*, 1983, ix.

36 *The Pursuit of Loneliness*, [1970] 1976, 167.

37 [d. 1930] "Pornography and Obscenity."

Nature

1 *The Philosophy of Fascism*, 1936, 41.

2 *Holy Bible*, Genesis 1:28.

3 *Sexual Personae*, 1990, 28.

4 *Libertarianism*, 1971, 276–77.

5 *Saturday Review*, Feb. 5, 1966, 27–28.

6 [1945] in *Quotations from Chairman Mao*, 1967, chap. 22.

7 *The Basic Writings of Bertrand Russell* 1961, 371.

8 *The Future of an Illusion*, 1927, 34.

9 *The Decline of the West*, [1932] 1965, 91.

10 *The Sense of Beauty*, 1955, 136.

11 in *North American Review*, Winter, 1974, 37.

12 *The Open Society and Its Enemies*, 1950, 195.

13 *The Dialectics of Nature* [1882], in *Marx/Engels Collected Works*, 1987, vol. 25, 460.

14 *Mein Kampf*, [1924] 1943, 287.

15 *The Greening of America*, 1970, 28.

16 *Silent Spring*, 1962, 85.

17 *The Warriors*, [1959] 1970, 237.

18 *The Fate of the Earth*, 1982, 111–13.

19 *Mankind and Mother Earth*, 1976, 20, 596.

20 *A Study of History*, [1934] 1972, 285.

21 *The Rebel*, [1954] 1967, 27.

22 *Existence*, 1958, 19.

23 *Civilization and Its Discontents*, [1930] 1961, 34–35.

24 *Order Out of Chaos*, 1984, 51.

25 speech of Dec. 3, 1939.

26 *Order Out of Chaos*, 1984, 218.

27 Ibid., 77.

28 *Science and the Modern World*, [1925] 1957, 80.

29 *Astronomy and general Physics considered with reference to natural Theology*, 1834, chap. 1.

30 *The Realm of Spirit*, 1940, 156.

Pages 255–62

31 *The Meaning of the 20th Century*, 1964, 152.
32 *The Concept of Mind*, 1949, 82.
33 in *The New Republic*, Feb. 9, 1921.
34 *The Quest for Certainty*, [1929] 1960, 248.
35 *Nature, Man, and Woman*, 1962, 62.
36 *The End of Nature*, 1989, 58, 211.
37 *The Real World of Technology*, 1990, 86–87.
38 *Philosophy in a New Key*, [1942] 1957, 278.
39 *Nature*, 1836, chap. 1.
40 *Where Is Science Going?*, 1932, 217.
41 *Economic and Philosophic Manuscripts*, [1844] 1964, 112.
42 *So Human an Animal*, 1968, 23.
43 *Gaia*, [1979] 1987, 148.
44 *Process and Reality*, [1929] 1978, 289.
45 *Sexual Personae*, 1990, 28.
46 *The Philosopher's Stone*, 1991, 52.
47 *The Open Society and Its Enemies*, 1950, 62.
48 *So Human an Animal*, 1968, 201.
49 *Tragic Sense of Life*, [1912] 1954, 150–51.
50 *Nature, Man, and Woman*, 1958, 49.
51 *Système de la Nature*, 1770, Part 2, chap. 1.
52 *Escape from Freedom*, 1941, 45–46.
53 *Man's Search for Himself*, 1953, 73.
54 *So Human an Animal*, 1968, 200.
55 *Man and His Symbols*, 1964, 85.
56 *Profiles of the Future*, 1982, 219.
57 *The Broken Connection*, 1979, 341–42.
58 *The Wooing of Earth*, 1980, 17–18.

Obedience

1 *The Need for Roots*, 1952, 13.
2 *The Imperial Animal*, 1974, 38.
3 *Works*, 1915, vol. 8, 17, 34.
4 *The Anatomy of Human Destructiveness*, 1973, 207.
5 *The Psychology of Dictatorship*, 1950, 237–38.
6 1946, Article 8.
7 quoted in *Trials of War Criminals* [1946–49], XI, 168.
8 at Nuremberg, quoted in *War and Morality*, R. Wasserstrom, 1970, 131.
9 quoted in *Sanction for Evil*, N. Sanford ed., 1971, 212.
10 *The Need for Roots*, 1952, 13.
11 *The True Believer*, 1951, 115.
12 *The Denial of Death*, 1973, 212.
13 "Some Thoughts on the Education of Children," 1752.
14 *Summerhill*, 1960, 156.
15 *International Journal of Law and Psychiatry*, vol. 6, 1983, 236.
16 *A Grammar of Politics*, [1925] 1938, 19.
17 *The Conservative Mind*, [1953] 1986, 67.
18 Ibid., 246.
19 *Guilt*, 1985, 216, 221, 240.
20 *The Revolt of the Masses*, 1932, 140.
21 *Considerations on Representative Government*, 1861, chap. 4.
22 *The Dangers of Obedience*, [1930] 1968, 13.
23 *Pacem in Terris*, 1963, 142.
24 *I Believe*, C. Fadiman ed., 1940, 22.
25 *The Revolution Betrayed*, 1937, 76.
26 *Ends and Means*, 1938, 57.
27 "Politics," in *Essays: Second Series*, 1844.
28 *The Arrogance of Power*, 1966, 25.
29 *An Inquiry into the Human Prospect*, 1975, 110.
30 *Obedience to Authority*, 1974, 2, 188
31 *Psychoanalysis and Religion*, 1950.
32 "Disobedience as a Psychological and Moral Problem," 1963.

Objectivity

1 *The Making of a Counter Culture*, 1969, 232.
2 *Personal Knowledge*, 1962, 264.
3 *The Making of a Counter Culture*, 1969, 208.
4 Ibid., 265.
5 *Signs*, Spring, 1982, 537–38.
6 *Sex and Power in History*, 1974, 70.
7 *Pornography*, 1989, 113.
8 *Aggression American Style*, 1978, 6–7.
9 *The Will to Power*, 1901, Book 2, sec. 425.
10 *Personal Knowledge*, 1962, 286.
11 *Psychology and Religion*, 1938, 3.
12 in *New Knowledge in Human Values*, A. Maslow ed., 1959, 160.
13 [1826] in *Goethe: Wisdom and Experience*, L. Curtis ed., 177.
14 "Looking Back on the Spanish War," 1943.
15 in *Quotations from Chairman Mao*, 1967, chap. 22.
16 *Phenomenology of Mind*, 1817, "Master and Slave."
17 *A Theory of Objective Self-Awareness*, 1972, 4.
18 *The View from Nowhere*, 1986, 139.
19 *The Passions*, 1976, 64, 75.
20 *Nature, Man, and Woman*, 1958, 44.
21 *Self-Esteem and Meaning*, 1984, 2.
22 *The Making of a Counter Culture*, 1969, 234.
23 *Ideas and Opinions*, 1954, 42.
24 *The Myth of Two Minds*, 1987, 224.
25 *The View from Nowhere*, 1986, 26.
26 *The Dancing Wu Li Masters*, 1979, 56.
27 *The Turning Point*, 1982, 87.
28 *The World As Will and Idea*, [1819] 1896, 166.
29 *The View from Nowhere*, 1986, 186.
30 *Man for Himself*, 1947, 105.
31 *Personal Knowledge*, 1962, 5.
32 *The Philosopher's Stone*, 1991, 47.

Other

1 *The Second Sex*, 1964, xvi.
2 *The Rebel*, [1954] 1967, 138.
3 *Being and Nothingness*, [1943] 1957, 263.
4 *The World and the Individual*, 1900, 379.

Pages 262–68

5 *Being and Nothingness,* [1943] 1957, 222.
6 *Guilt and Gratitude,* 1982, 196.
7 in *New Knowledge in Human Values,* A. Maslow ed., 1959, 186.
8 *Technology and Justice,* 1986, 39, 73, 75.
9 *Coming to Our Senses,* 1989, 24.
10 in *The Psychology of Women,* M. Walsh ed., 1987, 257.
11 *Political Ensembles,* 1985, 6.
12 in *Beyond Domination,* C. Gould ed., 1983, 66.
13 *Nature, Man, and Woman,* 1958, 49.
14 *The Nature of Woman,* 1980, 268.
15 *Positive Social Behavior and Morality,* vol. 1, 1978, 57.
16 *The Order of Things,* 1970, 328.
17 *Mind, Self and Society,* 1934, 154.
18 *The Politics of Experience,* 1967, 77–78.
19 *The Lonely Crowd,* [1950] 1965, 327.
20 *The Broken Connection,* 1979, 223.
21 *Beyond Psychology,* [1941] 1958, 168.
22 *The Image,* 1956, 74.
23 *The Integrity of the Personality,* 1963, 32.
24 *The Psychology of Self and Other,* 1985, 18.
25 *Self and Others,* 2nd. ed., 1969, 68.
26 *The Rebel,* [1954] 1967, 139.
27 *Symbols in Society,* 1968, 39–40.
28 *Coming to Our Senses,* 1989, 99.
29 *Experience and Nature,* [1925] 1958, 244.
30 *Youth,* 1932.
31 *Man for Himself,* 1947, 207.
32 *Self and Others,* 1969, 118.
33 in *Perspectives on Self-Deception,* A. Rorty ed., 1988, 400.
34 *Way to Wisdom,* 1951, 25.
35 quoted in *Psychology for Our Times,* P. Zimbardo ed., 1973, 204.

~ Parents ~

1 *The Absorbent Mind,* [1949] 1984, 42.
2 in *Moral Values and the Superego Concept in Psychoanalysis,* S. Post, 1968, 129.
3 *The Basic Writings of C. G. Jung,* 1959, 167.
4 *The Art of Loving,* 1956, 33–36.
5 *An Introduction to Social Psychology,* 1931, 143.
6 *Identity,* 1968, 103.
7 *The Psychology of Moral Behaviour,* 1971, 39, 66.
8 *Narcissism,* 1983, 106.
9 *Aggression,* 1962, 300.
10 *The Psychology of Moral Development,* 1984, 199.
11 *America As a Civilization,* 1957, 561–70.
12 *The Lonely Crowd,* [1950] 1965, 48–49.
13 *America As a Civilization,* 1957, 564.
14 Ibid., 567.
15 [1914], *On Narcissism* in *Works,* 1957, 91.
16 in *The Traitor,* A. Gorz, 1960, 15.
17 *The Drama of the Gifted Child,* 1981, 27.
18 *The Authoritarian Personality,* 1950, 387.
19 *Psychic War in Men and Women,* 1976, 3.
20 *The Self-Concept,* vol. 2, 1979, 351, 437.
21 *Positive Social Behavior and Morality,* vol. 2, 1979, 110.
22 *Woman and Socialism,* 1910, 145.
23 *Summerhill,* 1960, 103.
24 *Sociobiology,* 1980, 174.
25 *The Mermaid and the Minotaur,* 1976, 100–03.
26 in *77th Yearbook of the National Society for the Study of Education,* 1978, 325.
27 *The Culture of Narcissism,* 1979, 291.
28 *Culture Against Man,* 1965, 76.
29 *Baby and Child Care,* [1946] 1957, 4.
30 *The Lonely Crowd,* [1950] 1965, 48.
31 *Home Is Where We Start From,* 1986, 159.
32 *For Your Own Good,* 1984, 132.
33 *Democracy and the Student Left,* 1968, 14.
34 *Holy Bible,* Exodus 20:1.
35 *Cannibals and Kings,* 1977, 282.
36 quoted in *Beyond 1984,* R. Lazar ed., 1985, 3–4.
37 *Home Is Where We Start From,* 1986, 124.
38 *The Conquest of Happiness,* 1930, 198.

~ Patriarchy ~

1 *Understanding Women,* 1985, 3.
2 *The Sexual Revolution,* [1929] 1974, 10.
3 *For the Love of Life,* 1986, 22.
4 *The First Sex,* 1971, 135–36.
5 *Beyond Power,* 1985, 270, 296.
6 *A Choice of Heroes,* 1982, 11.
7 *Revolution from Within,* 1992, 259.
8 *Sexual Politics,* 1971, 45.
9 *The Inevitability of Patriarchy,* 1973, 32.
10 *Sex and Power in History,* 1974, 80.
11 *The Mothers,* 1927, vol. 3, 507.
12 *The Second Sex,* 1964, 73.
13 *Life Against Death,* 1966, 126–27.
14 *Woman and Socialism,* 1910, 33.
15 *Against Our Will,* 1976, 8.
16 *Gyn/Ecology,* 1978, 31, 39, 355.
17 *Right-Wing Women,* 1983, 121.
18 *Of Woman Born,* 1977, 38.
19 *The Nature of Woman,* 1980, 345.
20 in *Test-Tube Women,* 1984, R. Arditti ed., 367–68.
21 in *Beyond Domination,* C. Gould ed., 1983, 280.
22 in *International Journal of Law and Psychiatry,* vol. 6, 1983, 245.
23 *Beyond Power,* 1985, 294.
24 *The Wisdom of the Dream,* 1989, 119.
25 *The Mothers,* 1927, vol. 3, 515.
26 *Women and Love,* 1987, 764.
27 *Previews and Premises,* 1983, 11–12.
28 *Iron John,* 1990, 122.
29 in *International Journal of Law and Psychiatry,* vol. 6, 1983, 258.

Pages 268–74

PHILOSOPHY

1 *I Believe*, C. Fadiman ed., 1940, 79.
2 *Modes of Thought*, [1938] 1969, 63.
3 *Capitalism*, 1966, 254.
4 *The Ominous Parallels*, 1982, 313.
5 *Science and the Modern World*, 1925, x.
6 *The Public Philosophy*, [1955] 1989, 178.
7 in *The Republic*, by Plato, Book v.
8 *The Public Philosophy*, [1955] 1989, 177.
9 *New Organon*, 1620, Book 1, Aphorism 95.
10 *The Pessimist's Handbook*, [1893] 1964, 124.
11 *Supplements to "The World As Will and Idea,"* 1844, chap. 17.
12 *The Passions*, 1976, 4–7.
13 *Experience and Nature*, [1929] 1958, 7.
14 *The Philosophy of Moral Development*, 1981, 67.
15 *Beast and Man*, 1978, 169.
16 *The Realm of Spirit*, 1940, 159.
17 in *Alienation*, R. Schacht, 1970, xxvii.
18 *Essays*, 1580, Book 1, chap. 20.
19 *Life Against Death*, 1966, 108.
20 *The Sense of Beauty*, 1955, 236.
21 *An Anatomy of the World: The First Anniversary*, c. 1611, line 205.
22 *The World and the Individual*, 1900, 370.
23 [1816] *Introduction to the Reading of Hegel*, 1969, VI.
24 in *Self-Deception and Self-Understanding*, M. Martin ed., 1985, 282.
25 "On Old Age," 44 B.C.
26 *Meditations*, [c. 161–80 A.D.], Book 2, XV.
27 *The Age of Ideology*, 1956, 273.
28 *Life Against Death*, 1966, 157.
29 *Beyond Good and Evil*, [1886] 1907, chap. 1, par. 6.
30 [d. 1814] quoted in *Identity and Anxiety*, 1960, 540–41.
31 *Man in the Modern Age*, [1931] 1951, 179.
32 *Culture and Value*, [1931] 1980, 16.
33 *Personal Knowledge*, 1962, 267.
34 *The Quest for Certainty*, [1929] 1960, 34.
35 *The Death of the Soul*, 1986, 55.
36 *Tractatus Logico-Philosophicus*, [1921] 1961, 25, 4.112.
37 *Process and Reality*, [1929] 1978, 15.
38 *Philosophy in a New Key*, [1942] 1957, 293.
39 in *In Defense of Animals*, P. Singer, 1985, 13–26.
40 *A Memoir*, Appendix I.
41 *Process and Reality*, [1929] 1978, 10.
42 *An Essay on Man*, [1944] 1970, 78.
43 *A Concise Introduction to Philosophy*, 1967, 18f.
44 *Tractatus Logico-Philosophicus*, [1921] 1961, 25.
45 Ibid., 19, 4.003.
46 *Unpopular Essays*, [1950] 1976, 56.
47 *Eco-Philosophy*, 1981, 20.
48 *The Logic of Scientific Discovery*, [1934] 1968, 17.
49 Foreword to *Words and Things*, E. Gellner, 1959.
50 *Narcissism*, 1988, 192.
51 *Philosophy in a New Key*, [1942] 1957, 13.
52 *The Decline of the West*, [1932] 1965, 33.
53 *The Open Society and Its Enemies*, 1950, 183.
54 in *Inquiry*, 1977, vol. 20, 86.
55 *Third Eye Philosophy*, 1987, vi.
56 *The Logic of Scientific Discovery*, [1934] 1968, 15.
57 *Philosophy in a New Key*, [1942] 1957, 4.
58 *Meaning and Void*, 1977, 319.
59 *The Genealogy of Morals*, 1887, First Essay, s.17, note.
60 *The Quest for Certainty*, [1929] 1960, 37.
61 *Theses on Feuerbach*, 1845, XI.
62 *Man in the Modern Age*, [1931] 1951, 142.
63 *The Rebel*, [1954] 1967, 78.
64 *A History of Western Philosophy*, 1945, ix.
65 *Tragic Sense of Life*, [1912] 1954, 113.
66 *The Problems of Philosophy*, 1912, 161.
67 [1903] *The Basic Writings of Bertrand Russell*, 1961, 67.
68 *Orthodoxy*, [1908] 1959, 65.
69 *Capitalism*, 1966, 144.
70 *Creative Evolution*, [1907] 1944, 216.
71 *Science and the Modern World*, 1925, 55.
72 *Ends and Means*, 1938, 322.
73 *Tragic Sense of Life*, 1912, chap. 6.
74 in *The Stoic and Epicurean Philosophers*, W. H. Oates, [1940] 1957, 49.
75 *A Study of History*, [1934] 1972, 252.
76 *Eco-Philosophy*, 1981, 33.
77 *History of the Idea of Progress*, 1980, 353.
78 *The Closing of the American Mind*, 1987, 378.
79 in *Living Philosophies*, C. Fadiman ed., 1931, 33.
80 *Way to Wisdom*, 1951, 9.
81 *Man in the Modern Age*, [1931] 1951, 140–41.
82 *The Closing of the American Mind*, 1987, 208.
83 *The Quest for Certainty*, [1929] 1960, 255.
84 *Philosophical Sketches*, 1964, 151.
85 *Philosophy of Right*, 1821, preface.

POLITICS

1 *Politics*, Book 1, chap. 2.
2 *A Grammar of Politics*, [1925] 1938, 19.
3 *Power and Personality*, 1948, 160.
4 Second College Edition, 1974.
5 *Politics*, [1936] 1950, 16.
6 *Human Society in Ethics and Politics*, 1954, 10.
7 *Profiles in Courage*, 1957, 204.
8 *The Fable of the Bees*, [1724] 1970, 371.
9 in *Observations, Anecdotes, and Characters*, J. Spence, [1728] 1820, Anecdote 882.
10 *Public Opinion*, [1922] 1957, 291.
11 *Economy and Society*, [1918] 1968, 901–02.
12 *Politics Among Nations*, 1962, 260.
13 *The Open Society and Its Enemies*, 1945, vol. 2, 270.
14 *Twilight of Authority*, 1975, 153.
15 *The Education of Henry Adams*, 1907, chap. 28.
16 Ibid., chap. 1.

17 *Altruistic Love*, 1950, 50.
18 *A Self Portrait*, 1968.
19 [1938] in *Selected Works*, 1965, vol. 2, 153.
20 [1938] in *Quotations of Chairman Mao*, 1967, chap. 5.
21 *The Image*, 1956, 80.
22 *The Power Elite*, 1962, 171.
23 *Twilight of Authority*, 1975, 242.
24 [d. 1876] *Complete Works*, III.
25 *Politics Among Nations*, [1948] 1967, 25.
26 *Journal of International Affairs*, vol. 21, 1967, no. 1, 57–71.
27 *The Crowd*, [1895] 1960, 150.
28 speech, Nov. 3, 1774, in *Works*, 1883, vol. 1, 446.
29 *The Minimal Self*, 1984, 50–51.
30 *The Cult of Information*, 1986, 193.
31 *The Myth of the State*, 1946, 289.
32 "Politics and the English Language," 1946.
33 *The Image*, 1961, 249.
34 *The Lonely Crowd*, [1950] 1965, 213.
35 Ibid., 313.
36 in *Sexual Politics of Gender*, 1981, 66.
37 *The End of History and the Last Man*, 1992, XXI.
38 *Leadership*, 1978, 113.
39 *The Lawmakers*, 1965, 223–24.
40 *The Status Seekers*, 1959, 207.
41 *The Imperial Animal*, 1974, 127–28.
42 *Sexual Politics*, 1971, 277.
43 *The New Presidential Elite*, 1976, 379.
44 *Men in Groups*, 1970, 259.
45 *The Descent of Woman*, 1972, 215.
46 *Unfinished Democracy*, 1985, 166–69.
47 *Eros and Civilization*, [1955] 1966, xxv.
48 *Revolution from Within*, 1992, 16–17.
49 *The Human Problems of an Industrial Civilization*, [1933] 1960, 160.
50 in *Political Psychology*, M. Hermann ed., 1986, 332.
51 [1867] quoted in *Bismarck-Worte*, 1918, 19.
52 *The Rebel*, [1954] 1967, 302.
53 *The Conservative Mind*, [1953] 1986, 8.
54 *Folkways*, [1906] 1940, 402.
55 *Politics Among Nations*, 1962, 11.
56 in *Public and Private Morality*, S. Hampshire ed., 1978, 127.
57 quoted in *Man Alone*, E. Josephson ed., 1962, 47.
58 *The Political Illusion*, 1967, 221.
59 *America As a Civilization*, 1957, 356–57.
60 [431 B.C.] in *The History of the Peloponnesian War*, Thucydides, Book 2, par. 37–41.
61 *Capitalism, Socialism, and Democracy*, [1942] 1950, 262.
62 *The Triumph of Politics*, 1986, 14.
63 *Generation of Vipers*, 1942, 250.
64 *The Life of Reason*, 1954, 464.
65 *Nuclear Madness*, 1980, 70.
66 *Carnets 1935–42*, 1962, 99.
67 *The Republic*, by Plato, Book 5, 473.
68 *The Arrogance of Power*, 1966, 160.

~ Power ~

1 *Beyond Good and Evil*, 1886, chap. 1, par. 13.
2 *The Will to Power*, 1901, sec. 434, 702.
3 *Leviathan*, 1651, Part 1, chap. 11.
4 *Political Essays*, 1819, "The Times Newspaper."
5 *Human Society in Ethics and Politics*, 1954, 162–64.
6 *Letter to a Member of the National Assembly*, 1791, 12.
7 *The Education of Henry Adams*, 1907, chap. 10.
8 *Psychological Reflections*, [1953] 1970, 99.
9 *Power and Personality*, 1948, 39, 221.
10 *Escape from Freedom*, 1941, 184.
11 *Narcissism*, 1983, 98, 228.
12 Ibid., 75.
13 Ibid., 84–85.
14 *Being and Loving*, 1978, 31.
15 in *New York Times*, Jan. 19, 1971, 12.
16 *Beyond Power*, 1985, 180.
17 *Narcissism*, 1983, 90.
18 "The Bonds of Love," 1981, par. 65.
19 *The Power Elite*, 1956, 89.
20 *The Hero in History*, [1943] 1955, 235.
21 *Leadership*, 1978, 388.
22 *The Presidential Character*, 1985, 86.
23 *1999: Victory Without War*, 1988, 22.
24 Washington address, Feb. 20, 1987.
25 *Politics Among Nations*, [1948] 1967, 99.
26 *Mein Kampf*, [1924] 1943, 618.
27 *The Origins of Totalitarianism*, 1958, 137.
28 *The March of Folly*, 1984, 381–82.
29 in *The Voice of Destruction*, H. Rauschning, 1940, 279.
30 *The New Class*, 1957, 81, 169.
31 "Winston," in *1984*, [1949] 1977, 211–12.
32 *Saturday Review*, Feb. 5, 1966, 28.
33 *Escape from Evil*, 1975, 81.
34 *Life Against Death*, 1966, 251.
35 in *American Sociological Review*, 1965, vol. 30, 205.
36 *Sexual Politics*, 1971, 87.
37 *A Vindication of the Rights of Woman*, 1791, chap. 10.
38 *Moral Man and Immoral Society*, 1932, 33.
39 *The Spirit of Laws*, 1748, Book XI, sec. 4.
40 *On Civil Disobedience and Non-Violence*, [c. 1900] 1967, 272.
41 *Politics Among Nations*, [1948] 1967, 219.
42 *The Arrogance of Power*, 1966.
43 *Works*, 1899, vol. 4, 457.
44 *Folkways*, [1906] 1940, 71.
45 *Power Shift*, 1990, 10.
46 *The Cult of Information*, 1986, 67.
47 *The Politics of Lying*, 1973, 342.
48 *The Greening of America*, 1970, 307.
49 *The Mass Psychology of Fascism*, 1946, 280.
50 *Papers of James Madison*, vol. 2, 1073.
51 *Women and Power*, 1985, 82.
52 *On Liberty*, 1859, chap. 1.
53 *Beyond Power*, 1985, 545.

54 *The Greening of America*, 1970, 125.
55 letter in *Life and Letters of Mandell Creighton*, 1904, vol. 1, chap. 13.
56 [1928] quoted in *Alfred Adler*, J. Rattner, 1983, xiv.
57 *The Pursuit of Loneliness*, [1970] 1976, 165.
58 *The Passions*, 1976, 99–102.
59 *The Betrayal of the West*, 1978, 35, 131.
60 *Power*, 1938, 34.
61 *Vivian Grey*, 1826, Book 6, chap. 7.
62 *Power and Personality*, 1948, 110.
63 *Computer Power and Human Reason*, 1976, 259.
64 *The Myth of the Machine*, 1967, 3, 203.
65 *Of Woman Born*, 1976, 65.
66 *Technology—The God That Failed*, 1971, 160.

Progress

1 "A Death in the Desert," 1864, line 586.
2 *Mind, Self and Society*, 1934, 293–94.
3 *History of the Idea of Progress*, 1980, 4.
4 *Suicide*, [1897] 1951, 257.
5 *The Image*, 1956, 122.
6 *Entropy*, [1980] 1989, 43.
7 *The Rebel*, [1954] 1967, 102.
8 *Religion and the Rise of Capitalism*, [1926] 1961, 276.
9 *Modern Man in Search of a Soul*, 1933, 235.
10 *Mankind and Mother Earth*, 1976, 590.
11 in *From Max Weber*, H. Gerth, 1946, 140.
12 *The Wisdom of the Dream*, 1989, 148.
13 Motto of Sierra Club of U.S.
14 *Capitalism*, 1966, 21.
15 *Notebooks*, 1912, chap. 1.
16 *The Phenomenon of Man*, 1959, 50–51.
17 *The Life of Reason*, 1954, 83–84.
18 *Woman and Socialism*, 1910, 454.
19 *Against Method*, 1975, 167.
20 Ibid., 23.
21 *The Phenomenon of Man*, [1940] 1959, 230.
22 *The Betrayal of the West*, 1978, 197.
23 *Capitalism, Socialism, and Democracy*, [1942] 1950, 32.
24 *Life Against Death*, 1966, 16.
25 *The Peter Principle*, 1970, 148.
26 *Man and Superman*, 1903, Maxims: "Reason."
27 *Science and the Modern World*, 1925, 294.
28 *Suicide*, [1897] 1951, 364.
29 *The Informed Heart*, 1960, 75–77.
30 *The Genealogy of Morals*, 1887, Second Essay, sec. 12.
31 *Woman and Socialism*, 1910, 245.
32 *What Life Should Mean to You*, 1931, 252.
33 *The Basic Writings of Bertrand Russell*, [1931] 1961, 15.
34 *The End of History and the Last Man*, 1992, 6.
35 *Eco-Philosophy*, 1981, 67.
36 *The View from Nowhere*, 1986, 186.
37 *The Mind of Primitive Man*, [1911] 1938, 206.
38 *Cannibals and Kings*, 1977, 235.
39 *History of Europe*, 1935, vol. 1, preface.
40 *The Open Society and Its Enemies*, 1950, 462.
41 quoted in *History of the Idea of Progress*, R. Nisbet, 1980, 316.
42 *The Decline and Fall of the Roman Empire*, 1776–1788, chap. 71.
43 *History of the Idea of Progress*, 1980, 318.
44 *Profiles of the Future*, 1982, 12.
45 *Man for Himself*, 1947, 4–5.
46 *Orthodoxy*, [1908] 1959, 195.
47 *The End of History and the Last Man*, 1992, 7.
48 in *The International Journal of Ethics*, April, 1916.

Projection

1 *Being and Time*, [1931] 1962, 185–87.
2 in *The Psychobiology of Consciousness*, J. Davidson ed., 1980, 436.
3 *Life Against Death*, 1966, 154.
4 *The Natural Superiority of Women*, 1968, 22, 28.
5 *Human Society in Ethics and Politics*, 1954, 176.
6 [d. 475 B.C.] "Of Nature," *Xenophanes of Colophon*, 1992, 25.
7 *The Physical World of the Greeks*, 1956, 40.
8 *Sexual Personae*, 1990, 17.
9 *The Peaceable Sex*, 1987, 5–6.
10 *The Arrogance of Power*, 1966, 107.
11 *Childhood and Society*, [1950] 1963, 248–49.
12 *Modern Man in Search of a Soul*, 1933, 163.
13 *The Diaries of Anaïs Nin*, 1969, vol. 4.
14 *A Primer of Freudian Psychology*, 1954, 89–90.
15 *The Psychology of Moral Behaviour*, 1971, 36.
16 *The Authoritarian Personality*, 1950, 411.
17 *Psychology and Religion*, 1938, 60.
18 *Hitler's Ideology*, 1975, 90–91.
19 *Narcissism*, 1983, 24, 48, 51.
20 *For Your Own Good*, 1984, 86–87.
21 *Beyond Power*, 1985, 137.
22 *The Bonds of Love*, 1988, 67.
23 in *New Directions in Psycho-Analysis*, M. Klein ed., 1955, 504.
24 *Home Is Where We Start From*, 1986, 82.
25 *Psychology and Religion*, 1938, 101.
26 [1938] in *Collected Works*, vol. 11, par. 140.
27 *The Denial of Death*, 1973, 158.

Reality

1 *Tragic Sense of Life*, [1912] 1954, 39.
2 *The Philosophy of "As If,"* 1935, 350.
3 *Psychology*, 1892, chap. 13.
4 *Icon and Image*, [1954] 1965, 65.
5 *Home Is Where We Start From*, 1986, 25.
6 *Man in the Modern Age*, [1931] 1951, 178–79.
7 *Some Lessons in Metaphysics*, 1969, 155.
8 *The Heart of Man*, 1964, 66.

Pages 286–92

9 *Man's Search for Himself*, 1953, 32.
10 *The Sacred and the Profane*, 1959, 12–23.
11 *The Dragons of Eden*, 1977, 31.
12 *On Human Nature*, 1978, 74.
13 *The Third Wave*, 1980, 182.
14 *The Dancing Wu Li Masters*, 1979, 53–56.
15 *Atomic Theory and Human Knowledge*, 1958, 60.
16 *A Brief History of Time*, 1988, 139.
17 *The Politics of Ecstasy*, 1968, 239.
18 *The Tao of Physics*, 1975, 287.
19 *The View from Nowhere*, 1986, 26.
20 *The Phenomenon of Man*, [1940] 1959, 90.
21 *The View from Nowhere*, 1986, 85.
22 *Tragic Sense of Life*, [1912] 1954, 24.
23 *The Sense of Beauty*, 1955, 247.
24 *Process and Reality*, [1929] 1978, 310.
25 *The Passions*, 1976, xix, 14.
26 *Icon and Image*, [1954] 1965, 73.
27 *Order Out of Chaos*, 1984, 293.
28 *The Making of a Counter Culture*, 1969, 233.
29 *Being and Nothingness*, [1943] 1957, 180.
30 *The World and the Individual*, 1900, 348.
31 *Concluding Unscientific Postscript*, [1846] 1941, 107.
32 *Way to Wisdom*, 1951, 80.
33 *Insight and Responsibility*, 1964, 164–65.
34 *Self and Others*, 1969, 29.
35 *Coming to Our Senses*, 1989, 304.
36 *Love in the Western World*, [1940] 1956, 59.
37 "Wotan" [1936] in *Collected Works*, vol. 10, par. 387.
38 *Man for Himself*, 1947, 5.
39 Ibid., 90.
40 *Life Against Death*, 1966, 302.
41 *The Image*, 1962, 240–41.

~ Reason ~

1 *The Life of Reason*, 1954, 79.
2 *An Essay Concerning Human Understanding*, 1690, Book 4, chap. 19, sec. 4.
3 *Nicomachean Ethics*, Book 1, part 6.
4 *The Mind of Primitive Man*, [1911] 1938, 219.
5 *Mind*, 1967, vol. 1, 146.
6 *Aids in Reflection*, 1825, "On Spiritual Religion," Aph. VIII.
7 Ibid., "On the Difference in Kind of Reason and the Understanding."
8 in *Philosophical Review*, 1921, XXX, 5: 469–72.
9 in *New Knowledge in Human Values*, A. Maslow ed., 1959, 160.
10 *The Function of Reason*, 1959, 5.
11 *The Life of Reason*, 1954, 487.
12 *Meditations*, [c. 161–80 A.D.], Book III, par. 6.
13 *Civilization*, 1928, chap. 5.
14 *Science and the Modern World*, [1925] 1957, 27.
15 *The Life of Reason*, 1954, 73.
16 *Sceptical Essays*, 1928, 123.
17 *Capitalism*, 1966, 151.
18 *Eros and Civilization*, [1955] 1966, 111.
19 *The Essence of Security*, 1968, 109–10.
20 *The Wisdom of the Dream*, 1989, 38.
21 *Man and Superman*, 1903, Maxims: "Reason."
22 *Life Against Death*, 1966, 62.
23 in *Symposium on Love*, M. Curtin ed., 1973, 80.
24 *Computer Power and Human Reason*, 1976, 248–49.
25 *The Constitution of Liberty*, 1960, 38.
26 *The Crowd*, [1895] 1960, 116.
27 *Tragic Sense of Life*, [1912] 1954, 25.
28 *Mind, Self and Society*, 1934, 334.
29 *Psychology*, 1892, chap. 16.
30 *Critique of Pure Reason*, 1781, Second Division, chap. III, sec. 7.
31 *The Life of Reason*, 1954, 70.
32 *On Aggression*, 1966, 248.
33 *Human Society in Ethics and Politics*, 1954, 8.
34 in *Moral Development Foundations*, D. Joy ed., 1983, 153.
35 *Epistles*, "To Lord Bathurst," 1733, line 155.
36 *A Treatise of Human Nature*, 1739, Book 2, part 3, sec. 3.
37 *The Passions*, 1976, xvi, 127.
38 *The Revolution of Hope*, 1968, 40.
39 *The Informed Heart*, 1960, viii.
40 *Pensées*, 1670, Sec. 4, 267, 277.
41 Ibid., Fragment 81.
42 *The Conservative Mind*, [1953] 1986, 41.
43 in *Yale Law Journal*, June, 1974, 1329.
44 *The Culture of Narcissism*, 1979, 132.
45 *Los Caprichos*, 1799, plate 43 [title].
46 *Tragic Sense of Life*, [1912] 1954, 293.
47 *The Future of Mankind*, 1961, 213, 280.
48 *Man for Himself*, 1947, 40–41.
49 *My Belief*, 1974, 195.
50 *The Rebel*, [1954] 1967, 104.
51 in *Sanctions for Evil*, N. Sanford ed., 1971, 195.
52 in *Christian Century*, 77, Apr. 13, 1960, 439–41.
53 *The Nature and Destiny of Man*, 1949, vol. 1, 28.
54 *Table Talk*, 1569, CCCLIII.
55 *The Will to Power*, 1901, Book 1, I, sec. 12.
56 *Tragic Sense of Life*, [1912] 1954, 105.
57 *Psychological Reflections*, [1957] 1970, 160.
58 *The Mermaid and the Minotaur*, 1976, 109.
59 *Orthodoxy*, [1908] 1959, 32.
60 *Memories, Dreams, Reflections*, 1961, 302.
61 *The Fate of the Earth*, 1982, 156.
62 *Uncle Vanya*, 1897, act 2.
63 *One-Dimensional Man*, 1964, 169.
64 *The Closing of the American Mind*, 1987, 262.
65 *The Betrayal of the West*, 1978, 165–69.
66 Ibid., 149.

~ Religion ~

1 *Man's Search for Himself*, 1953, 210.
2 *The Unconscious God*, 1975, 13.

3 *Civilization and Its Discontents*, [1930] 1962, 23.
4 *Ideas and Opinions*, 1954, 42.
5 *The Sacred and the Profane*, 1959, 44, 106.
6 *The Varieties of Religious Experience*, [1902] 1958, 54.
7 *Science and the Modern World*, 1925, 275.
8 *The Life of Reason*, 1954, 262.
9 *Science and the Modern World*, 1925, 276.
10 *The Basic Writings of C. G. Jung*, 1959, 421.
11 *The Life of Reason*, 1954, 181.
12 *The Decline of the West*, [1932] 1965, 184.
13 *On Human Nature*, 1978, 169.
14 *The Study of History*, [1934] 1972, 295.
15 *Reflections on the Revolution in France*, 1790, 135.
16 in *Saturday Review*, Apr. 5, 1969, 24.
17 in *From Max Weber*, H. Gerth, 1946, 281.
18 in *Gesammelte politische Schriften*, 1921, 554.
19 "The Undiscovered Self" [1957] in *Collected Works*, vol. 10, par. 565.
20 *Summerhill*, 1960, 245.
21 *The Age of Ideology*, 1956, 230.
22 *Moral Man and Immoral Society*, 1932, 62, 257.
23 *The Duality of Human Existence*, 1966, 234–35.
24 *The Elementary Forms of the Religious Life*, 1912, 323.
25 *The Image*, 1956, 123–28.
26 *The Heart of Man*, 1964, 88.
27 *The Will to Believe*, 1896, sec. X.
28 *The Power of Positive Thinking*, 1952, 175.
29 *A Study of History*, [1934] 1972, 333.
30 *Self, God, and Immortality*, 1986, 194.
31 in *Living Philosophies*, C. Fadiman ed., 1931, 39.
32 *The Essence of Christianity*, [1841] 1957, 2.
33 *Dialogues of Alfred North Whitehead*, 1954, 134.
34 *Love in the Western World*, [1940] 1956, 67.
35 *The Mass Psychology of Fascism*, 1946, 125.
36 *The Psychology of Moral Behaviour*, 1971, 232.
37 *The War Myth*, 1967, 130, 137.
38 *Has Religion Made Useful Contributions to Civilization?*, 1930, 26.
39 *Pensées*, 1670, No. 813.
40 "Getting Married," 1911.
41 *On Human Nature*, 1978, 175.
42 *The Varieties of Religious Experience*, [1902] 1958, 263.
43 *The Influence of Darwin on Philosophy*, 1910.
44 *Home Is Where We Start From*, 1986, 14.
45 *Beliefs, Attitudes, and Values*, 1968, 193.
46 *Thoughts on Various Subjects*, 1711, line 1.
47 *A Vindication of Women*, 1792, chap. 12.
48 *The Naked Ape*, 1969, 158.
49 *Civilization and Its Discontents*, 1930, 21.
50 quoted in *The Philosophy of "As If*," H. Vaihinger, 1935, 318.
51 *The Art of Loving*, 1956, 67.
52 *The Minimal Self*, 1984, 164–66.
53 in *Explorations in Altruistic Love and Behavior*, P. Sorokin ed., 1950, 152.
54 *A Study of History*, [1934] 1972, 348.
55 *Process and Reality*, [1929] 1978, 16.
56 *Becoming*, 1955, 94.
57 *The World and the Individual*, 1900, 78.
58 *The Denial of Death*, 1973, 203.
59 *Signs of the Times*, 1829.
60 *I Believe*, C. Fadiman ed., 1940, 72.
61 *Psychology and Religion*, 1938, 75.
62 *A Contribution to the Critique of Hegel's Philosophy of Right*, 1843, introduction.
63 *Civilization and Its Discontents*, [1930] 1962, 28.
64 *The Social Brain*, 1985, 166–79.
65 *Group Psychology and the Analysis of the Ego*, 1929, postscript.
66 *The Hero with a Thousand Faces*, [1949] 1968, 164–165.
67 *The Triumph of the Therapeutic*, 1966, 34.
68 *The Myth of Mental Illness*, [1960] 1974, 255.
69 *The Politics of Ecstasy*, 1968, 223.
70 *Essays*, 1625, "Of Atheism."
71 *Collected Works*, 1958, vol. XI, 334.
72 *Folkways*, [1906] 1940, 103.
73 in *Christian Century*, 77, Apr. 13, 1960, 439–41.
74 *What America Means to Me*, 1947.
75 *Science and the Modern World*, 1925, 274.
76 Ibid., 270.
77 *The Savage Mind*, 1966, 221.
78 *Nature, Man, and Woman*, 1958, 33.
79 *The Quest for Being*, [1934] 1961, 125.
80 *Megatrends*, 1984, xxxi, 270.
81 *Understanding Media*, 1966, 144.
82 *The Sacred and the Profane*, 1959, 203, 213.
83 *Freud: The Mind of the Moralist*, 1961, 328.
84 *The Cultural Contradictions of Capitalism*, 1976, 30.
85 *The Varieties of Religious Experience*, [1902] 1958, 379.
86 *The Sacred and the Profane*, 1959, 210.
87 *The Changing Law*, 1953, 122.

Responsibility

1 *The Study of Man*, 1959, 71.
2 *Airman's Odyssey*, 1942, "Flight to Arras," chap. 22.
3 *Man's Search for Himself*, 1953, 276.
4 *The Constitution of Liberty*, 1960, 71–72.
5 *Obedience to Authority*, 1974, 11.
6 *Trials of War Criminals* [Nuremberg], 1946–49, XI, 303.
7 *Inside the Third Reich*, 1971, 19.
8 *Papers on the War*, 1972, 249, 295.
9 *Self-Deception*, 1969, 149.
10 *The Disowned Self*, 1971, 104, 111.
11 *Existentialism and Humanism*, 1948, 28.
12 *Being and Nothingness*, [1943] 1957, 553.
13 in *Determinism and Freedom in the Age of Modern Science*, New York University, 1961, 125.
14 *The Informed Heart*, 1960, 192.
15 *A Grammar of Politics*, [1925] 1938, 43.

Pages 298–305

16 in *Beyond Domination*, C. Gould ed., 1983, 55–56.
17 in *Psychology of Women*, 1985, J. Williams ed., 187–188.
18 *The Female Eunuch*, 1970, 19.
19 *The Power Elite*, 1956, 342, 353, 361.
20 *Preparing for the Twenty-First Century*, 1993, 64.
21 *Computer Power and Human Reason*, 1976, 241.
22 *The Structure of Evil*, 1968, 39.
23 *The Sacred and the Profane*, 1959, 93.
24 *The Greening of America*, 1970, 16, 74.
25 *Our Inner Conflicts*, [1945] 1966, 26.
26 *Post-Capitalist Society*, 1993, 97.
27 reporting to the "President's Commission for the Study of Ethical Problems in Medicine and Behavioral Research," 1982, 95 of "Splicing Life."
28 *Understanding Media*, 1966, 20.
29 *Personal Knowledge*, 1962, 309.
30 address to U.S. Congress, Nov., 1991.
31 *Post-Capitalist Society*, 1993, 13.

Sacred

1 *The Myth of the Machine*, 1967, 67.
2 *Twilight of Authority*, 1975, 78.
3 *The Sacred and the Profane*, 1959, 13.
4 *The Myth of the Eternal Return*, [1949] 1971, 11.
5 *On Civil Disobedience and Non-Violence*, [c. 1900] 1967, 258.
6 *The Sacred and the Profane*, 1959, 203.
7 *The Triumph of the Therapeutic*, 1966, 77.
8 *Capitalism, Socialism, and Democracy*, 1942, 144.
9 *The Technological Society*, 1964, 142–43.
10 *The Closing of the American Mind*, 1987, 214.
11 *Guilt*, 1985, 216.
12 *Eco-Philosophy*, 1981, 77.
13 *The Anatomy of Human Destructiveness*, 1973, 266.
14 *The Farther Reaches of Human Nature*, 1971, 279–89.
15 *The Cultural Contradictions of Capitalism*, 1976, 171.
16 *History of the Idea of Progress*, 1980, 357.
17 *Revolution from Within*, 1992, 314.
18 *My Life and Thought*, 1949, 271.
19 *I and Thou*, [1922] 1970, 128.
20 *The Anatomy of Human Destructiveness*, 1973, 197.

Sadism / Masochism

1 *The Anatomy of Human Destructiveness*, 1973, 233.
2 in *The Individual Psychology of Alfred Adler*, H. Ansbacher ed., 1956, chap. 4, sec. 3.
3 *The Heart of Man*, 1964, 32.
4 *Working Through Narcissism*, 1981, 63, 278.
5 *Political Ensembles*, 1985, 119.
6 *Escape from Freedom*, 1941, 165, 185.
7 *Working Through Narcissism*, 1981, 26, 42.
8 *Man for Himself*, 1960, 108.
9 *Maps of the Mind*, 1981, 50.
10 *For the Love of Life*, 1986, 121.
11 in *Maps of the Mind*, C. Hampden-Turner, 1981, 177.
12 *The Peaceable Sex*, 1987, 8–9.
13 *Gyn/Ecology*, 1978, 1978, 96.
14 *Human Aggression*, 1968, ix, 99.
15 *Identity*, 1968, 284.
16 *The Psychology of Woman*, vol. 2, 1945, 81.
17 *The Myth of Women's Masochism*, 1985, 9.
18 *The Psychoanalytic Review*, vol. 22, 1935, 62.
19 *Being and Nothingness*, [1943] 1957, 379.
20 *The Superego*, 1952, 47.
21 *Studies in the Psychology of Sex*, 1903, 94.
22 *Being and Nothingness*, [1943] 1957, 378.
23 *The Bonds of Love*, 1988, 72.
24 *Being and Nothingness*, [1943] 1957, 399, 405.
25 *The Anatomy of Human Destructiveness*, 1973, 194.
26 in *Sexual Politics of Gender*, 1981, 60.
27 *The Bonds of Love*, 1988, 69.
28 *Studies in the Psychology of Sex*, 1903, 126, 137.
29 *Working Through Narcissism*, 1981, 6.
30 *For Your Own Good*, 1984, 163.
31 *The Nature of Woman*, 1980, 44.
32 *Sand and Foam*, 1926, 56.

Science

1 *A Brief History of Time*, 1988, 9–10.
2 *The Logic of Scientific Discovery*, [1934] 1968, 15.
3 *The Origin of Consciousness in the Breakdown of the Bicameral Mind*, 1976, 435.
4 *The Decline of the West*, [1932] 1965, 190.
5 *Ideas and Opinions*, 1954, 46.
6 Ibid., 40.
7 *The View from Nowhere*, 1986, 9.
8 *The Image*, 1956, 164.
9 *Tragic Sense of Life*, [1912] 1954, 103.
10 *The Making of a Counter Culture*, 1969, 211.
11 *The Minimal Self*, 1984, 192.
12 *The Psychology of Science*, 1966, 139.
13 *Science, Liberty, and Peace*, 1946, 36–37.
14 *Order Out of Chaos*, 1984, 6.
15 *Life Against Death*, 1966, 303.
16 *The Stress of Life*, 1976, 460.
17 *Gargantua and Pantagruel*, 1534, Book 2, chap. 8.
18 *Self, God, and Immortality*, 1986, 5.
19 *Generation of Vipers*, 1942, 278.
20 *The Phenomenon of Man*, [1940] 1959, 52.
21 *The Basic Writings of C. G. Jung*, 1959, 90, 481.
22 attributed in *More Random Walks in Science*, R. Weber, 1982, 48.
23 *The Gutenberg Galaxy*, 1962, 276.
24 address at Washington University, St. Louis, October 5, 1954.
25 in *Science*, vol. 124, Nov. 30, 1956, 1062.
26 *Maps of the Mind*, 1981, 22.

Pages 305–11

27 *Motivation and Personality*, 1954, 6.
28 *Personal Knowledge*, 1962, 171.
29 *Scientific Autobiography*, 1949, 33–34.
30 *Against Method*, 1975, 296.
31 Ibid., 299.
32 *The Structure of Scientific Revolutions*, 1962, 150.
33 *The Image*, 1956, 71.
34 *Gaia*, [1979] 1987, vii.
35 *Marriage and Morals*, [1929] 1959, 184.
36 *The Logic of Scientific Discovery*, [1934] 1968, 281.
37 *The Will to Believe*, 1896, sec. VII.
38 *Mind and Nature*, 1979, 31–32.
39 *Process and Reality*, [1929] 1978, 274.
40 in *Intelligence in the Modern World*, J. Rattner ed., 1939, 359.
41 *The Politics of Ecstasy*, 1968, 299.
42 *The Quest for Certainty*, [1929] 1960, 310.
43 *The Mismeasure of Man*, 1981, 74.
44 *The Quest for Certainty*, [1929] 1960, 274.
45 *Education*, 1861, chap. 2.
46 in *Analysis of the Phenomena of the Human Mind*, J. S. Mill, 1869, vol. 1, VII.
47 quoted in *The Cerebral Symphony*, W. Calvin, 1990, 122.
48 *The Philosophy of "As If,"* 1935, 175.
49 *Man in the Modern Age*, [1931] 1951, 137.
50 *The Myth of the Machine*, 1970, 74.
51 *Order Out of Chaos*, 1984, 76.
52 *The Varieties of Religious Experience*, [1902] 1958, 391.
53 *John Dewey*, 1959, 22–23.
54 *Democracy and Education*, [1916] 1961, 189.
55 Ibid., 230.
56 *America As a Civilization*, 1957, 209.
57 *An Essay on Man*, [1944] 1970, 229.
58 *The Rich Nations and the Poor Nations*, 1962, 155.
59 *The Triumph of the Therapeutic*, 1966, 93.
60 *Order Out of Chaos*, 1984, 33.
61 *Life Against Death*, 1966, 317.
62 *Generation of Vipers*, 1942, 179.
63 *Where Is Science Going?*, 1932, 167.
64 *Ends and Means*, 1938, 268.
65 *Modes of Thought*, [1938] 1969, 44.
66 *Order Out of Chaos*, 1984, 55.
67 *Civilization*, 1969, 344.
68 in *Monthly Review*, May, 1949, "Why Socialism," par. 5.
69 *The History of Science and the New Humanism*, 1962, 185.
70 *Science and the Modern World*, 1925, 291.
71 *The Philosophy of Moral Development*, 1981, 30.
72 *Computer Power and Human Reason*, 1976, 14.
73 in *Man Alone*, E. Josephson ed., 1962, 287–88.
74 *Science and Human Values*, [1956] 1965, 70.
75 *The Division of Labor in Society*, [1893] 1964, 52.
76 *The Cosmic Code*, 1983, 311.
77 *The Psychology of Science*, 1966, xvi.
78 in *Science*, Jan. 28, 1910.
79 *Where Is Science Going?*, 1932, 169.
80 *Way to Wisdom*, 1951, 91.
81 *The Revolt of the Masses*, 1932, 84.
82 *Icarus, or the Future of Science*, 1924, 57.
83 *Eco-Philosophy*, 1981, 70.
84 *The Fate of the Earth*, 1982, 106.
85 *Marriage and Morals*, [1929] 1959, 181.
86 *Strength to Love*, 1963, chap. 7.
87 *Boredom or Doom in a Scientific World*, 1948, 16.
88 in *Living Philosophies*, C. Fadiman ed., 1931, 19.
89 *Gyn/Ecology*, 1978, 103.
90 *The Human Revolution*, 1972, 158.
91 Albert Einstein, in *Where Is Science Going?*, M. Planck, 1932, 209.
92 *The Science to Save Us from Science*, 1950, 33.
93 *The Will to Believe*, 1896, sec. IX.
94 *The Philosophy of Rudolf Carnap*, 1963.
95 *Newtonian Studies*, 1968, 23–24.
96 *Small Is Beautiful*, 1973, 87.
97 *The Philosopher's Stone*, 1991, 14.
98 *An Essay on Man*, 1970, 160.
99 *So Human an Animal*, 1968, 220–22.
100 *A Sand County Almanac*, 1949, 154.
101 *The Need for Roots*, 1952, 250.
102 *The Phenomenon of Man*, [1940] 1959, 284.
103 in *From Max Weber*, H. Gerth, 1946, 142–43.
104 *Against Method*, 1975, 298–99.
105 "The Philosophy of Science" in *British Philosophy in the Mid-Century*, C. Mace, 1957.
106 *Philosophy in a New Key*, [1942] 1957, 202.

Self

1 *The Minimal Self*, 1984, 20, 163, 184.
2 *How Does Analysis Cure?*, 1984, 143, 147.
3 *The Ego and the Self*, 1951, 82.
4 *Collected Works*, 1967, vol. 13, 45.
5 *Being and Time*, [1931] 1962, 312.
6 quoted in *Existence*, R. May, 1958, 69.
7 *Collected Works*, 1953, vol. 7, 238.
8 *Man in the Modern Age*, [1931] 1951, 196.
9 *The Birth and Death of Meaning*, 1962, 53.
10 in *New Knowledge in Human Values*, A. Maslow ed., 1959, 108.
11 *An Essay Concerning Human Understanding*, 1694, Book 2, chap. 27.
12 *The Dragons of Eden*, 1977, 98.
13 *Introduction to Psychology*, 1986, 189.
14 *Man in the Modern Age*, [1931] 1951, 182.
15 "John Galt" in *Atlas Shrugged*, 1957, 1030.
16 [1913] quoted in *The Human Soul*, K. Konig, 1973, 67.
17 *The Human Soul*, [1959] 1973, 68.
18 *The Conservative Mind*, [1953] 1986, 420.
19 [1974] in *The Search for the Self*, P. Ornstein ed., 1978, 757.
20 *Self-Esteem and Meaning*, 1984, 108, 194.

Pages 317–23

23 *The Ego and the Self*, 1951, 112.
24 quoted in *The Divine Supermarket*, M. Ruthven, 1989, 187.
25 Ibid., 189.
26 *The End of History and the Last Man*, 1992, 303.
27 "John Galt" in *Atlas Shrugged*, 1957, 1021.
28 *Being and Loving*, 1978, 80.
29 *Ethics*, 1675, Part 4, prop. 52.
30 *Revolution from Within*, 1992, 26.

Sex

1 *Studies in the Psychology of Sex*, [1897] 1936, vol. 1, xxx.
2 *The Sexual Revolution*, [1929] 1974, xxvi.
3 *The Basic Writings of C. G. Jung*, 1959, 534.
4 *The Stormy Search for the Self*, 1990, 32.
5 *The Politics of Ecstasy*, 1968, 231.
6 [d. 1930] "Fantasia of the Unconscious."
7 in Plato's *Symposium*, 205e.
8 *Birth Without Violence*, 1975, 62.
9 *Coming to Our Senses*, 1989, 44.
10 *The Mermaid and the Minotaur*, 1976, 60–61.
11 *What Do Women Want?*, 1983, 137–39.
12 *Thinking in the Shadow of Feelings*, 1988, 156.
13 *Love and Hate*, 1972, 151.
14 *The Myth of Two Minds*, 1987, 180.
15 *Tragic Sense of Life*, [1912] 1954, 137.
16 *The Mothers*, 1931, 51.
17 *Understanding Women*, 1985, 155.
18 *The Psychology of Woman*, vol. 2, 1945, 77.
19 *The Naked Ape*, 1969, 56–58.
20 *The Warriors*, [1959] 1970, 78.
21 in *The Vancouver Sun*, Oct. 2, 1993, sec. B6.
22 quoted in *Happiness in Marriage*, M. Sanger, [1926] 1969, 186.
23 *The Art of Loving*, 1956, 36.
24 *The Broken Connection*, 1979, 31.
25 *Sexual Personae*, 1990, 13.
26 *The First Sex*, 1971, 153.
27 Konigsberg lecture, 1775.
28 *A Vindication of the Rights of Woman*, 1791, chap. 4.
29 letter [June 14, 1860] in *Elizabeth Cady Stanton*, 1922, vol. 2, 82.
30 *Toward a Feminist Theory of the State*, 1989, 137.
31 *Right-Wing Women*, 1983, 144.
32 *Parisian Review*, Spring, 1967, 202.
33 *Toward a Feminist Theory of the State*, 1989, 140.
34 *The Rebel*, [1954] 1067, 44.
35 *Sexual Personae*, 1990, 22.
36 Ibid., 234.
37 *Sexual Politics*, 1971, 45.
38 *Sexual Personae*, 1990, 2.
39 *Right-Wing Women*, 1983, 83–84.
40 *The Mass Psychology of Fascism*, 1946, 74–75.
41 in *Partisan Review* 40, no. 2, 1973, 188.
42 *Right-Wing Women*, 1983, 91.
43 *The Culture of Narcissism*, 1979, 320.
44 *The Failure of the Sexual Revolution*, 1974, 54.
45 *Sex and Destiny*, 1984, 235.
46 *The Feminine Mystique*, 1963, 226.
47 [1913] in *Collected Works*, vol. 4, par. 440.
48 *Generation of Vipers*, 1942, 57.
49 in *Esquire*, Dec., 1970.
50 *The Most of Malcolm Muggeridge*, 1966, 35.
51 in *New York Times Magazine*, Mar. 24, 1968.
52 [1914] in *Collected Works*, vol. 4, par. 666.
53 *Sexual Personae*, 1990, 3.
54 Ibid., 98.
55 *On the Democratic Idea in America*, 1972, 36.
56 *The Unconscious God*, 1975, 86.
57 *Sexual Personae*, 1990, 19.
58 *Happiness in Marriage*, [1926] 1969, 20.
59 *The Unconscious God*, 1975, 89.
60 *A Vindication of the Rights of Woman*, 1792, chap. 13, sec. 6.
61 *The Feminine Mystique*, 1963, 261, 281.
62 *The Pursuit of Loneliness*, [1970] 1976, 92.
63 *The Problem of Being Human*, 1974, 161.
64 *Modern Man in Search of a Soul*, 1933, 138–39.
65 quoted in *On the Democratic Idea in America*, I. Kristol, 1972, 34.
66 *The Descent of Woman*, 1972, 247.
67 *Eros and Civilization*, [1955] 1966, xiii.
68 *Woman and Socialism*, 1910, 204.
69 in *I Believe*, C. Fadiman ed., 1940, 374.
70 *America As a Civilization*, 1957, 679.
71 *Folkways*, 1906, 297–98.
72 *Man in the Modern Age*, [1931] 1951, 185.
73 *Studies in the Psychology of Sex*, [1910] 1936, vol. 1, part 1, 310.
74 *The Pursuit of Loneliness*, [1970] 1976, 91.
75 *The Mass Psychology of Fascism*, 1946, 25–26.
76 *Ends and Means*, 1938, 316.
77 *Summerhill*, 1960, 206.
78 *Marriage and Morals*, [1929] 1959, 208.
79 *The Second Stage*, 1981, 310.
80 *The Primal Scream*, [1970] 1980, 285.
81 *Studies in the Psychology of Sex*, [1897] 1936, vol. 4, 132.
82 *Summerhill*, 1960, 214.
83 *Marriage and Morals*, [1929] 1959, 199–200.
84 in *The Vancouver Sun*, Oct. 2, 1993, sec. B6.
85 *Love and Will*, 1969, 107.
86 *The Second Sin*, 1973, "Sex."
87 *The Betrayal of the West*, 1978, 154.
88 *Love and Will*, 1969, 71.
89 *The Dialectic of Sex*, 1970, 68.
90 in *Saturday Review*, Mar. 26, 1966, 19.
91 *Narcissism*, 1983, 10.
92 *The Fall of Public Man*, 1977, 9.
93 *Narcissism*, 1983, 123.
94 quoted in *The Problem of Being Human*, L. Averill, 1974, 215.
95 *Totem and Taboo*, [1913] 1950, 144.

96 *Sociobiology*, 1980, 155.
97 [d. 479 B.C.] *Analects*, Book XV, 12.
98 *Tragic Sense of Life*, [1912] 1954, 133.
99 *The Eternal Now*, 1963, 16–17.
100 *Freud: The Mind of the Moralist*, 1961, 172.
101 *Supplements to the World as Will and Idea*, 1844, chap. XLIV.
102 *Complete Works*, 1957, vol. XI, 188–89.
103 *Understanding Women*, 1985, 156.
104 *Tragic Sense of Life*, [1912] 1954, 135.
105 *Marriage and Morals*, [1929] 1959, 134.
106 *Home Is Where We Start From*, 1986, 46.
107 *Technology and Justice*, 1986, 51.
108 *Nature, Man, and Woman*, 1958, 172.
109 *The Closing of the American Mind*, 1987, 106.
110 *Collected Papers*, [1912] 1959, vol. 4, 213.
111 *Death-Camp to Existentialism*, 1959, 100.
112 *Sexual Personae*, 1990, 20.
113 *Being and Nothingness*, [1943] 1957, 613–14.

Society

1 *Commentaries on the Laws of England*, 1765, Introduction, sec. 2.
2 *The Betrayal of the West*, 1978, 41.
3 *The Hero with a Thousand Faces*, [1949] 1968, 383.
4 *Meditations*, [c. 161–80 A.D.], Book 5, XV.
5 *Suicide*, [1897] 1951, 213.
6 *Politics*, Book 1, chap. 2.
7 *What Life Should Mean to You*, 1931, 8.
8 *Politics*, Book 1, chap. 2.
9 *Science and the Modern World*, 1925, 295.
10 *Auguste Comte and Positivism*, [1842] 1975, 270.
11 *Tragic Sense of Life*, [1912] 1954, 26.
12 *The Language of the Heart*, 1985, 270–75.
13 *A Study of History*, [1934] 1972, 43.
14 *Structural Anthropology*, 1963, 296.
15 *On Human Nature*, 1978, 156.
16 *Reflections on the Revolution in France*, 1790, 143.
17 *The Imperial Animal*, 1974, 80.
18 *Obedience to Authority*, 1974, 124.
19 *The Triumph of the Therapeutic*, 1966, 81.
20 *Woman and Socialism*, 1910, 367.
21 *The Fable of the Bees*, [1724] 1970, 81.
22 *Common Sense*, 1776, 1.
23 *Science and Human Values*, [1956] 1965, 44.
24 Ibid., 64.
25 *Motivation and Personality*, 1954, 321.
26 *The Denial of Death*, 1973, 45.
27 *Mind, Self and Society*, 1934, 327–28.
28 *The Study of Man*, 1959, 67.
29 *Woman and Socialism*, 1910, 401.
30 [1963] in *Quotations from Chairman Mao*, 1967, chap. 22.
31 *The Acquisitive Society*, 1920, 51.
32 in *Experimentation with Human Subjects*, P. Freund, 1970, 12.
33 *The Conservative Mind*, [1953] 1986, 68.
34 *Meditations*, [c. 161–80 A.D.], Book V, XXX.
35 *Eco-Philosophy*, 1981, 42.
36 *Reflections on Life*, 1952.
37 *The Greening of America*, 1970, 128.
38 *Sex and Destiny*, 1984, 76.
39 *The Meaning of the 20th Century*, 1964, 145.
40 "Science and Culture," 1880.
41 *The Fall of Public Man*, 1977, 314.
42 in *Women's Own*, Oct. 31, 1987.
43 *The Life of Reason*, 1954, 111.
44 *The Gay Science*, 1882, s. 356.
45 *Moral Man and Immoral Society*, 1932, 82.
46 *Democracy in America*, [1835] 1966, 488.

Soul

1 [1935] in *Collected Works*, vol. 9, Part I, par. 56.
2 *Metaphysics*, 6, 11.
3 *The Human Soul*, 1973, 15, 16, 70.
4 *Mankind and Mother Earth*, 1976, 19.
5 *Diary of a Writer*, vol. 1, Dec. 1876, chap. 1, sec. 3.
6 in *Crimes of War*, R. Lifton ed., 1971, 481–82.
7 *I and Thou*, [1922] 1970, 78–79.
8 *Tragic Sense of Life*, [1912] 1954, 80.
9 *Psychology*, 1892, chap. 12.
10 quoted in *The New Yorker*, Apr. 24, 1971.
11 *Modern Man in Search of a Soul*, 1933, 203.
12 in *The Wisdom of the Dream*, S. Segaller, 1989, 179.
13 *The Realm of Spirit*, 1940, 53.
14 *The Politics of Ecstasy*, 1968, 220.
15 *The Works of William James*, vol. 1, [1890] 1981, 332.
16 *The Decline of the West*, [1918] 1962, 159.
17 *The Realm of Spirit*, 1940, 16.
18 *Making Sense of Suffering*, 1990, 8.
19 *My Belief*, [1917] 1974, 44–45.
20 *Critique of Pure Reason*, 1781, Sec. Div., chap. III, sec. 7.
21 [1944] in *Collected Works*, vol. 12, par. 14.
22 *Good and Evil*, 1961, 130.
23 *The Human Soul*, 1973, 91.
24 *Foreign Review*, 1828, no. 111.
25 *Phaedo*, by Plato, 107.
26 *Nicomachean Ethics*, Book 1, 1098a, 16–20.
27 *And the Life Everlasting*, 1934, 204.
28 *Tragic Sense of Life*, [1912] 1954, 12.
29 *The Prophet*, 1923, 33.
30 [1903], *The Basic Writings of Bertrand Russell*, 1961, 71.
31 *Culture Against Man*, 1965, 393.
32 *Holy Bible*, Matthew 10:28.
33 *The Realm of Spirit*, 1940, 124.
34 *Generation of Vipers*, 1942, 7.
35 *The Gutenberg Galaxy*, 1962, 30.
36 [1944] in *Collected Works*, vol. 12, par. 126.
37 *Memories, Dreams, Reflections*, 1961, 333.
38 quoted in *Oui*, "Conversations with Indira Gandhi," 1975.

39 in *Living Philosophies*, C. Fadiman ed., 1931, 109.
40 *For Your Own Good*, 1984, 279.
41 *La Nouvelle Héloïse*, 1761, Part 2, letter 11.

Spirit

1 *The Sickness Unto Death*, [1849] 1944, 17.
2 *The Unconscious God*, 1975, 23.
3 *Experience and Nature*, [1925] 1958, 294.
4 *Holy Bible*, II Corinthians 3:6.
5 *Candida*, 1898, act 1.
6 *The Realm of Spirit*, 1940, 1.
7 *Works of Love*, [1847] 1962, 205.
8 "Woman in Europe," 1927.
9 *I and Thou*, [1937] 1970, 85–89.
10 Ibid., 89.
11 *The Sickness Unto Death*, [1849] 1944, 17.
12 *The Realm of Spirit*, 1940, 161.
13 *The Absorbent Mind*, [1949] 1984, 143.
14 *The Realm of Spirit*, 1940, 12.
15 *The Life of Reason*, 1954, 264.
16 *I and Thou*, [1922] 1970, 99.
17 *Holy Bible*, Galatians 5:22.
18 *Love in the Western World*, [1940] 1956, 238.
19 *Language and Myth*, 1946, 99.
20 *Science and the Modern World*, [1925] 1957, 29.
21 *The Realm of Spirit*, 1940, 251.
22 *My Life and Thought*, 1949, 268.
23 *The Farther Reaches of Human Nature*, 1971, 325.
24 *The Need for Roots*, 1952, 180.
25 *The Being of Man and His Future Evolution*, [1908] 1981, 59.
26 *The Stormy Search for the Self*, 1990, 1.
27 *The Road Less Traveled*, 1979, 193.
28 [d. 1930] "The Two Principles."
29 *The Stormy Search for the Self*, 1990, 40.
30 *The Aquarian Conspiracy*, 1980, 363.
31 *The Courage to Be*, 1952, 46.
32 "Woman in Europe," 1927.
33 *The Varieties of Religious Experience*, [1902] 1958, 195.
34 *Totem and Taboo*, [1913] 1950, 94.
35 *Tragic Sense of Life*, [1912] 1954, 9.
36 *I and Thou*, [1922] 1970, 103.
37 *Wealth and Poverty*, 1981, 216.
38 *Eco-Philosophy*, 1981, 10.
39 *The Stormy Search for the Self*, 1990, 1.
40 *The Sickness Unto Death*, [1849] 1944, 17.
41 *Modern Man in Search of a Soul*, 1933, 140.
42 *The Wish for Kings*, 1993, 189.
43 *The Absorbent Mind*, [1949] 1984, 261.
44 *The Realm of Spirit*, 1940, 14.
45 [d. 43 B.C.] *De Republica*, Book 6, chap. 26.
46 *Eco-philosophy*, 1981, 34–35.
47 *The Conservative Mind*, [1953] 1986, 211.
48 *The Being of Man and His Future Evolution*, [1908] 1981, 78, 94.
49 *I Believe*, C. Fadiman ed., 1940, 218.

State

1 [1921] in *From Max Weber*, 1946, 78.
2 *The Origin of the Family, Private Property, and the State*, 1894, 117–18.
3 *The State and Revolution*, 1917, chap. 2, part 1.
4 [d. 1896] quoted in *The Rise and Fall of the Third Reich*, W. Shirer, 1960, 99.
5 *Paroles d'un Révolté*, 1884.
6 *Twilight of Authority*, 1975, 154.
7 in *From Max Weber*, H. Gerth, 1946, 124.
8 *Philosophy of Right*, [1821] 1967, 241.
9 introduction to *On War*, [1832] 1976, 77.
10 in *Contemporary Political Philosophers*, A. Crespigney ed., 1975, 177.
11 *Escape from Evil*, 1975, 119.
12 *The Philosophy of History*, [1837] 1900, 39.
13 [d. 1939] *Works*, II.
14 *The Revolt of the Masses*, 1932, 171.
15 *Essays*, 1625, "Of Vicissitude of Things."
16 *Mein Kampf*, [1924] 1943, 534.
17 *Politics Among Nations*, [1948] 1967, 155.
18 *Ideas and Opinions*, [1948]1954, 150.
19 *Leviathan*, 1651, chap. 13, 17.
20 *A Grammar of Politics*, [1925] 1938, 20.
21 *Politics*, Book 3, chap. 9.
22 *The Philosophy of Mind*, 1817, 1981, sec. 433.
23 in *Signs*, 1982, vol. 7, no. 3, 644–45.
24 *The Female Eunuch*, 1971, 140.
25 *The Need for Roots*, 1952, 109.
26 *Woman and Socialism*, 1910, 51.
27 *Communist Manifesto*, 1848.
28 *Radical Priorities*, 1981, 137.
29 *The Revolt of the Masses*, 1932, 122.
30 *Post-Capitalist Society*, 1993, 121.
31 quoted in *The State and Revolution*, V. I. Lenin, 1917, chap. 3, part 3.
32 *Mein Kampf*, [1924] 1943, 387.
33 *The Fate of the Earth*, 1982, 134.
34 *The Greening of America*, 1970, 128.
35 *Anarchy, State, and Utopia*, 1974, ix.
36 *The Mass Psychology of Fascism*, 1946, 243.
37 in *Collected Works*, 1964, vol. 25, 468.
38 *The State and Revolution*, 1917, chap. 5, part 2.
39 Ibid.
40 *The Rebel*, [1951] 1956, 177.
41 *Ends and Means*, 1938, 58.
42 *The Wish for Kings*, 1993, 189.
43 *Capitalism*, 1966, 30–36.
44 *The Prospects of Industrial Civilization*, 1923, 4.
45 *Moscow New Times*, Nov. 26, 1947.
46 [1945] *Ideas and Opinions*, 1954, 120.
47 [1948] *Ideas and Opinions*, 1954, 147.
48 *A Grammar of Politics*, [1925] 1938, 45.

~ Suffering & Challenge

1 *On Death and Dying*, 1969, 15.
2 *The Myth of the Eternal Return*, [1949] 1971, 96.
3 in *New Knowledge in Human Values*, A. Maslow ed., 1959, 182.
4 *Ends and Means*, 1938, 306.
5 [d. 1900], *Works*, vol. XIX, 352.
6 *Suicide*, [1897] 1951, 201.
7 *Modern Man in Search of a Soul*, 1933, 275.
8 *On Population*, 1798, chap. 19.
9 *Love in the Western World*, [1940] 1956, 51, 211.
10 *The Prophet*, 1923, 52.
11 [d. 456 B.C.], *Agamemnon*, line 177.
12 *The Realm of Spirit*, 1940, 127.
13 *The Basic Writings of Bertrand Russell*, [1903] 1961, 69.
14 *Modern Man in Search of a Soul*, 1933, 278.
15 Ibid., 248.
16 *Adam Bede*, 1859, chap. 42.
17 *Man in the Modern Age*, [1931] 1951, 145.
18 *The Quest for Certainty*, [1929] 1960, 244.
19 *So Human an Animal*, 1968, 161.
20 in *The Literary World*, Aug. 17, 24, 1850.
21 *Tragic Sense of Life*, [1912] 1954, 131.
22 *The End of History and the Last Man*, 1992, 330.
23 *The Revolt of the Masses*, 1932, 99.
24 *The Realm of Spirit*, 1940, 71.
25 *Dear Theo: An Autobiography*, 1937, 20.
26 *The Realm of Spirit*, 1940, 66.
27 *The Moon and Sixpence*, 1919, chap. 4.
28 "The Transcendent Function," *Collected Works*, 1969, VIII, 73.
29 *Waiting On God*, 1951, 64.
30 *The Realm of Spirit*, 1940, 270.
31 *Autobiographies*, 1926, 234.
32 *The Road Less Traveled*, 1979, 16.
33 *The Sickness Unto Death*, [1849] 1944, 38.
34 *Tragic Sense of Life*, [1912] 1954, 43.
35 *The World As I See It*, 1934.
36 *The Rebel*, [1954] 1967, 207.
37 *The Power of Myth*, 1988, 160.
38 *De Profundis*, 1897.
39 *The Pursuit of Loneliness*, [1970] 1976, 158.
40 *Modern Man in Search of a Soul*, 1933, 108.
41 *Tragic Sense of Life*, [1912] 1954, 141.
42 *Culture Against Man*, 1965, 10.
43 *Tragic Sense of Life*, [1912] 1954, 212.
44 *The World and the Individual*, 1900, 381.
45 *Tragic Sense of Life*, [1912] 1954, 204.
46 *De Profundis*, 1897.
47 *Tragic Sense of Life*, [1912] 1954, 205.
48 *De Profundis*, 1897.

~ Symbols ~

1 *The Natural History of the Mind*, 1936, 279.
2 *Philosophy in a New Key*, [1942] 1957, 40–41.
3 *The Image*, 1956, 44.
4 *An Essay on Man*, [1944] 1970, 26–27.
5 *Icon and Image*, [1954] 1965, 122.
6 *The Condition of Man*, 1973, 9.
7 *Frames of Mind*, 1983, 300.
8 *Public Opinion*, [1922] 1957, 238–39.
9 Ibid., 235.
10 in *The Dehumanization of Man*, A. Montagu, 1983, 110.
11 *Philosophy in a New Key*, [1942] 1957, 290.
12 *Existence*, 1958, 75–76.
13 *The Quest for Certainty*, [1929] 1960, 161.
14 *The Sacred and the Profane*, 1959, 211.
15 *Philosophy in a New Key*, [1942] 1957, 200.
16 *Language and Myth*, 1946, 8.
17 *Science and Human Values*, [1956] 1965, 36.
18 *The Quest for Certainty*, [1929] 1960, 158.
19 *The Decline of the West*, [1932] 1965, 87.
20 *The Hero with a Thousand Faces*, [1949] 1968, 236.
21 *Being and Nothingness*, [1943] 1957, 579.
22 *Process and Reality*, [1929] 1978, 180.
23 *Mind, Self, and Society*, 1934, 181.
24 in *An Anthropologist at Work*, M. Mead, [1909] 1959, 116.
25 *Order Out of Chaos*, 1984, 312.
26 *Modern Man in Search of a Soul*, 1933, 129.
27 *The Hero with a Thousand Faces*, [1949] 1968, 251.
28 *The Life of Reason*, 1954, 223.
29 *The Broken Connection*, 1979, 293.
30 *Philosophy in a New Key*, [1942] 1957, 292.
31 *The Triumph of the Therapeutic*, 1966, 65.

~ Technology ~

1 *Entropy*, [1980] 1989, 94–95.
2 *Future Shock*, 1970, 387, 399.
3 *Maps of the Mind*, 1981, 59.
4 *The Broken Connection*, 1979, 430.
5 quoted in *Men Who Play God*, N. Moss, 1968, 20–21.
6 *The Technological Society*, 1964, xv, 14, 138.
7 from Nuremberg Tribunal documents, 1947–49.
8 *Megatrends*, 1984, 51.
9 *The Real World of Technology*, 1990, 24–25.
10 *Philosophy in a New Key*, [1942] 1957, 292.
11 in *Encounter*, Jan., 1968, vol. XXX, no. 1, 19.
12 *The New Left*, 1975, 142–45.
13 *Der Mensch und die Technik*, 1932, 14.
14 in *The Futurists*, A. Toffler ed., 1972, 304.
15 *Critical Path*, 1981, XXVII.
16 *Understanding Media*, 1966, 55, 64, 196.
17 in *Daedalus*, 1965, vol. 94, 223–44.
18 *For the Love of Life*, 1986, 29–30.

Pages 340–46

19 *Sweet Suffering*, 1984, 22.
20 *Coming to Our Senses*, 1989, 82.
21 *The Cultured Man*, 1958, 36.
22 *Saturday Review*, April 5, 1969, 24.
23 *The Pursuit of Loneliness*, [1970] 1976, 57–58.
24 *One-Dimensional Man*, 1964, 168.
25 *A Study of History*, [1934] 1972, 48.
26 *Technology and Empire*, 1969, 27.
27 *The Pursuit of Loneliness*, 1970, 26.
28 *The Informed Heart*, 1960, 62.
29 *Freud: The Mind of the Moralist*, 1961, 391–92.
30 *Love and Will*, 1969, 97.
31 *Understanding Media*, 1966, 33, 265.
32 *Crimes of War*, 1971, 574.
33 *The Greening of America*, 1970, 5.
34 *New Knowledge in Human Values*, 1959.
35 *Technology and Justice*, 1986, 32.
36 *Beyond 1984: The Vassar Symposium*, 1985, 1.
37 in *Science and Moral Priority*, R. Sperry, 1983, 142.
38 *Megatrends*, 1984, 36.
39 *Gaia*, [1979] 1987, 127–28.
40 *Future Shock*, 1970, 383.
41 *The Gutenberg Galaxy*, 1962, 254.
42 *The Real World of Technology*, 1990, 14.
43 *America As a Civilization*, 1957, 227.
44 *Computer Power and Human Reason*, 1976, 126.
45 speech to German Information Society, Stuttgart, Oct. 11, 1990.
46 *The Pursuit of Loneliness*, [1970] 1976, 58.
47 *One-Dimensional Man*, 1964, 248.
48 *Technopoly*, 1993, 179.
49 *The Pursuit of Loneliness*, [1970] 1976, 181.
50 in *Cyberspace*, M. Benedikt ed., 1991, 74.
51 *Ends and Means*, 1938, 8.
52 *The Myth of the Machine*, 1970, 435.
53 *The Future of Mankind*, 1961, viii.
54 *An Inquiry into the Human Prospect*, 1975, 168.

Truth

1 *The Need for Roots*, 1952, 35.
2 *Science and Human Values*, [1956] 1965, 29.
3 in *New Knowledge in Human Values*, A. Maslow ed., 1959, 56.
4 *The Monadology*, 1714, sec. 29.
5 *The Great Divide*, 1988, 3.
6 *Folkways*, [1906] 1940, 529.
7 *Science and Human Values*, 1965, 57.
8 quoted in *Gerald Ford and the Future of the Presidency*, J. Terhorst, 1974, 188.
9 "Voice of America," Feb. 26, 1962.
10 *Selected Works*, 1962, vol. 4, 176.
11 *The Problem of Neurosis*, 1929, chap. 2.
12 *Pragmatism*, 1907, 78.
13 *The Statue Within*, 1988, 15.
14 *In A Different Voice*, 1982, 104, 149, 166.
15 *Human, All-Too-Human*, 1878, s. 483.
16 *Becoming*, 1955, 17.
17 "The Coming of Age of the Origin of Species," 1881.
18 in *Alfred Adler*, J. Rattner, 1983, 18.
19 *The True Believer*, 1951, 80.
20 *The Broken Connection*, 1979, 20.
21 *Concluding Unscientific Postscript*, [1846] 1944, 181.
22 *The Will to Power*, [1901] 1967, 298–99.
23 "Ideals and Doubts," *Illinois Law Review*, vol. x, 1915, par. 4.
24 *The Gutenberg Galaxy*, 1962, 268.
25 *A History of Western Philosophy*, 1945, 37.
26 [d. 475 B.C.] in *Xenophanes of Colophon*, J. Lesher, 1992, 25.
27 *Ends and Means*, 1938, 7.
28 *The Image*, 1956, 169.
29 *The Culture of Narcissism*, 1979, 141.
30 *The Image*, 1962, 205.
31 in *Signs*, 1983, vol. 8, no. 4, 640.
32 *Principles of Philosophy*, 1644, Part 1, no. 1.
33 *The Will to Believe*, 1896, sec. x.
34 *Personal Knowledge*, 1962, 305.
35 to Thomas Poole, Mar. 28, 1801.
36 *Being and Time*, [1931] 1962, 263–69.
37 Ibid., 262.
38 *The World and the Individual*, 1900, 296.
39 *Tragic Sense of Life*, [1912] 1954, 104.
40 *Éloge de la Philosophie*, 1960, 137.
41 *What Life Should Mean to You*, 1931, 4.
42 *Pragmatism*, 1907, 218.
43 *Sceptical Essays*, 1928, 63.
44 *Leaves of Grass*, 1855, preface.
45 *De Profundis*, 1897.
46 "The Coming of Age of the Origin of Species," 1881.
47 *Annajanska*, 1919, 262.
48 in *New York Times*, Oct. 20, 1957.
49 *The Realm of Spirit*, 1940, 105.
50 *Tragic Sense of Life*, [1912] 1954, 23.
51 *The Need for Roots*, 1952, 242.
52 [c. 335–288 B.C.] *The Golden Mean of Tze-sze.*
53 *The Political Writings of Harold D. Lasswell*, 1951, 175.
54 *The Biological Origin of Human Values*, 1977, 315, 331.
55 *The New Left*, 1975, 107.
56 *Human Knowledge*, 1948, 111.
57 *The Origin of Consciousness in the Breakdown of the Bicameral Mind*, 1976, 435.
58 *The Monadology*, 1714, 33.
59 "John Galt" in *Atlas Shrugged*, 1957, 1017.
60 *Man's Search for Himself*, 1953, 252.
61 *Thoughts*, [1670] 1962, fragment 214.
62 *The Decline of the West*, [1932] 1965, 287.
63 *Works of Love*, 1847, chap. 10, par. 17.
64 *An Essay Concerning Human Understanding*, 1690, Book 4, chap. 19, sec. 1.
65 *The Realm of Spirit*, 1940, 242.
66 *Ideas and Opinions*, 1954, 42.
67 *The Metaphysic of Ethics*, 1796, Book IV, Part I, chap. 2, sec. 9.

68 *Good and Evil*, 1953, 7.
69 Introduction to his translation of Plato's *Republic*, 1871.
70 *Summerhill*, 1960, 148.
71 *Evolution and Ethics*, 1896, 146.
72 *The Need for Roots*, 1952, 93.
73 "Prudence," in *Essays: First Series*, 1841.
74 *Heart of Darkness*, [1902] 1963, 27.
75 "Ode on a Grecian Urn," 1820, stanza 5.
76 *Good and Evil*, 1953, 13.
77 *Critical Path*, 1981, XXXVII.
78 *The Making of a Counter Culture*, 1969, 236.
79 *Holy Bible*, John 8:32.

Unconsciousness

1 [1942] in *Collected Works*, vol. 11, par. 280.
2 *Modern Man in Search of a Soul*, 1933, 190.
3 *The Basic Writings of C. G. Jung*, 1959, 407.
4 *Works*, vol. 5, [1900] 1953, 613.
5 *Works*, 1953, vol. 19, 13.
6 *Beyond Power*, 1985, 377.
7 *The Hidden Persuaders*, [1957] 1980, 1.
8 *The Gutenberg Galaxy*, 1962, 244–45.
9 in *Emotion*, R. Plutchik ed., 1980, 133.
10 *The Conquest of Happiness*, 1930, 76.
11 *Folkways*, [1906] 1940, 68.
12 *Psychology and Religion*, 1938, 45.
13 *The Road Less Traveled*, 1979, 251.
14 *Modern Man in Search of a Soul*, 1933, 69.
15 [d. 1832], in *Goethe's World View*, 1963, 103.
16 [1927] "Mind and Earth," in *Collected Works*, vol. 10, par. 103.
17 *Journal*, Oct. 28, 1833.
18 *Structural Anthropology*, 1963, 18–21.
19 *The Order of Things*, 1970, 364.
20 [1952] *Symbols of Transformation* in *Collected Works*, 1953, vol. 5, par. 652.
21 *The Human Soul*, [1959] 1973, 127.
22 *Computer Power and Human Reason*, 1976, 280.
23 *The Road Less Traveled*, 1979, 282.
24 [1934] in *Collected Works*, 1953, vol. 16, par. 329.
25 *Life Against Death*, 1966, x.
26 *The Informed Heart*, 1960, 15–18.
27 *The Hazards of Being Male*, 1977, 97.

Understanding

1 *Ethics*, 1675, Part 4, Appendix.
2 *The Stress of Life*, 1976, XVII.
3 *The First Three Minutes*, 1977, 154–55.
4 *The Stress of Life*, [1956] 1976, 361.
5 *Computer Power and Human Reason*, 1976, 16.
6 *Post-Capitalist Society*, 1993, 217.
7 *For Your Own Good*, 1984, 3.
8 *Nicomachean Ethics*, Book 6, chap. 10.
9 Washington speech, 1968.
10 *God, Guilt, and Death*, 1984, 6.
11 *Intelligence*, 1960, 102.
12 *The Life of Reason*, 1954, 392.
13 *The Origin of Consciousness*, 1976, 52.
14 *Concluding Unscientific Postscript*, 1846, chap. 3, part 4.
15 *Being and Time*, [1931] 1962, 183–88.
16 *The Study of Man*, 1959, 21, 39.
17 *Characteristics*, 1831, par. 7.
18 *The True Believer*, 1951, 79.
19 *The Quest for Self-Control*, 1965, 3.
20 *The Division of Labor in Society*, [1893] 1964, 238.
21 *What Life Should Mean to You*, 1931, 203.
22 *Corinne*, 1807, Book 18, chap. 5.
23 *The Divided Self*, 1960, 35.
24 *Alfred Adler*, 1983, 108.
25 *Human Society in Ethics and Politics*, 1954, 197.
26 *Ideas and Opinions*, 1954, 53.
27 in *Yale Review* 49, 1959, 270.
28 *Modes of Thought*, [1938] 1969, 45.
29 *Cannibals and Kings*, 1977, 289.
30 *Wealth and Poverty*, 1981, 255.
31 *The View from Nowhere*, 1986, 10.
32 [1909] in *An Anthropologist at Work*, M. Mead, 1959, 116.
33 *The Philosophy of "As If,"* 1935, 171.
34 *Creative Evolution*, [1907] 1944, 218.
35 *Ethics*, 1675, Part 4, prop. 28.

Unity / Wholeness

1 *Ends and Means*, 1938, 303.
2 *The Powers of Evil*, 1975, 261.
3 *The Rebel*, [1954] 1967, 100–01.
4 *Holy Bible*, John 4:16.
5 Ibid., Galatians 3:28.
6 *A Study of History*, [1934] 1972, 197.
7 *The Philosophy of Moral Development*, 1981, 344–45.
8 *The Phenomenon of Man*, 1965, 31.
9 *Memories, Dreams, Reflections*, 1961, 324.
10 *Utilitarianism*, 1859, chap. 3.
11 [d. 1832] quoted in *Love, Altruism, and World Crisis*, J. Matter, 1974, 75.
12 *What Life Should Mean to You*, 1931, 9.
13 *The Concept of Dread*, [1844] 1946, 26.
14 *Meaning in Life*, 1992, 100.
15 in *Goethe: Wisdom and Experience*, J. Weigand ed., [1787] 1964, 213.
16 *Tragic Sense of Life*, [1912] 1954, 8.
17 quoted in *The Nature of Human Consciousness*, R. Ornstein ed., 1973, 40.
18 *Home Is Where We Start From*, 1986, 244.
19 in *C. G. Jung*, A. Jaffe ed., 1979, 228.
20 *Our Inner Conflicts*, [1945] 1966, 56.
21 *Home Is Where We Start From*, 1986, 61.
22 quoted in *Hitler's Ideology*, R. Koenigsberg, 1975, 14.

Pages 352–59

23 *The Art of Loving*, 1956, 15.
24 *Way to Wisdom*, 1951, 93.
25 *Collected Works*, 1953, vol. 16, 454.
26 *Escape from Freedom*, 1941, 287.
27 *The Varieties of Religious Experience*, [1902] 1958, 298.
28 *The Basic Writings of C. G. Jung*, 1959, 175.
29 *The Realm of Spirit*, 1940, 255.
30 *The Sane Society*, 1955, 25.
31 *The Bonds of Love*, 1988, 63.
32 *Solitude*, 1988, 197.
33 *The Pessimist's Handbook*, [1893] 1964, 620–21.
34 *The Minimal Self*, 1984, 20.
35 *The Betrayal of the West*, 1978, 165–66.
36 *The Realm of Spirit*, 1940, 224.
37 *The Phenomenon of Man*, [1940] 1959, 262.
38 *The Sense of Beauty*, 1955, 237.
39 *Mind and Nature*, 1980, 126.
40 *Memories, Dreams, Reflections*, 1961, 354.
41 *Meditations*, [c. 161–80 A.D.], Book 10: 6.
42 *The Turning Point*, 1982, 77–80.
43 *The Phenomenon of Man*, 1959, 41–44.
44 *A New Science of Life*, 1981, 206.
45 *Creative Evolution*, [1907] 1944, 14.
46 *Being and Time*, [1931] 1962, 225.
47 *The World and the Individual*, 1900, 413.
48 *Future Worlds*, 1979, 215.
49 *I and Thou*, [1922] 1970, 125.
50 Ibid., 138.
51 *Autobiographies*, 1926, 435–36.
52 *Mind, Self, and Society*, 1934, 144.
53 *Guilt and Gratitude*, 1982, 35.
54 *The Phenomenon of Man*, 1959, 35.
55 *Mind and Nature*, 1979, 19.
56 in *Stalking the Wild Pendulum*, I. Bentov, 1977, XII–XIV.
57 *The Image*, 1956, 114.
58 *Meditations*, [c. 161–80 A.D.], Book 7: 6.

Values

1 in *New Knowledge in Human Values*, A. Maslow ed., 1959, 187.
2 Ibid., 189.
3 *Thus Spake Zarathustra*, 1881, Book 1.
4 *The Voices of Silence*, 1953, 633.
5 *Being and Nothingness*, [1943] 1957, 38.
6 *Science and the Modern World*, [1925] 1957, 136.
7 *The View from Nowhere*, 1986, 209.
8 *The Futurist*, Aug. 1977.
9 *On Aggression*, 1966, 227.
10 *On Human Nature*, 1978, 5.
11 *The Peaceable Sex*, 1987, 68.
12 *Beliefs, Attitudes, and Values*, 1968, 159.
13 *The Nature of Human Values*, 1973, 20.
14 *The Biological Origin of Human Values*, 1977, 32, 386.
15 *After Virtue*, 1981, 25.
16 *The Constitution of Liberty*, 1960, 63.
17 *Meaning and Void*, 1977, 253.
18 *Twilight of Authority*, 1975, 162.
19 *Science and Human Values*, [1956] 1965, 55.
20 *The Virtue of Selfishness*, 1964, 19.
21 *The Nature of Human Values*, 1973, 216.
22 *New Knowledge in Human Values*, 1959, 123.
23 *Generation of Vipers*, 1942, 292.
24 in *Self-Deception and Self-Understanding*, M. Martin ed., 1985, 282.
25 *The Philosophy of "As If,"* 1935, XLVII.
26 *Ego Psychology and Adaptation*, [1937] 1958, 84.
27 *Understanding Human Values*, 1979, 49.
28 *The End of History and the Last Man*, 1992, 322.
29 *The Triumph of the Therapeutic*, 1966, 240.
30 *The Political Illusion*, 1967, 16.
31 *Technology and Justice*, 1986, 41.
32 *Capitalism and Freedom*, 1962, 167.
33 *Eco-Philosophy*, 1981, 59.
34 *The Real World of Technology*, 1990, 123.
35 *Soft Energy Paths*, 1977, 58, 147.
36 in *The Crisis of Our Age*, P. Sorokin, 1957, 255.
37 *A History of Western Philosophy*, 1945, 834.
38 *The View from Nowhere*, 1986, 136.
39 *The Revolution of Hope*, 1968, 96.
40 *The Biological Origins of Human Values*, 1977, 436.
41 *100 Pages for the Future*, 1981, 180.
42 *The Crisis of Our Age*, 1957, 321.
43 quoted in *The Age of Charisma*, A. Schweitzer, 1984, 219.
44 *Building a Sustainable Society*, 1981, 349–71.
45 *Our Common Future*, 1987, 111.
46 *Science and Moral Priority*, 1983, 5.
47 *The Will to Power*, [1901] 1967, 3–4.
48 *The Betrayal of the West*, 1978, 196–97.
49 *New Knowledge in Human Values*, 1959, vii.
50 *The Betrayal of the West*, 1978, 199.
51 in *New Knowledge in Human Values*, A. Maslow ed., 1959, 74.
52 *Science and Moral Priority*, 1983, 10–11.

War

1 *Leviathan*, 1651, chap. 13.
2 *The Hero with a Thousand Faces*, [1949] 1968, 238.
3 *Germany and the Next War*, 1912.
4 *Perpetual Peace*, 1795, Sec. 2, par. 1.
5 *Ends and Means*, 1938, 93.
6 *The Journal*, 1884, vol. 1, 101, 335.
7 *The Territorial Imperative*, 1973, 336.
8 in *Look*, May 5, 1964.
9 *The Myth of the Machine*, 1966, 220, 226.
10 letter to Albert Einstein, 1932, in *Collected Papers*, vol. 5, 1959, 808.
11 *The Nature of Human Aggression*, 1976, 265.
12 *Ends and Means*, 1938, 19, 99.
13 *The Imperial Animal*, 1974, 254.
14 *The Descent of Woman*, 1972, 219.

15 *Pornography*, 1989, 51.
16 *The Second Stage*, 1981, 311.
17 *The Naked Ape*, 1967, 153.
18 *Reading About the Social Animal*, 1984, 219.
19 *Human Nature and Biocultural Evolution*, 1984, 249.
20 *Communication and Social Order*, 1962, 131.
21 *Homo Ludens*, 1955, 91.
22 quoted in *The War Myth*, D. Wells, 1967, 162.
23 *The City in History*, 1961, 42.
24 *Tragic Sense of Life*, [1912] 1954, 280.
25 [d. 258 A.D.] *Epistle to Donatus*, par. 6.
26 *Ideas and Opinions*, [1952] 1954, 165.
27 *Works*, 1913, vol. 2, 35.
28 *Twilight of Authority*, 1975, 157–58.
29 *Pro Milone*, chap. 11.
30 *American Political Science Review*, vol. 55, 1961, 3.
31 *The Politics of Experience*, 1967, 83.
32 in *Civil Disobedience*, Center for the Study of Democratic Institutions, 1966.
33 *Dissent*, 1967, vol. 14, no. 3, 284.
34 press conference, Jan. 12, 1955.
35 *The Causes of World War Three*, 1958, 79.
36 *Politics*, 1896, vol. 1, book 1.
37 *A Grammar of Politics*, [1925] 1938, 63.
38 *The New York Times*, May 20, 1972, 2.
39 *The Life of Reason*, 1954, 127.
40 *The Rise and Fall of the Roman Empire*, vol. 2, 1235.
41 [1936] in *Quotations of Chairman Mao*, 1967, chap. 5.
42 *On The Law of War*, 1589, Book 1, chap. 6, par. 48.
43 *The Principles of Moral and Political Philosophy*, 1814, vol. 2, chap. 12.
44 *The Spirit of the Laws*, 1748, Book x, chap. 2.
45 *The War Myth*, 1967, 45.
46 *The Principles of Moral and Political Philosophy*, 1814, vol. 2, chap. 12.
47 speech to officers, Aug. 22, 1939.
48 *African Genesis*, 1961, 172.
49 "Looking Back on the Spanish War," 1943.
50 letter [Dec. 11, 1880] in *Helmuth von Moltke as a Correspondent*, 1893.
51 *Mutter Courage*, 1939, sec. 1.
52 *A Study of War*, [1942] 1964, 79.
53 *The Realm of Spirit*, 1940, 88.
54 *Understanding Media*, 1966, 101, 299.
55 *The Managerial Revolution*, [1941] 1960, 241.
56 *Tragic Sense of Life*, [1912] 1954, 111.
57 *The Power Elite*, 1956, 167.
58 *America As a Civilization*, 1957, 911.
59 *Capitalism, Socialism, and Democracy*, [1942] 1950, 128.
60 [1910] quoted in *War and Morality*, R. Wasserstrom ed., 1970, 5.
61 *The Theory of the Leisure Class*, [1899] 1934, 246.
62 speech, *Hansard* [U.K.], Nov. 23, 1945, col. 786.
63 *Le Diable et le bon Dieu*, 1951, act 1, tableau 1.
64 *The Prince*, 1513, chap. 14.
65 *King Arthur*, 1691, act 2, scene 2.
66 *On War*, 1832, preface.
67 *The End of History and the Last Man*, 1992, 255.
68 *Capitalism*, 1966, 35.
69 *The Aquarian Conspiracy*, 1980, 411.
70 *Love in the Western World*, [1940] 1956, 266.
71 [d. 1832] in *Goethe's World View*, 1963, 187.
72 *The Arrogance of Power*, 1966, 7.
73 *Home Is Where We Start From*, 1986, 34.
74 *Generation of Vipers*, 1942, 256.
75 *Nicomachean Ethics*, Book 10, 1176b, 5–6.
76 Address to Congress, Washington, Jan. 8, 1790.
77 *The War Myth*, 1967, 200.
78 *Ends and Means*, 1938, 89.
79 *Defended to Death*, 1983, 184.
80 *The Causes of World War III*, 1958, 149.
81 *Woman and Socialism*, 1910, 314.
82 in *Living Philosophies*, C. Fadiman ed., 1949, vol. 7.
83 quoted in *Fund for the Republic*, R. Gordis, 1959.
84 *The Crisis of Our Age*, 1957, 217.
85 *On War*, [1832] 1976, 103.
86 *Munich Rather Than War*, 1939, 174.
87 speech at Kettering, July 3, 1938.
88 in London *Observer*, May 4, 1930.
89 *The Meaning of the 20th Century*, 1964, 90.
90 in *The New Yorker*, Jan. 8, 1966, 93.
91 speech to United Nations, New York, Sept. 25, 1961.
92 *Essays*, 1903, 166.
93 Washington speech, June 10, 1963.
94 *The Late Great Planet Earth*, 1970, 138.
95 "Why War," letter to Albert Einstein, 1932.
96 *A Study of War*, [1942] 1964, 356.
97 *Who Speaks for Man?*, 1953.
98 *Generation of Vipers*, 1942, 257.
99 *Ideas and Opinions*, [1934] 1954, 103.

Will

1 *Beyond Good and Evil*, 1886, chap. 36.
2 *Ends and Means*, 1938, 210.
3 *Mein Kampf*, [1924] 1939, 391.
4 in *International Journal of Law and Psychiatry*, 1983, vol. 6, 241.
5 *The Meaning of Conservatism*, 1984, 99.
6 *Love and Will*, 1969, 285.
7 *The Mermaid and the Minotaur*, 1976, 166.
8 *The World As Will and Idea*, 1819, sec. 60.
9 *The Life of Reason*, 1954, 279.
10 quoted in *Love and Will*, R. May, 1969, 240.
11 *The World As Will and Idea*, [1819] 1948, vol. 1, 401.
12 *The Basic Writings of C. G. Jung*, 1959, 53.
13 *Waiting for God*, 1951, 126.
14 *The Realm of Spirit*, 1940, 68.
15 *On The Will in Nature*, [1836] 1992, "Comparative Anatomy."

Pages 363–69

16 *The Human Person*, 1954, 159.
17 "The Problem of Truth," 1911.
18 *Fundamental Principles of the Metaphysic of Morals*, 1797, Second Section.
19 *Principles of Psychology*, 1907, vol. 2, 567–68.
20 *Psychology*, 1892, chap. 26.
21 *Essay Concerning Human Understanding*, [1689] 1959, 367, n. 73.
22 *Will in Western Thought*, 1964, 235.
23 *Ethics*, 1677, Part II, prop. 48.
24 *The World and the Individual*, 1900, 327.
25 *Creative Evolution*, [1907] 1944, 261.
26 *Man for Himself*, 1947, 233.
27 *Positive Social Behavior and Morality*, 1978, vol. 1, 12.
28 *Agape and Eros*, [1932] 1982, 223.
29 *The Mystic Will*, 1930.
30 *Fundamental Principles of the Metaphysic of Morals*, 1785, First Section.
31 *The Evolution of Human Consciousness*, 1980, 324.
32 *The Will to Power*, [1901] 1967, 354.
33 *Physical Control of the Mind*, 1969, 136.
34 *Tractatus Logico-Philosophicus*, [1921] 1961, 70, 6.374.
35 *Suicide*, [1897] 1951, 373.
36 *An Outline of Philosophy*, 1923, 223.
37 paraphrase in *The World and the Individual*, 1900, 438.
38 [1940] in *Collected Works*, vol. 9, Part I, par. 276.
39 *Society and Solitude*, 1870, vol. 3, "Courage."
40 quoted in *Self-Deception and Morality*, M. Martin, 1986, 58.
41 *Being and Nothingness*, [1943] 1957, 442.
42 *Waiting On God*, 1951, 126.
43 *The Realm of Spirit*, 1940, 177.
44 *The Divine Comedy*, c. 1300, "Paradise," Canto 3, line 85.
45 *The Human Soul*, 1973, 29.
46 *Love and Will*, 1969, 244.

Wisdom

1 *Future Shock*, 1970, 229.
2 *The Informed Heart*, 1960, 86.
3 *Modern Man in Search of a Soul*, 1933, 261.
4 *Science and the Modern World*, 1925, 283–84.
5 *Generation of Vipers*, 1942, 242–43.
6 *The Structure of Evil*, 1968, 117.
7 *Small Is Beautiful*, 1975, 38.
8 quoted in *Philosophy*, J. Christian, 1990, 21.
9 *Human Society in Ethics and Politics*, 1954, 212.
10 *Essays*, 1625, "Of Cunning."
11 *Works of Love*, [1848] 1962, 265.
12 *Nicomachean Ethics*, Book 6, chap. 7.
13 *Nature, Man, and Woman*, 1958, 118.
14 *The Unconscious God*, 1975, 141–42.
15 *Twilight of the Idols*, 1888, maxim 5.
16 *The Principles of Psychology*, 1890, vol. 2, chap. 22.
17 *The Basic Writings of C. G. Jung*, 1959, 24.
18 *Small Is Beautiful*, 1975, 82.
19 *Nicomachean Ethics*, Book 6, chap. 7.
20 *Wisdom of the West*, 1959, 13, 26.
21 [d. 1274] *Summa contra Gentiles*, I, i.
22 *The Scientific Outlook*, 1931, x.
23 *An Inquiry into the Original of Our Ideas of Beauty and Virtue*, 1725, Treatise 1, sec. 5:16.
24 *The Passions*, 1976, 128.
25 in *Meno*, by Plato.
26 *Ethics*, 1677, Part 5, post. 42.
27 *The Analysis of the Self*, 1971, 328.
28 in *The Search for the Self*, P. Ornstein ed., 1978, 458.
29 *Émile*, [1762] 1979, 473.
30 *An Inquiry Concerning Political Justice*, 1793, Book 4, chap. 1.
31 *Some Turns of Thought in Modern Philosophy*, 1933, 98–101.
32 *The Analysis of the Self*, 1971, 327.
33 in *Man's Search for Himself*, R. May, 1953, 250.
34 *The Stress of Life*, 1976, 397.
35 *Holy Bible*, Ecclesiastes 9:16.
36 *The Greening of America*, 1970, 383–84.
37 Ibid., 383.
38 in *University of California Chronicle*, Dec., 1918.
39 *The Culture of Narcissism*, 1979, 360.
40 *Eco-Philosophy*, 1981, 38.
41 *Fables*, 1678, Book 8, "La Mort et la Mourant."
42 *Theory of Moral Sentiments*, 1759, Part VII, Sec. II, chap. 1.
43 *The Survival of the Wisest*, 1973, 121–22.
44 *The Making of a Counter Culture*, 1969, 238.
45 in *First Alcibiades*, by Plato.
46 *Holy Bible*, Proverbs 4:7.

Woman

1 *Revue d'Anthropologie*, 1879, 60–61.
2 *Human Paleopsychology*, 1987, 159.
3 *Myth, Religion, and Mother Right*, [1926] 1967, 112.
4 *The Decline of the West*, [1932] 1965, 355.
5 *Sexual Personae*, 1990, 12.
6 *The Longest War*, 1984, 258.
7 *The Power of the Positive Woman*, 1977, 17.
8 *The Total Woman*, 1975, 60.
9 *A Choice of Heroes*, 1982, 190.
10 *New Introductory Lectures in Psychoanalysis*, 1933, "Femininity," par. 2.
11 in *The Life and Work of Sigmund Freud*, E. Jones, 1961, 377.
12 interview in *New Republic*, Dec. 1, 1973.
13 *The Second Sex*, 1964, 75, 186.
14 *A Room of One's Own*, 1929, 60.
15 in *Signs*, Spring, 1982, 533–34.
16 *Émile*, 1762, Book v.
17 letter [June 14, 1860] in *Elizabeth Cady Stanton*, 1922, vol. 2, 82.
18 *Théorie des Quatre Mouvements*, 1808, vol. 2, chap. 4.

Pages 369–75

19 quoted in *Parade*, Dec. 1, 1963.
20 [1860] quoted in *Feminist Quotations*, C. McFee ed., 1979, 14.
21 *The Imperial Animal*, 1974, 150.
22 in *Signs*, Spring, 1982, 538.
23 "On Women," in *Studies in Pessimism*, 1893.
24 in *Popular Science Monthly*, 1895, 47, 212.
25 *Cannibals and Kings*, 1977, 61.
26 *Beyond Power*, 1985, 41.
27 *Woman and Socialism*, 1910, 58.
28 *International Journal of Psycho-Analysis*, 1929, vol. 10, 50.
29 *Woman As Force in History*, 1973, 288.
30 *Beast and Man*, 1978, 353.
31 [1925] *Collected Papers*, 1959, vol. 5, 196–97.
32 *In a Different Voice*, 1982, 16, 82.
33 in *New Society*, Aug. 23, 1979, 394.
34 *Myth, Religion and Mother Right*, [1926] 1967, 144.
35 *Reagan, God, and the Bomb*, 1985, 209.
36 *Women and Politics*, 1987, 81.
37 *The Inevitablility of Patriarchy*, 1973, 228.
38 *Beyond God the Father*, 1973, 61.
39 7th century B.C.
40 *Patriarchal Attitudes*, 1970, 45.
41 *Understanding Human Nature*, 1927, 131.
42 *Civilization and Its Discontents*, 1930.
43 *Don Juan*, 1819, Canto 1, stanza 194.
44 *The Sickness Unto Death*, [1849] 1944, 78.
45 *Vindication of the Rights of Women*, 1791, introduction.
46 Ibid., chap. 3.
47 in *Embodied Love*, P. Cooey ed., 1987, 166.
48 *The Female Eunuch*, 1971, 317.
49 [1913] *in An Anthropologist at Work*, M. Mead, 1959, 131.
50 *Eros and Civilization*, [1955] 1966, 161.
51 *Understanding Women*, 1985, 154.
52 *Love in the Western World*, [1940] 1956, 313.
53 *America As a Civilization*, 1957, 599.
54 *The Degradation of the Democratic Dogma*, 1920, 119.
55 *Anything But Love*, 1948.
56 *The Life of Reason*, 1905, "Reason in Society."
57 Senate speech, Washington, Sept. 30, 1918.
58 in *The Natural Superiority of Women*, A. Montagu, 1968, 166.
59 *The Pursuit of Loneliness*, [1970] 1976, 157.
60 *The Natural Superiority of Women*, 1968, 158–59.
61 *The First Sex*, 1971, 119.
62 *Fighting for Hope*, 1984, 37.
63 *The Power of the Positive Woman*, 1977, 17.
64 *The Basic Writings of C. G. Jung*, 1959, 315.
65 *The Natural Superiority of Women*, 1968, 103.
66 *The Inevitability of Patriarchy*, 1973, 227.
67 *Sexual Personae*, 1990, 296.
68 in *Young India*, Apr. 10, 1930.
69 *Woman and Socialism*, 1910, 243.
70 *Pedagogical Anthropology*, 1913, 259.

Work / Labour

1 *An Essay on Man*, [1944] 1970, 74.
2 *Life Against Death*, 1966, 130.
3 *Civilization and Its Discontents*, 1930, 46.
4 *The Division of Labor in Society*, [1893] 1964, 336.
5 *Psychological Reflections*, [1953] 1970, 146.
6 *The Human Problems of an Industrial Civilization*, [1933] 1960, 130.
7 *Brave New Workplace*, 1985, 1.
8 *Toward a Feminist Theory of the State*, 1989, 3.
9 *The Social Problems of an Industrial Civilization*, 1945, 111.
10 *The Acquisitive Society*, 1920, 67.
11 *The Imperial Animal*, 1974, 159.
12 *Men in Transition*, 1982, 65.
13 *A Grammar of Politics*, [1925] 1938, 142.
14 in *Psychiatry*, 1946, vol. 9, no. 1, 31.
15 *Guilt*, 1985, 21.
16 *Culture's Consequences*, 1980, 375.
17 *Work in America*, 1973, 13.
18 *What Life Should Mean to You*, 1931, 202.
19 *Technics and Human Development*, 1967, 162.
20 [1875] quoted in *Feminist Quotations*, C. McFee ed., 1979, 210.
21 *The Informed Heart*, 1960, 4.
22 *The Conquest of Happiness*, 1930, 219.
23 *News from Nowhere*, 1891, chap. 15.
24 *Democracy and Education*, [1916] 1961, 206.
25 in *International Journal of Psycho-Analysis*, 24, 1943, 118.
26 in *Beyond Domination*, C. Gould ed., 1983, 184.
27 in *Karl Marx*, T. Bottomore ed., 1964, 169–70.
28 *Eros and Civilization*, [1955] 1966, 105.
29 *The Need for Roots*, 1952, 52.
30 *Principles of Political Economy and Taxation*, 1817, chap. 5.
31 speech, June 16, 1933.
32 in *Living Philosophies*, 1931, C. Fadiman ed., 213.
33 *The Theory of the Leisure Class*, 1934, 40–41.
34 message to Congress, Washington, Dec. 3, 1861.
35 *A Modest Inquiry Into the Nature and Necessity of a Paper Currency*, Apr. 3, 1729.
36 *Critique of the Gotha Program*, 1875, part 1.
37 *The End of History and the Last Man*, 1992, 94.
38 *Woman and Socialism*, 1910, 370.
39 1918, Article 18.
40 *Democracy in America*, 1835, Second Book, chap. 20.
41 *Passages from the American Notebooks*, 1868.
42 *House of the Dead*, 1862, Part 1, chap. 1.
43 *Technics and Human Development*, 1967, 237.
44 Ibid., 242.
45 *The Cult of Information*, 1986, 179.
46 *The Technological Society*, 1964, 350.
47 *A Grammar of Politics*, [1925] 1938, 210–11.
48 *The Second Stage*, 1981, 241.

Pages 375–79

49 *Elites and Society*, 1964, 115.
50 "Looking Back on the Spanish War," 1943.
51 *The Meaning of the 20th Century*, 1964, 170–71.
52 *Global Reach*, 1974, 323.
53 *The Greening of America*, 1970, 292–93.
54 *America As a Civilization*, 1957, 334.
55 *The Need for Roots*, 1952, 77.
56 *Time and Tide*, 1867, letter 5.
57 in *Vocational Guidance and Human Development*, 1974, 21.
58 *Leaders We Deserve*, 1983, 205.
59 *The Mass Psychology of Fascism*, 1946, 250–2.
60 Ibid., 244.
61 *Bulletin of the Menninger Clinic*, 1942, 170.
62 *Work and Human Behavior*, 1985, 317–18.
63 *The Need for Roots*, 1952, 89.
64 *Understanding Media*, 1966, 129.
65 *The End of Ideology*, 1960, 368.
66 quoted in *The Presidential Character*, J. Barber, 1985, 91.
67 *The Prophet*, 1923, 26.
68 *The Need for Roots*, 1952, 93, 288.
69 quoted in *The Male Machine*, M. Fasteau, 1975, 115.

Youth / Children

1 *The Theory of Moral Sentiments*, 1759, Part 6, sec. 2 chap. 1.
2 *The Poetics of Reverie*, 1971, 126.
3 in *Essays on a Science of Mythology*, C. G. Jung, 1969, 213–24.
4 *The Beggar's Opera*, 1728, act 2, scene 4.
5 *Home Is Where We Start From*, 1986, 165.
6 *Table Talk*, 1821, Essay 33.
7 in *The Challenge of Youth*, 1965, 11.
8 *The Absorbent Mind*, [1949] 1984, 219.
9 *Explorations in Altruistic Love and Behavior*, 1950, 243.
10 *An Essay on the Education and Instruction of Children*, 1748.
11 *The Dialectic of Sex*, 1970, 117.
12 *How Children Fail*, 1964, 208.
13 [1932] in *Collected Works*, 1972, vol. 17, "Vom Werden der Persönlichkeit."
14 *Patterns of Culture*, [1934] 1960, 213.
15 in *Journal of Psychology*, 1949, vol. 28, 273–78.
16 *The Spying Heart*, 1989, 87.
17 *Mein Kampf*, [1924] 1943, 403.
18 *On Education Especially in Early Childhood*, 1926, 100.
19 *The Prophet*, 1923, "On Children."
20 *For Your Own Good*, 1984, xi.
21 *The Road Less Traveled*, 1979, 150.
22 *What Life Should Mean to You*, 1931, 65.
23 "My heart leaps up when I behold," 1807.
24 *The Psychology of the Child*, 1969, ix.
25 *The Heart of Man*, 1964, 51.
26 *The Goddess*, 1981, 225.
27 *The First Year of Life*, 1965, 300.
28 *Summerhill*, 1960, 160.
29 in *Psychological Issues*, 1959, vol. 1, no. 1, 100.
30 *Culture Against Man*, 1965, 205.
31 *The Road Less Traveled*, 1979, 26.
32 *Childhood and Society*, [1950] 1963, 235.
33 *On Aggression*, 1966, 263.
34 in *The Challenge of Youth*, 1965, 106.
35 *The Farther Reaches of Human Nature*, 1971, 376.
36 *Political Man*, 1963, 451.
37 *On the Democratic Idea in America*, 1972, 27.
38 *This Week Magazine*, Mar. 16, 1969, 7.
39 *Identity*, 1968, 257.
40 in *The Challenge of Youth*, 1965, 135.
41 Ibid., 94.
42 quoted in *The Moral and Political Thought of Mahatma Gandhi*, R. Iyer, 1973, 23.
43 *The Making of a Counter Culture*, 1969, 47.
44 *Eros and Civilization*, [1955] 1966, xxv.
45 *The Politics of Experience*, 1967, 49.
46 Ibid., 26.
47 *The Greening of America*, 1970, 360.
48 *The Mismeasure of Man*, 1981, 333.
49 *Childhood and Society*, [1950] 1963, 16.
50 *Homo Ludens*, [1950] 1955, 205.
51 *Culture of Complaint*, 1993, 8.
52 *Psychological Reflections*, [1953] 1970, 139–41.
53 *Holy Bible*, 1 Corinthians 13:11.
54 *Home Is Where We Start From*, 1986, 166.
55 *The Absorbent Mind*, [1949] 1984, 120.
56 *The Sibling Society*, 1996, 232.
57 quoted in *The Sexual Wilderness*, V. Packard, 1968, VII.

Author Index

Author Index